Government and Politics in Western Europe

Third Edition

Government and Politics in Western Europe

Britain, France, Italy, Germany

Third Edition

YVES MÉNY

AND

ANDREW KNAPP

First edition translated by

JANET LLOYD

OXFORD

UNIVERSITY PRESS

OXFORD
UNIVERSITY PRESS

Great Clarendon Street, Oxford OX2 6DP

Oxford University Press is a department of the University of Oxford.
It furthers the University's objective of excellence in research, scholarship,
and education by publishing worldwide in

Oxford New York
Auckland Cape Town Dar es Salaam Hong Kong Karachi Kuala Lumpur
Madrid Melbourne Mexico City Nairobi New Delhi Taipei Toronto
Shanghai

With offices in
Argentina Austria Brazil Chile Czech Republic France Greece
Guatemala Hungary Italy Japan South Korea Poland Portugal
Singapore Switzerland Thailand Turkey Ukraine Vietnam

Oxford is a registered trade mark of Oxford University Press
in the UK and in certain other countries

Published in the United States
by Oxford University Press Inc., New York

The first English edition was translated from an adapted version of the original French
publication *Politique comparée* © Éditions Montchrestien 1987
translated by Janet Lloyd © Oxford University Press 1990, 1993, 1998

First edition published 1990 in hardback and paperback
Second edition 1993
Third edition 1998

British Library Cataloguing in Publication Data

Data available

Library of Congress Cataloging in Publication Data
Mény, Yves.
Government and politics in Western Europe: Britain, France,
Italy, Germany / Yves Mény and Andrew Knapp; first ed. translated
by Jane Lloyd.—3rd ed.
Adapted translation of: Politique comparée. 1987.
Includes bibliographical references and index.
1. Comparative government.   2. Europe—Politics and
government—1945–   3. Europe, Western—Politics and government.
I. Knapp, Andrew.   II. Title
JF52.M36   1998   320.3'094—dc21   98–2539
ISBN-13: 978-0-19-878221-6
ISBN-10: 0-19-878221-7

7 9 10 8

Typeset in Minion
Printed in Great Britain
on acid-free paper by
Antony Rowe Ltd
Chippenham, Wilts.

PREFACE

Shortly after the death of John Smith and the election of Tony Blair as Labour leader in 1994, Professor Ivor Crewe altered the title of one of his regular guest lectures from 'Can Labour Win?' to 'Can Labour Lose?' The change bears witness to the capacity of seemingly personal, aleatory developments to confound the analyses and predictions of political scientists. Analysis and prediction cannot, of course, be ducked. But they are best undertaken with caution and humility; for political science has limits.

Of the major political developments that have taken place since the second English edition of this book went to press five years ago, few have been wholly unforeseen, but fewer still have lacked at least an element of surprise. Italy's established political parties were already in serious difficulty by the spring of 1992, but the ensuing meltdown of the party system after nearly half a century was unexpected, at least in its remarkable speed. The British Conservatives' failures early in their final term of office clearly offered Labour their best opening in thirteen years, but few anticipated the extent of Labour's victory in 1997. The disgrace of the French Socialists in the early 1990s was such as to offer a virtual guarantee of victory for the Right in the parliamentary elections of 1993 and the presidential race of 1995; but the speed of the Left's recovery, and the Socialists' early return to office in 1997, in 'cohabitation' with President Chirac, were largely unexpected. These developments are covered in the current edition, as are some of the more recent contributions to academic debate, such as Katz and Mair's concept of the 'cartel' party.

The fate of European integration has justified neither the brightest hopes raised by the Maastricht Treaty, nor the darkest fears provoked by the difficult referendums of 1992. The official creation of the three-pillar European Union in 1993 brought with it no spectacular growth of a European civic consciousness; the institutions remain, if possible, more baroque than ever in their complexity; the problems of eastward enlargement have been, at the most, partially addressed. But despite the uncertainties of voters, the assaults of the money markets, and the *atonie* of the continental economies of Western Europe in the 1990s, the project of Economic and Monetary Union remains, just, on course. And, crucially, the external policy priorities of any freshly elected government of a member state as it settles into office are increasingly headed by relations with the European Union. For this reason above all, two new chapters on the EU, one from a largely intergovernmental perspective and the other from an institutional one, have been added to this new edition.

My heartfelt thanks, finally, to Sara and Viveca Knapp for their forbearance and support during the preparation of this enlarged edition.

A.K.

November 1997

CONTENTS

DETAILED CONTENTS

Contents

Contents

Contents

ABBREVIATIONS

AER	Assembly of European Regions
BDA	Bundesvereinigung der Deutschen Arbeitgeberverbände (German Confederation of Employers' Associations)
BDI	Bundesverband der Deutschen Industrie (German Federation of Industrial Companies)
BHE	Block der Heimatvertriebenen und Entrechteten (Refugee Party)
BSE	Bovine Spongiform Encephalitis
CAP	Common Agricultural Policy
CBI	Confederation of British Industry
CDU	Christlich-Demokratische Union
CFDT	Confédération Française Démocratique des Travailleurs
CFTC	Confédération Française des Travailleurs Chrétiens
CGC	Confédération Générale des Cadres
CGIL	Confederazione Generale Italiana del Lavoro
CGT	Confédération Générale du Travail
CGTU	Confédération Générale du Travail Unitaire
CID-UNATI	Confédération Interprofessionnelle de Défense et d'Union Nationale d'Action des Travailleurs Indépendants (shopkeepers' organization)
CISL	Confederazione Italiana dei Sindicati dei Lavoratori
CNPF	Conseil National du Patronat Français
CNSTP	Confédération Nationale des Syndicats des Travailleurs Paysans
CODER	Comité de Développement Économique Régional
CONSOB	Commissione Nazionale per le Società e la Borsa
COPA	Comité des Organisations Professionnelles Agricoles
COREPER	Committee of Permanent Representatives
CP	Communist Party
CPRS	Central Policy Review Staff
CSU	Christlich-Soziale Union
DAG	Deutsche Angestellengewerkschaft
DATAR	Délégation à l'Aménagement du Territoire et à l'Action Régionale
DBB	Deutscher Beamten Bund
DBV	Deutscher Bauernverband (farmers' union)
DC	Democrazia Christiana
DGB	Deutsche Gewerkschaftsbund (German Confederation of Unions)

DIHT	Deutscher Industrie- und Handelstag (German Federation of Chambers of Commerce)
DKP	Deutsche Kommunistische Partei
DN	Destra Nazionale
DP	Democrazia Proletaria
EC	European Community
ECSC	European Coal and Steel Community
EDC	European Defence Community
EDF	Électricité de France
EEC	European Economic Community
EFTA	European Free Trade Association
EMS	European Monetary System
EMU	Economic and Monetary Union
ENA	École Nationale d'Administration
ETUC	European Trade Union Confederation
EP	European Parliament
EPP	European Peoples' Party
EU	European Union
FDP	Freie Demokratische Partei (= German Liberals)
FEN	Fédération de l'Éducation Nationale
FFA	Fédération Française de l'Agriculture
FLM	Federazione dei Lavoratori della Metallurgia
FN	Front National
FNSEA	Fédération Nationale des Syndicats d'Exploitants Agrícoles
FO	Force Ouvrière (full name: Confédération Générale du Travail—Force Ouvrière, or CGT-FO)
HOGS	Heads of State and Government
IGC	Intergovernmental Conference
IG Metall	Industrie Gewerkschaft Metall
IRA	Instituts Régionaux d'Administration
IRI	Istituto per la Reconstruzione Industriale
KPD	Kommunistische Partei Deutschlands
MEP	Member of the European Parliament
MODEF	Mouvement de Défense des Exploitations Familiales
MRP	Mouvement Républicain Populaire
MSI	Movimento Sociale Italiano
NFU	National Farmers' Union
NPD	Nationaldemokratische Partei Deutschlands
OAS	Organisation de l'Armée Secrète

Abbreviations

OECD	Organization for Economic Co-operation and Development
PAF	(Piccoli, Andreotti, Fanfani) Christian Democrat faction
PCF	Parti Communiste Français
PCI	Partito Comunista Italiano
PDM	Progrès et Démocratie Moderne
PDS	Partito Democratico della Sinistra
PDUP	Partito Democratico di Unità Proletaria
PES	Party of European Socialists
PLI	Partito Liberale Italiano
PME	Petites et Moyennes Entreprises
PMI	Petites et Moyennes Industries
PR	Parti Républicain
PRI	Partito Repubblicano Italiano
PSDI	Partito Socialista-Democratico Italiano
PSI	Partito Socialista Italiano
PSOE	Partido Socialista Obrero Español
PSU	Parti Socialiste Unifié
PSUP	Partito Socialista di Unità Proletaria
QMV	Qualified Majority Voting
RAI	Radiotelevisione Italiana
RATP	Régie Autonome des Transports Parisiens
RI	Républicains Indépendants
RPF	Rassemblement du Peuple Français
RPR	Rassemblement pour la République
SDP	Social Democratic Party
SEA	Single European Act
SFIO	Section Française de l'Internationale Ouvrière
SGCI	Secrétariat général du Comité interministériel pour les questions de coopération économique européene
SNP	Scottish National Party
SPD	Sozialdemokratische Partei Deutschlands
SVP	Süd-Tyrol VolksPartei (party of the German-speaking minority in Alto-Adige)
TUC	Trades Union Congress
UDF	Union pour la Démocratie Française
UDR	Union des Démocrates pour la Republique (Gaullist Party, 1968–76)
UIEA	Union of Industrial and Employers' Associations
UIL	Unione Italiana del Lavoro
UNR	Union pour la Nouvelle République

LIST OF FIGURES AND TABLES

Introduction

Comparative political studies

The goal of a study of comparative politics is to identify, analyse, and interpret the similarities and dissimilarities between different political systems, and its justification is that we may thereby arrive at an understanding of their fundamental processes that reaches beyond purely institutional formalism. Research of this kind proves particularly stimulating and rewarding when the political systems under consideration resemble one another sufficiently closely without being altogether similar. This is the case with the European democracies, for they share a number of characteristics but differ from one another in respect of their histories, myths, and values.[1]

Introduction

A priori, each of the four great West European democracies studied here has a well-defined personality of its own, and this is bound to complicate an overall comparison. France and Britain both have a long democratic tradition developed over the course of two centuries, whereas Italy had experienced only brief interludes of democracy before the establishment of the current republican system of government. The case of the Federal Republic of Germany is unique. In its ten Western *Länder* (plus West Berlin), the experience of democracy prior to its enshrinement in the post-war settlement had been as fitful as in Italy. In the five *Länder* of former East Germany, democratic processes were non-existent not only for the 12 years of Nazi dictatorship (as in the West) but also for over four decades of Communist rule prior to the unification of the two Germanies in 1990. But even between France and Britain there are many obvious differences: Britain is a model of stability and continuity, whereas since 1789 France has experimented with virtually every conceivable form of government; the French system is the product of a revolution, whereas Britain has been evolving with slow, progressive changes ever since the seventeenth century. In Britain it proved possible to establish democracy without breaking with the monarchy, whereas in most European countries setting up a democracy involved doing away with the monarchy.

The various political and constitutional paths that these different countries have followed have affected more than their respective systems of values and their political cultures. Each country's institutions, rules, procedures, and traditions are deeply marked by its past, even where that past has been forcibly repudiated. France, Italy, and Germany all owe much to their earlier political systems, even the least democratic of them, in sectors such as political and social economy, administrative structures, civil and penal legislation, and so on. The different paths that these countries followed towards democracy and their good or bad experiences along the way have also helped to shape their institutions and the fashion in which these are run.

Variations in institutions and in the organization of different interests and parties do not result solely from the similar or different experiences of the countries involved. They are also the product of each country's political culture, as it has been forged by its history and by past or present dominant ideologies. We may thus seek a society's distinctive and dominant characteristics as Almond and Verba did in their well-known work *The Civic Culture*. It is true that the dangers of subjectivity and schematization that such a venture implies make it a risky one, as does the exaggerated importance ascribed to cultural phenomena at the expense of other factors, particularly economic ones. But in a comparative study, such an approach has the merit of underlining the importance of this particular variable (namely, the political culture) in the functioning of the political system. Furthermore, some of the problems raised by resorting to the notion of a political culture may be palliated by complementing it with the concept of 'subcultures'. Within the political culture of Italy, for example, we can distinguish between two subcultures, one Catholic, the other Communist, which are all the more important since they are strongly rooted and territorially distinct: some regions are 'white', others 'red', though by 1992 the collapse of world communism and the drop in support for both Christian Democrat and Communist parties in Italy had reduced the sharpness of this distinction. The political cultures and subcultures of individual countries contribute in varying degrees to the similarities and dissimilarities between their political systems.

The common heritage

Nevertheless, these differences should not stand in the way of a comparative study for, despite all that separates them, the European democracies possess in common ideals and institutions which are peculiar to them as a group and so unite them. These may be listed under four main headings: the affirmation of pluralism, the specific mechanisms that allow for the expression of choice, the organization of balanced institutions with limited powers, and the subordination of the public authorities to higher rules (constitutionalism).

The affirmation of pluralism

The affirmation of pluralism lies at the heart of liberal democracy and operates in several spheres: the economic, the social, and, finally, the political.

Economic pluralism

A liberal democratic State allows different agents to operate freely in the market as entrepreneurs and traders, and does not itself seek to appropriate the means of production. There can be no doubt that in the past, as now, liberal democracy and a free market went hand in hand and developed in conjunction. However, the association between them does not go unchallenged and is not without its problems. Just as there is no such thing as an ideal democracy, no market is perfect: the economic pluralism of theory is often replaced by oligopolistic or monopolistic situations in practice; 'natural' mechanisms for regulating the market are impeded by obstructions and economic crises. In both cases, intervention on the part of the State has been seen to be necessary, and legitimate, not only by those imbued with progressive or socialist ideals, but by a more or less significant section of moderate conservative opinion.

The impact of such views has everywhere led the State to intervene in one way or another: as a regulator of production and trade, through legislation on product standards or on competition; as a distributor of the wealth produced by economic activity, through the complex mechanisms of the Welfare State; and as a direct producer of goods and manager of services, through public ownership of firms. To differing degrees, then, all the Western democracies—even the United States—are today countries with *mixed economies*, where the public and private sectors both operate, either in partnership or in competition. But debate on the need, advisability, and extent of such intervention, which runs contrary to 'pure' liberalism, is a constant factor in public life, not only in countries with an interventionist tradition (such as France), but also in those where *laissez-faire* doctrines have predominated (such as the United States).

Social pluralism

Social pluralism implies the acceptance of autonomous groups, which are considered as the normal, desirable means of organizing individuals. However, this form of the pluralist ideal has given rise to many dissenting views. In this domain, philosophers such as Montesquieu and Rousseau are in conflict, as are systems such as those of the United States and France: the notion of intermediary groups acting as the bases of democratic organization is opposed to that of the Jacobin view, according to which nothing at all should stand between a citizen and the State, between an individual's will and the general will. But despite these differences, it is generally accepted today that groups are a natural means of democratic expression.

Political pluralism

Political pluralism does not, in principle, depend upon the two other forms of pluralism, but it is difficult to see how it could exist without at least a minimum of economic and/or social pluralism. Political pluralism is identified, both historically and practically, with the affirmation of certain liberties, liberties that are at once economic, political, and social: freedom of assembly, freedom to form associations, religious freedom, the right to property. The affirmation of these liberties entails at least one important consequence: recognition of the freedom of choice and the right to defend this in an appropriate manner.

The expression of choice

The acceptance and recognition of political pluralism necessarily implies organized competitiveness and an acceptance of its consequences—both political and institutional. The organization of electoral competition must in the first place be governed by rules sufficiently strict and neutral not to appear to be electorally favouring one or another group. Excluded groups will be inclined to bring complaints against not only particular rules as they are applied, but the whole political system where it does not guarantee them an equal chance of acceding to power. The evolution of the Western democracies has been characterized, right from the start, by a long, slow progress towards processes favouring the expression of choices: lowering the voting age and the extension of suffrage to women, the control of constituency boundaries, the financing of elections, etc. But it should be emphasized that, despite all the improvements achieved, universal consensus on the rules of the game is still a long way off.

The acceptance of competition means more than simply agreement over the modalities of electoral battle. It requires the defeated to abide by the electoral results and to respect the majority rule. But the majority must, in its turn, tolerate the opposition and not exercise power exclusively to its own benefit. The archetype of a country where such mutual limitations are accepted is Britain, where the winner's right to exercise power is limited by the recognized rights of 'His/Her Majesty's Opposition'. France, in contrast, with its background of revolutionary struggle and strong ideological polarization, long found it very difficult to accept the idea that the defeat of the party in power leads naturally and ineluctably to the opposition's accession to government. The constitutional history of France has been punctuated by a series of attempts to manipulate the electoral system and by *coups d'état*. Uncertainties remained even under the Fifth Republic. Not until 1981 and 1986 did the practices of first alternation, then 'cohabitation' become confirmed, conferring upon the institutions involved their full legitimacy and political stability. It was this transformation of violent conflict into political competition which remained peaceful as a result of the recognition of the opposition's right to accede to power that prompted Robert Dahl to declare the institutionalization of the opposition to be 'one of the greatest and most surprising social discoveries of the human race'.[2]

The limitation of powers

At the centre of the liberal constitutional machinery lies the principle of the separation of powers, conceived as an instrument to check authoritarianism or absolute power.

People have often been amazed by how many different interpretations have been produced for the principle propounded by Montesquieu in the eighteenth century, and by all the different ways in which it has been implemented. The separation of powers is a fundamental principle upon which all the Western democracies rest but in none of them is it interpreted or, above all, 'lived' in the same way. That there are differences should not occasion surprise if one bears in mind that the principle itself promotes no logical or organizational advantages. It is dictated by a fundamental imperative: power must be checked by power. Adopting this as a central principle, it is perfectly possible to set up a whole range of different institutions which will vary according to the limitations deemed desirable and the balances—or imbalances—that one is seeking to promote. Checks and balances will play a more or less important role depending upon the political system, but they will always be central to the structure of liberal constitutions. From this point of view, France remains a system in which the imbalances strongly favour the executive in its relations with both the legislature and the judiciary. Furthermore, France—officially, at least—has so far implemented the principle of separation only partially, that is, as a separation between different functions. For many years it continued to resist any territorial division of powers that would go beyond purely administrative decentralization. Although the situation is more complex in practice, in general in France the territorial distribution of powers has never gone as far as in, for example, Germany.

Introduction

The separation of powers, both horizontally/functionally and vertically/territorially, remains the corner-stone of democratic liberalism. It is the principle upon which the new democracies of West Germany and Italy based themselves after the Second World War, and the basis upon which the Fifth Republic was built (particularly after the law of 3 June 1958), as were also the new democracies of Greece, Portugal, and Spain, following the demise of their dictatorships.

The rule of law and constitutionalism

The limitation of powers arose from an obligation imposed upon governments, and ultimately on legislatures too, to submit to a body of superior rules that guaranteed the citizen respect for his liberties and legal procedures. The rights gradually established by the British Parliament, the Amendments to the American Constitution, the *État de Droit* in France, and the German *Rechtsstaat* have together produced a whole panoply of more or less solemn laws (e.g. the Declaration of Human Rights, the General Principles of Law, Higher Law) that constitute a corpus of rules to which the Western democracies of today adhere and to which the countries of Europe have collectively given their approval, in particular through the European Convention on Human Rights.

But the *État de Droit* implies more than respect for individual liberties: it also involves the authority of a higher law that imposes its rules and constraints upon public powers as a whole. This policy of self-restraint accepted by the political power can be guaranteed by rigorous procedures and rules (such as those governing amendments to the Constitution) and, above all, by the conviction of citizens in general, and the élite in particular, that respect for higher law and the order that it establishes constitutes the essential basis of political consensus and stability. The virtues of the Constitution and the desire to preserve it as a means of welding together the social and political body— even if adjustments sometimes prove necessary—are particularly strong in countries such as Britain, where the Constitution, although informal and not entrenched, has long been held in respect (excessively so, in some views). The central importance of such a fundamental higher law was also manifested after the Second World War in Italy and West Germany where, following the experiences of Fascism and Nazism, it seemed more important than ever to provide the nation with a set of democratic rules that applied to everyone. Within this group, France often appeared to play an isolated and idiosyncratic part: the Fourth Republic provoked radical opposition from both the Right and the Left from the start; and the Fifth Republic seemed destined for a similar fate. Only very gradually did the Left come to accept the 1958 Constitution (the presidential election of 1965 was decisive in this respect) and it was not until later that it did so wholeheartedly. The cohabitation initiated in 1986 also had the merit of persuading politicians as a body to support the central importance of the Constitution despite the disagreements between their respective parties. 'The Constitution, the whole Constitution, and nothing but the Constitution' became the new leitmotif. By 1998, with France in her third period of cohabitation in little more than a decade, the former institutional curiosity had become a familiar, and widely accepted, feature of the French political landscape. The new support for constitutionalism was safeguarded further by the establishment of the Constitutional Council, which now effectively guarantees respect for the fundamental law. The Council is not simply an adjudicatory instrument: despite fleeting disagreements over particular issues, it has also become the most effective instrument of the general consensus that now presides over respect for the Constitution. One reason why the constitutional weaknesses of France could so often be laid at the door of the deep political and social divisions in the country was that, in the absence of some body capable of controlling those conflicts, they could so easily be exacerbated and get out of hand.

Challenges to democracies: the post-war generation and after

The Western democracies are based upon a variety of beliefs, myths, and values. However, this does not mean that a complete consensus exists among them, or that they are not subject to criticisms and even attacks that put them at risk. As the European democracies developed after the First World War, their internal fragility in the face of economic crises and political and social dissensus was palpable. For the generation after 1945, on the other hand, the chief threat to democracy in Western Europe appeared to be the external one of Soviet Communism, which the Second World War had vastly strengthened. The Soviet Union destroyed one functioning democratic regime, in Czechoslovakia, later demonstrating there, as well as in Hungary, East Germany, and Poland its readiness to crush opposition to the Communist system in blood. Soviet ideology preached that its system was superior to that of the West and destined to supersede it. And whether or not the West was ever really in immediate danger from a Soviet invasion, the troops massed along the Warsaw Pact's western frontiers lent credence to those who argued that it was. Moreover, in both France and Italy the Soviet Union was supported by powerful Communist parties, commanding up to a quarter of the vote and (at least initially) unstinting in their praise of 'really existing socialism'. In 1948 it did not appear a foregone conclusion that Rome or Paris would not go the way of Prague.

That did not happen, for many reasons: Soviet caution, the absence of anything approaching a pro-Soviet majority in the Western countries, the rapid construction of a Western military alliance, and the American money that helped rebuild Western European economies and subsidized anti-Communist parties and unions. For some, the Soviet challenge was a useful one: right-wing parties—Christian Democrats in West Germany and Italy, Gaullists and 'moderates' in France—thrived on it. More generally, common opposition to Communism actually helped to reinforce the legitimacy of democratic institutions, especially the new regime of West Germany, which needed it. Certainly the Western democracies in the post-war generation seemed increasingly confident (with some exceptions, notably France in the throes of colonial wars), protected from without by the American military umbrella and stabilized from within by an economic boom of unprecedented length and buoyancy. But that changed from the mid-1960s on, for several reasons: the coming of age of a generation that took democratic freedoms and economic prosperity for granted, and sought to express other aspirations; the enormous damage done to the image of the dominant capitalist power, the United States, and by extension to Western democratic institutions, by the Vietnam war; and finally, from the early 1970s, the end of the post-war boom and the social tensions that resulted. These developments engendered challenges to democracies, both old and new, that brought into question their very bases, namely: participation, representation, the nation state, state intervention, and legitimacy.

Participation

Conflict arose on two fronts. On the one hand criticism was aimed at the opportunities for electoral participation, which were declared to be limited, arbitrary, and reductionist. It was suggested that formal electoral participation should be complemented by participation that was 'real': concrete participation in the work place and the home. In both the United States and Europe, 1968 marked the climax of these utopian ideas. In France, where the most spectacular outbreak took place, governments were left haunted for a decade by fears of another 'social explosion'. But on the whole the institutional impact of such ideas was very slight, and even their effect on party systems, for example through ecological parties, has so far been limited. The second wave of criticism concerning participation was even more radical, since it rejected the very principle of elections as the democratic method of participation. The electoral scene was denounced as a 'spectacle'—a theatre of illusions designed to render ineffective the collective, revolutionary potential of the people. Although this leftist critique was often tempered by more moderate criticism of the inadequacies of electoral participation, some of its consequences were more serious. For over a decade after 1968, left-wing terrorists in some countries, most notably Italy and West Germany, actively sought to injure and assassinate leading figures of the 'capitalist class'. Their view was that they would thereby provoke reactions that would reveal to the people the 'objectively fascist' nature of capitalist society. They did provoke ugly reactions—repression in West Germany, a bloody outbreak of right-wing terrorism in Italy—and they did, in conjunction with economic difficulties, have an impact on both societies. But they did not get their revolution, and virtually the only long-term consequences of these shock waves was a clearer understanding of the limitations of electoral participation (but also of its indispensability) and a new stimulus to thought on the subject of democracy and its machinery.

Representation

The problem of representation raises the eternal question of the relationship between representatives and the represented. All the Western democracies have rejected the idea of a definite mandate binding on representatives, but none has gone so far as to declare total autonomy for the representative. In practice, the theory of the representative's mandate is counterbalanced by the role played by the political parties, which devise programmes and adhere to them, even when the mandate that they receive is due to an electoral system in which a minority of the electorate can produce a majority in Parliament. The problem becomes particularly acute when party programmes are radicalized. This happened in Britain between the late 1960s and the early 1980s, following a period of greater consensus described as 'Butskellism' (from the names of Butler and Gaitskell, the one a Conservative and the other a Labour Chancellor of the Exchequer). Such electoral and political swings become a source of tension; once invested with power, governments tend all too quickly to forget that it is only by convention that they have been entrusted to represent the nation as a whole, even if, in reality, they do not represent an absolute majority of the electors (as has been the case in both Britain and France ever since the Second World War). The conventions connected with the principle of majority rule can only function correctly and maintain acceptance if they are reconciled with the principles of respect for the opposition and moderation in the exercise of power.

However, the problems of representation are not limited to the meaning and scope of the representative's mandate. They also concern the more or less tenuous links that are established between representatives and represented. Since the dawn of the age of democracy in Europe there has been no shortage of voices raised against the diversion of popular power into the hands of an oligarchy (Robert Michels) or a restricted élite (Pareto, Mosca). Those who denounce this corruption of the democratic principle stress the extent to which power is concentrated in a few hands (see Burnham's analyses of the power of 'organizers', and the denunciation of the 'Iron Triangle' by Wright Mills and the American left) and the insidious osmosis that operates between various élites—political, economic, military, and so on. Such criticisms are rebuffed by the defenders of liberal democracy (Robert Dahl and Raymond Aron, for example), who, while recognizing the existence of powerful ruling élites, accept its inevitability (whatever the regime) and emphasize that in a liberal democracy those élites are never monolithic. They constitute a 'polyarchy' composed of elements competing with one another within and between given political and economic sectors. This situation tends to preclude domination by a restricted group. All the same, even if we accept the realistic pessimism of that analysis (that perfect and total democracy does not and cannot exist), the conclusion to be drawn must vary from country to country: the structure of élite groups, their recruitment, and their circulation differ from one Western society to another. The rifts that can develop between the élites and the people, or within the élites themselves, can give rise to tensions which are sometimes resolved by violent confrontation when the élites do not manage to engineer agreements and procedures which, while recognizing the existence of these conflicts, make it possible to contain them peacefully. The American Civil War, the tensions within the Weimar Republic and in Italy and Austria between the wars, and the 1871 Commune in France are all examples of the temporary incapacity of political systems to create a consensus on what the rules of the game should be. In contrast, some systems, sometimes described as examples of 'consociational democracy' (Austria, Holland, and Belgium), have, despite numerous and profound cleavages, devised sophisticated institutional arrangements and developed consensus between the various élite groups in such a way as to promote stability and civic peace.

Nation, region, and identity

All Western democracies claim to correspond to nation states in some way. But the nation state is an untidy and relatively new notion. Neither Italy nor Germany resembled nation states before the second half of the nineteenth century. As the result of the two world wars she had initiated, Germany suffered the amputation of part of her territory and ultimately a partition into two States that lasted over 40 years. France's tradition of zealous State-builders (Louis XIV, Napoleon, de Gaulle) is in part a reaction to the difficulties encountered by a country with no natural frontiers to the east and the persistence of very strong local identities; as Eugen Weber points out, as late as the 1860s 'French was a foreign language for a substantial number of Frenchmen, including almost half the children who would reach adulthood in the last quarter of the century.'[3] In the British Isles, the names of the different concentric units of statehood—England, Great Britain, the United Kingdom of Great Britain and Northern Ireland—and the persistence of different legal dispositions within these units indicate a less than perfect congruence between the State and a single nation. Not surprisingly, then, the different identities that make up 'the nation' in Western democracies are organized with varying flexibility.

National identity, expressed however imperfectly in the nation state in Western Europe, has faced three main challenges in recent years. The first is regionalism. Since the Second World War, economic, social, and territorial changes have provoked disputes, often of a radical nature, over the way in which power is organized and the balance established between the central power and the periphery. Throughout Europe, and particularly in 'peripheral' regions such as Scotland, Corsica, the Basque country, Brittany—or Northern Ireland—the 1960s and 1970s saw the emergence and growth of regionalist movements that challenged the institutions of the State and advocated replacing them with a 'Europe of regions'.[4] West European democracies were obliged to respond to this challenge by introducing reforms designed to change the relationship of regions to central government while keeping them firmly within the State. For although secession can take place peacefully, as Slovakia proved in 1992, it is often not so: from the United States to Nigeria to former Yugoslavia, its implications have been unpredictable and potentially bloody. Hence the concern of democratic politicians to keep regionalist demands within the reach of their own political control, even at the price of concessions, whether financial, constitutional, or both.

A second challenge to national identity, at least in the eyes of some, has arisen from the large-scale immigration from Africa and Asia that gathered pace from the 1950s onwards, and the resulting presence of ethnic minorities in Western Europe. In terms of the constitution of an 'ethnic vote' on the US model, this has so far had little impact. However, immigration, particularly at a time of economic crisis, has been seized upon as an issue by the far Right. Whether or not they indulge in overt racism, extreme right-wing parties reject the idea of a multi-racial society and argue that the presence of substantial ethnic minorities—particularly if black or brown—constitutes a mortal threat to national identity that should be reversed: 'La France aux Français', in the simple slogan of the most successful of far-right-wing leaders, Jean-Marie Le Pen. Mainstream politicians, with a few notable exceptions (such as Enoch Powell in Britain), have sought to exclude from the political agenda an issue that they see as potentially explosive. Their success has been variable: slight in France, where legislation has, if anything, fuelled the issue; greater in Britain, but at the price of particularly tough controls on immigration, or in Germany, but at the price of the tightening of traditionally liberal asylum laws.

Finally, national identity has been challenged by the growing importance of European institutions and the question of how much national sovereignty should be surrendered to Brussels. That dilemma has been most divisive in the two older nation-states, France and Britain, each of which had (rather inconclusive) recourse to the referendum as a means of settling European issues in the 1970s. Europe became divisive for left-wing parties because it could be seen both as an opportunity and as a threat to their goals. But it was, if anything, more contentious for conservative parties, torn between national sentiment and the economic attractions of European integration. Hence the profound divisions opened up by Europe among British Conservatives and French Gaullists: for each of them, Europe has rendered complex and problematic the formerly straightforward role of 'party of the nation state'.

The crisis of the Welfare State

The 1970s and 1980s have seen the development of two types of diagnosis and criticism of the situation of contemporary States—criticisms and diagnoses that also reflect the evolution of ideologies. At first, the Welfare State was criticized less for its excessive interventionism than for the bureaucratic and financial consequences of its policies. The governments of the Western democracies, it was argued, were turning into modern dinosaurs, rendered impotent by their interventionist excesses. Richard Rose's expression 'government overload' makes the point that it was the Welfare State's methods of intervention that were being brought into question rather than its ultimate aims. Along with the economic crisis of the 1970s, however, a more ideological, 'neo-liberal' body of criticism developed, voiced initially by a handful of political experts and economists such as Friedrich von Hayek and Milton Friedman. At the heart of their critique of the Welfare State was the argument that the demands it placed on the State—for health care, pensions, social security, and other public services, as well as for public employees' pay—were potentially without limit. To meet such demands, governments were constantly tempted to tax, to borrow, to print more money and thus depreciate the currency, or all three. In economic terms, that led to permanent, built-in inflation and an ever-rising share of national product being spent by government. Culturally, the work ethic and the personal rewards that went with it were diminished by higher taxation, and ultimately replaced by a habit of dependency on the State for jobs, housing, or simply handouts. Politically, the Welfare State distracted from the essential functions of government—law and order, diplomacy, and defence. New Right thinkers argued that the State should confine itself largely to these spheres and limit its economic role to defending a sound currency through tight control of the money supply, leaving the free market and individual enterprise to do the rest. The need for greater monetary discipline was acknowledged by the late 1970s even by moderate left-wing governments (notably that of James Callaghan in the United Kingdom, under pressure from inflation and from the International Monetary Fund). And the New Right found vigorous political converts in Ronald Reagan and Margaret Thatcher, both of whom addressed themselves enthusiastically to the tasks of 'deregulation' and of 'rolling back the State' in the 1980s. The practical results never went as far as the theorists would have liked (this was true even in Chile, where the Pinochet regime enjoyed great political freedom of manœuvre through being able to imprison, torture, and murder opponents of its New Right policies). But all governments in Western democracies, whether of the Right or the Left (even Italy, the most prone to spiralling public spending) have at least halted and in many cases reversed the persistent rise of economic and social intervention on the part of the State.

But over and above the vicissitudes of various policies and divergent views on whether State intervention in the economy is good or harmful, the fundamental question is that of the relation between the public and the private sectors. Given that liberal democracy in principle seeks a balance between the autonomy of the individual and government action, the difficulty is to determine where the dividing line should come. Many have considered excessive social interventionism to indicate an insidious transformation of liberal democracy. Valéry Giscard d'Estaing even settled, rather simplistically, on a level of public expenditure based on the gross national product in excess of which a system becomes socialistically inclined or even socialist, without imagining that even his own government would overstep that magic threshold. Since, in reality, no general agreement is possible between extreme 'libertarians', liberals, interventionists, and socialists, the dividing line is bound to be fluctuating and contingent, and to result from choices determined by democratic logic. It is probably this need to choose moderate policies that gives liberal democracy its value, but at the same time it creates certain difficulties; for it involves the permanent challenge of establishing a balance between the public and the private spheres, individual autonomy and State intervention, *laissez-faire* and economic or social interventionism. Practically speaking, the survival of liberal democracy can only be assured at the price of this kind of adaptation and compromise. These are the issues at the heart of political debate, and it is they that constitute the government's objectives and the *raison d'être* of the system. If the equilibrium necessary for the 'common weal' cannot be achieved, the legitimacy not only of the government but possibly of the system itself will be in danger of being called into question by those whom economic 'progress' and radical *laissez-faire* policies have abandoned.

Legitimacy and violence

The legitimacy of the Western democracies rests upon their citizens' acceptance of the rules and procedures for selecting their representatives, choosing their governments, and determining public policies. That legitimacy can be assessed both positively and negatively: by the people's participation in the political process and by the absence of any violent, systematic, and general rejection of the rules of the game. The most remarkable consequences of this legitimacy are the consensus from which the institutions benefit, the acceptance of turn and turn about, together with a rejection of violence as an instrument of change. Nevertheless, the balance necessary to democracies is fragile, at the mercy of groups that have no hesitation in resorting to violence or that see revolution as the only true instrument of change. The collapse of the Weimar Republic and the Austrian Republic between the two wars demonstrates the fragility of democracies in the face of violence. During the 1970s and the early 1980s, the European democracies—particularly Italy and West Germany—suffered attacks on their political systems from minority but determined groups, whose aim was to destabilize the system and force it to adopt repressive policies that would justify a posteriori accusations of 'Fascist State'.

In other cases, violence, though less organized and less conceptualized, is regarded by certain groups or individuals as the ultimate (or simply the most effective) means of obtaining satisfaction for their demands: such cases are widely diverse, ranging from race riots in Britain to the violent action of small groups (regionalists, for example) or professions that resort to action in the streets when negotiation fails to bring them satisfaction (farmers and small shopkeepers in France). Sometimes political violence and straightforward criminality become intermingled and reinforce each other. In Northern Ireland, the Irish Republican Army (IRA) has enjoyed significant political support among the Catholic population, but has also used protection rackets and bank robberies to survive materially. In Italy, the Mafia and its variants grafted themselves onto the political system and then resisted the judges and policemen who sought to bring them to justice by systematic, and often successful, assassination attempts. Social and political violence can become quasi-endemic despite the opposition of the vast majority. During the 1970s, violent challenges to the functioning of democracy gave rise to a current of pessimism that was fuelled further by international tensions and the economic crisis: in 1974, for example, Michel Crozier, Samuel Huntington, and Joji Watanuti prepared a report for the Trilateral Commission which underlined the fragility and ungovernability of Western societies and suggested limiting 'the excesses of democracy' in order to prevent the Western liberal political system from collapsing. Yet, despite their call for a 'well-tempered' democracy, the years 1970 to 1980 were notable for the vigour displayed by the Western democracies and the appeal that they had in countries subjected to authoritarian regimes: not only Spain, Portugal, and Greece, but also Argentina, the Philippines, Chile, and even the Eastern bloc.

Indeed, the remarkable extension of democracy into the Mediterranean countries of Europe in the 1970s, and, even more spectacularly, into Eastern and Central Europe after the fall of the Berlin Wall in 1989, raised the question of democracy's claims to be a universal model. Such claims should be treated with caution for three reasons. In the first place, the attractions of democracy do not only stem from its intrinsic merits. They may be enhanced by the failure of alternative models, or by its more or less close connection to the prosperity of advanced capitalist countries, or even by the prospect of international loans or trading agreements linked to the existence of at least the forms of a liberal state: all incentives which, on their own, are an unreliable basis for the emergence of a democratic culture. Secondly, not all countries even try to adopt democratic institutions as they emerge from authoritarian regimes. Iran, for example, overthrew a dictator and then embraced an Islamic theocracy as a successor regime, deliberately rejecting the tainted liberal values of the West. In former Yugoslavia the claims of ethnicity proved tragically stronger than the values of consensus or tolerance. Thirdly, as recently as the 1930s democracy has amply demonstrated its own vulnerability, being thrown back to its heartlands of Western Europe (where several democratic states were the centres of deeply undemocratic colonial empires), North America, and Australasia. One reason for this vulnerability lies among the very virtues of democracy: the moderation of power, the limitations set upon State intervention, the right of free expression, the recognition of the opposition's right to criticize and to exercise power, and the affirmation of civil liberties are so many weapons that may be used against democracy by its opponents. One of the central dilemmas of a democratic state concerns the degree of tolerance to be accorded to the enemies of tolerance. The search for an answer, somewhere between abandoning all attempts to protect democratic institutions, and reducing democracy and political freedom themselves to empty husks in the name of a struggle against their adversaries, is fraught with risks.

Despite these caveats, and despite its more or less shameful inadequacies and failings, democracy retains intrinsic merits that help account for its attractions to peoples living under dictatorial or authoritarian regimes. Two are worth stressing. First, democracy is perfectible, or at least improvable. At least in principle, it offers its citizens the chance to struggle peaceably to establish alternatives without incurring the threat of the dawn raid, the prison camp, or the unannounced bullet in the back of the neck. Second, democracy's founding principles are at once fundamental and capable of adaptation in both space and time. The liberal democracies offer a range of options: a greater or lesser separation or collaboration between the powers (functional fragmentation), a greater or lesser geographical dispersion of authority (territorial fragmentation), a greater or lesser degree of State intervention in the economic and social spheres. So, even within the democratic family, significant disparities do exist: between the Scandinavian social democracies and the economic liberalism of the United States; between the differing concepts of liberty and equality in France and in Britain; between German federalism and the unitary states of Britain and France; and so on. In short, the respective histories, cultures, economies, choices, and constraints of the various Western societies have made it possible for them to present many different ways of resolving the fundamental question of how to provide 'government of the people by the people and for the people', the quest for what was known in the ancient world as 'good government'. It is in the hope of reaching a better understanding of that quest, and its groping progress, that we shall now embark upon our comparative study of the political systems of four democracies which, because of their histories, their size and political and economic importance, and their contributions to the construction of a democratic ideal, have played and continue to play a primary role: the United Kingdom, the Federal Republic of Germany, France, and Italy. The complexities and pitfalls of such an undertaking are numerous. For that reason, and so as not to make the student's first steps in comparative analysis any harder than necessary, the method of presentation has been kept deliberately simple. The first three chapters consider the origins and the manifestations of pluralism—the political parties, the interest groups, the cleavages between them, and the mechanisms of representation and popular expression. This will lead on to a study of State institutions: parliaments, governments, bureaucracies, and the role of the judiciary as a counterbalance in some democratic systems. Finally it is necessary to examine the most sustained attempt made by all four of the states considered here at institutional improvement, the construction of the European Union, both as a process and as a set of institutions that hold the potential, although currently no more than that, to be transformed into a federal state.

NOTES

1. G. Almond and S. Verba, *The Civic Culture: Political Attitudes and Democracy in Five Nations* (Princeton, NJ: Princeton University Press, 1963). On the concept of political culture, see Y. Schemeil, 'Les Cultures politiques', in J. Leca and M. Grawitz (eds.), *Traité de science politique*, iii (Paris: PUF, 1985), 394.
2. R. Dahl, *Political Opposition in Western Democracies* (New Haven, Conn.: Yale University Press, 1966), xvii.
3. E. Weber, *Peasants into Frenchmen* (London: Chatto and Windus, 1979), 67.
4. Y. Mény and V. Wright (eds.), *Centre–Periphery Relations in Western Europe* (London: Allen and Unwin, 1985). An original example of a 'central' region rebelling against perceived domination by the 'periphery' is offered by the successes of the Lega Lombarda in the early 1990s.

CHAPTER 1

Politics and Society: cleavages

Every political society is split by cleavages whose origins, nature, and magnitude vary enormously.[1] They may be economic or social, sectorial or territorial, ideological or symbolic, long-standing or recent, deeply rooted or transient. It is important, at the outset, to assess their impact upon the formation of political attitudes and behaviour. For, while the whole range of cleavages that separate groups within societies and set them against each other is to be found virtually everywhere, the cleavages themselves vary greatly in intensity, distribution, and manner of combination. The ethno-linguistic division is crucial in Belgium, important in Spain, but no more than residual in Italy; economic divisions are deeper in Europe than in the United States; the religious divide, though still significant, has lost its importance. The intensity of any division varies from one country to another;[2] and it may also vary through time within a given society, for divisions may become less important as a result of changes in circumstances and in the ability of either masses or élites to mobilize their strength. Thus, in Belgium, the linguistic and regional issue was for a long time obscured, then played down by the agreement between the Flemish and Walloon élites to set up a centralized francophone system. Increasing opposition to that system brought the initial consensus into question again and eventually led to new modes of power-sharing and power division, which have in turn been called into question. Similarly, the urban–rural divide, which Sidney Tarrow has described as 'the fundamental division in French society', was particularly acute until the Second World War but after that became progressively less so, as urbanization increased and the rural population declined. Then again, the territorial divisions between the various fractions of a German Empire built up from a plethora of tiny kingdoms and states virtually disappeared in the maelstrom of the Second World War and the displacement of populations that followed it. Today, only Bavaria still preserves its own particular socio-political structure, whose major manifestation is the dominance of the CSU. The five *Länder* making up the former German Democratic Republic have a type of specificity, but this consists largely in the absence of the political landmarks familiar elsewhere in the country. The proportion of voters declaring no religious belief (two-thirds, against one-fifth in the West), combined—paradoxically—with the strong lead of the Christian Democrats among the working class, are two major examples of this contrast.

The distribution of cleavages and the ways in which they combine also exhibit great variety. Sometimes factors dividing off a group compound one another, reinforcing the group's specific individuality. When a minority linguistic group is concentrated in a particular, well-defined area where it practises its own religion, belongs to a particular social class (of peasants, for example), and identifies with a specific political party which represents it, all the makings of confrontation come together. To return to the case of Belgium, the Flemish community is concentrated in one half of the territory, and is Catholic and politically to the right, while the Walloons are francophone, more secular, and politically inclined to the left. Given, furthermore, that wealth and power were for a long time concentrated in the hands of a francophone élite, it is easy to see why the Belgian crisis has been—and remains—so difficult to resolve. The situation of Austria in the period between the two wars, where two opposed blocs, one Catholic, the other Socialist, adopted entrenched attitudes, presents an even more dramatic example in that it led to civil war (as did, even more tragically, the situations in Spain in the 1930s, in Lebanon in the 1970s and 1980s, and in successor states to Yugoslavia and the USSR in the 1990s). Another model is that of Northern Ireland, where a strong military presence and a corresponding loss of basic civil liberties helped to limit strife between Catholics and Protestants to 'an acceptable level of violence' even before the ceasefires of 1994 and 1997. It proves easier to mediate between the divisions that cut through a society when cleavages are 'cross-cutting' rather than 'overlapping'. Such is often the case in contemporary Western societies. Cross-cutting cleavages tend to off-set one another: for example, some Catholics are rich, others poor, some bourgeois, others workers, some rural, others urban, some more conservative politically, others less so. Cross-cutting cleavages of this kind help to create solidarities between different groups and reduce the likelihood of the conflict and violence that are so common where cleavages overlap.

Another important factor is the ability of the various political systems to overcome cleavages by *ad hoc* institutional means. Liberal democracies already by definition offer some kind of answer to this problem; their acceptance of different groups and of pluralism, and their legitimization of opposition and limitation of majority power provide so many means of converting social conflicts into political ones that may be peacefully resolved. In countries where cleavages are particularly acute and overlapping, however, the problem is harder to resolve.

A few democracies (Belgium, Austria, The Netherlands, and Israel) have attempted to overcome such divisions by setting up mechanisms or institutional arrangements that Arendt Lijphart[3] has labelled 'consociational democracy'. Lijphart stresses that the survival of such systems depends upon four preconditions: a capacity to recognize the dangers of this kind of fragmentation; a genuine will to preserve the system; the existence of élites capable of rising above the divisions; and the possibility of introducing appropriate solutions to satisfy the demands of subcultures.

But in the last analysis, whatever the intensity and structure of the cleavages, the capacity of political systems to overcome them will depend upon three factors: first, an ability to register the existence of new cleavages as they appear—socio-economic changes, international changes, whether military, political, or economic, and the emergence of new values; secondly, the ability of the social groups concerned to accept compromises and not regard certain of their own distinctive features as 'non-negotiable'; and thirdly, the ability of the political élite groups to prepare and organize political solutions rather than exacerbate conflicts and passions.

The solutions arrived at and the balances achieved will produce significant new political configurations, with far-reaching consequences. These will affect the structure of the political scene and the party system, the degree of conflict occasioned by the establishment of a political agenda, the organization of policy-making processes (e.g. the distribution of functions in Belgium, Holland, and Israel, 'transformism' in Italy, and so on), and the composition and functioning of the bureaucracy (i.e. the degree to which it is politicized, and whether appointments are proportionally divided between the parties). Shortage of space precludes our considering all the dimensions and implications of all the divisions that affect political systems. But let us concentrate upon three whose impact upon political behaviour has often been underlined: the class cleavage, the religious cleavage, and territorial and ethnic divisions.

Class and politics

Socio-economic divisions may not always be the surest indicators of political behaviour, but they are the most common to all Western societies. Whatever the variations in religious or territorial cleavages between countries, rich and poor, employers, the self-employed, and salary- or wage-earners are found in all of them. Nevertheless, the relationship between class and political behaviour (like that between any cleavage and political behaviour) is a complex one, for four reasons. First, its salience varies across space and time. Class is the main determinant of political behaviour in some societies, but is overshadowed by religious or territorial cleavages in others. Secondly, class structures themselves vary widely. The industrial working class, typically identified by political sociologists as a large, cohesive sector of society with a strong inclination to support left-wing parties, constituted a majority of the working population for just a few decades (or rather longer in Britain, where the industrial revolution was practically complete by 1900). In the early part of this century its efforts to win political power were held back in many countries by the continued existence of a large, and often much more conservative, population of peasants. Since the 1970s, on the other hand, de-industrialization has taken its toll as core industries such as coal, steel, textiles, or shipbuilding have shed labour or closed altogether. Many children of blue-collar workers found that their parents' jobs no longer existed, and either found white-collar or professional work or sank into a precarious existence of insecure jobs or no jobs at all. Thirdly, class identity is always composed of two elements: an objective one, most readily defined by occupation, and a subjective one, an individual's *feeling* of belonging to a given class. The relationship between the two may vary considerably, especially where upward or downward social mobility has affected the individual concerned. Fourthly, the action of political parties may make a difference, with some seeking to mobilize sections of the electorate on a class basis while others base their appeal precisely on a claim to transcend social cleavages. All of these reasons help to explain that indicators of class are useful but imperfect predictors of political behaviour. Thus, for example, while most workers in most contexts have voted, as they might be expected to, for left-wing parties, working-class support has also benefited conservative parties, such as the British Tories, the French Gaullists, the German or Italian Christian Democrats, or even far-right-wing ones, like France's Front National.

The French case brings the class correlation, and its limits, into sharp relief, because the second, decisive round of French presidential elections is a great simplifier of political competition: it is held between just two candidates, normally one on the right and one on the left. As Table 1.1 shows, a majority of blue-collar workers always vote for the left-wing candidate, while right-wing candidates can always count on the majority of votes among peasants and the self-employed. These findings are consistent with more general opinion-poll data. A survey carried out in 1978 showed that, on a left–right spectrum, 87 per cent of workers were on the left, and 13 per cent on the right; 26 per cent of farmers were on the left, 74 per cent on the right; and so on.[4] Guy Michelat and Michel Simon[5] have attempted to improve the predictability of this correlation by constructing a more sophisticated social indicator: this is an 'indicator of the objective membership of the working class' and it is composed on the basis of the socio-professional groups not only of the subject questioned, but also of the father and (in the cases of married women who were not the heads of their households) the head of the household. The conclusions of Michelat and Simon were clear: left-wing tendencies increased in proportion to the number of working-class attributes exhibited by the voter. It is also clear from Table 1.1, however, that the intensity of socio-economic

Table 1.1. **Voting behaviour of selected social groups at second ballots of French presidential elections, 1981–1995**

	Left (Mitterrand 1981 and 1988, Jospin 1995)			Right (Giscard d'Estaing 1981, Chirac 1988 and 1995)		
	1981	1988	1995	1981	1988	1995
All voters	52	54	47	48	46	53
Blue-collar workers	65	74	57	35	26	43
Farmers, peasants	32	29	32	68	71	68
Self-employed	36	31	30	64	69	70
Senior managers	45	46	50	55	54	50
Regularly practising Catholics	30	33	29	70	67	71

Source: SOFRES post-election opinion polls.

correlations can vary between elections. Strong in the 1970s, they had been weaker in the 1960s, when de Gaulle attracted many working-class votes, and became weaker from the 1980s, as more people began to identify themselves as 'middle-class' (up from 31 per cent in 1982 to 38 per cent in 1994) and fewer as 'workers' (down from 33 per cent in 1982 to 28 per cent in 1994), and as more and more people came to regard the notions of Right and Left as out of date (up from 33 per cent in 1981 to 57 per cent in 1994). The issue is further complicated by the rise of the far Right in the 1980s, and the readiness of some working-class voters to support Le Pen or the Front National at first ballots, before switching to left-wing candidates at the run-off.[6] It is also clear that the nature of political 'supply' is capable of altering voting behaviour, at least in part. Many senior managers, for example, reacted with alarm to the left-wing discourse of the 1970s, which readily preached the need to break with capitalism, but with relative equanimity to left-wing candidates of the 1980s and 1990s who were more inclined to proclaim their 'realism', albeit a realism 'of the Left'. Even the apparently simple French data, in other words, show that while a link exists between class and political orientation it is rarely a straightforward one.

A correlation between class and political behaviour seems to be established more firmly in Britain than anywhere else. Most British observers have emphasized that social class constitutes the fundamentally explanatory variable—or even the only one. Pulzer,[7] for example, writes that all other forms of explanation for electoral behaviour are simply 'embellishment and detail'. In 1938, Harold Laski noted that 'a party is essentially what is implied in the economic interest of its supporters';[8] and whereas, up to the beginning of the twentieth century in Britain, 'we have had, for all effective purposes, a single party in control of the State',[9] the birth of the Labour Party produced a fundamental break, introducing opposition based on class. The close correlation between class membership and political behaviour was explained by the homogeneous and urban nature of British society and also by the absence of other powerful cleavages that might have counterbalanced or weakened class oppositions. Samuel Finer, for example, wrote in 1970 that 'Class is important—indeed central—in British politics only because nothing else is.'[10]

That class voting is important in Britain is widely agreed. But its slow decline, or even its imminent demise, have been regularly announced for the past three decades. In his classic *Modern British Politics*, first published in 1965, Samuel Beer emphasizes that, compared with the period between the wars, British politics in the 1950s were characterized by a decline in class antagonisms.[11] During the same period, Butler and Stokes's study[12] revealed what they called 'an ageing of the class alignment'. Among socially stable electors, the strong class link to political behaviour persisted. But among the socially mobile, it was much weaker; and the 1970s were the years when Labour's traditional blue-collar electorate first began to suffer serious erosion. These changes at the depths of British politics were compounded by developments at the surface which further weakened the certainty and straightforwardness of class correlations. New divisions such as Scottish and Welsh nationalism, and Britain's membership of the European Community, intruded into the political debate. And the ideological positions of the two big parties became radicalized, with the Conservative Party leaning increasingly to the right after Mrs Thatcher's elevation to the leadership in 1975, and Labour's left-wingers, inside and outside the trade union movement, increasingly challenging the more moderate leadership. That polarization opened new space at the centre of politics: moderate Labour leaders defected to form the new Social Democratic Party, which then formed a close alliance with the Liberals, making both the 1983 and (to a lesser extent) the 1987 elections into three-way contests in which the SDP–Liberal Alliance attracted voters from all social classes in roughly similar proportions. However, the complication of political 'supply' that resulted from the creation of the Alliance tended to support rather than reverse the hypothesis of a decline in class voting. The most striking fact in this regard about the elections of 1983 and 1987 was that the Conservative Party enjoyed a clear lead, not only among non-manual occupational groups, but also among skilled manual workers. Even in 1992, when two-party politics had to some extent been restored, Labour's lead over the Conservatives in the skilled manual group was only of 41 per cent to 38 per cent (compared to 50 to 30 per cent among the unskilled). There were thus grounds for supposing that Labour was doubly doomed: by the destruction of its industrial heartlands, and by the much-diminished loyalty of the workers who remained, especially the skilled groups who had done so much to found the party a century earlier. This was not, it is true, a universally shared view;[13] and in Britain as in France, analysts have sought to move beyond simple class categories, and have focused on distinct but related aspects of social location such as trade union membership, degree of dependence on public services, housing (owner-occupier versus council-rented), and type of employer (public versus private sector).[14] Moreover, the 1997 result confounded the more incautious and sociologically deterministic claims that Labour was due to decline as inexorably as the rustbelt industries on which it had traditionally relied. The extent to which the victory of 'New' Labour confirms or invalidates arguments about the decline of class voting is, however, less clear. Part of that victory consisted in reviving Labour support among workers. On the other hand, Labour's old bastions also saw the lowest turnout in the country, tipping below 60 per cent in some cases. And Labour also benefited from direct middle-class defections from the Conservatives, and an apparently high level of tactical voting among former Liberal Democrat supporters seeking to unseat incumbent Conservatives. In Britain as in France, then, while the correlation between class and voting is indisputable in a very broad sense, the long-term tendency is more ambiguous, with the evidence in favour of its decline being balanced by data supporting a hypothesis of rises as well as of falls between elections; in other words, of 'trendless fluctuation'.

The same term could be applied to West Germany. Here, the Social Democrats (SPD) won 39 per cent of the overall vote and 54 per cent of the working-class vote in 1965. Three decades later, in 1994, the figures in the West were almost identical: 38 per cent of the total, 56 per cent of the working-class vote. But in between, the SPD's audience among workers had risen as high as 70 per cent (in 1972) and dropped as low as 46 per cent, barely ahead of the Christian Democrats, in 1990. The German experience is, however, complicated by the new Eastern *Länder*, where working-class voters have tended to shun the left-wing parties since 1990 and have given an absolute majority of their votes to Christian Democrats. In Italy, the 'subcultures' which underpinned electoral support for the Communist Party (PCI), the Christian Democrats (DC), and the secular parties of the Centre over the post-war generation, were always one step removed from direct class–voting correlations: the DC had large pockets of working-class support in the South and the Veneto, while the PCI counted small entrepreneurs as well as workers among its supporters in its heartlands of North–Central Italy. The dramatic renewal of the party system in the three elections of 1992, 1994, and 1996 accelerated a decline in the 'subcultures' which had already been under way for some two decades, further weakening the correlation between class and voting. Thus, although the PCI's two successor parties retained an electoral lead among the working class in 1996, this did not amount to a majority: new formations, including the Northern League, Silvio Berlusconi's Forza Italia, and even the Alleanza Nazionale, successor party to the Fascists, were major contenders for the workers' vote.

But even where, as is still more frequently the case, left-wing parties have retained, at least over a long time-span, something like old levels of support among workers, that support still counts for less in absolute terms with each election. For all left-wing parties face the long-term problem of the numerical decline of the traditional working class, compounded, notably in France and Germany, by the fact that a significant number of the remaining working-class jobs are done by voteless immigrant workers. As the workers' support offers less and less guarantee of a victorious election, so left-wing parties have faced the strategic necessity of casting their nets wider. That has meant addressing new groups of voters who are more highly qualified than the traditional working-class audience, better educated, more attuned to the values of post-industrial society (such as sexual equality or quality of life issues)—and more receptive to right-wing arguments in favour of economic efficiency and low taxation. For parties steeped in working-class traditions or myths this has been a painful transition, managed with varying degrees of success. Its interest for the student of politics lies in its illustration of how, after a more or less prolonged time-lag, changes in cleavage structures produce changes to political 'supply'.

The first major party to confront head-on the problem of reaching out beyond the working-class base was the West German SPD in 1959. Up until then, the SPD had pursued the line of the Social Democrats of the Weimar Republic: it continued to proclaim itself the party of the working class and, with its Marxist-tinged ideology, its share of the West German vote remained around 30 per cent. It did not break through the one-third barrier until after the Bad Godesberg Conference held in 1959, when a new programme and strategy were declared. The SPD now dropped its claim to be the party of the working class and instead became 'the party of the people', proclaiming its acceptance of the fundamental principles of the market economy and putting them at the service of justice and democracy. This volte-face paid off: in the 1960s the SPD consistently gained ground, becoming the leading party of West Germany in 1972. Bad Godesberg did not end debate within the SPD over the competing, at times contradictory, claims of working-class and middle-class voters when it came to framing election platforms, especially during the long period of national opposition that opened in 1982. But the debate was set on a different footing, in which the working-class audience had a major, but not an exclusive, claim to the SPD's attention.

In Britain, Hugh Gaitskell attempted a comparable transformation of the Labour Party in 1959–60. One of his main goals was to signal acceptance of the market economy by abandoning Clause IV of the Labour Party constitution, the long-standing commitment to 'the common ownership of the means of production, distribution, and exchange'. Gaitskell failed. In 1983, fully 20 years after his death, wholesale nationalizations were a major part of Labour's manifesto, soon to become known as 'the longest suicide note in history'. It took the shock of four successive election defeats before a Labour leader once again attempted an ideological *aggiornamento* on a comparable scale. Tony Blair's modernization of the Labour Party from 1994, while showing some points of continuity with his predecessors Neil Kinnock and John Smith, went much further: 'New Labour' dropped Clause IV, loosened organizational and financial links with the trade unions, actively sought business support, and openly identified with formerly right-wing goals such as economic competitiveness, labour market flexibility, and low taxation. This was a metamorphosis that owed at least as much to the experience of America's Democrats or the Labour Parties of Australia and New Zealand as to European models. In electoral terms, its result was striking: a gain of 8.8 points between 1992 and 1997, and the first Labour government in 18 years sailing into office on a parliamentary majority of 179. But it left 'old Labour' supporters, and not only those identified with the Left, concerned that the price of victory might be the abandonment of their party's long-standing commitment to redistribution as the necessary means to ensure social justice.

The cases of Italy and France are complicated by the presence of (at least formerly) strong Communist parties alongside the Socialists. In Italy, the Socialist Party (PSI) had started the 1950s committed to alliance with the Communists, but 30 years later it had become a near-permanent partner in the majority coalition, sloughing off any residual commitment to wide-ranging reform in favour of the simpler goals of replacing the Christian Democrats as the major party of government (an aim of which the PSI leader Bettino Craxi's unusually long premiership appeared to offer an earnest) and of maintaining the *conventio ad excludendum* which had kept the Communists out. But the PSI was one of the major victims of the elections of 1992, 1994, and 1996, and Craxi had to flee to Tunisia to escape the attentions of the judges and the police. Of more importance was the Communist Party (PCI), which typically won some 25 to 35 per cent of the vote compared with 10 to 15 per cent for the PSI. Although the PCI remained faithful up to 1989 to its original self-definition, the party of the working class, its organization, concepts, and strategy underwent many adjustments. By playing down democratic centralism, it was able to distance itself from the Leninist concept of the party. As Pasquino has pointed out, the arrival on the scene of new strata of non-manual workers and the lowering of the voting age to 18 in 1975 helped to change the 'party culture': 'Sheltered by the broad shield of Gramsci, the Italian CP had, over the years, been diluting the impact of cultures that were alien to it; but in the mid-seventies, this phenomenon made itself felt even at the heart of the party.'[15]

The PCI distanced itself further from traditional Marxism-Leninism with the strategy of 'historic compromise', involving support for Christian Democratic governments, which it adopted in the mid-1970s. This was prompted by the realization that not only was it difficult for the Left as a whole to win a majority but even with a majority of 51 per cent, it would not be possible for it to govern, given the national and international conditions in which communist parties come to power. (The PCI had been traumatized by the unfortunate experiences of Chile.) The party justified its new strategy by denouncing the illusion that 'in the event of the parties and groups of the Left succeeding in winning 51% of the votes and of the parliamentary representation, that fact alone would guarantee the survival and action of any government representing that majority'.[16] The 'historic compromise' brought the Communists increased support and office at local and regional level, but failed (partly because of the murder of Aldo Moro, their trusted partner in the Christian Democratic Party, in 1978) to achieve the critical breakthrough into national government, and was abandoned in 1980.

That did not, however, stop further moves towards liberalization, culminating in the PCI's transformation into the PDS (Partito Democratico della Sinistra) in 1990. The changes were accelerated by the fall of East European Communism (which prompted formerly ruling Stalinist Communist parties in these countries to change their names and policies in a similar way). Its detachment from Soviet-style Communism, undertaken from the mid-1960s on, did not fully protect the PCI or its successor from the consequences of the Soviet collapse: a hard-line faction, Rifondazione Comunista, split off from the PDS, which dropped 10 per cent to 16.1 per cent of the vote in the 1992 parliamentary elections. But it is arguable that the damage would have been even greater without the shift. And in retrospect, the long process of adaptation can be seen to have paid off. The reward came in 1996, when the PDS became Italy's biggest party in terms of votes and seats (with 21 per cent of the vote and 172 seats in the Chamber of Deputies), the nucleus of the victorious Olive Tree coalition, and, finally, a party of government. Even here, though, victory had its price: for the policies that the PDS was obliged to support in government included cuts to public spending that were far from welcome to its traditional supporters, whether active or retired workers.

France's left-wing parties have arguably been the most reluctant to cut loose from a class base. Thus the case of France's Communist Party, the PCF, is more or less diametrically opposed to that of its Italian counterpart. Like the PCI, the PCF started the post-war period as the larger of the two main left-wing parties, with as much as a quarter of the vote. Faced by the erosion of their working-class base and of the Communist 'counter-society' that had grown up around it, as well as by the emergence of a dangerous rival (and ally) in François Mitterrand's Socialists, France's Communist leaders flirted only briefly with the flexible brand of 'Eurocommunism' pioneered by the PCI, before retreating, during the late 1970s, into the old certainties: loyalty to the Soviet Union, workerism, and attacks on the Socialists. The result was disastrous, with a drop in the vote from over 20 per cent in 1978 to under 10 per cent ten years later; but even when modernization was attempted by a new leader, Robert Hue, after 1994, it was fiercely resisted by traditionalists within the organization. France's Socialist Party, the PS, has also been reluctant to shed an attachment to the working class which has often made up in ideology (in a residual commitment to Marxism) what it lacked in solid electoral or organizational support. Unlike their British, Italian, and German counterparts, the French Socialists were the main party in government during the 1980s, and as such took a series of decisions which destroyed the jobs and damaged the living standards of many French workers. Despite some rather hesitant attempts at modernization (for example, at Toulouse in 1985), no party congress was prepared to justify or underpin these policies by proceeding to an ideological repositioning in favour of the market. Indeed, as François Mitterrand's second presidential term drew to its close, party activists reacted strongly against the compromises of government, most notably at the congress held in 1994 at Liévin, a historic scene of past working-class struggles. Thus when the PS returned, earlier than expected, to government in 1997, it still bore a series of promises over traditional working-class issues—jobs, wages, and working conditions—which it would have difficulty in keeping.

The French experience should be set in the context of a globalized economy, in which the much enhanced mobility of capital has greatly reduced the bargaining power of labour. This context makes the choices available to left-wing parties in the face of the numerical decline of the working-class electorate doubly difficult. Modernizers run the risk of relegating the improvement of working-class conditions within and outside the workplace to the status of a marginal issue, thereby creating a section of voters without a real stake in the outcome of elections, and so ever more disposed to abstain. The danger of the French example, on the other hand, is that the raising of expectations in the hope of keeping faith is followed by too-frequent disappointments, creating a more active 'anti-system' vote: during the early 1990s, the place of France's premier working-class party was taken, albeit briefly, by Jean-Marie Le Pen's Front National. If these scenarios appear too pessimistic, the balance of probability nevertheless points towards a further loosening of the ties between left-wing parties and the working class that long represented one of the key features of the political sociology of Western Europe.

Religion and politics

As Alain Lancelot points out, 'in nearly all countries, religion and class are the most discriminatory of variables'.[17] It may seem a paradoxical observation to make at a time when Christian religious practice is on the wane everywhere in the Western world, whether the branch of Christianity is Catholic, Anglican, Lutheran, or Calvinist. Yet the influence of religion endures, as if the values connected with it persisted and were directing political behaviour despite the decline of religious practice and the weakening of institutional allegiances. A comparison between the various European democracies and the place held within each by one or several religions will help us to grasp the variations that may exist in the relations between religion and politics. In a study of these relations, there are three major elements to consider:

- the relations of Churches to the State,
- the relations of Churches to society,
- the relations of religious values to political values.

Church and State

The relations between Churches and the State cover a wide spectrum that ranges from the principle of total separation to quasi-identification between a dominant Church and the State apparatus. However, examples of these two extremes, which were still to be found in an almost pure form during the nineteenth and even the early twentieth centuries, have today given way to much more fluid situations which vary relatively little from one State to another. Two countries are marked by the tradition of a dominant religion: Italy and Britain. In Italy, that domination has been at once sociological, institutional, and political, whereas, in Britain, the Church of England's official status gave it a pre-eminence that has slowly been eroded in practice by the relative progress made by Catholicism, evangelical Protestant churches, and even Islam. The privileged position and national character of the Church of England explain how it was that, in the nineteenth century and even the early years of the twentieth, it looked as if it was one of the pillars of the political and constitutional system. (The abdication of Edward VIII in 1936 was the last and most spectacular manifestation of its influence.) The Church of England was so closely identified with the values of the ruling class that it was described as 'the Tory Party at prayer'. This is no longer quite the case: the long period of Tory government between 1979 and 1997 was punctuated by regular quarrels between the Anglican Church, which found the government's economic policies inhumane, and the Conservative Party, which considered that the Church was meddling in politics at the expense of its proper job, the cure of souls. The constitutional pre-eminence of the Church of England is largely symbolic. Both of its archbishops and twenty-four of its bishops (and no *ex officio* representatives of other religions) sit in the House of Lords, but play a strictly non-partisan role in debates and votes. The monarch is still the head of the Church of England (although the heir to the throne has publicly stated his reservations about such a role). Within the wider nation, the Church of England has suffered grievously from a general collapse in Christian practice, probably more so than its Nonconformist or Catholic rivals; and the fastest-growing faith in the country is probably Islam. The juridical pre-eminence of the Anglican Church, in other words, accommodates a full acceptance of religious pluralism, if not quite of religious equality.

Although religious influence is declining in Italy too, the history of the Catholic Church, its geographical placing, and its monopoly (95 per cent of Italians belong to the Catholic Church) all contribute to its predominant position. Its relations with the modern Italian State were initially fraught with conflict, however. From 1870, when Garibaldi's men took Rome, the centre of Christianity, and proceeded to make it the capital of the Kingdom of Italy, thereby completing the unification of the peninsula, until the Lateran Pact of 1929, the Church and the Catholics deliberately organized themselves outside, and even in opposition to, the liberal State. The Catholic world set itself up as a self-sufficient alternative power and was more concerned to bend the State to its will than to become an integral part of its structures. When the Fascist regime offered the Church a privileged status and considerable financial assistance, it neutralized a potential adversary, allowing it to develop within its own autonomous sphere. In 1947, when the Italian Constitution was drawn up, its creators sought to reconcile, on the one hand, the tradition of separation between the Church and the State desired by the fathers of Italian unity (Cavour: 'a free Church within a free State') and, on the other, the situation inherited from the Concordat established by Mussolini.

Hence the formulation of Article 7 of the Constitution, which declares that 'the State and the Catholic Church, each within its own order, are both independent and sovereign' but which goes on to make it clear that 'their relations are governed by the Lateran Pact'. The fact that many moves made by the Church were badly out of step with the evolution of Italian society gave rise to many tensions during the 1970s and 1980s until 1984 when the Vatican and the Italian government came to an agreement. The *aggiornamento* (bringing-up-to-date) of the Concordat was particularly concerned with religious teaching in schools (which now became optional), the financing of the Church by the State (which was now replaced by voluntary funding paid for by the people, as in Germany), and religious works (which now fell more or less under the common domain of Italian law). In short, despite certain historical and geographical links, relations between the Italian State and the Catholic Church have weakened. The crucifix continues to be displayed in public places (schools, administrative offices, law courts, etc.), but the State has secularized itself in recognition of the increasingly marked transformation of Italian society.

In Germany, relations between Church and State are characterized both by religious pluralism and by the change in the balance of faiths that took place after the Second World War. Before the war, the majority of the population were Protestant, but they were particularly affected by the partition of Germany, for most of the Catholics were concentrated in the south and west of the country. In West Germany, the Catholics thus moved from the position of a defensive minority to one of parity with the Protestants. A sense of oppression, or at least of being pushed aside has, nevertheless, helped to shape the behaviour of the Catholic Church: under the Empire and during the Weimar Republic, the Catholic Party was concerned to protect Catholics, as was the Vatican, particularly during the period of the Third Reich. The Concordat that the Church signed with Hitler in 1933 and its attitude towards the Nazis were both expressions of the particular kind of relationship that obtained, obscuring the need to defend more universal values and individuals who fell outside its authority. Alfred Grosser puts the point emphatically:

One cannot fail to be struck by the persistence of one particular theme in [Church] documents: it is first and foremost the Catholics who must be defended . . . And while, in Germany, the Church defended the Catholics first and foremost, one of the Pope's major preoccupations certainly also appears to have been the protection of the German Catholics.[18]

The Catholics were not alone in compromising themselves with Hitler. One section of Protestants supported him and tried to set up a Reich Church that would unite the twenty-nine German Protestant Churches. They were opposed by the members of the Confessional Church, born in 1934, which was hostile to Nazism. It was the activists in this movement who in 1945 reorganized the German Evangelical Church (EKD), which was no longer to stand for 'a specifically German type of Protestantism, but would be a German branch of world Protestantism'.[19] The painful Nazi experience had shown that the Christians had committed 'sins of omission' even if not 'sins of commission'. The better balance that now obtained between the religious forces was to make it possible to bring Catholics and Protestants closer together and to form an organization that included both groups, the CDU.

An important juridical and financial connection still exists between the State and the members of the Churches. As laid down by the Concordat, the government levies an ecclesiastical tax (the *Kirchensteuer*) amounting to between 8 and 10 per cent (depending on the region) of the taxes paid by citizens who have not explicitly declared their intention to leave the Church to which they have been attached. Despite the fact that regular church attendance is low among Catholics and extremely low among Protestants, almost 90 per cent of West German citizens continued to pay the Church Tax in the 1980s, thereby assuring the Churches in West Germany of substantial funds, more substantial than those received by the Churches of any other country apart from America. In the overwhelmingly Protestant East, the Church had had an ambiguous relationship of tightly monitored autonomy with the Communist authorities, but many Protestant pastors were active in the protest movements of the 1980s. After the breaching of the Berlin Wall in November 1989, such protest movements were less than enthusiastic about the option of early unification increasingly espoused by CDU Chancellor Helmut Kohl. But in the first all-German elections of the post-war era, in December 1990, the CDU easily won high levels of support in the East.

In France, relations between the Church and the Republic still bear the stigmata of past conflicts. Under the *ancien régime*, France's Catholic Church enjoyed a considerable freedom from intervention from Rome (the word 'Gallican' expresses this independence), but had an almost symbiotic relationship with the monarchy. After the Revolution, this status was not accepted by republican regimes, and relations were correspondingly tense: so much so that in 1905 the republican government terminated Napoleon's Concordat with the Vatican and formally separated the Church and the State. Twentieth-century French history has thus been marked even more than previously by pro-clerical and anti-clerical tensions, particularly since the religious divide coincided almost exactly with the Right–Left one. The First World War and the great movement of national unity prompted by the conflict with Germany made it possible for tensions to diminish and for less antagonistic relations to be established both with the Church of France and with Rome. However, the period between 1930 and 1960 was poisoned by a number of episodes: the fears that the Popular Front inspired among Catholics; reinforcement of the Left's mistrust by the support that most of the French bishops and clergy gave to the Pétain regime between 1940 and 1944; and recurrent clashes over the question of private schools (90 per cent of which are Catholic) have continued to the present day. Hostile crowds of up to a million greeted, and halted, the Socialist government's attempts to bring Church schools under tighter State control (in return for subsidies) in 1984; ten years later the secular lobby was galvanized into almost equally enormous demonstrations by the conservative Balladur government's attempts to supply more money to Catholic establishments. In other words, the almost uninterrupted decline in French religious practice since 1945 has not sufficed to defuse the issue.

Church and society

Political behaviour is also affected by the relations between Churches and society. Sometimes the Churches deliberately limit themselves to a strictly religious role, avoiding any competition with the State; sometimes, on the other hand, they establish an outright countersociety, reacting against the interventions of a State whose legitimacy or policies they challenge. Although counter-societies of this kind tend to be growing weaker today, they still manage to create subcultures whose impact on the vote may be crucial.

In Britain, nineteenth-century politics were periodically shaken by conflicts over Church–State relations which have left distinct, albeit slight traces. The ranks of the Liberal Party, and later of the Labour Party, were swollen by Nonconformists and some

Catholics who considered the privileged position of the Anglican Church as a major injustice, and identified the Conservative Party as the main defender of that privilege. In a country where, in the early part of the nineteenth century, crucial avenues of professional advancement such as the universities of Oxford and Cambridge were only open to Anglicans, religious distinctions naturally found expression in differentiated social institutions and networks. The importance of these diminished after the end of open discrimination against non-Anglicans later in the century. This is less true in the 'peripheral' parts of the United Kingdom than it is in England. In both Wales and Scotland, distinct religious identities (no established church and a high proportion of Nonconformists in Wales; an established Presbyterian Church in Scotland) have been linked to distinct national identities, so that it is hard to isolate the specifically religious dimensions of 'Welshness' or 'Scottishness' from their other aspects, such as Scotland's separate judicial and educational systems. However, the most striking case of religious divisions having a deep, institutionalized political effect is that of the Protestant/ Catholic divide in Northern Ireland. Even here, it is legitimate to wonder whether religion determines political divisions, or whether it serves as a token of even deeper social, economic, or even tribal sentiments, fuelled by ancestral memories of famine and oppression (for Catholics, Nationalists, or Republicans), and by fear of being ruled by Dublin, and thereby Rome (for Protestants or Loyalists). In England, on the other hand, the influence of religion makes itself felt more through a transfer of values into the political world than through the persistence of any network of ecclesiastical institutions. If Tony Blair, as Labour Party leader, has more than once gone out of his way to stress the Christian basis of his political values, it is partly because he believes that this will be well received by voters, including those who never set foot in a church.

France, Italy, and Germany, in contrast, do possess a tight network of institutions (mostly created by the Catholic Church), which provide a framework for the faithful and a basis for the party that represents their views, whatever their class. In such contexts, membership of the same faith may become an element which overrides all social differences, ignores economic disparities, and cements the organization of the entire group. This phenomenon is more highly organized within the Catholic Church on account of its desire to convey and put to work an influential message that relates to every aspect of both private and social life: education and sexual life obviously enough, but economic and social doctrines too. Furthermore, the existence of a hierarchy determined to maintain respect for the faith and its dogma leads to inflexibility and conflicts within the State. The anti-clericalism provoked by this kind of interventionism, both doctrinal and material, reinforces the embattled mentality of the Church and isolates Catholics from the rest of society. Such was the situation of Catholics in Germany in particular at the time of Bismarck's *Kulturkampf* policies, of French Catholics in the 1905 to 1920 period, and of Italian Catholics from 1870 to 1929 (throughout which period the Roman nobility even went so far as to wear mourning). The subculture produced by this isolation manifested itself in the proliferation of educational, social, and mutual-help institutions, and it is no accident that they are most numerous in the countries that have a strong Catholic tradition, such as France, Italy, Germany, Spain, and Belgium. The hold that these secular institutions controlled by the Churches maintained over all sectors of economic and social life fostered the tendency to consider every question in clerical or anti-clerical terms and to bypass class distinctions in the name of common membership of the same religion. The most striking example of the influence of this Catholic subculture on political behaviour is presented by the divisions relating to educational matters. For a long time, the problem of private schooling provided the cement that bonded the Catholics together—regardless of class—and it was this that constituted the most acute source of division between the political parties. Up until the late 1960s, this situation turned the Christian parties into conglomerations of Church members whose principal point in common was the faith that they shared. The Christian parties were expected to protect the doctrine and interests of the Churches and Christians were expected to vote for *their* party.

In France, the networks established by the Catholic Church were every bit as dense and active as those in Italy and Germany. Not only did the Church set up Catholic Action movements particularly among the young (young Catholic farmers, students, and workers) but up until the 1950s it managed to maintain its influence in many of its traditional sectors of intervention (for instance, the health and social sectors and, even more, in education); furthermore, it penetrated a number of sectors that were neglected by the State (agricultural training, for example). In the 1950s, the influence of the social framework provided by Catholicism was at its peak: everywhere, the Church controlled schools, hospitals, youth hostels, sporting and cultural associations, and even cinemas, quite apart from engaging in its more specifically ecclesiastical works. With the decline of the influence of Christianity and of religious vocational work, the importance of this network has diminished considerably. Nevertheless, the French Church has made a significant impact through its influence on the training of the ruling élites in many sectors of society, particularly among employers and in the trade unions.

However, instances of Catholic activism in support of a party have been becoming more circumspect and less common. In the first place, the Church found itself bound to recognize that Catholics no longer, as in the past, identified themselves as belonging to one *particular* party, even if it was that of the Christian Democrats. Their party loyalties were now spread more widely. Secondly, it was noticed throughout the dioceses, in the course of legislative campaigns (in 1972 in Germany) and referendums (on divorce and abortion, in Italy), that Catholic voters no longer accepted the precepts of the Church so unquestioningly or, at least, had no desire to impose upon society as a whole the beliefs and convictions of a small fraction of it, even if they happened to belong to that fraction. In the third place, it is always risky for the Church to declare undivided support for one particular political movement. Defeat for that party turns into defeat for the Church itself, as indeed proved the case for the Italian Catholic Church, which had totally committed itself to the campaign to repeal the law on divorce. Under the influence of currents of opinion extremely close to the Church and of the traditionalist Catholic movements (Communione e Liberazione, for example), the Christian Democratic Party took a risk in venturing into this campaign and was deeply traumatized by its defeat. The referendum showed that the Catholics were no longer in a position to impose their own choices and that some of the Christian Democrat electors were voting for the party more through conservatism and anti-Communism than through their religious faith. This set-back led, on the rebound, to a crisis in the relationship between the Church and the Christian Democrats that undermined relations that had remained stable for thirty years, despite all the changes in Italian society.

Religious values—social values

'Can we speak,' asks Alain Lancelot, 'of a decline in the "religious vote" as we speak of the decline in the "class vote"?'.[20] Any assessment of the continued intensity of political behaviour that is linked to a particular social cleavage has two distinct components: the power of the cleavage, where it is clearly present, to affect voting; and the extent to which the cleavage itself remains present within society (as measured by the number of blue-collar workers, or the number of regular churchgoers). On the first of these two questions, the answer as far as religion is concerned seems clear: despite the greater tolerance shown by churches to a range of political choices, religion has lost relatively little of its power to sway the vote of the faithful. Table 1.1 (p. 20) illustrates the French case perfectly: at the second rounds of presidential elections, right-wing candidates pick up at least twice as many votes from regularly practising Catholics as their left-wing opponents. In Britain the Conservatives, despite their quarrels with the established Church, still attracted the votes of 61 per cent of regularly practising Anglicans in 1992, compared with just 9 per cent for Labour; Nonconformists still vote disproportionately for the Liberal Democrats and Labour, and Catholics (a disadvantaged minority in Britain since the Reformation) for Labour. Among West Germans with strong church ties, 78 per cent of Catholics and 54 per cent of Protestants voted for the CDU–CSU in 1983.[21]

At the same time, however, the answer to the second half of Lancelot's question is equally clear and points in the opposite direction. For despite the often close relations maintained by the Churches and their respective States, despite the close-knit social framework organized by the Catholic Church, despite even the presence of 'charismatic' or revivalist movements within the churches, the most striking phenomenon of the past half-century or so has been the decline in church attendance throughout most of Western Europe (with Northern and Southern Ireland, for the moment, something of an exception). This has been of the order of from 40 to 50 per cent in the post-war years to 10 to 20 per cent in the 1990s: a more pronounced decline than the numerical shrinkage of the working class.

How, then, does this combination of plummeting religious practice with continued strong political loyalties among those who remain religious affect overall patterns of voting? Ronald Inglehart based his reply to that question on the example provided by the Netherlands, where a general weakening of religious practice preceded the dramatic decline of the religious vote in the 1970s.[22] His conclusion was that there is a more or less long delay between the decline of religious practice and any electoral expression of this detachment. That is a plausible interpretation, but other studies suggest the delay is more likely to be long than short. 'Catholic' Bavaria is still as dominated by the CSU as it was half a century ago, despite the thoroughgoing modernization it has undergone in the meantime. In France the geography of support for parties and candidates of the moderate Right has changed little since the post-war period, and even corresponds, with only a few discrepancies, to the map of the most Catholic parts of the country during the Revolution two centuries ago. Similarly, the heartlands of the PS continue to be in the traditionally anti-clerical south-west of France. To judge from these phenomena, it would appear that people's perceptions of real circumstances are often shaped by applying a virtually unchanging interpretative grid determined by a system of values or a cultural tradition so remote that it leaves hardly a trace and is barely remembered in any explicit terms.

Consequently, we may well wonder whether, despite the declining impact of Church institutions and personal Christian allegiances, Christian values have not become such an integral part of certain societies that they persist quite independently of the religious services and practices that expressed them in the past. The fact that the values preached by the Churches are recognized and accepted even by non-believers ensures that society remains affected by them even though religious practice has waned. Some social groups and regions maintain stable political modes of behaviour structured by Christian or conservative political parties despite the decline of the Churches. Or, to put it another way, as Gordon Smith does, if religion used to be a means of identifying with the dominant values of society, even now it still plays an important role as a constituent element in a wider social order: 'but the direction of influence is reversed: religion no longer determined political loyalties, the political loyalty was still supported by a religious value'.[23] Again, however, the question is for how long. For there are signs that, once they cease to be underpinned by regular religious practice, the Right's Christian bastions prove as open to challenge as the Left's working-class ones. Mitterrand and his Socialists made some of their biggest gains during the 1980s in the Catholic east and west of France. Alsace, formerly a bastion of the mainstream right, became a stronghold of the irreligious Front National from 1988 onwards. Italy's Christian Democrats were practically wiped out of the White Veneto and Lombardy by the Northern League in 1992, as soon as the Soviet threat that backed up their anti-communist appeal had disappeared; by 1994 they had collapsed and split into four different parties; in 1996, fewer than a quarter of Italy's practising Catholics voted for these successor parties. Other examples of the weakening religious cleavage work just as well, but in the opposite direction. Jacques Chirac earned his political spurs winning a foothold for the Gaullist Right in Corrèze, hitherto an anticlerical stronghold of the Left. Half a century of communism taught many East Germans to be irreligious, but that did not stop them from voting for the CDU after unification.

The links between present-day voting and what often appear as the myths, rituals, prejudices, and antagonisms of bygone ages are nowhere as striking as where religious cleavages are concerned. Yet the figures seem to indicate that *over the long term*, the force of habit is no substitute for regular churchgoing in fostering the continuation of political traditions from one generation to the next. If this is true, and if the churches continue to empty, then what is now a major social variable will eventually be relegated to a cleavage of merely residual importance in the determination of political behaviour.

Territory and politics

In a study on the evolution of the concept of territory, Gottman[24] notes that territory in itself is a neutral concept but that it acquires political significance through the interpretation and values that people ascribe to it (for a variety of reasons—ethnic, historical, linguistic, etc.). A territory may become the foundation of a society whose modes of organization and whose language, religion, and types of behaviour define its identity both positively and negatively (in contrast to neighbouring societies). It may thus become the symbol or indeed the very expression of an identity that is reinforced by all the mechanisms of political representation and also of symbolic representation. The importance of a territory for its people has always been great, for to organize a territory implies organizing power, given concrete form by structures, equipment, and frontiers. The myth of the frontier, and then of the 'New Frontier' in the United States, and all the squabbles and wars in Continental Europe testify to the power of the notion of territory, as do the survival of parishes and the resurgence of regionalism.

In Europe, the nation state has emerged out of conglomerations of various societies, all heterogeneous by reason of race, language, or religion. The example *par excellence* is represented by France, the model of a successful empire that turned 'Peasants into Frenchmen', to borrow the title of a study by Eugen Weber; but this was only achieved after centuries of intermittent wars from the later Middle Ages onwards, which had slowly enabled France's kings to join a patchwork of feudal holdings under their rule. Britain and Austria have gone through terrible upheavals that resulted, on the one hand, in Irish independence, on the other in the fragmentation of the Hapsburg Empire. Germany and Italy were constructed in the nineteenth century from a plethora of states, kingdoms, and principalities, whose respective cultural and, in some cases, political imprint is sometimes detectable even today. Furthermore, in Europe, both the late nineteenth century and the period between the wars were poisoned by the problem of nationalities, a problem that returned with alarming speed and violence to the eastern part of the continent after the collapse of Communism in 1990. Today, the map of Western Europe essentially corresponds to a map of nationalities, but the problems have not all disappeared: the principle of nationality as the basis for the construction of a nation state contains the seeds of its own destruction. Within every nationality, it is always possible for a minority, however small, to claim its own autonomy or even independence, in the name of its specifically individual characteristics: the 250,000 inhabitants of Greenland, the 200,000 Corsicans, and the francophone inhabitants of the Jura region can claim to deserve the same rights as the Danes, the island of Malta, and the canton of Berne. Such claims are usually asserted on a territorial basis, as is borne out by the creation of Israel, by the conquests of Hitler, or, alternatively, by the failure of claims put forward by the Gypsies.

When a minority organized on a territorial basis sets out to win recognition for its rights or, more modestly, its individuality, several possible strategies are open to it: the inhabitants of a given territory can make sure that it is represented by an autonomous political party; alternatively, it can see to it that the national party is divided along regionalist lines; or else, finally, it can manifest its specific individuality through political behaviour that diverges from that of the nation as a whole, behaviour that some observers have suggested calling 'sectionalism'.

The minority parties

The most radical non-violent means for a minority to express its own identity lie in organizing specific representation for itself and rejecting integration into the national party systems. (Violent forms of 'exit' such as bombs or assassination campaigns will not be considered here.) That identity, manifested by a language, a culture, or customs peculiar to the minority (or, at the very least, a sense of the need to defend its own par-ticular characteristics by opposing the dominant culture) may be expressed politically through a party whose aspirations and ambitions are organized on an infranational territorial basis. The emergence and survival of such parties are connected on the one hand with the existence of homogeneous, territorially concentrated groups and, on the other, with the forms of 'access' that are allowed by the institutional system. Thus, in West Germany, the destruction of local solidarities and the dispersion of local popula-tions as a result of the Second World War, and the absence of non-German-speaking groups made it possible for a homogeneous German society to emerge, a society in which nationalist parties seem pointless. (There is, it is true, a small Danish minority located along the Danish–German frontier, but its protection is assured by a treaty between the two bordering States.) In contrast, the 'peripheral' regions of France, Italy, and Britain, at least those with the most marked identities, have sometimes organized themselves politically around regional parties. Situations where the political parties are organized on a purely nationalist basis are potentially destructive to a State, as can be seen from the example of the Austrian Empire from the end of the nineteenth century onward, or that of Britain faced with the secession of Ireland. To a lesser degree, the very existence of political parties organized territorially constitutes a challenge to the Western representative systems. For in these systems—ideally—the parties are not supposed to represent specific interests of territories: such parties constitute dangerous competition for the political parties that are usually organized in relation to non-territorial cleavages.

Nationalist parties may of course position themselves either to the Left or to the Right on the political spectrum. For a long time, regionalist parties stood for conservat-ism and tradition and provided a means of expression for classes on the wane or other groups denied central power. The climax of that identification with right-wing values was reached in the Second World War, when many regionalist parties were willing to strike a pact with the Nazis.

But during the 1970s, the balance shifted to the Left or even the extreme Left, as regionalism rediscovered the voice of utopian socialism (as purveyed by Proudhon, for example) and teamed up with the ecologists and the advocates of self-management who emerged after 1968. Whether they incline to the Right or the Left, regionalist parties often tend to behave as if they held a hegemony, rallying—or attempting to rally—the entire local population to their banner. Two cases in point are the SVP (the German-speaking party of the Alto-Adige), which obtains over 60 per cent of the votes in its region, and the Unione Valdotana in the Valley of Aosta; and, in the period between the wars, to achieve a similar status was the ambition of Breton regionalists, who proclaimed that they were 'neither Red nor White, but Breton'. But not many regionalist parties succeed in seizing a dominant position in their 'own' territories. That is partly because non-territorial divisions (such as class and religion) usually tend to win out; and also because the regionalist parties have difficulty in reconciling their hegemonic pretensions with the persistent internal quarrels that tend to divide them.

A good illustration of these erratic movements is provided by the Scottish National Party (SNP), which in 1934 emerged from the fusion of two regionalist parties but in 1942 once more split, this time into the moderate devolutionists on the one hand, and those who favoured independence on the other; the latter took over the SNP. During the 1950s the SNP made little progress, but in the late 1960s it made a leap forwards, becoming (in terms of votes obtained) the second largest party in Scotland, in the 1974 elections. The size of the nationalist vote and the weakness of the Labour Party both encouraged the interests of the two organizations to converge, but that very strategy then helped to divide the SNP, which now oscillated between socialist options and a more moderate attitude. The failure of the devolution referendum of March 1979 and Labour's fall from power marked the beginning of a new period of decline: in the 1979 General Election the SNP won only 17.3 per cent of the Scottish vote, which produced two elected members of Parliament, and it slipped back into third place. This defeat was followed by an expulsion of 'leftists' from the party and further losses in the 1983 and 1987 elections. After the 1987 setback, the SNP returned to a more left-wing posture, and sought to woo traditional Labour supporters. The SNP's record since then has been more encouraging, thanks both to its own efforts and to outside circumstances. It acquired a young and able leader in Alex Salmond, who managed to stamp his authority on a normally fissiparous party. And it balanced attacks on Conservative government policy from the Left with repeated references to the central goal of independence (as a State of comparable size to Denmark) within Europe, in a manner that appeared both consistent and credible. It was helped by the fact that Scotland was ruled by a party which had won only a quarter of the votes north of the Border and only 10 out of 72 Scottish seats; by the insensitivity with which successive Conservative governments imposed unpopular policies devised in London on the unwilling Scots; and by the failure of the official opposition, Labour, to do much to stop it, after three successive election defeats. The direct benefit of this was no doubt limited: Salmond's SNP won 21.5 per cent of the Scottish vote in 1992 and just three parliamentary seats, and 23 per cent and six seats in 1997. More importantly, though, the capacity of the SNP to be taken seriously was one factor which led the Labour Party to include the promise of a Scottish Parliament in its 1992 and 1997 election manifestos. It was a promise on which Blair's Labour government moved rapidly after being elected. The referendum of 1997 on devolution was, unlike its predecessor of 1979, a resounding success for its supporters, with 74 per cent of voters favouring the creation of a Scottish parliament and 63 per cent agreeing to give it tax-raising powers. The SNP had campaigned for a Yes vote alongside Labour, but for diametrically opposed reasons: where the Blair government saw devolution as a means to contain demands for Scottish independence, the SNP saw a Scottish parliament as a forum in which to further them. While the issue of outright independence remained a very uncertain one, the new parliament appeared likely to guarantee the SNP against renewed marginalization in the immediate future.

The SNP's revival was more than simply an assertion of regional identity. It was fuelled not just by the argument that Scotland was being ruled by southerners who had little understanding or sympathy for Scotland's problems, but by claims that the country's wealth (in Scotland, notably North Sea oil) was being directed away from its people, and that with more and more national sovereignty being pooled in the EC in any case, independence for a small European country in the 1990s was a smaller, less risky step than it would have been a generation earlier. Some comparable claims were made by leaders of the most spectacular new expression of regionalist politics in the early 1990s, the Leagues of Italy. Leaders of the Leagues, and especially the federation of the Lega Lombarda and other groupings which came together as the Lega Nord in 1990, complained that the wealth created by Italy's productive, hard-working north was being squandered by a corrupt, indolent southern bureaucracy based in Rome. From a marginal position in Italian politics the Lega Nord achieved 8.4 per cent of the national vote (and over 20 per cent in Lombardy, and 17.3 per cent over the seven northern regions) in 1992, 8.6 per cent in 1994, and 10.1 per cent in 1996. In terms of its central aim, however, it had achieved rather little. The Lega Nord's brief experience of government in the Berlusconi coalition of 1994–6 was an unhappy one: the League was deeply out of tune with the pan-Italian chauvinism of its allies in the Alleanza Nazionale, and with the free-market preferences of Berlusconi's Forza Italia; its unpredictable leader, Umberto Bossi, rapidly became very critical of government policies; and its credentials as a clean, 'anti-system' party suffered damage. Out of office, Bossi organized demonstrations in favour of a 'Republic of Padania'; but direct action proved no more effective than participation in government at achieving the elusive goal of independence. The Lega Nord's main achievement may turn out to have been the making and the unmaking of the Berlusconi government.

At the end of the 1980s it made sense to describe territorial parties as almost a residual phenomenon, confined to a few small areas and having a limited impact on national politics. But the experiences of Scotland and northern Italy, as well as the success of the far right-wing Flemish Bloc in Belgium in 1991, all point to an increase in their importance from the early 1990s. The causes may be sought in reactions to the growing power of supra-national institutions in the EC: in the effects of the breaking wave of nationalism and micro-nationalism in post-Communist Eastern Europe; and in discontent with traditional parties at a time of world recession. The consequences will depend on economic recovery and on the success or failure of European governments in addressing the 'democratic deficit' that is the major political risk of greater European integration.

The federalization of national parties

The influence of territorial cleavages in politics may manifest itself in ways less radical than those offered by the nationalist parties but more effective than simply forming pressure groups within the parties. In between those two extremes, one comes across flexible solutions of a 'federal' nature in which minimal centralization is combined with a large measure of freedom of action for the various constituents of the group as a whole. Such is the case, for example, of the Liberal Democrats in the United Kingdom, who are organized as a federation of three separate and quasi-autonomous parties that correspond to the three territorial divisions of Britain (England, Wales, and Scotland; in Northern Ireland, they are effectively represented by the distinct Alliance Party); a comparable system applies to Britain's Green Party, though on a much smaller scale. This structure explains, in particular, how it was that the Liberal Party has proved particularly sympathetic to the claims of the nationalists.

But the most telling and important case is that of the CSU, the Bavarian Christian democratic party. Although we should remember that victory or defeat for the Christian Democrats depends upon the accumulated votes of the CDU and the CSU, the fact remains that the CSU is, for all that, a separate, autonomous party. Although the deputies of the CDU and the CSU admittedly sit together as a single parliamentary group, each party has its own organization. The autonomy of the CSU is reinforced by the fact that it truly does constitute a 'State party', being solidly anchored in Bavaria. The CSU has made one or two attempts to implant itself outside Bavaria (in 1957, for instance, it obtained two members of the Bundestag in Saarland); but these should be regarded more as manœuvres designed to intimidate the CDU than as a true nationwide strategy of expansion for the party. For, in principle, the CDU and the CSU each refrain from poaching in their partner's preserve. The two parties' agreements on cooperation include forming a single parliamentary group (or *fraktion*) in the Bundestag and fielding a common candidate for the post of Chancellor (an arrangement which in practice favours the CDU, but also gives the CSU a chance to negotiate and to apply pressure).

For decades, the CSU was identified not only with a single region, but with a particular right-wing ideology, and with a single leader, the impulsive, truculent, Franz-Josef Strauss. He was Christian Democrat candidate for Chancellor only once, in 1980, and undoubtedly put off some floating voters; indeed, many moderate CDU voters in the 1980s cast one of their two votes for the Liberal Party, which they saw as a counter-weight in the governing coalition to the CSU. Thereafter, two factors diminished the importance of the CSU in German politics; Strauss's death in 1988 blurred what had been an all-too-focused image, and unification two years later reduced the relative importance of Bavaria in the Federal Republic as a whole. It re-emerged, though, in the later 1990s, as Strauss's successor Edmond Stoiber sought to express the voice of conservative voters worried by the decline in religious values (the CSU displays cruci-fixes at its meetings) and by the threat to the Deutschmark posed by integration; his potential influence was increased after 1994 by the vulnerability of Chancellor Kohl's governing coalition, of which the CSU was a member.

Territorial specificities of political behaviour

The connection between territory and politics may also manifest itself in forms which, though less institutionalized, still have an important impact upon the way that institutions function. The determining character of one or another variable upon a particular territory sometimes imparts a homogeneous and stable political orientation to that territory. The influence of religion, the class vote, or a particular cultural tradition sometimes dictates the political and electoral configuration of a territory—and also of particular electoral constituencies. As Alain Lancelot points out, 'Behind all the statistics hides a society, with its network of interrelations, its currents of influence and its dominant ideas.'[25] When the political behaviour of a territory is particularly stable and homogeneous, the parties sometimes control veritable strongholds, whose survival may have nothing to do with the causes that created them. According to Klaus Von Beyme,[26] the electoral strongholds of the various parties tend to perpetuate themselves in two types of situation: '(1) in countries where the class conflict is more dominant than religious, language or regional differences (Great Britain); (2) in areas where traditional conflicts (the centre v. the periphery, or clericalism v. anti-clericalism) have been submerged in a subsequent class conflict in such a way as to survive in certain areas and provide party strongholds'.

Territorialized political behaviour and the persistence of its manifestations are to be found in all Western systems. In Britain, the Liberal Democrats are particularly strong in the 'Celtic fringe' of the kingdom, but the polling system makes it hard to convert this relative strength into electoral success (1997 was a partial exception to this rule, as tactical voting pushed the Liberal Democrat vote up where it counted most, allowing the party to double its parliamentary representation to 46 seats). But Labour also owes much of its strength to the periphery; indeed, one of the striking features of 1997 was the sparse distribution of Labour MPs across the English counties. This territorial skew makes Labour's pro-devolutionist stance, in the 1960s and 1970s and again in the 1990s, easier to understand: not only were nationalists seriously threatening Labour strongholds, but also demands for full independence have to be contained by Labour, because their fulfilment would deprive Labour of the means to win elections across

Great Britain. In Italy, the regional nature of political behaviour has been even more striking: the south and the Veneto were traditionally dominated by the Christian Democrats (in the Veneto, the Christian Democrat Party comes close to polling an absolute majority of votes), whereas the Italian Communist Party was the dominant party in central Italy, in the former states of the Holy See.

These 'sectionalist' phenomena (to borrow Jean Blondel's expression)[27] have certainly been persistent, but now, particularly under the impact of accelerating social change, they are beginning to be less so. For example, the strongholds of the French Communist Party around Paris were badly damaged in the 1980s, while those of the Radicals in the south-west have disappeared in all but a handful of localities. The electoral decline of Italy's Christian Democrats in the 1960s and 1970s was contained as long as they managed to hold up in their strongholds of the south and north-east. But when the 'White subculture' which had sustained these began to collapse in the late 1970s, the party's decline accelerated, leaving it increasingly vulnerable. The 1992 elections in Italy paradoxically saw the breakthrough of territorial parties—the Leagues—and the attenuation of a certain type of territorial politics, as Christian Democrats, Socialists, and Communists all saw support fall in their respective bastions.

There is thus an aspect to socio-political divisions that is both functional and territorial. On a territorial level, the centre–periphery division between on the one hand the élites and groups in power, on the other marginal territorial groups, must always be taken into account in the building of a nation state, and even in the oldest and most solidly constituted of States, the traces of that division have by no means disappeared. The functional dimension is apparent in the struggles involved in the share-out of economic resources and in clashes of values, ideologies, and religions. On the basis of this schema, Lipset and Rokkan[28] suggested an analysis of European political development that takes as its starting-point the great historical fractures that are the sources of the major divisions in European national societies and that, even today, still structure political life. Rokkan[29] emphasizes that those fractures were brought about by three different types of great revolution: the national revolution, the industrial revolution, and the international revolution.

The national revolution gave rise to the State–Church division and also to the division between the centre and the periphery (exemplified by conflicts between Rome and national Churches; and conflicts between central élites and ethno-linguistic peripheries). The industrial revolution of the nineteenth century constitutes the second critical phase in which industrial and urban interests on the one hand, and agricultural and rural ones on the other, came into opposition. The urban–rural divide was to dominate the political life of the nineteenth and early twentieth centuries. It was expressed chiefly through economic policies and conflicts between the partisans of Free Trade policies and those who supported protectionism through Customs and Duty tariffs. But the industrial revolution was also, and above all, to produce the division which set the holders of capital in opposition to the work-force, the division that even today determines one of the most fundamental and deeply anchored oppositions in political societies: namely, the Right–Left opposition.

Finally, Rokkan shows how the international revolution was to produce a division that essentially affected the workers, setting in opposition the partisans of an international revolutionary movement and those who opted for national integration, in other words, the communists from the socialists. Not all these splits have been sufficiently marked or enduring to constitute the basis of political formations which could be seen as embodying the effects of the divisions that had appeared in the course of these three major revolutions; for, as Lipset and Rokkan point out, while the political parties of the West may well express obvious or latent oppositions and divisions, their virtue is that they also make it possible to surmount some of them. In other words, the political parties that express and reinforce pre-existing cleavages are at the same time instruments through which negotiations may be held over conflicting demands, and compromise and agreement may be reached. Historical processes take different forms in different countries, depending on the capacity of élites to accept compromise and the persistence or eradication of ancient divisions. Each society is thus progressively structured by political parties which, even as they express certain divisions, repair others. The particularly paradoxical feature of political parties is that on the one hand they express oppositions and divisions (as the etymology of the word 'party' suggests), yet, on the other, they serve as an instrument of cohesion and co-operation, and also make it possible to bypass a certain number of antagonisms and divisions.

In order to understand how structural divides can be turned into party systems in this fashion, Lipset and Rokkan suggest that we should ponder upon the way in which protest movements and the representation of interests are expressed within each society, and they put forward the following hypothesis: the process of creating a party system depends upon crossing a number of 'thresholds', namely, legitimization (recognition—or not, as the case may be—of the right to criticism and opposition); incorporation (the inclusion or exclusion of individuals and groups in the choosing of representatives); representation (can new movements hope to win a place of their own or must they join pre-existing movements?); and the nature and extent of the power of the majority (are the powers of the majority that emerges from the poll limited, or can it implement major structural decisions that affect the system?).

The interest of Rokkan's 'genetic' analysis lies in the emphasis that it lays upon the interconnection between structural divides and political parties and the way in which it shows how, in the course of the historical process, the parties have helped to reinforce certain divisions and to attenuate others. In this way, it explains the persistence of political divisions that are anchored in oppositions that seem to be out of date and no longer of any relevance; indeed, in an argument now celebrated as the 'freezing hypothesis', Lipset and Rokkan argued that 'the party systems of the 1960s reflect, with few but significant exceptions, the cleavage structures of the 1920s'.[30]

Lipset and Rokkan's insights never did, however, add up to a total explanation of the political divisions expressed in voting behaviour, and their direct relevance has on the whole diminished with time. In previous pages we have seen that in the opinion of most observers, voting patterns characteristic of these types of major social cleavages—especially class and religion—and the territorial bastions that went with them, have tended to decline, without disappearing altogether. What should be put in their place? Two lines of argument stand out. One is that new cleavages have replaced old ones or have been superimposed on them. According to Inglehart, for example, many voters who grew up in the long post-war boom and reached maturity in the 1960s had different priorities from their parents, centred more on the environment and on the quality of personal life than on material well-being, which they took for granted.[31] That would explain the rise of ecology parties, and their difficulty in fitting into the conventional Left–Right spectrum. Another candidate for the status of a 'new cleavage' is Europe. The slow passage of a share of political sovereignty from national capitals to Brussels has proved deeply controversial, at least in some countries and at certain times; European integration generates winners and losers, a centre and a periphery; in short, Europe has the makings of a new 'revolution' to add to Lipset and Rokkan's series. Moreover, established political parties have great difficulty dealing with it: the British Conservative Party's damaging internal debates over Europe in the 1990s are an extreme case, but certainly not a unique one, of the controversies that plagued a wide range of parties of both Right and Left in the same period.[32] However, while both 'post-industrial' questions and the problem of European integration have certainly proved disruptive to established party systems, they have not, as yet, generated patterns of political behaviour stable enough and on a large enough scale to structure party systems in the way that the cleavage patterns that we have discussed earlier in this chapter clearly did. Nor have they given rise to the types of institution (trade unions or church organizations, for example) which helped to hold the old cleavages in place. Europe and the environment, in short, might be conceived, not as deep social cleavages, but as two 'issues', which, among others, help to structure choices on polling day.

This suggests a second hypothesis about what may have replaced the stable structures noted by Lipset and Rokkan. It is that *all* social cleavages have become less important in the shaping of political behaviour. On this view, the emptying of churches and the closure of mines, steelworks, or shipyards have eroded the communities on which the old cleavages were based, while the spread of television has given every household a source of information, and of political cues, independent of any such community. The result is a free electoral market. Thus, for example, Himmelweit and others see voters as individuals capable of choice, as consumers of the policies supplied by political parties, rather than as the passive products of their social environments. In this context, successful parties, like firms, must be able to develop products, or policies, to meet consumer demand as it turns up (or, better, very slightly earlier); and they will be 'catch-all' parties, in Otto Kirchheimer's phrase, eschewing exclusive ties with any single social group. Such a free market in policies and candidates is obviously no more a total explanation than Lipset and Rokkan; it ignores the sociological bases of electoral behaviour that persist, with however diminished an intensity, from one election to the next, or even return with renewed vigour after having been discounted. But the free-market idea does help to explain some of the changes in West European party systems since the 1960s.[33]

How long can cleavages stay frozen? A good test case is that of East Germany, which went from 1933 to December 1990 without a single multi-party election at national level. In 1932, much of East Germany had been a Social Democratic heartland, with many blue-collar industrial workers, no independent peasants, and very few Catholics. That led many to assume that the December 1990 elections would change the balance of party forces in the newly united Federal Republic to the benefit of the Social Democrats. In fact, the East surged to the Christian Democrats, who picked up some 42 per cent of the votes there compared to about 25 per cent for the Social Democrats. Possibly in the medium term more East German voters will recognize the Social Democrats as representing their fundamental values. But in the short term, the old loyalties were practically replaced by a blank slate, on which the Christian Democrats, as unifiers bearing the promise of prosperity, were well placed to make their mark. Few voters, after all, had the chance to go to the polls in both 1933 and 1990. More important, the institutions that reproduce cleavage structures across the generations in most countries—churches, trade unions, associations, and parties—had all been either co-opted or suppressed in the Communist East; as Peter Pulzer points out, 'sub-cultures . . . cannot survive for two generations if deprived of their institutional support'.[34] While cleavage structures may help to create or transform political parties, political parties are also vital to the perpetuation of cleavage structures.

Questions

- Has class declined as a determinant of voting in the major West European countries?

- Why has the impact of religion on political behaviour been so variable between different countries?

- Was political behaviour in late twentieth-century Western Europe more or less territorially fragmented than in the immediate post-war period?

- What is Lipset and Rokkan's 'freezing hypothesis'? How useful is it in explaining contemporary political behaviour?

NOTES

1. D. Rae and M. Taylor, *The Analysis of Political Cleavages* (New Haven, Conn.: Yale University Press, 1970). See also R. Dahl, *A Preface to Democratic Theory* (New Haven, Conn.: Yale University Press, 1956).

2. See A. Lijphart, 'Lingua, religione, classe e preferenze politiche: Analisi comparata di quattro paesi', *Rivista italiana di scienza politica*, 8 (1978), 78–111.

3. A. Lijphart, 'Typologies of Democratic Systems', *Comparative Political Studies*, 1(1) (Apr. 1968), 3–33.

4. G. Grunberg and E. Schweisguth, 'Profession et vote: La poussée de la gauche', in

Y. Capdevielle, E. Dupoirier, G. Grunberg, E. Schweisguth, and C. Ysmal (eds.), *France de gauche, vote à droite* (Paris: FNSP, 1981).

5. G. Michelet and M. Simon, *Classe, religion et comportement politique* (Paris: FNSP, 1977).

6. D. Boy and N. Mayer, 'L'Électeur français en questions', in CEVIPOF, *L'Électeur français en questions* (Paris: FNSP, 1990), 206–13; Sofres, *L'état de l'opinion 1996* (Paris: Éditions du Seuil, 1996), 175, 191.

7. P. G. Pulzer, *Political Representation and Elections in Britain* (London: Allen and Unwin, 1967), 98.

8. H. Laski, *Parliamentary Government in England* (London: Allen and Unwin, 1948), 63.

9. Ibid. 70, 72.

10. S. E. Finer, *Comparative Government* (London: Allen Lane, 1970), 142.

11. S. Beer, *Modern British Politics*, 3rd edn. (London: Faber and Faber, 1982), 242.

12. D. Butler and D. Stokes, *Political Change in Britain: The Evolution of Electoral Choice* (London: Macmillan, 1974).

13. The question of the class vote is one of the problems most fiercely debated by British political scientists, who disagree about its importance and also its evolution. One recent work emphasizes the persistence of the class vote (A. Heath, R. Jowell, and J. Curtice, *How Britain Votes* (Oxford: Pergamon Press, 1985)), but this thesis has been criticized (I. Crewe, 'On the Death and Resurrection of Class Voting: Some Comments on "How Britain Votes"', *Political Studies*, 34(3) (Sept. 1986)), and other recent studies have also underlined the relative decline of the class vote (R. Rose and I. McAllister, *Voters Begin to Choose: From Closed Class to Open Elections* (Beverly Hills, Calif.: Sage, 1986); M. Franklin, *The Decline of Class Voting in Britain* (Oxford: Clarendon Press, 1985)). A useful overview of the debate is given in D. Denver, *Elections and Voting Behaviour in Britain* (London: Philip Allan, 1989). The outstanding recent contribution is A. Heath, R. Jowell, J. Curtice, G. Evans, J. Field, and S. Witherspoon, *Understanding Political Change: The British Voter, 1964–1987* (Oxford: Pergamon Press, 1991).

14. P. Dunleavy and C. T. Husbands, *British Democracy at the Crossroads* (London: George Allen and Unwin, 1985).

15. G. Pasquino, 'Il Partito comunista nel sistema politico italiano', in G. Pasquino (ed.), *Il Sistema politico italiano* (Bari: Laterza, 1985), 140.

16. Ibid. 132.

17. A. Lancelot, 'L'Orientation du comportement politique', in J. Leca and M. Grawitz (eds.), *Traité de science politique*, iii (Paris: PUF, 1985).

18. A. Grosser, *L'Allemagne de notre temps*, Coll. Pluriel (Paris: Fayard, 1978), 440–1.

19. Ibid. 453.

20. Lancelot, 'L'Orientation du comportement politique', 394.

21. B. Cautrès, A. Heath, and D. Firth, 'Class, Religion and Vote in Britain and France', paper presented at the Franco-British conference on 'Electoral Behaviour in Britain and France', Maison Française, Oxford, June 1997; S. Padgett and T. Burkett, *Political Parties and Elections in West Germany* (London: C. Hurst, 1986), 273.

22. R. Inglehart, 'Changing Paradigms in Comparative Political Behavior', in A. Finifter (ed.), *Political Science: The State of the Discipline* (Washington: APSA, 1983), 443.

23. G. Smith, *Politics in Western Europe*, 4th edn. (London: Heinemann, 1983), 25.

24. J. Gottman, 'The Evolution of the Concept of Territory', *Social Science Information*, 14 (1975), 29.

25. Lancelot, 'L'Orientation du comportement politique', 404.

26. K. Von Beyme, *Political Parties in Western Democracies* (Aldershot: Gower, 1985), 278.

27. J. Blondel, *An Introduction to Comparative Government* (London: Weidenfeld and Nicolson, 1969), 53.

28. S. M. Lipset and S. Rokkan, 'Cleavages, Structures, Party Systems, and Voter Alignments: An Introduction', in S. M. Lipset and S. Rokkan (eds.), *Party Systems and Voter Alignments: Cross-National Perspectives* (New York: Free Press, 1967).

29. S. Rokkan, *Citizens, Elections, Parties* (Oslo: Universiteit Forlaget, 1970).

30. Lipset and Rokkan, 'Cleavages', 50. For an application of Rokkan's model to the European political parties, see D. L. Seiler, *Les Partis politiques en Europe*, 2nd edn., Coll. Que sais-je? (Paris: PUF, 1982).

31. Cf. R. Inglehart, *The Silent Revolution: Changing Values and Political Styles among Western Publics* (Princeton, NJ: Princeton University Press, 1977).

32. S. Hix and C. Lord, *Political Parties in the European Union* (Basingstoke: Macmillan, 1997), 26–7.

33. H. T. Himmelweit, P. Humphreys, and M. Jaeger, *How Voters Decide* (Milton Keynes: Open University Press, 1985): O. Kirchheimer, 'The Transformation of Western European Party Systems', in J. LaPalombara and M. Weiner (eds.), *Political Parties and Political Development* (Princeton, NJ: Princeton University Press, 1966). For a useful survey of the debates on voting behaviour, cf. M. Harrop and W. L. Miller, *Elections and Voters: A Comparative Introduction* (Basingstoke: Macmillan, 1987).

34. P. Pulzer, 'The German Federal Election of 1990', *Electoral Studies*, 10(2) (Aug. 1991), 145–54.

CHAPTER 2

Political Parties

The existence of political parties competing for power within a framework of rules that guarantee equal chances for all is one of the fundamental characteristics of pluralist Western democracy. With hindsight, it seems that this key element in the democracies of today is interconnected with the process that has shaped liberal democracy, even if the development of the political organizations known as the parties and that of the institutions of pluralist democracy have not always been in harmony.

To be sure, history provides many examples of political groups taking up arms in their struggle for power: the conflict between the Guelphs and the Ghibellines in Renaissance Florence, clashes between organized clubs during the French Revolution, the opposition between the Montagne and the Marais or the Jacobins and the Girondins all foreshadow party political forms involved in the political game. But at the end of the eighteenth century in Britain, political parties in the modern form began to emerge, in circumstances that were—admittedly—fraught with conflict. Men such as Burke defended the principle of organized parties: 'Party is a body of men united, for promoting by their joint endeavours the national interest, upon some particular principle in which they are all agreed,'[1] but the idea was generally criticized on the grounds that these 'factions' would introduce divisions in relation to the monarchy and the exercise of power. The debate was resumed in France, under the Restoration, in virtually the same terms, for the Ultras of 1815–16 (Chateaubriand) appealed to the English model as they attempted to impose their views on a monarch who was too moderate for their taste. But, despite the Anglomania felt on this score by a section of the political élite, it was relatively late in the day that France eventually came to accept a true party system. The contrasting evolutions of these two countries show that the birth of political parties is not always a natural concomitant of the extension of universal suffrage; and contemporary history demonstrates *ad nauseam* that party structures may be created and may develop and improve even when the practices of so-called universal suffrage amount to no more than a sham of democracy. The political party, as an instrument for winning and administering power, is essentially linked with a historical turning-point in Western democracy, as it developed in Britain.[2] But the determining factor was that, as the democratic system more or less modelled on Britain spread, there developed a conviction that *political parties are the instruments best adapted to political struggle.* That assumption was to find startling confirmation in Marxist and especially Leninist analyses and in the 1917 Revolution, which made the Communist Party the instrument through which the working class could first win and then administer power. At this point, the debate shifted: the question was no longer, as in the nineteenth century, whether there should be political parties, but whether the party system should be pluralist or monolithic. Thenceforward the whole debate was to concentrate upon the respective merits or flaws of multi-party and single-party systems; but the existence of party organizations was by now to some extent accepted as a constitutive element of the political system itself: thus the proliferation of States that followed the Second World War was accompanied by a corresponding proliferation of political parties. Institutional and political mimesis extends also to the creation of parties, although the imitations in some cases remain somewhat artificial. In developing countries, in particular, the parties created and organized often bear no more than a formal resemblance to the models claimed to inspire them, whether the framework be that of a single-party system or of a pluralist one.[3] This makes it much more difficult to establish comparisons, although

Political Parties

Table 2.1. **Parliamentary elections: France, 1958–1997 (% of first ballot votes)**

1958 (23 and 30 November)

Valid votes cast 75.22% of electorate of 27.2 million

Party	% of votes	seats
Communists (PCF)	18.9	10
Socialists (SFIO)	15.5	44
Radicals	9.5	39
Other Left	0.4	0
Non-Gaullist moderate Right	31.1	172
Gaullists (UNR)	20.6	207
Far Right	2.6	0
Others	0.5	0
Other Deputies (Algeria etc.)		105
Total	100.0	577

1962 (18 and 25 November)

Valid votes cast 66.57% of electorate of 27.5 million

Party	% of votes	seats
Communists (PCF)	21.9	41
PSU + other far Left	2.0	0
Socialists (SFIO)	12.4	66
Radicals	7.4	39
MRP + Conservatives	19.4	55
Gaullists (UNR)	33.7	233
Giscardians (RI)	2.3	35
Far Right	0.8	0
Others / Non inscrits	0.1	13
Total	100.0	482

1967 (5 and 12 March)

Valid votes cast 79.27% of electorate of 28.3 million

Party	% of votes	seats
Communists (PCF)	22.5	73
PSU + other far Left	2.2	4
Socialists/Left Radicals (FGDS)	18.9	121
Non-Gaullist Centre and Right	17.4	41
Gaullists (UDVe)	33.0	200
Giscardians (RI)	5.6	42
Far Right	0.6	0
Others / Non inscrits	0.1	6
Total	100.0	487

1968 (23 and 30 June)

Valid votes cast 78.60% of electorate of 28.2 million

Party	% of votes	seats
Communists (PCF)	20.0	34
PSU + other far Left	4.0	0
Socialists + allies (FGDS)	16.5	57
Non-Gaullist Centre and Right	12.4	33
Gaullists (UDR)	38.0	293
Giscardians (RI)	8.4	61
Far Right	0.1	0
Others / Non inscrits	0.5	9
Total	100.0	487

1973 (4 and 11 March)

Valid votes cast 79.48% of electorate of 29.9 million

Party	% of votes	seats
Communists (PCF)	21.4	73
PSU and other far Left	3.2	0
Socialists + Left Radicals	20.8	102
Other Left	0.4	0
Non-Gaullist Centre and Right	16.7	34
Gaullists (UDR)	26.0	183
Giscardians (RI)	7.2	55
Pro-Gaullist Centre (CDP)	3.9	30
Far Right	0.5	0
(Non inscrits)		13
Total	100.0	490

1978 (12 and 19 March)

Valid votes cast 81.63% of electorate of 34.4 million

Party	% of votes	seats
Communists (PCF)	20.6	86
PSU + other far Left	3.3	0
Socialists + Left Radicals	25.0	115
Other Left	1.4	0
Ecologists, feminists, etc.	2.2	0
Giscardians (UDF) + other Right	23.9	123
Gaullists (RPR)	22.8	154
Front National / Far Right	0.8	0
Others / Non inscrits	0.0	13
Total	100.0	491

Table 2.1. (*cont.*)

1981 (14 and 21 June)

Valid votes cast 69.85% of electorate of 36.3 million

Party	% of votes	seats
Communists (PCF)	16.2	44
PSU + other far Left	1.3	0
Socialists + allies (PS + MRG)	38.1	285
Other left	0.3	0
Ecologists, regionalists, etc.	1.2	0
Giscardians (UDF) + other Right	21.6	63
Gaullists (RPR)	21.0	88
Front National (FN)	0.2	0
Other far Right	0.1	0
Others / Non inscrits	0.0	11
Total	100.0	491

1986 (16 March: one ballot on PR)

Valid votes cast 75.08% of electorate of 36.6 million

Party	% of votes	seats
Communists (PCF)	9.7	35
Far Left	1.5	0
Socialists + allies (PS + MRG)	32.6	212
Ecologists, regionalists, etc.	1.3	0
Giscardians (UDF)	9.6	155
Gaullists (RPR)	11.5	131
RPR–UDF combined lists	21.0	—a
Various Right	2.7	
Front National (FN)	9.8	35
Other far Right	0.1	0
Others / Non inscrits	0.2	9
Total	100.0	577

1988 (5 and 12 June)

Valid votes cast 64.38% of electorate of 37.9 million

Party	% of votes	seats
Communists (PCF)	11.3	27
Far Left	0.4	0
Socialists + allies (PS + MRG)	37.5	276
Ecologists	0.4	0
UDF	18.5	130
RPR	19.2	129
Other Right	2.9	14
Front National (FN)	9.7	1
Other far Right	0.1	0
Total	100.0	577

1993 (21 and 28 March)

Valid votes cast 65.27% of electorate of 38.9 million

Party	% of votes	seats
Communists (PCF)	9.2	24
Far Left	1.7	0
Socialists + allies (PS + MRG)	19.2	65
Other Left	1.0	10
Ecologists	10.7	0
UDF	18.6	206
RPR	19.8	259
Other Right	5.6	13
Front National (FN)	12.4	0
Other far Right	0.1	0
Others / Non inscrits	1.7	0
Total	100.0	577

1997 (25 May and 1 June)

Valid votes cast 64.58% of electorate of 39.2 million

Party	% of votes	seats
Communists (PCF)	9.9	37
Far Left	2.2	0
Socialists + allies (PS + PRS)	26.6	266
Greens allied to Left	3.6	8
Other Left	2.0	9
Ecologists not linked to Left	2.7	0
UDF	14.7	109
RPR	16.8	139
Other Right	4.6	8
Front National (FN)	14.9	1
Other far Right	0.2	0
Others / Non inscrits	1.8	0
Total	100.0	577

a See above.

Note: French electoral statistics present problems of classification resulting chiefly from candidates who run under the label of a small party, or no party at all; who nevertheless enjoy the support of a larger party; and who may, after election, choose either to join that party's parliamentary group, or to stay outside a group, among *non inscrits*. All tables, including those of the Interior Ministry, thus involve an element of subjective judgement, at least at the margins. Here votes for 'others' and seats for 'non inscrits' do not necessarily correspond.

Sources: Adapted from the French edition of this book (Y. Mény, *Politique comparée*, 5th edn. (Paris: Montchrestien, 1996)); A. Lancelot, *Les Élections sous la Ve République*, 2nd edn. (Paris: Presses Universitaires de France, 1988); and *Le Monde*'s figures for 1997.

Table 2.2. Presidential elections: France, 1965–1995

5 & 19 December 1965 (electorate 28.9 million)

1st ballot: Valid votes cast 85.53% of electorate

Candidate	Party etc.	% valid votes
Mitterrand	United Left	31.72
Lecanuet	Christian Democrat	15.57
Marcilhacy	Moderate Right	1.71
Barbu	Independent	1.15
De Gaulle	Gaullist	44.65
Tixier-Vignancour	Far Right	5.20

2nd ballot: Valid votes cast 85.27% of electorate

De Gaulle		55.20
Mitterrand		44.80

1 & 15 June 1969 (electorate 29.5 million)

1st ballot: Valid votes cast 76.59% of electorate

Candidate	Party etc.	% valid votes
Krivine	Trotskyist	1.06
Rocard	PSU	3.61
Duclos	Communist	21.27
Defferre	Socialist	5.01
Poher	Centre	23.31
Ducatel	Independent Right	1.27
Pompidou	Gaullist	44.47

2nd ballot: Valid votes cast 64.43% of electorate

Pompidou		58.21
Poher		41.79

5 & 19 May 1974 (electorate 30.6 million)

1st ballot: Valid votes cast 83.46% of electorate

Candidate	Party etc.	% valid votes
Krivine	Trotskyist	0.37
Laguiller	Trotskyist	2.33
Mitterrand	United Left	43.25
Dumont	Ecologist	1.32
Muller	Centrist	0.69
Sebag	European federalist	0.16
Héraux	European federalist	0.08
Giscard d'Estaing	Centre-Right	32.60
Chaban-Delmas	Gaullist	15.11
Royer	Independent Right	3.17
Le Pen	Front National	0.75
Renouvin	Royalist	0.17

2nd ballot: Valid votes cast 86.16% of electorate

Giscard d'Estaing		50.81
Mitterrand		49.19

26 April and 10 May 1981 (electorate 30.6 million)

1st ballot: Valid votes cast 79.78% of electorate

Candidate	Party etc.	% valid votes
Laguiller	Trotskyist	2.30
Marchais	Communist	15.35
Bouchardeau	PSU	1.11
Mitterrand	Socialist	25.85
Crépeau	Left Radical	2.21
Lalonde	Ecologist	3.88
Giscard d'Estaing	UDF	28.32
Chirac	RPR	18.00
Debré	Gaullist	1.66
Garaud	Gaullist	1.33

2nd ballot: Valid votes cast 83.38% of electorate

Mitterrand		51.76
Giscard d'Estaing		48.24

24 April and 8 May 1988 (electorate 38.1 million)

1st ballot: Valid votes cast 79.74% of electorate

Candidate	Party etc.	% valid votes
Boussel	Far Left	0.38
Juquin	Alternative Left	2.01
Lajoinie	Communist	6.76
Mitterrand	Socialist	34.09
Waechter	Ecologist	3.88
Laguiller	Trotskyist	1.99
Barre	UDF	16.54
Chirac	RPR	19.94
Le Pen	Front National	14.39

2nd ballot: Valid votes cast 81.02% of electorate

Mitterrand		54.01
Chirac		45.99

24 April and 8 May 1995 (electorate 40.0 million)

1st ballot: Valid votes cast 76.17% of electorate

Candidate	Party etc.	% valid votes
Laguiller	Trotskyist	5.30
Hue	Communist	8.64
Jospin	Socialist	23.30
Voynet	Ecologist	3.32
Balladur	Centre-Right	18.58
Chirac	RPR	20.84
Le Pen	Front National	15.00
De Villiers	Anti-Maastricht Right	4.74
Cheminade	Independent	0.28

2nd ballot: Valid votes cast 74.92% of electorate

Chirac		52.63
Jospin		47.37

Table 2.3. Parliamentary elections: Germany, 1949–1994 (% of list votes)

	Electorate (m.)	Valid votes cast (% of electorate)	Bundestag seats (total)	Communists[a] % of vote	seats	Social Democrats (SPD) % of vote	seats	Greens[b] % of vote	seats	Free Democrats (FDP) % of vote	seats	Christian Democrats (CDU–CSU) % of vote	seats	German Party % of vote	seats	Bavarian Party % of vote	seats	Refugee Party % of vote	seats	Extreme Right[c] % of vote	seats	Neutralists % of vote	seats	Others % of vote	seats
1949	31.2	76.0	402	5.7	15	29.2	131	–	–	11.9	52	31.0	139	4.0	17	4.2	17	–	–	1.8	5	–	–	12.2	26
1953	33.2	83.1	487	2.2	0	28.8	151	–	–	9.5	48	45.2	243	3.3	15	1.7	0	5.9	27	1.1	0	1.1	0	1.2	3
1957	35.4	84.5	497	–	–	31.8	169	–	–	7.7	41	50.2	270	3.4	17	0.5	0	4.6	0	1.0	0	–	–	0.8	0
1961	37.4	84.5	499	–	–	36.2	190	–	–	12.8	67	45.3	242	–	–	–	–	2.8	0	0.8	0	1.9	0	0.2	0
1965	38.5	84.7	496	–	–	39.3	202	–	–	9.5	49	47.6	245	–	–	–	–	–	–	2.0	0	1.3	0	0.3	0
1969	38.7	85.3	496	0.6	0	42.7	224	–	–	5.8	30	46.1	242	0.1	0	0.2	0	–	–	4.3	0	0.6	0	0.2	0
1972	41.4	90.3	496	0.3	0	45.8	230	–	–	8.4	41	44.9	225	–	–	–	–	–	–	0.6	0	–	–	0.1	0
1976	42.1	89.8	496	0.3	0	42.6	214	–	–	7.9	39	48.6	243	–	–	–	–	–	–	0.3	0	–	–	0.3	0
1980	43.2	88.0	497	0.2	0	42.9	218	1.5	0	10.6	53	44.5	226	–	–	–	–	–	–	0.2	0	–	–	0.1	0
1983	44.1	88.2	498	0.2	0	38.2	193	5.6	27	7.0	34	48.8	244	–	–	–	–	–	–	0.2	0	–	–	0.1	0
1987	45.4	83.4	497	–	–	37.0	186	8.3	42	9.7	46	44.3	223	–	–	0.1	0	–	–	0.6	0	–	–	0.8	0
1990	60.4	77.8	662	2.4	17	33.5	239	3.9	8	11.0	79	43.8	319	–	–	–	–	–	–	2.1	0	–	–	–	–
1994	60.5	79.0	672	4.4	30	36.4	252	7.3	49	5.9	47	41.5	294	–	–	–	–	–	–	1.9	0	–	–	–	–

[a] KPD, 1949 and 1953; DKP, 1969–1983; PDS, 1990 and 1994.

[b] Greens + Bündnis '90 in 1990 and 1994; all seats in 1990 won in the East by Bündnis '90 list.

[c] DRP, 1949–1961; NPD, 1965–1987; Republikaner, 1990 and 1994.

Source: Adapted from Y. Mény, *Politique comparée* (5th edn., Paris: Montchrestien, 1996).

Table 2.4. Parliamentary elections: Italy, 1946–1992 (Chamber of Deputies)

	1946		1948		1953		1958		1963		1968		1972		1976		1979		1983		1987		1992	
	% of vote	seats	% of vote	seats	% of vote	seats	% of vote	seats	% of vote	seats	% of vote	seats	% of vote	seats	% of vote	seats	% of vote	seats	% of vote	seats	% of vote	seats	% of vote	seats
Far left	–	–	–	–	–	–	–	–	–	–	–	–	1.3	0	1.5	6	2.2	6	1.5	7	1.7	8	–	–
Rifondazione Comunista	–	–	–	–	–	–	–	–	–	–	–	–	–	–	–	–	–	–	–	–	–	–	5.6	35
Dissident Socialists (PSIUP)	–	–	–	–	–	–	–	–	–	–	4.5	23	2.0	0	–	–	–	–	–	–	–	–	–	–
Communists[a] (PCI / PDS)	19.0	104	31.0	183[b]	22.6	143	22.7	140	25.3	166	27.0	177	27.2	179	34.4	227	30.4	201	29.9	198	26.6	177	16.1	107
Socialists (PSI)	20.7	115			12.7	75	14.3	84	13.9	87	14.5	91[c]	9.6	61	9.7	57	9.8	62	11.4	73	14.3	94	14.3	92
Social Democrats (PSDI)	–	–	7.1	33	4.5	19	4.6	22	6.1	33			5.2	29	3.4	15	3.8	20	4.1	23	2.9	17	2.7	16
Republicans (PRI)	4.4	23	2.5	9	1.6	5	1.4	6	1.4	6	2.0	9	2.9	15	3.1	14	3.0	16	5.1	29	3.7	21	4.4	27
Liberals (PLI)	6.8	41	3.4	19	3.0	13	3.6	17	7.0	39	5.8	31	3.9	20	1.3	5	1.9	9	2.9	16	2.1	11	2.8	17
Radicals	–		–		–		–		–		–		–		1.1	4	3.4	18	2.2	11	2.6	13	1.2	7
Leagues	–		–		–		–		–		–		–		–		–		0.3	1	0.5	1	9.9	56
Greens	–		–		–		–		–		–		–		–		–		–		2.5	13	3.0	16
La Rete	–		–		–		–		–		–		–		–		–		–		–		1.9	12
Christian Democrats (DC)	35.2	207	48.5	305	40.1	263	42.4	273	38.3	260	39.1	266	38.7	266	38.8	263	38.3	262	32.9	225	34.3	234	29.7	206
Royalists	2.7	16	2.8	14	6.9	40	4.9	25	1.8	8	1.3	6											–	–
Far Right (MSI)[d]	5.3	30	2.0	6	5.9	29	4.8	24	5.1	27	4.5	24	8.7	56	6.1	35	5.3	30	6.8	42	5.9	35	5.4	34
Others	5.9	0	2.7	5	2.7	3	1.3	5	1.1	4	1.3	3	3.8	4	0.7	4	2.6	6	2.9	5	2.9	7	3.7	4
Turnout / total seats	89.1	536	92.2	574	93.8	590	93.8	596	92.9	630	92.8	630	93.1	630	93.1	630	90.1	630	88.3	630	88.5	630	87.2	630

[a] PCI to 1987, PDS in 1992.

[b] Communists and Socialists fought election jointly in 1948.

[c] Socialists and Social Democrats fought election jointly in 1968.

[d] Partito d'l'Uomo Qualunque in 1946 only.

Source: Adapted from Y. Mény, Politique comparée (5th edn., Paris: Montchrestien, 1996), and D. Hine, Governing Italy: The Politics of Bargained Pluralism (Oxford: Oxford University Press, 1993).

Table 2.5. **Parliamentary elections: Italy, 1994 and 1996 (% of list votes)**

Party	% of proportional votes	Proportional seats	Plurality seats	Total seats
1994: Valid votes cast 38.6 million				
Rifondazione Comunista	6.0	12	27	39
Ex-Communists (PDS)	20.4	37	72	109
Socialists (PSI)	2.2	0	14	14
Greens	2.7	0	11	11
La Rete	1.9	0	6	6
Alleanza Democratica	1.2	0	18	18
Other Left	0.0	0	16	16
Christian Democrats (PPI)	11.1	29	4	33
Patto Segni	4.7	13	0	13
Forza Italia	21.0	25	74	99
Right Christian Democrats (CCDI)	0.0	7[a]	22	29
Other Centre-Right	0.0	0		12
Far Right (Alleanza Nazionale)	13.5	22	87	109
Radicals (Lista Pannella)	3.5	0	0	0
Lega Nord	8.4	10	107	117
Others	3.6	0	5	5
Total	100.0	155	475	630
1996: Valid votes cast 38.6 million				
Ex-Communists (PDS)	21.1	26	147	172
Christian Democrats (PPI)	6.8	4	63	67
Dini lists	4.3	8	16	24
Greens	2.5	0	21	21
Total Olive Tree	34.7	38	246	284
Rifondazione Comunista	8.6	20	15	35
Leagues	10.1	20	39	59
Forza Italia	20.6	37	86	123
Far Right (Alleanza Nazionale)	15.7	28	65	93
Right Christian Democrats (CCDI/CDU)	5.8	12	18	30
Total 'Liberty Pole'	42.1	77	169	246
Radicals (Lista Pannella)	1.9	0	0	0
Far Right	0.9	0	0	0
Others	1.7	0	5	5
Total	100.0	155	475	630

[a] Seven seats allocated on Forza Italia contingent.

Source: Adapted from James L. Newell and Martin Bull, 'Party Organisations and Alliances in Italy in the 1990s: A Revolution of Sorts', *West European Politics*, 20/1 (January 1997), 81–109.

Table 2.6. Parliamentary elections: United Kingdom, 1945–1997

	Electorate (m.)	Turn-out (% of electorate)	Commons seats (total)	Communists % of vote	seats	Labour Party % of vote	seats	Liberal Party/ 'Alliance'/ Liberal Democrats[a] % of vote	seats	Conservative Party % of vote	seats	National Front % of vote	seats	Plaid Cymru % of vote	seats	Scottish National Party % of vote	seats	Northern Ireland[b] % of vote	seats	Others % of vote	seats
1945	33.2	72.7	640	0.4	2	47.8	393	9.0	12	39.8	213	–	–	–	–	–	–	–	–	2.5	20
1950	33.3	84.0	625	0.3	0	46.1	315	9.1	9	43.5	298	–	–	–	–	–	–	–	–	0.9	3
1951	34.6	82.5	625	0.1	0	48.8	295	2.5	6	48.0	321	–	–	–	–	–	–	–	–	0.5	3
1955	34.9	76.7	630	0.1	0	46.4	277	2.7	6	49.7	344	–	–	–	–	–	–	–	–	1.1	3
1959	35.4	78.8	630	0.2	0	43.8	258	5.9	6	49.4	365	–	–	0.3	0	0.2	0	–	–	0.6	1
1964	35.9	77.1	630	0.2	0	44.1	317	11.2	9	43.4	304	–	–	0.3	0	0.2	0	–	–	0.6	0
1966	36.0	75.8	630	0.2	0	47.9	363	8.5	12	41.9	253	–	–	0.2	0	0.2	0	–	–	0.6	2
1970	39.3	72.0	635	0.1	0	43.0	287	7.5	6	46.4	330	–	–	0.6	0	1.1	1	–	–	1.4	6
1974 Feb.	39.8	78.1	635	0.1	0	37.1	301	19.3	14	37.8	297	0.3	0	0.6	2	2.0	7	2.3	12	0.4	2
1974 Oct.	40.1	72.8	635	0.1	0	39.2	319	18.3	13	35.8	277	0.4	0	0.6	3	2.9	11	2.4	12	0.3	0
1979	41.1	76.0	635	0.1	0	36.9	269	13.8	11	43.9	339	0.6	0	0.4	2	1.6	2	2.2	12	0.5	0
1983	42.2	72.7	650	0.1	0	27.6	209	25.4	23	42.4	397	0.1	0	0.4	2	1.1	2	2.1	17	0.6	0
1987	43.2	75.3	650	0.0	0	30.8	229	22.5	22	42.3	376	–	–	0.3	3	1.3	3	2.2	17	0.5	0
1992	43.2	77.7	651	–	–	34.4	271	17.8	20	41.9	336	–	–	0.5	4	1.9	3	2.2	17	1.0	0
1997	43.8	71.5	659	–	–	43.2	419	17.2	46	30.7	165	–	–	0.5	4	2.0	6	2.5	18	4.0	1

[a] Liberals up to 1979; Social Democrat and Liberal Alliance, 1983 and 1987; Liberal Democrats, 1992 and 1997.
[b] Northern Ireland MPs are counted among British totals until 1974.

Source: Adapted from Y. Mény, Politique comparée (5th edn., Paris: Montchrestien, 1996) and D. Butler and G. Butler, British Political Facts, 1990–1994 (Basingstoke: Macmillan, 1994); the Times Guide to the House of Commons (London: Times Books, 1997) for 1997.

Table 2.7. The major political families

Country	Name	% vote at last election	No. of MPs	Members claimed
Communists				
France	Parti Communiste Français (PCF)	9.9	37	274,000
Germany	Partei des Demokratischen Sozialismus (PDS)	4.4	30	124,000
Italy	Rifondazione Comunista	8.6	35	150,000
Socialists				
France	Parti Socialiste (PS)	25.6	246	115,000
Germany	Sozialdemokratische Partei Deutschlands (SPD)	36.4	252	835,600
Italy	Partito Democratico della Sinistra (PDS)	21.1	172	712,000
UK	The Labour Party	43.2	419	401,000
Liberals				
France	Démocratie Libérale (part of UDF confederation)	approx. 6.5	41	33,000
Germany	Freie demokratische Partei (FDP)	5.9	47	75,038
UK	The Liberal Democrats	16.7	46	103,000
Christian Democrats				
France	Force Démocrate (part of UDF confederation)	approx. 6.5	43	40,000
Germany	Christlich Demokratische Union/Christlich Soziale Union (CDU/CSU)	41.5	294	847,000
Italy	Partito Popolare Italiano (largest fragment of ex-DC)	6.8	67	n.a.
Conservatives				
France	Rassemblement pour la République (RPR)	16.8	139	153,000
Italy	Forza Italia	20.6	123	n.a.
UK	The Conservative Party	30.6	165	400,000
The Far Right				
France	Front National (FN)	14.9	1	60,000
Germany	Die Republikaner	1.9	0	n.a.
Italy	Alleanza Nazionale	15.7	93	n.a.
Green Parties				
France	Les Verts	3.6	8	4,500
Germany	Die Grünen	7.3	49	48,600
Italy	Federazione dei Verdi	2.5	21	14,000
UK	The Greens	0.2	0	5,000

Source: Figures supplied from party offices and European parliamentary groups.

some interesting attempts to do so, such as those that Kenneth Janda[4] undertook in the 1970s, have made a fundamental contribution to our understanding in this area.

Limiting ourselves to the parties of the European democracies, we must remember that party systems stem from the combination and relative significance of a number of factors. They may not all be present in all the countries in question and they vary in importance from one to another. Among these factors we should include the structure and intensity of cleavages, the importance of historical divisions (in revolutions, and civil or religious wars), the impact of international events (such as the French Revolution of 1789 and the Russian Revolution of 1917), the nature of the system (presidential or parliamentary), the type of electoral system, and the ability of existing parties to adapt and thus discourage the emergence and development of new competitors. All these factors interact, determining the structure and evolution of the parties. Let us now study these interactions and their results from two different angles: first, from that of ideology, then from the point of view of the institutionalization and organization of the parties. The chapter concludes with an analysis of party systems.

Parties and their ideology

The term 'ideology', as used here, applies generally to the whole extensive system of ideas and values to which political groups claim to relate. These ideas and values may vary greatly in intensity within a single political system, from one political system to another, and from one period to another. In a system such as that of the United States, for example, the values to which each of the parties subscribes are so little differentiated that ideology appears to be of secondary importance in comparison to defending the interests championed by the respective groups. The role of ideology may also vary in importance from one political system to another: the ideological spectrum is more open-ended in France and Italy than in Germany or Britain. Finally, the intensity of ideology may vary from one period to another. In the early 1960s, many observers were hailing 'the end of ideologies', but subsequent events have proved that in reality it was a matter not so much of a collapse of ideology as of a realignment.

Some political observers have rejected the term 'ideology' in favour of concepts more indeterminate but, it is claimed, more appropriate to the diversity of the situations analysed: 'political temperament' (Siegfried), for example, or 'intellectual family' (Thibaudet). It is true that such expressions give a better idea of the orientation of parties such as the French Radicals or the various national versions of Christian democratic parties. Their disadvantage, however, is either to distinguish only in the broadest fashion between different groups (a left-wing temperament or a right-wing temperament), each of which may encompass several competing groups, or to lay so much emphasis upon the 'intellectual' element as to obscure the 'mixed' nature not only of the values but also of the interests promoted by the ideology.[5] Every political party has its own very individual history, and any classification is necessarily arbitrary. With that caveat, the following classification distinguishes seven major sets of parties: those representing liberalism, the conservatives, the far Right, the Christian Democrats, the wide spectrum of socialist parties, regionalist parties, and finally the ecologist groupings.

Liberalism

Liberalism in Europe can pride itself on a fine past and justly claim that Western democracy, in both its philosophy and its institutions, owes much to it. But precisely because the liberals have evolved the essentials of their original creed without managing to broaden the social bases of their support, their organized electoral power is now much reduced, even though their philosophy has by now penetrated the institutions and even the programmes of many of their rivals. It is difficult to determine the profile of a political group that is now much diminished despite its widespread influence.

The term 'liberal' first made its appearance in Spain at the beginning of the nineteenth century, when it was used to denote the promoters of the Cadiz Constitution of 1812. It then spread to Britain (through the writing of Bentham) and France, where men as diverse as Benjamin Constant and Chateaubriand flourished the torch of human liberties. But it was not until the mid-nineteenth century that the Whigs turned themselves into the Liberal Party, which remained powerful up until the First World War. In France, the liberals became influential under the July Monarchy[6] and during the Third Republic. In Italy, the liberals played a crucial role in the construction of the unified Italian State.

In the nineteenth century what all liberals shared was their hostility to the notion of absolute monarchy, their defence of individual liberties, and the stand that they took on broadening the basis of suffrage. In other words, the liberals favoured a constitutional system of government that would guarantee both individual liberties and property within the framework of a political system that was both moderate and balanced. However, beyond this consensus on general principles, liberals were divided over the methods, scope, and pace of reform. There were 'conservative' liberals, whose aims went no further than to protect the interests of the bourgeoisie for which they spoke (the Orleanists in France, for example); 'radical' liberals, hostile to all forms of monarchy, who had emerged from the republican movements of France and Italy in particular; and anti-clerical liberals, wherever the Church had become identified with the most reactionary forces, as in France and Italy (in Britain the Liberals, with a strong Nonconformist current, led the struggle to place non-Anglican churches on a more equal footing with the Church of England). Whether gathered into a single political formation or divided into several parties with different names, the liberal movement has always been weakened by the internal tension between change (liberties, suffrage) and conservatism (property). Herriot's description, 'heart on the left, wallet on the right', sums up the dilemma of liberals of all kinds, and also the contradictions within the bourgeois classes from which their members are mostly drawn. Today, having failed to reconstitute their social bases and win over new social strata, the liberal parties of Europe are everywhere divided or weakened. But that does not mean that their influence is by any means negligible.

In Germany, the small liberal party (FDP) has certainly played an essential role, as is shown by the fact that it has shared power continuously except from 1957 to 1961 (when the CDU–CSU had an absolute majority) and from 1966 to 1969 (when there was a grand SPD–CDU–CSU coalition). The FDP emerged from the reconciliation of its two branches, the left and the right (into which it had split during the Weimar Republic). The source of its influence and of its weakness too lies in what has been called its 'original sin in the face of power'. The constant temptation to share power multiplies the rifts and dissidences that undermine it, but at the same time gives it a strength and an influence quite disproportionate to its size. Due to the peculiar mechanisms of the German polling system, the FDP tends to hold the balance of power in German politics. Its committed supporters are estimated at a mere 3 per cent or so of the electorate, and its vote has repeatedly threatened to dip below the threshold of 5 per cent of voters necessary to win seats in the Lower House of parliament, the Bundestag (it managed 6.9 per cent in 1994). Yet it has also exceeded 10 per cent (for example, in the first all-German elections of December 1990), thanks in part at least to deserters from other parties, who are anxious to check the influence of their radical wings (the SPD left or the CSU). Despite the many phases of its evolution and the undeniable changes that have taken place within it, the FDP is still characterized by a number of fundamental features: a policy of openness towards Europe, and towards the Federal Republic's eastern neighbours both before and after the collapse of Communism; marked reservations over too close an association between Church and State (particularly in the area of education); a hostility towards interventionist economic policies such as 'co-management' (remarkably, the pro-European FDP actually voted against the Treaty of Rome because it was seen as too interventionist); and an unwavering support for personal liberties and State constitutionality. In short, over and above its incidental ups and downs and its sporadic adaptations to passing fashions and fleeting alliances, the FDP does its best to be a custodian of the traditional liberal patrimony.

In Italy, the liberal position was less rosy even before the political earthquake of 1992.[7] There, in the aftermath of Fascism and the Second World War, liberals failed to find themselves a satisfactory position between the Left (Socialists and Communists) and the Christian Democrats. The conditions in which the political parties came into being in Italy, particularly the Pope's ban on Catholics accepting political responsibilities (more or less effective up until 1919), thwarted the emergence of a great liberal or conservative party that could represent the interests of the bourgeoisie. Furthermore, the liberals in Italy are split into two parties, both of them small: the Liberal Party itself (PLI) and the Republican Party (PRI). To these should be added the PSDI, which, despite its title, was more democrat than socialist, competed for roughly the same voters, and thus compounded the divisions of the liberal family. The level of support for these parties of the 'secular Centre' never exceeded 14.5 per cent between 1948 and 1992, and was more frequently closer to 9 or 10 per cent: taken individually, therefore, they were fortunate if they reached 5 or 6 per cent. After the war, the PLI became the heir to Giolittian liberalism rooted, particularly in the south, upon its control over clienteles. However, having failed to seize the reins of central power, the PLI was soon forced to give way to the Christian Democrats in the south and attempt to recapture votes in northern and central Italy by approaching economic circles and reinforcing its links with businessmen. Its relations with the Christian Democrats were thus uneasy despite the fact that, from 1948 on, it frequently shared power with them in coalition governments. Such relations were against both the economic interventionism of the left-wing Christian Democrats (the nationalization of electricity, for example) and also the special relations with the Church. Meanwhile, the Republican Party, for its part, stood for republicanism and an attachment to the secular values of an enlightened bourgeoisie which rejected the philosophies of both the Socialists and the Christian Democrats. Aside from their (fairly unimportant) differences, all three of these parties owed their survival to the parliamentary arithmetic and to the pivotal position which frequently made them indispensable partners in government for the Christian Democrats. That relationship also brought them to the centre of the systemic corruption that characterized the 'first' Italian Republic of the post-war half-century. They fought their last election in 1992, before falling victim to the *tangentopoli* scandals and dispersing to the centre-left, the centre-right, or, in the case of some leaders, to the dock. 'Liberalism' was also invoked, in the most general terms, by Silvio Berlusconi to describe the ideas of Forza Italia, the party he conjured out of nothing (or rather, out of his television empire) to win the 1994 elections. But to apply even such a generally ideological term as liberalism to Forza Italia is at least debatable. For Forza Italia's prime purpose was to defend the business interests of its founder and to keep him safe from judicial investigation. To call it a liberal party is to reduce liberalism to the single dimension of the 'free' market—and to call markets free even where they are rigged.

In France, too, the liberal family has been divided, its members spread between several of the loose electoral alliances and parliamentary groupings that characterized the Third Republic. Perhaps more than in other countries, Liberalism in France has recently come to be identified—and not exclusively by its opponents—with the free-market Right. After winning the Presidency in 1974, Valéry Giscard d'Estaing called for an 'Advanced Liberal Society' in France, while attempting to position himself at the political Centre and in practice extending State intervention in response to economic crisis. But it was in the early- to mid-1980s, as ideas of the Anglo-American New Right gained influence in France, that almost the whole of the right-wing opposition to President Mitterrand and his Socialists discovered its 'liberal' beliefs and commitment to rolling back the State. Today, most French 'liberals' are to be found in Démocratie Libérale, (formerly the Parti Républicain), the biggest component of the Union pour la Démocratie Française (UDF) grouping founded by Giscard. The President of Démocratie Libérale, Alain Madelin, was actually dismissed from the Juppé government in 1995 for his outspoken free-market views, and in particular his calls for big cuts in civil service jobs. But not all Démocratie Libérale members share these opinions, and 'liberals' are also to be found in other parties.

The British Liberals were initially the most influential of European liberal parties. Now, as the Liberal Democrats, they are merely the most electorally strong, which is not at all the same thing. For extensive periods in the nineteenth century, and from 1905 to 1915, the Liberals governed alone. For roughly half the period between 1915 and 1945, they were in government, but always in coalition (the last Liberal Prime Minister, David Lloyd George, left office in October 1922). But there has been no Liberal minister since 1945. Bruised by internal conflicts and particularly clashes between Lloyd George and Asquith, the party was critically damaged by the extension of the suffrage in 1918, the reinforcement of class politics, and the resulting emergence of Labour as the main opposition to the Conservatives. Between 1935 and 1959, the Liberals never won over 9 per cent of the vote in a British election, and fell as low as 2.5 per cent in 1951. Since the 1960s, they have enjoyed a revival from these very low levels of support, winning 11.2 per cent of the vote in 1964, 19.3 per cent in February 1974, and, with their Social Democrat allies, 25.4 per cent in 1983. But this revival has alternated with downturns, with scores of 7.5 per cent in 1970, 13.8 per cent in 1979, 22.5 per cent in 1987, 17.8 per cent (as the Liberal Democrats) in 1992, and 17.2 per cent in 1997. And, crucially, the British first-past-the-post electoral system has denied Britain's Liberals the substantial parliamentary representation that a party with their support could have expected in most continental systems; whether alone or with allies, they never won even as many as 25 seats between 1945 and 1992. In this light, the 46 seats won in 1997, chiefly thanks to the tactical support of Labour voters in strong Liberal Democrat seats (a support reciprocated by Liberal Democrats in Labour's heartlands) were, not surprisingly, greeted as a triumph. The contrast with the FDP's strategic position at the heart of German politics on the basis of many fewer votes is remarkable. The Liberals' hopes of a breakthrough peaked in the 1980s. Public dissatisfaction with the two major parties' failure to deliver economic prosperity was widespread; the widening ideological gap between Conservative and Labour had opened up a space at the political Centre; and a split in the Labour Party offered the Liberals allies in the shape of the Social Democrats. But none of this was sufficient to deliver the one-third share of the vote required to win substantial numbers of seats for the Alliance. Ascribing their poor result in 1987 to their divisions, the two parties merged (apart from a handful of individuals on either side) to form the Social and Liberal Democrats, becoming the Liberal Democrats three years later. This may have helped avoid disaster, but in retrospect it appears that the reviving credibility of Labour after 1987 presented a greater, and largely intractable, problem. Neither unity nor the combative leadership of Paddy Ashdown prevented a further loss of support in 1992; nor did the collapse of Conservative support in 1997 hold any reward for the Liberal Democrats in terms of votes.

In policy terms, the Liberals and then the Liberal Democrats long suffered from the classic problem of a centre party—how to offer policies that are recognizably different from those of their big competitors, rather than merely something in between them. Their efforts to do so have taken four main forms.[8] In the first place, British Liberals have tried to reduce the concentration of power at all levels. During the 1970s, that meant a preoccupation with 'community politics' at local level, and with shared management in industry, though both of these were played down in the following decade. More recently, the party has consistently advocated both a federal structure for Britain and—faithful to its tradition of individualism—a Bill of Rights. Secondly, they advocate 'fair voting'—a change in the electoral system to some form of proportional representation. Clearly they themselves would be the principal beneficiaries of such a change. But it is also their claim that it would put an end once and for all to the 'confrontation politics' that they see as the main cause of Britain's decline since 1945. Thirdly, they campaign for a United Kingdom more open towards the outside world, and have been Britain's strongest pro-Europeans and most consistent advocates of greater co-operation with the United Nations. Finally, as a minority party, they can afford to take 'courageous' policy stances that could be unpopular in the short term—for example, much tighter environmental controls, or higher taxes to pay for improvements in State education. By 1997 many of these policies placed the Liberal Democrats not at the Centre but at the Left of British politics, chiefly because Tony Blair's New Labour had moved so far to the Right (promising, for example, to maintain levels of income tax and public spending set by the Conservatives). That, and the Labour victory of 1997, made the Liberal Democrats' problem different, but not any easier. For they now had to choose between becoming a principled, broadly left-wing opposition to the Blair government and its enormous parliamentary majority, or co-operating with Labour, as they were invited to do, in plans for constitutional change which held out the possibility of a change to the electoral system and with it a lasting transformation of their political prospects.

Despite the diversity of their interests and their political fortunes, the European liberal parties clearly share a number of preoccupations: commitment to personal liberties and property, distrust of 'big government' and its interventionism, and an inclination for open relations with the rest of the world, especially their European partners. And although they have not managed to set themselves up as majority parties, their political influence, whether in government or in opposition, is considerably stronger than might be supposed from their hold over the electorate. Although they have not been successful in renewing their social base, the parties that share liberal tendencies have managed to retain an important place in Western political systems, both through power-sharing and through their defence of an ideological inheritance that other political parties have to a large extent made their own.

The conservative parties

To delineate the conservative ideology, as defended by the conservative parties, is difficult for a number of reasons. In the first place, there are many conservative variants, all constantly evolving. Secondly, it is quite exceptional—and the important exception is Britain—for the conservative ideology to be purveyed by a single political party within a given political system.

The term 'conservative' appeared at the beginning of the nineteenth century, in reaction to the French Revolution. In 1817, Chateaubriand published a newspaper called *Le Conservateur*; and in 1835, Sir Robert Peel made his declaration of 'Conservative Principles'. After that, the Tories became the Conservative Party. But Britain is virtually the only country (with Denmark) where the Conservatives use that word to proclaim their identity. Everywhere else, particularly in France, the conservative tendency adopts a variety of other names. This is not—as might be imagined from the post-1945 ideological climate—because of a reluctance to identify with a discredited and unattractive banner. On the contrary, in the nineteenth century, some conservatives proudly proclaimed their support of counter-revolutionary values and were not afraid to attack liberals and radicals of every kind. The principal reason for the eclipse of the term 'conservative', particularly in France, lies in the split that developed among those faithful to the traditional values. The conservatives became divided in the first place over the extent of their commitment to the counter-revolutionary struggle, and secondly over the monarchist question. Alongside the Ultras, who followed the line of Bonald and De Maistre,[9] and the Ultramontanes, such as Lammenais,[10] the conservative tendency included many more moderate men (starting with Louis XVIII himself), who preferred compromise to the politics of confrontation, and conservative French gallicans, who were hostile to the sway of Rome. After 1830, the conservatives split into Legitimists and Orleanists, and the Second Empire further confused the situation, as it drew into the conservative camp some of the latter-day supporters and beneficiaries of Napoleon and the Revolution.

If the nineteenth-century conservatives in France and Spain were divided by the question of the monarchy, another rift was caused by the subject of relations between Church and State. In Italy, the Pope's interdiction forbidding Catholics to engage in political life (up to 1919) blocked the formation of a major conservative party. The right, in power from 1860 to 1876, was advantaged by a highly restricted suffrage that made it possible for it to govern despite the fact that it was very much a minority group. The practice of 'transformism', adopted by Depretis, constituted a new metamorphosis of conservatism. Gramsci, in his study of the *Risorgimento*, analyses the phenomenon as follows:

It is even fair to say that the whole of Italian political life from 1848 on . . . is characterized by transformism, that is to say by the formation of an increasingly broad ruling class within the framework that the moderates established after 1848 . . . through a progressive yet continuous absorption . . . of the more active individuals who had come either from allied groups or from opposed ones, that had previously appeared to be violent enemies.[11]

The creation of Don Sturzo's Popular Party and of the Christian Democratic Party after the war had the effect of confusing the situation still further, as this prevented the formation of a true conservative party. Even before their disintegration, the Christian Democrats still constituted a composite group that it would be wrong to define as a purely Catholic party. Notwithstanding this ambiguity, Mario Caciagli felt justified in declaring that 'despite its own protestations and those from a few other quarters, the Christian Democrats have always constituted the Conservative party of modern Italy. In the past, that was by virtue of its history and the place it held. Today, it is as a result of its social basis and the interests that it represents and defends.'[12] Similar phenomena can be observed at the end of the German Empire and during the Weimar Republic, when the Centre Party served as a refuge for many Catholics; and also under the Fourth French Republic, when the MRP, the Independents, and the Gaullists shared the conservative vote between them.

Attitudes towards the question of the nation, and nationalism in all its successive forms, constitute another component of the conservative tendency and also a cause of its internal divisions. Some conservatives are naturally drawn towards the idea of a State that respects the intermediary groups that revolutionaries tend to destroy and that are threatened by those who favour centralization at all costs. This group has included not only the Ultras of 1815 but also the conservatives of the German states hostile to Prussian domination (for example, the German Hanover Party, which opposed Prussia's annexation of Hanover in 1866, and obtained nearly 40 per cent of the vote there in 1881), the activists of Action Française and the Vichy regime, and the Italian Monarchists and Christian Democrats of 1945–6. On the other hand, circumstances can sometimes turn the vociferous partisans of a decentralized State into ardent nationalists: the right wing of the Italian Unità was Jacobin and nationalist in the same way that Bismarck was nationalist and Lincoln's Republicans were federalist. The British Conservatives were hostile to the independence of Ireland in the same spirit as that of the Bonapartists, who opposed provincial autonomy. Wars and defeats, colonial expeditions, and the subsequent disintegration of empires are all factors that upset usual classifications and usual allegiances. When the circumstances are sufficiently dramatic, the conservative nationalist tendency can transcend traditional political divisions. In 1870 and 1914, virtually the whole of France became nationalist, supporting the tricolour, even at the risk of allowing itself to be seduced by the partisans of the *coup d'état* (Boulanger). Similarly, defeat (as in Germany), or the frustrations of victory combined with an economic crisis (as in Italy) sometimes exacerbate conservatism to the point where it favours dictatorship. The shock produced by decolonization in France produced other reclassifications: the most extreme wing of conservatism opposed de Gaulle by every means possible, including repeated assassination attempts. More recently, conservatives have been deeply divided over European integration, viewed by some as necessary to the expansion of free markets and economic prosperity, but by others as an unacceptable threat to national sovereignty, or even, in Margaret Thatcher's words, as 'socialism by the back door'. Bitter feuding over Europe blighted the second half of the British Tories' 18-year period in office after 1979, contributing powerfully to the catastrophic defeat of 1997, when they saw their vote drop from 41.9 per cent to 30.7 per cent and lost nearly half of their parliamentary seats. In France, Jacques Chirac was so badly wrong-footed by President Mitterrand's announcement of a referendum on the Maastricht Treaty in 1992 that he refused to refer to the subject in public for a month (the electors of his party, the Rassemblement pour la République, voted two to one against Maastricht).

Conservatism has also long been characterized by its attachment to private property and to the principle of authority, and by its reservations regarding universal suffrage, whose development it generally (with exceptions, notably Disraeli's 1867 Reform Act) blocked or slowed down until the beginning of the twentieth century. But here again, the conservative group may at certain times and in certain of its sections be divided by considerably more than mere questions of emphasis. In principle, conservatives are certainly hostile to State intervention and fiercely defend the right to property. But in none of the Western countries has that prevented them from adapting to the needs of the Welfare State. All the Western democracies devote between 35 and 50 per cent of GNP to public spending; nor has this situation been brought about solely by socialist or social democratic policies. De Gaulle was responsible for the post-war nationalizations and he practised interventionist policies in the 1960s; and in 1979 it was Valéry Giscard d'Estaing who completed the gradual nationalization of the steel industry.[13] In Italy, the Christian Democrats inherited Mussolini's legacy of State industry and continued to expand it considerably until the end of the 1960s. The same ambiguity pervades conservative attitudes towards authority at every level of society. In this respect, too, the conservative group is profoundly heterogeneous, for while it is natural for it to welcome the paternal but firm authority of moderates, some tendencies (monarchists) dream of an absolute form of authority, unshared or even dictatorial.

In the last analysis, conservatism is primarily characterized not so much by a fixed and homogeneous body of doctrine, but rather by a *state of mind*:[14] pessimism as regards the individual, hence the need for authority; distrust of the idea of progress, although conservatives have themselves often been the instruments of economic and social change (de Gaulle and Margaret Thatcher, in very different ways); pragmatism, which makes them willing to make adjustments to their principles; and the defence of interests that are judged to be fundamental, such as the rights of private enterprise and property. In countries where conservatism is organized as a single force, the ambiguities and contradictions of this way of thinking can be reconciled within the party itself (as in Britain and, to a lesser degree, Germany, if one regards the CDU–CSU as a conservative party). However, in countries where historical circumstances did not permit unification, conservatism finds expression in many factions that are sometimes deeply hostile to one another and that can only be brought to co-operate in exceptional circumstances: the Gaullists and the extreme Right in France, for instance; and the Christian Democrats and the MSI (the neo-Fascist Italian Social Movement) in Italy.

Since the Second World War, however, ideological conflict within conservative parties has been largely on the wane, for a number of reasons. In the first place, the conservative parties are generally 'parties in office' which, if they are to act, are forced constantly to accept compromises and the 'legacy' of their opponents. Secondly, conservative parties are obliged by the relentless law of universal suffrage to go 'hunting' beyond the confines of their preferred preserves, namely the middle and lower bourgeoisie. Their electorate is—must be—popular too. Many workers are conservative in France, as they are in Germany, Italy, the United States, and Britain (the 'Tory worker') and the party must win or keep their votes if it is to avoid defeat. This has proven a hard discipline but a valuable one for conservatives, for the routine obligation to reach out to a wide range of social groups has made them less vulnerable than social democratic parties typically are to the decline of a core electorate. Finally, in the absence of any fixed doctrine, conservatism tends to be opportunistic, taking in whoever or whatever may be useful to it in the prevailing circumstances and the spirit of the moment. What would have been unthinkable in the nineteenth century—an alliance between liberals and conservatives, for instance—is commonplace today and the frequent practice of coalition government renders the ideological doctrines of political parties in general and the conservatives in particular more fragile and more fluid. During the 1950s, in Britain, this pragmatism was dubbed 'Butskellism'. In the 1970s and 1980s it was, however, replaced by a return to ideology, chiefly under the influence of the New Right. The neo-conservatives, whose torch-bearers were Ronald Reagan and Margaret Thatcher, have been emulated more or less everywhere, including France, where Jacques Chirac, as late as 1976, was claiming to speak for 'French-style Labour' and claiming that the Gaullists under his leadership represented 'the social-democratic tendency in French politics'. The common denominator is criticism of the all-pervading tentacles of the State. But the battle is only waged against one particular section of the State, the part which initiates intervention in the economic sphere and social matters. In contrast, the policing part of the State is more than ever called upon in the name of security, both internal and external. This return to the principles of the old conservatives is often more a matter of words than of deeds, but it nevertheless reflects the ideological evolution of Western societies concerning the role and place of the Welfare State.

The far Right

By the late 1930s, democracy in Europe was confined to the British Isles, Scandinavia, France, Benelux, Switzerland, and Czechoslovakia. Germany, Italy, the Iberian peninsula, and much of central, eastern, and south-eastern Europe were in the hands of Fascist or right-wing authoritarian regimes. Most of these were destroyed by the Second World War and the Allies' victory, which left central and Eastern Europe under Communist rule, a right-wing authoritarian enclave in Iberia (and, from 1967, in Greece), and democracy everywhere else. By the late 1970s, all three southern European dictatorships had managed a transition to democracy and governmental Fascism had been wiped off the European map. Moreover, as political movements Fascism and the extreme Right had been all but marginalized, except perhaps in Italy where the Movimento Sociale Italiano–Destra Nazionale (MSI–DN) claimed a membership of several hundred thousand and regularly polled between 4.5 and 8.5 per cent of the vote.

In the mid- to late 1980s, however, the far right grew and prospered in several West European countries. It is represented in France by the Front National (FN), in Italy by the Alleanza Nazionale (AN), successor to the MSI, in Germany by the Republikaner and the Deutsche Volksunion, and in Britain—albeit on a minute scale—by the National Front and the British National Party. It is also influential in some regionalist groups such as the Flemish Bloc in Belgium and some of the Italian Leagues.

If it is relatively easy to identify certain parties as being of the far Right, it is more difficult to define the values and policies that they have in common and that separate them from other groups, and in particular from more moderate conservatives. The inter-war Fascists sought, often successfully, to replace liberal democracies with more or less authoritarian dictatorships. Some far-Right groupings—the Deutsche Volksunion, the National Democratic parties (NPD) in Austria and Germany, and the British National Party—remain loyal to this heritage. But the more successful parties of the far Right, while fairly contemptuous of parliamentary government, tend to support changes to presidential regimes in terms that are on the face of it entirely compatible with liberal democracy and mainstream constitutional debate. Basic civil liberties—the right to free expression, or to strike, for example—are conspicuous by their absence from the preoccupations of the far Right; on the other hand, such liberties have also at times been eroded by conservative governments, and under certain conditions (for example, the Algerian War or the outbreak of left-wing terrorism in West Germany in the early 1970s) by social democratic ones. The far Right has always lambasted the rottenness, corruption, and incapacity of mainstream parties—but so have the Communists, some Greens, and, when they were out of power in the 1940s and 1950s (and identified as an extreme right-wing party by their opponents), the Gaullists. And in practice, far-right-wing parties have tended to knock insistently at the doors of the political establishment as soon as they acquire a reasonable share of the vote. Anti-communism has been a consistent theme of extreme-right-wing groups—but in this they scarcely outdid parties like the West German and Italian Christian Democrats. Nationalism, and suspicion or rejection of supra-national organizations like the EC, the UN, or NATO, is a fairly consistent feature of far-right-wing attitudes—but has been shared at times by both Gaullists and Communists in France, for example. A desire to return to a mythical *status quo ante*, where everyone knew their place and the complexities of twentieth-century industrial society did not exist, has been a common appeal of many far-right-wing parties, and notably the pre-war Action Française; but in practice, leaders like Hitler and Mussolini turned out to be ruthless modernizers in many respects. The left-wing origins of some pre-war Fascists (Mussolini in Italy, the Strassers in Germany, Mosley in Britain, Doriot in France), and the propensity of Hitler and Mussolini to extend the role of the State into all areas of national life, may be contrasted with moderate conservatives' suspicion of government intervention; but some contemporary far-right leaders such as Le Pen claim a commitment to economic 'liberalism' that makes Thatcher and Reagan look positively insipid. Finally, racism in general, and in particular the anti-semitism that found its ultimate expression in the Holocaust, is a characteristic of many parties of the far Right—whether openly as in the case of Britain's National Front, or more covertly and coyly in that of its larger French counterpart. However, as Klaus von Beyme points out, racism has been largely absent from fascist ideology in the Latin countries, while it is instructive to note that the break-up of the 'European Right' group in the European Parliament in 1992 resulted from objections to the racism of Le Pen and the Front National from the Republikaner contingent.[15] There is thus no perfectly homogeneous, distinct, body of ideology that characterizes the far Right in Western Europe, any more than there is for the other major political currents. Far-right parties are, however, likely to share more of the characteristics listed above than other parties, and to combine them with a preference for simplistic, demagogic solutions to complex problems—the birthright of extreme oppositions everywhere.

The failure of left- and right-wing governments successfully to address the problems of long-term mass unemployment, a crisis in the housing market arising from shortages or deterioration of the existing stock, and rising crime rates, have contributed to the revival of the far Right, which has tended to blame all three on immigration. These phenomena of urban decay have also allowed several far-right-wing parties to make inroads into the working class, especially young white men. But the situation varies considerably between countries. In Britain, the National Front, having done alarmingly well in a handful of local elections in the 1970s, then disintegrated into several warring splinter-groups with minimal support. Personality clashes played a role in this; but so did the successfully nationalist, ethnocentric, and authoritarian appeal of Margaret Thatcher's Conservatives. Germany's far Right has made episodic appearances since the fall of the Third Reich it created. As the NPD in West Germany, it drew on frustrations arising from the economic downturn of the late 1960s, and from the political cartel of the Christian and Social Democrats' 'Grand Coalition', to win 4.3 per cent of the vote in the 1969 Federal elections, thus coming close to the threshold needed to win Bundestag seats. Two decades later, it re-emerged as the Republikaner under the leadership of former SS officer Franz Schönhüber, and did well in several *Land* elections. Unable to compete with the CDU on the national issue in 1990, the Republikaner were practically submerged in the rush to unification, polling barely 2 per cent in the December elections. But the consequences of unification and of the collapse of the Soviet bloc were a gift to a far-right party: economic uncertainty and sacrifice in the shape of higher taxes, and a big influx of immigrants (whether ethnic Germans or others from Eastern Europe and elsewhere seeking to benefit from the Federal Republic's liberal asylum laws) putting increased pressure on housing and jobs. Some of the results over the following five years appeared to reflect that. In 1992, the far Right did impressively at *Land* elections in Bremen, Schleswig-Holstein, and Baden-Württemburg (where the Republikaner polled nearly 11 per cent in April 1992, and 9 per cent four years later). There is also some evidence to suggest that the far Right's rejection of European monetary union, against what had been a consensus among mainstream politicians, pulled other parties, and notably the SPD and even the CSU, in a more Eurosceptical direction. On the other hand, the federal elections of 1994 saw the far Right contained at 2 per cent. It appears unlikely that Germany's far Right will go away, in the current conditions. But equally, unemployment in the early 1990s does not appear to have benefited the Republikaner as it had benefited Hitler 60 years earlier.

Italy's MSI has been the most consistently supported extreme-right party in a European democracy since the Second World War, fluctuating between 4.4 and 8.7 per cent of the vote in parliamentary elections since 1953 and at times winning over 20 per cent in some southern cities. Its relationship with the established democratic system has been ambiguous. MSI members have been behind right-wing terrorist attacks including, in the opinion of many, a murderous, indiscriminate, bombing at Bologna station in 1980. But the MSI has routinely condemned such attacks, and its leader Giorgio Almirante multiplied friendly contacts with other parties (even paying a respectful visit to Communist leader Enrico Berlinguer—after the latter's death). Like the Italian Communists, the MSI under the 'first Republic' reached the threshold of government office, but no further; the Tambroni government's attempt to include it in a broadened DC governing majority ended in failure after popular demonstrations. Perhaps because of its long-standing position half-inside the Italian party system, the MSI initially reaped little benefit from the outbreaks of discontent with the major parties of 1992, when it actually lost half a percentage point. Such discontent was expressed more readily in support for the Leagues. That, however, changed after 1992, when the MSI's new, young, and telegenic leader, Gianfranco Fini, seized the opportunity afforded by the implosion of Italy's party system to stress the MSI's moderation, respectability, cleanness (above all), and fitness for government. The dividends were not slow in coming: a score of 13.5 per cent in the 1994 elections, taken not only from former Christian Democrat voters but also from former left-wing supporters, and five ministries in the Berlusconi government alongside Forza Italia and the Northern League. The failure of the Berlusconi experiment and his fall from power in December 1994 left Fini's party practically unscathed. With its name henceforth changed to Alleanza Nazionale (AN), and its identity distanced further, though not completely, from the Fascist past (notably by insisting on the specific and unrepeatable context of Mussolini's regime), it won 15.7 per cent of the vote in the 1996 elections, and support among the better-educated sections of the population as well as the excluded and disinherited. The AN's success in breaking into the mainstream of politics and, indeed, into government—the only far-right-wing party to do so in Western Europe since the Second World War—is open to two interpretations. It may be seen either as a reassuring sign that Italy's Fascists, at least, have been prepared to abandon their more extreme views and work within the democratic system, or as an alarming indication of the rise in Europe of a far Right which, despite having forsaken black shirts for Armani suits, has, at heart, given up few of its old beliefs and habits.

France's far Right, like Germany's, has had a far more episodic existence than the MSI, but since 1984 has provided Western Europe with its biggest extreme-right party in the shape of Jean-Marie Le Pen's FN. De Gaulle's followers in the Rassemblement du Peuple Français (RPF) of the late 1940s and early 1950s combined rabid anti-communism with fierce opposition to the Fourth Republic and to the European Defence Community; they were placed on the far Right by their opponents before being disowned by de Gaulle in 1953. The second right-wing surge party of the Fourth Republic, the Poujadists, started as a disorganized group of small traders (in sharp contrast to the heavily structured Gaullist organization), did well in the 1956 elections, but effectively disappeared as a political force with the change of Republic in 1958. The second half of the Algerian war saw the far Right turn to terrorism in the shape of the OAS before reverting, albeit unsuccessfully, to mainstream politics in the Tixier-Vignancour presidential candidacy of 1965, which was supported by many former colonists who had returned from Algeria to settle on France's Mediterranean coast. The FN was founded in 1972 and brought together both supporters of Tixier-Vignancour and activists from tiny, extreme groups of the late 1960s such as Occident and its successor Ordre Nouveau. But for the first decade, the FN's impact on French politics was negligible.

What caused the FN to break through in local elections in 1983, to win the support of 10 per cent or more of voters from 1984 onwards, and to reach 15 per cent at the 1995 presidential election and the 1997 parliamentary elections? Early explanations focused on right-wing voters' exasperation with the moderate Right, and its apparent inability to fight back after the Socialist victory of 1981; Le Pen did well in the smarter districts of Paris in 1984. But the FN has attracted more than traditional right-wing supporters; surveys carried out in 1988 showed the breadth of its cross-class support, while one poll dating from late 1991 put it as the leading party among France's working class. And some, at least, of the FN's supporters are more favourable to the left's economic policies than to those of the moderate Right.[16] Le Pen's electorate is held together by fear of immigration and immigrants—it is relatively small, for example, in conservative areas of western France with low immigrant populations. At earlier times of high growth and full employment, immigrants had not been a political issue. Nor were they even in the economic downturn of the 1970s, when the Left's claims to be able to end the economic crisis through a structural break with capitalism dictated the political agenda. Le Pen's opportunity was offered by the Left's failure to deliver once in power after 1981. That enabled him to argue that his proposals to send 'home' France's population of North African origin were the only 'solution' that had not been tried. And the use of proportional representation both for the European elections of 1984 and for the parliamentary elections of 1986 ensured that FN votes would produce FN parliamentarians in Brussels and Paris, who in turn won the party air-time and respectability.

The fact that the FN electorate of the early years was a 'soft' one, with little commitment to or identification with the party, suggested to optimistic observers that it might, like Poujadism, be no more than a temporary 'surge' movement. That has not been the case. Initially hesitant voters have turned into committed ones by virtue of repetition; the tendency of the French to favour local office-holders in all types of election has begun to benefit the FN, which now holds regional council seats, as well as four large towns in the south of France; and the regularity with which between a quarter and a third of poll respondents declare their agreement with Le Pen's ideas indicates a substantial electoral reserve. The FN's success in making itself an apparently permanent feature of the French political landscape is an unprecedented feat in the history of France's far Right. Whether it can be translated into an alliance with the more moderate conservative parties, and thence into national office, as some leaders both in the FN and even on the moderate Right would like, is less certain. But the underlying factors that have contributed to the FN's success—long-term mass unemployment, the alternation of economic policies between centre-left and centre-right within the tight constraints of the European and world economies, and constant pressure to immigrate from inhabitants of Western Europe's poorer neighbours to south and east—appear set to continue. They offer a potential source of support to the far right throughout Western Europe.

The Christian democrats

The Christian democratic parties are not exclusively Catholic (the CDU is a mixture of Protestants and Catholics and the Scandinavian Christian democratic parties are essentially Protestant in inspiration). Nevertheless, it is undeniably in predominantly

Catholic countries (Belgium, Italy, former West Germany, and France) that the Christian democrats are most firmly anchored.[17] But the birth and development of Christian democratic parties are themselves conditioned by other elements in the political picture, in particular by the existence of liberal or radical parties that constitute a direct threat to the Church and the Catholics. In this respect, the total failure of the Christian Democrats in post-Franco Spain is indicative, as is the fact that they are completely absent from Ireland, where all the parties proclaim their allegiance to the Church. As we have noted in our discussion of conservative ideology, since the 1960s particularly many overlaps have developed between conservative and Christian democratic doctrines. Christian democrats and conservatives may find themselves in agreement in a number of respects: pessimism as to human nature, attachment to the right of property, to non-extremist groups, and to the authority of those legitimately invested with it (heads of families, etc.). There is nothing surprising about this doctrinal agreement. Quite apart from the fact that the Catholic Church itself took up position in the die-hard conservative camp throughout the nineteenth century, the conservatives in part found their inspiration in the precepts of religion, whose natural defenders they considered themselves to be. 'The compact between throne and altar' was no mere figure of rhetoric. Nevertheless, the European Christian democratic movement was born from a twofold 'dissidence': first, towards the most hardened conservatives, who were totally unresponsive to the 'social question'; secondly, towards the Church itself, which was initially hostile to the formation of Catholic political parties which would collaborate in the establishment of a democracy. For democracy was itself condemned as one of the 'errors of our times' by a whole succession of popes up until Leo XIII. In 1832, Gregory XVI, naming no names, condemned Lammenais together with all those who 'under the cover of religion are everywhere attempting to ignite the flames of innovation and revolution'. It is true that, in 1892, Leo XIII, in his encyclical 'In the Midst of Solicitudes', recommended that French Catholics should accept the Republic, but papal support for socially involved Catholics continued to be extremely measured, as is attested by the papacy's condemnation of the 'Sillon' movement of Marc Sangnier, who later founded the Popular Democratic Party, and of the post-war movement of 'worker-priests'. The papacy continued for a long time to attempt to dissuade Catholics from taking an active part in politics, trying to persuade them, instead, to concern themselves solely with charitable works. It was only out of necessity (for the Church was losing influence) and because the experience of the German Zentrum had not proved altogether negative (the Centre Party had, after all, made it possible to put up some resistance to the *Kulturkampf* and the persecutions of Bismarck) that the Pope made a few concessions: in the elections held before 1914, a few Catholic candidates came forward (winning 4 per cent of the vote in 1909 and 6 per cent in 1913), but it was not until after the First World War that Don Sturzo was allowed by the Vatican to launch himself fully into Italian politics, provided he agreed to a division of tasks: Catholic Action, placed under the authority of the Pope, would be responsible for providing a social and religious framework for Catholics; meanwhile, the party would organize them, more autonomously, on the political level.

The conditions in which the Christian democratic parties made their appearance and the strong influence of Church doctrine certainly explain some features of Christian democratic ideology and policies. But it cannot be denied that, as they have evolved, these parties have considerably modified their original exclusive orientation.

One characteristic feature of Christian democratic ideology is a forthright rejection of the extreme doctrines put forward by capitalism on the one hand and Marxism on the other. Both represent forms of materialism that run counter to most teaching of the Church. It was characteristic of their desire to establish a distance from both types of materialism that the title given to the programme that the CDU elaborated in 1947 should be 'CDU überwindet Kapitalismus und Marxismus' (the CDU outdoes capitalism and Marxism). The 1945–6 programmes of the Italian Christian Democrats and the French MRP were inspired by a similar distrust. The position that they adopted reflected the hierarchy of Christian democratic values inspired by Church doctrines: the spiritual comes before the material and economics should be put to the service of mankind. It is on this basis that the Christian democrats dissociate themselves from the conservatives, for whom social interests take second place to the dictates of the economy. This Christian democratic order of priority had a number of concrete political consequences, particularly after the Second World War: policies favouring families and economic planning in France; support for craftsmen, shopkeepers, and smallscale farmers in Italy; and a policy of shared management in the mining sector and the steel industry in West Germany were all products of that humanist and social conviction. But the Christian democrats could not maintain their position of equidistance from capitalism and communism for long. The post-war success of the Christian democrats stemmed as much from the collapse of the traditional right-wing parties, ostracized after the fall of the authoritarian regimes of Italy, France, and Germany, as it did from the intrinsic appeal of the new political groups themselves. No doubt they did constitute the party for Christians, but they also spoke for the moderate Right. The Christian democratic parties were, from the start, torn between, on the one hand, those doctrines that distanced them from the Right and, on the other, their electorate, which was more conservative than the party leaders. Those that remained more faithful to their ideals than to the tendencies of their voters, such as the MRP in France, paid the price for doing so. First they were weakened, then they collapsed. In contrast, with the Cold War delivering them the anti-Communist vote, the CDU–CSU and the Christian Democrats in Italy succeeded in playing down their initial anti-capitalism and became converted to the market economy (conveniently renamed 'the social market economy' in West Germany, where it was represented by Ludwig Erhard, an enthusiastic proponent of economic liberalism).

Secondly, Christian democratic parties since the Second World War have been resolutely pro-European. Perhaps the fact that their leaders belonged to a supranational Church and their common faith made them readier than others to overstep national boundaries. At all events, it was undeniably men such as Alcide de Gasperi, Konrad Adenauer, and Robert Schuman who were the builders of Europe, 'Vatican Europe', as the Communists stigmatized it in the 1950s. This is also the domain in which Christian democrats have been the most consistent and tenacious, whatever the compromises made elsewhere in the economic or social domains. For the Italian party it was a costly choice: their instinctive reaction in favour of European monetary union entailed a degree of rigour in public finance that rapidly undermined their client base. For Helmut Kohl and the CDU, the unification of Europe was a logical sequel to that of Germany, and one which—given the reluctance of Germans to give up the mark—entailed political risks that were at least comparable.

The third characteristic of the Christian democratic movement is the importance that it attaches to the values of education and morality. For a long time, Christian democratic parties were expected to adopt the Catholic Church's position on such matters (the Protestant Churches meanwhile took a more liberal line), and this no doubt delayed their secularization. In West Germany, Italy, and France, the pressure for denominational teaching remained considerable and the ways in which it was organized and financed and the manner in which it functioned often provoked violent conflict. Compromise solutions on the issue of relations between Church and State were not found until relatively late in the day and were frequently a source of acrimony in political life. The Fourth French Republic was in a constant state of agitation over the schools controversy, which was not resolved until 1958. But between 1981 and 1984, and again in 1994, the country was shaken by new upheavals on this issue, a clear enough indication that the battle over schools was now a clash no longer between Catholics and the State, but between the Right and the Left. In West Germany, up until the late 1960s and despite the Concordat of 1933, there were many clashes in the *Länder* on account of their responsibility for educational policies, and not until 1983 did religious instruction become optional in Italian schools.

Family and moral questions were also for many years central to Christian democratic doctrine: marriage, divorce, contraception, and abortion were so many areas where Church law became Christian democratic programme. Only gradually did some Christian democrats come round to the idea that personal religious convictions should be kept separate from the party programme. As in the sphere of economic matters, the change was a product of necessity, that is to say it was brought about by constraints that stemmed from the changing nature of the electorate. For although as many as 90 per cent of French, German, and Italian adults are ready to declare themselves Christians of one sort or another, regular churchgoers now number only between 10 and 15 per cent of the adult population. The rest have become less and less receptive to the teachings of the Pope or of other religious hierarchies, and the Christian democratic parties have accordingly been obliged to adapt to their voters. Legislation on contraception and abortion and less stringent divorce procedures were introduced in France by governments that included 'centre' politicians from Christian democratic parties; and in Italy, the same reforms were brought about, willy-nilly, by governments that were dominated by the Christian Democrats. It is true that in Italy the reforms were carried out somewhat reluctantly and many Christian Democrat Deputies first opposed them in Parliament and subsequently insisted upon a referendum in the hope of repealing them. However, the result of this inflexible line was disastrous for the Christian

Democrats. When the referendum on divorce was held in 1974, those in favour of repealing the law (the Christian Democrats and the MSI) obtained no more than 40.7 per cent of the vote although the Christian Democrats, on their own, had been oscillating around the 39 per cent mark ever since 1963. The collapse of Christian Democratic support showed that a proportion of the 'secularized' bourgeois electorate now preferred to vote for a small secular party rather than for a conservative 'Catholic' party. The Christian Democrat Party was faced with a crucial choice: should it be a Catholic party, a party of and for Catholics, or a moderate conservative one? In this respect, as in the economic domain, the Christian democratic parties moved closer to the conservatives. Indeed, it could be said that in the countries where they dominate a large section of the political spectrum, that is, Italy (before 1992) and Germany in particular, they have, under the pressure of circumstances, become *the* conservative party.

A new challenge faced the major Christian democratic parties with the collapse of the Soviet empire, since, particularly in the earlier post-war years, they had always based some of their support on anti-communism. The contrast between the German and Italian experiences here is striking. Germany's Chancellor Kohl seized the opportunity offered by the piercing of the Berlin Wall to unite his country, ensuring his place in history as the 'unification Chancellor', acquiring a degree of personal electoral invulnerability (at least until the Germans began to pay for unification), and extending his party's electoral audience into the atheistic lands of the former Democratic Republic. For the Italian party, on the other hand, the end of Soviet Communism removed a vital source of electoral appeal, just two years before the public financial underpinning for its clientelistic base became unsustainable, the judicial investigations of the *Mani pulite* operation began to reveal the extent of its involvement in corruption, and the electoral reform gave politics a bipolar tendency which it had previously lacked. The result, in 1993, was that the Italian Christian Democratic party disintegrated. The mainstream renamed itself as the Italian People's Party (PPI), attempted to hold the centre ground in a bipolarizing party system in 1994, and finally reconstituted the 'historic compromise' in alliance with the former Communists of the PDS in what became known in 1996 as the 'Olive Tree' coalition. A right wing allied itself with the Alleanza Nazionale and Berlusconi's Forza Italia, but was itself split into two components, the Christian Democratic Centre and Christian Democratic Union. Between them, the former Christian democratic formations mustered 15 per cent of the vote in 1996, roughly half what they had achieved four years earlier. It is true that the Prime Minister appointed in 1996 at the head of the Olive Tree coalition, Romano Prodi, was a former Christian Democrat; that their very dispersal across the political spectrum virtually ensured the presence of Christian Democrat ministers in any possible government; and that some Christian Democrats, especially those outside the majority coalition, dreamt of reconstituting a 'broad centre' that would revive the fortunes of their former party. But the Christian Democrats' return to the dominant position of the 'first Republic' appeared to be precluded, in the medium term, by the bipolarization of the party system after 1994.

The divided Left

The birth of socialism in Europe in the nineteenth century marked a new departure in the relationship of political parties to voters and institutions and also in their relations between one another. Socialist parties claimed to work for one particular class, the working class, and they took up the struggle against bourgeois institutions, organized themselves into an 'International', and consigned both the liberals and the radicals, considered until then the 'revolutionaries', to the camp of the supporters of the established order. For many liberal parties, the advance of the socialist parties was to spell decline, even obliteration. Yet, initially, the main strength of the socialist parties came not from their militancy or their parliamentary representation—which until the turn of the century remained quite derisory; rather, it lay in their programmes' destabilizing effects upon the bourgeois monarchies and republics of the late nineteenth century. Nevertheless, the socialists, the 'reds', the 'sharers' (*partageurs*), and other 'communards' were, from the start, divided by their own internal quarrels and their constant clashes over ideology and policies at both international and national level.

This was principally because of the large number both of key doctrines and of founding fathers of different *kinds* of socialism: the 'utopian communism' of men such as Proudhon and Fourier and the reformism of Louis Blanc and Pierre Leroux in France were opposed by the vigorous critical analyses of Marx and Engels, who propounded a 'scientific' socialism. The 1848 *Manifesto* was not simply a revolutionary proclamation; it was also a condemnation of all the forms of socialism that Marx and Engels deemed worthy of rejection. For they also condemned Lasalle's state socialism (see *The Critique of the Gotha Programme* (1875)) on the grounds that it compromised with nationalism and with the bourgeois State (particularly in the creation of production companies controlled by the proletariat but dependent on State aid). Their condemnation of Bakunin and the anarchists was even stronger: they were guilty of attacking the State without first tackling the causes which brought it into being and which continued to justify its existence (capitalist accumulation). Over and above these early clashes and the excommunications that tore socialism apart, we should take into account the many individual modes in which socialism took hold in the various countries and the manner in which Marxist theories became known there. Germany and France present two strongly contrasting examples of the reception that Marxism received from local socialists. In Germany, the thought of Marx and Engels was widely diffused and discussed, thanks to the unified Social Democrat Party created in 1875, and also through Karl Kautsky and Rosa Luxemburg. In France, on the other hand, it became known later and even then only in a limited fashion (very few editions and translations into French were published before the end of the century). In the hands of the Guesdists, it was, furthermore, transformed into an often simplistic and doctrinaire vulgate. The situation was compounded by the many factions into which socialism had split in France, for it was not until 1905 that they were belatedly drawn together in the SFIO. Jaurès had to pay the price for this unification, and claimed that he too derived his inspiration from Marxism, but this was more a matter of convenience than of true conviction. Far from easing these tensions, the 1917 Revolution exacerbated them throughout Europe. When the Third International was formed under the aegis of Lenin, it produced a deep and lasting split among socialists, dividing them into reformist socialists on the one hand, and communists hostile to 'bourgeois democracy' and committed to Moscow on the other.

At the level of organizations designed to rally the working-class masses, the contrasts are equally striking. As early as 1890, the powerful German SPD won 1,400,000 votes and 35 seats in the Reichstag; by the eve of the First World War, it counted 110 Reichstag seats, and a million party members supported by three million trade unionists. In France and Italy, on the other hand, socialist movements were uncoordinated at both the political and the trade union levels. The Italian Socialist Party did not take shape until 1891, the SFIO not until 1905, and the trade unions did not organize themselves into a confederation until 1906 in France (the CGT), and 1907 in Italy (the Confederazione Generale Italiana del Lavoro: the CGIL). Furthermore, political structures and party organization remained separated by a wide gulf. In France, the Amiens Charter officially rejected setting up links between the trade unions and the party (in contrast to the situation of British trade unionism).

Britain, along with Belgium, is the world's oldest industrial society, with the longest-established working class and the longest tradition of working-class activism. But it was not until the end of the nineteenth century, after three extensions of the suffrage, that this activism made the jump from trade unionism to the creation of a political party. In 1899, the Trades Union Congress decided to set up a 'Labour Representation Committee'. It came into being in 1900 with the purpose of ensuring parliamentary representation for the workers by co-ordinating the various political groups: to wit, the Independent Labour Party (with 13,000 members), the Marxist Social Democratic Federation (with 9,000 members), and the Fabian Society which, despite its small membership (861 in 1900), had a huge intellectual impact on the constitution and doctrine of the party.

The socialist parties born at the beginning of the century, together with the Western communist parties, are certainly those that most strongly proclaim their commitment to an ideology, a doctrine, and a programme. But precisely because their ideological positions were the most uncompromising, their conflicts, crises, and histories have been the most dramatic. It would not be possible to describe the history and processes of evolution of socialist ideology in the limited space at our disposal. The most we can hope to do is sketch in the broad outlines of development in a few key areas such as the economy, access to power and the exercise of it, and internationalism.

The contrast between the SPD's early embrace of the social market economy at Bad Godesberg in 1959, and Labour's tardier (but almost unnervingly enthusiastic) acceptance of capitalism under Tony Blair has been referred to earlier (above, p. 23). The behaviour of the French Socialist Party that rose from the ashes of the SFIO and the clubs of the Left in the 1960s was more hesitant. There can be no doubt that nationalization was only desired by the left wing of the party and many voters, activists, and leaders did not really consider that aspect of Socialist Party doctrine to be of fundamental importance. But two other considerations pushed the Socialist Party into the policy of large-scale nationalization that it eventually carried out in 1981–2. One was the tactical necessity to come to an agreement with the French Communist Party, which was determined to make nationalization the corner-stone and goal of any government of a united left. The second was the relative disregard—not to say lack of understanding—shown by most socialists towards the economy and the market. Not until 1983 did François Mitterrand voice praise for the mixed economy, not until 1984 did the process of gradual and partial denationalization begin, and it was 1985 before the Socialists, at the Toulouse Congress, qualified their choice of a State-administered economy. Although France's corruption scandals of the early 1990s revealed the extent to which the Socialists had relied materially on kickbacks from firms (particularly building companies seeking contracts), relations with private business continued to pose an ideological problem for many activists and even leaders.[18] The issue of even a partial privatization of a State-owned enterprise like France Telecom remained a controversial one for the French Socialists supporting the Jospin government in 1997. In Italy, on the other hand, the Christian Democrats' appropriation of large parts of the public sector for their own personal and party ends made the advantages of a nationalized or State-controlled economy appear much less obvious in the eyes of the Left. That led the reformed Communists of the PDS, once they were in government after 1996, to accept privatizations with some enthusiasm, even if such measures were less well received by the Rifondazione party, which had stuck more closely to Communist principles, and which sought at least to bargain its support for privatizations for concessions on the welfare budget.

The question of access to power and the exercise of power is unquestionably one of the crucial points that for many years divided socialists from communists. For the socialists, winning power was a matter of legality and elections; for the communists, right up until the Second World War, participation in electoral competition to gain access to Parliament was motivated above all by a desire to subvert bourgeois institutions. Their ideal remained the revolution, as achieved by the model brother party of the Soviet Union.

The threat of Nazism and Fascism, and the Spanish Civil War changed the attitudes of Western communist parties, for they now learned a lesson from the socialists of Germany and Italy, who refused to collaborate with the bourgeois parties to oppose Hitler and Mussolini. The strategy of the Popular Front in France and Spain was adopted with the blessing of Stalin, who was becoming worried by the rising power of Nazi Germany. In 1936, the French Communist leader Maurice Thorez justified this apparent acceptance of the bourgeois democratic game by proclaiming:

Perhaps History will declare that one of the great merits of the Communist Party in France is, to borrow Nietzsche's words, to have given all values a new value. We have readopted the Marseillaise and the banner of our forefathers, the soldiers of Year Two. We have readopted those verses on liberty . . . We have behaved as Marxists, rejecting dead slogans but retaining the living content that certain things, even legacies of the past, express.[19]

The Second World War and the Resistance made it possible for the Italian and French Communist parties to become integrated into new institutions by taking an active part in their creation and establishment. The French and Italian parties were both active partners in government before the outbreak of the Cold War and the spring of 1947, when they both found themselves suddenly removed to a spell in opposition that lasted till 1981 for the French party and till 1996, as a result of what is known as the *conventio ad excludendum*, for the Italians. The two parties' development since 1947 can be divided into three periods: from 1947 to the early 1960s, from the early 1960s until the mid-1980s, and from the mid-1980s to the present day. The first period, roughly corresponding to the worst of the Cold War, was for both parties one of near-total exclusion from mainstream politics at home, despite high levels of electoral support (over 22 per cent in Italy, and over 25 per cent in France until 1958).

During the second period, opening with a modest thaw in the Cold War, both parties became more integrated into their respective political systems. But the paths of the French and Italian parties diverged in many important respects. The Italians were increasingly prepared, in the context of a parliamentary system where inter-party bargaining was the norm, to work with the 'system' and vote bills through parliament, in a strategy that found its ultimate expression in the 'historic compromise' of the 1970s. This strategy failed to win them national office and was abandoned in 1980, but the Italian Communists ended the period electorally stronger than they had begun it, with their vote running at some 30 per cent and peaking at 33.3 at the European elections of 1984, in a wave of sympathy after the death of their popular leader Enrico Berlinguer. The French party, on the other hand, while probably less inclined than the Italians to move closer to the system, was none the less almost forced by the institutional dynamic of the Fifth Republic to join a strategic alliance with the Socialists, in opposition to the ruling right-wing coalition. The 'Union of the Left' improved the support of their allies, but left the Communists stagnating in the region of 20 per cent of the vote, a figure that fell to 15.4 per cent in the 1981 presidential election. Unlike their Italian counterparts, the French Communists did enter government, but only after their own crushing defeat had indirectly contributed to Mitterrand's victory. The four Communist ministers whom Mitterrand appointed had no influence on the key policy decisions, and left office in 1984 after a further dramatic slump in PCF support to 11.2 per cent in the European elections (prompting one French commentator to observe that Berlinguer dead had done three times as well as Marchais alive).

The most recent period has seen both the Italian and the French Communists return to government, the Italians in 1996 and the French PCF in 1997. But the return was effected under very different conditions in the two cases. For the Italians, it was the culmination of a long and tortuous process of organizational and ideological renewal, which included three election defeats (26.6 per cent of the vote in 1987, a drop of over 3 points on 1983; 16.1 per cent in 1992; and 20.4 per cent in 1994, before the marginal upturn to 21.1 per cent in 1996 which propelled the PDS into government as the major party of the new centre-left Olive Tree coalition); two changes of leader (from Alessandro Natta to Achille Occhetto in 1987, and from Occhetto to Massimo d'Alema in 1994); an almost continuous process of ideological revision from Eurocommunism to social democracy, with the high point of the change coming with the change of name in 1990; one major split, as the committed communists left to form Rifondazione Comunista in 1991; and one false entry into government, in the 1993 Ciampi ministry. The main task of the Prodi government was to implement the austerity measures necessary for Italy to meet the criteria to join Europe's single currency in 1998. This was a goal to which the PDS was sufficiently committed and ideologically prepared that it supported the measures, despite their implications for many long-standing left-wing supporters; indeed, even Rifondazione, which had stayed out of the government, did not go as far as outright opposition.

France's Communists, on the other hand, entered Lionel Jospin's left-wing government in June 1997 with many more misgivings. The party vote had stagnated at 10 per cent or less since 1986, making the PCF very much the junior partner to the Socialists, who had over twice that level of support; the process of internal reform after 1994 engaged by the new Communist leader, Robert Hue, had been undertaken with great caution; the Party's memories of participation in government with the Socialists in the past, in 1944–7 and particularly in 1981–4, were not happy ones; and both the election and the left's victory had been unexpected. Moreover, it became clear within weeks that Jospin, like Prodi, was intent on qualifying his country for monetary union, a goal to which the PCF, unlike the PDS, was officially opposed. It was perhaps not surprising that within three months of the election victory Hue should come under pressure from the PCF's hardliners to return to opposition.

The problem of Communist or former Communist parties entering government in coalition with larger socialist and 'bourgeois' partners, in an economic context that renders impossible the realization of any substantive Communist aims (indeed, it might be argued, of any substantive left-wing aims), is really the most recent version of a dilemma that socialist parties themselves encountered in the past: how far to compromise socialist principles in order to win and retain office in an increasingly globalized capitalist economy. As we have seen, both the West German SPD and (much later) Britain's New Labour chose to make their peace with capitalism, in the expectation both that this would be attractive to the voters and that the gap between expectations and performance in government would thereby be narrowed. In Italy and France the issue was complicated by the need to join alliances in order to win, but this imperative pulled the two Socialist parties in opposite directions. The Italian Socialists began a *rapprochement* with the Christian Democrats in the 1960s which earned them the prestigious intellectual approval of the philosopher Norberto Bobbio, who wrote:

The Socialist Party is a median party, that is, a classic party of coalition, be it with the right, the left or the centre, either in government or in opposition. Like it or not, a median party is a coalition party, that is, it can only make its influence felt by entering into a coalition.[20]

That logic, however, led the PSI into the heart of Italy's corrupt political establishment, and thus ultimately to its downfall. For France's Socialists (the PS), on the other hand, the problem, once they had jettisoned any serious notion of joining a centre-left grouping (which they had done by 1970), was that the Communist alliance in the 1970s and again, albeit to a lesser extent, after 1993, acted as a leftward pull on policy-making. This explains in part the expectations which the Left had to face on arrival in power in 1981, and the bitterness among many left-wing voters when they were dashed. Whether the same will be the case with Jospin in 1997 remains to be seen.

One distinctive feature of the socialist movements was the way in which, from the outset, they banded together to form a workers' International. The First International was created in London, in 1864, when the International Association of Workers was set up. But constant clashes with the supporters of Proudhon, Mazzini, and above all Bakunin caused Marx to transfer the association's headquarters to New York in 1872. The disintegration of the First International made in possible to set up the Second International in 1889, marking the centenary of the French Revolution. But although these associations were based upon the idea that 'proletarians do not have a country' and that nationalism was a product of bourgeois culture, they foundered utterly when the First World War broke out. Numerous pacifist moves were initiated but they were a total failure as the French, British, and Belgian socialists refused to sit down at the same table as the German ones. The informal conference held at Zimmerwald in Switzerland in 1915 was also a failure, although its delegates did agree to refuse to follow the radical line defended by Lenin (namely, that of 'turning this imperialist war into a civil war'). The Second International managed to survive despite the divisions that appeared between socialists, along lines defined by the belligerent States, and also the internal rifts caused by some of the individual choices made by its members. (For example, Mussolini was excluded from the Socialist Party on the grounds of his ardent support for Italy's entry into the war, after having earlier been an equally determined pacifist.)

However, all this dissension certainly heralded future rifts. In 1920 and 1921, Blum with his followers in France and Turati with his in Italy were excluded by the party's left wing, which remained faithful to Lenin and the Soviet Communist Party. Relations between the socialist and the communist parties in Europe were appalling for most of the inter-war period: the German Communists, whose uprising in 1918–19 had been suppressed by a Social Democrat government, fought mercilessly against their former SPD comrades, sometimes even going so far as to join forces with Nazi groups. Up until 1934, the French Socialists were similarly dragged through the mud, being denounced as 'social Fascists'; and the periods of reconciliation in 1934–8 and 1941–7 were short-lived. The outbreak of the Cold War revived the atmosphere of hatred, mutual insults, and dirty tricks. The reformist Force Ouvrière (FO), broadly supportive of the Socialists, split off from the pro-Communist CGT. Nenni's refusal to burn the bridges between the Socialist Party and the Italian Communist Party in 1947 resulted in Saragat's departure to form a dissident Social Democrat Party, the PSDI.

The Second International had been powerless to prevent nationalistic rifts. The Third International then proceeded to split the socialist movement definitively into social democrats on the one hand and communist parties on the other. A true International, which would certainly override national divisions, did exist, but not so much for the benefit of the world-wide working class as for that of a pitiless and unprincipled dictatorship.

Not until the 1970s did the links of Western Communist parties with Moscow begin to loosen. It took no less than the repression in Berlin and Budapest, the Khrushchev report, the invasions of Czechoslovakia and Afghanistan, and further repression both in Poland and elsewhere to undermine that mechanical alignment of all brother communist parties. The attempt that the Italian, Spanish, and French Communists made to create a 'Euro-communism' hung fire, faced with Moscow's hostility and as a result of the unequal determination of the three parties involved in this strategy for autonomy. After 1979 and the revival of the Cold War, conditions for a broadening of Communist influence in Western Europe were hardly propitious, and as support for the Spanish party collapsed, while the Italians broke their links with Moscow and the French renewed them, the Western Communists' brief window of opportunity of the mid-1970s closed firmly shut.

Meanwhile, the socialist parties have managed, by dint of adapting their ideology, to quit their role of eternal opposition and to become government parties (in France, Italy, Spain, Austria, and Greece as well as Britain). The socialist and social democratic parties of Western Europe are also loosely bound together in a Socialist International (which, apart from its name, has very little in common with the early Internationals). They have become the defenders and engineers of the kind of democracy that their fathers used to deride. As for the heirs to the original socialism, now as then they are divided and weak: the limited number of activist troops of the extreme left throughout Europe has not deterred them from indulging in esoteric and sectarian squabbles. Their intellectual influence has been by no means negligible for all that, particularly in the late 1960s and the 1970s. But even in that peak period, neither in West Germany, nor in France, nor in Britain, was the extreme left able to overcome the obstacles of electoral legislation and win parliamentary representation. Italy is the only country where, because of the former extremely proportionalist electoral system, it has been possible for representatives of this kind of socialism, which is supported more by intellectuals than by the working class, to find a place at Montecitorio (the seat of the Chamber of Deputies). Even here, the decision of the last survivor of these groups, Democrazia Proletaria, to join the (relatively) mainstream Rifondazione Comunista in July 1991 signalled the end of an era.

Territorial politics and regionalist parties

Most European nation states are the untidy products of historical accident, and as such fail to satisfy the aspirations felt by some of their inhabitants to a distinct territorial identity. It is true that great empires were dismantled, initially in the nineteenth century and again following the First World War, in the name of the principle of nationality, but the treaties that redrew the map of Europe in 1919–20 created at least as many discontented minorities as satisfied nationalities. The Second World War introduced a new batch of territorial tensions, and the manner of their resolution was in many cases brutal: consider the massive displacement of peoples and the rigid domination of the Soviet Union in Eastern Europe. That strong territorial identities can survive even the most determined and autocratic rule from the centre, possibly even thriving on repression, was strikingly demonstrated by the emergence of the USSR and its former satellites from Communist rule. In many cases, the assertion of such identities took priority for populations and for successor governments over the mundane business of rebuilding shattered economies.

In Western Europe, territorial politics were held of little importance for two decades after the Second World War, but they re-emerged in the 1960s to take all the specialists by surprise, provoking a plethora of analyses and explanations. The first point to note is that while the regionalist phenomenon has affected almost all West European countries, and particularly Spain, Belgium, the United Kingdom, Italy, and France, the ways in which it has found political expression have varied considerably. It produced terrorist movements in Northern Ireland, the Basque Country, Corsica, and (more ephemerally) in Brittany. In other areas, regionalist parties are non-existent or insignificant but electoral behaviour has or has had a strong regional profile (e.g. the Christian Democrat vote in Alsace and Brittany); elsewhere, in contrast, political parties are organized on a specifically regional rather than national basis (as in Belgium). Between these two extremes, many intermediate situations are possible, such as those where regionalist parties have either acquired a dominant position (as in the Alto-Adige, the Valley of Aosta, and the Basque region) or else are at least competitive (as in Scotland or Corsica).

Thus regionalist ideology may be expressed by political parties but, given their electoral weakness in most cases, is not expressed solely by them. Regionalist parties are single-issue parties: they focus almost exclusively on *a single* problem, and all other questions are perceived from that angle and treated in relation to it. Virtually everywhere, the regionalist parties are minority parties: invariably so at a national level, and frequently also at a regional or even local level. However, the electoral impact of these minority parties does not provide a fair reflection of the influence of the regionalist ideology in most European countries. This ideology has varied considerably from one period to another and often differs profoundly from one country to another. In France, regionalism remained, up until the 1950s, a right-wing movement, frequently reactionary in character, and certainly nostalgic for past forms of culture, economy, and administration. But, with the passing of time, the regionalist movement has become more radical, sometimes adopting the language and methods of action of the Left or the extreme Left, identifying with more or less Marxist doctrines, so that it has eventually convinced the parliamentary Left that regionalism amounts to more than just a struggle on the part of reactionary country yokels. The themes of 'internal colonialism' and 'dependence' were taken up in both France and Britain, where part of the Scottish and Welsh nationalist movements adopted a radical position as they began to express the views of certain intellectual strata and sections of the urban middle classes. In Italy, regionalism stands for something rather different. In 1946–7, the Christian Democrats regarded it as a democratic 'guarantee' that would stand in the way of the extreme kind of centralization that tends to foster dictatorships; but when they gained power, their attitude soon changed. Now it was the Left, in particular the PCI, that laid claim to pockets of regional power, in order to oppose the Christian Democrat hegemony. Furthermore, regionalism took on a quite distinctive character in the three frontier regions (the Valley of Aosta, the Alto-Adige, and the Friuli–Veneto–Julian Alps region) and the two islands (Sardinia and Sicily) that still possess marked linguistic, cultural, and economic identities. A further twist is given to the Italian problem by the fact that the political and economic centres of the country are not the same, as they clearly are in the United Kingdom and France. The successes of the Lega Nord in the 1990s, in obtaining over 10 per cent of the all-Italian vote (in 1996), in briefly entering government (in 1994), and even in mobilizing supporters in demonstrations for the bogus 'Republic of Padania', owed much to the conviction of some voters in the rich northern regions that they were being misruled from the centre (Rome) by a corrupt bureaucracy originating chiefly from the poor south.

During the 1970s, observers pondered upon the roots of regionalist ideology and also the reasons for its success. Many factors were suggested but none provided a general explanation: neither language, nor religion, nor culture, nor economic under-development can on their own account for the birth of the regionalist ideology. To do so, any analysis of these factors needs to be complemented by a number of observations. First, through the emphasis that it lays on defending a particular territory, a regionalist ideology has a 'catch-all' character. Secondly, generally speaking, regionalist ideology has developed from the conjunction of two factors: on the one hand the existence of a particular identity (in some instances cultural, in others religious, in others economic), on the other an upheaval that affects the economic and social structures. These social changes, whether negative (an economic crisis) or positive (change and growth), often constitute the stimulus that triggers a series of regional claims and the development of a more or less widely diffused regional ideology. Regionalism may, in this way, become one of the best ways of promoting a number of different interests on a territorial basis. Regionalist ideology often smacks to some extent of indiscrimination, but despite—or perhaps because of—that eclecticism, the considerable success that it has enjoyed in Europe is quite remarkable. Today, most of the countries of Western Europe[21]—with the exception of Britain—are to some extent regionalized, with even Britain, for long the exception, finally setting itself on that road with the successful referendums favouring a Scottish Parliament and a Welsh Assembly in 1997; yet, except in Belgium, their national parliaments incorporate no more than a handful of regionalists.

Green parties

Can Green parties, like the regionalists, be treated as single-issue parties? Better-established opponents often dismiss them on precisely this ground. Such an assessment deserves some scepticism, for three reasons. First, if ecological parties are primarily obsessed with a single issue, it is a very large issue indeed, involving the survival of human life on the planet. The fulfilment of their ultimate aim, the creation of an environmentally sustainable economy and society, would entail a definitive break with the 'productivist' logic which, they argue, has driven the economic policies of all other parties, whether of the Right or the Left. That in turn would mean major changes in every policy area covered by mainstream political debate. Secondly, Green parties, as opposed to environmental defence groups such as Greenpeace or Friends of the Earth (both of which operate internationally), have been assiduous in drawing up a wide range of policies on many issues—though their early documents in particular tended to be little more than wish-lists of dubious practicality. Thirdly, as Thomas Poguntke points out in a Europe-wide comparative analysis,[22] almost all Green parties have espoused a variety of causes that grew out of the 'New Politics' of the 1960s, whether closely linked to Green issues (nuclear disarmament and defence of the Third World) or more remote (feminism, the defence of civil liberties, and ethnic or sexual minority rights).

Do Green parties belong to the Left or the Right? A common Green answer is 'neither'. Brice Lalonde campaigned as Ecology candidate in the 1981 French presidential elections under the slogan 'En Vert et Contre Tous'; Antoine Waechter, the Green candidate in 1988, claimed that his party was 'neither to the Right, nor the Left, nor the Centre'. But if Greens reject the economic 'productivism' of left-wing parties and their acceptance of big central government, they are even more distant from the free-market ideology of the right. And the Greens' major excursion into foreign and defence questions, in the last freeze of the Cold War, put most of them on the same side as leftists and even Communists as energetic campaigners against the West's nuclear weapons. Green conservative parties, concentrating on countryside conservation, do exist, but are rare; Poguntke identifies just two in his survey of sixteen, and even these cases are problematic.[23] Lalonde's own decision to gravitate rightwards with his Génération Écologie movement in 1995 was, in a sense, the exception that proved the rule, for Génération Écologie practically disappeared as a result. The French 'Chasse, Pêche, Tradition' lists, whose claim to concern with nature sits ill with their central assertion of a universal right to shoot songbirds in springtime, are another such marginal case. Individual conservatives may be active in Green politics, but rarely last in high-profile leadership positions: a prominent example was that of Herbert Gruhl, a former CDU politician who resigned from the West German Green Party shortly after its creation in 1980. More representative individual leaders are France's Dominique Voynet and Germany's Joschka Fischer, both of whom come from the far Left. Among Green supporters, sympathies lie largely, though not wholly, with the Left. Thus at the second ballot of the French presidential elections, François Mitterrand attracted 53 per cent of Lalonde supporters in 1981 (compared with 26 per cent for Giscard, the right-wing incumbent), and 63 per cent of Waechter voters (compared with 20 per cent for Mitterrand's challenger Chirac) seven years later. Similarly, polls among West German Greens in the 1980s showed strong support for alliances or coalitions with the SPD; in practice, these have been the only alliances the party has entered.

The question of alliances highlights the problems of Green parties operating in Western democratic systems. These problems are threefold. The first concerns the Greens' relation to national politics itself. Environmental destruction is no respecter of national frontiers: green policies thus tend to be necessarily global (merely national cuts in emissions of chemicals that deplete the ozone layer, or cause global warming or acid rain, make a minimal difference to the world environment), or very local (stopping specific nuclear power stations or motorway projects, or cleaning up particular rivers). The lack of fit between Green issues and the politics of nation states is one factor that lays the parties open to the charge of being no more than single-interest pressure groups. Secondly, Green parties have an organizational problem. Most of them reject the hierarchical patterns of organization of other parties, and prefer more egalitarian, decentralized forms of decision-making that reflect the type of society they wish to create. A striking expression of this was the attempt by the West German Greens, after winning seats in the Bundestag for the first time in 1983, to rotate their representation by making each of their parliamentarians cede his or her seat to a colleague after two years. This may have been effective at displaying the Greens' refusal to be drawn into the clubbishness typical of a Western parliamentary assembly, but it reduced their chances of exercising real influence, for example through committee work over extended periods. More generally, it is not clear that a party represented by a variety of spokespersons is well placed to compete in the media, and especially on television, with parties offering clearly identifiable leaders. And ultra-democratic structures may prove bad at resolving conflicts. As Sara Parkin, a sympathetic observer (and identifiable leader *manquée* of the British Greens), put it in 1988, 'Die Grünen have a quite proper commitment to basic democracy and its implied checks on abuse of power, but the system is simply not working'.[24]

The Greens' third problem in relation to Western democratic systems is strategic. It arises from the Green parties' electoral weakness in relation to established parties and their slim chances of winning government office as anything other than a minority coalition partner. The problem may be summarized as the conflict between Germany's *Fundis* and *Realos*, which in practice surfaces in every ecological party. *Fundis* seek to offset electoral weakness through building strength at the base of civil society, which they see as an essential counterweight to conventional politics; they are acutely suspicious of the compromises that would be implied by any firm alliance with an established party. *Realos* see established party politics as effectively 'the only game in town' and are thus readier to seek allies, in practice Socialist ones. This is an argument that the *Realos* have tended to win once the Greens attain significant political representation. In Germany, the Greens' leader Joschka Fischer persuaded his party, at the Kassel congress in November 1997, to commit itself to a national version of the 'red–green' alliance with the SPD that already governed four *Länder*. In France it was actually one of the Verts, supposedly the more independent wing of the ecology movement, who first won the presidency of a French regional council (Nord-Pas-de-Calais) in 1992, with Socialist support. That heralded a more general integration of the Verts into an alliance with the Socialists, culminating in the election of eight deputies in 1997 and the appointment of their leader, Dominique Voynet, to the Jospin government.

Since their creation out of environmentalist pressure groups in the 1970s or early

1980s, ecology parties everywhere have found their readiest support among young, well-educated, voters of the new middle class. No European country has been short of ecological issues on which to mobilize: nuclear reprocessing in the United Kingdom, an enormous nuclear power station programme in France, environmental disasters such as Seveso in Italy, and acid rain as well as a concentration of nuclear weapons in Germany. But levels of support vary substantially between countries. One source of this variation has been the different 'opportunity structures' afforded by different political, and particularly electoral, systems. That structure may have proved particularly favourable to the German Greens. Under Germany's proportional representation system, a party needs 5 per cent of the national vote to win seats in the Bundestag. According to E. Gene Frankland,[25] this threshold is about right—low enough to be attainable, high enough to force coalitions between different 'alternative groups'—including, most recently, East Germany's former dissidents of Bündnis '90. The Greens won West German Bundestag seats in 1983, at the second Federal election after their foundation as a party. Public funding of political parties means that votes and Bundestag seats bring much-needed money. Germany's federal structure has allowed Greens to win seats in most of its *Länder*, and in some cases to govern with other parties—the SPD or, more rarely, the FDP. Like all German parties except the FDP and the CDU, the Greens were caught unawares by reunification, only winning seats in December 1990 as it were by proxy, thanks to the respectable showing of their Bündnis '90 allies in the East. But the solidity of their hold on a small part of the electorate was confirmed four years later, when the Green–Bündnis '90 alliance won 7.3 per cent of the vote and 49 seats. In Italy the electoral system operating till 1992, proportional representation with a low threshold, offered easier opportunities to small parties, but this may have contributed to a fragmentation of the 'alternative' vote. The Greens' main competitors were the Radicals, who, while not remarkable for their sensitivity to the environment, occupied the ground on other issues, such as civil liberties and minority rights, which are also of concern to Green voters. Italy's Greens have regularly won between 10 and 21 seats in the four elections of 1987, 1992, 1994, and 1996, but without exerting the same pull on the political system as their German counterparts.

The United Kingdom boasts Western Europe's oldest Green party (founded in 1973) and the highest nationwide score of any Green party at a national election—some 15 per cent in the 1989 European election. But that result was achieved on a very low turnout at an election regarded by most voters as an inconsequential opinion poll. The first-past-the-post electoral system used in all British elections makes votes for small parties particularly hard to translate into seats, and Britain's Greens proved wholly unable to turn their 1989 performance into any form of lasting political influence.

It is perhaps not surprising that in France's semi-presidential system, Green politics have been to some extent presidential politics. Ecological or Green candidates have run in the last three presidential elections, but have never achieved a score of even 4 per cent. France's Greens have also, like other French parties, been prone to division, notably, in the early 1990s, between Lalonde's Génération Écologie, founded with President Mitterrand's support in 1990, and the somewhat more independent Verts. Yet France's ecology movement has also, at times, occupied a strategic position in the French political landscape, as a place of refuge for discontented Socialists (the various ecology groupings attracted 10 per cent of the vote in the 1993 parliamentary elections), and most recently as indispensable allies of the Left, leading to parliamentary seats and a ministry in 1997.

It should also be noted that the influence of Green parties on national policy does not necessarily depend on national office-holding. In the German case the party has brought Green issues onto the national agenda both by building its national strength steadily over two decades and by governing at *Land* level; but it has never been part of a Bundestag majority. Other cases are more striking still: governments in Holland or Denmark have weak Green parties but a relatively strong environmental record, while, on the other hand, the parliamentary seats won by Italy's Greens have had no significant impact on public policy. Those Greens who have been less successful can take consolation from their movement's achievement in opening up a debate that barely existed a generation ago, and from the fact that the issues which mobilize them are not likely to go away in the foreseeable future.

The institutionalization and organization of parties

Political parties are now part of the Western 'political scene', indeed one of its essential elements. A democratic system without political parties or with a single party is impossible—or at any rate hard—to imagine. But this was not always the case, for initially political parties were considered to undermine democracy and were suspected of being either divisive (where parties = factions) or hardly in keeping with the democratic ideal (where parties = oligarchies). A dominant phenomenon of today, however, is the *institutionalization* of political parties as powerful *organizations* that seek to monopolize mediation between the governed and those who govern.

The institutionalization of parties

There are several aspects of the concept of party institutionalization. From a sociological point of view, it involves transforming associations that are structured to a greater or lesser degree into genuine organizations that are managed with a view to winning and exercising political power. This kind of institutionalization implies a combination of 'objective' elements (the parties being firmly established as institutions) and 'subjective' ones (acceptance of the parties, recognition of their legitimacy). From a more juridical point of view (inspired mainly by the ideas of Kelsen), institutionalization involves recognition for the political parties and their constitutional integration within the political system. The most recent and often controversial type of institutionalization has been the establishment, in many countries, including France, Germany, and Italy, of direct State financing of parties.

In his study of political parties, Janda establishes the degree of a party's institutionalization on the basis of three parameters: its age, the depersonalization of its organization, and its organizational differentiation. He investigates fifty or so countries and 158 parties considered to be representative of all the different parties noted throughout the world. It emerges from his study that the degree of a party's institutionalization depends firstly upon its age, which, in its turn, is connected with the development and age of the State in which it exists and that State's institutions. It is, then, not surprising that two of the most fully institutionalized parties turn out to be the American Democratic Party (founded in 1828) and the British Conservative Party (founded in 1832). In contrast, the French parties became institutionalized relatively late in the day (more or less at the dawn of the twentieth century), as if the instability of France's political institutions had delayed or prevented the organization of the various groups even though they had been clearly identifiable throughout the nineteenth century. The relatively long-standing institutionalization of some of the political parties of the Western democracies has another, negative consequence for party organizations of more recent date: it makes it difficult for new party organizations, not so much to emerge, but to develop, as they strive to find a place for themselves in the political spectrum. Only rarely do new parties manage to win places in parliament and even more rarely do they survive there. In the United States, third parties are excluded from the political game, and the European states have been almost as unwelcoming towards them. Few of the new parties that have attempted to take hold have been successful: the FN in France and the Greens in Germany are rare examples of parties that have succeeded in overcoming the institutional and political barriers. But even they have not been able to end the domination of the older political formations whose pedigree goes back to the revolutionary upheavals of the nineteenth century or of 1917. The case of Italy in 1992–6 (Fig. 2.1) is a unique one among West European democracies in this respect, with a meltdown of the party system resulting from an exceptional combination of events (a changed electoral system, a State financial crisis, and corruption scandals). Even here, though, a number of the 'new' formations that emerged (though not, for example, Forza Italia) were the old ones in new clothes (Fig. 2.1).

In truth, most of the 'new' parties to be found on the political map have resulted either from transformations of earlier declining formations or from the reunification of groups split asunder in the past by some political crisis or another. Italy aside, it is in France that the party system has undergone the most fundamental recomposition, by very reason of the low level of institutionalization there in the past. Up to the 1980s the various manifestations of Gaullism facilitated the formation of a vast movement incorporating all the components of the authoritarian Right and, in the 1960s and early 1970s, most of the rest of the Right as well. In contrast, the UDF has so far produced no more than an undisciplined federation of various liberal and centre-right sects. As for the Socialist Party, it became the leading French political party by dint of building upon

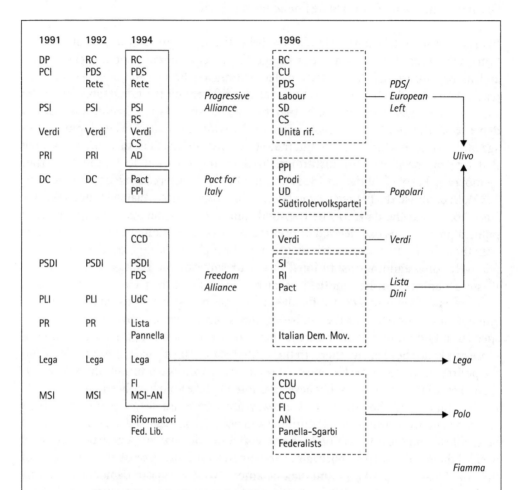

Fig. 2.1. The transformation of the Italian party system, 1991–1996

Key: DP = Proletarian Democracy; PCI = Italian Communist Party; PSI = Italian Socialist Party; *Verdi* = Greens; PRI = Italian Republican Party; DC = Christian Democrats; PSDI = Italian Social Democratic Party; PLI = Italian Liberal Party; PR = Radical Party; *Lega* = Northern League; MSI = Italian Social Movement; RC = Communist Refoundation; PDS = Democratic Party of the Left; *Rete* = Network; CS = Social Christians; AD = Democratic Alliance; Pact = Pact for National Renewal; PPI = Italian Popular Party; CCD = Centre Christian Democrats; FDS = Democratic Socialist Federation; UdC = Union of the Centre; *Lista Pannella* = Pannella List; FI = *Forza Italia!*; AN = National Alliance; *Riformatori* = Reformists; *Fed. Lib.* = Liberal Federation; CU = United Communists; SD = Social Democrats; *Unità rif.* = Reformist unity; UD = Democratic Union; *Südtirolervolkspartei* = South Tyrolese People's Party; SI =Italian Socialists; RI = Italian Renewal; Italian Dem. Mov. = Italian Democratic Movement; CDU = Christian Democratic Union; *Fiamma* = Tricoloured flame.

Source: James L. Newell and Martin J. Bull, 'The April 1996 Italian General Election: The Left on Top or on Tap?', *Parliamentary Affairs*, 49.4 (October 1996), 630.

the ruins of the 'old firm', the SFIO, and by federating the many organizations of the nebulous 'New Left' (ranging from the PSU to the clubs of the Convention of Republican Institutions).

There is a second criterion for assessing the institutionalization of a political party: depersonalization. It is a point that Monica and Jean Charlot have emphasized:

This indubitably constitutes an essential condition for the continuity of an organization, to the extent that it allows it to outlive the lifespan of its founder, however prestigious he may be. Until a party (or any association) has surmounted the crisis of finding a successor to its founder, until it has drawn up rules of succession that are legitimate in the eyes of its members, its 'institutionalization' will remain precarious.[26]

In this respect, the Gaullist party provides a rare example of recent institutionalization for a major political party in the West. Its survival and force are the more remarkable in view of the fact that, at the outset, the 'party' consisted of no more than a vast 'gathering' cemented together by the personality of General de Gaulle. Once over the periods of uncertainty occasioned first by the political retirement, then by the death of the founder of the Fifth Republic, the Gaullist party, under the leadership of Georges Pompidou and then of Jacques Chirac, managed to turn itself into a powerful party machine.[27]

Thirdly, the institutionalization of a political party depends upon how successfully it is organized as an instrument for mobilizing political support and winning power. In most Western countries there exists no *ad hoc* structure specially designed for political parties, so these tend to take shape within the legal frameworks that cater for other organizations, that is, associations generally. But the particular category of political parties does possess specific organizational characteristics, both as regards means (the recruitment of activists, party organization, the selection of candidates at election time) and as regards methods. A political party is different from a simple association, a group with common interests or a club, although it may borrow or preserve some of the features of those types of organization. Generally speaking, parties only survive if they can depend upon rigorous organization whose structures are defined in relation to particular ends and needs. The so-called parties that fail to set up such organizational systems are bound to vanish. The party of l'Uomo Qualunque in Italy (the Man-in-the-Street's party) after the Second World War, the Refugee Party in West Germany, the Poujadist party in France, were in reality no more than sectional protest organizations and all disappeared through want of being able or knowing how to turn themselves into true party organizations. This organizational element is developed to a greater or lesser degree in all the various Western States, but it is undoubtedly in the United States and France that it took the longest to evolve.

Although political parties have become an essential element of Western democracy, their existence is not always 'constitutionally recognized'. This was generally true of pre-war constitutions and remains so in countries such as the United States and Britain. However, many post-war democratic constitutions sought to give the political parties a constitutional status. The German Basic Law, the Constitutions of Italy and of the Fifth French Republic (and equally the Spanish Constitution of 1978, the Portuguese Constitution of 1976, and the Greek Constitution of 1975) all give political parties a status, a status that may be defined—albeit in imprecise terms—both negatively and positively. Furthermore, in these States, and also in those which do not explicitly recognize a constitutional status for political parties, ordinary laws and Supreme Court decisions have delineated the political parties' role and place within the political system.

The Italian Constitution was the first to move towards constitutional recognition for the political parties when it declared in Article 49: 'All citizens have the right to associate freely in parties so as to contribute, in accordance with the democratic method, towards the determining of national policies.' This somewhat elliptical formulation was the result of a laborious compromise between the various forces that had emerged together from the Resistance but did not share, for instance, a common vision of democracy. It was for this reason that the National Constituent Assembly rejected all amendments designed to impose 'the democratic method' in the *internal* as well as the external dealings of the parties. It was, of course, chiefly against the Communist Party, with its own particular set of rules, that such amendments were aimed. In 1958, the French Communist Party was the object of a similar amendment (also rejected) which attempted to ensure that 'the parties be obliged to respect the democratic principles contained in the Constitution'.

The West German Basic Law, on the other hand, was more insistent, but such differences can be explained by the political contexts peculiar to each system: whereas France and Italy had to take into consideration powerful Communist Parties, which respectively represented close on one-quarter and one-third of voters, West Germany sought to guard against the Communist Party, which was dominant in the Soviet zone, and also against the rebirth of a neo-Nazi party. Article 21 of the Basic Law stipulates that the political parties' 'internal organization must correspond to democratic principles'.

The objectives attributed to the political parties also vary from one system to another. The most restrictive concept of these was that adopted by the Fifth French Republic—which is hardly surprising in a Constitution stamped with the seal of General de Gaulle. It declares that 'the parties aim to express the suffrage of the people'. In West Germany, their role was defined in a more ambitious manner: they 'co-operate to form the political will of the people'. Finally, the Italian parties are declared to help 'to determine national policies'—a formula which attributes to them an essential function close to that which Article 20 of the French Constitution allots to the government ('the government determines the policies of the nation'). As Pierre Avril points out, 'Herein lie the beginnings of a basis for a partitocratic state.'[28]

Another consequence of such constitutional stipulations is that, while parties may be freely created, they do not hold a monopoly over representation. The text of Article 49 of the Italian Constitution does not refer to parties *per se* ('All citizens have the right to associate . . .') and the text of the French Constitution mentions 'parties and political groups'. The text of the West German Basic Law might have given rise to a restrictive interpretation, but the Constitutional Court always ensured that the parties of the

Bundestag did not claim any monopoly and, in the law of 24 July 1967 on the political parties, 'party' was given a relatively wide definition. But while the law dispelled the shadowy zones of misunderstanding that might have been engendered by Article 21, at the same time it turned the parties into true public organizations (the Constitutional Court described them as *Staatsorgane* (organs of the State), whose structures, rules of functioning, and finance are all strictly controlled by the State).

Although the creation of political parties is, in principle, free in the European states, there are many restrictions and prohibitions. In some cases the restrictions are more or less symbolic (as, for example, in Article 4 of the 1958 French Constitution, which declares that parties 'must respect the principles of sovereignty and democracy'), but it may be that the more insidious they are, the more effective.

Over and above such more or less visible restrictions built into the political system, measures of a more severe nature may restrain the activities of the parties, even to the point of banning them. In France, the Republic has a long-standing 'Republican tradition' of banning parties hostile to the 'Republican form of government', a regime that a series of constitutions since the Third Republic have declared it to be impossible to revise. These prohibitions affect all associations that 'strike at the integrity of the [national] territory' and 'the Republican form of government' and they are sanctioned not only by the 1901 law but also by a new law adopted on 18 June 1936, at the time of a struggle against extreme right-wing leagues. These vague formulas have effectively been used to dissolve many political groups—associations, movements, and parties of every kind. Successive governments have struck in turn or simultaneously at the extreme right, the extreme left, overseas nationalist movements, many regionalist movements within France itself, and so on. The imprecise phrasing even made it possible for the Vichy Government to order many dissolutions in the name of the 'Republican form of government'—at a time when most of France was under Nazi occupation! There are no statistics on the total number of associations dissolved; but it would seem from a few soundings taken in connection with protests against administrative decisions of dissolution that, since the Second World War, several dozen groups have been banned from official activity. One is bound to regard the procedure as shocking both because of its scope and because of the inadequacy of the guarantees provided: decisions of the government can take effect with very little warning and are subject to very limited controls. Furthermore, the question of whether it is effective remains in doubt.

As for West Germany, in Article 21.2 of its Basic Law, it tackled unambiguously the very principle involved in the banning of extremist parties: 'Those parties which, according to their goals and the attitudes of their membership, seek to strike at the fundamental free and democratic order, to topple it or to compromise the existence of the Federal Republic of Germany, are unconstitutional. The Federal Constitutional Court is empowered to rule on the question of unconstitutionality.' The federal government has sought to ban extremist parties on two occasions: first, the neo-Nazi Sozialistische Reichspartei, on 19 November 1951; then the Communist Party (KPD), on 22 November of that same year. In the case of the party of the extreme Right, sentence was quickly passed, on 23 October 1952, but in that of the KPD it was much delayed both by procedural battles and also by indecision on the part of the court. Sentence was eventually pronounced on 17 August 1956, in a document of over 300 pages. With the passing of time, and as the West German State became more confident, the existence of a Communist party was no longer considered a threat. In October 1967, the *Länder* Interior Ministers decided to tolerate the creation of a new communist party. However, to get round the earlier decision of the Constitutional Court, the party's name was changed and it became the Deutsche Kommunistische Partei (DKP); also, the statutes were adapted in such a way as to take account of the motivation behind the 1956 sentence. Similarly, the extreme Right resurfaced in the late 1960s, taking care to steer clear of doctrines and language that were too reminiscent of Nazism. Neither party had much electoral impact, however; the NPD won some successes at *Land* level in the late 1960s, but failed to break through the 5 per cent barrier nationally. Outbreaks of racist arson and murder raised the question of banning again in 1992, and one far-right group, the Nationalist Front, was outlawed in November.

European political systems all, to a greater or lesser degree, favour the integration of parties recognized to be compatible with the values of democracy as defined by their constitutions, and the rejection of parties that do not fit into the system. It is unquestionably in Germany and Italy that political parties are the most fully integrated into the State, constitutional recognition there being but one—albeit the most solemn—of the forms taken by that integration. *Parteienstaat* and *partitocrazia* may not be completely realized concepts yet, but the two expressions testify to what Gerhard Liebholz calls the tendency of parties to identify with the people.

Although the forms of integration are less fully developed—and are, indeed, much criticized—in countries such as France and Britain the fact remains that the parties in the system are the necessary avenues of communication between the governed and the government, and that their roles have tended to grow in importance. Concurrently, 'outsider parties' have been confined to the touch-line by electoral legislation. Italy is probably the most open country in this respect, adopting an extremely liberal attitude towards access to Parliament, but the price it has had to pay for this has been high: small groups within the party system have proliferated; there have been constant operations of political 'transformism' designed to integrate parties outside the system and, as a matter of principle, the Italian Communist Party was excluded for half a century from a central governing role (the famous *conventio ad excludendum*).

Party organization

Party organization is a problem that has given rise to a series of monographs and reflections that must be accounted some of the most stimulating works in political science. They range from Robert Michels's *Political Parties: A Sociological Study of the Oligarchic Tendencies of Modern Democracy* (1914) to Maurice Duverger's classic work *Les Partis politiques* (1951) and include many analyses on party organization and the explanatory force of organization as a variable.

Maurice Duverger, in particular, considers organization to be a key element for the understanding not only of parties themselves but also of Western political systems in general. In the preface to the 1981 edition of his book, he acknowledges that his model is 'centred on [party] organization'.[29] In other words, each type of party has its own particular method of organization, and this constitutes its essential characteristic. Since Duverger set up that paradigm, many critical studies of it and variants to it have been put forward. Let us take a brief look at them before analysing how the tension between democracy and oligarchy that persists within the parties may be resolved.

By way of a summary, let us note that Duverger draws a contrast between two major types of political party, cadre parties and mass parties, and he stresses that the distinction has nothing to do with whether the parties are large or small; it is not a matter of the size of their membership. It is not size but structure that is important. He explains that cadre parties cannot be defined by reference either to their statutes or to the official statements of their leaders. On the other hand, he is inclined to believe that the absence of any register of members and of any regular levying of dues and a vagueness in quoted statistics may well constitute significant characteristics. A mass party, by contrast, is characterized by the register of its members, its levying of dues, and its autonomous funding during elections. The first of these two groups is composed of the 'bourgeois' parties, the second of the socialist, communist, and Fascist ones although, quite apart from their ideology, the latter differ from one another on a number of counts. But Duverger recognizes that

several types of party do not fit into this general schema: namely, the Catholic and Christian democrat parties, which occupy a position more or less midway between the old parties and the socialist ones; the 'Labour' parties based on unions and co-operatives, with an indirect kind of structure . . . ; agrarian parties that display a wide diversity of types of organization and are only operative in a limited number of countries; and parties of an archaic or prehistoric type . . .[30]

Duverger's typology provoked a stimulating debate still not exhausted and of such wide scope as sometimes to obscure the essential question. One of his most acid critics was Aaron Wildavsky, who produced a methodological critique and attacked Duverger on the basis of his falling victim to four 'illusions': the illusion of one-dimensional history (belief in the existence of forces that lead to identical historical experiences despite the diversity of cultures); a mystical illusion (belief in the natural, binary nature of certain phenomena); the illusion of formal demonstration (Duverger's presentation of an abstract schema impossible either to attack or to verify); and the illusion of a representation that is divorced from reality (all exceptions that contradict the model are ignored).[31] However, most of Duverger's critics have taken up their positions on his own terrain, pointing out the inadequacy and incompleteness of his typology and suggesting possible additions or modifications to it. Duverger's typology has thus been expanded for example to include the catch-all party defined by Kirchheimer, the voters' party (Jean Chariot), and Eldersveld's stratarchic party (inspired by the American model, where power is held at every level of organization).

In a debate which rather readily transforms concrete, organizational questions into abstract, theoretical categories, it is worth returning for a moment to the material underpinning of Duverger's distinction. Cadre parties are the product of the typical conditions of nineteenth-century politics: a suffrage often limited to property-owners (and always to men); a ballot that was rarely secret; primitive conditions of communication; societies which retained large (and often over-represented) rural populations, where traditional hierarchies were still important. In these conditions, what candidates needed to win parliamentary seats were long purses and wide social networks; party organization, on the other hand, while helpful in achieving common goals within the legislature, was barely necessary on the hustings. Mass parties, by contrast, were the tool developed by the urban working classes (with the German SPD being very much the prototype) to make the most of the opportunities offered by a wider suffrage. Membership dues—small amounts, but paid by many people—were the substitute for the personal or business finance of bourgeois politicians. Trade union links, or simply party members knocking on doors to get the vote out, replaced the networks of traditional notables; and the more these were reinforced by a range of 'satellite' organizations, whether women's or youth groups, or sports clubs, the firmer party loyalties would be. The result constituted a formidable challenge to the cadre parties, which were forced, to a greater or lesser degree, to adapt, by taking on at least the basic forms of extraparliamentary organization, membership, and programmes. This is, of course, an oversimplified, generalized narrative; many of Wildavsky's remarks are pertinent in this respect, and national histories vary enormously. In Britain, for example, both Conservative and Liberal Parties grasped the importance of a fast-urbanizing society and progressive extensions of the suffrage (which they both, at different times, furthered), and organized nationally, well before the birth of the Labour Party. French parties, by contrast, have always had more difficulty than most in sustaining a sizeable membership for any length of time. What is essential, however, is the notion of party organization as a material and financial means to the end of winning office, and the varying capacity of parties and their leaders to learn from competitors and adapt their organization, as well as their policies, to new circumstances.

Since the immediate post-war period in which Duverger first formulated his typology, the most striking change in the operating conditions of parties has been a communications revolution which has brought television into almost every household and generated exponential growth in the advertising and public relations industries. The public meeting held by national but also local politicians, once an important source of political cues, has been marginalized by the almost constant appearance of national party leaders on television. In this new context, politics have become more 'capital-intensive'; parties have a competitive edge if they can command, and use effectively, the services of professional (and expensive) media consultants, advertising agencies, polling experts, conference organizers, and producers of video clips. Traditional mass parties, relying on more labour-intensive (and more amateur) techniques, have begun to look as antiquated and as slow as the dinosaurs—and equally doomed to extinction, given the erosion of the working-class communities from which they drew their lifeblood. The new organizational context has also had consequences for policy: the ideologically flexible catch-all party, able to deliver and package a nationwide message that promised something for everyone, has had an advantage over parties focused on the needs of their traditional core communities. These were conditions that favoured 'bourgeois' parties, able to mobilize money and long accustomed, by virtue of the fact that under universal suffrage the wealthy are never the majority, to pitching for a broad electorate. It was the left-wing parties' turn to adapt.

The notion of a 'capital-intensive' party begs two questions. First, if (as the case of the United States appears to prove) there is potentially no limit to the propensity of candidates to spend, where is the money to come from? Secondly, is there still any point in recruiting members? One possible answer to the first question is: the State can be made to provide cash, whether legally or illegally. The Italian case is an object lesson in this respect: before 1993 all major parties, including the Communists (but not the far right, or not to the same extent), were systematically financed by corrupt means from Italy's very large public sector; the introduction of legal State funding for parties in 1974, supposedly to remove incentives for corruption, merely added an extra source of money; and the public's disgust at this system, and the vote to change the party finance laws in 1993, were a major factor in the implosion of the party system. In France the situation is comparable, even if the scale of corruption is much smaller. All major parties have drawn finance from corrupt sources, typically, but not exclusively, from percentages on building contracts delivered by local or national government; and there is no certainty that the arrival of public finance in the laws of 1988 and 1990 has ended such practices. The spread of official public finance of parties (it has also operated in Germany since the 1960s) is one element that inspires Katz and Mair's concept of the 'cartel' party. According to their model, a handful of parties are able to rig the political market by awarding themselves exclusive, or at least privileged, access to State funding, sharing power (whether through alternation or through coalition) amongst themselves and thus marginalizing competitors.[32] An alternative answer to the issue of political finance is supplied by the case of Silvio Berlusconi's Forza Italia, which has drawn generous financial support from Berlusconi's own companies and enjoyed unlimited television coverage on stations owned by Berlusconi himself.

Both the cartel model and Forza Italia can be considered as perversions of democracy, the former because it confiscates public goods for private purposes, the latter because it represents an attempt to buy political power. It can also be argued that both help to delegitimize democracy by cutting off parties, which are among democracy's major actors, from members and thence from ordinary voters. The question of the role of party members in a world where politics has become capital-intensive is a complex one. Anecdotal evidence is certainly not lacking to suggest that, given the chance, party leaders would rather dispense with rank-and-file members altogether. Alain Peyrefitte, former secretary-general of the Gaullist party, is on record as saying that activists 'bored him rigid'; Alan Clark spoke of the members of his local Conservative association as 'boring, petty, malign, clumsily conspiratorial, and parochial to a degree that cannot be surpassed in any part of the United Kingdom.'[33] At the same time there are plenty of indications, albeit of an unscientific kind, that an active, mobilized membership helps win votes. One of the features of Britain's 1997 election was Labour's success in bringing its total number of individual activists above 400,000 for the first time in two decades; although the Conservative numbers were roughly equivalent, they were dwindling (the party had claimed a million members in the early 1990s), ageing (with a majority of over-60s), and discouraged by what they saw as long-term neglect of the rank and file. In France, the fratricidal battle between the two Gaullist candidates, Jacques Chirac and the Prime Minister Édouard Balladur, in the first round of the 1995 presidential election, turned to Chirac's advantage in part because, although Balladur was Prime Minister, Chirac had retained control of the party organization. In Italy, Forza Italia owed part of its success to its allies, the Alleanza Nazionale, who had a much better organization on the ground. The uses of party members have certainly changed. No large modern party expects significant numbers of its activists to engage in the intense doctrinal debates of the ideal-type Socialist party section, or to spend Sunday mornings selling the party press at local market-places; the credit-card donation, the occasional visit to cheer at a professionally stage-managed (and televised) party rally, the even more occasional act of door-to-door canvassing, are more frequent, if less educative, forms of activism. But they are still activism of a sort. So far, neither the access to public finance under advantageous conditions afforded to the cartel party, nor the massive private finance mobilized by Berlusconi, have led parties to believe they can dispense with members altogether. Parties still need an effective structure that will get the best out of the 'base' as well as from parliamentarians and leaders, whatever the potential conflicts between them.

No parties, whatever their nature, are monolithic organizations, even in cases where their methods of organization tend to turn them into docile and disciplined instruments (communist parties, for example). Party organizations comprise a number of facets, in principle all complementary but in practice often antagonistic or at least differentiated. Most parties consist of three separate essential components: the party apparatus, *stricto sensu,* which organizes the party at every level; the 'party in office', that is, the group which holds or shares power or has done so in the past (members of parliament, ministers, and even those elected by subsidiary bodies); and the party-in-the-electorate.[34] Each of these three has its own interests and strategies which sometimes coincide with those of the other two but sometimes do not. As Pierre Avril puts it, the party

cannot be reduced to a structure built up in the form of a pyramid, nor to a juxtaposition of concentric circles. Rather, it is defined by the interaction between the electoral, the social, and the State domains: operating three-dimensionally, it can never quite be reduced to any of these three planes. Rather, you could say, it occupies the whole of their geometric space.[35]

Both the business of engineering agreements and that of resolving disagreements raise the fundamental problem of democracy within the party. The problem was posed remarkably acutely at the beginning of the century by Robert Michels, who based his observations on the example provided by political parties in Germany, in particular the SPD. Noting that democracy cannot exist without organization (for he harboured no illusions about direct democracy), Michels nevertheless recognized that democratic practices tend to become deflected in organizations such as trade unions and political parties, to the benefit of the leading party members who control the apparatus. He wrote as follows: 'The party, as an external formation, a mechanism or machine, is not necessarily identified with the register of members as a whole, even less with a particular class. As it becomes an end in itself, developing goals and interests of its own, it gradually moves away from the class that it represents.'[36]

The tensions between the various components of a party and those within its apparatus determine a series of complex interrelations which we may try to classify under three main headings: relations between the apparatus and the electorate, relations between the apparatus and the 'party in office', and relations within the apparatus itself (i.e. internal democracy).

Relations between the party apparatus and the party electorate are marked firstly by the various kinds of distance that tend generally to separate the masses from élites. On the one hand there are the professionals who control communications, monopolize statements, and formulate political promises—professionals who, through their cultural, social, and professional attributes are clearly distinguishable from the mass of citizens in general and from their own electorate in particular (although communist parties are careful to try to prevent such a gap developing). Then there is an electorate whose only means, in many cases, of making itself heard is through an infrequent poll, while its means of control are limited and its demands often distorted if not ignored. The few studies that have been devoted to 'electoral promises and demands' point out clearly the lack of correspondence that often occurs in electoral campaigns between the latent demands of the citizens and the parties' electoral promises. This mismatch frequently occasions considerable embarrassment for the party apparatus, especially in electoral competitions in which every party seeking power has to try to win over members of the electorate quite alien to its own particular ideologies and programmes yet possibly open to persuasion. Once the beguilements of the election are over, party apparatuses are often extremely hard put to it to hang on to their electoral base, as the German Social Democrats learned to their cost in 1983 and the French Socialists in 1986 and 1993. The parties' basic task is to maintain the support of their voters and to avoid disputes and desertion, or, as Hirschman put it in his tripartite scheme, to maintain *loyalty* and avoid *voice* and *exit*.

For not only in organizations where the ideology is all-important, but in 'catch-all' parties too, voters are easily lost once they become aware of the disparity between their expectations and the reality. In circumstances such as these the French Communist Party has been called a 'sieve' and Malraux's definition of Gaullism realistically reflected similar fluctuations: 'Everybody is, has been, or will be Gaullist'! Hence the constant, more or less successful attempts either to adapt the apparatus to the voters or, on the contrary, to maintain it unchanged at any cost, even if it means changing its electorate or losing it altogether. Social democratic and bourgeois parties have generally favoured the former option, extreme parties the latter, in the name of the ideological purity that the apparatus defends and embodies.

But as well as being marked by certain ideological and social disagreements, the relationship between the party apparatus and the electorate also depends upon *quid pro quo* arrangements that sometimes afford the latter a measure of control. The *quid pro quo* mechanisms (patronage as opposed to ideology) that Max Weber[37] regarded as an essential element in the typology of political parties, amount to more than simply offering the voters certain material advantages in return for their votes, although such practices, frequently used by the Democratic Party in the United States, were also common in Europe so long as suffrage remained limited. However, with the advent of universal suffrage, patronage shifted from the individual to the collective level. While the practice of offering advantages to individuals may not have disappeared, those advantages were 'dematerialized'. They now tended to take the form of small services such as bringing influence to bear or exerting pressure to obtain certain favours. The fact is though that, short of cutting themselves off from their bases, political parties cannot unilaterally decide what their political offers will be. Even if the political programmes that they elaborate 'activate vigorous and clear-cut solutions that in many cases have not been called upon earlier', they are not in a position to ignore the demands of society in general, for, if they do, they are in danger of severing the links between the party apparatus and the citizens and of provoking negative reactions on the part of the electorate.

Where there are few or no institutional possibilities for channelling that pressure, there is a danger that it will be brought to bear upon the parties through the development of violent means (terrorism, extreme right-wing or left-wing movements), anti-system parties (such as the Poujade movement and the RPF in France, the Uomo Qualunque party in Italy), or new parties which take up some of the electorate's unsatisfied demands (the nationalist and the Social Democrat parties in Britain, the FN in France, the Greens in West Germany).

The 'party in office' is constituted by the group of party members who hold (or have held) office within the State institutions. They may include members of parliament, ministers, and even, to varying degrees, those elected to local office. The relations between this fraction of the party that exercises (or has exercised) power and the party apparatus (where the influence of activists makes itself felt more strongly given that many of their leaders are distracted by the administration of power) are often marked by tensions and conflicts that stem from the different nature of their respective roles. The intensity of these conflicts is itself determined by a whole series of complex factors. Chief among them are: the degree of flexibility or inflexibility of the party ideology and apparatus; the relative importance of elected representatives and activists, and the *practical* possibilities of acceding to power. Clearly, the danger of friction is greater in cases where the party has a firmly rooted ideology, a powerful apparatus, and a large number of elected representatives with responsibilities to exercise than it is in flexible organizations, in cadre parties whose programmes and ideologies amount to little more than a few vague general declarations of intent, or in small doctrinaire parties where there can be no clash with the elected representatives since none exist. The fact is that tensions are likely to arise in the debate between those with responsibilities to exercise and those who remain outside the decision-making circles of the State. The French Communist Party, for example, was traditionally so keen to ward off 'municipal cretinism', that is to say, a managerial dilution of its elected representatives, that as far as possible it avoided putting up Communist mayors of large cities to stand in national elections (though this policy has been modified somewhat as PCF leaders came to realize that well-known and well-liked mayors were among the Party's last remaining electoral assets). The governments of Mauroy and Fabius, for their part, found it very difficult to explain to the Socialist Party why they favoured a 'pause' in essential reforms and policies to gain acceptance for these ideas; and Jospin, too, faced bitter opposition from a section of his party within weeks of taking office in 1997. Under the aegis of Chancellor Schmidt, the SPD–FDP coalition also frequently clashed with the left wing of the Social Democratic Party, which was deeply hostile to the installation of missiles in West Germany. But the classic case of tension between a party apparatus and its office-holders was that of the British Labour Party, especially in the 1970s and early 1980s. There, clashes occurred constantly between the National Executive Committee, where local party members and trade unionists are dominant, and the 'Parliamentary Labour Party', which includes Labour members from both Houses. The conflict became very intense after Labour's 1979 election defeat, when the Left sought to circumscribe the powers of Labour Members of Parliament both by requiring them to submit to a mandatory reselection process to become candidates for the next general election, and by breaking their control over the choice of the party leader. Attempts by moderates to safeguard the independence of the parliamentary group were largely in vain; at Labour's Wembley conference in January 1981, it was decided that at future leadership elections, the trade unions should control 40 per cent of the votes and local constituency parties and the parliamentary group 30 per cent each. That provoked a split within Labour as moderates who opposed putting the parliamentarians in a minority chose to secede and form the new Social Democratic Party.

It might be supposed that in cadre parties, whose ideology and apparatus are both more flexible than in mass parties (the socialists in particular), conflicts would be unlikely to break out. Yet even here they are not absent. For example, in 1956, the tensions within the West German FDP brought into collision those who supported Adenauer's policies (in particular, the FDP Government ministers) and those who opposed them. This led to a split. In 1962, a similar situation arose in France where, on the occasion of the referendum on the direct election of the president, some ministers of the Independent party rallied to General de Gaulle and, led by Valéry Giscard d'Estaing, formed a party of Independent Republicans.

All the same, it would be exaggerated to suppose that these conflicts are invariably expressed in clashes between the group of elected representatives on the one hand, and the party apparatus on the other. In truth, the dividing lines are far more complex and, just as the party in office finds support and co-operation in the party apparatus, the latter is not without its own champions within the parliamentary group or amongst the elected representatives in general.

Depending upon the circumstances and the problems involved, conflicts sometimes take place between the government and a section of the parliamentary group which may be drawn from a number of elements in the party: back-benchers, rank-and-file representatives, and *franchi tiratori* (the Italian deputies of the majority who would take advantage of the old system of secret parliamentary ballots to vote against the government) are sometimes recalcitrant or even, in extreme cases, rebellious when the policies followed by the government that they support seem to them too far removed from the programme that they themselves have promised to adopt and fight for.

In these complex and shifting relations, the most one can do is recognize the existence of a wide spectrum of possibilities that range from the strictest discipline to the widest autonomy. The old-style communist parties are at one of these extremes, adamantly proclaiming their allegiance to the party apparatus: consider the case of the French Communist ministers who in 1947 voted against the proposals of the government of which they were themselves members. During the 1970s and 1980s, however, such tensions between elected officials and party apparatchiks became more intense and less discreet, for the most part ending with either the departure or the exclusion of those in dispute. Next in line after the communist parties come the extremist parties of both the Right and the Left, whose discipline tends to be more inflexible the more limited their chances of exercising power. Next come the socialist parties and the bourgeois or Christian democratic ones. In these, the problem is frequently complicated by the existence of many well-organized factions. Finally, the American parties are positioned at the opposite extreme. Here, the party apparatus is so incapable of imposing any line of conduct that there is virtually no conflict to speak of. Whereas the free vote is becoming the exception in European parliaments (where it is tolerated more or less only on questions such as the abolition of the death penalty or abortion), in the United States House of Representatives a straight vote opposing the two party majorities is often rarer than cross-party voting.[38]

All parties seek to appear to the outside world as organizations united around a programme, with a team or a leader to guide them. Unity is claimed all the more emphatically when the party concerned declares itself to be the sole spokesman for a particular group or social class: divisions must be unacceptable when a party regards itself as, for example, *the* party of the working class (just as certain trade unions profess to be *the* workers' or *the* farmers' trade union). The logic behind this monopolistic and unitarian attitude is quite simple: unity must be guaranteed by iron discipline, even at the cost of exclusions and expulsions. Admittedly, the objective is seldom achieved. Only communist parties, through their use and abuse of the principle of democratic centralism, have succeeded here. Small parties of the extreme Left and occasionally of the extreme Right and a few regionalist parties have also endeavoured to guarantee their unitarian purity, but at the cost of periodic 'purges' and splits that have in many cases drained them of all life.

Other political parties have been obliged, willy-nilly, to accept their internal divisions in the name of the democracy that they claim to represent, but that process is not an easy one. The reluctance to accept divisions within a party is certainly understandable. How far can pluralism go without producing centrifugal and potentially destructive tendencies? The political vocabulary reflects the ambivalence of attitudes towards the phenomenon of fragmentation. Up until the nineteenth century the word 'party' denoted a 'faction', but the latter term then took over from 'party' with derogatory connotations, while 'party' came to be accepted and used to denote the various political groups. In English, the word 'faction' continues to be used (although Sartori suggested replacing it by 'fraction'). The French use the terms *courants* (currents) (particularly to refer to the Socialist Party) and *tendances* (tendencies) more or less indiscriminately. The Italians speak of a *corrente*, or sometimes an *area*.

The causes and the scope of factionalism within the parties vary greatly and a general interpretation of the phenomenon would be hard to find. It clearly occurs in widely diverse parties: cadre parties and voter parties, mass parties and mini-parties, pragmatic parties and ideological ones. The formation of factions is encouraged by factors of various kinds: some are of an ideological, others of a 'charismatic' nature, while yet others are related to clientship or electoral problems. They combine in forms that vary from one party to another, but in most parties they are all at work to some degree.

Ideological factors

Parties which are endowed with strong ideologies but still accept debate and diversity are likely to contain factions which clash over the more or less dogmatic interpretation of the party creed. They frequently represent the whole range of divisions that arise in the political world in general between the left wing, the right wing, the centre, radicals, and so on. For example, in Britain, before the creation of the SDP, the Labour Party included a right wing, to wit the Social Democratic Alliance (which broke away in 1981), the revisionists of the Manifesto Group (set up in 1974), the moderates led by William Rodgers under the banner 'Campaign for a Labour Victory', as well as the left-wing Tribune Group and far left Militant Tendency. The German SPD[39] was also divided into groups representing the Centre Right (Vogel Kreis) and the Centre Left (Frankfurter Kreis). Electoral defeat in 1983 and competition from the Greens led to increasing assertiveness from the SPD New Left, particularly in the area of nuclear policy, both civil and military. In France, the Socialist Party revised its regulations in 1978 to admit the legitimacy of different tendencies (it imposed some limits, most importantly on the autonomy of funds, though these have been widely circumvented). The party then organized itself around the various 'currents', each of which set out its own political strategy and the programme promoted by its own leader (Mitterrand, Mauroy, Rocard, and Chevènement). Following Mitterrand's presidential election victory in 1981, the currents desisted for several years from parading their differences at party congresses. But as Mitterrand started his second presidential term, the party's leaders began manœuvring in preparation for the succession, and the resulting Rennes congress of spring 1990, embodying faction fighting with barely a pretence of serious policy differences, did more damage to the Socialists than any attacks from the opposition. Since their catastrophic defeat in the 1993 parliamentary elections, the Socialists have taken care to give their factions a more muted public expression, though few would deny the continued intensity of party rivalries beneath the surface.

The 'charismatic' factor

Leadership struggles and personal rivalries are not the exclusive preserve of the French Socialists in their post-Marxist period. In right-wing parties they are generally more common than ideological clashes. But it would be simplistic to suppose that factionalism is inspired on the left by ideology and policies, and on the right by personalities. For example, Michael Heseltine's challenge to Margaret Thatcher for the leadership of Britain's Conservative Party in 1990 was at least dressed up as a policy difference between Thatcher's free-market zeal and Heseltine's stress on the need for a more positive government-led industrial policy. The truth is that there are no factions without leaders, whatever the party, and that even within the most ideological factions, leadership is always an essential cause of internal divisions.

Of course, personality clashes are more marked in cadre parties where the different tendencies are not strongly organized and may amount to no more than vague allegiances (seldom formalized by voting) to the principal personalities of the party. For instance, in the case of the Radical Party under the Third and Fourth French Republics, one can hardly speak of factions or tendencies, for the internal divisions were essentially determined by clashes between the leading personalities in the party.

On the other hand, the Italian Christian Democrat Party provides a good illustration of a party where there is a mixture of strategic, or even ideological, divisions together with others established by the various faction leaders. In 1976, for example, six different factions could be distinguished: Area Zac (named after the former party secretary, Zaccagnini), which brought together men such as Marcora, Rognoni, De Mita, and Andreatta; the Dorotheans (Piccoli, Bisaglia, and Gaspari); the Fanfanians; the supporters of Andreotti; those of Donat-Cattin, Rumor, and Colombo; and, finally, the little group known as *Proposta* or *Amici di Prandini*.

In 1982, these factions, while continuing to exist, came together in coalitions reacting, in different ways, to the new Secretary-General, De Mita, and the political line that he was adopting. Area Zac joined up with the PAF group (Piccoli, Andreotti, and Fanfani), which included the Dorotheans and the Fanfanians. Together, these two factions accounted for 65 per cent of the votes at the Christian Democrat Congress and it was they that set up the new De Mita leadership. Then there was the 'opposition' group (known as 'Preamble', as it was insisting on an explicit declaration to the effect that the Italian Socialist Party would be the Christian Democrats' preferred choice for a partner).[40] Both these factions were dominated by strong personalities, but they certainly reflected many aspects of the Christian Democrat Party: its divisions over strategy and alliances, its different sensibilities, and its general internal pluralism.

Factors connected with clientship

The strength of a faction or tendency does not depend solely on the originality of its political line and the magnetism of its leader. Also to be taken into account is the support that the faction and its principal personalities can attract through practices of patronage or clientship both inside and outside the party. Inside the party, a particular faction and its leader will win over considerably more supporters if they are in a position to offer rewards—whether or not of a symbolic nature—to their faithful followers. Factions must also be able to guarantee their supporters candidacies in the national and local elections (giving rise, for example, to the battle over candidacies in the French Socialist Party, in 1985–6), posts in the administrations and town halls that they control, and in the public, semi-public, or even private sectors (such as associations), and also rewards within the party apparatus itself (posts as party officials, advisers, experts, and so on). The existence of factions certainly has the effect of inflating the number of posts and titles, as new ones are created to keep pace with 'demand'. (It should be pointed out, however, that the phenomenon also exists in parties which do not tolerate fractional organizations, such as the French Communist Party, in which one in every four members is a 'cadre'). Needless to say, it is a phenomenon that is accentuated in cases where a party has a real chance of acceding to power. In Italy, many a place for a party activist has been found in the regional bureaucracies, as also in Germany, where the *Länder* have been so accommodating that the close intermingling of bureaucrats and politicians is sometimes referred to as *Verfilzung* (interweaving).[41]

Of course, these practices of patronage are just one facet of a wider policy of clientship that reaches beyond the party itself and enables a leader and his faction to establish their own local and regional strongholds. In the waning years of the Italian Christian Democratic Party, Fanfani was solidly established in Tuscany, Donat-Cattin in Liguria, De Mita in Apulia, and Colombo in Basilicata. Similarly, Johannes Rau was for many years the SPD's strong man in the Rhineland, while his successor in the leadership, Oskar Lafontaine, is solidly established in Saarland and Rudolf Scharping in Rhineland-Palatinate. In France, the two federations of the Nord-Pas-de-Calais (under Mauroy) and the Bouches du Rhône (under Defferre) were for many years the dominant factions in the SFIO and are still extremely powerful in the Socialist Party. The remarkable political survival of Jacques Chirac, who suffered two presidential defeats in 1981 and 1988 but who remained as leader of the Gaullist party right up to his successful bid for the presidency in 1995, owed much to his control of the Paris Town Hall and the enormous patronage opportunities that went with it (the allocation of building contracts by the City of Paris has been under judicial investigation since 1993).

Electoral factors

The polling system is not the major element in determining configurations of power within a party. But in the context of political parties, as in the overall political system, it does affect the line-up of factions and helps to establish a particular set of rules for the political game. The evidence of all the different political parties of Europe shows well enough that the polling system is not an essential factor: for factions exist everywhere, whatever the country's polling system may be, and a party's modes of internal organization and voting are no sure indication of whether or not it is divided into factions. Nevertheless, the introduction of proportional representation does help to develop and reinforce factions, particularly when combined with other divisive elements, such as those connected with policies, personalities, or clientship. It then becomes a means of stabilizing the respective strengths of the various ideological currents, personal clans, and more or less regionalized groups that are in conflict inside the party.

Thus, the percentage of votes obtained by the various factions in the Italian Christian Democrat Party was essential in determining the extent to which they should be represented on electoral lists, the formation of the government, and the distribution of public posts and functions. Allocations were worked out strictly in proportion to the results obtained, in accordance with the 'Cencelli' rules (so-called after the name of the Christian Democrat official responsible for devising the rules of this 'division of spoils'). For example, Area Zac, which won 30.2 per cent of the vote in the Party Congress of 1982, obtained 30 per cent of the government posts reserved for the Christian Democrats in the Craxi Government, in 1983. The PAF faction, which had won 34.6 per cent of the vote, received as its share 35 per cent of the Christian Democrat ministries, and the opposition (Preamble) group was also allocated a percentage of portfolios that tallied with its results at the Congress (35 per cent). As a journalist noted in the *Corriere della sera*, the 'Cencelli handbook' had been 'respected'.[42] What caused the Cencelli manual to appear (and to be) so cynical was the underlying assumption that the Christian Democrats would always be in power, and that they could therefore allow their own factional balances alone to dictate the composition of the government without the slightest regard for any wider political considerations, let alone for the ability of the individuals concerned to serve their country with competence or honour. The contrast with the formation of the 1996 Prodi government, when the PDS deliberately chose to serve a form of apprenticeship and accept fewer ministerial posts than its electoral weight entitled it to, is significant. Whether this return to the letter of the Italian constitution (requiring that the Prime Minister choose the government) will last beyond Prodi is, of course, a more open question.

Party systems

By party system, we mean 'the whole collection of parties as they interact in a given political system'. In Western countries, the fundamental characteristic of this structure of interrelationships is party pluralism. There are two reasons for this. One is the belief that democracy cannot be achieved through a single organization holding a monopoly; the other, the *de facto* circumstances (all the Western democracies do include several parties). But the number of parties varies greatly from one country to another and for a long time political analysts tended to regard that as an essential factor in the understanding of a party system. They would contrast two-party systems, for which Britain constituted the model, with multi-party systems, for which France provided a good illustration. Meanwhile, single-party systems could be observed in the socialist countries or in those where totalitarian regimes insisted upon unquestioning obedience.

The two-party or the duopolistic system?

Two-party systems are associated with English-speaking countries—most typically Britain and the United States—and with the first-past-the-post electoral system. The first-past-the-post electoral system does not completely rule out the formation of third parties, as was seen in the United States in 1860 or 1912, but it does discourage it. It also makes a third-party breakthrough extraordinarily difficult; Labour's replacement of the Liberals as Britain's main opposition party in the 1920s is the unique case in the twentieth century, and it followed a big extension of the suffrage, scarcely a frequent event. Under normal circumstances, the political supremacy of the two established parties is assured.

Yet a purely two-party system is more of an ideal concept than a reality. In the United States, while it is true that Democrats and Republicans between them usually win almost all the popular votes and legislative seats, it is also the case that traditional southern Democrats have often had little in common with their northern colleagues, and party has frequently been an unreliable guide to the policy coalitions that form in the House and Senate. In Britain, Conservative and Labour successfully shut out competitors in the eight post-war elections, up to 1970, leaving the Commons dominated by a single-party majority facing just one serious opposition party. But in 1974 the situation changed; neither of the two elections of that year produced a secure government majority, and so the Labour governments that won them were obliged to take account of small parties in the parliamentary arithmetic. Although outright two-party domination returned to parliament in 1979, it did not quite return to the country; a quarter or more of the voters have regularly taken their support elsewhere. Thus even if government whips have rarely needed to take account of smaller parties in parliament since 1979 (the case of John Major's government, divided internally, governing without a majority, and having to court the Ulster Unionists to stay in power after 1995, is the major exception), party campaign managers certainly need to include them in their electoral calculations.

It would therefore be more accurate to borrow an expression from the realm of economics and speak of 'duopolies', to underline the essential point, for this is not so much the number of parties (which, in reality, is *never* limited to two), but rather the fact that one of those two duopolistic parties holds power for periods of varying length, alternating with the other major party and without help or support from any third party. Even that profile is a great deal tidier than the reality. In the United States, the Democrats controlled the House of Representatives continuously from 1954 until 1994; and for 20 of the 40 years after 1952 a Republican in the White House coexisted with Democrat majorities in Congress. In Britain the growth of third-party support helped to ensure four consecutive election victories for the Conservatives and thus their sole domination of the political system for close to two decades. The alternation in power generally associated with two-party systems does not exclude very long periods when a single party controls one or other, or even all, of the levers of government.

Multi-party systems

What distinguishes pluralist party systems from duopolistic ones is thus, in principle at least, not so much the number of parties involved as the dominant position of two of them. The dividing line between the two types of party system is thus a flexible one, for the balance between the various parties depends upon the changes that affect ideologies, polling systems, prevailing circumstances, and so on. A number of variants to Duverger's typology have accordingly been suggested, to take account of such swings of the pendulum and intermediate situations (e.g. party realignment). To reflect hybrid situations, Jean Blondel suggests a typology with four components: two-party systems, systems with two-and-a-half parties, multi-party systems in which one party is dominant, and pure multi-party systems.[43] This has the advantage of conveying a better idea of the real situation. The drawback to it, however, is that it was worked out chiefly on the basis of the West German movement towards a two-party system during the 1960s and 1970s and it has been somewhat invalidated by the developments of the early 1980s. A few years later (in 1976), Sartori made a useful contribution to the analysis of party systems by making a distinction between *categories* (defined by fragmentation) and *types* of systems (determined by the *ideological distance* between the parties and the degree of their polarization).[44] By taking this new variable into account, Sartori is able to distinguish, within multi-party systems, between moderate pluralistic systems and polarized systems in which the parties are separated by a wide ideological gap (given that some of them are anti-system parties, as Sartori argued was the case in France and Italy). Of course, any new typology attracts criticism, debate, and suggestions for readjustments of various kinds. We shall not, for example, go into the clash between Sartori, who defined the Italian party system as a 'polarized pluralist system', and Giorgio Galli, who regards it as an 'imperfect two-party system'.[45] We shall limit ourselves to describing first the pluralist systems in which the political 'market place' is divided between parties that are relatively evenly balanced, and then those in which one political group holds a dominant position.

According to Sartori's typology, centripetal pluralist systems are defined principally by three features:

- a small ideological gap between the principal parties;
- a propensity to form coalitions between different parties, even when they favour different programmes;
- essentially centripetal competition.

In contrast, the polarized pluralist model is characterized by:

- a wide ideological gap between the parties;
- the existence of anti-system parties;
- competition of a centrifugal nature.

At first sight, the democracies that correspond most closely to the centripetal model would appear to be the countries sometimes described as 'consociational' (Switzerland, Holland, and Belgium—until, that is, regionalist and federalist parties made their appearance there). However, it would be exaggerated to assimilate consociationalism and centripetal pluralism, for the latter model lacks some of the characteristics of consociational systems, namely, the religious and linguistic divisions that underlie the political culture of those States. Rather, centripetal pluralism can be said to be embodied in States where, by reason of the contradictions and heterogeneity of both the Right and the Left, the competition is played out at the Centre. The role of the centre is crucial, not because of its own intrinsic strength, but on account of the weakness of both the Right and the Left.

Paolo Farneti has pointed out that the dynamics of this system result from the competition between parties all of which aim to forge an alliance at the centre, since the price to pay for being permanently in opposition is greater than that involved in participating in a mixed coalition.[46] On the basis of these characteristics, France under the Fifth Republic may be considered as an example of centripetal pluralism. On the other hand, Sartori, who was deeply suspicious of the Italian Communist Party, balked at classifying Italy in this category, presenting it instead as an example of polarized pluralism comprising centrifugal and anti-system parties in the form of the MSI and, above all, the Communists. On this point, Paolo Farneti's view is less extreme and more realistic. For him, Italy constituted a polarized pluralist system from 1944 to 1961, but as from 1965 fell into the centripetal pluralist category. And Farneti interprets the historic compromise of the 1970s as a refusal on the part of the Communist Party to destroy the existing centripetal tendencies at work. It preferred this course to the option of radically changing the system by bringing in a left-wing coalition—which would, anyway, have been of a heterogeneous nature. All the same, the price to be paid for such centripetal tendencies may be a heavy one, involving a widening gap between the general electorate and élite groups, a simultaneous isolation of right-wing or left-wing minorities that are tempted to embrace radicalism, and a depoliticization of public opinion.[47]

Farneti's application of Sartori's model seems more in line with the ideological and political evolution of Italy than Sartori's own interpretation. Many studies have shown that in the course of the 1970s, ideological polarization[48] became less acute, and all observers of Italian political life agree that the Italian Communist Party ceased to be an anti-system party well before its name-change and final renunciation of the Communist tradition. That its chances of acceding to power were very slight, that it was confined to the periphery, did not alter its fundamental integration into the system.

Party pluralism may be inegalitarian when the political scene is dominated by a party that is not only powerful but also central to most alliances. A dominant party cannot be defined simply in terms of size: the French Communist Party under the Fourth Republic and the Italian Communist Party were respectively the strongest and second strongest forces in their own political systems, but neither was in a dominant position. To be so, a party must also be the key element in the constitution of any political coalition: this was true of the Italian Christian Democrats, who held a central position. No government could be formed without them since there was no leftist alternative.

Being in a dominant position is not necessarily a lasting situation, despite what the Italian example might suggest, for in the first place the word 'dominant' may be applied to a whole collection of different situations varying from hegemony (as in the case of the Christian Democrats during the 1950s) to far more competitive situations such as those that were a feature of the relations between the secular Italian parties and the Christian Democrats during the 1980s. Secondly, multi-party systems with one dominant party sometimes evolve into duopolistic or even quasi two-party systems. West Germany up until the early 1960s was characterized by the domination of the CDU–CSU and the steady weakening of small parties, so that by 1961 only the CDU–CSU, the SPD, and the FDP remained in the Bundestag. What developed over the next 20 years appeared to observers to constitute a genuine two-party system, or at least a 'two-and-a-half party system', in Jean Blondel's terminology, with all three parties tasting both government office and opposition. The 1980s, on the other hand, were marked by a more centrifugal pattern—the temporary weakening of the FDP, the Greens' breakthrough into the Bundestag, and the re-emergence of the far Right, chiefly in the form of the Republikaner, to win seats at *Land* level and in the 1989 European elections. That left the CDU–CSU still on top, though, and unification did not appear, judging by the first all-German election in 1990, to effect any radical change to the party system. Four years later, however, the position looked rather less stable, with the Green–Bündnis '90 alliance back in force with 49 seats, the former East German Communists, now renamed as the PDS, installed as a significant force with nearly 20 per cent of the votes in the Eastern *Länder* and 30 Bundestag seats—and the CDU–CSU–FDP majority reduced to just ten. This could no longer be classified as a 'two-and-a-half-party' system.

Under the Fifth Republic, France also went through a decade when one party predominated (1962–73). But de Gaulle's resignation in 1969 and his successor Pompidou's death in 1974 heralded the end of the Gaullists' supremacy under the impact both of the non-Gaullist right (which regrouped as the UDF in 1978) and of the Socialists, who won back left-wing voters temporarily seduced by the General. The very strong institutional positions of the Socialists themselves in the 1980s do not, however, qualify them as a dominant party; they were unpopular for too much of the time, lost too many local elections, and above all faced a reasonably determined right-wing opposition that won a parliamentary majority for two years in 1986–8 and inflicted a crushing defeat on the Socialists in 1993. Today, pluralist systems with one dominant party are very much the exception in Western democracies: the fate of the Italian Christian Democrats, not to mention the Spanish Socialists or the British Conservatives, are illustrations of the fragility of dominant status.

Fragmentation, concentration, coalitions

As we have seen, any classification of parties in particular political systems is bound to fluctuate and change, given that those parties will always be affected by new developments. Fragmentation or, conversely, concentration are constantly recurring features in the life, development, and demise of political parties. Such developments tend to fall into three main patterns: in the first the number of parties increases, in the second it decreases, while in the third it remains more or less stable but the parties' relative strengths change. In the early 1990s there was a widespread tendency towards fragmentation, at least in Germany, Italy, and France, though it is not certain that this will last; in earlier periods, developments varied greatly between different systems.

Until recently the clearest example of fragmentation was that of Britain, the homeland of the 'two-party system'. From the end of the Second World War up until the 1974 elections, the Labour and Conservative parties' combined share of the vote never fell below 87.5 per cent and was more frequently well over 90. Since February 1974, on the other hand, the two big parties have only exceeded 75 per cent of the vote between them in three of the seven elections, and they have never managed more than 81 per cent. The initial beneficiaries of the disaffection from the two major parties were sometimes the centrifugal parties (in October 1974, Plaid Cymru and, especially, the Scottish National Party, which won 11 seats), and sometimes parties of the centre, whether old (the Liberal Party, which won 13 seats in 1974 and 11 in 1979) or new (the SDP which, in alliance with the Liberals, won 23 seats in 1983). But the relatively modest change in seats conveys only a weak reflection of the shock to the party system caused by the Labour split of the early 1980s: in 1983, while the Labour Party polled just 27.6 per cent of the vote (its worst result in half a century, but one which gave it 209 seats), the Alliance pressed hard on its heels with 25.4 per cent. Since 1983 Labour's initially slow and painful, then rapid recovery (30.8 per cent in 1987, 34.4 per cent in 1992—and 43.2 per cent in 1997) has halted fragmentation; but even the 1997 result appeared to presage a regular one-quarter of the vote going to parties outside the former duopoly.

West Germany up to the 1980s, on the other hand, exemplifies the tendency towards concentration. Between 1953 and 1983, the multi-party system turned into a three-party system[49] or even a virtually duopolistic one, as a result of the decline of the FDP in the late 1970s. When the Federal Republic held its first elections, the CDU–CSU and the SPD together accumulated only 60.2 per cent of the vote. But in 1953, they won 74 per cent (totalling 83.5 per cent together with the FDP), and between 1957 and 1987 they scored over 80 per cent. The Communist Party (15 seats in 1949), the extreme Right (2 seats), and the Bavarian Party (17 seats) had all been eliminated by 1953. The only survivors from this political massacre were the Deutsche Partei and the Refugee Party, but the latter also fell victim to the 1957 elections. Only the Deutsche Partei went on to win 17 seats in 1957, but that was because it had allied itself to the CDU, which had refrained from opposing its candidates in its strongholds of Lower Saxony and north-eastern

Germany. When it tried to become autonomous in 1961, however, the German Party bought its own one-way ticket out of the electoral scene. The supremacy of the two major parties has remained strong, due in part to a polling system that is most unfavourable to small political groups, but since 1980 the position of the two major parties has weakened. Between them, they shared 90.7 per cent of the vote in 1972 and 91.2 per cent in 1976, but this fell to 87.4 per cent in 1980 and to 87 per cent in 1983. By January 1987 they polled a 'mere' 81.3 per cent, and in the united German elections they polled 77.3 per cent in 1990 and 77.8 per cent in 1994. With just three parties represented in the Bundestag in 1980, but five in 1994 (or six, if Bündnis '90 are separated from the Greens), the earlier concentration in the German system appeared to have gone into reverse.

The third pattern is one where the number of parties remains stable, but the balance of their relative strengths shifts in a quite striking fashion. Italy up until the late 1980s provides a good example. For some 35 years, Italian politics were characterized by the long, slow slide of the Christian Democrats and the equally slow, and uneven, rise of the Communists. The Christian Democrats managed an exceptional result in 1948 (48.5 per cent), then stabilized at about 40 per cent in the 1960s before losing further ground to reach 34.3 per cent in 1987. The Communists, on the other hand, had started immediately after the war as the weaker party of the left, with 18.9 per cent of the poll in 1946 compared to the Socialists' 20.7 per cent. They then overtook the Socialists (in 1953), and built steadily to their best-ever result in a parliamentary election two decades later (34.4 per cent in 1976). At the 1984 European elections, the death of their leader Enrico Berlinguer helped to make the Communists Italy's largest party, by a very short head, in terms of share of the vote (33.3 per cent to the DC's 33.0). That, however, was an ephemeral success, and the Communists faced Bettino Craxi's increasingly aggressive Socialist Party attempting to build towards 15 per cent and uninterested in a left-wing alliance. At the 'earthquake' of the 1992 elections, fragmentation hit the Italian system: both of Italy's big parties recorded their worst post-war results, with 29.7 per cent for the DC and 16.1 per cent for the PDS, the renamed Communist party. The reasons were different in each case: the DC was hurt by the Northern Leagues' success in exploiting discontent with a corrupt party that had run Italy since the Second World War, while the Communists were damaged by the events in the East and by the secession of Rifondazione Comunista, who went on to steal 5.6 per cent of the vote in 1992. That 'earthquake' was, of course, only the prelude to the greater upheavals of 1994 and 1996, which swept the post-war party system away. This process is probably unfinished, but there appears at least a possibility that the inclusion of a majority component in the electoral system will fix a more or less bipolar structure on the party system and allow for a measure of consolidation.

The system that displays no long-run tendency (but which shares with Germany and Italy the tendency to fragmentation in the early 1990s) is that of France. Changes in the British, Italian, and German systems have usually (though not always) been slow, spread over several elections. One reason for this is that in all three countries, parties have been fairly well rooted in society and the ground rules of electoral competition have changed only slightly (in all EC countries, a new level of competition was added with direct elections to the European parliament in 1979). In France, on the other hand, change has often been sudden. This may be partly explained not only by the comparatively poor entrenchment of most parties in terms of membership, but also by frequent changes to the rules of the game. Since the Second World War, French politicians have had to accommodate a change of constitution (in 1958); four major changes to the parliamentary electoral law (in 1951, 1958, 1985–6, and 1988); and the addition of three new levels of electoral competition (the European parliament from 1979, regions from 1986, and most importantly, the directly elected Presidency from 1965). The French can vote at six different types of election, each of which is habitually regarded as a major test of national party strengths; of the 20 years after de Gaulle's resignation in 1969, there were only three (1975, 1980, and 1987) without either an election or a referendum, while the single year 1988 saw presidential, parliamentary, and cantonal elections, and a referendum. Electoral systems, and thus patterns of party competition, vary between different types of election: currently, some form of two-ballot majority system is used for presidential, parliamentary, cantonal, and (in towns) municipal elections, while proportional representation applies for regional and European polls.

Many types of election and frequent changes to the rules have made for change and complexity in the French party system. Fourth-Republic France corresponded rather well to Sartori's 'polarized pluralism' model, with four 'system' parties (Socialists, Radicals, MRP, and Independents and Peasants) squabbling amongst themselves but managing to shut out their 'anti-system' competitors (the Communists on the Left, and on the Right the Gaullist RPF in 1951 and the Poujadists in 1956). With de Gaulle's return and the foundation of the Fifth Republic in 1958, observers identified first a 'dominant-party' system, as the Gaullists and their Giscardian allies gave France her first taste of majority government, and then a 'bipolarized' system as the Centre parties were squeezed between the governing Right and a Left that was slowly reorganizing as an opposition alliance. With the weakening of the Gaullists in the early 1970s, that produced what Duverger called the 'bipolar quadrille': a clear division between the majority and the opposition, but two intensely competing political forces within each—on the left the Communists and the Socialists, and on the right the Gaullists and Valéry Giscard d'Estaing's UDF, a loose coalition of Christian Democrats, liberals, and the non-Gaullist Right. The victors of this competition were the Socialists, who had overtaken the Communists as the stronger party of the Left by the mid-1970s, and went on to win the Presidency and a single-party National Assembly majority in 1981. What might have appeared then as the start of a new dominant-party period quickly became something more complex. The major new development of the 1980s was the rise of Le Pen's FN, which helped to fragment the Right and to keep the more moderate right-wing parties out of power for most of the decade. More than ever, party competition split between different levels; in particular, the FN, while almost excluded from Parliament (thanks to the electoral system, it won just one National Assembly seat in 1988 and 1997, and none in 1993), occupies strategic positions on regional councils and plays a key role in setting the terms of national political debate. On the Left, while the

Communists' decline has been confirmed, the Socialists' new position as France's 'natural party of government' has not. The Socialists suffered a catastrophic drop in popularity in the early 1990s, losing four-fifths of their parliamentary seats in 1993; their victory of 1997, while remarkable, was still achieved with little more than a quarter of the first-round votes, and they needed all the support they could muster from Communists and Greens to form a parliamentary majority. It was more than ever the case, in the French system towards the turn of the millennium, that no party was safe.

Fragmentation and realignment almost always make it necessary to set up coalitions in order to form governments. Government of a country by a single party (normally with a majority but sometimes with only a minority) is the rule in Britain, which has avoided coalitions since 1945, but the exception in other European states.[50] In France it has happened only twice since 1945, with the Fabius Government from July 1984 to March 1986 and with the Rocard, Cresson, and Bérégovoy Governments during the 1988–93 parliament: and given the inclusion of some of the Socialists' close Left Radical allies in each of them, even these were only 'single-party' governments in the sense that they did not involve a formal coalition of two or more major parliamentary parties.[51] The same goes for West Germany and Italy. The CDU–CSU was in a position to govern alone for only four years, from 1957 to 1961, and the only periods when the Italian Christian Democrats headed an undivided minority government (a government of a single shade) were from August 1953 to January 1954 (the Pella Government), from May 1957 to June 1958 (the Zoli Government), from February 1959 to February 1961 (the second Segni Government, the Tambroni Government, and the third Fanfani Government), from June to November 1963 (the Leone Government), from June to November 1968 (the second Leone Government), from August 1969 to February 1970 (the second Rumor Government), and from March 1974 to August 1979 (the Moro Government and Andreotti's government of national unity): this adds up to about eight years over the 1945 to 1989 period. In truth, of all the countries studied, Britain is alone in having escaped the arithmetical or political need to resort to coalition governments since the Second World War.

In 1962, William Riker tried to establish a theory of coalitions,[52] which was followed by Dodd[53] and Budge and Farlie.[54] These formal theories, founded for the most part upon criteria of size but also upon ideological disparities and the types of policy adopted, fall a long way short of providing a completely satisfactory explanation for the variety of existing coalitions, no doubt because they postulate rational behaviour (by no means a safe assumption to make), and their record as a basis for prediction is not particularly impressive. For example, Riker's concept of a 'minimal winning coalition', which assumes that coalitions are formed in such a way as to exclude all members not essential to the constitution of an absolute majority, is only partially substantiated by the facts and does not account for either minority governments or coalitions that are far wider than is arithmetically essential, such as, for example, the grand CDU–CSU–SPD coalition in West Germany that governed from 1966 to 1969.

It is clear that some coalitions are deliberately constructed to include more groups than are strictly necessary from the point of view of the parliamentary balance of power, and even that parties which, on their own, already hold a majority sometimes enter into coalitions with small parties. One instance in point was the grand coalition in West Germany mentioned above, but plenty of other examples are provided by the many Centre-left coalitions in Italy during the 1960s, and the *Pentapartito* coalition of 1983 to 1989. For instance, in 1983 the majority necessary was 316 votes but the actual majority amounted to 366, while the three small secular parties controlled respectively 29 (PRI), 23 (PSDI), and 16 (PLI) seats. Theoretically, it would have been possible to do without one, or even two, of those parties and still obtain the 'minimal winning coalition' of Riker's theory.

Even more paradoxically, a party with an absolute majority sometimes chooses to form a coalition with a small allied political group. Such was the situation in West Germany in 1957, when Adenauer included representatives of the small Deutsche Partei in his government despite the fact that the CDU–CSU had obtained an absolute majority. De Gasperi proceeded in similar fashion between May 1948 and June 1953, even though the Christian Democrats had won more than 50 per cent of the seats. The French experience is also instructive in this respect. The Gaullists included their Independent Republican allies in their governments from 1968 to 1973, although they enjoyed France's first-ever single-party National Assembly majority. President Mitterrand, although commanding France's second such majority, did bring Communists into the governing coalition in 1981, when they were arithmetically unnecessary but politically useful; seven years later he left them out as a political liability—although in arithmetical terms they would have made the difference between a minority and a majority government; and in 1997, on Jospin's appointment to the premiership, they were brought back in as a political and an arithmetical necessity. How should we interpret these situations? We must fall back upon explanations of a political nature to discover the logic of behaviour that appears irrational from a purely formal point of view.

One possibility is that periods of serious crisis are likely to produce large coalitions. They constitute a form of government of national unity. Such an interpretation might explain, in particular, the grand coalition formed in West Germany at a time of serious economic crisis (even if, looking back, it looks relatively minor in comparison to the crisis of the 1970s).

A second explanation might be that an arithmetically weak majority that is theoretically adequate for the purposes of government may be threatened by the insufficiency of legitimacy that results from the narrowness of that majority and the 'quasi-victory' of the opposition. This was Berlinguer's justification for the historic compromise: he pointed out that a left-wing majority needs more than 51 per cent of the poll in order to govern. The gap between an arithmetical majority and true legitimacy is often accentuated, in continental Europe at least, by the obvious discrepancy that exists between a parliamentary majority and an electoral minority. The CDU–CSU obtained no more than 50.2 per cent of the poll in 1957, the Christian Democrats only 48.5 per cent in 1948, the Gaullists only 43.65 per cent on the first ballot in the 1968 election, and the Socialists only 37.51 per cent in 1981 (also on the first ballot). Increasing the parliamentary majority is a way of calling for wider support from the electorate and public opinion.

A third explanation may lie in the relations that obtain between parties that might conceivably form a coalition, given their ideological proximity and electoral alliances. For parties allied out of necessity but hostile and competitive by nature, sharing power in a coalition may be mutually advantageous: the dominant party draws in those that are less dangerous to it when included in a coalition than when left out (as Mitterrand's Socialists did to the PCF from 1981 to 1984); meanwhile, it is in the interest of small minority parties to band together so as to be integrated all together into the coalition, even when they are not all strictly needed in order to create an absolute majority (as in the case of the Italian *Pentapartito*). In these types of situation, it is essential to distinguish between two kinds of party whose individual characteristics might be conveyed by the labels 'support parties' and 'pivot parties'. Support parties are the parties that are necessary to convert a relative majority into an absolute one (the Independent Republicans in France between 1962 and 1968, for instance, or the FDP in West Germany). Pivot parties are parties around which coalitions cluster, and may also be dominant parties (the UNR in 1962, or the Christian Democrats).

The opposite situation is created—in flagrant contradiction to the theory of democracy—by minority governments, whether formed by a single party or by a coalition. Unknown in Britain (except from February to October 1974, when the Labour Government could count on only 301 votes out of 635) and Germany, minority governments can only survive with the support of a parliamentary majority (not included in the government). Such situations have frequently arisen in France under the Fourth Republic, and in Italy. In these circumstances it seems as though the implicit coalition agreed within parliament can only be set up on condition that it is not reflected in the composition of the government. In polarized systems, such paradoxical situations are more likely to occur in the presence of a party or parties which, it is felt, cannot at any cost be allowed to accede to power (the Communist Party and the FN in France, the PCI and the MSI in Italy). Another possibility, in Fifth-Republic France, is that the Constitution allows for a minority government to survive provided no clear anti-government majority is constituted: this explains the persistence of minority Socialist governments from 1988 to 1993.

Since they do not operate actively and visibly within the government, parties which simply support a government in parliament carry no formal responsibility for its decisions. Sometimes an even more complicated situation is created by the establishment of parliamentary coalitions which are not reflected in the composition of the government, as is demonstrated in the case of the Government of National Unity in Italy from 1976 to 1979: as always during the Cold War, the Communist Party was excluded from the ministerial team, but this time it was fully associated with government policies at a parliamentary level. Although the participation of the PCI was not official, the effect of it was reflected in the quasi-unanimous support—at parliamentary level, at least—that was given to the policies adopted during this period. The PCI subsequently paid a heavy price for that 'support without participation': its percentage of the vote fell from 34 per cent in 1976 to 30.4 per cent in 1979 (whereas the Christian Democrats forfeited only 0.4 per cent, dropping from 38.7 to 38.3 per cent).

The functions of political parties

Political parties are one of the fundamental elements in contemporary liberal democracies. The place that they occupy is itself a consequence of the very concept of democracy, founded upon the pluralism of interests, the unanimous rejection of a single-party system, and political competition in the choosing of leaders and policies. But over and above that fundamental and crucial choice, Western political parties appear to be playing an increasingly important role as a consequence of the functions that they assume in the life of liberal political societies. It is fair to say, without exaggeration, that the political parties 'control' the entire political process from the raising of political consciousness to the elaboration of policies and their implementation. Admittedly, the political parties are by no means the only agents involved (not only is the party system pluralistic, but the parties themselves hold no monopoly over the exercise of some of their functions), and their role, furthermore, varies from one country to another. But they are usually the essential agents in political life. Let us review the major functions that the political parties discharge, for this will make it possible to gauge their impact within Western political systems.

Integration and mobilization

The evolution through which the liberal democracies progressed from a concept of individualistic and uncoordinated political participation to a more realistic acceptance of communal action within the framework of *ad hoc* organizations had, by the nineteenth century, made it possible for parties to emerge, parties capable of organizing and expressing the choices of citizens who shared common ideals and interests. But the decisive phase in this evolution came with the creation and development of workers' parties that specifically proclaimed themselves to speak for a particular class and possessed a powerful, unifying ideology together with an apparatus comprising militants and grass-roots organizations set up to mobilize electoral support. To defend themselves against this kind of apparatus and these potentially destabilizing modes of mobilizing support, the bourgeois parties were obliged to improve their own powers of integration and mobilization. It is significant that it should be the American parties (which have never been confronted by the 'challenge' of workers' parties) that are the least efficient in this respect and face the most vigorous competition from the *ad hoc* organization of interest groups. But even where the parties constitute the major means of mobilizing and integrating support, they may at any time face competition and need to revise their methods.

Political Parties

Disenchantment was especially widespread in the 1980s, when disaffection or out-right disgust with established parties spread across several West European countries. In Italy they were the prelude to the 1993 referendum which withdrew the public money which had been made available to parties for two decades, and to the collapse of the party system as a whole. In France, disenchantment with the Socialist and Communist Parties after their entry into government found expression in falling membership rolls, and all parties were suffering from negative opinion poll ratings by 1991. In Britain, the Labour Party, whose particularity had always been the millions of trade unionists who were affiliated to the party without being direct members, inevitably suffered from the decline in the trade union movement—and individual membership suffered from the party split at the start of the decade, falling from over 600,000 in 1979 to under half that four years later. In the United States, some of the foremost students of parties produced a comparative work entitled *When Parties Fail.*[55]

There is certainly no shortage of reasons to explain the decline of political parties, and particularly the decline of their capacity to integrate and mobilize, to form a link between government and ordinary citizens. Among such explanations may be cited a growing disinclination to join mass organizations, which may also be seen to extend to churches and trade unions; a sense, in a globalizing world where the constraints of the market matter more and more, that party politics is less and less effective as a means to affect events; the decline of the communities or the subcultures, whether industrial or ecclesiastical, which had sustained and reinforced party activity; even a lessened sense, among party leaders, that having a mass membership really mattered. There is also, however, plenty of evidence to suggest that, in Europe at least, no satisfactory alternative structure has been found that would allow the parties to wither and die. In the first place, revival appears to be both possible and sought after by politicians under the right circumstances. Britain's Labour Party, which counted over 400,000 members by the time of Tony Blair's election in 1997 and which had given them new, if largely symbolic, tasks such as voting on the party's election manifesto, is a case in point. Secondly, alternative organizations rarely seem to mount effective challenges. East Germany's Bündnis '90, for example, the 'Forum'-type movement built by former dissidents who had opposed Communist rule before the Berlin Wall came down, might have been expected to do well in the 1990 elections. In fact, it was effectively sidelined by the big parties as early as March 1990, and only survived in the December elections in alliance with the Greens; it was the established, professional CDU–CSU that moved into the East and started putting down roots in its new territory. In Italy, the collapse of the parties of the post-war 'first Republic' was immediately followed by the creation of new parties. In France, de Gaulle's claim to be 'above parties' looked less and less sustainable as the 1960s advanced, and by 1966 at the latest, his Prime Minister Pompidou had made a priority of building a strong party structure to perpetuate the General's inheritance into *l'après-de Gaulle*. In the same period, the profusion of newly emerging left-wing political clubs were seen as substitutes for the parties (especially the moribund SFIO) that had failed to win over voters to the non-Communist left. But the non-Communist Left only really became a serious contender for power when it had reconstituted itself as the new Socialist Party at Épinay in 1971. More recent attempts by politicians of the centre-right like Michel Noir or Alain Carignon to set up looser, alternative groupings have been no more effective as vote-catchers than the Left's clubs. The French example is particularly interesting, for it shows that in Western countries, even in unfavourable circumstances, only parties can mount an effective challenge to parties as instruments of political mobilization. Passing crises may shake them but, so far, nothing has succeeded in calling their supremacy in question. Only the American parties find themselves in a seriously competitive situation, being confronted by powerful interest groups, whose legitimacy as a rule goes unchallenged.

Influencing voting patterns

In the area of mobilizing and integrating supporters, the political parties do face a measure of competition from other groups. But when it comes to electoral promises, their monopoly is virtually absolute. In the nineteenth century and at the beginning of the twentieth, candidates for election were frequently 'Independents' and their chances of success were by no means negligible. Today, a wide range of Independents still stand as candidates but their chances of election are virtually nil. Even when a candidate's links with his party are weak (as they tend to be in the United States and in France, in the case of cadre parties such as the Radicals and the Republicans), to stand a chance of being elected it is important to be recognized by some party, to carry a party 'label': a sort of trademark guaranteeing some form of name recognition, and often, like a MacDonald's hamburger franchise, requiring discipline and sacrifice from the individual acquiring it. As we have seen, in connection with the party identification of voters and the typology suggested by Parisi and Pasquino (who speak of 'a supporter's vote', 'an opinion vote', and a 'bargaining vote'), to degrees that vary depending on the country, the time, and the parties, electoral behaviour is dictated by the voters' support for particular parties and by a preference for one candidate rather than another that has nothing to do with individual personalities.

Of course, the parties' hold over the way that people vote is disputed and by no means unwavering. The party monopoly may be challenged both politically and ideologically. A political challenge arises when, from time to time, groups or individuals seek to break the monopoly by organizing anti-party movements. But this usually amounts to no more than a flash in the pan or a total flop (the Poujade movement, l'Uomo Qualunque). 'Ideological' challenges are rooted in the liberal constitutional tradition, which started out by rejecting political parties as the instruments of political structuring and subsequently refused to recognize their monopoly: in West Germany in 1967, the Federal Court rejected a proposal that the 5 per cent elimination clause should be applied in the financing of electoral campaigns; in Italy, the mode of polling in principle makes it possible for an extremely wide range of groups and individuals to win seats; in France in the past, the rules that applied to the presentation of candidates for presidential election were designed to prevent the parties from controlling all candidacies (although that is no longer the case).

Yet if the parties' hold over voting patterns is undeniable, it should also be remembered that it is not altogether unwavering. Voters sometimes change their minds and the volatility of the electorate can become a major problem for the political parties. They have to try to maintain the loyalty of their voters by means of the ideology that they purvey (and are obliged to adapt as circumstances and voters change: something that the French Communist Party failed to do), the programmes that they put forward, and the advantages that they promise (and deliver if ever they accede to power).

Recruitment of political personnel

This is another area where the parties' monopoly is virtually total, at least in so far as central institutions are concerned. At a local level, the parties' sway is usually less general, particularly in France. But the most fundamental aspect of the situation lies not so much in these differences but in developments which here, too, at the local level, have tended to give the parties a quasi-monopoly over the recruitment of political personnel. In truth, what is implied by the 'nationalization of political life', or 'politicization', is the growing influence that the political parties are acquiring even at an infranational level.

As regards the executive personnel, the situation differs from one system to another, depending on whether it is presidential, semipresidential, or parliamentary. In parliamentary systems, the political parties certainly do hold an almost absolute monopoly, for parliamentary tradition dictates that ministers be members of parliament. However, under the Fifth Republic, in France, more than a quarter of the ministers, on average, have been picked from outside Parliament. In such a case, the influence of the parties at first sight seems more limited, but it could well be that, on the contrary, by penetrating the upper administration they considerably extend their political monopoly. It should be added that the parties, either directly or indirectly, control many appointments in a number of areas: these include the judiciary (the Constitutional Courts), public administration (the German and French 'spoils' systems), the non-departmental government agencies (the *sotto-governo* in Italy), the economic sector (public or partly State-owned businesses), culture (public or subsidized theatres, museums, foundations, etc.), and health (particularly in Italy). State expansion to a large extent entails expansion of the political parties, although it is sometimes difficult to judge exactly which comes first.

Elaboration of policies

It is probably in this area that the parties' position is weakest, however loud and emphatic their claims. With very few exceptions, political parties generally present themselves as potential 'parties in office', that is to say, parties which either aspire to the exercise of power, or currently exercise it, or have done so in the past. In the West, the communist parties are virtually alone in rejecting, or claiming to reject, the constraints that the function of government in Western capitalist countries would impose (although the emphasis of such claims varies considerably from one communist party to another). To exercise power or seek to do so, political parties must put forward programmes and policies to the voters and undertake to implement them if they accede to government. And although most politicians, once in office, try to retain as much freedom of political manoeuvre as they can (and secretly agree with A. J. Balfour's remark that he would rather take advice on policy from his valet than from a Conservative Party conference) they are generally obliged at least to pay lip-service to the manifesto of the party that brought them to power. But the business of devising a programme and putting it into operation is affected by many conditions and subject to many pressures. In the first place, it is conditioned by the international situation as well as the political, economic, and social structures of the country concerned. The space for manoeuvre available to political parties is much more restricted than their ideology may suggest. The evolution of the European socialist parties testifies to their recognition of that fact and also to the limitations that may be imposed upon political aspirations. But above all, even though the political parties may to a large extent control the electoral game, in the economic, social, and administrative spheres they come up against many other agents whose power in their own particular sectors is frequently much greater. Large firms disposing of unprecedented freedom to locate factories, and jobs, anywhere in the world, and financial institutions disposing of a similar freedom to move capital and obliged, for the sake of their own survival, to move their investments away from countries and currencies that are seen as bad risks, are two examples. Even where political parties are capable of putting forward more or less ambitious programmes, they face strong competition from interest groups of all kinds and from bureaucracies which play an essential part in drawing up and implementing public policies.

Even so, despite these limitations, the parties play a significant role. Their contribution to the construction of a political programme is decisive, for only they can turn latent, diffuse, and hitherto rejected claims into government programmes: for example, the issue of abortion was bound to remain an ethical, social, and judicial problem until such time as the political parties identified themselves with the more or less clearly expressed desires of society. The parties, whether they are in the majority or in opposition, play an equally important part in channelling and satisfying demands. However, this can be a risky business for a political party, particularly if it is more concerned to represent particular interest groups than to mediate and synthesize conflicting public demands. Finally, the parties also help to fulfil a 'feedback' function, establishing channels of communication between the citizens and the government and thereby helping to temper and modify government policies.

Of course, we cannot overlook the fact that these functions are fulfilled by parties of many different kinds, operating within political systems that offer them a variety of opportunities. But, on the whole, the European democracies all provide relatively similar frameworks for the operations of their political parties: the parties hold a virtual monopoly as regards the organization of the electoral game and political life generally (although it is a monopoly that is occasionally disputed); but they operate in a far more pluralist and competitive context when it comes to carrying out their mandate, that is, in the whole process of policy-making. Here their claim to legitimacy is not nearly so strong, and this leaves room for other modes of organization, influence, and action to operate: the role and functions of interest groups are defined by the context of this pluralist competition.

Questions

- Why has governmental office posed particular dilemmas for Socialist and Communist parties, and how have they generally reacted to these difficulties?

- Can any useful distinctions still be made between the ideology of Christian democrats, liberals, and conservatives?

- Can the rise of (1) the far Right and (2) ecology parties in many European countries since the 1980s be explained by any common causes?

- Has change in European party systems over recent years resulted more from changes in society, or from the behaviour of political actors?

- How relevant is Maurice Duverger's distinction between 'cadre' and 'mass' parties to the present-day organization of political parties?

- In what ways can political parties still be seen as essential to the democratic process?

NOTES

1. Edmund Burke, *Thoughts on the Cause of the Present Discontents*, 2nd edn. (London, 1770), 110.
2. M. Duverger, *Les Partis politiques* (Paris: Colin, 1951); L. D. Epstein, *Political Parties in Western Democracies* (New York: Praeger, 1967).
3. J. LaPalombara and M. Weiner (eds.), *Political Parties and Political Development* (Princeton, NJ: Princeton University Press, 1966).
4. K. Janda, *Political Parties, a Cross National Survey* (New York: Free Press, 1980).
5. D.-L. Seiler, *Partis et familles politiques* (Paris: Themis (PUF), 1980).
6. Moderate bourgeois and parliamentary monarchy established after the July Revolution of 1830, which brought down Charles X.
7. See G. Galli, *I Partiti politici* (Turin: UTET, 1974).
8. V. Bogdanor (ed.), *Liberal Party Politics* (Oxford: Clarendon Press, 1983).
9. French counter-revolutionary ideologists.

10. A priest who defended Catholic teaching and social policies to favour the disadvantaged.

11. A. Gramsci, *Il Risorgimento* (Turin: Einaudi, 1949), 70.

12. M. Caciagli, 'Il Resistibile declino della Democrazia Cristiana', in G. Pasquino (ed.), *Il Sistema politico italiano* (Bari: Laterza, 1985), 103.

13. M. Anderson, *Conservative Politics in France* (London: Allen and Unwin, 1974); J. Charlot, *Le Phénomène gaulliste* (Paris: Fayard, 1970).

14. R. Kirk, *The Conservative Mind* (Chicago: Gateway, 1960).

15. K. von Beyme, 'Right-Wing Extremism in Post-War Europe', *West European Politics*, 11(1) (1988) (special issue on the far Right), 5; S. Hix and C. Lord, *Political Parties and the European Union* (Basingstoke: Macmillan, 1997), 107.

16. F. Haegel, 'Le Lien partisan', in CEVIPOF, *L'Électeur français en questions* (Paris: FNSP, 1990), 195–6; D. Boy and N. Mayer, 'L'Électeur français en questions', ibid. 221; *Le Monde*, 25 Oct. 1991.

17. R. E. M. Irving, *The Christian Democratic Parties of Western Europe* (London: Allen and Unwin, 1979).

18. Cf. A. Bergounioux and G. Grunberg, *Le Long Remords du pouvoir: Le Parti socialiste français 1905–1992* (Paris: Fayard, 1992).

19. M. Thorez, Eighth Congress, Villeurbanne, Jan. 1936.

20. N. Bobbio, 'La Questione socialista', *Monde Operaio* (1976), 41–51.

21. Y. Mény (ed.), *Dix ans de régionalisation en Europe* (Paris: CUJAS, 1982).

22. T. Poguntke, 'The "New Politics Dimension" in European Green Parties', in F. Müller-Rommel (ed.), *New Politics in Western Europe: The Rise and Success of Green Parties and Alternative Lists* (Boulder, Colo.: Westview Press, 1989), 184–5: cf. also R. Inglehart, 'Post-Materialism in an Environment of Insecurity', *American Political Science Review*, 75(4) (1981), 880–900.

23. Poguntke, ' "New Politics Dimension" ', 190.

24. S. Parkin, *Green Parties: An International Guide* (London: Heretic Books, 1989), 138.

25. E. G. Frankland, 'Federal Republic of Germany: "Die Grünen" ', in Müller-Rommel (ed.), *New Politics in Western Europe*, 63–4.

26. M. and J. Charlot, 'Les Groupes politiques dans leur environnement', in J. Leca and M. Grawitz (eds.), *Traité de science politique*, iii (Paris: PUF, 1985), 437.

27. 'Le RPR', *Pouvoirs*, 28 (1984), *passim*.

28. P. Avril, *Essai sur les partis* (Paris: LGDJ, 1986), 109.

29. Duverger, *Les Partis politiques*, 10.

30. Ibid. 46.

31. A. B. Wildavsky, 'A Methodological Critique of Duverger's Political Parties', *Journal of Politics*, 21(2) (May 1959), 305 ff.

32. Y. Mény and M. Rhodes, 'Illicit Governance: Corruption, Scandal and Fraud', in M. Rhodes, P. Heywood, and V. Wright (eds.), *Developments in West European Politics* (Basingstoke: Macmillan, 1997), 95–113; R. S. Katz and P. Mair, 'Changing Models of Party Organization and Party Democracy: The Emergence of the Cartel Party', *Party Politics*, 1(1) (1995), 5–28; M. Rhodes, 'Financing Party Politics in Italy: A Case of Systemic Corruption', *West European Politics*, 20(1) (1997), 54–80.

33. A. Knapp, *Gaullism since de Gaulle* (Aldershot: Dartmouth Publishing, 1994), 33; A. Clark, *Diaries* (London: Phoenix Paperback edn., 1994), 123.

34. See F. J. Sorauf, 'Political Parties and Political Analysis', in W. N. Chambers and W. D.

Burnham (eds.), *The American Party System: Stages of Political Development* (Oxford: Oxford University Press, 1967).

35. Avril, *Essai sur les partis*, 69.

36. R. Michels, *Political Parties: A Sociological Study of the Oligarchic Tendencies of Modern Democracy* (New York: Free Press, 1962), 289.

37. M. Weber, *Wirtschaft und Gesellschaft* (Tübingen: Mohr, 1922).

38. D. McKay, *American Politics and Society*, 2nd edn. (Oxford: Basil Blackwell, 1989), 161.

39. K. Von Beyme, 'I Gruppi dirigenti nella SPD', *Città e regione*, 3 (1983), 21–40.

40. A. Zuckerman, *The Politics of Faction: Christian Democratic Rule in Italy* (New Haven, Conn.: Yale University Press, 1979); G. Sartori (ed.), *Correnti, frazioni e fazione nei partiti italiani* (Bologna: Il Mulino, 1973); G. Pasquino, *Degenerazioni dei partiti e riforme istituzuionali* (Bari: Laterza, 1982).

41. K. Dyson, *Party, State and Bureaucracy in Western Germany* (London: Sage, 1977).

42. V. Ciuffa, 'Rispettato il "manuale Cencelli"', *Corriere della sera*, 5 Aug. 1983.

43. J. Blondel, 'Party Systems and Patterns of Government in Western Democracies', *Revue canadienne de science politique*, 1(2) (June 1986), 183–90.

44. G. Sartori, *Parties and Party Systems* (Cambridge: Cambridge University Press, 1976).

45. G. Galli, *Il Bipartismo imperfetto: Comunisti e Democristiani in Italia* (Bologna: Il Mulino, 1966).

46. P. Farneti, *The Italian Party System*, ed. S. E. Finer and A. Mastropaolo (London: Frances Pinter, 1985), 184.

47. Ibid. 185.

48. R. D. Putnam, R. Leonardi, and R. Y. Nanetti, 'Polarization and Depolarization in Italian Politics', *American Political Science Association Conference*, New York, Sept. 1981.

49. F. Pappi ('The West German System', *West European Politics*, 7(4) (Oct. 1984), 7–27) suggests that there have been two main phases to the West German system. The first, 1948–61, involved a diminution in the number of parties; the second, 1961–83, the stabilization of a three-party system.

50. E. Pappalardo, *Partiti e governi di coalizione in Europa* (Milan: Fageli, 1978).

51. The first Mauroy Government, between the presidential and parliamentary elections of 1981, was similarly 'monochrome'—though again, with some left Radicals. The Socialists' widely expected 'opening to the Centre' of 1988 was limited to the appointment of a few centrist ministers, who did not, however, mobilize their parties' support behind them.

52. W. Riker, *The Theory of Political Coalitions* (New Haven, Conn.: Yale University Press, 1962).

53. L. Dodd, *Coalitions in Parliamentary Government* (Princeton, NJ: Princeton University Press, 1976).

54. I. Budge and D. Farlie, *Explaining and Predicting Elections: Party Strategies and Issues. Outcomes in Twenty-Three Democracies* (London: Allen and Unwin, 1983).

55. K. Lawson and P. Merkl (eds.), *When Parties Fail* (Princeton: Princeton University Press, 1988).

CHAPTER 3

Interest Groups

The formation of groups is a phenomenon common to all societies, for the individual relation between the voter and power, as elaborated in theory by certain schools of political thought, does not in reality find full expression anywhere. The countless different groups in which individuals gather together and interact range from more or less extended families to tribes or ethnic groups and from informal groups to powerfully structured organizations.

All these groups are formed in the name of common interests of one kind or another: affective, family-based, ideological, corporative, professional, or convivial, etc. In the widest possible sense of the expression, all are in some way interest groups. But as used in political science, the expression has acquired a narrower and more precise meaning. It refers to those groups which, in a wide variety of forms, seek to promote their own particular interests *vis-à-vis* the political authorities. Conversely, the political authorities enter into relations with these groups, occasionally to ban them, sometimes to control them, frequently to associate them with their own actions. An interest group is thus distinguished from other groups by the fact that it interacts in some way or other with the State institutions and the parties engaged in the struggle to win and exercise power.

The modes of interaction vary, being more or less structured (the unemployed, pensioners, women, and consumers all constitute vast heterogeneous groups, which even today are often hardly organized at all); moreover, they are affected by the attitudes and ideology of those who hold political power. A group's access to those in power is facilitated or impeded depending upon its relative proximity to them: for example, it was easier for employers than for unions to obtain the ear of the Major Government. But a government's attitude is often ambivalent: as President, General de Gaulle professed a loathing for the world of finance ('the policies of France are not created in the inner enclosures of the Bourse'). Yet his Governments maintained close relations with economic groups, mainly in the context of planning. Finally, though groups mainly seek to exert pressure on particular territorial or functional segments of the State, their influence does not stop there: a consumer group may boycott a particular product or brand; pensioners, as a group, influence political decisions through the sheer weight of their numbers, and so on. Groups do thus have the power to exert pressure on the State, to influence market economies, and to use the market to exert pressure on the State. (Consider the pressure exerted, with some success, upon investors by anti-apartheid groups in the United States during the 1970s and 1980s, in an effort to influence the policies of the major banks and the American Government.)

From this point of view it is possible to establish a kind of spectrum within the category of interest groups, in which they can be classified according to the intensity of their modalities of action and organization. But in any such attempt at classification we should exclude on the one hand groups that—as such—have no relations at all with politics and, on the other, those whose declared purpose is to win political power, in other words the political parties; for both categories are different in kind from interest groups that are set up to influence those in power. As we make those exclusions, however, we should not underestimate how tenuous the dividing lines sometimes turn out to be: any group, however unconcerned to influence the politico-administrative power, may from time to time or in particular circumstances be prompted to take action to obtain advantages or to oppose decisions contrary to its particular interests; even the most anodyne of friendly societies can become an interest group if it mobilizes its forces under the influence of a leader and/or in reaction to some event that affects it. And equally, an interest group may try to organize itself in such a way as not simply to influence those in power but to try to win power for itself and exercise it. Such a group tries to turn itself into a party by stepping squarely into the politico-electoral arena: one example is provided by the Refugee Party in West Germany in the 1950s. But it is a difficult change to make, as is shown by the failure of the Poujade movement in France and the abortive attempts of Italian employers to set up a political group to represent their interests directly. The principal exceptions to this rule are constituted by the British Labour Party, formed, in the first instance, to give political expression to the interests of the British working class and its trade unions; and, less conclusively, by the various ecology movements which have transformed themselves into Green parties across Europe since the 1970s.

As is shown by these examples of unorganized groups turning to activism and interest groups turning into parties, in the context of political science the definition of an interest group rests upon both *organizational factors* and *modalities of action* designed to influence (but not to win) political power. The action that interest groups aiming to influence the political authorities take is likely to be criticized by some and applauded by others, but it is central to the definition of democracy whatever its form: pluralist, oligarchic, or neo-corporatist.

Organizational factors

In the name of their attachment to pluralism, liberal democracies today recognize both the existence and the legitimacy of these groups in society. However, that has not always been the case. France, by reason of its hostility to *ancien-régime* corporations and in the name of a popular sovereignty that tolerated nothing that stood between the State and the individual, was the country which most virulently declared its aversion to such groups with so-called common interests. It was only by virtue of the irresistible pressure of circumstances (in particular, the organization of trade unions to defend the working class) and a struggle on the part of those who favoured intermediary bodies (often recruited in circles hostile to the Revolution) that the existence of groups became first tolerated, then accepted and recognized. In this respect, France was relatively late in coming to accept all the implications of political liberalism, in particular the pluralism of interests, for it did not do so until the end of the nineteenth century. But even when the other Western democracies accepted the legitimacy of groups in principle, they still excluded organizations considered suspect or a hazard to social order: everywhere trade unions had to fight for a legal and official existence and, in this respect, Britain, the United States, and France differed hardly at all from the more authoritarian regimes of Germany and Italy at the end of the nineteenth century. But the distrust of groups that States manifest does not always take its most radical form, namely, banning. It may be expressed in a wide variety of rules and restrictions to limit the groups' field of action or to control their activities, or even, more subtly, in the sort of absence of legal recognition that long deprived British trade unions of any sanction against those of their officers who chose to pocket for their own use the hard-earned dues of trusting comrades. As a result, the organization of interest groups is subject to twofold constraints: first, those inherent in any form of action, which make it necessary to adapt the organization of the group to the achievement of its objectives; secondly, those imposed by the political authorities, which sometimes force groups to adopt institutional forms and predefined structures.

Constraints on action

Almond and Powell, in their *Comparative Politics*,[1] suggested distinguishing four types of interest group, according to their modes of organization: those without rules, those that do not take the form of associations, those that are institutional, and those that are associations. Only the last two categories are sufficiently highly organized to be considered as interest groups that aim to exert some influence on political authorities. Institutional groups such as public administrations, the Churches, and the Armed Forces possess structures not originally designed for the purpose of promoting their own particular interests but, when necessary, they can make use of their strong organization to bring influence to bear upon political and administrative decisions. Groups that take the form of associations, on the other hand, are specifically constituted to organize the interests or causes that they represent (trade unions, professional groups, associations, etc.).

The primary function of bureaucracies is not the promotion and defence of their own particular interests. All the same, quite apart from or even to the detriment of their primary functions, these organizations can become powerful interest groups capable of influencing or determining policies to the advantage of their own sectional or personal interests. If that happens, a kind of symbiosis develops between the interest groups and certain segments of the State apparatus which, together, use their privileged means of access to the public authorities for their own ends. In these circumstances, the administrative service concerned, instead of working for all and sundry, gradually becomes primarily preoccupied by its own interests and those of its members, blocking or completely undermining any government reforms that affect it. The Ministry of Education in France has often been cited as the prototype of the kind of bureaucracy that is concerned more with the interests of the teachers of whom it is composed than with the educational policies that are its *raison d'être*. More generally, the *Grands Corps de l'État* in France, the Civil Service in Britain, the *Dirigenza* in Italy, and the senior civil servants of Germany often manage to impose their own views on matters that affect their personal or sectional interests. In many cases, the institutions that they direct have their own internal associations or friendly societies and these constitute the official organs for the expression of their own particular interests, but we should not be misled by this. The group's real influence stems from its internal control of the bureaucracy, and from the networks and the knowledge that go with it. Another example is that of the US military during the Cold War, which regularly overestimated the Soviet threat in order to be quite sure of commanding what they considered to be adequate levels of manpower and weaponry.

But institutional interest groups are not formed solely to defend the personal interests of their members or to block reforms that would affect them adversely. They are also there to influence the decisions of other institutions and other segments of the bureaucracy: it is, for example, worth noting that in all Western countries, locally or regionally elected representatives have organized themselves into powerful federations or associations on the basis of a 'united front' in which all distinctions of size, political affiliation, and ideology are wiped out.

The Association of the Mayors of France provides a good illustration of this kind of local institutional group, set up to exert pressure on the central government. It is striking that the Association's Gaullist president, Jean-Pierre Delevoye, did not hesitate to deliver sharp public criticisms of the treatment of municipal authorities by the Balladur and Juppé governments between 1993 and 1997, even though they were headed by members of his own party. Associations of a similar type are to be found in Britain (although they are less influential than in France): the Association of Metropolitan Authorities, for example, (before 1986) and the County Councils' Association. In Germany these are powerful associations by very reason of the development of co-operative federalism (for example, the Association of German Towns, the Deutsche Städtetag, is extremely influential). In Italy, the Association of Regions, although formed recently, has acquired considerable political influence, together with a permanent representative body in Rome whose task is to do the rounds of the ministerial offices, the corridors of Montecitorio (the Chamber of Deputies), and the Palazzo Madama (the Senate).

Equally, alliances are sometimes set up between institutional interest groups and others that take the form of associations, when their respective interests converge. These may constitute veritable 'policy communities' in which administrations and specific groups find themselves in a position of mutual dependence as they attempt to influence policy-making. An example is provided by the relations between farmers' associations and Ministries of Agriculture.

This confusion may come about all the more easily when, as in France, the bureaucracy tends to present itself as embodying the public's general interest. Its decisions acquire a high juridical and political status the effect of which is to obscure the private interests that are involved at a second level. The shift that then takes place away from the general interest that the administration is supposed, in principle, to represent to the selfish interests of the civil servants involved comes about all the more easily given that the definition of the general interest does not emerge from public debate but is itself proclaimed unilaterally by the administration.

Organization is crucially important if interests are to be co-ordinated, expressed, and defended. Interests that are diffuse and unorganized are usually ill-protected. Such was for a long time the plight of consumers and equally of the unemployed, for until the unemployment crisis prompted greater awareness, with the result that various measures were taken on their behalf, the unemployed, for whom no trade union really assumed responsibility, were without protection. The need to organize is both social and juridical: only with at least a modicum of organization will an interest group acquire cohesion and make its voice heard. It is that requirement that, in France, for instance, explains the success of the 1901 Law on Associations.[2]

A major reason for the proliferation of groups must be the expansion of State interventionism, whether in the form of rules and regulations or of financial interference. These days, few sectors remain unaffected by State action and this encourages the crystallization of interests hitherto diffuse and unorganized. The area in which the creation of such groups has been the most spectacular is that of the environment, where nowadays any development plan, however local, gives rise to defence movements.

Sometimes these groups have proved to be extremely powerful, not so much as groups capable of determining what is ultimately decided, but rather as 'veto groups' strong enough to block and prevent public action (e.g. halting the construction of nuclear plants in Italy, West Germany, and the United States).

A second reason for the proliferation of *ad hoc* groups is that the central, federal organizations find it difficult or even impossible to preserve their monopoly of the representation of interests. In France, for example, the CNPF has often been reproached by small and medium-sized firms for ignoring *their* specific problems in its negotiations with the State. Gérard Nicoud's CID-UNATI was set up as a reaction against the Chambers of Commerce, which were accused of neglecting the needs of small businessmen. In Italy, the famous Bresciani steel producers dissociated themselves from the dominant steel-industry group controlled by the IRI, reckoning that they were being sacrificed in Brussels on the altar of the State-owned steel industry. As Suzanne Berger points out:

The first of the conclusions that emerge from the apparent political opportunism and organizational volatility of the interest groups representing the traditional middle classes is that the economic and social demands of these strata can be expressed in a variety of different types of organizations. Because the range of organizational variation extends from groups that push their claims in violent and illegal opposition to the state to groups that collaborate in essentially corporatist arrangements, the issue of which organizational groups predominate at any time is a highly consequential one for other actors in the system and for the prospects of stability or transformation.[3]

A number of mammoth groups stand out from the heterogeneous collection of associations: the confederations of employers, the trade unions, and the agricultural organizations. In all the Western countries, these groups have special access to the public authorities, if only by reason of their size and powerful organization.

Employers' organizations

Even without group organization, business exerts a powerful influence on government simply by carrying on its day-to-day activity; it will invest and create jobs in a favourable environment, and disinvest and create unemployment—or cease trading altogether—in an unfavourable one. The globalization of the economy and the ability of multinational corporations to shift production between plants in different countries has enhanced this form of 'automatic' pressure, which governments ignore at their peril. But in addition, business interests in every country are represented by at least one if not several national organizations. In Germany, the Confederation of Employers' Associations, known as the BDA, the diversity of whose members prevents it from concluding pay agreements and imposing its own directives, sometimes comes into conflict with the powerful Confederation of German Industry, the BDI, which is comprised solely of industrialists. In 1977, these two organizations, without merging, sought to co-ordinate their respective policies by appointing a common Chairman, Hans-Martin Schleyer (kidnapped and assassinated in the autumn of 1977 by the Red

Army Faction). Finally, the strong Federation of Chambers of Commerce (DIHT) lends its support to both these groups, which are divided more along professional lines than by any fundamental divergences. In Italy (although for different reasons), a similar division along professional lines separates the Chambers of Commerce, Confindustria, which represents private employers, and Intersind, which co-ordinates the public sector.

In Britain, the Confederation of British Industry (CBI) resulted in 1965 from a merger between the Federation of British Industry and other smaller organizations,[4] with the notable backing of George Brown, then Minister for Economic Affairs and keen to introduce overall planning. In France too, the CNPF[5] and the Chambers of Commerce (which in France are compulsory organizations for all employers, with tax-raising powers) are very influential, although in the 1970s their authority met stiff challenges from many small and medium enterprises and from the Nicoud movement. Nevertheless, it is important to note that following the nationalizations of 1982, firms in the public sector continued to belong to the CNPF, possibly in the secret hope of counterbalancing the groups within that organization that were deeply hostile to socialist policies.

No government can afford to ignore groups that are not only powerful but also indispensable to the elaboration and implementation of its economic, fiscal, and social policies, etc. But the traditions and nature of the relations between public authorities and major employers' groups vary from one system to another. In France, the interventionist tradition and overall planning policies turned the employers' spokesmen into special partners in State policy-making. In Germany, similarly, the influence of the employers' federations is strong, and they are frequently quite naturally consulted by the State, for Germany has a long tradition of co-operation between the political authorities and the economic powers in the country. As in France, the expression 'social partner' (*Sozial Partner*), which conveys an image of solidarity (virtually unknown in the value systems of English or American businesses), and the institution, since 1951, of co-management (*Mitbestimmung*) in the coal and steel sectors testify to the 'corporatist' style of the relations that exist between representatives of the economic sector on the one hand and the public authorities on the other. Traditions such as these account for the preference that some States show for negotiation with a limited number of responsible partners. In Mrs Thatcher's Britain, on the other hand, a government that prided itself on its 'pro-business' stance was nevertheless capable of keeping the CBI at arm's length, to the point where one CBI Director-General promised (somewhat unconvincingly, it is true) a 'bare-knuckle fight' against the tight-money policies that were suffocating many of his members' firms. Paradoxically, the credibility of the CBI suffered under Conservative government, and many smaller employers' organizations lost members or disappeared altogether.

Even employers' organizations that enjoy the status of State partners often have to face competition from businesses or groups big enough to operate outside centrally co-ordinated associations. This is or frequently has been the case with the most powerful of industrial federations (such as the Chambre Syndicale de l'Automobile in France, and, in the past, the Chambre Syndicale de la Sidérurgie) or companies such as ICI in

Great Britain. In Italy, relations between Confindustria and the giant Fiat company have not always been good on account of the strong Christian Democrat influence among the employers, and it was only in the early 1970s that they began to improve, when Agnelli was elected Chairman of the Confederation. But whatever the relations between Fiat and Confindustria, there remains the basic fact of the influence and impact of a single firm that holds virtually a national monopoly in its own sector. Similarly, German banks (which are privately owned) and Italian ones (which were, until recently, nationalized) and, even more, the banking and financial circles of the City of London constitute veritable States within States.

The employers usually seek to present a united front to the outside world, particularly in their dealings with the public authorities. However, they are themselves heterogeneous and divided. Clashes often occur between small and big businesses, between the sectors that are protected and those that are competitive, between the industry and the service sectors, between liberals and corporatists, and between socially minded employers and authoritarian ones. The strength of the larger organizations stems in part from the fact that their own interests *as organizations* frequently coincide with those of the public authorities, who are often happy negotiating with a limited number of partners, all in a position to guarantee that agreements will be respected and that the anticipated co-operation will be forthcoming. A further and growing possibility of friction among the ranks of employers is represented by the rise of the multinational firm, which may be disinclined to join national employers' federations, preferring either to talk to government directly or else to concentrate an increasing proportion of its efforts in the European Union rather than in individual nation states.

Trade unions

Apart from the employers' organizations, the trade unions constitute the other most powerful collection of interest groups. But the trade unions differ from the employers in that they are far more divided, if only because their organization often depends upon an ideological or political programme: they may be split between reformist, social democratic, and revolutionary tendencies; they are often to varying degrees linked with particular political parties; and they may be out to promote either purely professional objectives or, alternatively, vast social projects. Furthermore, as interest groups, the trade unions are obliged to fight on two fronts at once: the world of business and employers, and the public authorities responsible for social regulations and frequently also for wage policies and the arbitration of disputes.

The 1980s and 1990s faced the unions with large new challenges. The dismantling of the rustbelt industries which had been their traditional heartlands everywhere, and the appearance of long-term mass unemployment; the tilting of the global balance of industrial power away from labour, as capital became more mobile and markets freer, allowing business to deploy globally but leaving unions to try and defend their members nationally; and the pressure on governments to contain public spending, whether in order to control inflation, to limit taxes, or to prepare their countries for EMU, all left the unions struggling to keep in touch with their rank and file while at the same time find new ways to promote their interests.

A preliminary evaluation of trade-union power within individual countries may be made on the basis of the unions' fragmentation. It is in France that the unions appear to be the most divided, because they are both numerous and quarrelsome. The Confédération Générale du Travail (CGT, close to the Communist Party), the Confédération Française Démocratique du Travail (CFDT, more or less close to the Socialists), Force Ouvrière (FO, notionally apolitical, formerly close to right-wing parties but now truculently independent), the Fédération de l'Éducation Nationale (the FEN, itself now split into two tendencies, one closer to the CGT and the other to the CFDT), and Confédération Générale des Cadres (CGC) compete with one another and also with the many autonomous unions in each sector to attract members for whom there is no particular advantage in joining anyway (except in a few closed shops, such as publishing or the docks). Their division, and habitual mutual distrust, frequently leads union leaders either to try to outbid each other in their demands, or to seek a special recognition from government denied to their competitors. But their numerical weakness, with total membership below 10 per cent of the workforce, often limits unions' bargaining power (except in certain public services such as the post office or the railways, where they are stronger and can cause great disruption) and leaves leaders out of touch with rank-and-file workers. The recent history of the French trade union movement is littered with strike calls that have fallen flat—but also with 'days of action' that have released the pent-up frustrations of workers and triggered unexpected movements lasting weeks, such as the revolt against the Juppé social security reform in 1995.

Italy, too, has generally corresponded to what has been called the 'Mediterranean model' of fragmentation, except that there have been longer periods of co-operation, first in the 1970s, when it even took a loose institutional form in the Federazione Unitaria that grouped the main union confederations, and more recently since 1992. The Confederazione Generale Italiana del Lavoro (CGIL), which was close to the former Communist Party, includes a minority of Socialists and Christian Democrats (a reflection of the initial consensus established in June 1944 between the three main parties in the 'Rome Pact') and is the most powerful confederation. As in France, the Cold War led to a split in the union movement: in 1948, the Christian Democrats left the CGIL to form a 'free' CGIL, which two years later became the Confederazione Italiana dei Sindacati dei Lavoratori (CISL). In 1950, the trade unionists close to the Social Democratic Party (which had separated from the Italian Socialist Party (PSI) in 1947) also formed their own trade union, the Unione Italiana del Lavoro (UIL). These three unions, which frequently took common action between 1968 and 1985 (when, in the spring, divisions between them became apparent in the referendum on the indexing of wages) are unquestionably the most powerful trade union organizations and the ones that can count on the ear of the Italian public authorities. But they are frequently outnumbered—particularly in the public sector—by the collection of small, autonomous unions whose strength lies, not so much in the overall size of their membership, but rather in the virtual monopoly that they hold over a number of key professions or sectors (civil aviation pilots, train drivers, etc.). They were also plagued by their political divisions, not only between each other but within the CGIL, which even after the splits of 1948 and 1950 retained a big Socialist minority. This proved especially problematic in the 1980s, when conflict between the (governing) Socialists and the (opposition) Communists was acute. However, the fall of the Berlin Wall and the collapse of the party system have proved beneficial to trade union co-operation. The CGIL has chosen to distance itself somewhat from all parties (a move started by its Communist current, which dissolved itself in 1990), and the three main confederations were drawn together by their common opposition to the economic policies of the Berlusconi government, finding themselves, rather to their surprise, at the head of a social movement that brought a million and a half people out to demonstrate on the streets of Rome.

Germany presents a contrast with 'Mediterranean pluralism', as trade unions, while close in their general sympathies to the SPD, are nevertheless separate from parties and so not divided on political lines; competition between the three main organizations is largely confined to the sector of the public services and employees. The Deutsche An-gestelltengewerkschaft (DAG), whose creation in West Germany in 1945 was prompted by hostility towards the principle of unions formed on the basis of professions, is essentially composed of employees from both the public and the private sectors, but is somewhat in decline. The Deutscher Beamten Bund (DBB) is a federation of civil servants; this union includes rather more public employees than its rivals and enjoys a dominant position in the highest echelons of the Bund civil service. Finally, the Deutscher Gewerkschaftsbund (DGB) is a powerful confederation of seventeen unions, one-third of whose members belong to the metalworkers' union (IG Metall). However, despite its great power and the monopoly that it holds over the representation of many sectors of industry, even this confederation is not proof against many internal rifts between the various individual federations that compose it. As regards the public authorities, the DGB is an interlocutor that cannot be ignored. But its authority is limited by the strength of the seventeen individual unions, all of which energetically defend their own autonomy.

On the face of it, the British unions present an image of strength in that nearly all gather together under the banner of the Trades Union Congress. In reality, however, divisions abound. These result, in the first place, from the considerable disparity between the size of different unions. Another divisive factor is the disparity between the various unions' organizational structures: some are fragmented, allowing a large measure of autonomy to local sections, while others are very centralized, granting their general secretaries powers that are extremely wide—virtually dictatorial, some critics would claim. A third source of conflict lies in the unions' relations with the Labour Party: some belong to the Party *en bloc*, while others allow their members to make their own individual decisions. Then there are classical oppositions between unions of public employees and those from the private sector and, more recently, between blue-collar unions (in decline) and white-collar ones. These tensions sometimes run very high indeed and may be exploited either by the government (as in the miners' strike, which did not gain the support of the rest of industry) or by employers. The Thatcher Governments were adept at exploiting divisions within the labour movement and a general hostility, even among many union members, to what was seen as 'trade union militancy'. No fewer than six Employment Acts, in 1980, 1982, 1984, 1988, 1989, and 1990 limited the legal immunities of trade unions, effectively outlawed the closed shop, gave legal guarantees to non-strikers, and required secret ballots to elect union leaders and to call strikes. Tony Blair's Labour Government showed little inclination to reverse any of them when it came to power in 1997.

The strength of trade unions may also be gauged from the size of their memberships and, above all, from their membership density—the percentage of the total numbers of wage-earners that they represent. For a majority of the workforce to be unionized has always been unusual, and is now exceptional. In the European Union, this state of affairs applies only to the Scandinavian countries: membership density in 1995 was 79 per cent in Sweden, 80 per cent in Denmark, and 91 per cent in Finland. These figures are almost twice as high as those for the most highly unionized of the remaining EU countries, Italy (44 per cent, with signs of an upturn following the demonstrations of 1994) and Austria (41 per cent). The trade unions of France, on the other hand, are the weakest in Europe, with a combined membership of roughly 2.5 million (including 700,000 each for the CGT, CFDT, and FO) and a membership density of some 9 per cent (15 per cent in the public sector and a mere 6 per cent in private firms). Membership has fallen by over a third since 1981 (with the CGT losing half of its members), a development that has damaged already inadequate material resources. In Germany, membership density has remained much higher, at 29 per cent, but this total has fallen, and includes details which must give unionists cause for concern about the future. In the first place, unification, which had brought the DGB's membership up from 7.9 million in 1989 to 11.2 million in 1992, was followed by an enormous shake-out in the inefficient industries of the East, resulting in a drop in DGB membership to about 9 million by 1996. Secondly, white-collar workers, who now represent some 50 per cent of the workforce, are only 20 per cent unionized. Thirdly, workers aged under 25 are only 13 per cent unionized. In Britain, where membership density was just under a third in 1995, the ravages of the 1980s—in terms both of unemployment and of a loss of confidence within the labour movement—took a heavy toll of trade unions. Membership had reached a peak, both in absolute figures (13.3 million, of whom 12.1 million were in TUC-affiliated unions), and in membership density (54.5 per cent) in 1979, the year of Mrs Thatcher's election. By 1990, there were just 9.9 million members, of whom 8.1 million were TUC-affiliated, and by 1997 the TUC-affiliated membership had declined further to 6.8 million. A country's level of union membership will depend on its industrial relations traditions and culture, on the economic climate, and also, crucially, on the legal environment. In Britain, a 'closed shop' system made trade union membership compulsory for many jobs, but was effectively outlawed by the Thatcher Government of 1987–90. However, both in Britain and in Germany union dues are still, in many cases, deducted from wages at source and paid over directly to the union. Some unions can thus rely on resources which enable it to provide its members with services and strike pay far in excess of anything that their French or Italian counterparts can expect. Finally, in Britain,

Germany, and Italy—but not in France—the practice of collective bargaining within the various industries is far more common; and the effect of this is to strengthen the unions, which alone are empowered to negotiate with employers and so are in a position to obtain tangible benefits for their members. In contrast, negotiation procedures in France tend to minimize the role of the unions at plant level, promoting instead that of the individuals who make up the confederal leadership. It is the latter who negotiate at top level with their opposite numbers from management or from the government.

Trade unions throughout Western Europe ended the twentieth century in a battered state, but not without influence. The political divisions between Communists and Socialists had, at least, all but disappeared. Other divisions, though, remained: whether to campaign on wages, hours, or defence of jobs (a problem that the DGB found especially acute in the East, where its instinctive preference for industry-wide wage rates came up against their likely effect on jobs in the vulnerable Eastern firms); how far, if at all, to collaborate with governments in regulating industrial relations (as the Italian unions did in 1990, when a law governing them in the public sector was passed with the support of unions worried by rank-and-file militancy); and how to offer a range of benefits and incentives to keep members inside organizations which right-wing political parties were all too willing to present as outdated and irrelevant.

Agricultural organizations

These present a particularly interesting example of interest groups. In the first place, they display features that are reminiscent of both employers' associations and trade unions. Secondly, they continue to wield great influence, despite the unchecked demographic decline of agricultural areas as if, in politics, the land and its primary occupants, the farmers, were deemed to deserve special treatment.

At this point an observation of a general nature seems in order. The agricultural world is disappearing fast. If Britain is the exception in this respect, it is only because the proportion of farmers and farm labourers in the total population had already dropped below 10 per cent by 1900 (in 1992 it was barely more than 2 per cent). In France, the proportion fell from a third on the eve of the Second World War to a quarter in 1954 to barely 5 per cent in 1992; in Italy, from 17.2 per cent in 1971 to under 8 per cent in 1992; in the Western *Länder* of Germany, from 6 per cent to 3.5 per cent (or under a million people) between 1980 and 1992.

However, this demographic decline has certainly not been reflected in a parallel loss of influence. On the contrary. In Italy in particular, the small landowners (the *coldiretti*) were defended assiduously by the Christian Democrats, for whom they constituted a privileged group of clients. In France, too, relations between the farmers and the Gaullist Governments were always marked by intense collaboration, notwithstanding outbreaks of violence from time to time: the notoriously unpopular 'drought tax' of 1976 was regarded by public opinion as typifying the preferential treatment given to the farmers. Similar analyses can be applied to West Germany, where successive Agriculture Ministers (such as Josef Ertl, who held the job from 1969 to 1982) tended to behave as the farmers' delegates in national government (and in Europe) rather than as ministers responsible in the first instance to a wider population. Other politicians might find this degree of influence exasperating or distasteful: Alan Clark, for example, observed that 'nothing, no one, not even "Claimants' Unions", can be as bad as farmers'.[6] But they still accepted it. The extreme sensitivity of the Major Government to the plight of the beef industry at the time of the 1996 BSE crisis, contrasting with its relative indifference to the concerns of consumers or the families of victims, is one indication of this.

There are many reasons for the disproportionate degree of influence that farmers wield over politicians. The following points are worth noting: (1) many constituencies are predominantly rural and here the farmers constitute the most homogeneous and influential group because of the economic impact of their activities; (2) in the collective national consciousness, the issue of the countryside and nature tends to be a highly emotive one; (3) farmers hold an important position at a local political level as a consequence of the continuing division into separate communes of France and Italy, for example, and until the 1960s of West Germany also; (4) the Common Agricultural Policy, Europe's first common policy to be fully operational, removed an element of control, and of accountability, from national governments, concealing part of the vast costs of farm subsidies in the European budget, to which few politicians before Mrs Thatcher paid much public attention.

But the crucial factor seems to be the particular structure of this social group and the way in which it is organized. In general, farmers band together under umbrella organizations that include agricultural producers of every kind: small-scale and large-scale, tenant farmers and landowners—organizations that look essentially to the State for support. Whereas industrial employers and trade unions must defend their interests in the face of their partners-cum-adversaries as well as the State, farmers, whatever their legal status, seldom need to fight on two fronts at once. Furthermore, because of the specific nature of their activities which, until quite recently, were not subject to the mechanisms of the market economy (or were only partially so), farmers, more than other social groups, have tended to be taken under the State's wing. Agricultural interests are frequently represented by a single, powerful organization, and the usual procedures adopted in their defence include negotiation, consultation, and institutional integration. This is certainly the case in Britain, where the National Farmers' Union (the NFU) represents 90 per cent of all British farmers,[7] in France, where the FNSEA, despite challenges from both the Left and the Right, can still claim with at least residual credibility to represent the whole of the agricultural sector, and in Germany, where the Deutscher Bauernverband (DBV) represents virtually all the country's farmers. Here, furthermore, as in France and Italy, Chambers of Agriculture constitute a further essential source of support as well as an institutionalized instrument of communication between the economic and the political spheres.

The power of the agricultural organizations is such that, as Grosser notes, 'Liberalism is discounted in all countries that lay claim to a market economy'.[8] But that power seems to have peaked in the late 1970s. Since then, the economic crisis and the demographic decline of the agricultural sector have combined to check the effectiveness of agricultural interest groups. It is significant in this respect that, since 1980, government measures at both European and national levels have been designed to stem the flood of excess produce and the aid that gave rise to it, by reforming the mechanisms for supporting the market.

The influence of public authorities

Interest groups must be organized if they wish to make themselves heard. But the public authorities that are their primary target are themselves by no means passive. Sometimes they ban groups (as did the Le Chapelier law of 1791 in France) but more often they seek to contain or control them by regulations, or even to limit the pressure that they bring to bear by integrating and institutionalizing them. Most solutions involving control through regulations are essentially liberal, while those involving integration are of a more corporatist inspiration.

Even in systems that are the most favourable to group action and that are prepared to accept groups as a constitutive element of liberal democracy, it sometimes proves necessary to intervene to limit jungle law and shady deals.

One example of this kind of control was provided in West Germany, where the law of 21 September 1972 established the procedure for groups seeking to enter into relations with Parliament and the government. All such groups must register with the President of the Bundestag, indicating their social purpose and their structure and stating the names of their leaders and representatives. Through this formality (which nearly 1,000 organizations observe), the group representatives gain admittance to the Bundestag, where they can make the necessary contacts and exchange information and, in some cases, may be invited to take part in hearings organized by parliamentary commissions. As can be seen, the obligation to register is hardly a stiff requirement, and it has had very little effect except in so far as group organizations have become more public. The German registration system was inspired by American legislation, but it is less complex and detailed, though it is true that in Germany lobbies are not as omnipresent as they are in Congress.

Public authorities sometimes adopt a more interventionist attitude towards interest groups, seeking to integrate them, either by formally associating them in the decision-making process, or by turning the groups into quasi-public institutions.

At all events, they tend everywhere to consult interest groups, for it is no longer possible to administrate and impose regulations unilaterally. The continental European countries have frequently sought to set up a system of official consultation with the government's major 'social partners'. No doubt such attempts may be seen as stemming from the streak of corporatism and anti-liberalism by which the systems of Germany, Italy, and France are all to varying degrees affected. But they could also be interpreted as a quest for social and political consensus.

In Italy, consultation often takes place through public bodies which incorporate a selection of private interests. As Marco Cammelli writes: 'There is quite a marked tendency to integrate these interests into the politico-administrative circuit rather than have them apply autonomous and specific pressure from outside.'[9] In West Germany, consultation with social partners from the economic sector was given official status by the 1967 Economic Stabilization Law, under the label of 'concerted action', (*Konzierte Aktion*)—a move that was facilitated by the grand coalition between the CDU–CSU and the SPD at that time. However, its achievements were limited and, during the 1970s, interest in formal consultation of this kind waned. It was revived in the economic crisis of the mid-1990s, when, in the face of a burgeoning budget deficit, faltering growth, and growing worries about German competitiveness, the 'Alliance for Jobs' won union and employer support for a package including a wage pause and welfare cuts in return for promises on employment; but the deal had broken up in some acrimony by 1997, with unions accusing Chancellor Kohl of reneging on his side of the bargain. The lack of success of such consultations was particularly striking in Britain where the Conservative Chancellor of the Exchequer, Selwyn Lloyd, set up the National Economic Development Council, composed of six trade unionists and six representatives from the employers' confederation, in 1962. In the event, the institutionalization of consultation (inspired by the French model of overall indicative planning at this time, credited with responsibility for the economic boom) failed to supplant the system of 'government by committee' through which the public authorities took concerted action with their partners.[10] And the NEDC was abolished by Mrs Thatcher, who was wholly out of sympathy with its 'corporatist' implications.

Despite the somewhat disappointing results produced by integrating groups into consultative organs on more or less equal terms, France has remained faithful to 'administrative polysynody' and continues to set up countless committees and commissions of all kinds both within the State apparatus (personnel commissions) and in its dealings with groups. There is no systematic record of them all, but they are generally reckoned to run into many thousands. As Miriam Golden notes in connection with Italy, where these practices are also common,

the innumerable committees of experts established to back up central and local administrations are part of a proliferation of representative bodies, all with a common purpose: namely to increase the number of institutionalized interpreters of social interests; and also to profit from their implicit political legitimacy which provides them with new ways to express themselves.[11]

The French administration tends to be selective about its partners, bestowing the label of 'representativity' and according 'official recognition' (and, often, financial aid) to those with whom it feels most comfortable and excluding others with which it is out of tune, or which have proved obstructive, violent, or politically unsympathetic in the recent past.[12] Such was the case, for example, when the committees for economic expansion were set up in the 1950s or when associations for the protection of the environment were recognized by the environment law of 1976. For many years prior to 1981 the government tended to limit its relations with trade unions to FO. Such a strategy may be beneficial to both parties, but it is not without its risks. In May 1968, for example, as a near-general strike took hold of France, the Pompidou Government found itself obliged to talk to the CGT, but lacked any established channels through which to open the dialogue. It is also the case that powerful groups may impose themselves as the government's partners, even to the extent of forcing it to shut out their rivals. A notable example here is the farmers. Until 1981, the FNSEA had succeeded in monopolizing the agricultural world's contacts with the government, not just in regular meetings with officials and with the minister, but in the control at local level of aspects of farm policy and of social insurance for farmers and farm workers. The attempts of the left-wing government elected in 1981 to bring minority agricultural unions (MODEF, FFA, and CNSTP) into the consultation process were vigorously resisted by the FNSEA, which brought out its members in fierce, at times violent, demonstrations, of a type more often tolerated when organized by farmers than when they involve, for example, trade unionists. By 1983, these tactics had worked: the minister's door was closed to the minority unions, despite their having won a third of the vote in that year's elections to the Chambers of Agriculture, and the FNSEA was back as the farmers' 'sole' representative.

Institutional integration takes many different forms and is produced by a whole spectrum of juridical and organizational instruments ranging from groups that are only minimally integrated to others that assume the form of public organizations.

The first level of institutionalization is to arrange for the representatives of particular interests to operate as such within political bodies. It is a form of institutionalization that is not highly regarded in the liberal models of Britain and the United States. In continental Europe, on the other hand, it constitutes an unfortunate reminder of the corporatism of Fascist regimes, even though its roots are older than that. All the same, a few systems modelled on this way of organizing interests still operate in Italy, Germany, and especially France. In Germany, it is worth noting the handful of 'Chambers of Workers' in the *Länder* of Saarland and in Bremen, but these are exceptional examples and the system is unlikely to be extended to the rest of the country. The post-war constitutions of Italy and France set up Economic Councils (in France, the Conseil Économique et Social, in Italy, the Consiglio Nazionale dell'Economica e del Lavoro). Their function is to advise the government on economic and social matters, but in both countries the influence of these assemblies has remained marginal. France carried the experiment a little further, setting up the Comités de Développement Économique Régional (CODER) in 1964 and the Comités Économiques et Sociaux Régionaux, which took over from them in 1972. But de Gaulle's 1969 proposal to introduce changes in the Senate and to set up regional councils, in the form of assemblies where politicians could come into contact with the representatives of various interests, met with strong resistance and was rejected at the referendum of 27 April 1969.

The next level of institutionalization is reached when a private organization is granted public prerogatives or is made responsible for the management of public bodies. This often happens in France, where many associations are entrusted with public duties together with the prerogatives that go with them (the power to raise taxes and impose special regulations). But it also happened in Italy where, until the health reforms of the 1970s were introduced, the agricultural union, Coldiretti, a body that came under the law pertaining to the private sector, was empowered to manage the bodies that dealt with the social security of agricultural workers. Finally, in countries with civil law, certain groups are integrated by being brought under public-sector regulations. Here, Chambers of Commerce represent the best example. In Britain and the United States, the function of these is simply to co-ordinate and express the interests of their members. But the Chambers of Commerce of Italy, Germany, and France all have the status of public institutions. French Chambers of Commerce, for example, are Napoleonic creations with the power to raise taxes from their (compulsorily enrolled) members and to undertake a wide range of activities, including vocational training and major infrastructure projects. Another example of the curious osmosis that takes place between the private and the public sectors is provided by professional groups such as doctors and lawyers in France, or by the German body responsible for ensuring that the regulations are observed in the recruitment of labour and with respect to working conditions, Ordnung des Berufsstandes. The situation is similar in Italy, where, amid the veritable jungle of some 41,000 *enti pubblici*, the function of about 2,000 of them is to supervise the ordering and management of various sectors of economic and social life.

While the regulating and controlling function of some of these bodies is similar to that of the independent agencies and commissions of the United States, the structures of the two types of organization differ substantially. The orders or *enti* invested with the prerogatives that pertain to public services provide public organization for private interests; whereas in the case of the American agencies, the boards of directors are appointed by the public authorities according to the criteria of expertise, independence[13] (tenure of office is, as a rule, not renewable), and pluralism (the board members are, in principle, drawn from diverse walks of life).

Interest groups and the political system

One reason why it is particularly difficult to apprehend the phenomenon of interest groups is that they are organized in so many different ways. Another is that they operate in so many different sectors—wherever power is held by the State—and that they do so in so many different forms. Let us try to sort out this confused picture by examining how interest groups operate in relation to two main parameters: the structure of the State and the politico-administrative characteristics of the system, both of which help to shape and direct the interest groups' modes of action. In conclusion, we shall examine the ways in which interest groups affect the functioning and nature of the political system.

Where interest groups apply pressure

In Western democracies, power is divided both functionally and territorially. The division of responsibilities between the executive and the legislative, and between central and local authorities, is dictated by a country's constitutional patterns and historical heritage and by the relative power of various institutions at any given moment. Since the purpose of interest groups is to influence the public authorities and to prevent decisions that would be unfavourable to them, it is hardly surprising that they adopt modes of action that are closely related to the structure of public power, adapting these when shifts of power take place either within the central State apparatus or in the institutional balance between the centre and the periphery or, most recently, between national governments and Europe. To put it another way, interest groups try to 'shoot where the ducks are' (and may also, on occasion, mistake their targets and blast away to little useful purpose).

The legislature

For a long time parliaments provided the best places for interest groups to operate, because of their prestige and symbolic value. The decision to treat parliament as the major target was natural enough: it was where power both seemed to, and often did, lie; besides, members of parliament were the most accessible elements in the system. Take, for example, the Third and Fourth French Republics. Alongside the political parties and parliamentary groups, many *ad hoc* groups were created to defend some specific interest or other. Despite the fact that, under the Fourth Republic, the rules of the National Assembly forbade 'the constitution, in the Assembly, of groups purporting to defend particular local or professional interests', such groups continued to operate in the guise of friendly societies or committees of inquiry: the interests of home distillers, private schools, forestry workers, and farmers were among those most vigorously championed in the French Parliament.

Although the British Parliament no longer has the power it once had, interest groups still subject it to intense lobbying. One of the many factors contributing to the Conservatives' defeat in 1997 was the extent and manner of this practice, and notably the clear evidence that Conservative MPs were being paid retainers by firms, groups, or most frequently professional lobbyists, to further their or their clients' interests, whether by speaking in their favour or asking questions in the Commons, or by arranging meetings with ministers. There is little evidence of legislation being fundamentally affected as a result; it is, after all, rare for laws voted in Parliament to be substantially different from the bills that the executive has prepared in advance to present there. But the revelations of 'sleaze' served as a reminder that the House of Commons, and its members, were still seen to matter by some groups at least. In the Italian Parliament groups exert pressure mainly upon the committees which, under certain conditions, are empowered to pass laws (known as *leggine*, or 'little laws'). The specialized nature of these committees and their members and their relatively unpublicized activities make for an ideal structure for the promotion of specific interests, even if recent research has shown that not all so-called *leggine* live up to their reputation as essentially minor laws tailored to the needs of specific firms or groups.

The pressure exerted by groups within parliaments is thus conditioned by the degree of autonomy that the parliaments concerned have retained in relation to the executive, the strategies that the groups adopt (discreet action or maximum publicity), and the greater or lesser degree of public access to the committees in which most negotiations take place. Finally, the influence wielded by pressure groups is also determined by the socio-professional origins of members of parliament. Without taking a sociologically deterministic view, it must be said that a parliament's composition is bound to affect the degree of ease with which particular groups gain a hearing. In the parliaments of the French Third and Fourth Republics, the liberal professions were over-represented; now it is the turn of state employees, in particular teachers from the public sector. When certain British trade unions chose to sponsor Labour MPs, it was in the hope that they would further their interests, or at least those of the labour movement as a whole; initially at least, they preferred to select men drawn from their own ranks to do this.

The executive

The primary targets of interest groups everywhere are the executive and its administration, as these have become the essential organs of decision at every level, from preparing the ground for a policy through to implementing and monitoring it. In France under the Fifth Republic, the central focus of pressure groups has shifted from the legislature to the executive and the administration. Civil servants have an ambivalent attitude: they hold considerable reservations where 'pressure groups' are concerned, considering them to be illegitimate, but are better disposed towards the recognized institutional spokesmen, who are indispensable when it comes to gathering information and ensuring that policies are correctly implemented.[14] Contacts between the administration and these recognized groups are constant, sustained, and frequently intimate, the more so as such dialogue is encouraged by the common education, recruitment, and careers of the élites involved. The attitudes that élites, both public and private, share, because of the training that they have all received in prestigious establishments of higher education and in the grandes écoles, are reinforced by the 'old-boy network' that operates within those same sectors. A public administrator becomes a private one and finds it easy to enter into dialogue with his colleagues, who have risen along with him in their careers. It would no doubt be mistaken to leap to conclusions of corruption, connivance, and collusion, but the visible facts in France emphasize the high degree of interpenetration between the political, administrative, and economic élites. This transformation of the role played by the administration in relation to the sectors under its control is not solely attributable to causes external to it, such as the intensity and efficacy of the action of interest groups. To a large extent it also results from the desire of each administrative section to defend its own preserve against other sections that threaten its power and influence. By protecting the groups that depend upon it, each section of the administration is to some extent protecting its own patrimony against encroachments from adjacent sections. Clearly, the relations between the administration and interest groups are far from one-sided. The groups certainly exert pressure but they are also treated as 'instruments' by the administrative sections involved, which use them to defend their own policies and interests. It is, after all, not uncommon to see a French or German

Minister of Agriculture jubilating over farmers' demonstrations which, they say, are bound to strengthen their own position in negotiations with Brussels. Furthermore, it would be mistaken to regard the relations that obtain between administrations and interest groups as relations between two homogeneous worlds. In reality, administrations are every bit as fragmented, competitive, and divided as interest groups themselves are.

Europe

An increasing amount of group activity has shifted, or has been extended, to the institutions of the European Union: chiefly the Commission, but also the European Parliament, and even the Court of Justice. This will be discussed in more detail below (p. 433).

Politico-administrative cultures and modes of action

The concept of a politico-administrative culture relates to the body of rules and values that particular societies produce—rules and values that do not necessarily tally perfectly with those to which the system overtly subscribes. A good illustration is provided in France by the contrast between general, impersonal regulations and individual practice—all the 'arrangements' that make it possible for the system to function and that are consequently accommodated and accepted not only by society but also by the administration. The modes of action that interest groups adopt are determined by a number of specific factors: the nature of the group, its strategies, the means at its disposal, and the openings that the system affords it; and either they fit into the framework of the national politico-administrative culture or they are at odds with it. In other words, a group's modes of action are essentially determined by the means available to it and the extent to which the influence exerted by interest groups is tolerated by the political system and by society in general.

There are many possible modes of action for interest groups, but they are unevenly distributed, and vary according to the country concerned (its administrative culture) and time (the general sympathy of the government in power). The exchange at the basis of interest-group dealings with government is a fairly simple one. Groups want access to government; the opportunity to present a case for policies favourable to themselves, whether they involve regulation, or funding, or a particular position in an international (or European) negotiation; and ultimately the chance to determine, or at least to influence, those policies. The government ministers, or officials, or parliamentarians, who talk to groups, want something in return. What groups can offer in return may be classified under three headings: the avoidance of trouble; knowledge and technical expertise; and, in some cases, money.

The avoidance of trouble

The avoidance of trouble is the most diverse of the incentives for dialogue that groups have to offer. Firms and their associations are perhaps the most strategically placed in this respect. Even if they have no other case to put forward, they can argue that the prosperity upon which the government's electoral prospects to a great extent depend requires a favourable business environment. Governments can be more or less sensitive to such appeals, but few can ignore them altogether; in a global marketplace, the sanction can be more or less massive disinvestment. Trade unions are in a more delicate position, but also have something to offer a government prepared to talk to them: the chance of social and industrial peace. What such peace means in practice has changed over time, as the bargaining power of trade unions has declined. In the 1970s, when it was still great, industrial peace meant the avoidance of economically ruinous and politically damaging strikes. More recently, with the decline of industrial disputes and of union bargaining power, it has meant a willingness to negotiate measures to render the labour market and wages more flexible, or the welfare state less costly, or both, in an effort to improve the conditions for job creation on which every government's future depends to a greater or lesser extent.

Governments are, of course, free to judge whether the 'avoidance of trouble' that a group can deliver is worth the trouble of talking to it. Those judgements will differ from one government to another. Britain's Labour governments of 1974–9, for example, founded much of their policy around their capacity to talk to trade unions, and to tie them into a 'social contract' that would ensure industrial peace. These hopes were dashed in the 'Winter of Discontent' of 1978–9. Margaret Thatcher, on the other hand, based much of her electoral appeal on her ability *not* to talk to trade unions, and indeed to cut them out of the policy process altogether. For groups that are excluded, however, there remains the possibility of 'direct action', in the form of peaceful or violent mass demonstrations, tax revolts, attacks on public buildings, obstruction of transport or other public services, and so on. In such a context, the avoidance of trouble for governments is synonymous with the preservation of public order. Direct action is often the resort of weak groups with more or less marginal constituencies, but not always. In France, especially, where despite the profusion of avenues for dialogue it is still notoriously difficult to secure consent across the board for controversial policies, governments of both Left and Right have regularly had to bow to the mass demonstrations of Catholic or secular educational organizations, the motorway barriers of truck drivers, or the more or less riotous and incendiary protests of fishermen and farmers.

Expertise or technical skill

Expertise or technical skill can also be an invaluable resource in the hands of groups, since no government's servants can command all the knowledge it needs to frame policy in every eventuality. There are at least two ways in which groups can deploy such expertise: either they can get the public authorities to recognize them, as such, and thus win legitimacy and the right to dialogue as equals with the administration; or they can use their skills or influence in a particular area to operate in another field, that of politics, for example. In the first case, the interest group's impact upon the government and the administration is plain to see, for the public authorities are dependent upon or even prisoners of the groups that possess the necessary information and knowledge. Dramatic examples of such situations are provided by the United States, where the oil and gas companies withheld from President Carter the information that he needed to implement his energy policies, and by France, where the government found itself in a position of dependence upon the steel industry's association.[15] Other examples are provided by the numerous cases of over-investment provoked by optimistic forecasts made by groups with a vested interest in doing so (for example, the nuclear lobby in France, the 'cathedrals in the desert' in southern Italy). It is also possible for groups to intervene at the parliamentary level simply by drawing up a bill that some member of parliament is willing to introduce. This is common practice in the United States but it occurs to some extent in all parliamentary systems. Finally, there is now another way for groups to make use of their skills or status outside their normal and legitimate field. It is a practice that is becoming increasingly frequent as political life is more and more affected by the media: artists, scientists, and university professors are mobilized for causes of the most heterogeneous nature, causes which in many cases have very little to do with their own specialist fields. Nowadays any group that wants its voice to be widely heard may be tempted to engage in such tactics.

Money

Money is a third way for groups to influence the political process, and it can be deployed in at least four ways. The first is to hire professional lobbyists for their contacts, their knowledge of the corridors of power, or their skill at presenting a case. The second is to undertake campaigns in the press or television over a particular issue, though this is rarely considered cost-effective by groups that enjoy access to government. The third is to finance political parties. This is a notoriously delicate area, since even where such donations from business or other groups are perfectly legal, as they are, for example, in Britain, they are intended to be free gifts representing a general agreement with the party's policies, and certainly not a fee for specific services, nor even, in principle, a payment to secure access. In France, by contrast, business contributions to parties have been illegal, except for a brief period between 1990 and 1995, but they were still widely practised, especially in order to secure public contracts. The French Socialist Party, for example, was very largely financed by this type of payment to the various town halls it controlled throughout the 1970s and 1980s; the discovery of the 'Urba' network in 1991 was a major cause of the party's drop in popularity that year. This leads to the fourth way in which groups can use money to further their aims: by buying politicians. This practice has been frequent: Italy's President Leone (the Lockheed scandal), West German Finance Minister Count Otto Lambsdorff (the Flick scandal), and the two former French ministers Michel Noir and Alain Carignon are merely a handful of names that have appeared in numerous West European corruption cases since the 1980s. In Italy the phenomenon has been so systematic that one can hardly speak of the corruption of politicians by groups, so symbiotic was the network of corrupt relationships between politicians, parties, private firms (especially in the construction sector), and state-owned enterprises. One should add that such systematic corruption invariably creates the need to launder money and thus to seek the services of those who do this best: the world of organized crime is never far away, whether or not Italy's former Christian Democrat Prime Minister Giulio Andreotti was himself a member of the Mafia.

Pluralism, corporatism, and policy networks

As was suggested at the beginning of this chapter, attitudes towards interest groups and their role have varied greatly between different countries. Although individual governments and politicians have some freedom of choice about whether and under what conditions to allow groups into the policy-making process, their behaviour in this area will also correspond, in most cases, to an existing national model. At one extreme in this respect is the United States, where the rather open organization of interest groups in their relation with government is considered both to demonstrate and to guarantee the country's social and political pluralism. The British case is generally seen as close to this liberal model. The political traditions of France and Italy, on the other hand, have tended to express mistrust at the intervention of private interests in politics (with good reason, one might add, in the light of recent events). In the former case, the general interest is held to result from the confrontation and conciliation of numerous conflicting private interests. In the latter, more *étatiste* tradition, the general interest is to be served by the representatives of the people (in effect, the government and its administration), with groups participating, if at all, within a fixed, constraining institutional framework.

Pluralism and its critics

Interest groups, those associations of citizens so admired by Tocqueville, are considered by a whole current of liberal thought—particularly in America—as a fundamental element of pluralist democracy. It was A. F. Bentley who proclaimed that credo the most forcefully:

The great task in the study of any form of social life is the analysis of these groups. It is much more than classification, as that term is ordinarily used. When groups are adequately stated, everything is stated. When I say everything, I mean everything.[16]

The thesis is important because of the emphasis that it lays upon processes rather than structures, but it goes much too far when it reduces all political activity (including that of the State) to the interaction of groups all considered to be more or less equal. The 'group' theory of political life was taken up half a century later by David Truman, who also tended to set all groups on the same footing, thereby to some extent recasting the classical democratic theory according to which all individuals, as citizens, are free and equal: Truman replaces 'individuals' by 'interest groups'. Not until the 1960s did attention shift to the differentiation and inequality between groups. But over and above these different assessments of the status of groups, it was generally agreed that the action of groups was good for democracy. This positive view was founded upon a notion of the healthiness of competition between groups, and also upon the realization that individuals may belong to a number of different groups that partially overlap (with cross-cutting divisions). This means that both affinities and differences exist between group members and these make for stability and consensus (because of the practical need for compromise). Of course, this optimistic but by no means groundless view is reinforced by the assumption that the capacities and statuses of the various groups are all comparable. This pluralist model was subsequently disputed, particularly in the United States, on the grounds, not so much of the group theory *per se*, but rather of the question of the concentration or pluralism of élites (for example, the disagreement, in the 1950s and 1960s, between those who regarded the United States as being controlled by an oligarchic élite (Floyd Hunter, C. Wright Mills) and those who maintained that it was a polyarchic pluralism (Robert Dahl, in particular)).

Although the optimistic view of groups has predominated in the United States, it has never been a universal one, as is shown by the attempts during the 1930s to bring the lobbies of Congress under control, and the trenchant criticisms voiced by many politicians and political theorists such as Ted Lowi.

But one of the most vigorous critiques of the 'group theory' was put forward by Mancur Olson[17] in his work *The Logic of Collective Action*. Olson challenged the central assumption in the theory, namely, that economic groups take action to defend the interests of the group and the individuals who compose it, to the personal benefit of the latter. Olson reckons that in *large* groups individuals are not usually prepared to make sacrifices in order that the group as a whole should attain its objectives, even if the result obtained by collective action would in the long run prove to be to the advantage of each individual. He shows that large economic groups (consumers, for instance) are much less powerful than small groups of industrialists that are organized and strongly structured. In other words, the existence of a common interest is not enough to set up a group that comprises all or virtually all those who are its potential members and that is capable of taking collective action. The case of the trade unions is typical of this paradoxical situation. Although their actions help to win advantages for all wage-earners, most of them attract the membership of only a small percentage of their potential supporters. And this discrepancy is even more striking in the case of consumer groups.

The dilemma of corporatism

In France and in much of the rest of continental Europe, criticism of the relations between public authorities and interest groups takes a number of different forms. One line taken is Jacobin and revolutionary in spirit: in the name of the State, it rejects all intervention on the part of groups, and even goes so far as to condemn their existence. It cannot be denied that this analysis contains the seeds of anti-democratic and totalitarian developments in the name of a State with a tendency to absorb everything into itself.

Another critical approach is not directed against groups in general, only against those of them that can control political power through a tight-knit oligarchy or pluto-cracy. This kind of criticism, from traditionalist and anti-republican circles, does not reject groups as such—on the contrary, for these constitute the intermediary bodies of which they so much approve. What it condemns is the control that a small handful of individuals hold over the reviled democratic system. In the eyes of these critics, the way to make society healthier is to bring back groups and to organize them—to the detriment of the individual—under the aegis of the State, the summit of this edifice of collective bodies. The corporatist experiments of the 1930s and 1940s in Germany, Italy, France (the Vichy regime), Spain, and Portugal testified to the collapse of the liberal democracies that had been founded upon the idea of 'free individuals, all equal before the law' and signalled the establishment of a new order in which groups, far from constituting an expression of pluralism, became no more than so many cogs in the State machinery. In a corporatist concept of society, groups are expected to play a deter-mining part in the exercise of power, for the representation of organized interests takes the place of traditional political representation based on universal suffrage. Although all the European political systems that embraced this concept have disappeared, there can be no doubt that vestiges of that recent past still survive (the professional orders in France, the obligation to renegotiate collective contracts every three years in Italy).

However, the expression 'neo-corporatism', which acquired considerable popularity in the 1970s, does not refer to those survivals so much as to new forms of co-operation between the State and various groups. What is neo-corporatism? We should do well to refer to the original definitions given by the leaders of this school, for although the theory has enjoyed considerable success, the concepts involved have not been expressed at all clearly and, furthermore, its field of application has been greatly expanded (meso-corporatism, micro-corporatism, etc.). For Philippe Schmitter, one of the chief promoters of the theory,

Corporatism can be defined as a system of interest representation in which the constituent units are organized into a limited number of singular, compulsory, noncompetitive, hierarchically ordered and functionally differentiated categories, recognized or licensed (if not created) by the state and granted a deliberate representational monopoly within their respective categories.[18]

The same author contrasts this neo-corporatist model with the pluralist model, which he defines as:

A system of interest representation in which the constituent units are organized into an unspecified number of multiple, voluntary, competitive, nonhierarchically ordered and self-determined (as to type or scope of interest) categories which are not specifically licensed, recog-nized, subsidized, created or otherwise controlled in leadership selection or interest articulation by the state and which do not exercise a monopoly of representational activity within their respective categories.[19]

As abstract models, the pluralist and the neo-corporatist options are clearly distinct and stand in contrast to one another. In truth, it is hard to see in what respect the definition of neo-corporatism distinguishes it from the classic corporatism tried out by the Fascist regimes, except in so far as it suggests it to be possible for the classic system of representation (parliaments) to coexist with a system designed for the representation of interests. Two questions then arise: first, can the neo-corporatist model be empirically verified? and secondly, is neo-corporatism compatible with the maintenance of classic liberal democracy?

The first question prompted a spate of empirical research in the 1970s and 1980s particularly in the countries of northern and central Europe (Scandinavia, West Germany, Austria, and Switzerland), but also in Italy, Britain, and France. But, despite the abundance of literature on the matter, the answers are far from clear, for the degrees of corporatism may vary greatly from one country to another and even within a single State. It is generally recognized that the neo-corporatist model is inapplicable to the systems of group representation in the USA, Britain,[20] Italy, and France. Nevertheless, in France, for example, there are certain sectors, such as agriculture[21] and education, where in its essential components the model may be applicable.

On the other hand, Austria, Germany, and especially Sweden do appear to fit the neo-corporatist model, for it is one that tends to find favour when power is held by social democratic parties that are close to the unions and prepared to support them as the primary negotiators with their partners, the employers, and to sanction the agreements that are reached. The essence of the neo-corporatist system seems to lie in the public status conferred upon these organizations and the agreements that they reach. The various agents involved in the negotiations confer legitimacy upon one another and guarantee to fulfil their mutual commitments. Problems nevertheless remain. In France, for instance, many features of the neo-corporatist model are detectable (where the structure and status of 'peak organizations' are concerned, for example). Yet these institutional elements do not lead to neo-corporatist policies even under the most favourable conditions (as between 1981 and 1986, when the Socialist Party was in power). In Britain the 'social contract' of the 1970s between a Labour government and the trade unions was criticized on the ground (among others) that it was replacing a liberal regime of group representation with a corporatist one, in which free democratic processes were giving way to deals done with union leaders over 'beer and sandwiches at Number 10'. Yet the extraordinary difficulty encountered by union leaders in getting their rank and file to stick to the deal, and its disintegration in 1978, indicate its true nature: a conditional agreement in specific circumstances, rather than a system, even a partial system, of group representation. Furthermore, since consultation and the conclusion of agreements are, in principle, indicative of neo-corporatist practices, it has sometimes been assumed, on the strength of such indicators, that a neo-corporatist model applies. That may be an altogether false assumption, particularly when it is suggested that the model applies not at the topmost levels, as in the original definition of neo-corporatism, but at intermediate levels (meso-corporatism) or local levels (micro-corporatism). The real situation thus appears to be extremely diverse, combining elements of both pluralist and neo-corporatist representation. But at this point it seems reasonable to ask: what is so 'new' about all this? In liberal democracies, interests have always been represented and, to varying degrees, organized and protected, for it is not as if liberal democracy ever existed in a pure state in some golden age before the appearance of corporatism. We know what pluralist democracies, with all their imperfections, are; and we are also familiar with the particular characteristics and vices of authoritarian corporatism. The question is, is there any place for a neo-corporatism, that might combine traditional political representation with a new system for the representation of interests?

Lehmbruch believes there is. He has pointed out that neo-corporatism was not an alternative to pluralist democracy, but could interact with it in various forms.[22] Such a view seems open to only two interpretations: either it is unrealistic, or else it strips the neo-corporatist theory of most of its interest. For the distinctiveness of corporatism depends precisely on absolutes. Where, as is the case in the West European democracies, membership of a specific group is not compulsory (even though it may be advantageous), or where a single group enjoys predominant, but not monopoly representation in its area, we have not corporatism, but a variant of pluralism. It is fair to say that the idea of a compromise between, on the one hand, pluralist democracy and, on the other, forms of organization and intervention by interest groups that are fundamentally constricting, authoritarian, and oligarchic is unrealistic. If the neo-corporatist model is fully applied in practice, we should not beat about the bush but speak quite simply of corporatism. That way, there is no danger of conferring legitimacy upon an authoritarian way of exercising power. On the other hand, if no more than dispersed and unsystematized corporatist elements are present, there is no need to construct a theoretical model which no longer explains what the liberal democracies of today really are: namely, confirmed pluralist systems within which it is possible for many heterogeneous elements bequeathed by each country's own particular history and traditions to coexist. In the democracies of the West, the aftermath of recent or less-recent corporatist experiments lives on here and there, in Economic and Social Councils, or Napoleonic Chambers of Commerce, or certain practices carried over from the *ancien régime*; but these 'foreign bodies' exist alongside other elements that are equally 'impure' from the point of view of classic democratic theory. Such elements include, for example, the representation of specific territories in upper chambers, the maintenance of traditional practices (such as inherited parliamentary membership in the House of Lords), and the persistence of community solidarities that win out over the political individualism of liberal constitutions. The wave of neo-corporatism may have stimulated interesting speculation, but it is fair to wonder whether it really helps to interpret or explain the evolution of Western democracies, either individually or collectively. To quote from Schmitter's more recent work, 'I have become less and less convinced that corporatism—with or without one of its multiple prefixes or adjectives—will survive'.[23]

Policy networks

The most interesting aspect of the neo-corporatist theory is that it has revealed and demonstrated that, contrary to American theories of the group-based nature of politics, groups certainly are not all equal and their functions are exceedingly diverse, ranging from the expression of particular interests to the formulation, determination, and implementation of public policies. The concept of 'policy networks' is one approach that seeks to reconcile some of the basic tenets of pluralism—multiple, competitive groups, existing outside the direct control of the state—with some of the clearest objections to 'classic' pluralist theory, such as unequal access to the policy process, or the symbiotic and exclusive relationship that can develop between certain parts of government and some interest groups. A policy network can be defined, in its most basic form, as a group of bureaucrats and interest-group representatives, plus, in some cases, politicians and experts, meeting regularly to develop policies in a particular area to their mutual advantage. One attraction of this very general definition is its flexibility: there is more than one possible style of policy network, and different styles can coexist between different policy domains within the same political system. This variety of possible styles can be expressed as a continuum. At one end of the continuum is what is often known as a policy community. The partners here consult regularly over a period of years, or even decades, in more or less formalized contexts; they are able to keep out groups perceived as a threat or an inconvenience; and it takes a very determined initiative to separate them or to give a radical new turn to policy. Obvious examples would be the relations between farm lobbies and ministries of agriculture, characterized by regular, long-term, and instutionalized consultation between civil servants and a single 'peak' organization with high membership density. Other interested parties, such as consumers or environmentalists, are marginalized; the leading group may play a role in implementing policy, and will certainly be active in framing legislation; and the minister frequently behaves as a spokesman for the group (and, indeed, may be a former member of the group himself).[24] This is clearly close to the pattern of relations described as corporatist, but it differs from corporatism, at least on the Schmitter definition quoted above, by virtue of its voluntary character: group membership is advantageous but not compulsory, and it remains possible in principle for the state autorities to co-opt new interlocutors, or for either partner to walk away from the table. At the other end of the policy network spectrum are more open and *ad hoc* groupings, sometimes known as issue networks. These are typically much less exclusive than policy communities, and may bring together apparently unlikely alliances of groups—for example, feminists and churches joining forces against pornography; focused on specific issues rather than broad policy areas, they are likely to be fairly tactical and temporary. Between these two extremes are any number of types of policy network, more or less institutionalized, more or less open to a variety of groups, more or less wide-ranging, more or less permanent. Their character will depend on a variety of factors, including the newness of the policy area concerned, the number of potential players involved, the policy priorities of government, and so on. A second attraction of the policy-networks approach is that it allows for a degree of autonomy for the policy network in relation to the political direction of the system. This recalls the regular complaints of ministers at the difficulty of implementing policies if they conflict with a *modus operandi* (including relations with partners) established in a department over many years. It is also consistent with academic research: Marsh and Rhodes, for example, argue that the existence of policy networks was crucial in blunting the radical-ism of some of the more extreme Thatcherite policies.[25] Yet while the policy-networks approach rightly stresses the capacity of bureaucrats and interest groups to deflect or modify, or even determine the policies of an elected government of right or left, it does not discount (as fully developed corporatism would appear to do) the importance of parliamentary representation. For, despite all its limitations and the constraints on its actions, the democratically elected legislature remains an indispensable component of liberal democracy.

Questions

- What can the behaviour of interest groups show about the distribution of power within a political system?

- Under what circumstances are trade unions best able to exert influence within a political system?

- Can any generalizations about the most effective forms of group organization be made from the case of the farm lobby in Western Europe?

- To what extent have national politico-administrative styles affected the relations of different governments with groups?

- What criticisms can be made of pluralism as a framework for understanding the role of interest groups within a political system?

NOTES

1. G. A. Almond and G. B. Powell, *Comparative Politics: A Developmental Approach* (Boston: Little, Brown, and Co., 1966).
2. This law encouraged the organization of groups by allowing them to acquire an extremely liberal juridical status merely by declaring themselves.
3. S. Berger, 'Regime and Interest Representation: The French Traditional Middle Classes', in S. Berger (ed.), *Organizing Interests in Western Europe* (Cambridge: Cambridge University Press, 1981), 99.
4. The National Union of Manufacturers, created in 1916, and the National Confederation of Employers' Associations, founded in 1919.
5. H. Weber, *Le Parti des patrons: Le CNPF, 1946–1986* (Paris: Seuil, 1986).
6. A. Clark, *Diaries* (London: Phoenix paperback edn., 1994), 307.
7. P. Self and H. Storing, 'The Farmers and the State', in R. Kimber and J. Richardson (eds.), *Pressure Groups in Britain* (London: Dent, 1974).
8. A. Grosser, *L'Allemagne de notre temps*, Coll. Pluriel (Paris: Fayard, 1978), 346.
9. M. Cammelli, *L'Amministrazione per collegi* (Bologna: Il Mulino, 1980), 240.

10. In Britain, the CBI, in its 1983 Annual Report, mentions that it took part in a wide range of committees, about seventy in all, including the National Dock Labour Board, the Health and Safety Commission, the Commission for Racial Equality, the Genetic Manipulation Advisory Group, etc.

11. M. Golden, 'Neo-corporativismo ed esclusione della forza-lavoro dalla rappresentanza politica', in G. Pasquino (ed.), *Il Sistema politico italiano* (Bari: Laterza, 1985), 254.

12. Y. Mény, 'La Légitimation des groupes d'interêt par l'administration française', *Revue française d'administration publique*, 39 (1986), 99f.

13. In practice, however, the interpenetration of American élites may make board members over-sensitive to the interests that they are responsible for controlling.

14. See E. Suleiman, *Politics, Power and Bureaucracy in France* (Princeton, NJ: Princeton University Press, 1974).

15. J. Hayward, 'The Nemesis of Industrial Patriotism: The French Response to the Steel Crisis', in Y. Mény and V. Wright (eds.), *The Politics of Steel: Western Europe and the Steel Industry in the Crisis Years (1974–1984)* (Berlin: De Gruyter, 1987), 502.

16. A. F. Bentley, *The Process of Government* (Evanston, Ill.: Principia Press of Illinois, 1949), 208. According to Bentley, government and its policies result *purely* from the pressures exerted by various groups. He writes, for example: 'the balance of the group pressures *is* the existing state of society' (pp. 258–9).

17. M. Olson, *The Logic of Collective Action: Public Goods and the Theory of Groups* (Cambridge, Mass.: Harvard University Press, 1965).

18. P. Schmitter, 'Still the Century of Corporatism?', *Review of Politics*, 36 (1974), 93.

19. Ibid. 85–93.

20. A. Cox and J. Hayward, 'The Inapplicability of the Corporatist Model in Britain and France', *International Political Science Review*, 4(2) (1983), 217–40.

21. J. Keeler, 'Corporation and Official Union Hegemony: The Case of French Agricultural Syndicalism', in Berger, *Organizing Interests in Western Europe*.

22. G. Lehmbruch, 'Liberal Corporatism and Party Government', *Comparative Political Studies*, 10 (Apr. 1977).

23. P. Schmitter, 'Corporatism Is Dead! Long Live Corporatism!', *Government and Opposition*, 24(1) (1989), 54–73.

24. Cf. M. J. Smith, *The Politics of Agricultural Support in Britain: The Development of the Agricultural Policy Community* (Aldershot: Dartmouth, 1990). In France, the former FNSEA leader, François Guillaume, was made Agriculture Minister in the 1986 Chirac government.

25. D. Marsh and R. Rhodes (eds.), *Policy Networks in British Government* (Oxford: Clarendon Press, 1992).

CHAPTER 4

Voters, Elections, and the Elected

The Western democracies are all founded upon election, for it is this that confers legitimacy upon power. But, as political and constitutional history teaches us, a declaration of intent may be a far cry from its realization, just as a constitution may be an imperfect guide to political practice. Sartori[1] has wittily remarked that 'election means selection', and it is quite true that for a long time the Western democracies retained devices designed to eliminate certain potential electors even in countries where suffrage was claimed to be universal. The trouble is that, as with any other idealistic principle, if power is to be attributed to the people or nation, certain juridical and political mechanisms are necessary and these may distort or even destroy the initial objective.

Electoral systems

Political democracy expresses itself partly by giving most of the population the right to vote. But the conditions in which that right is exercised, in particular the procedures of electoral competition, mould and determine the conditions in which democracy is played out. Even if the purpose of the 'rules of the game' observed by Western democracies is to transform the violence and conflicts inherent in social relations into a symbolic battle, the partners and parties concerned must also accept that transformation: the object is to settle peacefully upon a winner who will govern but do so under the best possible conditions for freedom and fairness. There is plenty of scope for disagreement as to which precise mechanism will best serve this purpose. While the principles of liberty, justice, and efficiency are all regularly invoked to promote or to defend different electoral systems, they are only partially compatible with one another. Every electoral system is the result of a trade-off, which will depend on the traditions, values, political and social cleavages, and ideologies of the political world surrounding it. It will also result from the calculations of politicians, whose disinterested conduct can be counted on in this extremely sensitive area even less than in other aspects of policy.

The principle of liberty

Between the ideal of men legally 'free and equal' and the reality, there is, as everyone knows, a vast gulf that electoral rules can only partly make good. Guaranteeing the formal conditions for the exercise of liberty is certainly the first step. Establishing measures that offer the voter the maximum degree of freedom of judgement, freedom from pressures, and freedom to express his preferences is quite another matter.

In most Western democracies, formal guarantees to safeguard the right to vote such as the secret ballot were established only in the late nineteenth or early twentieth century. In the United States, secret balloting was achieved only gradually, state by state, from 1888 onwards; in Italy, after the First World War; in Britain, in 1872; and in France, in 1913–14. In Italy, voters may choose whether to vote in a private polling booth, whereas in France they are required to do so. In Germany, the secret ballot was established in 1919. Most ballot-papers are now standardized and bear only the names of official candidates.

But freedom also means the right not to take sides, the right to abstain, to leave the ballot-paper blank or to spoil it. In Germany, Britain, and France, voting is not obligatory, as it is in Belgium. But the assumption that one has a 'duty' to vote is stronger in some countries than in others. Italy occupies an intermediate position in this respect. Non-voting is noted in voters' civil and criminal records; no punishment is applied beyond that; but until recently, many Italians believed that non-voting was subject to material sanctions. Italy therefore generally saw turn-out figures of 85 to 90 per cent in the past, and drops of even a few percentage points provoked much expression of anxiety in the media and among politicians. Indications from the most recent elections are that this (not wholly spontaneous) sense of civic duty has declined: a turnout of 86.2 per cent in 1994 was accompanied by a huge number of spoilt ballots (2.8 million), giving a total percentage of valid votes of just 80.3, a proportion that dropped to 76.9 per cent in 1996. The percentage of valid votes has also fallen, albeit over a longer period, in Britain and France, where it is often closer to 65 per cent in parliamentary elections than to the 75 or 80 per cent typical in the 1970s. The level also varies between different types of elections, ranging from 75 per cent at the run-off ballot of a French presidential race to a mere 30 to 40 per cent in a British local election. Although there is room for concern over what these generally falling figures show about the public's confidence and sense of a stake in elections, it should also be stressed that abstention and blank or spoilt ballot-papers are one manifestation of the freedom of the electorate and are a necessary—if not sufficient—condition for democratic expression to function satisfactorily. Elections where 99 per cent participation is claimed are not invariably totally corrupt, but the massive polls of Eastern bloc socialist countries were always dubious, as have been comparable phenomena in some Third World states. The emergence of Eastern Europe to democracy was almost invariably accompanied by a drop in turn-out from levels of Communist days, sometimes a very large one. In the case of East Germany, indeed, there was a drop from earlier Western levels. The addition of the East brought turn-out in the Federal Republic of Germany down from an Italian-style 84.4 per cent (in 1987, the last West German parliamentary election) to a British- or French-style 74.7 per cent in the unification election of 1990.

It would, however, be hasty to conclude that abstentions and blank or spoilt ballot-papers necessarily indicate the existence of a satisfactory freedom of choice. On the contrary, such manifestations of the voters' discontent or indifference often reflect their frustration in the face of the choices that are forced upon them and that they prefer to reject. This was the point that Khrushchev was making—although he was certainly in no position to preach—in his quip to American journalists as they pressed him with questions about the one-party Soviet system: 'I have never seen the difference between a donkey (Democrat) and an elephant (Republican).' One of the most telling criticisms levelled at the single-ballot majority system, especially in a context where two parties dominate, as in Britain and the United States, is that even quite large minorities can be deprived of a voice over large parts of the country. This is true of the Greens throughout the United Kingdom, and of Liberal Democrats in most of England. Even in France, where the two-ballot system limits the scope of this objection, moderate voters may find themselves forced to choose at the run-off between one candidate from the Communist Party and another from the National Front.

Proportional-list systems do not escape objections of this kind: under the system used in France in 1986, for example, the voters had no way of influencing the choice of candidates listed or their order on the list. To mitigate such constraints mechanisms are sometimes introduced into list systems whereby the voters themselves select the candidates. This is the traditional procedure followed in small French communes, but only for municipal elections (and, since 1982, only in communes of less than 3,500 inhabitants). The voter is allowed to strike off certain names and to 'mix in' names from rival lists. In small, local communities, this is all greatly facilitated by the voters' personal and direct knowledge of the candidates. All the same, it is not a common procedure and the French electoral reforms of 1985 made no provision for any personalized mechanisms of the type used in Germany and Italy.

In Germany, seats are allotted on a proportional basis but still partly according to the principles of a one-vote ballot producing a relative majority. Effectively though, the voter has two votes to cast. With the first, he helps to choose a candidate at local constituency level; with the second, he expresses his preferences on a party list at *Land* level. The voter thus uses his first vote to choose a candidate, then either confirms or corrects that choice by casting his second vote either for the same party or a different one. This type of election makes it possible to introduce local and personal considerations into a ballot on the basis of a proportional list which, without that opportunity for correction, would leave the political parties with a free hand. Recent elections to the Bundestag showed that German voters are fully aware of all the possibilities that the system offers them. The FDP, with few local roots or charismatic leaders, was nevertheless regarded as an indispensable counterbalance to the dominant party of the moment: the SPD in 1980, the CDU–CSU in 1983 and 1987. The FDP was able to weigh in against the left wing of the Social Democratic Party in 1980 and Franz-Josef Strauss's right-wing CSU in 1983 and 1987. It thus helped to push the positions of first Chancellor Schmidt, then Chancellor Kohl towards the Centre. Voters used the 'split ticket' to reflect both their personal and their political preferences, showing that they knew perfectly well how to make the most of the system. Rudolf Hrbek writes:

In 1980, the liberal constituency candidates only won 48.5 per cent of the second votes for their party, while 35.5 per cent of the FDP voters cast their first vote for the SPD candidate. In 1983, only 29.1 per cent of FDP voters also cast their first vote for the FDP candidate, while 58.3 per cent chose the CDU candidate. In both cases voters wanted their votes to influence the composition of the coalition.[2]

In this light, the personal success of FDP leader Hans Dietrich Genscher in December 1990, when he managed to win a constituency seat in his native town of Halle, in the Eastern *Land* of Saxony-Anhalt, was a break with tradition, and reflected both a general rise in the FDP vote and an increase in 'double' votes for the FDP. The 1994 elections showed that the less experienced East Germans were more hesitant about splitting their tickets than their Western compatriots, at least where the FDP was concerned. Whereas in the West the FDP won 3.4 per cent of personal votes but 7.4 per cent of party votes, the figures in the new *Länder* were 3.0 and 4.0 per cent respectively.

Italy, for its part, had, till 1992, a system of preference voting which, in theory at least, ought to correct the predominance of the political parties. The voter could choose whether to vote for the list as it stood or for a list that he could 'reconstruct' by changing the order of the candidates' names, provided they all appeared on the same list. In constituencies of sixteen or more seats, each voter could express four choices (in smaller constituencies, only three). With his preference vote, he could vote for the candidates of his own choice, disregarding the order of names fixed by the party. In the south, more voters (40 per cent) took advantage of the possibility of expressing a personal preference than in central and northern Italy (less than 20 per cent on average) and more voters from the Christian Democrats and the Italian Socialist Party did so than from the Italian Communist Party. The preference vote chiefly reflected local interests and internal struggles between different party factions and came in for virulent criticism on that account. Such criticism was well formulated by Giuliano Amato (Professor of

Constitutional Law, Bettino Craxi's *éminence grise*, and Italy's Premier from June 1992 till April 1993):

the fear of increasing the strength of the parties at a moment when their stock is low stands in the way of reform for the time being. Yet there can be no doubt that the preference vote produces two negative effects. In the first place, it very often makes Deputies dependent upon local or corporatist support, as when, in order to amass enough preference votes, they put themselves at the service of organized groups that are in a position to guarantee these to them: hospital employees, railway workers, Post Office employees. Secondly, it encourages the most powerful élite figures to rope themselves together with an entourage of unknown and weak candidates who, thanks to this 'double bet', achieve a success that they could never have won on their own.[3]

The case put here by Amato 'won' when a referendum held in June 1991 cut the number of possible preference votes to one, on a turnout of 62.5 per cent and a Yes vote of 95.6 per cent—despite the mobilization against it of both Christian Democrats and Socialists. This referendum was the start of the electoral break-up of the Italian party system. Ironically, it was another referendum on the electoral system, introducing a strong majority element into elections for the Senate, that signalled Amato's own departure from the premiership in 1993.

The secret ballot, formal guarantees, the right to abstain or to spoil the ballot-paper or leave it blank, and the possibilities for expressing a choice rather than simply voting for what is proposed are all examples of the kinds of liberty that the European democracies guarantee, in varying degrees, to their electorates. But it is worth pointing out that even the whole collection of them hardly does more than ensure a 'formal' liberty—though in itself no mean achievement—and does not guarantee any concrete exercise of it. If it did, the situation would be utopian and probably tyrannical. Concrete liberty would presuppose such specific and precise intervention on the part of the public authorities that their good intentions would soon be cancelled out by the conditions necessary for their realization. The most an observer can do is point out any overt or insidious infractions of the freedom of voters, recognizing that whatever remedies or palliatives may be introduced, they can never eliminate *all* the many pressures that are inseparable from the exercise of power and the constraints of social life.

The principle of justice

How should the Western democratic ideal summed up by the slogan 'one person, one vote' be translated into the representative system? In the contemporary period, Western democracies have sought to draw closer to the ideal of justice in two specific ways: either by adopting proportional representation or, within a framework of majority voting systems, essentially by redefining constituency boundaries in a more equitable fashion.

On the whole the tide is flowing in favour of proportional representation, leaving the United Kingdom, the United States, and Canada almost alone in using the 'first past the post' single-ballot majority system in its pure form. PR has generally been favoured by countries emerging into democracy—Spain, Greece, and Portugal in the 1970s, the former Soviet-bloc countries more recently. New Zealand has forsaken the 'first past the post' system it had used for over a century in favour of PR. Even the British are likely to adopt PR for European elections, and may even consider it for parliamentary ones. Only Italy, with nearly five decades' experience of the drawbacks of PR, has moved in the opposite direction. As a result of this general drift towards PR, democratic representational systems have tended to evolve towards their ideal, that is, towards a system in which it is possible for representatives faithfully to express and mirror the social body that chose them. The switch to proportional representation stems from a methodological and ideological assumption: namely, the idea that 'good government' more or less explicitly reflects not only a society's current opinions but also the particular characteristics of its social structure. Studies in political or administrative sociology frequently betray a yearning for a complete parallel between representatives and represented, pointing out, for example, that there are too many peasant mayors, not enough worker deputies, too many sons of the bourgeoisie in power, and so on. Some seem inclined to overlook the dangers inherent in such total parallelism. The quest for justice generally has spread beyond electoral systems themselves to many other sectors of political life—the administration, party organization, and so on. It has prompted the introduction of 'proportionalization' across the board: racial quotas; 'affirmative action'; systematic *proporz* for Flemish and French speakers in Belgium; quotas designed to protect the German-speaking minority in Italy's Alto-Adige region; quotas of women in the higher echelons of the political parties; and so on. The proportional voting systems of Germany and Italy abide by the unwritten rule whereby all parties must present lists of candidates that are 'balanced' from the regional, professional, social, etc. points of view. Few countries, however, have gone so far as to institute overall proportional representation, as has Israel, where the entire country constitutes a single constituency.

German proportional representation

Because of the way it works, the German electoral system has often—wrongly—been described as a mixed system, that is, one that combines a majority voting system with proportional representation. This is not correct: the German system is strictly proportional,[4] but the distribution of seats is determined partly on the basis of a single-vote ballot. The German voter actually has two votes. With the first he can vote for a candidate in one of the 328 electoral constituencies of the country. With the other he can vote, at *Land* level, from a list of names (*Landeslist*). Some of the listed candidates are also constituency candidates, but the voter is free to divide his vote favouring, for example, an SPD candidate and a FDP list. The list votes that are cast determine the number of seats allocated to each party. When all the votes won by the various parties at the federal level are added up, they are allocated according to the d'Hondt, or highest average, system (which gives an advantage, albeit a small one where so many seats are involved, to the strongest list), and the seats are distributed amongst the *Länder*. Now each seat can be allotted to an individual. The first to be named are the 328 who came first in the constituencies. Then, in the case of each party, the number of seats thus obtained is deducted from the total due to it according to proportional distribution. The 328 seats reserved for candidates from the lists are therefore distributed in such a way that each political group receives a number of seats proportional to the number of votes cast for its list. If a group suffers in the first allocation because hardly any of its candidates came top, the second allocation makes it possible to redress the injustice.

As can be seen, the German system clearly manifests a desire for fairness but retains a personalized ballot that is characteristic of majority systems. However, the principle of fairness is to some extent affected by an exclusion clause: the only parties included in the allocation of seats are those which either obtained at least 5 per cent of the second votes (for the *Länder* lists) at the federal level, or which managed to win a seat in at least three constituencies. (Up until 1957, the requirement was 5 per cent of the vote at *Land* level or one constituency seat.)

The effect of this clause upon German political life and the constitution of coalitions is considerable, despite its seemingly modest character (particularly in comparison with the exclusion clause of 12.5 per cent of the electorate affecting candidates in the second ballot in France). In West Germany, the Refugee Party, which won 4.6 per cent of the vote in 1957, despite its 27 seats in the preceding Bundestag, was thus eliminated. The extreme right-wing NPD, which won 4.3 per cent of the vote in 1969, suffered the same fate. On the other hand, in 1983 the Greens, with 5.6 per cent of the vote, won 27 seats. A few decimal points less would have eliminated them altogether, leaving Helmut Kohl with an uncomfortable absolute majority in harness with his rival/ally, Franz-Josef Strauss. Another indication of the system's occasional unpredictability came in the unification election. Following a ruling by the Constitutional Court, the West and East were treated, for the December 1990 elections only, as separate zones for the application of the 5 per cent threshold. The Green/Bündnis '90 alliance chose to run separate lists in each zone, fell below the threshold in the West, and thus only won seats in the East. As their result over the whole of Germany just exceeded 5 per cent, they would have won considerably more seats with a single list. The 5 per cent clause thus constitutes a slight abuse of the principle of justice, but compared with most other Western electoral systems that of Germany is one of the most equitable.

France: 'majoritarian' PR

The French have changed electoral system even more than they have changed regime, and various PR systems figure among the many options they have chosen. A 'dose' of PR is used at municipal level, while at European elections French voters have been invited to choose among national lists of candidates (each with 87 names on it, corresponding to the French representation in the Strasbourg parliament). Where PR has been used in parliamentary elections, however, as it was under the Fourth Republic and again, once only, in 1986, it has taken the form of *proportionnelle départementale*, with each of France's *départements* becoming a multi-member constituency. As there were 96 *départements* in mainland France in 1986 (there were 90 under the Fourth Republic) for

555 seats, most constituencies only elected five Deputies or fewer; some depopulated rural *départements* only elected two (which, on a strictly demographic calculation, was still one too many). In an election with an absolute minimum of four lists present in each *département* (Communists, Socialists, moderate right, and National Front), this did not allow for a very proportional distribution.[5] And while, as in Germany, a 5 per cent threshold was also applied, it was irrelevant in all but the two *départements* with over 20 seats. This delicate balance between PR and a majority system was quite intentional. The PR component limited the impact on the governing Socialists of their expected (and inflicted) electoral defeat, while the small constituencies penalized the extreme parties (each of which won just 35 seats with 10 per cent of the vote). The concern here was not so much abstract justice as electoral expediency.

Italy: from PR to a modified majority system

Italy is unusual in having two chambers of equal standing, elected, both before and after the electoral reforms of 1993, by two similar but not identical systems. The Chamber is composed of 630 Deputies. Up until 1963, the Constitution ruled as follows: 'The Chamber of Deputies is elected by direct universal suffrage, with one Deputy for every 80,000 inhabitants or for any fraction of over 40,000.' This ruling was later revised, and seats were distributed among the constituencies by dividing the number of inhabitants of the Republic according to the latest census by 630, and allocating seats in proportion to the population of each constituency on the basis of full quotas and the highest remainders. The boundaries of constituencies within the separate regions respected regional boundaries but might incorporate two or more provinces. Except for the Aosta Valley, which had only one seat, all the constituencies were allotted at least three seats. There were striking disparities: 5 constituencies had fewer than 10 seats each, 15 had between 10 and 19, 7 had between 20 and 29, and 4 large, densely populated constituencies had from 37 to 57 seats. As can be seen from this list, the Italian electoral constituencies were much larger than the French ones were in 1986. The system for the Italian Senate was similar to the one for the Chamber: Senators were elected in each region on the basis of a quota obtained by dividing the total electoral population by 315. With the exception of the Molisa region, with only 2 Senators, and the Aosta Valley, with only 1, the constitution allocated at least 7 senators per region.

As for the division of seats between the parties, Italian law settled for the method of the corrected quota, known as the *Imperiali* formula:

Quota = total number of votes cast in the constituency/number of seats + 2

This 'n + 2' formula limits remainders to a minimum and these were then transferred to a single national college. This arrangement was particularly advantageous to small political groups that would be incapable of obtaining the minimal quota in any constituency. All the same, to be included in this national redistribution, they had to have obtained at least one seat in a constituency and a minimum of 300,000 votes nationwide. It is worth pointing out that this was by no means an exorbitant requirement since it corresponds to less than 1 per cent of the whole electorate (which numbers nearly 40 million).

The allocation of seats in the constituencies was determined by dividing the number of votes obtained by each party by the electoral quota. Remainders were transferred to the national college. Given the extremely low threshold, which eliminated only the very smallest groups, some tiny ones obtained representation through having won one seat in one constituency. For example, in 1976, the Proletarian Democracy Party, the Liberals, and the Radical Party with, respectively, 1.5, 1.3, and 1.17 per cent of the vote, managed to win parliamentary representation by obtaining one whole quota in a single constituency. In contrast, in 1972, the Italian Socialist Party of Proletarian Union (the PSUP), with a better score (1.9 per cent of the votes), was unable to obtain a full quota because its votes were more widely dispersed throughout the country.[6]

A different system operated for the Senate before 1993. Candidates presented themselves to single-nomination colleges, where they had to win at least 65 per cent of the vote in order to be elected. As no more than one or two candidates scored highly enough, the operation then moved on to a second, more complicated stage. Within each region, the total number of votes obtained by each party was added up and seats were allocated according to the d'Hondt formula of greatest remainders. Once this distribution between the parties had been completed, seats were allotted to individual candidates on the basis of the fraction of the quota that he or she had won. The paradox of the situation is that it allowed several candidates to be elected in the same constituency despite the fact that in principle there should be only one. This happened when two or three parties happened to achieve their highest scores within one and the same constituency.

As we have seen, these two systems of proportional representation allowed the various parties involved to be represented as accurately as possible.[7] The criticisms that were made of them focused on anomalies shared by majority systems—and notably the advantage given to small parties with strong local bases over larger ones with more diffuse support—rather than to the principle of PR itself.[8] Little by little, however, the electoral system became the focus of mounting attacks on the chaotic way in which Italian politics worked. A cross-party movement for reform, including both former Communists and Christian Democrats (notably Mario Segni), put forward a number of referendum proposals aimed at abolishing the existing legislation, and the results of the April 1993 referendum on the voting system for the Senate, which was passed by an 82 per cent Yes vote (on a 77 per cent turnout), gave a decisive impetus to the movement to replace Italy's scandal-ridden élites. Amato, though not unsympathetic to reform, could not hold the line against this, and resigned. His successor, the former governor of the Bank of Italy Carlo Azeglio Ciampi, who headed a government of 'technicians' (in fact, of university professors), committed himself to reforming the electoral system in his investiture speech on 6 May 1993. The result was a hybrid electoral law, dictated at once by the demands of the public, which now favoured and got a first-past-the-post majority system, and the concerns of sitting parliamentarians (loyal, as parliamentarians usually are, to the system under which they had been elected), who secured the continued use of PR for a quarter of all the seats. The details for this proportional quarter vary between the Chamber, where seats are shared out on a national basis, using the highest-remainder system (which favours smaller lists), but with a 4 per cent threshold, and the Senate, where they are allocated regionally, on the highest-average system, and with no threshold. This new system certainly sacrificed the principle of 'justice', or at least of strict proportionality, to the goal of ridding Italy of a system associated with a corrupt political class. In 1996, for example, the former Communists of the PDS won 50 more seats than their nearest rival, Forza Italia, thanks to a strong performance in the constituency-based seats, although they were only half a percentage point ahead on the proportional part of the ticket. But the distortions were limited, and the representation of many parties preserved, by the actions of the parties themselves. The bipolarization which majority systems tend to produce took the form of electoral pacts (the 'Olive Tree' on the Left, the 'Freedom Pole' on the Right), but within those the allied parties shared out constituency candidacies among themselves, allowing nine party groups to be constituted in the Chamber. Very broadly speaking, this compromise between fairness and stable majorities is also sought in the constitutional plan agreed by Italy's parties in June 1997 and likely to be submitted to referendum within the following year. Under this system the Chamber would be elected on two ballots. At the first round, 80 per cent of the Deputies would be elected, 55 per cent of them by a majority vote and 25 per cent on PR. The two parties or coalitions that led at this ballot would then compete for the remaining 20 per cent of the seats at a run-off. In principle, this system would offer clear choices and clear majorities, while still leaving room for smaller groupings to survive. Its critics, on the other hand, claim that it still leaves too much power to the parties.

Redefining constituency boundaries

Although majority voting systems do not precisely represent society's expressed opinions, they do try to correct inequalities by improving the demographic balance between constituencies. The combination of a majority ballot and unequal constituencies is likely to produce the greatest injustice. Quite apart from nineteenth-century Britain where, in 1831, the electors of Cornwall returned forty-two Members of Parliament, while large cities such as Manchester and Birmingham elected none at all, it is worth remembering that, under the Fifth Republic in France and since 1945 in Britain, no parliamentary majority has been backed by an absolute majority of votes. The Conservative and Labour 'landslides' of 1983 and 1997 were both won with the support of fewer than 44 per cent of the voters and less than a third of the registered electorate. In 1981, the French Socialist Party obtained an absolute majority in the National Assembly on the strength of no more than 36 per cent of the vote at the first ballot, yet that did not prevent it from governing alone from July 1984 to March 1986. The growing discrepancy between votes and results indicates a need for corrective measures that could take only one of two forms: the adoption of proportional representation, which was the course taken by France in 1985–6; or a redefining of constituency boundaries.[9] The latter is the course periodically taken by the British and the Americans: it was also taken by France in 1986.

In Britain, the quest for more balanced constituencies began in 1944 with a law that created four Boundary Commissions, one for each nation in the United Kingdom, with the purpose of avoiding population variations of over 25 per cent. It was severely criticized, for if discrepancies of such magnitude were tolerated the reform was meaningless. A new law passed in 1958 accordingly referred to no specific percentage, leaving it up to the commissions to find the best kind of balance possible. In theory, the Speaker of the House of Commons presides over these commissions, but they are in fact placed under the authority of a High Court judge and chaired by Circuit Court judges. The other two members of each commission are not supposed to be members of the House of Commons. Every fifteen years at least, the commissions are required to put forward proposals or suggest revisions in a report accompanied by a projected Order in Council to be put before Parliament. Parliament is free to accept or reject the proposals. As a result, no changes were made from 1954 to 1970, since the Labour Party was reluctant to make changes that might affect its level of representation. Even after the reforms effected in 1970, serious discrepancies remained. The largest constituency numbered 96,380 electors, the smallest only 25,000. Before the 1983 elections, the Thatcher Government embarked upon sweeping reforms, which left only 66 constituencies unaffected and increased their number from 635 to 650. In vain the Labour Party opposed a redefinition of boundaries that took account of the decline of inner cities and, as a result, threatened Labour strongholds. Furthermore, the reform reduced the representation of Scotland and Wales, hitherto over-represented and dominated by the Labour Party. Although the number of seats allocated to them was retrospectively increased from 71 to 72 in the case of Scotland and 35 to 36 in that of Wales, this was more than offset by the creation of 15 extra seats. The ratio of electors to Members of Parliament was certainly considerably improved in 1983, but disparities were not eliminated altogether. Islands pose a special problem, owing to the difficulty of reconciling strictly arithmetical claims with the demand that constituencies should reflect communities as far as possible: hence the 101,680 voters of the Isle of Wight, but the 22,963 of the Western Isles. But the most widespread problem in Britain has been the depopulation of inner cities. This has been the main focus of recent redistrictings, and will no doubt continue to be so: nine out of the ten Glasgow constituencies, for example, have fewer than 55,000 voters, against a national average constituency size of 66,500. It is a trend under which Labour has most to lose. Despite the progress made, the British system guarantees neither perfect equality nor a process of adaptation altogether independent of the parties. The majority party is obliged neither to take action nor to accept the commissions' conclusions. 'Self-restraint' and the pressure of public opinion are virtually all that can be relied upon to limit possible excesses on the part of the parties.

There were even fewer safeguards when France switched from *proportionnelle départementale* to single-member constituencies and the two-ballot majority system in 1958, and proceeded to the first post-war redistricting. The job was given to the executive, to which the parliament of the moribund Fourth Republic had assigned full powers; it was done without any judicial or parliamentary control at all, with a certain amount of gerrymandering being the almost inevitable result, and favouring the Right. This advantage was accentuated over time by urbanization, which led to rural over-representation (a classic trump card in the hands of conservative parties in industrial-izing societies) in many parts of France. The Left denounced this state of affairs when in opposition, but undertook no redistricting after winning power, preferring instead to switch to PR in 1985. It was therefore left to Jacques Chirac and his right-wing govern-ment, who came to power in 1986 having promised a return to the majority system, to redraw constituency boundaries for the first time in nearly three decades. This time, although the Interior Minister Charles Pasqua certainly approached his task with polit-ical advantage in view, the controls were much tighter. First, although the government attempted to pass the redistricting by ordinance, thus avoiding awkward parliamentary questions by Deputies worried about their chances of re-election, François Mitterrand, who remained President, refused to sign the ordinance, obliging the government to use normal legislative procedure. Once that was complete, the Constitutional Council found itself empowered to exercise a measure of control which, although limited, nevertheless marked a profound change in French political mores.[10] The Constitu-tional Council was twice called upon to demonstrate its methods of control. On the first occasion, faced with the law that authorized the government to alter electoral boundaries by ordinance, the Council produced a whole list of conditions to be observed in the redetermination of constituency boundaries. Subsequently, in response to the law that adopted the boundaries (after President Mitterrand had refused to sign the ordinance), the Council declined to claim 'general powers of assessment and decision identical to those of Parliament', and went on to declare 'that, in view of the variety and complexity of local situations that may call for different solutions even in respect of the same demographic regulation, it did not consider that the decisions of the legislature fell noticeably short of constitutional requirements'.[11] The control that a constitutional judge can exercise is thus clearly imperfect and incomplete; nevertheless, substantial progress *has* been made in imposing some check upon arbitrary govern-ment action.

The majority principle

There are two aspects to the majority principle. First, the candidate who is elected is the one with either a relative majority (the 'first past the post') or an absolute one; secondly, it means that the government of the country is entrusted to those who hold a majority in parliament. The second factor is one that is common to all systems, but in systems of proportional representation it is undeniably considered less crucial than in majority voting systems. In the former, fair representation is a higher priority than efficiency—even if it means that no party can hold a majority. In the latter, the simplicity of an opposition between a majority and a minority is deemed preferable to the political advantages of electoral equity. Or, as Duverger remarks with remarkable dogmatism,

One cannot seriously present PR as a moral and fair system, and the plurality and majority systems as immoral techniques, because they are alleged to be unfair. On the contrary, one must clearly state that PR generally weakens democracy and that plurality and majority systems strengthen it, which, in the final analysis, makes the latter more moral and just. The first duty in the development of morality and justice in political relationships consists of reinforcing democracy and weakening dictatorship.[12]

Adherence to the majority principle makes for efficiency but does not do away with ambiguities. In Britain, for example, the parliamentary majority more often than not masks an electoral minority. Since 1918, the only governments to win a majority of votes have been the 1931 National Government and the Conservative Government of 1935. Neither the Labour Party in 1945 and 1966 nor the Conservatives in 1959 and 1983 could claim to have obtained an absolute majority of votes, despite their overwhelming parliamentary majorities. But that is not the only artificial aspect to the system. It sometimes—but fortunately, seldom—happens that the party with the majority of votes holds a minority of seats (usually as a result of winning with over-large majorities in some constituencies while the rival party won with tiny majorities in a larger number of marginal constituencies). In 1951, for instance, the Labour Party obtained only 294 seats with its 13,948,605 votes, while the Conservatives won 321 with only 13,717,580 votes. In 1974, it was the Labour Party's turn to benefit from this anomaly, when it won 4 seats more than the Conservatives despite the fact that the latter obtained 240,000 more votes than Labour.

As Max Beloff and Gillian Peele have pointed out, the drawbacks of such a situation cannot be fully appreciated simply in terms of the comparative electoral strengths of the parties involved. The anomalies are heightened by the 'mandate' doctrine according to which 'a political party which secures the right to form a government thanks to the electoral system also claims the right when in power to put through any legislation it thinks fit so long as it is based on some policy statement contained in the party's election manifesto'.[13] Beloff and Peele point out that this 'mandate' theory is used as a justification even when the ruling party has only just managed to scrape a victory: 'The Labour governments of 1974–9 took office with the support of 37.1 per cent and 39.2 per cent of the voters at each election; but the rhetoric of the mandate persisted when the government's legislative proposals were discussed in Parliament and the country.'[14]

The persistence of such an unjust system can only be explained by the fact that it favours the interests of the two dominant parties, notwithstanding prevailing public opinion. It produces clear results and is a means of choosing governments, selecting representatives, and so on. Nevertheless, the English majority voting system gives rise to many protests, particularly from those whom it eliminates or marginalizes: the Welsh and Scottish Nationalist parties, the Greens, and especially the Liberal Democrats, are all whittled away by the system. The British two-party system is not so much the result of a dual division in society, but rather a product of the constraints of the electoral system. In 1974, the Liberals obtained only 14 seats out of 635, despite winning 19.8 per cent of the vote. In 1983, the Conservatives walked off with 397 seats out of 650 with no more than 42.4 per cent of the vote; Labour obtained 209 seats with 27.6 per cent of the vote; but the Alliance, despite a very good score of 25.4 per cent—almost as high as Labour's—had to settle for 23 seats. Despite the protests occasioned by the injustice of these results, the dominant parties still clung to the system. Only when first-past-the-post seemed to be benefiting two parties, Conservative and Labour, in terms of seats, but only one, the Conservatives, in terms of government office, did Labour begin to move hesitantly away from its whole-hearted support of the old system. In 1990 the Labour Party set up a committee to discuss electoral reform (and to avoid intra-party conflict breaking out over the issue), and promised in the 1992 campaign that this would develop into a Royal Commission when Labour won power. The Liberal Democrats campaigned aggressively for proportional representation, insisting that in the absence of a single-party majority in the Commons, they would refuse to vote for a government that was not committed to it. The 1997 election result brought the possibility of reform closer than at any time since the Royal Commission of 1918, with proportional representation as part of the agenda of a joint Labour–Liberal committee on constitutional reform. This was at first sight paradoxical: the majority system had just served Labour well, giving the incoming majority 64 per cent of the seats in the Commons for 43 per cent of the popular vote. But in the first place the consideration, though not the commitment, that Labour had put into the issue of electoral reform before polling day could not simply be set aside as a result of an unexpectedly large majority without laying the party open to charges of cynicism. Secondly, the more far-sighted of Labour politicians might consider possible future elections, when the tide would not run so strongly in their favour, and when their Scottish heartlands might look less secure and above all less profitable as a result of cuts in the number of Scottish seats. That was the most powerful practical argument for PR that its supporters could put, after 1997, to the probably larger number of sceptics.

France is the only European country that uses a majority voting system with two ballots. Its choice of this system was largely a consequence of its rejection of both the other available options: the single-ballot majority system had always been considered as a 'guillotine' that eliminated third parties and was consequently unacceptable to a country in which the consensus is too fragile to allow only the two principal parties to emerge from the election. As for proportional representation, used often under the Third Republic and constantly under the Fourth, it became so closely equated with ministerial instability that most French voters became disenchanted with it. The compromise constituted by a single-name two-ballot voting system functions as follows. For the first ballot, all parties can put up candidates, in the hope of obtaining over 50 per cent of the vote or at any rate the best possible result. Candidates who win an absolute majority are elected. Where none manages this, there is a second ballot in which the winner is the candidate who obtains either an absolute or a relative majority. But the chances of winning are best for candidates from the Left or the Right who have managed to persuade the candidates closest to them who have done badly in the first ballot to stand down. If, for example, two left-wing candidates, one Socialist, the other Communist, both stand against a single right-wing candidate, they are both likely to be beaten by their opponent, who will attract all the votes from the Right, while they are obliged to share the votes from the Left. The incentive to regroup between the first and the second ballots is, accordingly, strong. In the first ballot, the competition is frequently between as many as five or six candidates, but the second becomes a battle between the Left and the Right in almost all constituencies. In principle, the candidate with the best chance of winning benefits from the withdrawal of allies who originally stood as rivals in the first ballot. Furthermore, French electoral law increases the pressure to withdraw since it stipulates that candidates who at the first ballot fail to win the votes of 12.5 per cent of all persons on the electoral roll must stand down. As a result of this regulation, it can even happen that a *single* candidate remains since all his rivals have been eliminated, as happened, for example, in several constituencies in 1988.

The French system is less flagrantly unjust than first-past-the post, and offers voters the combination of a wide choice of candidates at the first ballot with the opportunity to take a final decision at the second. It allows for both the identification of two opposed blocks as the majority and the opposition, and at the same time the retention of a pluralist party system. That said, its workings are not necessarily 'fairer' than first-past-the post in terms of the relation between (first-ballot) votes and seats. The FN, in particular, has complained of being shut out of the National Assembly, or left with just one seat, despite having won 10 or even 15 per cent of the vote. The moderate Right, on the other hand, emerged from the 1993 parliamentary elections with 84 per cent of National Assembly seats, despite having won just 44 per cent of first-ballot votes (four years later, when the Right's vote dropped 8 per cent, it lost half its seats and the majority, causing some of its leaders to support an alliance with the FN). Nor is the two-ballot system necessarily a guarantee of majority government. True, between 1958 and 1981, and again in 1993 and 1997, it proved possible to establish a majority despite the existence of six or seven parties that are at once autonomous (from the point of view of their respective programmes and strategies) and at the same time dependent (from the point of view of elections and the formation of a government). However, with better-balanced electoral constituencies and public opinion split more or less evenly between the two blocks, it sometimes happens that no party or coalition can put together a majority. Such was the situation of the Socialist Party in 1988, when it was obliged to govern with no more than a relative majority. However, although such a situation may be difficult in principle, it is less precarious than might be supposed, since the Constitution of the Fifth Republic provides the government with a number of trump cards (see Chapters 5 and 6).

Candidates and elected representatives: from selection to election

Election is a technique whereby citizens choose their representatives in accordance with mechanisms fixed by the constitution or the established government. Like many other institutional and political mechanisms, election is a 'modern' procedure to the extent that, formally at least, it has taken the place of other, older modes of selection (co-option or heredity, for example) and is to be found in all contemporary political systems. However, the democratic element in this by now virtually universal procedure varies enormously. Even in Western countries, where elections come closest to the ideal of free and open competition, much could be said about the inadequacies and imperfections of the system. A clearer idea of the strengths and weaknesses may be gained by examining the modes of selecting candidates and the sociological characteristics of those who are elected.

The selection of candidates

How does one become a candidate? It is tempting to reply: 'First, by wanting to be one,' if only to undermine the French myth of politicians who are 'urged to come forward by their friends', 'pressed to do so by public opinion,' or who 'respond to the call of duty'. But wanting is not enough. Whatever the system, it is also necessary to surmount a number of barriers and undergo certain rites of passage. The forms taken by the selection of candidates vary from one country to another, but we may synthesize them around two contrasting possibilities. Selection may be, to varying degrees, national or local; and, to varying degrees, open or closed.

There are very few countries in which selection is effected on a purely local level or a purely national one. But it is rare to find an even balance of the two. Most countries evolve in such a way that the national level comes to assume more importance than the local. This is certainly true of Italy and Germany, and to a lesser extent Britain. In the case of the United States, the opposite is true. In France, despite progressive centralization in the recruitment of candidates, local influences remain important.

On a spectrum of modes of selection ranging from local to national, France holds an intermediate position. For a long time, the selection of candidates for general elections remained in the hands of local élites, particularly in parties of the Right. Only the Communist Party eschewed this localism, taking care to avoid what Maurice Thorez called 'municipal cretinism' by preventing most Communist mayors from presenting themselves as candidates in national elections. Even the SFIO included local leaders and faithful supporters who were impervious to the influence of the party's national organization. For centre and right-wing parties (particularly the Radicals and Independents) individual personalities and local standing regularly constituted determining criteria in the selection of candidates.

With the advent of the Fifth Republic, accompanied by a progressive bipolarization of political life and a restructuring of political parties, national considerations gradually grew in importance compared to local ones in the selection of candidates. Deputies who were recalcitrant or too independent-minded were hauled back into line and forced to knuckle under or else to face the challenge of candidates 'parachuted' in from above. The Gaullist party (UNR) led the way in the adoption of a centralized and disciplined strategy, favoured as it was by the two trump cards that it held: the fact that it was already in power, and the authority of its charismatic leader. Thanks to the support forthcoming from an electorate fed up with unstable governments and parliamentary indiscipline, Deputies were soon forced to recognize that the impact of personality was declining in elections, as the national aspects of political life became more important. Nevertheless, it would be mistaken to conclude that the 'local factors in national political life' (to borrow Albert Mabileau's expression) disappeared completely. Central-party intervention most frequently takes place when a strong lead is needed, whether to resolve a conflict at the local level or to persuade a worthy but ageing incumbent to pass on the torch. Otherwise, central party offices tend to ratify local choices. For them to do otherwise would entail a range of possible costs: the demobilization of the local party section, or the risk of deselected candidates with good local support standing as independents, dividing the voters, or even winning themselves. The French position is thus a delicate balance. Most independent notables, however deep their local roots, find it hard to survive more than one or two elections without a party label. On the other hand, French parties are organizationally weaker than many of their counterparts elsewhere in Europe, and cannot afford to disregard the situation on the ground.

The British case can be seen as one or two degrees more centralized than the French. In the first place, local roots count for less: while independents and party defectors may win the occasional by-election, they are invariably defeated at general elections (unless they have joined another party in the meantime). As Monica Charlot writes,

When voters go to the polls, they are more concerned with political labels than with the personality of the candidates. For an aspiring candidate, the most difficult task is to secure selection as the Conservative or the Labour candidate for a seat that is not impregnable. In the electoral race in Britain, it is far harder to qualify as a candidate than to win in the grand finale.[15]

Secondly, many constituencies are normally (barring landslides, as in 1983 or 1997) considered safe for one party or another: Labour's strongholds in Scotland and Wales, the Conservatives' bastions in rural and south-east England. Thirdly, each of the major parties holds a national list of approved candidates: while it is generally quite long, certainly longer than the number of safe or even winnable seats available (especially in the case of the Liberal Democrats), almost every aspiring candidate is obliged to go through a national selection process as the first step to adoption as a candidate. Fourthly, there are well-documented cases, at least on the Labour side, of the party's National Executive Committee, which is ultimately responsible for candidate selection, stepping in to deselect a candidate it does not like (notably members of the so-called Militant Tendency, especially in the 1980s).[16] Labour also has special rules allowing party headquarters to choose candidates in by-elections, which are considered to be especially sensitive by virtue of the national media attention they attract. Yet despite all of these elements pointing towards centralization, a significant measure of local autonomy remains, with local party selection committees normally being more or less free to choose between several candidates from the national list.[17] This can have consequences that the national parties regret, quite aside from the inevitable choice of a handful of incompetent or unsuitable candidates in every intake. For example, while Conservative Central Office would have liked, in the abstract, to see more women candidates, nine out of ten Tory selection committees in 1992 and 1997—many of them, ironically, run by women—chose a (generally white, middle-aged) man to run. For Central Office to have taken any serious steps to change this would have involved a degree of direct central intervention that went against the party's traditions.

More control, finally, is afforded to parties under proportional systems, where the positioning of candidates on big nationwide or regional lists is crucial to their chances of victory, and rebel lists are almost always doomed to failure. The term *Parteienstaat* in Germany and *Partitocrazia* in Italy reflects this among many other phenomena. Von Beyme clearly demonstrates that election to the German Bundestag is a matter for professionals.[18] Since 1953, not a single independent candidate has won a seat in Parliament, despite the fact that the German Constitutional Court has pronounced favourably on the subject of political pluralism (declaring that the parties should not monopolize the public finances available for elections and that all candidates who have obtained at least 1.1 per cent of the vote should also receive State subsidies). A further sign of the power of West German parties came in October and December 1990. In the context of a dearth of East German politicians untainted by association with the old regime, a number of Western politicians stood in Eastern seats at *Land* and federal elections, one getting elected Prime Minister of Saxony.[19]

However, despite the predominance of national organizations, selection is not and has not been totally centralized. In Germany, among the members of the Bundestag elected within the constituency framework (half of the total), the advantage goes to candidates who can count on strong local support. In pre-1992 Italy all the parties had to take account of the 'barons' who controlled the major strongholds, and to satisfy the internal factions (especially within the Christian Democrat organization) which were themselves to a large extent territorial. Before 1992, furthermore, the preference vote which made a personal choice possible counterbalanced party influence, at least in the cases of those seeking re-election; there is reason to suppose that the nursing of the new single-member constituencies will have an effect at least comparable, even if, in 1994 and 1996, the move to local candidate choice that might be expected to result from the move to single-member constituencies was to some extent balanced by the role of parties in the intense pre-poll negotiations necessary to fix alliances.

The formal procedures set up by the parties mask a more fundamental reality. To a large extent, the selection of candidates has already taken place very early on, and the jockeying for position within the political parties is simply the last stage in a sequence of more subterranean processes of elimination.

Those processes are partly of a political nature. The first point to note is that, in the major European parties at least, the competition is limited to a small fraction of citizens, namely voters who are also party activists. In other words, while it is true that election to parliament often leads to those elected becoming political 'specialists', that election is itself very often preceded by a period of training that turns the candidate into a party or political professional. Giuseppe Di Palma and Maurizio Cotta produced an interesting study of this phenomenon, in the form of a longitudinal analysis of the Italian Parliament from 1948 to the end of the 1970s. It shows that the number of Deputies without any previous party experience fell sharply (from 22 per cent up to the third legislature to 11 per cent up until the 1970s, and thereafter to 4 per cent). Meanwhile, an increasing number of Deputies had held some party post before the age of 25 (50 per cent each in the case of the Christian Democrats and the Socialists, 76 per cent in that of the Communists). Given that the average age on election had not dropped since 1948, the study gives some idea of the length of the path that might eventually lead to the goals of selection and election. The authors conclude as follows: 'The average deputy is increasingly often an individual who has completed a long party apprenticeship.'[20] The same phenomenon is to be found in many other countries, particularly in left-wing parties, where selection is the ultimate reward for party activism.[21] There are a handful of exceptions to this general rule. In France, the main parties of government have all recruited non-party figures (ranging from the former European Commissioner Raymond Barre to the founder of Médecins sans Frontières, Bernard Kouchner) directly to government, asking them to work their way into a constituency only after the event. Communists have also sought 'fellow-travellers', sympathizers well-known in other fields, to carry their banner and improve their image in a handful of areas. And Silvio Berlusconi had to bring together a mixed bag of candidates, including his own employees, media personalities, managers, and members of the liberal professions when he launched Forza Italia just months before the 1994 elections.

Finally, long before it ever comes to official procedures, selection is also a social matter. The importance of the position of a member of parliament is such that all candidates are expected to possess special qualities and attributes, or at least ones that are *judged to be so* by all concerned, from the parties and candidates themselves down to the party activists and the voters. The fact is that, unlike working-class parties, which seek to identify their representatives with those represented, most political parties and voters have a more or less hierarchical concept of political representation. The representative is expected to possess qualities and skills that render him *worthy* to be put forward. On top of all this, the voter has a traditional (if stereotyped) image of a 'good' candidate for parliament or the presidency.[22] A mysterious alchemy is at work here, in which objective, structural, and historical elements are complemented by subjective views, and the latter frequently make all the difference.

Elected representatives

The modes of recruitment for Upper House members of parliament are so varied that it would be pointless to try to compare the Italian and the French Senates, the Bundesrat, and the House of Lords. On the other hand it *is* possible to sketch a rough portrait of a 'typical' Western member of parliament. For despite the diversity of national electoral systems, there are striking similarities in the sociological profile of those elected, similarities that are, furthermore, progressively being reinforced. The typical Lower House member of parliament in a European democracy reappears everywhere, with remarkably few variants: he is male, mature, middle-class, well educated, and nowadays increasingly likely to be a professional politician.

Female members of parliament are few, but their numbers are growing. In Britain, where as recently as 1983 there were a mere 23 women out of 650 MPs, the figure had risen to 60 by 1992, and then doubled to 120 (over 100 of them Labour) in 1997. In France, the Left's victory in the 1997 elections brought the number of women to 63 (42 of them Socialists) out of 577, breaking through the 10 per cent barrier for the first time. In Italy, the proportion of women in the Chamber was limited to 8 per cent on average between 1948 and 1983, but had reached 15.1 per cent by 1994. In Germany, where the percentage (in the West) was just 10 in 1983, women won 26 per cent of the Bundestag seats in 1994. The precise reasons for this quite rapid increase since the mid-1980s are uncertain, but two points stand out. First, growth has been disproportionately concentrated among left-wing parliamentarians, primarily socialists (and also, in Germany, the Greens, the only party in which women parliamentarians have outnumbered their male colleagues). And it has coincided with a period when the role of male, unionized, industrial communities in their recruitment has declined. Secondly, growth has resulted from deliberate party policy. In Britain, Labour's attempt at requiring some constituencies to draw up all-women shortlists was unsuccessful in narrow terms, but almost certainly encouraged selection committees to move in this direction. In France, Lionel Jospin let it be known that he was considering a (somewhat problematic) constitutional amendment to give women parity of representation. In Germany the task was made rather simpler by the national list system, allowing a more incremental move to a 'balanced ticket'. Whether these changes will be confirmed in future is uncertain, and depends in great part upon the right-wing parties; but it is at least worth considering that, were the mathematical rate of increase prevailing since the mid-1980s to be sustained, women would achieve parity in parliaments within a generation.

European members of parliament are mostly mature. The youngest citizens (18–25) and the oldest are largely absent from parliamentary Assemblies, most of the elected members falling into the 40–60 age group. Forty per cent of the German Deputies are less than 45 years old, and another 45 per cent are between 45 and 55. In France the average age of elected representatives in 1978 and 1981 was, respectively, 51 and 49 (while the average age of candidates was, respectively, 46 and 48: yet another illustration of the preference given to the older men in this career).

Identical situations obtain in Italy and Britain. In Britain, however, there was for a long time a marked difference between Conservative and Labour Members of Parliament. Conservatives, who came from privileged circles, won their seats in Parliament at an earlier age and were, on average, seven years younger than their Labour counterparts. For the latter, as Monica Charlot has pointed out, a seat in Parliament was 'in most cases the accolade granted in return for previous activism'.[23] However, the process of change amongst the political personnel of the Labour Party over the last 20 years has virtually eliminated that difference.

From the point of view of their level of education, members of parliament differ greatly from the citizens whom they represent. Their qualifications are no doubt particularly important in a profession that has traditionally depended largely on an ability to communicate and be articulate. In any event, politicians are not only educated but increasingly well educated. In 1976, Robert Putnam published a study of élite groups in Europe.[24] On the basis of the sample studied, it showed that 88 per cent of the members of Congress in the United States, 65 per cent of Members of Parliament in the United Kingdom, 76 per cent of Italian Deputies, and 69 per cent of members of the Bundestag in West Germany held university degrees. All the studies, whether based on wider samples or on parliamentary groups alone, come to the same conclusions, even if the results show a few variations. Furthermore, all the evidence points to a rising level in the education of members of parliament, so far as can be seen from the examinations that they have passed. In 1951, only 57 per cent of British Members of Parliament held university degrees. But that figure had risen to 68 per cent by 1979 and to 79 per cent by 1983 (when 36 per cent held degrees from either Oxford or Cambridge). In the Bundestag, the percentages of members with a university education rose from 52.3 per cent in 1953 to 70.5 per cent in 1980.[25] Roland Cayrol *et al.*[26] have revealed a similar situation in France, as has Maurizio Cotta in Italy.[27]

This continuous progression is to a large extent a result of the increasingly homogeneous nature of the circles from which members of parliament are recruited. In other words, what Giovanni Sartori has called the 'rule of distance' (meaning the distance that disadvantaged citizens have to cover before they can be selected as parliamentary candidates) has progressively narrowed. Thus in Italy, Maurizio Cotta, who estimates the number of Italian Deputies between 1946 and 1976 to have attended a university at 73 per cent, goes on to draw attention to inter-party disparities. 70 per cent of the Socialists and 84 per cent of the Christian Democrats held university degrees, as against 43 per cent of the Communists. A similar imbalance was noticeable between the Conservative and the Labour parties in the British House of Commons up until the mid-1960s, at least. However, among the Italian Communists, the British Labour Members of Parliament, and the German Social Democrats alike, the percentage of representatives with no university education has fallen. In 1970, for example, 53.7 per cent of Labour representatives as against 63 per cent of Conservatives held university degrees, whereas up until the late 1950s a difference of 20 per cent had separated the two parties.

Given the high level of education of members of parliament, it is not surprising to find that most belong to the highest socio-professional categories. This holds good for the Western parliaments in general, all of which—we are bound to recognize—are almost totally inaccessible to the most disadvantaged social categories. Manual workers, in particular, are noticeably absent from the parliaments of the Western democracies. In the Bundestag, the political personnel comprises an estimated 1 per cent of workers;[28] in France 2–3 per cent of Deputies come from the working class.[29] However, working-class representation has been higher in Italy, thanks to the Italian Communist Party, and also in Britain, thanks to the Labour Party. Maurizio Cotta estimates that Italian Deputies of working-class origin account for 17 per cent of the total (36 per cent of

Communist Party representatives) in the 1946–76 period. In Britain, MPs with a background as manual workers accounted for nearly 20 per cent of the Labour Party total (but only 1 per cent of Conservatives) as late as 1979. But such MPs, like their counterparts in the French and Italian Communist parties, have generally left behind manual jobs for full-time union or party activity years before being elected to Parliament. Going straight from manual labour to a seat in a legislature has been almost unknown in Western European countries since the Second World War. Except in Britain from 1930 to 1950, even the wider group of those with manual or working-class backgrounds has been consistently and colossally under-represented in Western parliaments.

On the other hand, it is fair to draw attention to the political decline of the highest social classes, in particular the aristocracy and the *grande bourgeoisie*. In Germany and Italy they have virtually disappeared, partly as a result of their compromises with these countries' totalitarian regimes, but in France, too, their decline has been continuous ever since the nineteenth century, and in Britain it has been particularly rapid since Lords have had to renounce their titles in order to sit in the House of Commons. The House of Lords is certainly a bastion of the aristocracy but its political role is limited. The same goes for the other two groups that used, in the past, to be dominant: the military and the clergy. In Britain, soldiers must resign or retire before becoming eligible to the Commons, and Church of England or Roman Catholic priests must resign; but without such restrictions, soldiers and priests are also virtually absent from other Western parliaments, even if the Church and the military continue to wield considerable influence.

Most members of parliament come from what Colette Ysmal calls 'categories with a high social status'.[30] The profile of this group is certainly by no means sharply defined, but the description at least identifies the category as a whole better than even vaguer terms such as 'middle class' or 'bourgeois'. Analyses of the composition of the parliamentary group show that its members are essentially drawn from what might be called the 'privileged' professions. The 'privileges' involved are of many kinds and also vary in degree from one political system to another, but we can at least survey them rapidly. Some, of course, are financial privileges, but others are social (membership of the social élite), professional, or to do with status (membership of the Civil Service). The profile of members of parliament varies from one system to another depending on the dominant values and the scope of the privileges involved, but the essential point is that most come from well-to-do categories. The following socioprofessional categories stand out among the dominant groups.

Civil servants

Civil servants constitute a major group in the parliaments of mainland Europe, especially if teachers are included in this category (as, technically, they are, in terms of employment status, in France, Germany, and Italy). This was true particularly of West Germany, where the percentage of public employees rose from 16.8 per cent in the first legislature to 49.8 per cent in the eighth.[31] In France, on average 30 per cent of Deputies came from the public sector between 1958 and 1978, a percentage that has continued to rise: 31.5 per cent in 1973, 40.7 per cent in 1978, and 53.1 per cent in 1981—though this last figure was exceptionally high and may be attributed to the landslide of the teacher-ridden Socialist Party. In both countries, the increasing strength of public employees may be partly explained by the statutory facilities (leave with job security and sometimes a salary) available to civil servants, but it is also due to the prestige of the higher echelons of the bureaucracy who are allowed to move freely in and out of politics if they choose. On the other hand, in Italy, where public employees enjoy similar facilities, the percentage of civil servants is lower and on the wane, chiefly due to the poor reputation of the Italian bureaucracy.[32] They account for barely 2 or 3 per cent of the total number of parliamentary representatives, but to this should be added the 18 per cent of professors, whose numbers are also falling. In 1994, 9 per cent of Italy's Deputies were university professors, 10 per cent were other teachers, and 9 per cent were other public servants. However, this relative weakness of the public sector is made up for by the increasing number of professional politicians who have emerged from the various parties and trade unions. They are truly the bureaucrats of the political apparatus and their entire careers have evolved within these organizations. During the sixth legislature, 89 per cent of the Communist Deputies, 81 per cent of the Christian Democrats, and 66 per cent of the Socialists had begun their careers with duties at a local level[33] (and 60 per cent of Deputies had been party activists before the age of eligibility, which is 25).

In Britain, in contrast, serving civil servants and members of the armed forces are barred from engaging in political activity. The obligation to resign one's job before even becoming a candidate is a powerful disincentive from embarking on a political career; few (Foreign Secretary and former diplomat Douglas Hurd being a notable exception) have been inclined to take the risk. Teachers and university lecturers, on the other hand, do not enjoy the status or suffer from the constraints of civil servants in Britain, and under the (tiny or relative) Labour majorities of the 1970s these groups actually overtook lawyers briefly to become the largest occupational category in the Commons.

Industrialists, businessmen, and members of the liberal professions

This is the second most important group, somewhat heterogeneous, but its members possess at least one common characteristic, namely, assured economic independence. In 1981, for example, the French National Assembly included 6 per cent of industrialists and businessmen (17 per cent in 1978) and 16 per cent from the liberal professions (28 per cent in 1978: the decline in 1981 again reflecting that year's Socialist landslide).

In Germany, professional nomenclature makes it difficult to establish any precise comparison with France. However, of the members of the ninth West German Bundestag (1980–3), 5.6 per cent came from the legal profession, 9.6 per cent from independent professions, and 2.3 per cent from the world of journalism. In Italy, roughly one-third of parliamentary representatives came from independent professions (whether the liberal professions, industry, or trade) before 1992. With the entry of Forza Italia onto the scene and the decline of Christian Democracy this proportion rose to nearly 43 per cent, of whom some 16 per cent were business people or managers and 26 per cent lawyers or other professionals. In the United Kingdom, business people dominate the Conservative Party in Parliament (193 MPs, or 51.5 per cent of the total elected in 1987), but are rare among Labour MPs (just 11 of the 1987 group, or 4.8 per cent of the total). The professions (including university teachers but excluding journalists) are much more evenly balanced between the parties (125, or 33.3 per cent for the Conservatives in 1987, and 94, or 41.0 per cent for Labour)—though within this total, there are likely to be more lawyers among the Conservatives and more teachers in the Labour ranks.[34]

Professional politicians

In Germany and Italy, the number in this group is on the increase. One-third of Italian and German parliamentary representatives may be classed in this category. The proportion is probably lower in France and Britain (by reason, in particular, of a voting system that is more uncertain for candidates who have emerged from the political apparatus), but here too there is a trend towards political professionalism. The requirements of the job now make it difficult for parliamentarians to engage actively in another career while serving in parliament. It is also the case, however, that the frontiers between professional backgrounds are often unclear, and parliamentarians frequently do not fit into single categories. For example, an MP who gives his or her profession as journalist, or researcher, or local government officer, may in reality have long been a professional politician learning the trade. Similarly, individuals may become lawyers because they aspire to be legislators, and value both the professional apprenticeship and the relative freedom to dispose of one's time that the legal profession offers. These uncertain boundaries between professions may amount to no more than statistical pitfalls awaiting the sociologist of élites, but they may, in some cases, correspond to something else: to a confusion between public office and work aimed at the accumulation of private wealth. This was an important issue in the Major government in Britain, where the tendency of many Conservative MPs to use their position in the Commons to run business 'consultancies', at times taking fees for work done in the Commons, led to numerous opposition allegations of 'sleaze', and some well-publicized lying by MPs and junior ministers. This type of problem is unlikely to go away, particularly as the gap between the high and rising pay available to private-sector managers and the relatively modest salary of an MP continues to grow.

The sociological profiles of the elected members of parliament in the various Western democracies thus present more similarities than profound differences. The first feature to note is an increasing professionalism that calls for those elected to devote themselves full-time to politics. Nowadays, an elected member of parliament lives *for* and *by* politics. This is a consequence of the growing importance and influence of the political parties, but meanwhile the parties themselves are strengthened by the professionalism of their personnel. The age of the 'amateur' in politics has given way to that of the professional. And, more and more, the professional politician is required also to be an expert in the field of communications, capable of operating within the media and making the most of the means of political marketing.

One area in which the European democracies differ from one another, however, is the local affiliations of their politicians and the avenues open to them to achieving national election. In Britain, a local political career and a national one are not generally complementary; either they are sequential, with local office serving in effect as an apprenticeship, or they develop along parallel lines. A stint as a local councillor remains an asset for the aspiring MP: 57 per cent of the Conservatives first elected in 1992, and two-thirds of their Labour counterparts, had local government experience. But this experience was not always anywhere near the constituency: only 22 per cent of Conservative MPs elected in 1992 had this experience of local government close to the constituency, for example. And most MPs resigned from their council posts or scaled down their activities upon election. The local loyalties of MPs are therefore relative, the more so if, as is often the case, they are geographically mobile. The case of the former Conservative Home Secretary, Michael Howard, born in Wales, a graduate of Cambridge, and a practising lawyer in London, who fought an impossible seat in Liverpool before getting a safe one in Folkestone, is by no means exceptional. However, constituency work is more and more necessary if MPs wish to maintain support among the local electorate.

A system more different from that which obtains in France would be hard to imagine, for here, on the contrary, the accumulation of elected offices (*cumul des mandats*) constitutes one of the most solid cultural and political conventions of political life, with between 75 and 85 per cent of Deputies in the last four National Assemblies holding local office, 50 per cent as mayors. The reforms introduced in December 1985 to check the practice of accumulating elected offices only partially limited the excesses of a phenomenon that remains unique, without equivalent in the other Western democracies, all of which either prohibit such practices legally or discourage them culturally. The practice of accumulating responsibilities can certainly be advantageous: it provides an antidote to the excessive centralization of power, makes it possible to reconcile the antagonistic views that may be held by the centre and by the periphery, and encourages the consideration of local views at the level of parliamentary and governmental decision-making. But on balance, its negative points weigh heavily. Too much power and influence are concentrated in a few hands; real power tends to be transferred to technical experts or non-elected right-hand men, since the Deputy himself cannot manage to be in two places at once; the *deus ex machina* type of local boss, who constitutes the linch-pin between local and central affairs and between the political and the administrative spheres, acquires an exaggerated importance.

Such is the strength of these local leaders, deeply entrenched in their local strongholds, and discharging a series of interdependent functions, that attempts to introduce reforms that might threaten their status have all failed, including plans to reform the Senate, to merge communes, and to reorganize department boundaries. The fact that the limitations set on the *cumul des mandats* were eventually unenthusiastically accepted can only be explained by the coincidence of two factors. One was the creation of a fourth electoral level (the region), which made it impossible for local Deputies to discharge every single function at every single level; the other was the need, in 1985–6, for many Socialist Deputies to make sure of a few seats at regional level, in default of seats in Parliament.[35] More recently, the *cumul des mandats* has been proved to have been a crucial element in the system of corruption which has financed French political parties over recent decades. As local and regional government accounts for well over half France's total non-military investment, the opportunities available are obvious. France's decentralization reforms, which were set in motion in 1982, probably contributed to the development of local corruption, by removing some of the State controls on the activities of municipalities, *départements*, and regions; but they were certainly not at the origin of the problem. The (almost certainly unfinished) series of corruption scandals that shook France in the early and mid-1990s brought the *cumul des mandats* back to the centre of public debate, and Lionel Jospin has promised to restrict it further. Whether this would be allowed by the Senate, which is composed of men who owe their seats to electors from among mayors and local councillors, is uncertain. For the moment, the *cumul* is sufficiently ingrained in French political mores for the reaction to Jospin's plea to his own ministers to resign from their local government posts to have been broadly hostile—even from his own side.

Such accumulation of responsibilities is extremely rare in Italy and Germany, since here the general system of proportional representation and the control over the political system wielded by the various political parties make it necessary for electoral rewards to be distributed as widely as possible among party activists at both local and national levels. Political careers thus evolve under the aegis of the party and in progressive stages, moving on from the local to an intermediate level (province, region, or *Land*, as the case may be) and in some cases from there to the national level. In Germany, particularly, since half the members of the Bundestag are elected within the constituency framework, where it is possible for the voters to indicate their choices for particular individuals, representatives have the opportunity to develop deep local roots. However, careers at local and national levels have tended to progress successively, rather than simultaneously.

Questions

- Can any one electoral system be said to be more 'moral' than the alternatives?

- Compare and contrast the circumstances of France's changes of electoral system in the 1980s with Italy's in 1993.

- Why is the social recruitment to legislatures so restricted? Is this state of affairs likely to continue?

- Why is selection as a candidate so often the same as election as a parliamentarian in Western democracies?

NOTES

1. G. Sartori, *Théorie de la démocratie* (Paris: Colin, 1973), 84.
2. R. Hrbek, 'La Réalité du mode de scrutin allemand', *Pouvoirs*, 32 (1985), 67–82.
3. G. Amato, 'Le Système électoral', *Pouvoirs*, 18 (1981), 49–58.
4. Apart from the elimination clause of 5%.
5. e.g. in a department with two seats at its disposal, the votes obtained by all the lists apart from the top two are 'lost'. If the two elected share between them 70% of the votes (40% and 30% respectively), the remaining 30% of voters remain unrepresented. Cf. A. Knapp, 'Proportional but Bipolar: France's Electoral System in 1986', *West European Politics*, 10(1) (Jan. 1987).
6. See G. Pasquino, 'I Sistemi elettorali', in G. Amato and A. Barbara (eds.), *Manuale di diritto pubblico* (Bologna: Il Mulino, 1981).
7. F. Lanchester, *Sistemi elettorali a forma di governo?* (Bologna: Il Mulino, 1981).
8. Amato, 'Le Système électoral', 52–3.
9. In West Germany, the Constitutional Court monitored the rule according to which a constituency population was not supposed to exceed or fall short of the average constituency population figure by more than 25%. In its decision of 22 May 1963, the Court declared: 'The constituency boundaries have become unconstitutional in that they clearly no longer correspond to the distribution of the population, and it is no longer likely that the distortion will rectify itself. The federal legislator is consequently to proceed to change the constituency boundaries during the present legislature.'
10. The Constitutional Council had already marked out the guidelines for its jurisprudence in a decision relating to New Caledonia in 1985—ironically, in a ruling requested by the Right when in opposition.
11. Decision no. 86.208 of 1/2 July 1986, and 86.218 of 18 July 1986.
12. Maurice Duverger, 'Which is the Best Electoral System?', in A. Lijphart and B. Grofman (eds.), *Choosing an Electoral System* (New York: Praeger, 1984), 35.
13. M. Beloff and G. Peele, *The Government of the UK: Political Authority in a Changing Society*, 2nd edn. (London: Weidenfeld and Nicolson, 1985), 169.
14. Ibid.

15. M. Charlot, *Le Système politique britannique*, Coll. U (Paris: Colin, 1976).

16. P. Paterson, *The Selectorate: The Case for Primary Elections in Britain* (London: MacGibbon and Kee, 1967).

17. A. Ranney, *Pathways to Parliament: Candidate Selection in Britain* (London: Macmillan, 1965); M. Rush, *The Selection of Parliamentary Candidates* (London: Nelson, 1969); P. W. Buck, *Amateurs and Professionals in British Politics, 1918–1959* (Chicago: University of Chicago Press, 1963).

18. K. Von Beyme, 'The Role of Deputies in West Germany', in E. Suleiman (ed.), *Parliaments and Parliamentarians in Democratic Politics* (New York: Holmes and Meier, 1986), 156.

19. K. Von Beyme, *The Political System of the Federal Republic of Germany* (Farnborough, Hants: Gower, 1985), 28; K. Von Beyme, 'Electoral Unification: The First German Elections in December 1990', *Government and Opposition*, 26(2) (Spring 1991), 167–84.

20. G. Di Palma and M. Cotta, 'Cadres, Peones and Entrepreneurs: Professional Identities in a Divided Parliament', in Suleiman (ed.), *Parliaments and Parliamentarians in Democratic Politics*, 57.

21. Charlot, *Le Système politique britannique*, 105.

22. D. Butler and D. Stokes, *Political Change in Britain: The Evolution of Electoral Choice* (London: Macmillan, 1974).

23. Charlot, *Le Système politique britannique*, 105.

24. R. D. Putnam, *The Comparative Study of Political Élites* (Englewood Cliffs, NJ: Prentice Hall, 1976).

25. All these figures are taken from a study of 'The Political Class in European Parliamentary Regimes (France, Belgium, West Germany, Britain)', carried out by J.-P. Caille within the framework of the DEA de sciences politiques of the University of Paris II, Feb. 1985 (unpublished).

26. R. Cayrol, J.-L. Parodi, C. Ysmal, *Le Deputé français* (Paris: FNSP, 1973).

27. Cotta, *Classe politica e parlamento in Italia*.

28. H. Haack, *Die Personnelle Struktur des 9 Deutschen Bundestages: Ein Beitrag Zur Abgeordnetensoziologie* (Bonn: Z Parl 1981), 185.

29. Cayrol *et al.*, *Le Deputé français*; R. Cayrol, 'Beaucoup plus d'enseignants, moins d'industriels et de paysans', *Le Monde*, 23 June 1981.

30. C. Ysmal, 'Élites et leaders', in J. Leca and M. Grawitz (eds.), *Traité de science politique*, iii (Paris: PUF, 1985), 616f.

31. H. Neumann, *Zur Machtstruktur in der Bundesrepublik Deutschland* (Munich: Knoth, 1979).

32. Di Palma and Cotta, 'Cadres, Peones and Entrepreneurs', 53.

33. Ibid. 57.

34. M. Rush, 'The Members of Parliament', in M. Ryle and P. G. Richards (eds.), *The Commons under Scrutiny* (London: Routledge, 1988), 25.

35. J. Becquart-Leclercq, 'Cumul des mandats et culture politique', in A. Mabileau (ed.), *Les Pouvoirs locaux à l'épreuve de la décentralisation* (Paris: Pedone, 1983), 207–39; A. Mabileau, 'La Limitation du cumul des mandats: Illusion électoraliste ou modernisation démocratique?', in *Annuaire des collectivités locales 1986* (Paris: LITEC, GRAL, 1986); A. Knapp, 'The *Cumul des Mandats*, Local Power and Political Parties in France', *West European Politics* 14(1) (Jan. 1991).

CHAPTER 5

Parliaments

If there is one symbol that stands for a representative system, it is certainly that of the Assembly, a collegial body through which the will of all (or part) of the population is expressed. As such, it is indissociable from the liberal democracies: all are constructed around the Assembly or on the basis of it. Any attack against the organization, composition, or functioning of the representative Assembly is seen as an attack or blow against democracy. We should remember that, in France, the right of dissolution lapsed under the Third and Fourth Republics until 1955, because it was considered to encourage potential *coups d'état*. Nor should we forget the way in which classic parliamentary structures have been debased or eliminated under Fascist, Nazi, Francoist, and other authoritarian regimes. However, while the fundamental place of parliament in democratic symbolism may be undisputed, its real role and influence are more debatable. John Locke's opinion was that parliament 'holds the supreme power of the commonwealth', but that view no longer seems appropriate even in Britain, where the saying 'Parliament can do anything except change a man into a woman' survives more out of habit than any desire for accuracy. So should parliaments now be regarded purely as 'rump' Assemblies, theatres of illusion, or even mere 'rubber-stamp chambers'? Or ought we, rather, to take Pierre Avril's[1] view that the transformations undergone by Western parliaments constitute a realignment, an adaptation to the new political and social conditions that obtain in the Western democracies as a whole?

The latter seems a more accurate and realistic interpretation than those that emphasize the inexorable decline of Western parliaments. For we should recognize that the decline to which they point is a relative one. It is true that today most of the laws that parliaments pass have been prepared by the executive. But parliaments possess other means of influence: they can introduce amendments, apply pressure through the majority party or coalition, mobilize public opinion, and so on. Admittedly, their powers of control over the executive appear to have declined. But are we not here confusing the issues of agitation and instability with that of democratic control? In France, in particular, diagnoses of her Parliament's decline are too often based on comparisons with the Third and Fourth Republics, despite the fact that these can hardly be claimed to provide satisfactory models. Furthermore, comparison with what some consider to have been the Golden Age of parliamentarianism, that is to say, the nineteenth century, is not convincing either. Given the changing modes of electing Assemblies (limited suffrage, incomplete universal suffrage, the existence of rotten boroughs in England, non-secret voting, the exclusion of women: all are features of the past) and the differences in means of communication and in economic and social structures, any comparison in this area calls for extreme prudence. It would, after all, not occur to us to bewail the decline of modern executives on the grounds that they have become less authoritarian than they used to be in the nineteenth century. Parliaments have undeniably changed and evolved (there have even been initiatives in recent years, such as the reforms to the French Parliament undertaken by the National Assembly President Philippe Séguin after 1993, to reinforce them). But, as we assess the transformations that have taken place, we should take care not to compare them to an idealized version of the past.

In the theory and practice of the representative system, parliaments have been assigned three functions: representation, decision, and control over the executive. Each of these functions has gone through considerable changes during recent years and within each country.

The function of representation: one or two chambers?

In principle, the theory of representation seems incompatible with the idea of more than one chamber of representatives. How is it possible for the people as a whole to be represented by two or three different Assemblies? Yet, in fact, a large number of Western States organize their parliamentary representation using two chambers: the United States, Germany, Switzerland, Holland, Britain, Italy, Spain, France, etc. However, the origin, justification, and powers of the second chamber differ. By and large, it is possible to distinguish between two groups: on the one hand States in which the second chamber is a product of a federal or regional structure, on the other those in which the upper house is a survival from the country's constitutional past (Britain and France, for example). Generally speaking, the powers of the upper chamber are far less extensive than those of the lower; this is certainly the case of the French Senate, and to an even greater extent of the British House of Lords. In Italy, by contrast, the powers of the two chambers are identical and the modalities by which their members are elected are so similar that neither could claim to be any more representative or more democratic than the other. The US Senate is something of an exception in that it is in some ways *more* powerful than the House of Representatives, having specific responsibilities in foreign policy and in the appointment of high-ranking federal officials (though the House has the monopoly on initiating finance bills). The German Bundesrat, finally, occupies an intermediate position, lacking legislative equality with the Bundestag but wielding powers to block some legislation that its British or French counterparts do not have. The survival of such an anachronistic and unrepresentative institution as the British House of Lords results in large part from its own policy of 'self-restraint' and the application of what, since 1945, has been known as the 'Salisbury doctrine', after the then Conservative leader of the Lords. According to Lord Salisbury, it would have been unseemly, after the Labour victory of 1945, for the Conservatives to use their majority in the House of Lords to oppose the manifesto policies on which the Labour Party had won a majority in the Commons. To adopt any other attitude would have been suicidal. Half a century later, however, even self-restraint appeared insufficient to preserve the Lords from the Blair Government's programme of constitutional reform, starting with the end of voting rights for hereditary peers.

The French Senate, whose representative character also leaves much to be desired, has not adopted the same acquiescent attitude to government policy as the British House of Lords. Senators are elected by universal suffrage, but only at one remove: their major electors are themselves elected locally, but the rural areas are over-represented and most of the major urban electors are selected by local representatives, in other words by local élites or by the party apparatuses. Furthermore, Senators, who are elected for a period of nine years, survive politically despite the changes that may come about in the electoral college. Under de Gaulle, they remained recalcitrant to Gaullism (and it was a failed attempt to reform the Senate that triggered the General's departure). After 1981, the upper house (which has *never* had a clear left-wing majority) became the main bastion of resistance to the Socialists. Yet the fact that the representative nature of a Senator's mandate is progressively diluted by reason of the very length of its duration is an issue that is seldom raised. Some historical accidents (such as the seven-year tenure of a French President) end up by becoming facts of life that are highly resistant to change.

Historical survivals are also detectable—but in a more marginal fashion—in the Italian Senate which, alongside the Senators elected by majorities and by proportional representation, includes five Senators appointed for life by the President of the Republic. The fact that the Senate is representative and possesses powers similar to those of the

Chamber of Deputies creates political and constitutional difficulties comparable to those posed by the Senate of the Third Republic in France. Furthermore, its very existence and *raison d'être* are in question. After all, what is the point of having two chambers which, apart from the minor differences in the modalities of electing their members and the greater ages required both for voters and for candidates for election in the Upper House, are bound to be identical? There have been many proposals on ways of giving it a function and complexion of its own that would mark it out from the Chamber of Deputies. Attempts have been made to turn it into a Senate for the regions, a territorial chamber that would constitute the apex of the regional structure established during the 1970s. Under the constitutional changes discussed in June 1997, on the other hand, the Senate was to ensure the correct functioning of Italy's institutions. Both ideas reflect the preoccupations of their different times.

It is worth pointing out, though, that the composition of the upper chambers of federal States varies considerably from one system to another. In the United States, Senators, like Representatives, are elected by direct universal suffrage, but there are only two for each state, irrespective of size and population. Alaska, with its 400,000 inhabitants, has the same number of elected Senators as California, with its 24 million citizens, so as to maintain strict equality between all the members of the federal State and to prevent domination by the most highly populated states.

In Germany, on the other hand, the members of the Bundesrat are not 'Members of Parliament' in the *strict* sense of the expression. Article 51 of the Basic Law stipulates that they should be 'members of the *Länder* governments'. Their mandate comes to an end when their governmental functions do. The composition of the Bundesrat thus changes in step with reshuffles, resignations, and changes in the majority of coalition governments. Seats in the Bundesrat go to all *Land* Minister-Presidents, *Land* Ministers of Finance, Home Affairs, and Justice, *Land* representatives to the Bund, and any *Land* Minister affected by a problem being debated by the Bundesrat. However, regardless of how many of its representatives are present, each *Land* also has at its disposal a number of votes calculated on the basis of the size of its population and now (since unification) fixed by the Constitution as follows: 6 each for Bavaria, Baden-Württemberg, Lower Saxony, and North Rhine-Westphalia; 5 for Hesse; 4 each for Rhineland-Palatinate, Berlin, Brandenburg, Saxony, Saxony-Anhalt, Schleswig-Holstein, and Thuringia; 3 each for Saarland, Bremen, Hamburg, and Mecklenburg-Western Pomerania. The presidency of the Bundesrat is subject to equally strict regulations. It is assumed for the period of one year by the Minister-President of each of the *Länder*, according to a system fixed by the Königstein agreement of 30 August 1950. Like the United States Senate, the Bundesrat has an important role to play in the legislative process. But, as the Federal Constitutional Court pointed out in 1974, it does not possess the full legislative powers that are held by the Bundestag. Depending on the issue in question, the Bundesrat may hold either an absolute power of veto or merely the power to suspend proceedings. During the 1970s, the role of the Bundesrat increased in importance, as the CDU–CSU made the most of their majority in the Upper Chamber to mount as energetic as possible an opposition to the policies of the SPD–FDP coalition, in power from 1969 to 1982. In this fashion, the Bundesrat's role of territorial representation for the federated states was in part superseded by a more classically political kind of representation in which the clash of interests between the majority and the opposition is played out. Although the CDU–CSU's majority in the Bundesrat was ended in 1990, the SDP faces some difficulties in putting the upper chamber to similar party-political use; for, by 1996, the SPD was governing five *Länder* in coalition with parties of the national majority: with the FDP in Rhineland-Palatinate, and with the CDU in Berlin, Bremen, Mecklenburg-West Pomerania, and Thuringia. Nevertheless, the importance of the Bundesrat's role, even in financial matters (from which the British House of Lords, for example, has been largely excluded for almost a century) was well demonstrated in 1997, when despite lengthy negotiations it refused to agree to the ambitious tax reform programme presented by the Kohl government.

None the less the lower house is, except in Italy, pre-eminent to a greater or lesser degree by very reason of its strictly representative character. Because it is the best means of expression for the democratically declared will of voters as a whole, the lower house holds wider powers and prerogatives that almost always afford it the final word. This is certainly the case in France and of course Britain, where the official two-chamber system masks what in effect virtually amounts (at least where ordinary legislation is concerned) to a one-chamber system.

The 'privileges' of the lower chambers are justified by their representative character. In reality, as we have seen in Chapter 4, the quality of that representativeness may vary enormously. In the nineteenth century it was minimal, because the masses were largely shut out of the electorate and women were totally excluded. Today, majority electoral systems penalize small parties, while party selection processes, despite a degree of recent feminization, tend to favour white, middle-aged, middle-class men. This unrepresentativeness has been an object of criticism for over a century. One of the purposes of the Labour Representation Committee, founded in 1900 and a predecessor to Britain's Labour Party, was, as its name implied, to get working men into Parliament in the belief that they would further the interests of their class there (they did, but were also increasingly prone to upward social mobility once in the Commons). More recently, initiatives in Britain have sought to bring more ethnic minorities into the legislature and, in Britain, France, and Germany, to increase the representation of women both in legislatures and in governments and party leaderships. One of the arguments underlying such attempts is that the legislature should more closely reflect the sociological balance of society. There are obvious attractions to such a view, even beyond a general notion of 'fairness'. A political system is in danger of losing its legitimacy if too many people believe that no-one at the top is capable of understanding their problems or representing their interests. But it should be stressed that such a mimetic concept of parliamentary representation is no guarantee of good government, or even of representative government. In Germany, for example, an almost perfectly proportional electoral system regularly produces a Bundestag where the decision as to who is to govern Germany depends on which way the little FDP chooses to jump (even if, in practice, the FDP has tended to announce its choice of preferred colour of co-alition partner in advance). Italy's use of almost equally perfect PR over half a century spawned Western Europe's most detested political class, thanks to a succession of elections in which the connection between voter choice and executive outcome was all but severed, leaving the electorate with no apparent way to sanction poor and corrupt government. The attraction of a majority system, for Italians in 1993, was not its repres-entativeness but the unaccustomed chance it offered to make clear political choices.

Legislation

The decision-making role of Assemblies stems from a rational concept and a notion of the division of tasks inspired by anthropomorphic images. According to the democratic concept of representation, sovereignty lies with parliament, which alone has the right to vote on the law. The law is supposed to satisfy a number of essential criteria. It should have priority over every other kind of norm; and it should condition all the decision-making and practical activities of bodies that are inferior or subordinate to parliament, starting with the government itself.

This sublime view of the law finds its fullest expression in the traditions of Britain and France. These assert the absolute supremacy of the law and of any body that ad-ministers it, and the absolute right of parliament to pass laws without any interference from either judges or constitutional texts. Since the Second World War this fine edifice of juridico-political theory has lost some of its lustre. In the first place, the existence of disciplined party majorities has made parliaments appear as rubber stamps that offer legitimacy to 'elective dictatorships': as Gordon Smith put it, 'The processes of legis-lation may seem to be a surviving piece of symbolic ritualism.'[2] Secondly, in both countries, constitutional or quasi-constitutional controls on legislation have appeared: explicitly in France, through the actions of the Constitutional Council (Italy and Germany also have constitutional courts), and implicitly in all European Union coun-tries as a result of the willingness of the European Court of Justice to behave like a constitutional court.

Such developments invite the suggestion that parliaments have fallen from omni-potence to impotence, or at best to a situation in which they enjoy a marginal power of control alongside an executive that takes most of the decisions and a judiciary ready to strike down the unconstitutional ones. What is the situation in reality? Is it true that the Fifth French Republic is characterized by an abasement of Parliament, whereas one outstanding feature of the Italian system is the *centralità del parlamento*? Is the British Parliament still the linch-pin of the political system? What is the role of the Bundestag? A comparison of the decision-making role of these various Assemblies may enable us to gain a less simplistic view of their current situation. Let us consider three different aspects: the division of tasks, the organization of work, and the rules of the game.

The division of tasks

The history of each country has had a powerful effect on the ways in which legislative tasks are divided between parliaments and other bodies. In the French and British models, Parliament has been conceived as central, both functionally and territorially. Parliament was *the* legislator: not only was the executive by definition subordinate to it, but no other authority was empowered to legislate within the national territory. Thus the French Revolution laid the ghosts of the *parlements* of the *ancien régime* when it denied judges any role in the creation of laws; thus, too, the Act of Union between England and Scotland resulted in the abolition of the Scottish Parliament for nearly three centuries. By contrast, in post-war West Germany, and to a lesser extent Italy, the experience of Fascism and Nazism had a substantial, if rather differentiated, institutional impact. In the first place, legislative power was dispersed territorially, in the Federal Republic of Germany especially, but also in Italy to a lesser extent. Secondly, the role of parliaments was conceived in the light of painful inter-war experiences. Parliament became 'central' to the new Italian constitution, as a putative safeguard against Fascism, while in Germany the Bundestag, though very important, was subject to constitutional constraints aimed at avoiding both the paralysis typical of the Weimar years and the possibility of another handover of power to a dictator. Aside from these often idiosyncratic legacies of the past, however, one development common to all Western democracies has had a profound impact on parliaments: the modern State has come to do more things than could possibly be debated or determined adequately in a classic legislative assembly conceived for the more limited activities of bygone centuries. This combination of national histories and cross-national pressures has produced, in each state, a particular division of tasks between parliaments and other actors in the political system: between the legislature and the executive in the first instance, but also between the national legislature and various territorial levels.

The fundamental flaw in the classical system of dividing tasks between the legislature and the executive lies in the rational and hierarchical concept of the process of decision that it implies. The legislative authority decides, the government executes; the first operation necessarily conditions the second. As State intervention has increased in both volume and technicality, that hierarchical vision has turned out to be both impractical and inappropriate. More and more modifications have had to be introduced into the traditional concept of the separation of powers: either tasks are quite simply transferred to the executive, or the executive takes the place of the legislature when it comes to determining the formulation of the rules formally adopted by parliament.

The transfer of powers from the legislature to the executive came about as a consequence of the progressive incapacity of parliaments to cope with crisis situations or, quite simply, with the development of the Welfare State. But different constitutional arrangements deal with these changes in different ways. The Italian case is a fairly extreme example of reluctance to make allowances for them; the result has often been shown to be dysfunctional and, indeed, self-defeating. It repeatedly makes provision for what is known as a *riserva di legge*, that is, certain areas—particularly those concerned with public liberties—which can only be regulated by law. On the other hand, circumstances in which legislative powers may be delegated are also envisaged, albeit with considerable reserve and circumspection. Delegation can only take place once Parliament has laid down principles and guidelines in relation to the delegated material. A time limit is set and an objective carefully defined. Finally, if the government does wish to adopt certain rules, giving them the force of laws, it must bring them before the Chambers on the very same day (but may only do so in cases of absolute necessity and emergency). Such decrees lapse if they are not converted into laws within 60 days of their adoption. But in practice constitutional safeguards have been progressively swept aside. The number of decree-laws has been increasing rapidly: from 29 during the first legislature to 124 during the sixth, 167 during the seventh, and 265 during the eighth. Moreover, the limitations imposed by the Constitution have either been rendered pointless or adroitly sidestepped. For example, in order to avoid its decrees lapsing when the 60-day period is up, the government simply adopts a new, identical decree, to postpone the fateful day for another two months. Similarly, the 'necessity' or 'emergency' required by Article 77 of the Constitution is frequently a matter that goes unverified.

Let us recall the principles involved. In theory, parliament holds overall power. But, despite that power, checks and delays tend to accumulate. For example, in the matter of transmitting European Community directives, Italy constitutes an almost pathological case. In 1981, one-third of the directives were not applied because Parliament never incorporated them into Italian law. To resolve the problem, on 9 February 1982, Law no. 42 was passed, authorizing the government to take the necessary steps for applying ninety-seven directives. So it is Parliament's own inability to come to decisions that causes it to be dispossessed of its powers. Its theoretical rule—of that famous *centralità del parlamento* so often invoked by the Communist Party at the time of the *Unione nazionale*—is replaced by an admission of impotence. Similarly, activism on the part of the government[3] is partly provoked by procedures that prevent it from fully exercising the powers that the Constitution recognizes it to possess. Although it may take the initiative in proposing laws, the fact that the Assemblies control the agenda places the executive in the same position of weakness as that of the government of the Fourth French Republic. It accordingly uses its decree-laws as a means of forcing Parliament to discuss government proposals. They may be treated to a rough ride in the course of the debates on ratification, and if they are rejected this may lead to a governmental crisis. But at least they will have been discussed. As a result, Parliament's supreme authority over both the content and the form of its agenda is doubly undermined. This is the price that has had to be paid for an exaggerated and outdated concept of Parliament's powers of decision.

The situation explains the interest shown in Italy in a 'rationalization of parliamentarianism' of the type introduced in France under the Constitution of the Fifth French

Republic. The distinction drawn in Articles 34 and 37 of the French Constitution between legislation and regulations, and delegation by means of a system of ordinances, have all been closely studied with a view to possibly transposing them into the Italian constitutional system. So far, however, no such proposals have been successful, partly because the French system was considered to give too much power to the executive, and partly because it appeared inaccurate. As Pierre Avril has pointed out, the separation of the sphere of law from that of regulations was presented as the cornerstone of the normative system of the Fifth Republic until it was noticed that the declared revolution of Articles 34 and 37 had never, in fact, taken place.[4] At any rate, in respect of the cumbersome workings that safeguard the impression of sovereignty given by Parliament, the Italian system is more or less in line with the other systems of Western Europe. Nearly everywhere—with a few exceptions, such as Sweden and Denmark—the executive plays an essential, if not dominant, role in the elaboration of laws. That is, bills are presented to Parliament as drafts prepared by the government after a more or less lengthy process of consultation between officials, interest groups, and ministers. In the Fifth French Republic over 90 per cent of all laws started out as government bills. In Germany the proportion is three-quarters, a comparatively low figure, but this is partly to be explained by the fact that bills starting in the Bundestag are presented by party groups, and are often disguised government legislation. The practice of Western parliamentary systems generally is thus broadly comparable with that of the 'mother' of them all, namely the British Parliament.

In Britain, the essential legislative initiative has long lain with the government. Over 95 per cent of the bills proposed by the executive are adopted, and 82 per cent of all laws are initiated by the government. In fact, these figures almost certainly understate the true dominance of the executive, for most private members' bills only pass because the government has chosen to make parliamentary time for them, and even to give their private backers the benefit of its advice, adopting the bills, in effect, as its own.[5] The British parliament is also in the unusual habit of admitting legislation that originates neither with the government nor with MPs, but with external bodies (such as local authorities) or even individuals. Such 'private legislation' must be proposed, according to procedures fixed by the House of Commons, by non-members of the House, who must be prepared to defend their bills when challenged. Such bills grew in number in the 1980s, prompting misgivings about the subordination of parliament and its scarce time to well-financed private interests, and a select committee report that recommended reforms. 'Hybrid' bills, finally, are the product of two procedures, for they can only be proposed in accordance with the procedure followed for 'public' bills, but all 'private measures', that is to say those that affect specific interests, must also undergo an examination in the course of which those 'for' and those 'against' more or less fight it out in debate.

Nevertheless, over and above all these formal distinctions, the executive still holds the real power of initiative, either directly or through Members of Parliament who are persuaded to support the government. We should remember, furthermore, that the executive exercises a crucial influence within Parliament itself: the members of the government constitute a close-knit group of about 100 (almost one-quarter of the majority), all of whom, by definition, support all government proposals.

Finally, through the device of 'delegated legislation', important prerogatives are made available to the British government. The expression masks a relatively heterogeneous mode of intervention that corresponds in part to the classic regulatory powers of executives. The legislation is said to be 'delegated' because the fiction of Parliament's omnipotence has prevailed for so long, at least at the level of terminology. But this attribution of regulatory activities to Parliament is more the result of the absence of any rigid hierarchy of norms such as exists on the Continent, than of any real transfer of the domain of law to the government, in the sense in which, for example, the French and the Italians would understand it. These conceptual and organizational differences account for the apparently extensive use of 'delegated legislation' (which has produced, on average, 2,000 Rules and Orders each year since the Second World War). At least in principle, delegated legislation is of secondary importance, designed to implement what Parliament has already agreed to in principle (and indeed in some substance), and therefore more analogous to France's routine ministerial decrees than to the ordinances of the French or the decree-laws of the Italians. The danger, however, lies when a minister abuses such delegated legislative power to make new policy without presenting it to Parliament. This tendency has exercised the Commons for some years, and well illustrates the difficulty of making hard and fast distinctions in this area, as well as the executive's tendency to try and push back the limits to its own power.

In France and Britain, regional and local authorities do not possess any legislative power, and few concessions are made to these countries' strictly centralized systems. In the case of France, certain territories and regions (essentially the overseas possessions and Corsica) are allowed to express their opinions and desires and in some cases adaptations are made—but always by centrally controlled means. In Britain, the loudly proclaimed sovereignty of Parliament may be modified by certain pragmatic concessions: a virtually federal system operated in Northern Ireland up until 1972; particular arrangements, including special parliamentary committees, exist for Wales and Scotland (and will, following the referendum results of September 1997, be amended to allow Scotland a Parliament to legislate on internal affairs, as well as a Welsh Assembly with more limited powers); while the various small offshore islands enjoy great autonomy, not technically being part of the United Kingdom at all. However, with the exception of the new Scottish Parliament, the ideology of national sovereignty together with the solemnly proclaimed sovereignty of Parliament have ensured that these palliatives stop short of recognizing federal or regional Assemblies to possess any legislative powers.

In contrast, the post-war settlements in both Italy and West Germany explicitly envisaged the territorial division of legislative tasks. In Italy, the Constitution recognizes the legislative authority of all the regions but grants wider powers to the five with special status (Sardinia, Sicily, Alto-Adige, the Aosta Valley, and the Friuli–Julian Alps–Veneto region) than to the fifteen regions with ordinary status which were established later, after 1970. The Constitution recognizes the latter to possess legislative powers in all matters as defined in Article 117 (in particular those relating to agriculture, local crafts, tourism, town planning, and so on), always providing they respect 'the fundamental principles fixed by the State laws' and providing 'they do not conflict with the national interest or that of other regions'. For several years, the central apparatus's reluctance to get these 'law frameworks' adopted paralysed activity in the regions. Now, however, the Constitutional Court has ruled that, despite the absence of any specific law on the matter, the 'principles' of the arrangement were implicit in the existing body of legislation; and this has made it possible for the ordinary regions to pass laws within their particular fields of competence. The laws are subject to the 'supervision' of a regional commissioner (or prefect) appointed by the government. If he withholds his approval, the government informs the region of his reasons for opposing the proposal and requires it to make the appropriate changes. If the region persists in its attitude, the government can refer the matter either to Parliament or to the Constitutional Court, depending on whether the clash is of a political or a juridical nature. Seeking to avoid political clashes, the government has in practice tried to turn political conflicts into juridical ones and has transferred to the Constitutional Court the responsibility for pronouncing on all conflicts.[6]

West Germany was spared the hesitations and procrastinations that bedevilled Italy's progress in its construction of a regional State. Both the Allies and the political forces present favoured a system in which powers were apportioned on a territorial basis, for some thought that this would prevent a repetition of dictatorial developments, while others (in particular the French occupying forces) reckoned that the German State would thereby be weakened. The Basic Law provided for a system in which the *Länder* hold a residual measure of legislative power. Article 70 lays down that the *Länder* have the power to pass laws in areas where the present constitutional law does not specifically assign legislative power to the Federation. Furthermore, even where the Federation does hold such powers, the *Länder* have the right to legislate 'so long as and to the extent that the Federation makes no use of its right to legislate' (Article 72). The basic law recognizes the Federation's right to take over from the *Länder* in three sets of circumstances:

- if a question cannot be settled satisfactorily by the various *Länder*,
- if the legislation of one *Land* may affect the interests of others,
- if it is necessary to protect the juridical and economic unity of the country.

As may be imagined, these 'limitations' are not very rigorous and it is hard to see how any area could, in the long run, elude intervention from the Bund. However, the *Länder* do carry exclusive responsibility for education, the organization of local communities, and policing. The fact that these areas are 'reserved' for the *Länder* can, on occasion, cause problems, particularly when *Länder* policies clash with undertakings made by the Bund (particularly at international level). For example, in 1955, the federal government appealed to the Constitutional Court, claiming that the educational legislation adopted by Lower Saxony was incompatible with the Concordat concluded in 1933 between the Vatican and the Third Reich. In 1957, the Court decided that, in view of the *Länder's*

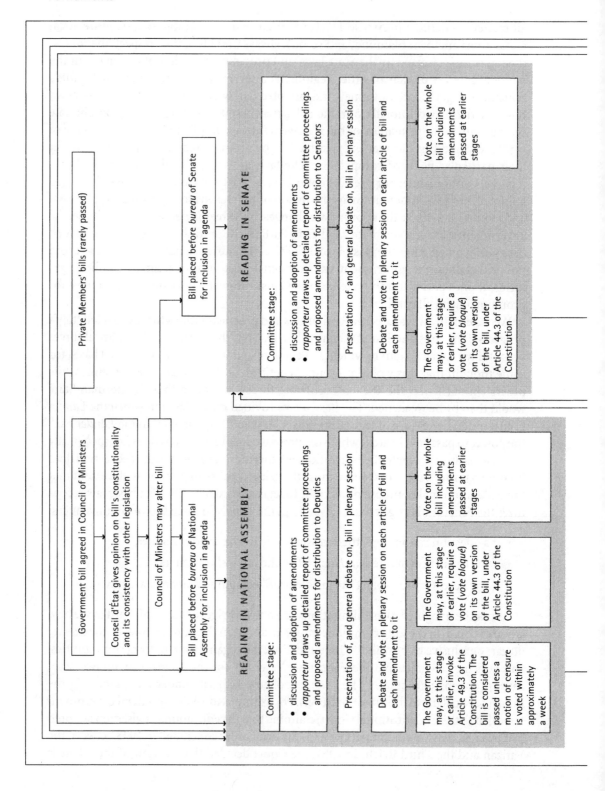

READING IN SENATE

Committee stage:
- discussion and adoption of amendments
- *rapporteur* draws up detailed report of committee proceedings and proposed amendments for distribution to Senators

Presentation of, and general debate on, bill in plenary session

Debate and vote in plenary session on each article of bill and each amendment to it

The Government may, at this stage or earlier, require a vote (*vote bloqué*) on its own version of the bill, under Article 44.3 of the Constitution

Vote on the whole bill including amendments passed at earlier stages

READING IN NATIONAL ASSEMBLY

Committee stage:
- discussion and adoption of amendments
- *rapporteur* draws up detailed report of committee proceedings and proposed amendments for distribution to Deputies

Presentation of, and general debate on, bill in plenary session

Debate and vote in plenary session on each article of bill and each amendment to it

The Government may, at this stage or earlier, invoke Article 49.3 of the Constitution. The bill is considered passed unless a motion of censure is voted within approximately a week

The Government may, at this stage or earlier, require a vote (*vote bloqué*) on its own version of the bill, under Article 44.3 of the Constitution

Vote on the whole bill including amendments passed at earlier stages

Private Members' bills (rarely passed)

Government bill agreed in Council of Ministers

Conseil d'État gives opinion on bill's constitutionality and its consistency with other legislation

Council of Ministers may alter bill

Bill placed before *bureau* of Senate for inclusion in agenda

Bill placed before *bureau* of National Assembly for inclusion in agenda

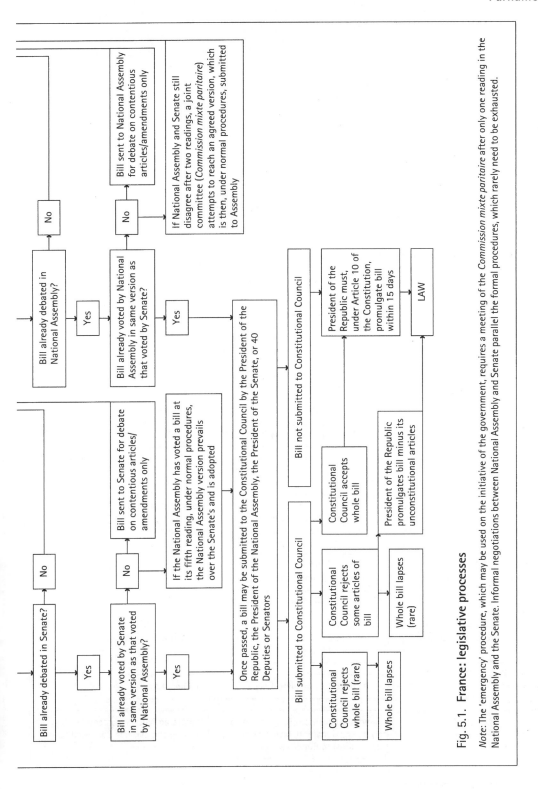

Fig. 5.1. France: legislative processes

Note: The 'emergency' procedure, which may be used on the initiative of the government, requires a meeting of the *Commission mixte paritaire* after only one reading in the National Assembly and the Senate. Informal negotiations between National Assembly and Senate parallel the formal procedures, which rarely need to be exhausted.

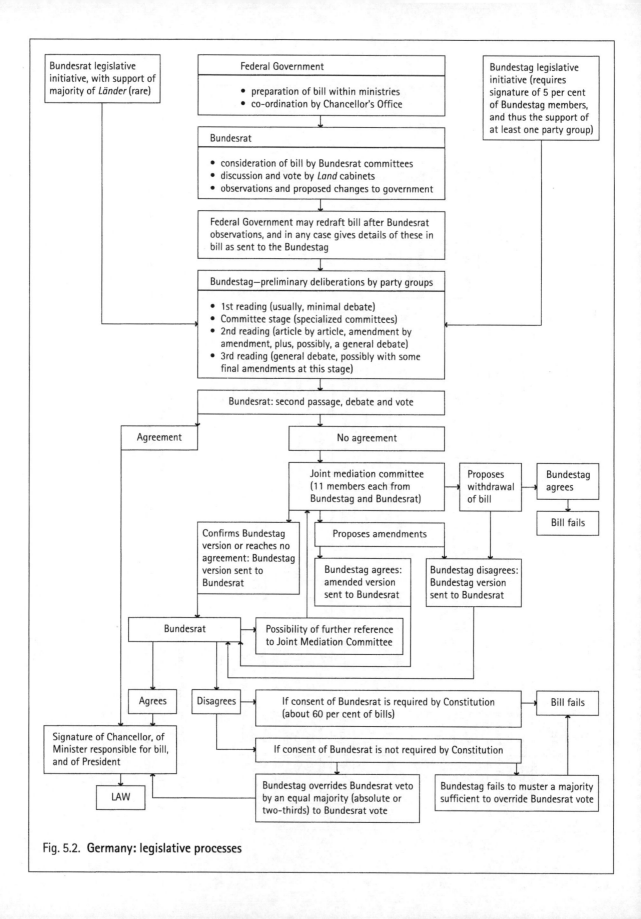

Fig. 5.2. **Germany: legislative processes**

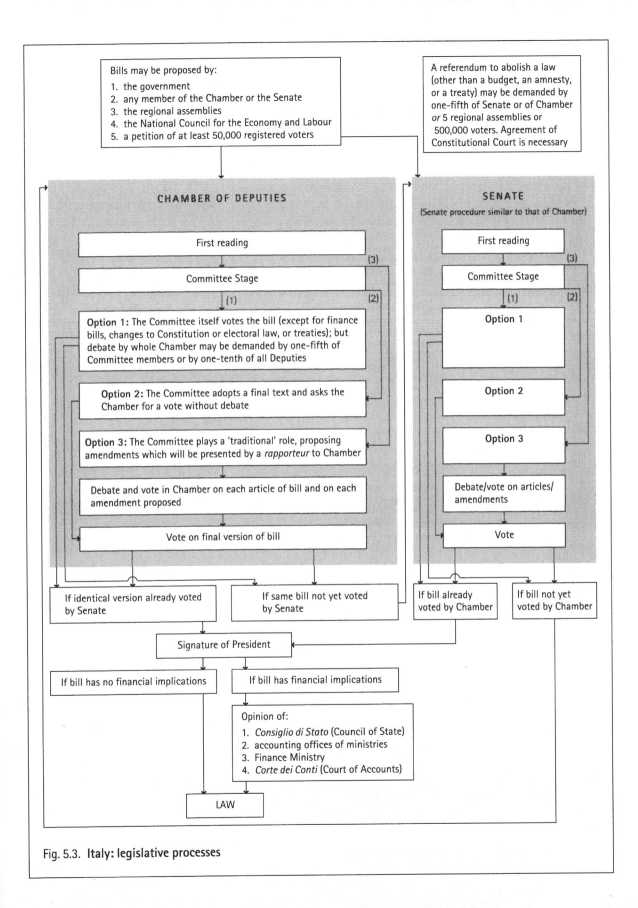

Bills may be proposed by:

1. the government
2. any member of the Chamber or the Senate
3. the regional assemblies
4. the National Council for the Economy and Labour
5. a petition of at least 50,000 registered voters

A referendum to abolish a law (other than a budget, an amnesty, or a treaty) may be demanded by one-fifth of Senate or of Chamber *or* 5 regional assemblies or 500,000 voters. Agreement of Constitutional Court is necessary

CHAMBER OF DEPUTIES

First reading

Committee Stage (3)

(1) (2)

Option 1: The Committee itself votes the bill (except for finance bills, changes to Constitution or electoral law, or treaties); but debate by whole Chamber may be demanded by one-fifth of Committee members or by one-tenth of all Deputies

Option 2: The Committee adopts a final text and asks the Chamber for a vote without debate

Option 3: The Committee plays a 'traditional' role, proposing amendments which will be presented by a *rapporteur* to Chamber

Debate and vote in Chamber on each article of bill and on each amendment proposed

Vote on final version of bill

SENATE
(Senate procedure similar to that of Chamber)

First reading

Committee Stage (3)

(1) (2)

Option 1

Option 2

Option 3

Debate/vote on articles/amendments

Vote

If identical version already voted by Senate

If same bill not yet voted by Senate

If bill already voted by Chamber

If bill not yet voted by Chamber

Signature of President

If bill has no financial implications

If bill has financial implications

Opinion of:

1. *Consiglio di Stato* (Council of State)
2. accounting offices of ministries
3. Finance Ministry
4. *Corte dei Conti* (Court of Accounts)

LAW

Fig. 5.3. Italy: legislative processes

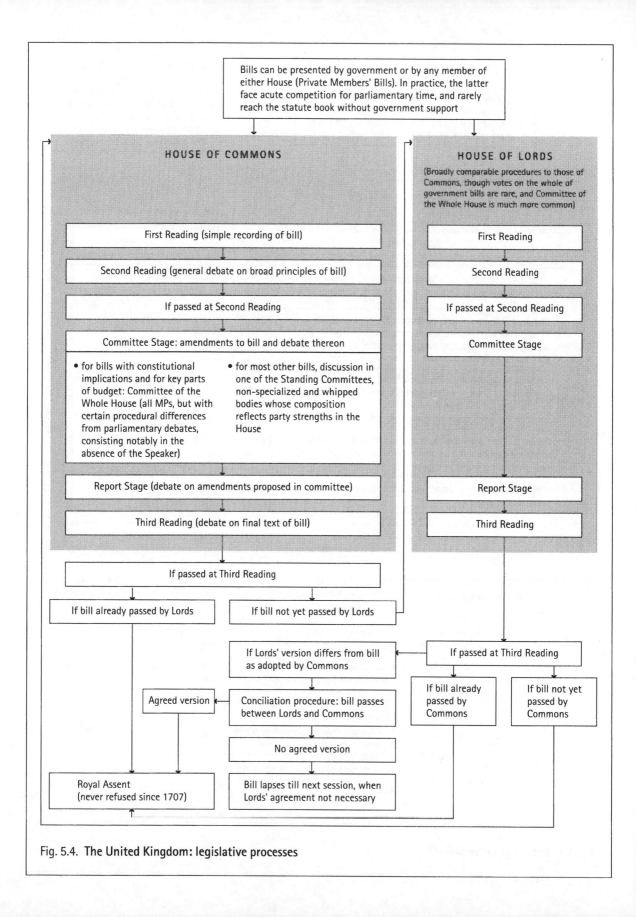

Bills can be presented by government or by any member of either House (Private Members' Bills). In practice, the latter face acute competition for parliamentary time, and rarely reach the statute book without government support

HOUSE OF COMMONS

HOUSE OF LORDS
(Broadly comparable procedures to those of Commons, though votes on the whole of government bills are rare, and Committee of the Whole House is much more common)

First Reading (simple recording of bill)

First Reading

Second Reading (general debate on broad principles of bill)

Second Reading

If passed at Second Reading

If passed at Second Reading

Committee Stage: amendments to bill and debate thereon

Committee Stage

- for bills with constitutional implications and for key parts of budget: Committee of the Whole House (all MPs, but with certain procedural differences from parliamentary debates, consisting notably in the absence of the Speaker)

- for most other bills, discussion in one of the Standing Committees, non-specialized and whipped bodies whose composition reflects party strengths in the House

Report Stage (debate on amendments proposed in committee)

Report Stage

Third Reading (debate on final text of bill)

Third Reading

If passed at Third Reading

If bill already passed by Lords

If bill not yet passed by Lords

If Lords' version differs from bill as adopted by Commons

If passed at Third Reading

If bill already passed by Commons

If bill not yet passed by Commons

Agreed version

Conciliation procedure: bill passes between Lords and Commons

No agreed version

Royal Assent (never refused since 1707)

Bill lapses till next session, when Lords' agreement not necessary

Fig. 5.4. **The United Kingdom: legislative processes**

exclusive powers in the domain of education, the federal government could not apply the Concordat regulations, despite the fact that they were still in force.

Parliamentary autonomy in the legislative process

In the past, parliaments could, no doubt fairly, be defined as bodies responsible for making laws. Nowadays it would be more accurate to call them instruments for converting bills (elaborated elsewhere, more often than not) into written laws. The decision-making powers of parliaments lie not so much in their initiating—or sometimes blocking—legislation, but rather in their revision of drafts that have been prepared elsewhere.

The degree of a parliament's autonomy largely depends upon the procedures through which the work of legislation is organized. Let us now try to assess the degree of autonomy possessed by each of the parliaments that we are discussing, by examining the principal stages of their respective parliamentary processes.

Fixing the agenda

One indication of the independence of a legislature is the extent to which it can control the use of its own time. Broadly speaking, the British House of Commons and the French National Assembly are kept on quite a tight rein by their executives, while their German and Italian counterparts enjoy more autonomy. In Britain the work of Parliament is quite strictly organized, in such a way that, while the rights of the opposition are guaranteed, government action is effective. In principle, the House of Commons meets from 2.30 to 10.30 p.m. (except on Fridays, when the hours are from 9.30 a.m. to 3 p.m.), and its business is organized so as to avoid night sessions as far as possible. The hours between 3.30 and 10.30 p.m. are reserved for 'public business', that is, both projects decided by the government in Cabinet meetings and presented by it, and Private Members' bills. In the case of the latter, priority goes to the twenty Members of Parliament whose motions head the ballot taken at the beginning of each session. However, the number of these bills that are both registered and subsequently adopted is, as we have seen, low. In the course of the 1979–83 Parliament, for example, 379 Private Members' bills were introduced, of which only 44 were passed (13 per cent), whereas over 95 per cent of government bills were successful. Furthermore, the government can organize debates before making their proposals, for example, by scheduling sittings after the normal closing time of 10 p.m.

The French Constitution of 1958 was influenced by British parliamentary procedure but imposed even stricter discipline upon the Assemblies. Under the Third and Fourth Republics, the Assemblies had been responsible for determining their own agendas, but Article 48 of the present Constitution reverses that situation, ruling that the government takes priority in determining agendas. Whatever time remains—if any—is organized by a President's conference attended by the Presidents and Vice-Presidents of the two

Assemblies, the presidents of committees and parliamentary groups, and the general spokesman for the budget, in the form of a complementary agenda. As a result, laws of parliamentary origin are subject to both qualitative and quantitative limitations. They represent barely 10 per cent of all laws, and most are of secondary importance.

Germany and Italy both allow a large measure of autonomy to their Parliaments, but it is applied differently in the two countries, since their political party structures differ. In Germany, the agenda is decided by a 'council of elders' (Ältestenrat) composed of the President and Vice-Presidents of the Bundestag together with a number of delegates from the various parties in proportion to their respective strengths. Up until 1969, the rulings of this council had to be agreed unanimously, but since the parliamentary reforms adopted in that year, that has no longer been the case. Nevertheless, the procedure for fixing the agenda remains largely consensual and makes it possible to respect the rights of the opposition. The relative autonomy of the Bundestag—which the personal prestige of its President sometimes reinforces—is reflected in a greater openness towards bills originating from its members. Of the 4,269 bills passed in the Federal Republic between 1949 and 1992, 77 per cent originated with the government, 19 per cent with the Bundestag, and 3 per cent with the Bundesrat. But according to the Bundestag's internal regulations, such bills must be proposed by at least 5 per cent of its members; in other words, they must have the backing of one or other of the party *fraktionen*, which may mean the federal government acting behind the scenes.[7]

In Italy, where Parliament enjoys an institutional role of central importance, the agenda and scheduling of parliamentary tasks are fixed by a conference of parliamentary party group presidents, whose decisions must be unanimous. When such agreement proves impossible to reach, the agenda is fixed by the President of the Lower Chamber (or of the Senate). But, as Antonio Baldassare points out, the President 'must not refuse to attempt to mediate between the various positions expressed in Parliament'.[8] The supremacy of the Italian Parliament's role certainly affects legislative 'input' and 'output'. Laws proposed by Parliament are more numerous (but often of less importance) than those of government origin and, to get round the obstacles of access and delays, the Government has increasingly been forced to resort to the practice of decree-laws some, but not all, of which are subsequently ratified by Parliament.

Parliamentary committees

In France, Germany, and Italy (though not, or rarely, Britain) committees can be seen as the place where the essential work of legislation is accomplished. It is here, far more than in plenary sessions, that bills can be discussed and amended article by article, line by line, in an atmosphere sheltered from both media attention and party competition, allowing a degree of collaboration between technical experts who may share a common commitment to the quality of the final legislation. In principle, and with some possibility of exceptions in the Italian case, committees can only recommend amendments to the parliaments of which they are a part; it is for the plenary sessions to pass the final legislation. In practice, committees may enjoy a degree of autonomy that makes them into potentially powerful legislators, rather than mere technical devices for moving business forward.

In France, the 1958 Constitution limited the number of committees to six, but other parliamentary and presidential systems leave their Parliaments free to organize their own committee work and hence also to decide how many committees are necessary. In West Germany, for example, the number tended to vary depending upon political considerations. For example, the first Bundestag set up 39 committees, the second 36, and their membership varied by a factor of four. The most 'sensitive' committees (for example, those concerned with European security) were also the smallest, so as to avoid having to include the smaller parties, in particular the Communist Party. After the marginal parties began gradually to disappear and a *de facto* three-party system developed, the number of committees oscillated between 15 and 20. One of the most unusual Bundestag Committees is the 'petitions committee', which receives the complaints that citizens may address to Parliament under Article 17 of the Constitution.

In Italy, the Chamber of Deputies includes 14 permanent committees, the Senate 12, and special committees may also be created. As they are quite large (about 45 Deputies and 25–30 Senators to each committee), they are divided into internal committees, permanent *ad hoc* Chamber committees, and Senate committees and subcommittees, sometimes supplemented by other study groups. As a result, close liaison is established both with the ministerial departments that the committees follow and also with the interest groups involved, each of which is represented by a spokesman with specialized knowledge of the situation. By contrast, Britain's standing committees are neither permanent, nor closed to media attention, nor specialized. They are set up by the House of Commons as and when need arises and are given no specific names, being known quite simply as Committee A, B, C, and so on. Each is generally composed of eighteen members, all appointed by a selection committee. Britain also sometimes employs a special type of committee known as a 'committee of the whole House'. When it is decided to set up such a committee, the House no longer observes the rules that apply to plenary sessions. The Speaker leaves his seat and places his mace under the table, thereby indicating that the procedures that usually apply have been suspended. For instance, in these circumstances, a Member of Parliament is allowed to speak more than once on a single subject. It is a procedure that is used particularly when the problem under consideration is too extensive for a single committee to handle on its own and, above all, when the government commands only a small majority that would be further reduced by the few members engaged in standing committees.

The composition of Italian and German committees, like French and British ones, is proportionally representative of the various political groups. However, in France, the majority tends to monopolize the chairmanships. In Germany, the composition of committees is proportionally representative of the various political groups but, as we have already noted, it has sometimes proved possible, by juggling the numbers of members, to eliminate the smallest and most undesirable groups (*Fraktionen*) from committees that are considered to be of crucial importance. The chairmen of these committees are appointed by the Ältestenrat on the basis of a consensus that respects the political equilibrium: the Christian Democrats and the SPD divide the lion's share between them, in accordance with the election results. However, the FDP has never been excluded—not even when its support was not indispensable to the formation of a coalition. In Italy, the rule of proportional representation applies to the composition of committees, but the political groups themselves decide upon which of their members to appoint to which of them. None can belong to two at once (except members of the Senate, where the smaller parties are allowed to appoint the same Senator to sit on two committees at the same time). Posts of president (or chairman) are allotted in relation to the existing balance of political forces and reflect the consensus that prevails in Italian parliamentary life whatever political quarrels and passions are current.

In Britain, the rules are dictated by the traditional two-party system and the relationship between the majority and the opposition. The chairman of a standing committee is appointed (in the case of each separate law) by the Speaker on the recommendation of what is known as a 'chairman's panel', a group of about ten Members of Parliament who are themselves endorsed by the Speaker, on the recommendation of Government and Opposition whips, at the beginning of each parliamentary session.

The committees to which bills are submitted by the executive, parliamentary groups, or individual parliamentarians have three essential functions: to gather information, the better to legislate; to amend and revise the drafts that are submitted to them; and, in the Italian case, actually to pass laws.

The gathering of information may be done by organizing hearings. This practice became increasingly successful in West Germany and in Italy from the 1970s, and was initiated in France in 1991. Apart from their normal sessions, which are not public, German committees may organize meetings that are open to the Press and the public, during which experts and the representatives of interest groups may have their say. Up until the 1970s, such hearings were relatively exceptional; but since then the Bundestag has increased their number. Similarly, in Italy, the 1971 reform of Assembly regulations (in particular Article 143 of the Chamber of Deputies' regulations and Article 47 of those governing the Senate) opened up the possibility of more hearings in the American style. As a result, many more hearings and inquiries are now conducted by permanent parliamentary committees. As in the United States, the way in which the presentation of problems is staged has become as important as the collection of information.[9] In Britain, although select committees responsible for monitoring the administration organize hearings, the standing committees set up to discuss bills do not; the provision in 1979 for 'special standing committees', empowered to take evidence before considering a bill, has in practice been used on only a handful of occasions.

The second task of committees is to table amendments and in some cases to redraft bills. However, their powers vary from one political system to another depending on the degree of authority enjoyed by the executive through its control over the parliamentary majority. In Britain, party control places very severe limits indeed on the real possibilities of amendment. The exception to this general rule occurs when changes to a bill are backed by a groundswell of opinion in the Commons (and especially in the majority party), in which case the government may accept, or more often propose, amendments in committee. But as Andrew Adonis remarks, Commons standing committees are 'a microcosm of the House itself, complete with front and back benches, whips, and division bells'. Party discipline thus applies here as much as anywhere else. The consequences (outside the exceptional conditions of 1974–9, when the government had first a tiny majority and then none at all) are a caricature, not just of majority, but of executive dominance. In the debates on water and electricity privatization in 1988–9, for example, 114 amendments were carried, of which one was moved by a Conservative backbencher and 113 by ministers; not one of the opposition's 227 amendments was carried.[10] The combination of non-specialization, long-drawn-out proceedings, and partisanship on standing committees has drawn withering attacks from political diarists: the procedure was 'utterly futile . . . utterly debilitating' for Richard Crossman in the 1960s, and 'like bad "discussion-therapy" in a loony-bin' for Alan Clark 20 years later.[11]

Party control is also important in Germany, but it is balanced both by the very much greater specialization and expertise of the Bundestag's committees, and by the Bundestag's self-image as an *Arbeitsparlament*, whose main task is processing legislation, rather than a *Reteparlament*, a debating parliament (an identity far more readily associated with the House of Commons). Committees are therefore expected to amend, but not to destroy, government bills, and often undertake at least part of their job on a bipartisan basis. In Italy, by contrast, Members of Parliament may completely reconstruct government proposals in such a way as to render them unrecognizable.

In France the right of amendment is strictly controlled. In particular, the government can reject all amendments as a result of which funds would be depleted or public expenditure increased. A rule such as this enables a hostile government to reject virtually all amendments that are not to its liking. Furthermore, having rejected them, it can request its majority to adopt the law as drafted, using the 'blocked vote' procedure of Article 44 of the Constitution. The governments of the Fifth Republic have, however, adopted a more conciliatory attitude over the years, particularly where amendments are tabled in committee. The privacy of these meetings allows the government to take the temperature of its majority, which is almost always more composite than in the British case, and make adjustments accordingly. There is even scope for co-operation and complicity to develop between majority and opposition. Under these conditions, committees can play a decision-making role which the casual observer of the rare references to them in the constitutional texts could only guess at. For as Paul Cahoua's study of 'committees as legislative workshops' notes, '26.2 per cent of the amendments registered are proposed by committees. They represent 64.4 per cent of all amendments passed, and 88 per cent of the proposals made by committees are adopted.'[12] This success rate does not hold, however, for amendments tabled in plenary sessions. Their purpose is more frequently to attract attention to the proposals and criticisms of the opposition, or simply to slow the passage of legislation. And they pass much more rarely.

In Italy, however, parliamentary committees may perform a third function: they exercise legislative power directly. Committees may adopt the famous *leggine* (or 'little laws'), on the basis of Article 72 of the Constitution, subject to two restrictions. First, the Constitution does not allow them to intervene in matters of constitutional or electoral reform, legislation relating to finance, the ratification of international treaties, or in connection with the delegation of legislation. Secondly, either the government or one-tenth of the members of the Chamber, or one-fifth of the members of the Committee itself may, so long as the bill has not yet been finally approved, require that the whole text be returned to the plenary Assembly. It is interesting to note the political effects of this combination of factors: in the first place, Italy is in the paradoxical position of being able to 'produce' many laws but few 'reforms', since most of the texts are given limited application. Secondly, the fact that special committees hold decision-making powers particularly encourages systematic intervention on the part of interest groups, since their influence is thereby brought to bear upon a restricted circle of individuals (whose inclusion in a particular committee in the first place results from pre-existing interests in the sector concerned), besides which their debates usually receive minimal publicity. Thirdly, the fact that it is at any point possible to return a text to the plenary Assembly for further discussion turns the whole procedure into a system of complex bargaining and negotiation between the government and the other Members of Parliament, the majority coalition and the minority (essentially the Communist Party), and within the coalition. It is significant that, during the 1970s, the Italian Communist Party voted in favour of three-quarters of the *leggine*, abstained in 5 to 10 per cent of the cases, and opposed the remainder. What this shows is that, while it is in the plenary sessions of the Assembly that the major dramas are played out, the committees, thanks to their decision-making powers, act as the system's 'clearing-houses'.

Parliamentary debates

The organization of the debates of parliamentary plenary sessions poses various problems. The first is of a purely practical nature, and the order of debates varies from one country to another. The second relates to the Assembly's right to table amendments and also to engage in obstructive policies or filibustering.

Italy's approach to the method of discussing legislation resembles that of the French Parliament. Once the committee representatives have had their say, a general debate is held, followed by a discussion of the bill, article by article, in the course of which amendments may be tabled by parliamentary groups or even by individual Deputies or Senators. The Assembly then proceeds to adopt the overall text. It should be noted that the regulations governing the two Italian Chambers make it possible, at this stage, through an operation of 'final co-ordination', to correct any contradictions that have crept in as each article of the bill was voted upon. It is a useful procedure that is clearly necessary, but it sometimes lends itself to dubious interpretations and manipulation.

Procedures used in Britain and in Germany differ from those described above, and are broadly similar to each other, though in Germany all government bills go first to the Bundesrat for its opinion before being introduced into the Bundestag. Once a motion is entered on the agenda, a general debate is organized on the legislation as drafted. The draft is then passed on to the committees appointed to discuss it, then debated once again on the basis of the amendments proposed by those committees. At this stage amendments may be introduced both by the government and by members of parliament.

The right of members of parliament to table amendments is particularly important, especially in the European parliamentary democracies, where Assembly members have virtually lost the power of legislative initiative, whether they belong to the majority or to the opposition. The tabling of amendments affords the majority party or coalition a chance to 'correct' government proposals, and the opposition an opportunity to make its voice heard or even to put forward counter-proposals by a systematic tabling of amendments; although, as we have seen, amendments presented in committee have a better chance of adoption.

In Italy, the practice of parliamentary obstructionism has given rise to some particularly tense situations, albeit with a peculiarly Italian style. Because the tabling of amendments is often the surest means of obstruction, the regulations governing the Italian Assemblies have, since 1981, stipulated that there should be one discussion only to cover all the amendments to a single article. Furthermore, in the course of this, each Deputy may speak once only, even if he is the author of a whole series of amendments or additional articles. This rule is part of the arsenal of regulations that the Italian Assemblies have introduced in order to guard against the obstructionism of determined parliamentary groups, such as the Radicals, who in the late 1970s managed on several occasions to block the legislative machine. Up until 1971, the rules allowed the Assembly to bring debates to a close with a vote. In that year, a reform introduced two corrections, limiting the time allowed for each intervention and, in some debates, allowing only one speaker from each group. But that same reform undermined its own effectiveness by opening up the possibility of more flexible methods. In 1981, the Chamber rules were again made more rigorous: now, each speaker was in theory allowed no more than 45 minutes (although, it is true, he could overrun his time, providing he did not exceed 90 minutes). These measures made it possible to put an end to the most flagrant abuses, in particular the obstruction engineered between 1976 and 1980 by the Radicals, who became champions of filibuster and of amendments. However, it is not possible, nor indeed advisable, to prevent all obstructions, for these remain the last weapon of the minority. In view of the degree of power held by the political parties within the Italian political system, a compromise between democracy and efficiency has been devised. It involves transferring to the parliamentary groups part of the responsibility for their own self-discipline: the rule of 'one spokesman per group' makes it possible to limit abuses and to appeal to the sense of responsibility of the parties that are represented in the two Assemblies. But none of these have been willing to submit themselves to too many restrictions, knowing full well that at some time or other they have all needed to resort to obstructionism—the Left in 1949 and 1953 against the Atlantic Pact and the infamous electoral law proposed by Minister Scelba, the Right in 1970, when the regional institutions were finally being set up.

As the 'Mother of Parliaments', Britain has considerable experience in the matter of controlling amendments and limiting obstructionism. When the British House of

Commons discusses a text that has been amended by the relevant standing committee, the government resumes its full powers and can force its majority to accept either its own amendments or, alternatively, the elimination of the amendments adopted by the committee. Of course, every government must take account of its own majority party and the moods of its back-benchers, but an analysis of the legislative process in Britain shows clearly how limited an impact ordinary Members of Parliament make. Studies carried out in the 1960s indicated that the government's power to get its way was almost limitless, and the power of back-benchers negligible. However, the early 1970s saw an upsurge of independent back-bencher activity, which had particularly striking effects under the wafer-thin, and then non-existent, Labour majorities of 1974–9. This greater assertiveness survived into the Thatcher years, and while bigger majorities made it easier to contain, the government often took care to anticipate and to head off trouble on the back benches.[13] John Major's fairly narrow majority from 1992 made his government more vulnerable than his predecessor's to back-bench pressures.

The government's control over the processes of Parliament is equally firm when it comes to attempts at obstruction on the part of a minority. There are three instruments for avoiding filibusters. The first device is a motion to close the debate, first used by Gladstone in 1881, to counter the filibusters of the Irish Nationalists. According to this procedure, which is now the subject of Standing Order no. 31, a member of the Commons, usually a whip, can request that a motion to close the debate be put to the vote. With the proviso that the Speaker agrees that there has been sufficient debate (to some extent a guarantee for the minority), the motion is proposed. To be adopted, it must obtain a majority, collecting a minimum of 100 votes.[14] A similar procedure is followed in France. A second means of preventing possible blockages in the work of legislation is constituted by the so-called 'kangaroo' technique of selecting for discussion only the most important of the amendments in cases where it looks as though debating every single one will take too long. The selection is made by the Speaker (or the committee chairman, as the case may be). The third instrument is the guillotine procedure (also introduced in 1881), which allows the government to close debate on any individual item in a bill. When the government considers a bill to be particularly important and the debate over it drags on, it can move an 'allocation of time order,' allowing a limited period of time for the discussion of each item of the bill still to be debated. Since such 'guillotine motions' are always passed if there is a stable parliamentary majority (though they must be debated, which itself takes up parliamentary time), the government can thus impose a strict schedule upon the debate. When the period of time allotted has elapsed, the debate is halted and the House must vote on the bill, including articles that have not yet been adopted and all government amendments, but not those tabled by ordinary Members of Parliament. The parties—in particular the opposition—are forced to make a drastic choice: either to slow down the process at the risk of debating only a small part of the bill, or to co-operate with the government by debating only the most important points and persuading their supporters to speak briefly or not at all.

In this area, too, the French Constitution has followed the British example and provided the government with extremely effective deterrents, which were brought into use even before the advent of truly filibustering behaviour. Parliamentary obstructionism only became a serious problem in the late 1970s during Giscard d'Estaing's presidency. At this point the Socialists became experts in the art of filibustering, but the Right also learned from their example and, in its turn, adopted the same techniques after Mitterrand and the Socialists had come to power. The opposition has a number of means of slowing down the legislative process. It can claim that the proposed legislation is inopportune or unconstitutional (declaring it to be unacceptable, raising preliminary questions, tabling motions of adjournment or of censure, appealing to the regulations, demanding public votes or that the session be suspended, etc.) and once these preliminary obstacles are cleared away, it can table quantities of amendments. In 1983, for example, 2,204 amendments were tabled when the law on higher education was debated; in 1984, 2,598 on the proposed law relating to the Press. The government, for its part, has three principal means at its disposal. It can refuse to consider amendments that have not been tabled in committee. It can use Article 44.3 of the Constitution to require a 'blocked' vote in parliament on a complete text, including only those amendments the government approves of. Or it can invoke Article 49.3, under which the government makes a bill an issue of confidence. In this case, the bill is considered passed if no motion of censure is passed within 72 hours by an absolute majority of the Assembly's members. This is an absolute weapon that makes it possible for even a minority government to get its own way, for the opposition is seldom sufficiently strong and united to get a motion of censure adopted. Between 1958 and 1981, this article was called into use only 15 times, but between 1981 and 1986 it was used 6 times. The Rocard Government established in June 1988 declared itself hostile to excessive use of this procedure, but since it did not control an absolute majority in the National Assembly, it was nevertheless forced to resort to it 27 times on 14 bills in the three years of its life.

The effects of bicameralism

The existence of two chambers complicates the legislative process, since the bills must be studied, and some of them approved, in exactly the same terms by Assemblies whose modes of recruitment, social composition, and ideological affiliation are—or may be—quite different. The relations between the two branches of the legislature vary depending on whether the two chambers involved stand on an equal or an unequal footing.

In France, Italy, and Britain, government proposals may be tabled before either chamber, but the lower chamber is usually the first to discuss the draft prepared by the executive. Indeed, this is obligatory for finance bills. Proposals are generally laid before the Senate or the House of Lords either as a matter of courtesy or for reasons of timing and, in Britain in particular, the House of Lords tends to receive such drafts as are not likely to give rise to much disagreement, a fact that eases the pressure in the Upper House as the parliamentary session draws to a close. The German Basic Law, in contrast, stipulates that 'the Federal Government's legislative proposals *must* in the first instance be tabled before the Bundesrat, which has the right to take three weeks to decide what should become of them'.

When bills have been debated and adopted by the first Assembly to receive them, they are passed on to the other chamber which, in its turn, examines them. It is at this stage that any disagreements between the two chambers must be resolved on the basis of the superiority of the one or negotiation between the two. The British House of Lords is undoubtedly in the weakest position of all the upper chambers, since it has no powers at all in financial matters and can only block other bills temporarily. In principle, by refusing to adopt a bill, the House of Lords plays a decisive role, for if a bill is to be adopted by the House of Commons on its own, this can only be done in the next parliamentary session. Several months may thus elapse between the two debates, during which time it may prove possible to mobilize opposition and cause the proposal to founder. At the end of a parliament, opposition from the Lords could mean the 'loss' of the whole bill, which would need to be reintroduced after the general election. In practice, however, the Lords have respected Lord Salisbury's doctrine and have not voted down whole bills. Their role is most active in amending legislation, either by improving the drafting or, more rarely, by altering the text on a point of substance (for example, the decision to charge for dental and eye examinations on the National Health Service) and thus facing the government with a difficult choice between overriding the amendment or allowing it to stand.

In France, agreement between the two Assemblies is effected by means of shuttling the proposed text between the two for repeated examination, for such time as it takes to obtain complete and definitive unanimity. If the government wishes to block a text proposed by one Assembly, all it has to do is manipulate the other so as to avert a compromise: the proposal then founders. Furthermore, *only* the Government has the power to unblock the situation when the two Assemblies fail to reach agreement. Once a proposal has been given two readings in each Assembly (or just one, if the government declares the matter to be urgent), the Prime Minister can convene a mixed committee of seven Deputies and seven Senators in all, to represent both the majority and (since 1981) the opposition. This committee must endeavour to elaborate a compromise text that the government is at liberty to put to the vote in both Chambers, including only such amendments as it finds acceptable. If the two Chambers fail to agree over this compromise text, the government is empowered to request the National Assembly to pronounce definitively either upon the text produced by the committee or upon the latest version adopted by the Assembly (which may be revised in the light of amendments made by the Senate). This mechanism is ingenious, for it makes it possible for the government to block or unblock the process at will, choosing, according to the prevailing political circumstances, either to give the Senate parity with the National Assembly or to make it subordinate. In 1958, for instance, General de Gaulle reckoned that he would not obtain a majority in the Assembly but that the Senate would support him. (As it turned out, the reverse was true, for from 1962 to 1969 the Senate opposed de Gaulle.) However, in any event, the government is in a winning position since it can either block the National Assembly with the aid of the Senate or, alternatively, dispense altogether with the Senate's approval. In other words, the two-chamber system provides the executive with an extra means of implementing its own decisions.

The position of the German Bundesrat is strong in some respects, weak in others. If the bill being debated concerns the federation as a whole, opposition from the Bundesrat constitutes a veritable veto. In other strictly federal matters, opposition from the Upper Chamber can be overridden by a Bundestag vote with an absolute majority of its members (or with a two-thirds majority of voting members if more than a two-thirds majority was obtained in the Bundesrat). In Italy, on the other hand, the matter may continue to be shuttled between the two Assemblies, with neither gaining the upper hand. The only constraint imposed upon the two Chambers is of a procedural nature: at a second reading, each can only pronounce upon the amendments tabled by the other, and only amendments that have undergone such modifications may be accepted. The hope is that, by restricting the field of discussion, piecemeal agreement may eventually be reached between these two strictly equal Assemblies. Curiously enough, no formal arbitration procedure has ever been established although mixed commissions are frequently set up, either through the Constitution (such as the commission for regional questions) or as a result of ordinary legislation (such as committees for radio and television, and for southern problems). The functioning and role of the Senate were, however, an important element in the constitutional talks of June 1997.

In Germany, by contrast, as in France, mixed committees are used to settle differences between the two Chambers. Composed of eleven members of the Bundesrat and an equal number of Deputies chosen for their personal qualities, the *Vermittlungsausschus* (mediation committee) was invoked 507 times between 1949 and 1989 to resolve differences. Such committees have no powers of decision, and can only propose compromises for the two Chambers to vote on. However, since the rejection of such compromises usually (in the case of federal laws, at least), means that the bill in question will be quashed, the recommendations of the *Vermittlungsausschus* were followed on all but 52 occasions in the Federal Republic's first 40 years.

Controlling the executive

From the point of view of constitutional theory, the modes of control of a classic parliamentary system and those of a presidential regime have nothing in common. In the former, members of parliament may topple the government by refusing it a vote of confidence or voting a motion of censure, whereas in the latter model two forces, the executive and the legislature, counterbalance one another, blocking each other's moves, without involving the political responsibility of any ministry. Thus, the United States and parliamentary systems seem to represent two strongly contrasting models which apparently share virtually nothing in common. This may be a true opposition at the level of constitutional theory and political philosophy, but it bears little relation to reality or to the manner in which parliaments' modes of control over their executives have evolved ('executives' being, in truth, a misnomer, given the degree of authority that they have acquired). The ambiguity is reflected in the move made, under the Fifth French Republic, to maintain ministerial responsibility of the classic type, even though true power (except in the periods of 'cohabitation', from 1986 to 1988 and 1993 to 1995, and since 1997) was concentrated in the hands of a President whose actions could not be challenged by Parliament. The function of parliaments has changed, as have their means of control over their executives. It is from this point of view that we shall now examine the evolution and transformation of the ways in which parliaments and governments interact.

The persistence and limits of traditional forms of control

The Western parliamentary democracies possess one ultimate instrument for controlling their governments: the vote of confidence or of no confidence. It is a means of control that is still in use and that has been considerably improved, but its importance, in real terms, has been considerably diminished.

In parliamentary systems, parliaments theoretically hold the power of life or death over governments. In practice, however, even if the procedures that constitute the very essence of parliamentarianism do still exist, they are used less and less. For example, Britain, which 'invented' the principle of ministerial responsibility, seldom uses a House of Commons vote of no confidence to unseat a government. And on occasions when it succeeds (as in 1979, when James Callaghan's Labour Government was beaten by a single vote), it does so because the party in power commanded only a composite or extremely small majority anyway. In general, political crises and the implementation of the principle of responsibility manifest themselves not in constitutional forms but internally, within the majority party. When a government finds itself in difficulties, following repeated defeats and disagreements with its majority, it is sometimes forced to resign without any vote of no confidence (as was Chamberlain's Government, in 1940). The dissatisfaction of its back-benchers is expressed through pressures within the party and by acts of 'rebellion' (such as abstentions or hostile votes), which seldom amount to a defeat of the government in strictly constitutional terms. Nevertheless, the Prime Minister may be obliged to take account of dissent within the governing party and either accept the resignation of ministers who have lost the confidence of back-benchers (such as Leon Brittan during the Westland affair early in 1986, or David Mellor in 1992) or take the ultimate step and present his (or her) own resignation. Eden was obliged to do this in 1956 (over the Suez affair), as was Macmillan in 1963 (over the Profumo scandal)—though both also claimed ill-health at the time. Margaret Thatcher left in 1990 because her personal unpopularity had convinced many Conservative MPs that she would lose the next general election; failing to win outright at the first ballot of a party leadership election forced by a challenge from Michael Heseltine, she stood down and then helped to ensure the defeat of Heseltine by her Chancellor of the

Exchequer, John Major.[15] In other words, the classical principle of political responsibility before Parliament has been replaced by a mechanism that allows the party in question to make its own choices and to keep its leader under surveillance.

In Italy, we find a similar discrepancy between constitutional theory and practice, albeit for different reasons and taking different forms. In principle, the government may be called into question whenever a vote of confidence or a motion of no confidence occurs (Article 94). The remarkable solemnity of these procedures is manifested in particular by the fact that every individual Deputy is called upon to cast a public vote. This is no doubt one reason why, to date, only one Italian government has been toppled by these means. Political crises tended to become manifest when disagreements arose over secret votes on government bills (eliminated for the most part in 1988 by a parliamentary reform). The *franchi tiratori* (the deputies of the majority who voted against the government in secret ballots) made the most of such situations to record either their own personal disagreement or the unacknowledged misgivings of their party as a whole. For example, in 1980 the Cossiga Government was forced to resign after two hostile votes on bills that it was proposing when it had barely managed to secure an absolute majority of votes. In June 1986, Bettino Craxi suffered the same fate. In this respect a comparison between Britain and Italy is particularly interesting, for both systems possess mechanisms to facilitate the formation of governments; but in the one case they reinforce government stability while in the other they undermine it. In Britain, the government comprises about 100 members (one-third of the minimum majority), who automatically vote in its support. In Italy, in contrast, governments have a habit of resigning even when they are not constitutionally obliged to do so, and this plays into the hands of those who seek to obtain a minister's portfolio by devious means. However, in both cases the situation may be said to be 'extra-parliamentary', as the Italians put it, in the sense that it becomes an internal problem to be faced by the majority party or coalition. Accordingly, the solemn techniques for registering confidence in the government are increasingly often deflected from their initial objective. Votes of confidence, in Italy, and Article 49.3 in France, for example, are increasingly employed to halt obstructionism on the part of the opposition (or even within the majority), thereby becoming the functional equivalents of the motions to close debates, or the guillotine, that are used in Britain.

Italian governments have also been known to come into being and survive on the basis of a *non sfiducia* (a non-no confidence vote). The Andreotti Governments (claimed to be Governments of National Unity) were supported by the entire constitutional spectrum of political parties, with the exceptions of the MSI on the right and the Radicals and the PDUP on the left. All the parties involved supported a vote of confidence in the Government, with the exception of the Communist Party, which abstained, thereby helping to stabilize the Government and actively collaborating in the elaboration of its policies.

Only one motion of no confidence has been passed in Italy since the war, only one in Britain (in 1979) since 1929, only one in France (in 1962) since 1958. The use of the 'absolute weapon' has become so exceptional that it can no longer be called a parliamentary means of controlling the government. Even in West Germany, where the mechanisms for expressing confidence and no confidence were elaborated in a sophisticated fashion, the Constitution was deflected from its original intentions. Article 67 establishes an unusual mechanism frequently described as a 'constructive vote of no confidence'. According to the Constitution, the Bundestag can only censure and bring about the fall of a government if an absolute majority of its members votes for a new Chancellor to succeed the one just toppled. It is a procedure only used in exceptional circumstances (for example, in 1982, to topple Chancellor Schmidt and replace him by Chancellor Kohl). The truth is that, as in Britain and Italy, many political crises arise and are resolved outside the parliamentary framework. Adenauer's departure in 1963 was largely due to pressure applied by the CDU and the FDP; and his successor, Ludwig Erhard, suffered a similar fate in 1966, having failed to imbue his party with the new impetus that it needed. Brandt's resignation in 1974 was connected with the discovery of an East German spy in his immediate entourage (the Guillaume affair) and consequently had nothing to do with any hostile vote on the part of the Bundestag. But the Chancellor had in any case lost his influence over both his party and his Government and it would have been impossible for him to remain in power. A similar 'deflection' of the constitutional rules takes place if Parliament is dissolved following a vote of no confidence. Even when a majority is so weak or a coalition so divided that it is reduced to impotence, it may still prove impossible for the opposition to appoint a new Chancellor. For example, in April 1972, Barzel, the CDU candidate, obtained only 247 of the necessary 249 votes. In such cases, Article 68 of the Constitution allows the Chancellor to call for a vote of confidence and, if he is defeated (by an absolute majority), to ask the President of the Republic to dissolve the Bundestag within three weeks, if a new Chancellor is not elected within that period. Thus, on 22 September 1972, the Bundestag passed a motion of no confidence in the Brandt Government by 248 votes to 233. That vote was only obtained because of the organized defection of a few members of the majority, which made it possible to satisfy the juridical conditions for a dissolution of Parliament. Similarly, in 1983, although the Kohl Government had enjoyed a comfortable majority since the CDU–CSU–FDP coalition had been set up in the autumn of 1982, it resorted to a dissolution of Parliament to enable the German electorate to ratify the political changes that had taken place following the resignation of the FDP ministers of the Schmidt Government. As in 1972, it proved necessary to 'organize' a vote of no confidence within the majority itself in order to meet the constitutional conditions for a dissolution as laid down by Article 68.

A reversal of the traditional hierarchy: the primacy of unsanctioned controls

Modes of control other than motions of censure and votes of no confidence do not necessarily immediately lead to that highly symbolic event, the fall of a government. For that reason, they were for long—and often still are, even today—considered to be instruments of secondary or minor importance. The role played by these mechanisms of control varies from one country to another, but everywhere the tendency now is to reinforce them, and those countries with the richest panoply of methods of this kind now tend to 'export' them. Let us consider three of the major ones: parliamentary questions or request for information, committees of inquiry and control, and hearings.

The institution of 'Question Time' developed in Britain in the second half of the nineteenth century, at a time when Members of Parliament were less rigidly controlled by their parties. During Question Time (which usually lasts for one hour each day except Friday), Members of Parliament may ask up to two questions each, per day, provided they have given the relevant ministers 48 hours' notice of their intention to do so (in practice this may mean several weeks, as individual ministers' appearances to answer questions are organized by rota). Questions that have not been answered orally by the end of the session subsequently receive a written answer. As in France, the technique of putting questions may have either a practical purpose (to find out more about the administration's position *vis-à-vis* a particular subject) or a political one (to embarrass the government). In Germany, the technique of asking questions is also much in use. About 5,000 questions are asked each year, most of which receive a written reply, the procedure being similar to the British one. Every plenary session (of which there are sixty each year) includes one hour set aside, during which ministers answer about twenty questions. However, in Germany, the role of questions seems on the whole less important than in Britain (although there have been exceptional instances: in 1962, the West German Minister of Defence, Franz Josef Strauss, was obliged to resign following questions put to him over the Spiegel affair). In 1965, 'current questions' (*Aktuelle Stunde*) were introduced, making it possible for the Bundestag to debate the most pressing problems of the moment for one hour every day.

In France, there are two kinds of oral question, those that are not accompanied by a debate and those that are. In the case of the former, the Deputy asks a brief question (lasting no longer than 2 minutes in the Assembly, 5 in the Senate). Following the relevant Minister's answer, he is allowed a maximum of 5 minutes in which to respond. In the case of oral questions accompanied by a debate, the restrictions are less stringent. To explain the problem put before the government, the speaker has between 10 and 20 minutes in the Assembly, 30 minutes in the Senate. Following the Minister's reply, in the Senate each registered speaker is allowed 20 minutes, in the Assembly as long as the President of the session deems fit. The limiting nature of these procedures has provoked two types of reaction. In the first place, in order to secure more time for discussion, the opposition may table a motion of censure even if it has no chance of being adopted, with the sole object of obtaining a debate worthy of the name. Secondly, in 1970 in the Assembly, 1982 in the Senate, a time for 'current questions' was introduced, to give more animation and interest to the dialogue between the executive and the legislature. In 1974, these came to be known as 'Questions for the Government'. This Question Time takes place on Wednesday afternoons in the Assembly. As the session is televised, it produces flights of oratory and dramatic skirmishes which may give the public a somewhat distorted impression of the normal behaviour of Deputies. Wednesdays, furthermore, are the days when the level of attendance is at its highest. In general, the level of parliamentary absenteeism is deplorably high on account of the tendency for Deputies each to accumulate a whole collection of responsibilities at both national and local levels.

Oral questions unaccompanied by a debate are frequently asked (an average of 200 per year), but questions accompanied by a debate are very rare (only 5 in the course of the seventh legislature, which lasted from 1981 to 1986). It is also worth noting that many written questions are asked (17,000 to 18,000 in the Assembly, 5,000 to 6,000 in the Senate, each year). But these questions hardly constitute a means of control over the government. Essentially, their function is practical: to obtain from the Minister an official interpretation of a text or an administrative practice that may then be imposed from above upon his administration as a whole.

In Italy, the practice of Question Time is also much in use and, since the reform of the Chamber's regulations in 1971, Deputies have been able to put their questions not only during plenary Assemblies but also in committees. The number of questions put orally in the Chamber of Deputies rose from 5,458 during the first legislature (1948–53) to 7,886 during the eighth (1979–83), while the number of written questions increased from 12,472 to 20,204 over the same period. But the rate at which replies are forthcoming is low (only 23 per cent of oral questions received a reply in the course of the eighth legislature, chiefly because there were altogether too many to cope with and because of the system of collecting connected questions into a single group). In Italy the Chamber of Deputies organizes times for 'current questions', resembling those in France, Britain, and Germany, once a week, on Wednesdays. During these sessions, the questions are answered immediately and the exchange between the Minister and the Deputy is replaced by a real dialogue. When the Minister concerned has made his reply, five Deputies from different groups are allowed to request further explanations. This practice thus constitutes an intermediate procedure between that of a traditional Question Time and that of what is known in the French Parliament as 'interpellation'.

The practice of interpellation was prohibited under the Fifth French Republic, but is still much in use in other parliamentary systems. In Italy, interpellations, unlike questions, are limited to sessions of the Assembly and are not allowed in commissions. If the author of an interpellation is not satisfied by the reply given by the Minister, he is allowed, according to Article 138 of the Chamber's regulations, to move that there be a 'discussion on the explanations provided by the government'. As with questions, the relatively low percentage of replies received by interpellations (between 12 and 49 per cent, depending on different legislatures) may be partly explained by the increasing use of this procedure (2,546 instances between 1979 and 1983) and by the 'self-sufficient' nature of the parliamentary interpellation, which may be formulated not so much in order to elicit a response and a debate, but rather to sound out public opinion on both the issue concerned and the standing of the Deputy involved.

In Germany, the formula of the 'minor interpellation' (*Kleine Anfrage*) has been extremely successful. It differs from other forms of interpellation in that it is constituted by written questions posed by at least twenty-six Deputies (the minimum required to make up a parliamentary group or *Fraktion*). A reply must be given by the Minister or government within a fortnight, and is usually expected to contain detailed answers, the purpose of which is not to give rise to a debate but to provide the parliamentary group concerned with as much information as possible; as many as 400 to 500 minor interpellations are made each year. Interpellations in the classical form (*Grosse Anfragen*) allow the opposition to force a Bundestag debate on a major policy issue. Their use declined from about 40 a year in the early years of the Federal Republic to ten or eleven in the 1960s and 1970s. However, thanks in part to an influx of combative Green Deputies, the number of *Grosse Anfragen* rose sharply to 175 for the 1983–7 Bundestag, returning to levels of the early 1950s.[16]

In Britain, the interpellation takes the form of what is known as a 'motion of adjournment' made by back-benchers of the government or of the opposition. When Question Time is up and before Parliament turns to the matters listed on its agenda, any member of the House of Commons has the right to table a motion to debate 'a specific and important matter that should have urgent consideration'. However, he must have the backing of forty other members and convince the Speaker of the interest of such a debate. Since the reform of Standing Order no. 9, in 1967, the Speaker has been relieved of all constraints of precedence and must simply decide whether the subject is 'proper to be discussed'. If the motion is accepted, the debate is organized for the following afternoon and is brought to a close after a maximum of three hours. More frequent, and more brief, are the half-hour adjournment motions at the end of the main business of the Commons, when back-benchers who have entered a ballot may raise questions. In all these possible circumstances which (with certain variants) are common to all parliamentary systems, the control exercised by the chambers depends not so much upon the sanctions that they may impose, but rather upon the continuing pressure that they apply to the government and the administration, and the publicity that this attracts. These new modes of control have acquired a progressive importance due to the work of the media that publicize them and possess the power to turn any question raised by a member of parliament into a national debate. It is the formidable impact of the media that makes these controls without sanctions so powerful.

Committees of inquiry are part of the parliamentary tradition but, as a result of American experiments and practices, here and there other forms of parliamentary monitoring have been developed, in particular taking the shape of investigations and hearings.

France is probably the country in which committees of control or inquiry possess the least influence. In the first place, as we have seen above, the National Assembly may set up no more than six permanent committees, the effect of which is to turn them into veritable mini-Assemblies comprising, on average, about 100 members. The only possibility left for Deputies is to set up temporary committees of inquiry and control (whose duration is limited to six months). These committees, composed on the basis of proportional representation of the various party groups, are in effect dominated by the majority, which generally seizes the key posts of chairman and 'spokesman' and is thus in a position to draw up the report that suits it, while the minority has no chance to express its views in a dissenting report. Under the Fifth Republic, this bipolarization has undermined the credibility of these inquiries to such a degree that, in some cases (the *Rainbow Warrior* affair of 1985, for example), the opposition has given up pressing for the creation of special committees. It is, for example, significant that between 1981 and 1986, a period marked by considerable political tension, only 3 committees of inquiry were set up (though 61 were requested) and not a single committee of control (2 were requested). It should also be noted that the proceedings of these committees were until recently secret and the committees may decide not to publish their reports. Furthermore, they may not be set up (or must cease their activities) when a judicial inquiry is set up to deal with the same question. As can be seen from all these restrictions, committees of inquiry or control in France have so far played little more than a marginal role. Only the senatorial committees of the 1960s (a period when the Senate was opposing de Gaulle) truly fulfilled the functions of monitoring and inquiry that one might expect from a parliamentary Assembly. There has been some sign of this changing under the 1988–93 Parliament, under the influence of an activist President of the National Assembly (former Prime Minister Laurent Fabius) committed to reinforcing its activities. Thus in 1991 a committee of enquiry chaired by an opposition Deputy, Pierre Mazeaud, investigated the sensitive issue of party finance—and did so in public, publishing its proceedings. In practice, however, it was unable to persuade many of its witnesses to talk in sufficient detail, and so did not constitute a decisive break with the past pattern of ineffectiveness.

In Britain, the 1979 measures taken to reform committees created fourteen select committees to follow up matters connected with their respective areas of responsibility. The number of these committees and the degree of their specialization makes it possible for them to keep a close eye on the functioning and policies of each of the various Ministries (except, till 1991, the Lord Chancellor's department and the government's law officers), and their power of control is strengthened by the fact that the Ministers themselves and their parliamentary private secretaries, that is to say the Members of Parliament who assist them, are excluded from the relevant committees. The backbenchers consequently play a considerably more important role in these committees than they do in the business of legislation, particularly since the parliamentary 'prima donnas' who are not in the government tend to rule themselves out through lack of time. These select committees may hear all persons necessary for the completion of their tasks and produce reports which give a general account of the information received in the course of these hearings. Their effectiveness is open to question, however, for three reasons. Firstly, they share a general problem with the House of Commons in that they are badly understaffed, compared not only with the committees of the United States Congress, but even with their European counterparts. This limits their investigative power. Secondly, although select committees are supposedly free of partisan loyalties, a means for the Commons to act as a check on the executive, there are few guarantees that the power of party discipline, so invasive elsewhere in the House of Commons, will stop at the committee-room door. This became a particularly contentious issue in 1996, when one of the Conservative government's whips, David Willetts, was found to have recommended exploiting the 'good Tory majority' on the Commons Standards and Privileges Committee investigating corruption allegations relating to a former Conservative minister, Neil Hamilton. The episode resulted in the resignation (as Whip) of Willetts, but suspicion was widespread that his memo, albeit with an unusual absence of discretion, reflected common practice.[17] Thirdly, even where a Select Committee produces an all-party report that is highly critical of the Government, as has happened, the matter may remain there after perhaps half a day in the national headlines; fewer than 5 per cent of select committee reports are ever debated in the Commons.

West Germany seems to have had difficulty in putting the committees of inquiry (*Untersuchungsausschuß*) prescribed by the Constitution to positive and intensive use. In his study of Western Germany, Gordon Smith[18] interprets this relative weakness on the basis of the peculiar characteristics of the Bundestag, which are indeed very different from those of the House of Commons. As he sees it, whereas the House of Commons is essentially a forum, the Bundestag is a legislative body. It is an *Arbeitsparlament*, which devotes most of its time to committee work rather than to plenary Assemblies, and most of its energies to drafting and amending laws rather than, strictly speaking, monitoring the administration. We should also note that Germany's extremely strong juridical tradition, which includes juridical controls, makes parliamentary monitoring less essential.[19] Consequently, no more than a score or so of committees of inquiry have been set up since 1949 and few of these have reached any satisfactory conclusions, probably because they are over-politicized. From this point of view, the situation resembles that of France, where the majority frequently seeks to prevent inquiries of an embarrassing kind from taking place, and where the opposition sometimes settles for a boycott rather than participation.

Article 82 of the Italian Constitution rules that every Assembly may conduct inquiries into affairs of public interest through committees formed on the basis of proportional representation of the parliamentary groups and 'holding the same powers and subject to the same limitations as those of the judicial authority'. In practice, special laws are passed to set up these committees, in which both Chambers are usually represented. It is a way of extending the powers attributed by the Constitution. (For example, certain secrets that may not be divulged even to the judiciary must be revealed to a committee established by the Constitution.) The enhanced role of these committees of inquiry is a consequence of the political and social trauma that Italy suffered during the 1970s. The proliferation of scandals, terrorism, and Mafia operations underlined the degree to which the political, administrative, judicial, policing, and financial apparatus had become corrupt. In the course of the eighth legislature, for example, the two Chambers had to set up inquiries into affairs such as the assassination of Aldo Moro, the Sindona scandal (tragically concluded in March 1986, when the banker was discovered poisoned to death in his cell), and the P2 Masonic Lodge. Some of the inquiries were so extensive as to involve years and years of investigation, and even so the questioning of hundreds of individuals did not always lead to altogether conclusive results. The P2 affair, for example, which had exploded so publicly, was wound up correspondingly discreetly, but no clear conclusions were ever reached, no action ever taken (despite the most insistent protests from the Italian Communist Party). Furthermore, the existence of these committees poses certain delicate problems regarding their relations with the judicial authorities—problems that were only partially resolved by Decision no. 231 made by the Constitutional Court in 1975. The Court was of the opinion that the committees should agree to pass on to the judiciary all the evidence and information that they had collected, except for those that they considered it necessary to keep secret in order to be able to fulfil their tasks. Furthermore, the increasingly penal nature of these committees raises the problem of what guarantees to offer to the individuals interrogated. It has been agreed that those interrogated on matters that could lead to penal sentences for them may claim legal assistance, but also that the committee may proceed to arrest a witness in a case of false evidence or a refusal to collaborate. This shift from the political to the legal domain is risky, for a good system of justice needs serenity, rules, and guarantees that the committees of inquiry can provide only partially, if at all. Perhaps not surprisingly, the task of exposing the corruption at the heart of the Italian political system was finally carried out, not by parliamentary investigations, but by a judiciary which had, unlike many parliamentarians, remained outside the circle of plunder.

Conclusion

How should we evaluate the role of contemporary parliaments and their place in the institutions of their respective countries?

To answer this question, we must start by dismissing the myth that usually obscures the issue, namely, that there ever was some kind of parliamentarian Golden Age when parliaments which expressed the democratic will were the corner-stone of the constitutional system, exerting effective control over the government and dominating the legislative process. It is true that the power and influence of parliaments have been greater in particular periods and in particular countries (Britain, the United States, and France, in particular). However, a number of qualifications are called for. In the first place, the power of parliaments has frequently been exaggerated, for strategic reasons, by those seeking to create a freer, less authoritarian society. In France, for instance, the myth of British parliamentarianism has been fostered in the interests of certain political groups or parties. Secondly, even when they were powerful or appeared to be, parliaments no more than imperfectly fulfilled their first duty, namely, to represent the people as a whole: limited suffrage, rotten boroughs, electoral corruption, pressures exerted by the existing authorities, etc. were not the exception, but the rule. Thirdly, it is all too often forgotten that the 'decline' of parliament that is nowadays so much lamented has been going on for an extremely long time. It has been pointed out that Bagehot's classic work *The English Constitution*, celebrating the British Parliament, describes a situation that no longer obtained even at the date of its publication (1867). In similar fashion, the critics of the Fifth French Republic are evoking largely mythical parliaments when they contrast the 1958 Parliament to the Assemblies of the Third and Fourth Republics. All too often they confuse unrest with influence, and the ability to topple governments with that of bringing some influence to bear upon the course of events. There can be no better illustration of the parliamentary decrepitude of the Third and Fourth Republics than their respective capitulations, in 1940 and 1958, when the Assemblies placed themselves totally in the hands of two men of destiny, first Pétain, then de Gaulle, in order to set up new institutions. If we recognize that the erstwhile so-called power of parliaments is illusory, the present-day situation appears less dramatic than it is often made out to be.

The first point to emphasize is that parliaments have seldom been more representative than they are today. Suffrage is more or less universal, guarantees to ensure that elections are free from corruption are constantly being improved, and the drawing of constituency boundaries, while not always perfect, is also becoming fairer and better monitored in the European democracies.

Secondly, parliaments remain the forums of political life *par excellence* and, seen from this point of view, their audience, far from shrinking, has increased, thanks to the Press, television, and radio, all of which are mediators and broadcasters of the parliamentary debate.

Thirdly, parliaments, in Europe at least, are still the places where government members tend to be recruited (or at the very least legitimized). In Italy and Germany (and elsewhere too), nobody becomes a Minister until he has proved himself as a Member of Parliament. Even in France, where General de Gaulle tried to separate the functions of Ministers and Deputies, tradition proved stronger than his political will. In Britain, although junior ministerial posts are given to peers to be the government's spokespersons in the Lords, and ministers may occasionally be appointed from outside parliament and then found a peerage or a safe Commons seat, the core of the government still consists of experienced Commons performers. Only the United States differs in this respect. Furthermore, the ever-increasing importance of political parties helps to consolidate the links and interchanges between governments and parliaments, encouraging the professionalism of politicians and making for the reconciliation of the antagonistic views of different groups.

Fourthly, the 'input' of a parliament cannot be reduced to the passing of bills. At an earlier stage, it also involves deciding upon party programmes, fixing the political agenda, and negotiating with the executive over legislative proposals. For governments cannot afford to ignore parliamentary advice and opinions, even as they prepare their own proposals. Indeed, very often government bills are the fruit of a synthesis of legislative proposals that have already been tabled (one example in France being the proposals to legalize abortion).

Fifthly, while the impact of party discipline, in Britain but also elsewhere, has done much to blunt the use of formal modes of parliamentary activity both in legislation and control, party is a two-way street. It is at their own peril that governments ignore the concerns of their parliamentarians about their re-election prospects (as Mrs Thatcher found to her cost in 1990); yet such concerns may not find expression in any formal procedures of legislation or scrutiny.[20]

Sixthly, parliamentary decline is often claimed to be particularly dramatic in the area of controls. But, while parliaments frequently do find it extremely difficult to exercise control, here, too, the scale of parliamentary decline has been exaggerated as a consequence of the prevailing notion that control boils down to votes of confidence or motions of censure. Yet it is quite possible for controls to be effective even without involving any 'political responsibility' in the parliamentary sense, as the example of the United States reminds us. And meanwhile the case of Italy makes the point that the game of toppling governments in which its Parliament indulges is really more a way of paying off old party scores than a means of imposing effective control over the actions of the executive. Parliamentary control limited to the formal procedures of the legislature can indeed be ineffective, even if formally successful. On the other hand, parliamentary control as one link in a chain involving the media and public opinion can be devastating, even if the impact on formal procedures is slight. That, of course, imposes an obligation on the media and public opinion, as well as on parliamentarians, to behave as if it mattered.

The pluses and minuses are thus much more evenly balanced than may at first sight appear, if we bear in mind that parliaments today avail themselves of their modes of intervention within an institutional, political, and social framework that is very different from that in which Assemblies were originally conceived. That is emphatically not to deny the need for reforms on a wide range of issues, such as the designation of upper houses (especially in the United Kingdom and France) or the absurdity of the standing committees in the British House of Commons. It is, on the other hand, to deny the view that parliaments no longer matter. For as Polsby[21] observes, parliaments are more than ever 'multi-purpose organizations' with a role of central importance to play in democracies of the Western type, and their influence is by no means limited to the closed space of the formal political arena.[22]

Questions

- In what sense should legislatures 'represent' voters?

- Do parliaments in Western Europe legislate?

- What roles do committees play in West European parliaments, and how important are they?

- How much can the analysis of formal rules and procedures tell us about the powers of legislatures in Western Europe?

- What evidence does Western Europe offer of a 'decline of Parliaments' since 1945?

NOTES

1. P. Avril, 'L'Assemblée d'aujourdhui', *Pouvoirs*, 34 (1985), 9.

2. G. Smith, *Politics in Western Europe*, 4th edn. (London: Heinemann, 1983), 171.

3. F. Cazzola and M. Morisi, *L' Alluvione dei decreti* (Milan: Giuffre, 1985); R. Motta, 'L' Attività legislativa dei governi 1948–1983', *Rivista italiana di scienza politica*, 15(2) (1985), 255–92.

4. Avril, 'L' Assemblée d'aujourdhui', 5.

5. These figures represent the average since 1945. See J. Dutheil de la Rochère, 'L'Inflation législative et règlementaire en Grande-Bretagne', in C. Debbasch (ed.), *L'Inflation législative et règlementaire en Europe* (Paris: CNRS, 1986), 106. Cf. also A. Adonis, *Parliament Today* (2nd edn.; Manchester: University Press, 1993), 110.

6. See Y. Mény (ed.), *Dix ans de régionalisation en Europe* (Paris: Cujas, 1982).

7. O. Jouanjan, 'L'élaboration de la loi en République fédérale d'Allemagne', *Pouvoirs*, 66 (1993), 89.

8. A. Baldassare, 'Le "Performances" del parlamento italiano nell'ultimo quindecennio', in G. Pasquino (ed.), *Il Sistema politica italiano* (Bari: Laterza, 1985), 313. Intervention by the President of the Chamber of Deputies was made possible by a change in the regulations introduced in 1981. (The President of the Senate had held that prerogative since 1971.)

9. G. De Vergottini, *Les Investigations des commissions parlementaries en Italie*, i (Paris: RDP, 1985), 37 ff.

10. Adonis, *Parliament Today*, 154.

11. Crossman quoted in G. Drewry, 'Legislating', in M. Ryle and P. G. Richards (eds.), *The Commons under Scrutiny* (London: Routledge, 1988), 129; A. Clark, *Diaries* (London: Phoenix Paperback Editions, 1994), 66.

12. P. Cahoua, 'Les Commissions, lieu du travail législatif', *Pouvoirs*, 34 (1985), 37–49.

13. J. A. G. Griffith, *Parliamentary Scrutiny of Government Bills* (London: Allen and Unwin, 1974); Philip Norton, 'Parliament in the United Kingdom', in id. (ed.), *Parliaments in Western Europe* (London: Frank Cass, 1990), 17–18.

14. The same procedure may be adopted when the House is sitting as a 'committee of the whole

House', and also in standing committees (in the latter case, provided the motion is supported by one-third of the committee).

15. The Conservative Party has also been known to encourage its leaders to resign following electoral defeats. Sir Alec Douglas-Home was forced to resign in July 1965 under pressure from back-benchers and whips who were convinced after the Conservatives' 1964 defeat that Home could not lead them to victory. Edward Heath, having lost two general elections in 1974, went on to lose the Conservative Party leadership election to Margaret Thatcher in 1975. She won three elections in succession, but still became vulnerable when it appeared unlikely that she would repeat the feat a fourth time. John Major's departure from the leadership in 1997 was a foregone conclusion, which he accepted gracefully as soon as it became clear that he had lost that year's election. Defeated Labour leaders have had more control over the timing of their departures: James Callaghan took over 18 months to resign as leader after Labour lost power in 1979, but both Michael Foot in 1983 and Neil Kinnock in 1992 were quicker—Kinnock leaving three days after Labour's fourth defeat.

16. See N. Johnson, 'Questions in the Bundestag', *Parliamentary Affairs*, 16(1) (1962–3); T. Saalfeld, 'The West German Bundestag after 40 Years: The Role of Parliament in a "Party Democracy"', *West European Politics*, 13(3) (July 1990), 68–89.

17. D. Leigh and E. Vulliamy, *Sleaze: The Corruption of Parliament* (London: Fourth Estate, 1997), 240–52.

18. G. Smith, *Democracy in Western Germany: Parties and Politics in the Federal Republic* (London: Heinemann, 1979).

19. It should also be pointed out that Germany has particular methods of control that fulfil an important function: among them, the right of citizens to petition the Bundestag (over 12,000 petitions are currently presented each year), the right of all individuals to apply to the federal Constitutional Court over a violation of basic human rights, and the creation, in 1956, of a kind of ombudsman for military matters, etc.

20. Cf. e.g. J. Brand, *British Parliamentary Parties: Policy and Power* (Oxford: Clarendon Press, 1992).

21. N. Polsby, 'Legislatures', in F. I. Greenstein and N. W. Polsby (eds.), *Handbook of Political Science*, v (Reading, Mass.: Addison, Wesley, 1975), 301.

22. F. Baumgartner, in a recent study ('Parliament's Capacity to Expand Political Controversy in France', *Legislative Studies Quarterly*, 12(1) (Feb. 1987), 33–54) concludes his assessment of the role of Parliament in France as follows: 'The French Parliament is not the center of policy making by any stretch of imagination. It is the center of politics, however, and politics can have a great impact on policy.'

CHAPTER 6

Presidents and Governments

While the political systems of the democracies may all be founded upon common principles such as the separation of powers and popular representation through Parliament, there are substantial differences between one country and another in the procedures of constitutional machinery set up to achieve these objectives. The purest and, at the same time, most strongly contrasting systems are those of Britain and the United States. Britain represents the model of a parliamentary system, the United States that of a presidential one. Between these two extremes of constitutional classification, there exists a whole range of variants which are the delight of typology specialists. In view of all the profound organizational and structural differences that even a cursory examination reveals, to attempt to compare government institutions may thus seem a risky venture. Nevertheless, one fact is bound to strike the observer over and above the many marked institutional differences: namely, the central character of the function of government virtually universally. This is as true of primitive societies as it is of the most developed ones, and of liberal democracies as well as of the most bloodthirsty dictatorships. No other political institution is so common a feature of all political systems: a government is, as it were, the very incarnation of power. Henri Lefebvre has spoken of the 'catholic' nature of the State, underlining the formidable expansion of this particular form of organized power, and Jean Blondel, in his turn, similarly points out the remarkable 'universality of the phenomenon of government'.[1]

The fact is that, over and above the diversity of institutions in different countries, a fundamental need for command and coercion emerges, even if the Western translation of that need has led to a differentiation and limitation of the organs of power (a separation of powers). Beyond the differences engendered by different histories and cultures, common objectives and functions truly do seem to exist. Besides, we should not exaggerate the importance of institutional differences between the various Western systems, for they are often more formal than substantial and tend to become less striking as a result of 'contamination' from one system to another. Furthermore, similar constitutional structures (for example, those of Germany, Italy, and Britain) may coexist with highly varied political practices. Consequently, it is only through a more detailed analysis that we may seize upon the ways in which the European executives differ from or resemble one another and the roles they play in their respective political systems.

The executive

There is no unanimously accepted term to denote the function of government. Montesquieu used the expression 'executive power' but, following Rousseau, the lustre of that expression was dimmed by France's Revolutionaries, who resorted instead to anthropomorphic images, assimilating an executive to a simple executor: the legislature was the head of the system, the executive simply the hand that executed its orders. In the United States, the term 'executive' applies to the President and his collaborators, but de Gaulle insisted that the adjective 'executive' applied solely to the government. In Britain, the word 'executive' generally refers not only to the government itself, but also to the administration placed under it. On the other hand, the term 'government' may equally apply to the whole collection of institutions, rules, and procedures by which the country is run. Here, it is the word 'Cabinet' that most closely corresponds to the French *gouvernement* or the Italian *governo*. However, neither in France nor in Germany nor in Italy does there exist any expression that adequately conveys the dual nature of an executive power that is divided between a President and a head of government.

In parliamentary systems, dual executives are the end-product of a slow evolution in the course of which the prerogatives of the monarch have been transferred to the government and the Prime Minister. The transformation of the role of the monarchy, which has become increasingly symbolic and ceremonial, has made it possible to transfer to a system in which the Head of State embodies the continuity of the State and its institutions, without holding the power or means to devise or implement policies of his or her own. Moreover, by avoiding even a formal concentration of power within the hands of a single executive figurehead, the dual solution incorporates both political and constitutional advantages which may well account for its success among European democracies such as Greece, Spain, and Portugal that have recently emerged from dictatorships.

The Head of State

Let us begin with the grand exception (though an exception which may find Italian imitators). In the French Fifth Republic, the head of State is the institutional 'keystone', to borrow the words of one of the constitution's authors (and de Gaulle's first Prime Minister), Michel Debré. In a Constitution bearing many of the marks of a parliamentary system, this presidential power is something of a paradox. Its extent is barely contested: there is a strong case for claiming that, from 1958 to 1986 (which saw the beginning of the 'cohabitation' between the Right and the Socialists that lasted up until 1988), no Western Head of State or Prime Minister—not even the President of the United States—held such extensive powers. These powers were reinforced by the fact that, since the 1962 reform,[2] the French Head of State has been elected by universal suffrage, which confers upon him greater legitimacy than that possessed by any other politician, a legitimacy as great as that of the National Assembly itself. The mechanisms of election were indeed deliberately elaborated in order to reinforce that legitimacy. Candidates must be put up by 500 'sponsors' hailing from thirty departments (Deputies or local elected officials). In the first ballot of the election, they compete freely. However, to be declared the winner it is necessary to obtain an absolute majority of votes. If no candidate obtains such a majority (and none ever has, yet), only the two candidates who head the poll may stand for a second ballot. This guarantees that, whatever the outcome, the victor will have been elected by an absolute majority of all votes cast. In France, the political consensus is too fragile to allow the appointment of a minority President (as has been known in the United States), or for a President elected by a small fraction of the population to be politically acceptable.

Armed with his prestige (in the case of de Gaulle) or 'consecrated' by the vote, a President of the Fifth Republic holds considerable powers even though he carries no political responsibility and is elected for a very long term of office (seven years), the only justification for which is the tradition established under the Third Republic. The Constitution bestows numerous powers upon him: he appoints the Prime Minister, presides over the Council of Ministers, signs decrees and ordinances, appoints three members of the Constitutional Council (including its President), and also senior civil servants. But in addition, he is Commander-in-Chief of the Armed Forces and head of the Diplomatic Service; he can call a referendum, and he can dissolve the National Assembly (a right which de Gaulle used with success in 1968, as Mitterrand did in 1981 and 1988, but which led to a major defeat for Chirac when he did the same in 1997). Finally, in exceptional circumstances (war or rioting), Article 16 gives him the right to exercise a kind of 'legal dictatorship': for such time as he deems necessary, he may assume all powers necessary for dealing with the situation. (These measures were clearly prompted by President Lebrun's inability, in 1939–40, to manage events when de

Gaulle, for his part, announced his intention of continuing the struggle from a London base.)

As listed above, these powers are already startling enough. But it should also be noted that, from 1958 to 1986, they were further extended by two factors: the 'conventions' created by the practices of de Gaulle and his successors; and the combination, over almost thirty years, of the presidential and the parliamentary majorities. The Head of State thus had at his disposal a generally docile majority and also a government completely at his service, and was thereby in a position to adopt an extremely wide interpretation of his powers. In practice, there was no limit to the problems to which the President could address himself: agricultural negotiations in Brussels, fiscal policies, decisions regarding one particular group or another. There is probably no other Western country where a President could have the last word on the route to be taken by a regional line of the Paris Underground (de Gaulle), or decide to create a cultural centre (Pompidou), a Parisian museum (Giscard d'Estaing), or to undertake a whole series of major public building projects (Mitterrand). In effect, the Elysée has often operated as a substitute for Matignon (the seat of the government) to the extent that technical councillors and the heads of presidential missions had systematic access to the files of every Ministry and frequently also the last say in decisions on these matters. One of the characteristics of the French system is that the *éminences grises* (the high-ranking civil servants on the staffs of the President, the Prime Minister, and other Ministers) often have far more influence and power than the political or administrative personnel who are in principle responsible for devising and elaborating policies.

This quasi-monarchical system was disrupted by the victory of the Right in the parliamentary elections of 1986, at a time when François Mitterrand, the Socialist President, was to continue as Head of State until 1988. This was the start of the first period of what journalists and politicians refer to as 'cohabitation'. It was the first time that such a situation had arisen under the Fifth Republic and it promised to be an explosive one, since relations between the majority and the opposition in France have in the past traditionally been atrocious. Ever since 1789, a series of governments have collapsed or ended abruptly as a result of *coups d'état* or civil wars, having failed to convert the Constitutional text into a political and social pact. As it turned out, however, the constitutional experiment ran its course without too many upsets. This was certainly not because of any unexpected personal rapport between Mitterrand and his unchosen Premier, Jacques Chirac; on the contrary, their relations were visibly poisonous by the end of the two years. The explanation lies firstly in the fact that a presidential election was imminent; secondly in the probability, understood by both men, that they would be candidates; and thirdly in the public's generally favourable reception to the division of powers that results from cohabitation, and the logical corollary to that, the threat of deep unpopularity falling upon the first of the two adversaries to break the appearance of collaboration based on the letter of the Constitution. Two further cohabitations have followed since 1988, each under rather different political circumstances. From March 1993 till May 1995, Mitterrand was in a far weaker position than seven years earlier, because the Left had been practically swept away in a landslide of the parliamentary elections and because he himself was terminally ill. The second of his right-wing Prime Ministers, Édouard Balladur, could therefore encroach more on the presidential domain than Chirac had ever done, notably in foreign policy. Finally, from June 1997, Chirac himself, now elected President, had to appoint a Socialist Prime Minister, Lionel Jospin, in a situation that was especially unpredictable because no elections, presidential or parliamentary, were officially due until 2002.

Compared with the way in which institutions operate during periods of agreement between the President and the Assembly, cohabitation considerably reduces the powers of the Head of State.

Once the President has entrusted the premiership to a Prime Minister from the opposite 'camp', he is obliged to leave him a large measure of freedom in the choice of his Ministers. Between 1958 and 1986, the composition of governments was affected more by the choices made by the President than by proposals coming from the Prime Minister. In a period of cohabitation, however, it is the Prime Minister who forms his government (as the Constitution states he should) to a large extent at his own discretion. All the same, it was noticeable that in the Chirac Government of March 1986, the appointments of two Ministers (Foreign Affairs and Defence) resulted from a measure of consensus between the President and the Prime Minister, a fact accounted for by the sweeping powers that the Constitution allots to the President in these two areas. Furthermore, in periods of cohabitation, when the government and the National Assembly stand in opposition to the President, it is difficult for the latter to call for a referendum or to institute a revision of the Constitution; for the Head of State may only take those two decisions when the government or Parliament proposes that he should do so.

Apart from the power to dissolve the Assembly, that of implementing Article 16, and the right to tender his resignation, a President in a period of cohabitation thus loses most of the freedom of manœuvre available to him in a period of consensus, for he is deprived of the support afforded by a government appointed largely by himself and that of a majority in the Assembly. In these circumstances, it is well and truly the government, on the strength of its majority in the Assembly, that 'determines and directs the policies of the nation' (Article 20 of the Constitution).

The constitutional and political influence of the Head of State is much weaker in the other parliamentary systems. In Britain, the Head of State, who is also Head of the Church of England, is designated according to the hereditary principle. In Germany and Italy, the President of the Republic is elected according to a procedure that confirms both the national and the federal or regional nature of the political system. In Germany, the electoral college is composed of members of the Bundestag and an equal number of delegates elected on the basis of proportional representation by the various *Landtage*. Each *Land* contributes a number of delegates in proportion to its population, but, unlike the system for the Bundesrat, in which the *Länder* representatives represent the existing *Länder* governments, in a presidential election the delegates are representative of the various political forces (CDU, SPD, etc.). Italy has hitherto displayed an approach comparable to Germany's, although the modalities of selection are somewhat different (and constitutional reform may result in a major switch to direct universal suffrage). A President of Italy is elected by the two Chambers in a common Assembly chaired by the president of the Chamber of Deputies. These Deputies are joined by three delegates from each region (but only one from the Aosta Valley) at least one of whom, usually, does not belong to the regional majority. In both countries the relative strengths of the parties are crucial, even if this is, in principle, tempered by the fact that voting is secret. The result has therefore generally been a fairly predictable one, even if, in a multi-party system, it has sometimes taken several ballots to reach. Recent elections in both countries, however, have been exceptions in this respect. Italy's choice of president in May 1992 was deeply perturbed by the destabilization of the party system in the parliamentary elections which had just taken place; these resulted in even more convoluted party negotiations than usual, which only ended after the public's revulsion at the assassination of Judge Falcone made them appear grotesque. In Germany in 1994, Chancellor Kohl's preferred choice for the post, Steffen Heitmann, faced such wide-spread criticism for his views on women, and for his claim that Germany could now draw a line under the Nazi past, that he was forced to withdraw, leaving the job open for the less alarming Roman Herzog.

In all three countries, the modalities of acceding to power condition the extent and nature of the responsibilities and functions involved. These may be summarized under three headings: the symbolic function, the function of providing a constitutional guarantee, and the function of maintaining balance.

1. The symbolic function may seem the least significant, but in reality it probably constitutes one of the most important elements of a Head of State's powers, since it is this that authorizes and legitimizes his or her intervention in domains in which, in principle, the powers are no more than nominal. The Heads of State who possess the widest room for manœuvre are those who have most successfully managed to symbolize the country's identity, being seen as the incarnation of all the public and private virtues of their people. It is that identification that makes it possible for the British sovereign to symbolize the unity and permanence of the State (the Crown) over and above all political divisions. The Queen is so totally neutral that she speaks as is demanded, as the mouthpiece of either the Labour or the Conservative Party when she delivers the Queen's Speech, which is written by whoever is the current Prime Minister. Her position is far above party and parliamentary antagonisms: Her Majesty's Government has to coexist alongside Her Majesty's Opposition. Her international prestige is what provides the tenuous but nevertheless solid link between the various components of a widely disparate Commonwealth. She is also the Head of the Church of England. All these attributes combine to make the British sovereign's political role the model for all monarchs and even for parliamentary Heads of State. In the republican States of Italy and Germany, the mission of the President of the Republic is analogous, but is subjected to additional constraints. Given that the parties play such an important role in selecting the Head of State, the political nature of the candidate and the appointment inevitably

weaken his position as a symbol of national unity to some extent. Every newly elected President is obliged to try to erase the memory of his erstwhile party allegiances. That requirement is not always an easy one to fulfil, particularly when the elected President's past gives rise to polemics (Lübke in 1967–8, Leone in 1978, and Waldheim, elected President of Austria in 1986). The personality of a Head of State and his general *savoir-faire* are thus essential ingredients in the construction of the presidential image. The first President of West Germany, Theodor Heuss, and the popular Sandro Pertini of Italy are both remarkable examples of Presidents who had the ability to create a powerful presidential image—as was Francesco Cossiga, though in a way successors may not wish to emulate.

2. In parliamentary democracies, Heads of State also stand as guarantors of the country's institutions. This function is to some extent a counterpart to their declining role as effective focuses of power, for, as can be seen from the example of the Fifth French Republic, this function of guardian of the country's institutions is materially guaranteed by the measures that assure the Head of State a longer term of office than other institutions (in particular, Parliament). The Italian President is elected for seven years, the two Chambers for only five; the German President for five years, the Bundestag for four; and the British monarchy is still officially grounded upon the continuity symbolically expressed by the cry of 'The King is dead. Long live the King!' Given the weakness of their powers, however, it seems fair to wonder whether these Heads of State really do effectively guarantee the continuity of the State. In light of the 1939–40 disaster in France and Lebrun's attitude at the time, de Gaulle's response at the Liberation was negative; and in 1958, René Coty, in his turn, contributed to the move towards a change in the political system rather than defend the Fourth Republic which, it must be admitted, was already moribund.

However, the attitudes of French Presidents from 1939 to 1958 and their individual failures in their fundamental mission could not, on their own, justify the establishment of a President with extensive powers. The German and Italian experiences of the interwar period would indeed warn against such a move. Neither the considerable powers nor the strong influence of the Heads of State in the Weimar Republic and the Italian monarchy were capable of preventing the corruption of their countries' political systems, nor the rise of Hitler and Mussolini.

3. Heads of State have a third, equally delicate mission: to act as arbiters. In Britain, this function is seldom called upon, although in difficult circumstances the monarch may make his or her influence felt. This happens when a general election results in no absolute majority and, discreetly, sometimes in other circumstances too. In 1945, for example, Attlee acted on the 'advice' of George VI, and chose Bevin as Foreign Secretary rather than Hugh Dalton: and in 1986, the British Press suggested that the Queen, as Head of the Commonwealth, may have tried to persuade Margaret Thatcher to adopt a firmer attitude towards South Africa. This role of maintaining balance, by 'exerting influence', as President Vincent Auriol of France was so often claimed to have done under the Fourth Republic, also depends more upon a Head of State's personality than upon the specific powers allotted to him by the Constitution. For example, the first President

of the Italian Republic, Luigi Einaudi, managed to create for the post of President, for which there was no historical precedent, an autonomous political 'space', particularly when it came to appointing members of the Constitutional Court, dissolving Parliament, and even choosing a President of the Council. (Pella, for example, was chosen without any consultation.) Between 1948 and 1955 the parties had a chance to assess the importance of the post of President and that was no doubt what sparked off the ferocious battles to gain control of it. Gronchi tried, unsuccessfully, to make the double post of Head of State and President of the Council approximate more closely to that of an American-style President, while the election of Segni, President from 1962 to 1964, was the price that the left wing of the Christian Democrats (who favoured a centre-left government) had to pay to the party's conservative wing. For that very reason, and also because he did not approve of the existing coalitions, Segni, in two short years of office, made more use than any of his predecessors of the Head of State's power to refuse to ratify adopted laws when the funds necessary for their application had not been voted.

His successor, Giuseppe Saragat (1964–71) took his role as a guarantor of the centre-left formula so seriously that he steered the formation of all governments in that direction, thereby exceeding the strict terms of his institutional mandate. The subsequent election of Giovanni Leone (1971–8) marked both a return in force of the Centre-Right and at the same time a more discreet interpretation of the role of President. Leone was obliged to tender his resignation six months before the end of his presidential term (as a result of being compromised in the Lockheed scandal), but while in office he had helped to give the post of President a lower profile that was more in keeping with the model envisaged by the Constitution. The election of Pertini meant a return to presidential activism and independence for the Head of State. Pertini, who was elected by a combination of all the parties included in the constitutional spectrum (that is, the parties that had emerged from the Resistance), revealed himself, like Einaudi, to be extremely independent of the influence of all political parties. Unlike the first President of the Italian Republic, however, he could depend upon widespread popularity. He manipulated public distrust of the political parties to his own advantage in a sometimes demagogic fashion; exploited his past as a member of the Resistance, and his great age; and spoke up against things that no other politicians dared to mention. He took both the government and the political parties to task, admonished both the Left and the Right, and filled the role of 'father of the country/father of the family' in all the many assassination attempts, catastrophes, and national calamities by which Italy was beset. Politicians were secretly exasperated by this inconvenient figure, whose exceptional popularity allowed him to play the iconoclast, and they were becoming alarmed at the prospect of a second term (which they were powerless to prevent) for an aged and intractable President who would continue to stir things up. But Pertini spared them, and stepped down in favour of Cossiga, a supporter of the policy of reconciliation with the Italian Communist Party, at a time when the historic compromise was in fashion. Elected in 1985, Cossiga acted far less as an intermediary, and allowed the parties to regain lost ground. A notable example of this was the La Staffeta agreement specifying a form of rotation of the premiership, struck between the Christian Democrats and the

Socialist Party. This effectively left the choice of the President of the Council—in theory a presidential function—in the hands of two parties. When Cossiga did break out of his passive role, in 1991, he did so in spectacular fashion, by a succession of vigorous televised attacks against the Christian Democrats, the former Communists, and the Italian system generally, provoking the PDS to call (unconstitutionally) for his impeachment. Whatever the system's faults, these outbursts did little to reinforce the role of the President as guardian of Italy's institutions. Cossiga resigned after the 1992 parliamentary elections, to be replaced—after a humiliatingly long tussle in the new Parliament, running to sixteen ballots—by another Christian Democrat, Oscar Luigi Scalfaro. Scalfaro's major attraction was his (exceptional) reputation for integrity, as a Christian Democrat politician without a clientele. He was also a declared opponent of 'presidentialism' and defender of the prerogatives of parliament. Thus while he supported the Amato Government's severe austerity package of autumn 1992, he prevented (on grounds of unconstitutionality) the Premier from taking emergency powers to impose it, necessitating a wider consultation with trade unions and other interested parties than would otherwise have been the case. He also, in April 1993 and January 1995, played an important role in the appointments of the 'governments of technicians' of Ciampi and Dini, as well as resisting the call made by Berlusconi for new parliamentary elections in December 1994. This refusal provoked cries of betrayal from Berlusconi, who believed, probably rightly, that he would have won had the elections been held then. In the future Constitution discussed between the parties in 1997, the president's role would be much enhanced and would include the right to appoint the Prime Minister; and since the President himself would be elected for six years by direct universal suffrage, he would have the political clout to exercise this right of appointment effectively.

The experiences of West Germany also underline both the limits and the potential of the role of Head of State as a constitutional arbiter. In reaction against the excesses of the Presidents of the Weimar Republic, the formal powers of the Head of State were largely whittled away, and the political evolution of West Germany more or less precluded any informal modification of those limitations. Indeed, the trend is rather the reverse: for example, the Head of State is in principle supposed to choose a candidate for the post of Chancellor and to put his name forward to the Bundestag. But in fact he does no more than pass on to the Bundestag the name proposed to him by the majority party or coalition. As would be expected, the same goes for the appointment of Ministers and senior civil servants. When Heinrich Lübke tried to dismiss Gerhard Schröder from the Ministry of Foreign Affairs in 1965, his intervention was condemned almost unanimously as being misjudged and contrary to the Constitution. The President's powers are equally limited when it comes to the dissolution of the Bundestag. In this domain, the powers of the President, conferred upon him by Articles 63.4 and 68 of the Constitution, are in practice subordinated to the decisions reached by the parties and (in the case of Article 68) by the Chancellor. Thus, in 1983, when Chancellor Kohl organized an artificial crisis so that the voters would ratify the new alliance between the CDU–CSU and the FDP, the President expressed his misgivings over what amounted to a distortion of constitutional procedure, but ended up by bowing to the Chancellor's request. It is thus only in a state of crisis that the German Head of State might be in a position to play a significant role—though the back seat taken by Richard von Weizsäcker in the rush to unification suggests this is far from inevitable. West Germany's, and more recently Germany's, Presidents have in general performed their functions with dignity. (The one who attracted the most criticism, Lübke, retired several months before his time was up, ostensibly so as to avoid a clash between the presidential and the parliamentary elections, but really because his position during the Second World War was giving rise to more and more controversy). However, their principal role has been to act as a symbolic embodiment of the State. To discover where the real power lies, we must turn to the complementary element in the system, that is, the government and its leader—known either as the Prime Minister or (in Italy) as the President of the Council.

The government: the selection and appointment of ministers

The process of selecting and appointing Ministers is more complex in parliamentary systems than in the American presidential system, since one essential stage must first be completed—that of the choosing of the Prime Minister by the Head of State. That expression 'choosing' is, however, ambiguous, for the freedom of choice of a Head of State is limited to varying degrees, depending upon the country's Constitution, the prevailing political circumstances, and so on.

Today, it is exceptional for a Head of State to enjoy total autonomy in the procedure of choosing a Prime Minister, and very few examples of such a situation can be found. Up until the mid-eighteenth century, the British monarchs certainly chose their Prime Ministers to suit themselves, but in 1746 and 1757, George II was forced, whether he liked it or not, to call upon Pitt, the majority leader. In France 120 years later, MacMahon learned to his cost of the limits of a Head of State's powers in a parliamentary system. Faced with a Republican parliamentary majority to which he was hostile, he called new elections, the result of which was to reinforce the Republicans further. At this point he had just two choices, as the Republican leader Gambetta pointedly argued— 'to submit or to resign'. MacMahon chose the second option. King Victor Emmanuel III in Italy and Hindenburg in Germany failed to oppose the rise of Fascism and Nazism by refusing to appeal to the respective leaders of those two movements—a fact that was later held against them. Today, no Head of State holds discretionary powers in the choice of a Prime Minister, for the limitations to which he is subject encapsulate the very principle of the parliamentary system: namely, to replace the arbitrary authority of one individual by the popular will as expressed by the parliamentary majority.[3] In this respect, the history of the Fifth French Republic is significant. It has often been said and written that the President could choose whoever he liked. That seems fair comment given both the nature of the political system (not strictly parliamentary) and also the

230

practice of a succession of Heads of State: the Prime Minister chosen was never the leader of the majority, but became it; sometimes he had been elected to Parliament, but even that was not obligatory, as is shown by the appointments of Georges Pompidou in 1962 and Raymond Barre in 1976. Just as significant have been the occasions when the President has dismissed a Prime Minister with whom his own personal relations had deteriorated, as happened when Pompidou sacked Chaban-Delmas in 1972, or when Mitterrand obtained Rocard's resignation in 1991. The President's right to dismiss a Prime Minister does not appear in the Constitution, and neither Chaban nor Rocard had sustained a serious reverse in Parliament (indeed, Chaban had just won a big vote of confidence in the National Assembly). The two cases thus illustrate that under 'normal' conditions, a Prime Minister who has lost the President's support is finished. However, that freedom of choice was only made possible by the coincidence of the presidential and the parliamentary majorities, and by the fact that the Prime Minister chosen was generally acceptable to that existing majority. Moreover, certain taboos could not be violated. After his defeat at the polls in 1967, Maurice Couve de Murville was not appointed Prime Minister. And by 1978, Valéry Giscard d'Estaing was making it clear that he would call upon François Mitterrand to be Prime Minister in the event of a victory for the left. As President, elected as a Socialist, Mitterrand was himself faced with a precisely similar situation with the victory of the right-wing RPR–UDF coalition at the parliamentary elections of March 1986. Less than 48 hours of consultations after the election results served to confirm to the President that the new majority would only accept one candidate for the Premiership, RPR leader Jacques Chirac, and that to try and appoint anyone else would merely add a political defeat to an electoral one. Mitterrand, in effect, had no alternative, and the Fifth Republic thus found its way back to the strict canons of classic parliamentarianism, as it did again in 1993, when Mitterrand had to appoint Balladur, and in 1997, when Chirac was forced to accept Jospin.

The opposite extreme from the 'normal' French case is the situation of a Head of State who has absolutely no room for manœuvre at all, but is obliged to appoint the Prime Minister chosen, *de facto*, by others. The most remarkable example of such subjection for the Head of State is represented by Britain, where the monarch's 'choice' amounts to no more than the ratification of a double process of pre-selection: first by the party, which chooses its own leader; then by the electorate, which gives victory to one particular party together with its leader. Nevertheless, a Head of State's lack of autonomy is also affected by the coincidence of specific circumstances: the presence of a leader whose position is uncontested, and an electoral victory that is indisputable. If either or both of these factors is missing, the Head of State regains some of the monarchy's old powers of influence. For example, in 1923, when the Prime Minister, Bonar Law was obliged to retire for reasons of health, George V called upon Stanley Baldwin to head the Government, although he had been expected to choose Lord Curzon. In 1931, George V again played a significant role in choosing Ramsay MacDonald, the Labour leader, who thus became Prime Minister in a minority government. When he resigned as a result of dissension within the Labour Party, which was divided over the

measures to be taken to deal with the economic crisis, the King consulted the Conservative and Liberal leaders and then decided to call upon Ramsay MacDonald to form a
Government of National Unity. This 'class collaboration' caused a crisis in the Labour
Party; but in October 1931, the country ratified that option by giving 554 seats to the
supporters of the National Government, as against 52 to the Labour candidates who
had kept faith with their party's traditional positions. In general, though, the role of the
British monarch is extremely limited and the sovereign can only affect the choice of
Prime Minister in quite exceptional circumstances.

The situation of Germany is, in this respect, very similar to that of the sovereign of
the United Kingdom. Each party is headed by a leader who, in the event of his political
group winning the election, is naturally destined to become Chancellor. Alfred Grosser
underlines this point, recalling to mind how, in 1959, Adenauer, prompted by a desire
to thwart the chances of his Deputy Chancellor, Ludwig Erhard, to whom he was
antipathetic, briefly stood as candidate for the presidency of the Republic. Adenauer left
for his holidays, telling journalists that his bedside reading would consist of the
Constitution, in which—as Grosser ironically suggests—he no doubt discovered the
bitter truth: namely, that, as President, he would no longer be in a position to impose his
own choice for the post of Chancellor. This marginalization of the Head of State's role
was prompted by the unfortunate experience of the Weimar Republic. In response to
what Von Beyme has called 'the Hindenburg allergy' and to prevent the Chancellor
from becoming what Gordon Smith calls the President's 'scapegoat' and avoid a repetition of untimely presidential interventions and dissolutions in the style of the Weimar
Republic, the Constitution of the Federal Republic insists that the Chancellor be elected
by the Bundestag, leaving to the Head of State a purely formal role in this domain.

Between these two possible extremes, there are some cases in which the Head of State,
either as ruled by the Constitution or as a result of a fluid political situation, does enjoy
significant powers: in the Fourth French Republic, for instance, and in the Italian
Republic today, particularly when the Head of State can rely on the support of public
opinion. Vincent Auriol and Sandro Pertini both, in the absence of a political majority,
used their own personal popularity to influence the choice of Premier. They did so
either by organizing consultations very much under their own aegis or by proceeding to
'nominate' a potential Prime Minister who would only be appointed if he managed to
form a government. Practices such as these sometimes made it possible to make use of
certain potential but controversial candidates before eventually settling upon the one
whom the Head of State secretly favoured all along. The situation in the Fourth Republic nevertheless differed from that which obtained in Italy at least up to the election of
Sandro Pertini in 1978. In contrast to the situation in almost all the other parliamentary
democracies, in France the President of the Fourth Republic was never bound by any
rule stipulating that, in the absence of an absolute majority, the Prime Minister (called,
at the time, the President of the Council) must be chosen from amongst the members
of the largest party, the party holding a relative majority. The picture established by
Jean-Claude Colliard in his study of contemporary parliamentary democracies shows
quite clearly how unusual the French situation was: not one of the twenty-one

Presidents of the Council came from the largest political party, namely, the Communist Party, considered to be 'beyond the pale'. Colliard comments as follows:

In other countries, as a rule, the higher the position of a party (on a classificatory scale ranging from 1 to 8, and based on the relative size of the various parties), the more chance it has of forming a government. In the case of the Fourth Republic, the reverse appears to have been true and the most propitious position for becoming President of the Council seems to have been membership of a small party ranking fourth or fifth on the scale.[4]

In Italy, on the other hand, the Head of State has been allowed less room for manœuvre, despite the appearance, there too, of the procedure of 'nomination' (*presidente incaricato*). Until Sandro Pertini's election, the convention—always hitherto respected—was that the Premier should be selected from the party which held a relative majority, in other words from the Christian Democrat group. And, even within this framework, the President's hands were tied except when the Christian Democrats had failed to put forward any specific suggestions. It became possible to flout the convention only when the development of a more fluid political situation (as a result of the decline of the Christian Democrats) coincided with the advent of a President of Pertini's charisma. Having called in vain upon first the Republican La Malfa, then the Socialist Craxi to form a government, the Head of State turned to Giorgio Spadolini, who thus managed to become the Italian Republic's first Prime Minister from one of the secular parties (although Parri had also qualified for that description during the transition period of the Liberation). After the 1983 elections, the President appealed to Craxi, the leader of the small Socialist Party (with 12 per cent of the vote), who eventually broke the record for longevity for a government leader: not until April 1987 was he obliged to tender his resignation. It may seem surprising that the Christian Democrats of the 1980s should have tolerated the flouting of a constitutional convention so favourable to them. Two explanations may be adduced for this, apart from the strength of Pertini's personality. In the first place, the Christian Democrats saw this retirement from the centre of the stage as a possible period of sorely needed rejuvenation. Secondly, the Italian Communist Party, pressing hard upon the heels of the Christian Democrats, was gaining strength, even emerging from the European elections of 1984 as the leading party. If that situation were confirmed and the constitutional convention maintained, it would be necessary to select a Prime Minister from the ranks of the Communist Party. Rather than draw attention to the *conventio ad excludendum*, the Christian Democrats accepted what they hoped would be no more than a temporary setback, until the return of better days. In 1985–6, the Christian Democrat Secretary General, De Mita, was already pointing out the advantages of 'rotation'. And the La Stafetta agreement of July 1986 did indeed envisage the post of President of the Council passing to a Christian Democrat. However, that was reckoning without Craxi's Machiavellian manœuvrings and his proposal to hold referendums in future. This split the majority so deeply that the next parliamentary elections had to be brought forward to June 1987. The political crisis that opened in 1992 gave a degree of freedom back to the President because the parties had become too weak to impose a candidate, even after the most protracted horse-trading. Thus it was that in April 1993, President Scalfaro appointed the first non-parliamentarian to hold the premiership in the history of the Italian Republic. A former governor of the Bank of Italy, Carlo Azeglio Ciampi came from almost the only Italian institution not to have a reputation for corruption and had the double advantage of being attractive both to public opinion and to the money markets, giving him the authority to make a start on political and economic reforms. Again, in January 1995, Scalfaro was instrumental in choosing to appoint a second 'technician', Berlusconi's former treasury minister Lamberto Dini, to the premiership, in preference to Berlusconi's preferred option of a dissolution of parliament. Dini's gravitation to the centre-left Olive Tree coalition was crucial in its electoral victory of April 1996.

But in more normal times, it would appear that the Head of State's role in selecting a Prime Minister in the parliamentary democracies we have considered is marginal. Only France stands out as an exception. But if the coexistence of a President with an Assembly whose opinions diverge from his becomes a more frequent phenomenon, the Fifth Republic will fall more closely into line with neighbouring democracies. And in that case, as in Britain, Germany, and Italy, the choice of Ministers would similarly become a prerogative of the Prime Minister rather than of the President of the Republic.

When it comes to the appointment of Ministers, whoever the formal authority belongs to (the Head of State, for instance), essentially the power belongs to the Prime Minister. The only real exception is constituted, once again, by the Fifth French Republic, by reason of its bicephalous executive system. However, as a result of the experience of cohabitation between 1986 and 1988, the situation in France has fallen more closely into line with those of its neighbours.

In the American presidential system, many Ministers are chosen from outside Congress, and are the 'President's men'; those from within Congress resign their seats there on confirmation of their Cabinet appointment. In France, where the system is a hybrid one, a considerable proportion of government Ministers, including two Prime Ministers (Pompidou and Barre), have been selected from outside Parliament. It has even happened that Ministers who, after appointment, have tried their luck at the polls (Messmer and Couve de Murville in 1967) have been retained in their ministerial posts despite having suffered humiliating electoral defeats. However, tradition demands that most 'experts' recruited in this way should, sooner or later, enter the political arena to receive confirmation in their posts from universal suffrage. There is nothing of this kind in purely parliamentary systems, for here it is an unwritten rule that a Prime Minister should choose his Ministers from the ranks of Members of Parliament. Here and there, one could cite cases where appointments have gone to individuals outside Parliament, but they are certainly exceptional. In Italy there were barely a dozen cases in the 45 years after the foundation of the republic in 1948 (though the Ciampi and Dini governments clearly altered that record); while in Germany experts are easily turned into members of the Bundestag because of the system of electoral lists and proportional representation. In Britain, a few individuals from outside Parliament have from time to time been appointed as Ministers, but they have had to stand for Parliament (and be elected) at the next by-elections held in the country.[5] The convention is an implicit but natural consequence of ministerial responsibility, both individual and collective. How could Parliament possibly exercise political control over Ministers who had no connections with it? The rule becomes even more stringent and specific in countries where the government is responsible to both Chambers, as in Italy. The President of the Council is bound to allocate a few portfolios to Senators. Similarly, in Britain, despite the minor role played by the House of Lords, there is still a rule that a Minister may only address the House of which he is a member. In practice, this means that the British government is bound to include a few Lords so as to be in a position to present and defend its policies before the Upper House. For example, in July 1978, the Callaghan Government was composed of 113 individuals, only 97 of whom were members of the House of Commons, and in February 1984, the Thatcher Government numbered 101 individuals, only 79 of whom were members of the Commons.

But the essential constraint in any parliamentary system can be summed up in one word: balance. Whether the parliamentary majority is composed of a single party or emanates from a coalition, the Prime Minister must take account of internal equilibrium, factions, and rivalries, and, contrary to what a rapid and simplistic assessment might suggest, the correct balance is not necessarily easier to achieve in a single party than in a coalition. Jean-Claude Colliard, who has made a systematic study of this question in connection with the practices of Western parliamentary democracies, emphasizes that although 'the key to allocation is, in principle, a simple arithmetical rule', in the real world the situation is far more complex. He distinguishes five different patterns for the allocation of ministerial posts where coalitions are involved: proportionality, over-representation for the larger parties, over-representation for the smaller parties, over-representation for the Prime Minister's own party, and parity for all the parties concerned. In practice, the first and the last options are seldom used, for rigid arithmetic is hardly compatible with the subtleties of politics. Thus Colliard cites only one case of proportionality in France under the Fourth and Fifth Republics (the third Pompidou Government, composed of 22 UNR and 3 RI), and only one instance of parity (the Barre Government). No such situation of strict proportionality or egalitarian balance in a single coalition has ever arisen either in Britain or in West Germany before 1990, or in unified Germany since.

In Italy, on the other hand, the allocation of posts, in both the parties and governments, corresponded under the system prevailing until 1992 to a relatively strict arithmetical calculation.[6] In this connection, Hugues Portelli writes:

the famous Cencelli handbook on the allocation of posts—both generally and specifically within the party—institutionalizes this practice. The various posts are distributed proportionally on the basis of the results of each faction at the last national party congress: the posts of President of the Republic and President of the Council, Ministers and Under-Secretaries of State, the Presidents of the two Chambers, and posts of responsibility within the party. When the first Craxi Government was set up, the rule was applied to the letter, producing a spectacle in which one of the minority factions of the Christian Democrats blocked the formation of the

Government until such time as it got its own way. When it is also remembered that the Cencelli handbook—itself a Christian Democrat creation—is now generally applied to all the factions and sub-factions of all the parties that go to make up the majority, it becomes clear just how unfair the apportionment of power has become.[7]

The system was inevitably perturbed by the post-1992 crisis, by the arrival of governments of technicians, and by the decision of the PDS (for tactical and interested reasons as well as altruistic ones) to accept less than its full share of posts in the Prodi government. One sign of Italy's return to business as usual, pre-1992-style, would be the revival of the practices codified by Cencelli.

The other patterns noted by Jean-Claude Colliard all constitute situations of imbalance that favour either one dominant party or, alternatively, the party or parties whose support is necessary if a majority is to be obtained. In situations such as these, the political balances achieved bear little relation to strict arithmetical calculations. The number of ministerial posts allocated to particular groups reflects the degree of pressure and influence that they can respectively bring to bear, as does the *quality* of those posts (the titles and importance of the various portfolios and the opportunities they afford for patronage). There is one particular pattern that often applies to coalitions in which one or several small parties are absolutely indispensable if a parliamentary majority is to be obtained. This was the case, quite spectacularly, of the second Adenauer Government (1953), in which the CDU–CSU held only 11 of the 19 portfolios (despite having won over 45 per cent of the votes), while the FDP with 9.5 per cent obtained 4 posts, the BHE 2 posts for its 3.9 per cent of the vote, and the DP also 2 posts for its 5.9 per cent of the vote. However, the distribution of posts does not necessarily convey a true picture of the balance of power, as is shown by the Christian Democrat/FDP coalition of 1961: the FDP certainly obtained a slightly higher proportion of posts than their electoral score allowed them to hope for, but above all they managed to impose two draconian conditions: first, that Adenauer should retire before the end of the legislature; and secondly, that a 'coalition committee' should discuss government proposals before the Cabinet adopted them, to prevent FDP Ministers from being manipulated or overwhelmed by the Chancellor's blandishments. The situation in the CDU–CSU–FDP coalition after 1982 was in some ways comparable. The FDP, with about a quarter or less of the CDU–CSU's level of support still managed to corner for itself the ministries of Justice, Economic Affairs, and Foreign Affairs. When Hans Dietrich Genscher resigned from the latter post, Chancellor Kohl made it clear that he would accept the FDP's choice of a successor. (After some hesitation, the FDP chose its leader Klaus Kinkel, who had only joined the party in 1991).

Similarly, in Italy the smaller parties have managed to capitalize on their strength as necessary partners: the second Moro Government, for example, distributed most posts between the PSI, the PSDI, and the tiny Republican Party, so that it would be possible to continue the centre-left experiment started six months earlier, in December 1963. The same phenomenon was frequently to recur and was a feature of the second Craxi Government, formed in August 1986. In this, the tiny Liberal Party obtained 2 portfolios, the PRI and the PSDI 3 each, and the PSI 6, as against the 16 that went to the

Christian Democrats. In other words, dominant parties have to pay for the collaboration of minority parties, and the latter sometimes subject them to a veritable process of blackmail. This has seldom happened under the Fifth French Republic, as the secondary partners of the majority have possessed no more than limited means of exerting pressure upon the coalition as a whole since this has been clearly dominated by the principal party, that of the President. On the other hand, when the President came from one of the smaller parties, as did Valéry Giscard d'Estaing from 1974 to 1981, the 'dominant' party found itself in a weaker position and was less heavily represented in government in both the Chirac and the Barre Cabinets; and Balladur, notionally a Gaullist, inaugurated a new practice as Prime Minister in 1993 when he appointed a government with a near-majority of centrists, betraying an ambition to build an alternative power base outside his own party, which was dominated by his rival, Chirac. However, in some situations, the pressure from the smaller parties is not at all unwelcome to the leader of the dominant party, especially if the latter is of a heterogeneous or even composite nature, as in the case of the CDU–CSU. Brandt and Schmidt were quite glad of the pressure exerted by the FDP as this tended to keep their left wings in check. Similarly, Chancellor Kohl must certainly have been relieved that the absence of a homogeneous majority spared him a resounding individual clash with Franz-Josef Strauss, the 'Bull of Bavaria'.

All the variants described so far underline the advantages that pivot parties are adept at deriving from the necessity of coalitions, for they are in a position either to use their power of veto (since without them no government can possibly be formed) or their destructive powers (since if they resign they bring down the government). However, in certain circumstances small parties that take part in government nevertheless derive scant advantage from this. A relatively exceptional situation of this kind arises when the small parties concerned are in no position to exert pressure on the dominant party. One case in point, in France, was that of Giscard's RI from 1962 to 1968. Had they engineered a crisis, it would have resulted in the Assembly being dissolved and elections, in which they, as a party, would probably have foundered. Small parties are even more clearly incapable of exerting pressure on a dominant party when the latter, no doubt partly due to the voting system, itself controls an absolute majority. Then, the reason for its forming a coalition has nothing to do with the needs of parliamentary arithmetic; rather, it is because it is seeking a majority consensus in the country as a whole. Neither the Gaullists in 1968[8] nor the Socialists in 1981[9] were obliged to share power with, respectively, their Giscardian and Communist allies. But de Gaulle and Pompidou, and, similarly, Mitterrand, were well aware of all the difficulties that would face a majority party that attempted to govern on its own without having received an overall majority of votes. In circumstances such as these, it is the minority party that finds itself in a delicate position: virtually the only choice open to it is between knuckling under or resigning, as the Communists discovered between 1981 and 1984.

Nevertheless, the above remarks, based on quantitative data, need correcting from a qualitative point of view. In the first place, distributing appointments of Ministers and Secretaries of State is but *one* of the means by which a head of government can satisfy factions and parties. On a qualitative level he can also play upon the degrees to which a purely honorific or, alternatively, an essential value is attached to those appointments. Hence the creation of the posts of Deputy Prime Minister (not always provided for by the country's Constitution) and of new Ministers of State with or without portfolio, and the proliferation of Secretaries of State and Parliamentary Secretaries, all of which are a means of distributing many small satisfactions at no great cost. Furthermore, a subtle and detailed examination would be needed to gauge the real impact of the smaller parties, or at least of their leaders. Should the influence of the RI, in France, be measured by their number or by the position of their leader at the Ministry of Finance? Should we concentrate upon the size of the FDP, or its influence upon economic policies, or the decisive parts played by Scheel and Genscher in the domain of foreign policy, in particular *Ostpolitik*? From the opposite point of view, the diminishing number of Italian Christian Democrat Ministers under the Socialist leadership between 1983 and 1986 was perhaps not as significant as the figures and the loss of the Presidency of the Council might have suggested. After all, the Christian Democrats had retained not only the Vice-Presidency, the Ministry of Foreign Affairs, the Interior Ministry, the Ministry of Justice, and the Treasury, but also the Ministries most involved in clientship, in particular those concerned with large numbers of jobs, or whose social and economic impact was particularly important: Education, the Postal Service, Health, the Civil Service, State-Run Industries, Southern Italy, etc.

Secondly, we have so far only considered the constraints affecting the choice of individuals to fill certain posts, not those that affect policy-making. But we should not forget that this aspect is often crucial and that parties upon which the majority is dependent may well be influential even if they do not formally belong to the government. For example, the devolution policy for Scotland and Wales was proposed by Callaghan's Government in order to retain the support of the nationalist parties; and the stalemate in the Ulster peace process in the later months of the Major Government was widely attributed to his having to depend on Ulster Unionist support in Parliament to retain a majority. Similarly, from July 1976 to August 1979, the minority but homogeneous Christian Democrat Government in Italy was supported by every party in the constitutional spectrum, most importantly the Communist Party, whose influence upon the country's major economic and social reforms during this period was crucial.

Government leadership

Governmental cohesion

The problem that confronts all governments, whether presidential or parliamentary, is how to reconcile each Minister's autonomy in discharging his departmental responsibilities with the unity necessary for all government action.

In parliamentary systems, Prime Ministers hold two essential trump cards that the

American executive lacks: the constraints that stem from ministerial responsibility and the existence of firmer and more disciplined party structures. The archetype of this kind of executive leadership is constituted by the British Prime Minister. The parliamentary system invented by Britain requires, in the name of the government's collective responsibility before Parliament, that the Cabinet should present a united front so as to maintain the cohesion of its majority. This also applies to all junior Ministers, whips, and even the parliamentary private secretaries (the so-called 'payroll vote', although the last group are not, in fact, paid). This institutional constraint has certainly undergone considerable modification over the years, but it was extremely useful at a time when the Prime Minister was still considered simply as 'the first among equals' in the government.

In Britain, the principle of collective responsibility no longer welds the executive together as it did in the past (although the notion of the individual and collective responsibility of Ministers remains far stronger than on the Continent). The task of maintaining cohesion now falls to the Prime Minister, who truly has become the keystone of the Cabinet. In the post-war period, the role of the Prime Minister has assumed such importance in the institutions of Britain that it has sparked off considerable controversy over the apparent transformation of Cabinet government into 'presidential government'. All Prime Ministers since 1945 have made full use of their freedom, in effect, to hire and fire their colleagues. In July 1962, Macmillan carried out a veritable purge in a (largely unsuccessful) bid to resume a firm hold over his Government, sacking seven Ministers, including the Chancellor of the Exchequer and the Ministers of Defence and Education. Yet despite being his first victims, the Ministers affected were the first to recognize the Prime Minister's 'life or death' powers.[10] With Margaret Thatcher's election in 1979, any doubts remaining on the role of the Prime Minister as leader of the government were soon dispelled. The 'Iron Lady' not only exploited to the full the prerogatives granted her by the Constitution and by convention; she imbued the role of Prime Minister with her own personal decisive and authoritarian style, engineering successive reshuffles in such a way as to promote those loyal to her (the 'dries') and ease out the Ministers classed as 'wets', who did not invariably share her views. According to Michael Lee,

Mrs Thatcher seems to have extended the authority of the Prime Minister beyond the limits respected by her predecessors. . . . She does not simply take the initiative in Cabinet discussions, but also tends to 'short-circuit' it by organizing external pressures when she comes up against internal resistance. Furthermore, the Ministers responsible for economic and industrial questions feel obliged to consult her on a regular basis.[11]

In July 1989, she reshuffled her Cabinet, replacing twelve out of twenty-one Ministers after the Conservative losses in the June European elections.

The role of the British Prime Minister is the product of a long political and constitutional evolution whose peculiar nature becomes easier to understand when it is compared to those of its German and Italian counterparts. These two countries have adopted the framework and canons of the parliamentary system but, in the absence of all the ingredients used in the British recipe, they have introduced a number of differences inspired by their own particular histories or designed to allow them to evolve in new directions. Both Germany and Italy constructed their political systems in the aftermath of the war, upon the ruins of their dictatorships. Yet the institutional consequences that they have drawn from their past experiences differ substantially. In Italy, a decree issued as early as 1944 introduced the expression 'President of the Council of Ministers' as a replacement for the title 'Head of Government', which had been established by a law passed in 1925. The semantic change reflected not only a rejection of an authoritarian style of government leadership but also a desire to prevent a recurrence of such mistakes by introducing *ad hoc* institutional mechanisms designed for that purpose. The President of the Council, deprived of power and means and unable really to choose and fire his Ministers, was supposed to be no more than the first of the Ministers, and on the face of it that reform appears to have proved successful, to judge—that is—by the titles of two books by specialist observers of the Italian political scene, the British Percy Allum's[12] *Italy, Republic without Government?* and the Italian-American Giuseppe Di Palma's[13] *Surviving without Governing*. Italy and France (in 1945) both learned the same lesson from their experiences of authoritarian and non-democratic governments: weaken the executive and make Parliament the central point of the Constitution and political life in general.

The reactions of post-war West Germany were different. While the country sought to guard by every means against any resurgence of Nazism, it was aware that it was the deficiencies of the Weimar Republic that had in part been constitutionally responsible for the birth of the Nazi regime. In the light of past experience, it was clear that until Hitler arrived upon the scene, the Chancellor had been made (to borrow Gordon

Table 6.1. **France: Presidents and Prime Ministers under the Fifth Republic**

	Prime Ministers	PM's party		Presidents
January 1959–April 1962	Michel Debré	Gaullist	January 1959–April 1969	Charles de Gaulle
April 1962–June 1968	Georges Pompidou	Gaullist		
June 1968–June 1969	Maurice Couve de Murville	Gaullist		
June 1969–July 1972	Jacques Chaban-Delmas	Gaullist	June 1969–April 1974	Georges Pompidou
July 1972–May 1974	Pierre Messmer	Gaullist		
May 1974–August 1976	Jacques Chirac	Gaullist	May 1974–May 1981	Valéry Giscard d'Estaing
August 1976–May 1981	Raymond Barre	Giscardian		
May 1981–June 1984	Pierre Mauroy	Socialist	May 1981–May 1995	François Mitterrand
June 1984–March 1986	Laurent Fabius	Socialist		
March 1986–May 1988	Jacques Chirac	Gaullist		
May 1988–May 1991	Michel Rocard	Socialist		
May 1991–April 1992	Édith Cresson	Socialist		
April 1992–March 1993	Pierre Bérégovoy	Socialist		
March 1993–May 1995	Édouard Balladur	Gaullist		
May 1995–June 1997	Alain Juppé	Gaullist	May 1995–	Jacques Chirac
June 1997–	Lionel Jospin	Socialist		

Table 6.2. **Chancellors of the Federal Republic of Germany, 1949–1997**

	Chancellor	Chancellor's party
September 1949–October 1963	Konrad Adenauer	Christian Democrat
October 1963–November 1966	Ludwig Erhard	Christian Democrat
December 1966–October 1969	Kurt Georg Kiesinger	Christian Democrat
October 1969–May 1974	Willy Brandt	Social Democrat
May 1974–October 1982	Helmut Schmidt	Social Democrat
October 1982–	Helmut Kohl	Christian Democrat

Table 6.3. **British Prime Ministers, 1945–1997**

	Prime Minister	PM's party
July 1945–October 1951	Clement Attlee	Labour
October 1951–April 1955	Winston Churchill	Conservative
April 1955–January 1957	Sir Anthony Eden	Conservative
January 1957–October 1963	Harold Macmillan	Conservative
October 1963–October 1964	Sir Alec Douglas-Home	Conservative
October 1964–June 1970	Harold Wilson	Labour
June 1970–February 1974	Edward Heath	Conservative
March 1974–April 1976	Harold Wilson	Labour
April 1976–May 1979	James Callaghan	Labour
May 1979–November 1990	Margaret Thatcher	Conservative
November 1990–May 1997	John Major	Conservative
May 1997–	Tony Blair	Labour

Table 6.4. **Italian heads of government and government coalitions, 1946–1997**

Prime minister	Coalition	Duration
Parri	DC–PCI–PSI–PLI–PDL–Pd'A	June–Dec. 1945
De Gasperi I	DC–PCI–PSI–PLI–PDL–Pd'A	Dec. 1945–July 1946
De Gasperi II	DC–PCI–PSI–PRI	July 1946–Feb. 1947
De Gasperi III	DC–PCI–PSI	Feb.–May 1947
De Gasperi IV	DC–PLI–PSLI–PRI	May 1947–May 1948
De Gasperi V	DC–PLI–PSLI–PRI	May 1948–Jan. 1950
De Gasperi VI	DC–PSLI–PRI	Jan. 1950–July 1951
De Gasperi VII	DC–PRI	July 1951–July 1953
De Gasperi VIII	DC	July–Aug. 1953
Pella	DC	Aug. 1953–Jan. 1954
Fanfani I	DC	Jan.–Feb. 1954
Scelba	DC–PDSI–PLI	Feb. 1954–July 1955
Segni I	DC–PSDI–PLI	July 1955–May 1957
Zoli	DC	May 1957–July 1958
Fanfani II	DC–PSDI	July 1958–Feb. 1959
Segni II	DC	Feb. 1959–Mar. 1960
Tambroni	DC	Mar.–July 1960
Fanfani III	DC	July 1960–Feb. 1962
Fanfani IV	DC–PSDI–PRI	Feb. 1962–June 1963

Table 6.4. (*cont.*)

Prime minister	Coalition	Duration
Leone I	DC	June–Dec. 1963
Moro I	DC–PSI–PSDI–PRI	Dec. 1963–July 1964
Moro II	DC–PSI–PSDI–PRI	July 1964–Feb. 1966
Moro III	DC–PSI–PSDI–PRI	Feb. 1966–June 1968
Leone II	DC	June–Dec. 1968
Rumor I	DC–PSI–PRI	Dec. 1968–Aug. 1969
Rumor II	DC	Aug. 1969–Mar. 1970
Rumor III	DC–PSI–PSDI–PRI	Mar.–Aug. 1970
Colombo	DC–PSI–PSDI–PRI	Aug. 1970–Feb. 1972
Andreotti I	DC	Feb.–June 1972
Andreotti II	DC–PSDI–PLI	June 1972–July 1973
Rumor IV	DC–PSI–PSDI–PRI	July 1973–Mar. 1974
Rumor V	DC–PSI–PSDI	Mar.–Nov. 1974
Moro IV	DC–PRI	Nov. 1974–Feb. 1976
Moro V	DC	Feb.–July 1976
Andreotti III	DC	July 1976–Mar. 1978
Andreotti IV	DC	Mar. 1978–Jan. 1979
Andreotti V	DC–PSDI–PRI	Jan.–Aug. 1979
Cossiga I	DC–PSDI–PLI	Aug.–Mar. 1980
Cossiga II	DC–PSI–PRI	Mar.–Sept. 1980
Forlani	DC–PSI–PSDI–PRI	Sept. 1980–July 1981
Spadolini I	DC–PSI–PSDI–PRI–PLI	July 1981–Aug. 1982
Spadolini II	DC–PSI–PSDI–PRI–PLI	Aug. 1982–Dec. 1982
Fanfani V	DC–PSI–PSDI–PLI	Dec. 1982–Aug. 1983
Craxi I	DC–PSI–PSDI–PRI–PLI	Aug. 1983–Aug. 1986
Craxi II	DC–PSI–PSDI–PRI–PLI	Aug. 1986–Apr. 1987
Fanfani VI	DC	Apr.–July 1987
Goria	DC–PSI–PSDI–PRI–PLI	July 1987–Apr. 1988
De Mita	DC–PSI–PSDI–PRI–PLI	Apr. 1988–Aug. 1989
Andreotti VI	DC–PSI–PSDI–PRI–PLI	Aug. 1989–Apr. 1991
Andreotti VII	DC–PSI–PSDI–PLI	Apr. 1991–June 1992
Amato	DC–PSI–PSDI–PLI	June 1992–Apr.1993
Ciampi	'Technicians', cross-party support	Apr. 1993–Apr. 1994
Berlusconi	FI–MSI–LN–CCD	Apr. 1994–Dec. 1994
Dini	'Technicians', Left-supported	Dec. 1994–May 1996
Prodi	PDS–PPI–Lista Dini–Greens	May 1996–

Notes:

1. *Period of office*: During a political crisis, prime ministers are generally requested to stay in office until their successors are sworn in; the periods given thus often include some weeks of 'caretaker' rather than 'effective' government.

2. *Coalitions*: Parties named are those holding office in the Council of Ministers; other parties are from time to time essential elements of the parliamentary coalition on which the government depends.

3. *Abbreviations*: DC: Christian Democracy; PCI; Communist Party; PSI; Socialist Party; PSLI and PSDI; early and subsequent initials of the Social Democrat Party; PRI: Republican Party; PLI: Liberal Party; FI: PPI; Christian Democrats, post-1993; Forza Italia; MSI: Neo-Fascists; LN; Lega Nord; CCD; Right-wing Christian Democrats, 1994; PDS: post-Communists, after 1990; the PDL (Democratic Labour Party) and Pd'A (Action Party) were casualties of the Cold War and did not outlive the 1940s.

Source: Updated from D. Hine, *Governing Italy: The Politics of Bargained Pluralism* (Oxford: Oxford University Press, 1993), 283–4.

Smith's expression)[14] the 'scapegoat' of the Reichstag and the President of the Reich. To prevent such an erosion of the Chancellor's role, the Federal Constitution switched to the Chancellor powers that were essentially transferred from the former domain of the President. It also conferred pre-eminence upon the position of Chancellor by stipulating that the Bundestag itself should elect him, thereby reinforcing his position as leader of the executive. As in Britain, the mechanisms of ministerial responsibility have been largely deflected from their original purpose. Nevertheless, in Germany too the executive as a whole is subject to similar parliamentary constraints that operate to the advantage of the Chancellor. For even if the Bundestag, *as an institution*, does not have much say in the choosing of a Chancellor, the majority party or the parties in the coalition must come to an agreement on a candidate, and if they should eventually come to disapprove of the one whom they elect, the mechanisms of 'constructive no confidence' still constitute a serious limitation to any rebellious inclinations they might have. Consequently, once elected, the Chancellor finds himself in a strong position and, furthermore, a seldom-flouted convention requires that he be appointed for the duration of the legislature. With the exceptions of Adenauer's retirement in 1963 and the resignations of Brandt and Schmidt, it is certainly by now traditional that the government is headed by the same leader throughout the duration of each legislature. Between 1949 and early 1998, the Federal Republic of Germany had no more than six Chancellors: Adenauer, Erhard, Kiesinger, Brandt, Schmidt, and Kohl.

This institutional characteristic of West Germany was further reinforced by the strong influence that Adenauer had in the shaping of the style and role of the Chancellor, an influence that, particularly until the late 1950s, rested upon his extraordinary popularity. As Grosser notes, 'The real political impact of the Head of Government has varied considerably, depending upon individual personalities and circumstances.'[15] Nevertheless, the lack of leadership provided by his successor, Erhard, did not result in any loss of prestige for the post of Chancellor; indeed, for a long time ironic remarks about the *Kanzlerdemokratie*, the 'Chancellor's democracy', continued unabated. All the same, as Gordon Smith points out, the circumstances that had permitted the exceptional political longevity of the first Chancellor, Konrad Adenauer, soon disappeared. In Smith's opinion, Adenauer's pre-eminence had been promoted by three elements: the role that he had played in constructing the CDU, the particular nature of the electorate, most of whom owed their first acquaintance with democracy to the Christian Democrat leader, and the international status of West Germany, whose evolution had been largely determined by the actions of Adenauer. With these elements gone, the Chancellor's role as leader of the Government became more subject to institutional and party factors and less a matter of personal charisma.

A head of government's power to lead his team is still determined by what are, in effect, political factors connected with the party system and the role played by the parties in the interaction of institutions. If we compare the three 'pure' parliamentary systems of Britain, the Federal Republic of Germany, and Italy, it becomes immediately clear that, although these three systems in principle belong to the same 'family', the political conditions in which they operate are substantially different. In the period since the war, Britain has never had a single coalition government (though the Callaghan Government from 1976 to 1979 was a minority government dependent upon the parliamentary support of the Liberals or the Scottish and Welsh Nationalists or both). In contrast, *every* West German and all-German government has been a coalition, even when it was not arithmetically necessary that it should be. In Italy, despite the seemingly permanent Christian Democrat dominance from the war to 1993, single-party governments were the exception rather than the rule, and most governments included small right- or left-wing groups to support the dominant party. It is accordingly impossible to gauge a Prime Minister's freedom of movement in leading his government without taking into account his relations with his own party and with the other groups included in the coalition.

British Prime Ministers owe their dominant position to the party that chose them as leader, and as such they are automatically considered as the person to head the government if the party wins the election. Moreover, while in opposition, a party leader acts as the head of a 'shadow cabinet', and this by anticipation places him in the position of head of a future government team. However, the ways of choosing a party leader and hence also a possible future Prime Minister vary from one party to another, and to a certain extent determine his room for manœuvre in government. So, inevitably, does the popularity in public opinion of the individuals concerned. In the Conservative Party, Members of Parliament alone chose the leader up until 1997 (when William Hague's ratification of his leadership election by the party membership was the prelude to larger-scale reforms). In the Labour Party, on the other hand, the trade unions had a 40 per cent share of the vote in the election as leader of Neil Kinnock in 1983, John Smith in 1992, and Tony Blair in 1994 (though the possibility, widely considered when this system was introduced in 1980, that it would produce a leader more radical than the parliamentary party, has not been realized). Potentially more important, on the face of it, is the fact that Labour Members of Parliament elect their party's shadow cabinet. Although a Labour leader still allocates the various shadow cabinet posts among the successful candidates, and can dilute this group with additional front-bench appointees of his own, and although Labour Prime Ministers can reshuffle the government as they please once in office, the potential is clearly present for the leader to be obliged to work with colleagues of views strongly opposed to his or her own. Yet there is also a sense in which the Labour Party's apparently constraining procedures merely formalize processes that go on in any party. Thus Margaret Thatcher, though technically free to choose her colleagues as she pleased, was obliged to accept, not only in her shadow cabinets, but even in her first government in 1979, a majority of colleagues who did not share her monetarist economic views; her hold on the party was simply not strong enough for her to follow a different course. John Major, even having called and won a special leadership election in June 1995 to outface his Eurosceptical critics in the Conservative Party, was still too politically weak to remove such critics (whom he had referred to as 'bastards') from his Cabinet. Tony Blair, on the other hand, although subject to shadow cabinet elections, was so clearly instrumental in improving his party's position in the opinion polls after winning the party leadership in 1994 that he had little trouble in getting MPs to surround him with like-minded colleagues. It is also the case that the drive to unity in the Blair leadership of the Labour Party served to highlight the break with a past when Labour had been deeply divided. The high point of these divisions came in 1974–5, when the Wilson Government organized a referendum on Britain's continued membership in the European Community in order to get round his cabinet's inability to take a collective decision on the issue. Onlookers were presented with the unprecedented sight of Ministers campaigning vigorously in both the 'yes' and the 'no' camps, regardless of the principle of the cabinet's collective responsibility. The true extent of Blair's break with the past might perhaps be demonstrated in the event of a further referendum, under his premiership, on Britain's entry into European monetary union.

The role of a Prime Minister who heads a coalition would seem to be even more problematic. However, it is hard to generalize since his or her ability to lead the government successfully is bound to depend upon the nature of the coalition. In the 1950s, Adenauer governed with the support of small right-wing parties (in particular, the Refugee Party), which were virtually extensions of the dominant party and could always be counted upon to support the Chancellor. In 1961, the situation was quite different: only three parties now remained in the Bundestag and the FDP was in a position to lay down, as a condition for their participating in a coalition Government, that Adenauer should retire half-way through his term of office. Kiesinger, Chancellor of the grand coalition of 1966–9, was more concerned to mediate than to lead from the front, particularly since some of his Ministers (Schiller and Strauss, for example) disagreed over policy and were on execrable personal terms. Similarly, the last two years of Helmut Schmidt's Government were marked by arguments between the Social Democrats and the FDP that increased in intensity until the latter changed allies in 1982.

Furthermore, the Chancellor frequently has to cope with divisions among his own troops over particular aspects of his policies. Adenauer was forced by his majority to accept an 'Atlantic' clause, as a condition of their ratification of the Franco-German treaty. When Brandt was elected Chancellor for the second time after his party's triumphal success in the 1972 elections, he failed to make the most of this chance. His hesitations allowed a certain vacillation to creep into the party and deprived the Government of an assured leadership (a situation for which he tried to compensate by increasing the politicization of the higher echelons of the Civil Service, in the hope of ensuring efficient execution of government decisions). Helmut Schmidt, for his part, appeared to be a victim of the FDP defection in 1982; but his fall was also brought about by deep rifts within the SPD, divisions that the head of the Government had been powerless to overcome since they were, by their very nature, irreconcilable (ecologists against trade unions, pacifists against strong NATO supporters, and so on).

In other words, however strong the position of a German Chancellor, it depends upon his own personality, the nature of the coalition, and the prevailing political circumstances. And, except during the period of Adenauer's chancellorship, the Chancellor's power has never smacked of the authoritarianism that the Presidents of the

Fifth French Republic have led the French to expect (and perhaps to relish). A German Chancellor has to enter into discussions, negotiate, and accept such compromises as the institutions and the parliamentary majority impose upon him. For the Chancellor's leadership is always modified and held in check by the rule of *Ressortprinzip*, according to which each Minister is solely responsible for his own department. This, too, will depend on popularity, and thus on the extent to which the Chancellor is judged indispensable by the majority parties. As 'unification Chancellor' in 1990, Helmut Kohl could do almost no wrong, but the situation was very different in his periods of deep unpopularity in 1989, 1993, and 1996.

The 'Italian miracle'—to use the expression fashionable in the 1960s (albeit at the time applied to the economy)—is a quite different matter. As we have seen, initially the President of the Council in principle had only a minor role to play. His Ministers were generally imposed upon him by the parties, his authority over them was virtually non-existent, his powers for co-ordinating the government team were minimal, and his means of operation laughable—on paper at least. However, the paradox is that the Italian President of the Council, like the Third Estate of 1789, from being 'nothing' has definitely become 'something'. Although he enjoys very few of the powers and means at the disposal of his foreign counterparts, he has progressively strengthened his position 'not by reason of his own functions', as Cassese points out, 'but because he is situated in a position where he is able to influence and reconcile all the different fragmentary subsystems'.[16] Cassese goes on to describe him as 'the catalyst for all the other elements that need to be united'.[17] In a system as fragmented as the Italian one, the President of the Council becomes the key piece in the political game and also the point from which the interplay of the many administrative and para-administrative agents may be co-ordinated. In a sense, his role rises above the chaos engendered by the theoretical autonomy of each of the many centres of decision-making, the constant conflicts between various political or bureaucratic lobbies, and the external need for a central reference point. It is true that the powers of an Italian President of the Council are a far cry from those possessed by Prime Ministers in other parliamentary systems. However, quite apart from the fact that his role has grown considerably more important since the war—without any institutional changes being made—it is necessary to gauge the 'performance' of a President of the Council on the basis of the characteristics of Italian political life and the processes by which political decisions are made. Italian politics are a long way from the politics of authoritarianism, *decisionismo*, and radicalism. They proceed via endless debate, compromise, consensus, and piecemeal reforms. Transformism, that is, the ability of political groups to absorb ideas and even people from other, hostile groups, is part of the tradition of united Italy: the country was developing the art of 'incrementalism' long before British and American scholars popularized the expression. In short, only the vices and virtues of Italian political life can provide a yardstick by which to gauge the evolution of the role of the President of the Council. The Craxi phenomenon provides a good illustration of the changes that had taken place over the past forty years. Despite the fact that, during the 1970s, Craxi's Socialist Party represented no more than 13 per cent of the electorate, its leader managed to turn the post of President of the Council into the central pivot of the whole system. It is symptomatic that Craxi (who beat the records for political longevity, since his Ministry was the third longest in the entire history of united Italy) strengthened his personal position as a political leader through the role that he played as President of the Council, and thereby helped his party to strengthen its position to over 14 per cent in the elections of June 1987. On the whole, the signs are that the President of the Council will emerge reinforced from the crisis of Italian politics in the mid-1990s, because of a greater personalization of his role. This pattern was set by Berlusconi, but the more presidential style was to some extent taken up by Prodi, who certainly behaved in the media as the 'locomotive' of the Olive Tree. Much, though, will depend on the constitutional proposals discussed in June 1997, and on what relationship between President and Prime Minister emerges from them.

Even in the context of the heterogeneity and diversity of the experiences of the Western democracies as a whole, the French situation stands out as one of the most unusual, since here the government leadership has, practically speaking, been shared between the President of the Republic and the Prime Minister. The situation, which is in principle a cumbersome one, was to some extent created by the Constitution, but was subsequently shaped and reinforced by practices that de Gaulle introduced and that his successors have maintained. For the most part, potential conflicts have been stifled by the supremacy of the Head of State (considered to be the country's guide or captain), whose strength has rested on his strong claim to legitimacy and his two majorities, the one parliamentary, the other presidential. Conscious of the conditions necessary to preserve partnership and harmony in the government leadership, politicians and the public alike continued for a long time to view the prospect of an antagonistic diarchy with alarm, the effect of which was no doubt to defer any change in the situation. However, following the Socialists' defeat in the elections of 1986, a new balance was struck. The President's role shifted. From being the quasi-monarch that practice over recent years had made him, he became more of an arbiter, as prescribed in Article 5 of the Constitution. His powers were reduced to the veto (over ordinances but not laws), the purveying of advice (the guide became an oracle), and arbitration (the power to dissolve Parliament). His role in government leadership was now limited to the fields of defence and foreign policy; and it should be remembered that, even in the realms of 'high politics', nowadays more and more of the agreements concluded are of a technical or sectorial nature. A President can certainly give a lead on general lines of orientation, but much of contemporary international relations is largely a matter of agreements on transport, taxation, the immigrant work-force, and so on, and these are the province of the Ministries with technical expertise rather than the presidency. In all other respects, government leadership passed, in accordance with Article 20 of the Constitution, into the hands of the Prime Minister. It was he who decided and implemented the policies of his government. This situation, which turned out to be less awkward than most observers predicted, probably gained acceptance from the various protagonists only because it was regarded as provisional, the prelude to a revival of presidential pre-eminence. In fact, the presidential omnipotence that had reigned before 1986 has never really returned. Mitterrand's Socialists lacked an overall parliamentary majority even after 1988, and then became very unpopular, reducing the President's freedom of man-œuvre. President Chirac in 1995 was weakened by his low score (under 21 per cent) at the first round of the presidential elections, and by the deep unpopularity of his Prime Minister, Alain Juppé. More importantly, though, cohabitation became almost routine, with the Gaullist Balladur governing under Mitterrand in 1993–5, and the Socialist Jospin under Chirac from 1997. In both cases, conflict was kept within manageable proportions. In each of them, the Prime Minister was more powerful than Chirac had been in 1986 (in Balladur's case because of his enormous parliamentary majority, in Jospin's because of the deep political damage President Chirac had inflicted on himself by calling snap elections which the Left had unexpectedly won), and encroached more on the President's domain, especially on European issues; and in each case the public appeared fairly satisfied with the checks and balances that the system offered.

Determining policies

As we have noted above, a head of government's powers as leader of his team are particularly crucial when it comes to determining choices, co-ordinating policies, and supervising the way in which decisions are implemented. In other words, a government may be considered either as a team or, alternatively, as a collection of individual Ministers each essentially responsible for his own department.

The most formalized system in this respect is that of Germany, whose constitution makes arrangements—somewhat conflicting, in some cases—relating to the collegial or autonomous position of Ministers. Article 65 of the Constitution allots to the Chancellor what Article 20 of the French Constitution, under the Fifth Republic, attributes to the government ('the government determines and directs the nation's policies'). According to this provision, the Chancellor has the right to decide upon 'the general political line' (*Richtlinienkompetenz*). Of course, this theoretical duty varies according to the nature of the coalition, the personality of the Chancellor, and the influence of certain of his Ministers. Adenauer certainly played a determining role in tying the Federal Republic to the West, just as Brandt was responsible for opening up relations with the East, and Kohl took the lead in unifying East and West Germany faster than anyone had thought possible or desirable when the Wall came down. But Erhard's influence was probably greater when he was simply the Minister credited with creating the German miracle than when he became an increasingly controversial Chancellor. Similarly, the SPD–FDP coalitions frequently produced scenes of stormy disagreement over economic and foreign policies. On the whole, observers of German politics agree that Chancellors from 1949 truly were in a position to direct the policies of their country, but they point out that the steering of the governmental vessel is an increasingly difficult task which may threaten the Chancellor's power at any moment.[18] The fact is that the Constitution also states that Ministers should manage their own portfolios autonomously, which seems somewhat at odds with the other provisions of

Article 65. We shall examine later how, and by what means, potential clashes have been avoided.

In Italy, in contrast, the President of the Council is in no way empowered to direct the policies of his Ministers. According to the Italian Constitution the 'king' is stripped bare, so the President of the Council can only influence the activities of his Government by *political* means: that is, by referring it to the programme negotiated with the other parties in the coalition, by making full use of any collateral support forthcoming from Parliament or the media, by playing off the disagreements between one Minister and another, by employing the powerful brake constituted by the Treasury, and finally, in the most difficult cases, by using his veto[19] to block certain moves on the part of his Ministers. Over the past two decades, the gravity of the problems facing Italy has afforded the President of the Council the chance to strengthen his influence over policies, particularly through financial control of public bodies and semi-public ones and through the crucial role that he has played in the area of security and public order (particularly since 1977). However, the increasing importance of the role of the President of the Council is limited by the decisional powers of the Italian politico-administrative system.[20] There can be no doubt, for example, that many of the reforms introduced during the 1970s constituted no more than implementations of the measures dictated by the Constitution that had been 'frozen' ever since its adoption, while the sweeping projects announced when the Ministries were set up were in reality more a matter for debate than for practical implementation. Here again, much will depend on the implementation of the constitutional reforms agreed in principle in June 1997.

In this respect, the situation in Britain is the opposite of that in Italy. In Italy, the parties lay before the voters programmes that, without a single-party majority, they are likely to find it hard to implement; the voter has no way of knowing what kind of post-election alliances will be formed or what their composition will be. By contrast, British voters are presented with programmes, frequently clearly defined, which the victorious party, by virtue of its theoretical 'mandate', considers itself committed to implementing. Some observers have regarded this commitment to the party programme to be the source of many of Britain's difficulties: they have pointed out how ridiculous these radical swings sometimes appear, particularly in the economic sphere. The Prime Minister is thus invested with a precise mission which he or she can invoke in the event of his or her Ministers proving recalcitrant. In return, when it is the Premier who drags his feet in the implementation of party policy, the party has a right to remind the executive of its electoral promises. Such situations have been quite common in the Labour Party, in which, up until the 1980s, the unions exercised a dominant influence. Tensions between the demands of grass-roots activists and the constraints to which a government party is inevitably subjected were endemic in what has come to be known as 'Old Labour', and the party's decline was in part a consequence of the free rein given to activists after 1979 and the resulting failure to attract votes from the Centre. The remedy adopted, in a contest when much of the party was in any case ready to accept a measure of ideological dilution in order, finally, to win an election, was a composite one: to recruit more middle-class, and often moderate, activists; to create new policy forums in which the voice of Labour's traditionalists was not heard as strongly as elsewhere; and finally to go into the 1997 election campaign with a manifesto, approved by the rank-and-file membership, that contained few radical promises that would become hostages to fortune. But Labour's difficulties in the 1960s and 1970s are a typical instance of the dilemma that faces all left-wing parties faithful to the ideals of reforming society and standing by their commitments. Another example was the French Socialist Government's 1984 schools reform. An initially prudent bill was radicalized by a series of strongly secularist amendments which the Prime Minister, Pierre Mauroy, had found it impossible to refuse. This revived the spectre of the historic schools conflict, dormant in French politics since 1959, and led to the massive right-wing demonstrations of June 1984. The pragmatism displayed by Mauroy's successor, Laurent Fabius, indicated a switch to a 'party-government' attitude: that is to say, to more flexible practice that allowed the Prime Minister to steer his government's policies bearing in mind present or future needs in so far as these could be assessed, always in the light of changing circumstances.

In France, the direction of government activity under the Fifth Republic has, as we have seen, been decided for the most part by the Head of State. This had always been the case in areas considered to be of essential importance (decolonization, defence, foreign policy, and European affairs), and even in more technical or less crucial sectors in which presidential arbitration was deemed necessary. From 1958 to 1986, 1988 to 1993, and 1995 to 1997, given the coincidence of the presidential and the parliamentary majorities, the Head of State's interventions into government affairs were subject to no check apart from his own discretion and political circumstance. During cohabitation periods, by contrast, the government is in a position to make full use of its powers without subjection to the President, except in the areas of defence and foreign affairs. After June 1988, Mitterrand adopted a less interventionist line, relinquishing to the Prime Minister responsibility for most policies (and also for their possible unpopularity), though Mitterrand stepped more readily into the fray in 1991, owing to Prime Minister Cresson's plummeting popularity and apparent inability to give a clear direction to government policy. The division of tasks thus depends essentially upon contingent conventions rather than constitutional rules. It varies according to the protagonists involved, the circumstances, and, in the last analysis in most cases, the President's own decision on whether or not to intervene in government action.

For a long time, the Prime Ministers of parliamentary systems were more or less without means of either an administrative or a financial nature, or in terms of personnel. To have at his disposal at least a minimal infrastructure, it was traditional for the Prime Minister or President of the Council to combine his functions with those of another Minister, usually that of Finance or Foreign or Home Affairs. In France, it was not until the emergence of the Popular Front in 1936 and the premiership of Léon Blum that the leader of the government began to acquire the trappings of a support system. Similarly in Italy, up until the 1950s, the office of President of the Council was provided with neither staff nor means, not even with an official headquarters. The Presidency of the Council constituted as it were an extension of the Ministry of the Interior (usually the responsibility of the President of the Council himself), which provided him with the necessary material means of operation. The virtual absence of logistical means at the disposal of the President of the Council corresponds to his theoretically slender responsibilities. But once again, appearances are deceptive. In principle, the presidency of the Council commands no budget or staff of its own. It may call upon the services of up to 340 staff seconded from other Ministries or offices (a significant force) and can make use of Treasury funds for its own expenses. In practice, though, the scene looks rather different: quite apart from this personal staff, usually headed by a Councillor of State, the President of the Council can count upon the services of an Under-Secretary (either a senior civil servant or a Member of Parliament), who has his full confidence and acts as his closest collaborator and spokesman. To understand the importance of this post, we should remember that it is one that has been held by a number of top-level figures such as the future Premiers Andreotti (from the fourth to the eighth De Gasperi Governments) and Giuliano Amato (under Bettino Craxi). As regards the administrative organization of the President of the Council's office, practice and theory are, again, at odds. In the first place, immediately after the war, the President's staff was about 50 strong; by 1963 it had risen to 300. Since then the number has increased perhaps twentyfold. In its report of August 1986, the Audit Office estimated the members of the office of the President of the Council (which also includes the members of the offices of Ministers without portfolio) at 1,586[21] and the total number of staff employed at the Palazzo Chigi at 3,828 (ten times more than the official allocation). Expenses show a similar discrepancy between appearances and reality. The original budget for the Presidency was 1,995 thousand million lire, but in reality expenses have more than doubled (to 5,022 thousand million).[22] However, the Audit Office recognizes in its report that these anomalies are due to the mismatch that has developed between obsolete regulations and financial provisions, on the one hand, and the increasing importance of the Presidency, on the other. In its conclusions, it emphasizes that the bill to reform the Presidency (finally adopted in 1988) would constitute a step forward and 'an important stage in the implementation of the Constitution'.

It would appear that, in Italy, the increasing size of these staffs is an institutional and structural reaction to the constraints of a system that is diffuse, fragmented, and multipolar. This impression is confirmed when we compare Italy to Britain and Germany, where the staffs of Prime Minister and Chancellor are far more modest, despite the key roles that these figures play. Margaret Thatcher, despite her inclination to maximize the power of the Prime Minister, saw no reason fundamentally to alter the existing, small-scale, arrangements at No. 10 Downing Street. The British Prime Minister's Office (a term first officially used in 1976) has five components. The private office consists of five or six private secretaries, young, exceptionally able civil servants seconded from their departments for a period of roughly three years, who act as the immediate link between the Prime Minister and the government departments. The Prime Minister's political adviser and assistants in the political office constitute a link with the governing party and the Prime Minister's constituency that completely bypasses the Civil Service. The No. 10 Policy Unit, first set up by Harold Wilson in 1974, is staffed by political appointees from both outside and (since Margaret Thatcher's arrival) within the Civil Service, and supplies the Prime Minister with both long-term and, if necessary, immediate policy advice. The Prime Minister's Parliamentary Private Secretary, a backbench MP, is in charge of liaison with the government majority in Parliament. Finally, the Press Office, typically headed by a politically loyal former journalist, handles press relations generally and in particular the regular and controversial No. 10 'lobby briefings' in which newspapers are fed information and rumour on the understanding that they will not reveal their source. To these five should be added one addition of Margaret Thatcher: the Efficiency Unit, set up to advise on improved management of the machinery of government, and located in Whitehall, not Downing Street. As Anthony King notes, 'The total prime-ministerial staff comes to between two dozen and about thirty people, of whom perhaps seventeen or eighteen are intimately concerned with policy and the politics (and presentation) of policy.'[23] It is a small, flexible, shifting community, in which personal relationships are all-important, divisions of labour between different branches more notional than substantive, and the risk of entrenched, institutionalized, viewpoints and procedures building up are minimal. The Prime Minister is strong enough, as leader of the governing party and (usually) of a solid, stable, parliamentary majority, not to need the extra complication of a bureaucratized parallel administration as an instrument of decision. Indeed, the Prime Minister's Office proper was never intended to house all the tools required to do the Prime Minister's job. The function of policy co-ordination, similar to that carried out by the General Secretariat of the government in France, is assured by the Cabinet Office—in principle at the service of the whole Cabinet, in practice beholden chiefly to the Prime Minister, the Cabinet's chairman. The Cabinet Office plays a role of fundamental importance in determining policies, since its members loom large in all the ministerial committees in which the various departments try to harmonize their respective points of view. The Treasury (of which the Prime Minister has the title of First Lord) allocates resources between departments. After 1968, management of the government machine was the responsibility of a separate Civil Service Department, but in 1981 Margaret Thatcher abolished it and divided its functions between the Treasury (resource allocation) and the Cabinet Office (personnel management). She also abolished the Central Policy Review Staff, a Cabinet Office 'think tank' set up by Edward Heath in 1970. The CPRS had been designed to develop, on behalf of the whole Cabinet, long-term policy options and a framework for planning in an atmosphere free of political contingencies and inter-departmental rivalries. Mrs Thatcher always preferred to use an expanded, more political, No. 10 Policy Unit and a number of special advisers such as Sir Alan Walters (on economic policy) and Sir Anthony Parsons (on foreign affairs), and in 1983 simply scrapped the CPRS altogether.

In Germany, the Chancellor's staff is neither as large as those available to his counterparts in the United States and Italy, nor as minimal as the British Private Office. By virtue of the tasks assigned to it and its size, the Chancellor's Office (Bundeskanzleramt) most resembles the office and staff at the disposal of the Prime Minister of France. As in many other areas, the powers acquired by this structure stem to a large extent from the measures taken by Konrad Adenauer. He was so keen to have at his disposal an efficient instrument for implementing decisions that up until 1955 he went so far as to combine his functions of Chancellor with those of the Ministers of both Defence and Foreign Affairs. For ten years, from 1953 to 1963, the Chancellor's office was run by Hans Globke, Adenauer's adviser and a remarkable organizer, whom the Chancellor backed and retained in his post despite his past as a high-ranking civil servant under the Third Reich (in which capacity he had written the official commentary on the Nuremberg laws). Globke left his mark at the organizational level just as Adenauer left his at the political level, and the Chancellor's Office has retained all its importance despite the subsequent presence of secretaries in whom less confidence was placed and who lacked Globke's managerial skills (Grabert, for example, appointed by Brandt at the beginning of his second Government). The Office is organized into six functional divisions, each one under the management of a senior civil servant (a ministerial *Direktor*), appointed at the discretion of the government. These are the only appointments, apart from the Secretary of State[24] or Minister who is the Head of the Office, that can be described as political, for although successive Chancellors have managed to politicize the Office when new appointments were being made,[25] their opportunities to do so more generally are limited, since most of the civil servants who man the Office are appointed on a permanent basis. In other systems this situation might produce tensions, but in this case it does not give rise to too many difficulties because of the political consensus, the tradition of coalitions, and a concern to appoint first and foremost civil servants of high calibre. At present, the Chancellor's Office comprises a staff of roughly 500, of whom about 100 belong to the highest echelons of the Federal bureaucracy. A measure of flexibility is introduced into the personnel management by the presence of many contractual staff (about 40 per cent of the total).[26] Apart from being served by the Office itself, the Chancellor has at his disposal a Press Office with a huge staff (of about 800), described by Grosser as 'gigantic as compared to what exists in other pluralist states'.[27] The Chancellor is thus provided with an efficient instrument to promote co-ordination and collegiality. During the months following the breach of the Berlin Wall, it proved highly influential in the policy-making that led to unification. In contrast to the British Cabinet Office, however, its staff is stable and more loyal to the Chancellor than to the Ministry from which they may be seconded. The fact that the chief of staff has, since 1984, held the rank of federal minister also enhances the political weight of the office. Moreover, despite the fact that the German system is a fragmented one due to its federal structure and the persistence of coalition governments, the Chancellor's Office has so far—apart from the Press Office—resisted the inflationary trends displayed by the American Executive Office and the Italian Office, both of which have now assumed the dimensions of veritable central administrations.

The limited expansion of the Chancellor's staff is partly explained by the wide powers held by the *Länder*, which are responsible for virtually all administration. But the chief reason for it is the strong measure of autonomy possessed by the various German Ministries (*Ressortprinzip*), which prevents the Chancellor from direct intervention into the current business of each of them. Although he must verify and guarantee the application of the measures announced in his general policy statement (*Regierungserklärung*), he is not expected to interfere in his Ministers' handling of their respective sectors. This is totally different from the situation in France or Britain, where it has sometimes been known for an adviser to the Prime Minister (or the President) to overrule a Minister. Such a state of affairs would be inconceivable, even scandalous, in Germany.

It is true that in France, under the Fifth Republic, the services at the disposal of the executive have presented two unusual features. In the first place, both the President's staff and the Prime Minister's wield considerable influence over the actions of Ministers and the administration. Secondly, the staff of both heads of the executive always comprise two different groups, the one more concerned with political action, the other responsible for steering and co-ordinating the administrative machine (although, in practice, the two functions often appear inextricably intermingled). The presidential Secretariat (composed of between 15 and 30 people) and the General Secretariat of the government (about 100 strong) are the principal cogs in the administrative machine. But whereas the latter is a venerable institution with long-standing links with the parliamentary system (and, indeed, with monarchical roots), the former was set up in its present form by General de Gaulle, his predecessors of the Fourth Republic having been served by no more than a handful of individuals with little influence. The main tasks of the General Secretariat of the government are to organize meetings of interministerial councils and committees, to supervise the preparation and implementation of legislation, and to ensure the co-ordination and continuity of ministerial action—in short, to assist the Prime Minister in his general functions as leader and as head of the 'college' constituted by the government. Some members of this secretariat may be appointed at the discretion of the Prime Minister, but the general stability of these civil service posts, which constitutes a guarantee of State continuity, is considerable, even in the case of the one that is most in the public eye, namely, that of the Secretary-General to the Government. When, in 1986, Jacques Chirac dismissed the Secretary-General who had been appointed by the Socialists in 1981, this was regarded as a break in what had become a well-established tradition of the Republic. In 1988, on the other hand, Michel Rocard retained the Secretary-General whom his right-wing predecessors had appointed. At the Elysée, where no such traditions exist, the President himself appoints his men at his own discretion, and here the turnover is far more rapid (two or three Elysée Secretaries in the course of a seven-year presidential term of office). The importance of these posts is attested to by the fact that many of their incumbents (Jobert, Balladur, François-Poncet, Bianco) have been appointed to major ministerial duties following a period working at the Elysée.

The other component of the Elysée and Matignon staffs, that is, the directly political element, consists of offices (*cabinets*) whose members, for the most part senior officials seconded from the prestigious *grands corps* of the French civil service (the Council of State, the Court of Accounts, and the Inspection des Finances), operate as *chargés de mission* or technical advisers. The members of these *cabinets* are recruited on the basis of their sympathy for the existing authorities and, in theory, their duties are to advise the Prime Minister or Head of State and to supervise the activities of the sectors for which they have special responsibility. In reality, they are frequently more influential than the Minister in charge of the sector concerned, if only because they are afforded constant access to the decision-makers at the top (whereas a Secrétaire d'État, for example, may only come face to face with the President once or twice a year). However, the power of these *éminences grises* varies according to the ability of the Minister in question to impose or defend his own views and also the conceptions that the President or Prime Minister may entertain of their respective roles. At all events, conflicts and 'guerrilla' operations abound, including some between the two *cabinets*. The hostility of Georges Pompidou and his closest advisers towards the members of Jacques Chaban-Delmas's *cabinet* was one of the causes of Chaban's downfall in 1972.

The collective work of government is organized in councils or committees. Constitutional literature and political symbolism represent the council of ministers or the Cabinet (in the English sense of the word) as the centres, *par excellence*, of collective decision-making and policy determination. But in fact that is seldom a true picture, for the discussion and determination of government policies cannot possibly be limited to brief weekly or fortnightly meetings lasting two or three hours and with fifteen to thirty participants. In reality, in parliamentary systems a Council of Ministers is a symbol of the principle of collegiality sanctioned by ministerial responsibility. Accordingly, it is at these meetings that the government's essential actions are approved or 'decided': the adoption of bills and regulations, budgetary decisions, the orientation of internal or foreign policies, personnel appointments, and so on. But the meeting itself is hardly more than a final formality in a long process of decision-making, which has taken place elsewhere involving negotiations between the various partners in a coalition, internal arbitration within the party or parties in power, interministerial compromises and decisions, and policies adopted by the administration after extensive consultation with interest groups. However, the processes leading to these collective decisions and the extent of the head of the executive's authority in the resolution of conflicts vary from one country to another.

In France, the Council of Ministers formally ratifies decisions taken elsewhere. It is unusual for the Head of State chairing the meeting to consult each Minister present and even rarer for the meeting to provoke any clash (as happened in 1967, when Edgard Pisani tendered his resignation in protest against the use of ordinances). The meetings of the Council of Ministers are preceded by smaller and more informal meetings of Ministers and senior civil servants, and it is in these that most decisions are taken. Up until 1986, ministerial or interministerial committees were presided over by the Prime Minister or his representative, except when the President called meetings at the Elysée, in which the general policies of the government tended to be determined. Meanwhile, permanent interministerial councils were presided over by the Head of State, and it fell to them to deal with problems considered to be either of crucial importance (e.g. Algeria, or African or Madagascarian affairs) or areas of potential sensitivity at the time (e.g. the Central Planning Council created in 1974 or the Nuclear Policies Council in 1976). Jean Massot has illustrated the progressive presidentialization of the system by showing the extent to which councils (based in the Elysée) took over from committees (based in Matignon).[28] But between March 1986 and June 1988 and in other periods of cohabitation, the situation has been totally reversed since now it is the Prime Minister who holds the essential power to call and chair committee meetings. The Head of State is reduced to chairing the Defence Committee and the Council of Ministers (the latter being a more or less formal role). Meetings of the Council of Ministers become more than ever a rubber stamp under such conditions: the President still takes the chair, and the Prime Minister, his political opponent, seeks at all costs to avoid any revelation of discord within the government that could provide political ammunition to the enemy. One meeting held in 1987 was timed at just 15 minutes by one of the ministers present.

It is in Germany that rules for organizing the work of government are the most strictly codified. Although every Chancellor can impose his own style upon the management of government, the essentials are determined by legislation adopted in 1951 (and revised in 1970) on the basis of Article 65 of the Constitution. It is this that determines the procedures of decision-making, in particular the rules applying to Cabinet voting. But it has been relatively rare for the Cabinet of the Federal Republic to take a vote. Often, disagreements are resolved and decisions taken in a context that is more informal and also, given the prevalence of coalitions, more party dominated. For example, during the period of the grand coalition led by Kiesinger, rifts were frequently repaired and contradictions resolved at Kressbronn, near Lake Constance (hence the name 'the Kressbronn Circle' given to these periodic meetings). But conflicts cannot always be resolved politically, for many of them are not specifically related to the parties. As Renate Mayntz[29] points out, some antagonisms are 'structurally determined, reflecting the conflicting interests and inclinations of Ministers and their respective clienteles'. In such situations, only the Chancellor's personality and his gifts of mediation and persuasion can produce agreement over policies that accommodate the different views of his Ministers. By reason of the Constitution and the practices established by Adenauer, the powers that the Chancellor possesses are thus far from negligible, but they are limited by the increasingly important part played by the parties in the formation of coalitions and the determination of government policies. His prerogatives are restricted by the general policy declaration that he makes to the Bundestag, a declaration that is itself conditioned by the agreements reached between the various parties included in the coalition government (*Koalitionsvereinbarung*). Finally, in accordance with the Constitution, which allows Ministers a very large measure of independence (*Ressortprinzip*) in the running of their Ministries (as regards both political decisions and the organization of their departments), the Chancellor only has the right to intervene if a Minister's decisions do not seem to conform to the general orientation of government policies. As can be seen, especially if the Chancellor is weak, the head of the German executive does not enjoy such sweeping powers as his French and British counterparts.

In Britain, as in other parliamentary systems, 'full Cabinet' meetings give official expression to a more important process of decision-making that is already completed.

Essentially, this takes place in Cabinet committee meetings, whose importance is such that they are sometimes said to constitute the fundamental element in the United Kingdom's process of governmental decision. These committees fall into two main categories, the permanent (or 'standing') committees, which deal with questions such as foreign affairs, defence, and so on, on a regular basis; and *ad hoc* committees. The creation, composition, and agendas of these committees are decided by the Prime Minister, who also chairs the most important of them. The committees are not supposed to take decisions that are the province of the 'full Cabinet'. In practice, though, the Prime Minister's control over the committee structure is a powerful prerogative. During her early years as Prime Minister, Margaret Thatcher was almost certainly in a minority in Cabinet on key questions of economic policy, but her power to appoint the key economic committees—as well as the divisions among the opposition to her—allowed her monetarist views to win through. Cabinet committees have traditionally been subject to a Civil Service blackout, and when Margaret Thatcher admitted the existence of four of them (out of a total of some 160) in 1979, 'she was going much further than any Prime Minister in recent times'.[30] Peter Hennessy published a list of 72 of them in 1986, but the list will change frequently, as new committees are created and others fall into disuse.[31] And their composition, as well as the decisions that they take, are kept secret, for reasons of confidentiality, but also so as to maintain the fiction of collegiality and ministerial solidarity. Obviously, this excessive secrecy is impossible to maintain, and as well as the lists in academic books on government, the Press takes mischievous delight in publishing all kinds of information and reporting on many controversies that are in theory cloaked in secrecy. In a sense, however, the greater the extent of politico-administrative secrecy and the more limited the consensus reached over political decisions, the more 'leaks' there tend to be. Within the Cabinet, the Prime Minister provides strong leadership, not so much as a result of his (or her) constitutional prerogatives but rather as leader of the majority party. Occasionally, the Prime Minister may call for a vote in Cabinet, but only does so in very exceptional circumstances (although the procedure was more common under the Labour governments of the 1960s and 1970s, partly because of Labour's more formal procedural style and partly owing to divisions within the Labour Party at the highest level). Usually, decisions are reached by consensus, possibly after the Prime Minister has consulted each Minister individually. The object is to avoid crystallizing the existence of a minority within the government by taking a formal vote.

In Italy, as we have seen, the President of the Council is both weak, by reason of the role that the parties play in coalition governments, and, at the same time, central to the system, in that he is one of the few cogs in the machine in a position to free some of the others in the system and thus to make it run more smoothly. The position of the President of the Council is seen rather differently by different observers. Some, Merlini, for example, stress that all too many ministerial committees are placed under the authority of one or other of the Ministers themselves.[32] Others, such as Cassese, point to the progressive extension of the powers of the President of the Council. (For example, the co-ordination of regional affairs and the regions' conference have recently been placed under his direction.) What should also be pointed out is that, as in all countries, but particularly in Italy, the President of the Council must always reckon carefully with whoever is in charge of the Treasury, especially if the latter happens not to belong to the same party or faction as the President of the Council himself.

However, as in all systems, more or less formalized procedures have been devised to improve the processes of decision. One case in point has been the attempt to associate party secretaries with the government so as to resolve crises from the inside rather than from outside the Cabinet. Another has been the constitution of very small crisis Cabinets. (For example, to cope with the Achille Lauro affair, Craxi conferred with the Ministers of Defence and Foreign Affairs.) This is also fairly common practice in Britain, where 'inner Cabinets' are frequently set up (either to deal with ongoing problems or in crisis situations such as the 1982 Falklands War). In such situations, the Prime Minister presides over a group of Ministers selected either on the grounds of their particular responsibilities and skills or because of the confidence that the head of government places in them. Thus the crisis Cabinet set up during the Falklands War included Cecil Parkinson, not—obviously enough—because he was Chancellor of the Duchy of Lancaster, but as Chairman of the Conservative Party and a faithful ally to Mrs Thatcher. All these processes and structures provide added proof of the gap that has developed between constitutional theory, according to which the Council of Ministers or Cabinet is the central organ of decision, and current political practice, which is remarkably different.

Conclusion

The government today, whether parliamentary or presidential, is the central element of a political system. The centrality of its role stems from a number of factors. In the first place, as has already been emphasized, governments and the apparatuses that they control have benefited from an expansion of functions, means, and staff that is unparalleled in other 'branches' of power. In the early nineteenth century, in Britain, the number of staff employed by the central government was roughly equivalent to that employed by Parliament. Today, any comparison between the two would be pointless, except to stress the vast discrepancy between the means available to the legislature and those enjoyed by the executive.

Secondly, contemporary processes of decision-making, which call for rapid action and reaction often kept secret until they are officially reported, render the roles played by the political parties and their leaders more important and reinforce the power of teams that are kept small, or even of individuals, to the detriment of decision-making machinery such as Parliaments. Even in Italy, where the executive (apart from a few exceptions) is weak and unstable, the expression *centralità del Parlamento* reflects only one side of the political reality: Parliament, as everywhere, certainly remains the primary forum for political debate, but even the formal power of decision-making is increasingly slipping from its grasp and passing to the government (which can pass decree-laws) and to the administration.

Thirdly, the reciprocal checks that legislatures and executives used to be able to impose upon each other have become more and more unbalanced. Ministerial responsibility is no longer an issue or, when it is (taking forms that are frequently semi-constitutional), as in Italy, it is not so much a matter of Parliament attempting to apply controls as of disagreements between the parties or between different factions within a party. Ministerial responsibility in the classic sense of the expression plays such an insignificant role that, beneath all the turbulence caused by the rapid succession of governments, Italian Ministers in fact continue to display a remarkable degree of political stability. In contrast, the means of control and constraint available to the executive are both powerful and widely used. They include, for instance, procedures to expedite decisions (such as Art. 49.3 in France and the guillotine in Britain), as well as other constitutional constraints.

Finally, the growing power of party leaders and the increasingly important role played by the political parties provide Presidents and heads of government with extra trump cards. Ordinary members of parliament are more likely to be dependent upon the executive than vice versa. This reversal of roles can be seen quite clearly if we look back at the situations in which leaders of the executive have found themselves in difficulties over recent years: Nixon and Brandt were undermined by revelations in the Press, de Gaulle by a referendum; Eden, Macmillan, Adenauer, and Erhard were all, more or less unceremoniously, put out of action by their own parties, while (with the exception of Jacques Chirac in 1976) French Prime Ministers have suffered the same fate at the hands of their respective Presidents but not those of Parliament as such, and so on. Only the Italian situation is (to some extent) an exception to the rule.

However, it would be excessive to conclude that the executives of today have become all-powerful. They continue to be subject to both internal and international constraints and to pressures exercised by the political parties, other groups, and their own administrations, all of which constitute so many considerable limitations to their authority. Nowadays, particularly in the West, societies are complex and unwieldy entities that in many cases can only be steered into making changes of a marginal nature. The process of globalization has compounded the economic constraints, while the growing power of the European Union has reinforced the political ones. Notwithstanding the undeniable charisma of certain leaders (Reagan, Thatcher, and Mitterrand, for example), governmental power is limited by the plurality of the agents involved in all policy-making and the recalcitrance of facts. It is altogether in accordance with the logic of things that it should be the very elements supposed to possess the most power and authority (the government and its administration) that should be the most subject to *external* pressures, now that internal limitations upon the exercise of power have been eroded or have become obsolete.

Questions

- Should the function of Head of State in West European democracies be considered a largely ceremonial one?

- How, and under what conditions, can prime ministers exercise leadership in West European governments?

- What is the function of staffs of heads of government, and why do they vary so much in size?

- Is anything of importance decided at full meetings of Cabinets or governments in Western Europe?

- 'The legislature is the least important constraint on the activity of the executive branch in Western Europe.' Discuss.

NOTES

1. J. Blondel, 'Gouvernements et exécutifs: Parlements et législatifs', in J. Leca and M. Grawitz, *Traité de science politique*, iii (Paris: PUF, 1985), 355.
2. The 1958 Constitution had initially made provision for the President to be elected by a college of notables (Deputies, locally elected representatives, and representatives from overseas territories), numbering about 75,000 individuals. The system was devised, on the one hand, so as not to be solely dependent upon Deputies and senators (who used to elect the President under the Third and Fourth Republics) and, on the other, to avoid direct universal suffrage. The memory of the *coup d'état* of 2 Dec. 1851 by Louis Napoleon Bonaparte (the only President to be elected by direct universal suffrage until 1962) prompted fears that the same might happen again. It was only in 1962, at the end of the Algerian War, that General de Gaulle was able to hold a referendum to get the Constitution revised and establish presidential elections by direct universal suffrage.
3. e.g. in twentieth-century Britain, there has existed a firmly established tradition that the Prime Minister must be a member of the House of Commons. In 1963, Lord Home submitted to this 'convention' by renouncing his hereditary rights and getting himself elected to the House of Commons in a Scottish by-election.
4. J.-C. Colliard, *Les Régimes parlementaires contemporains* (Paris: FNSP, 1978), 130.
5. Unless they are made members of the House of Lords, which makes things rather easier (e.g. Lord Young).
6. M. Dogan, *How to Become a Cabinet Minister in Italy: Unwritten Rules of the Political Game*, European University Institute Working Paper, 1983.
7. H. Portelli, 'La Proportionnelle et les partis', *Pouvoirs*, 32 (1985), 87.
8. The RI obtained three ministerial portfolios and one Secretary of State portfolio in the Couve de Murville Government, four ministerial and three Secretary of State posts in the Chaban-Delmas Government (which also included three Centre PDM Ministers).

CHAPTER 7

Central Administrations,
Local Governments

The sector that has changed the most over the last century in the Western democracies is probably that of central administrations. The change is primarily one of size, reflecting the remarkable expansion of the functions assumed and the services rendered by the various branches of the State apparatus. The 50,000 officials of the Italian central administration at the end of the nineteenth century have increased fortyfold and today number almost 2 million.[1] Britain, which in the early nineteenth century employed only 20,000 in the central administration, today employs about 500,000.[2] The figures are slightly lower in Germany (just over 300,000 in West Germany in 1980)[3] on account of the essential administrative role of the *Länder*, but overall the tendency is the same.

Central Administrations, Local Governments

It is extremely difficult to establish statistical comparisons between different countries, on account of the differences between their respective staffs and functions (public in some countries, private in others). It is nevertheless clear that, once the various levels (central and local) and fragmentations of the administrations concerned have been taken into account, the ratio of civil servants to members of the public works out to be remarkably similar in all the Western countries.

The changes that have taken place also concern the functions assumed by administrations. Here, expansion has been continuous ever since the nineteenth century. The formidable explosion of the Welfare State and 'Big Government' was checked (but not totally halted) only by the economic crisis of the 1970s. Today, European democracies use, on average, over 40 per cent of the gross national product for running costs and the redistribution of national wealth. The management of taxation and redistribution and of investment in the State requires a whole army of staff, massive funding, and increasingly numerous and sophisticated regulations and procedures. For the tasks of bureaucracies have not only proliferated; they have also changed in kind, calling for new methods, instruments, and modes of management. And in cases where the traditional administration has not proved capable of encompassing the necessary changes, new structures have developed alongside, using the new methods that the many new functions demand.

Other transformations have been of a more fundamental nature. First, in every case, the body known—for the sake of convenience—as 'the administration' is extremely heterogeneous. When necessary, the whole conglomeration presents a united front to the external world and is sometimes believed by the public to be indeed united. However, in reality it constitutes a severely divided world of separate departments in which much energy is devoted to pre-empting one's neighbours, empire-building, angling for judicial guarantees for organizational or functional claims of one kind or another, and defending one's own responsibilities and prerogatives. There is nothing particularly scandalous about that, nor is the phenomenon peculiar to public organizations. However, it is all a far cry from the myth of a united administration under the control of the political authorities or from the Weberian model of bureaucracy. The internal conflicts of administrations are recognized to varying degrees in different countries: in Italy, they are an integral part of the politico-administrative scene; in Germany, the force of *Ressortprinzip* to some extent legitimizes the autonomy of the different departments. In France, where the Revolution, using materials left by the monarchy, built such a fine theoretical edifice, the majesty of power is less prone to such cracks in its façade. Nevertheless, in reality the situation is no different from elsewhere.

But it does not follow from this heterogeneity that all the agents involved stand on an equal footing. Everywhere, the financial administrations dominate: their strategic position, their direction of taxation and finance, which gives them control even over the policies of each government that enters office, and the strength and calibre of the élites who make up their staff are all factors that combine to turn the Ministries of Finance into 'States within States'. The fortunes of other Ministries depend upon current circumstances, political decisions taken by the government, and social pressures.

Ministries in charge of technology, the education sector, and culture (in France and Italy) have greatly expanded. Despite budget cuts following the end of the Cold War, defence retains an important position, particularly in countries such as France and Britain where it is concerned with issues that are diplomatic and political as well as military, and with strategies that have global implications. On the other hand, some Ministries are currently in a relative state of decline (Foreign Affairs) or have yet to establish themselves firmly (the Environment, in its strict sense of environmental protection). Within each individual Ministry, furthermore, technical staff sometimes clash with general administrators, as do political appointees with personnel recruited on the grounds of personal merit, 'insiders' vie with 'outsiders', and so on. In short, there could be no better way of debunking the myth of the 'State' with a capital 'S', be it that of the Jacobins, the Marxists, or the *philosophes*, than by noting the multiform, fluctuating, and antagonistic nature of Western States viewed from the inside.

There is a second point to make that also applies to all the Western democracies. Nowadays, each of their bureaucracies plays a role of crucial importance in public policy-making. According to Western tradition, and also to the Cartesian view of the processes of decision-making, the role of administrations is to implement decisions taken elsewhere, usually by the political authorities. But, as many studies have shown, that view has not for some time corresponded to the real state of affairs. Nowadays, bureaucracies are involved at every stage in public policy-making.

1. They help to shape the political agenda, that is, they elicit demands of which the political authorities have been unaware, suggesting bills, reforms, and changes to them. Or, alternatively, they help to set aside demands that are 'fantastic', 'unrealistic', 'too expensive', or 'completely impractical'. Thus, they operate as 'sifting agents', even if they do not monopolize that function and if, in most cases, they allow the political authorities to appear to be active in that capacity.

2. They are the gatekeepers of the State and the main point of contact between the political authorities and interest groups. Shaping the agenda does not only mean selecting and shaping ideas and policies; it involves talking to interest groups or closing the door to them. Of course, ministers and parliamentarians also have contacts with representatives of groups, and can and do take political decisions about which groups should be listened to; but most of the discussions from day to day take place at official level. These regular contacts, if pursued for long enough, shape what have come to be known as 'policy networks' (cf. above, p. 149); a 'departmental view' of a particular policy area is usually shaped, not only by the department's own accumulated wisdom, but by the groups that give it advice. And the absence of certain groups from the circle of consultation shapes the 'non-decision-making', the omission of certain questions from the agenda, that is as important as the policies that are developed.

3. They help to determine the substance of political decisions by drafting bills conceived or accepted by the political authorities. Policies are frequently initiated by a written text (a law or a ruling), a financial grant, an *ad hoc* choice of instruments, or the selection of particular procedures. At all these levels, bureaucracies are necessary,

indeed essential partners. Only they can provide the expertise to enable the political authorities to realize their plans. But this 'assistance' from the civil servants often places the authorities formally responsible for decision-making in a position of dependence: as is frequently acknowledged, 'it is impossible to govern against one's bureaucracy'.

4. Bureaucracies are, furthermore, responsible for implementing the government's policies. This, indeed, is normally considered their *raison d'être*. As we have noted, their function extends far beyond what is frequently and simplistically claimed for them, namely, that of executive agents. Moreover, the way in which a policy is implemented may have very little to do with faithful execution of the plans of those who conceive it. All policies affect not only those whom they immediately concern and those who benefit from them, but also those who apply them. Policy implementation invariably involves adjustments, distortions, unexpected effects, and changes that are quite beyond the control of whoever originally decided upon the policy. Long before the 'policy studies' of today abundantly confirmed the fact, Tocqueville, in his *L'Ancien Régime et la révolution*, noted that 'Rules are rigid, but practice is flexible.' The truth is that the dichotomy between decision and execution is quite artificial. 'Execution' involves the juxtaposition and/or accumulation of a whole set of 'decisions' not recognized as such and in many cases neither formalized nor legitimized, yet which effectively transform the original decision. Execution means decision 'continued by other means' and with other decision-makers, however much philosophical, political, and juridical discourse persists in turning a blind eye to that mutation.

5. Finally, bureaucracies, as the instruments and means of expressing the continuity of the State, have an inherent interest in pursuing and maintaining the policies to which they have committed themselves. Institutional and structural pressures 'justify' this. Everything combines to encourage them in doing so: the guarantees afforded by the status of civil servants, the techniques for renewing the funding of services that have been approved, competition between one Ministry and another, and pressure from 'clients' (the regulated) working in unison with them. The resulting policy networks are typically committed to defending the policies that they initiated and from which they benefit. Recent neo-liberal policies may have brought into question such conduct, amplified as it has been by the Welfare State. However, it has proved extremely difficult to put the clock back, to 'roll back the State'. In both Britain and the United States it has been proved that in the course of a decade of governments determined to reduce public expenditure, it has been possible to do no more than than halt its relative progress. The 40 per cent of GDP accounted for by public spending in the United Kingdom in 1996, after 17 years of Conservative government, was barely lower than the proportion that Mrs Thatcher had found on taking office in 1979.

The principle according to which the continuity of the State should be ensured whatever the changing fortunes of the political authorities places considerable power in the hands of bureaucracies. Despite the rhetoric about the subordination of the administrative branch to the political, the experience of the Western democracies confirms that, at the very least, such subordination is far from automatic. The power of administrations lies in a number of factors: in the limited room for manœuvre (political, financial, and psychological) available to politicians in applying their policies, the difficulties involved in steering this huge apparatus in the desired direction, and the ability of civil servants to organize themselves into powerful pressure groups that are capable of resisting government decisions or of imposing their own views.

There are thus many similarities between the Western bureaucracies, despite all the differences caused by history or by the particular position of each administration within the framework of its country's system as a whole. And today they are complemented by yet another unifying factor: Western democracies all face the same problems, are all subject to similar constraints, and are all engaged in continual interactions which lead them to seek similar solutions. By reason of these common constraints and experiences, there exists today a veritable market in methods of administrative reform, in which ideas are exchanged about new structures, new methods, and new modes of management. National administrative training centres, the use of an 'ombudsman' or independent commissions, means of access to administrative documents, and techniques for combating terrorism are just a few examples of the subjects of common interest to the administrations of the liberal democracies today. And beyond that limited circle, they are also of interest to countries which, for historical or ideological reasons, tend to use the liberal democracies as administrative models.

Administrative structures

Whatever the country under consideration, one general point is clear: bureaucracies are extremely complex and the administrative unity so dear to Weber turns out to be a myth. There have been many attempts to rationalize the situation, many denunciations of the creeping tentacles of bureaucracy, many 'hatchet committees' and other attempts at radical reform. But, for all that, many responsibilities continue to be duplicated, many posts are in reality redundant, and the statuses of different administrative departments are largely unstandardized. However, to give a simplified picture of a complicated situation, let us concentrate our analysis upon four levels which, to a greater or lesser extent, are discernible in all the systems that we are studying: central bureaucracies, local and regional authorities, autonomous or specialized bodies, and the public economic sector.

Central bureaucracies

Central administrations are in principle placed under the authority of a Minister and organized as Ministries or Departments. But there are exceptions to that general rule, particularly in the United States, where it has proved politically difficult to set up Ministries (in 1987, there were still no more than thirteen in all, five of which had been created since 1953), and where the gap is filled by Agencies, Boards, or Authorities. But even in countries with less strong political and psychological reservations about the creation of new Ministries, governments may prefer to resort to structures that are the functional equivalent of Ministries without being formally organized as such. So it was in the cases of regional development (DATAR) in France, the environment (up until 1986) in West Germany, the Commissariat for civil protection in Italy, and so on. Another factor differentiating one country from another is the degree of public interventionism tolerated (a permanent, well-established Ministry of Culture would be virtually inconceivable in Britain where the Culture Minister is chiefly concerned with spending lottery money, and has a much lower profile than French counterparts like André Malraux or Jack Lang) or national peculiarities (the Commonwealth for Britain, the refugees for Germany, the southern problem for Italy, the Overseas Departments and Territories for France, and so on). Finally, the number and size of Ministries and the services that they provide also depend upon the country's degree of administrative deconcentration or decentralization.

All Ministries are organized hierarchically, on the model of a pyramid, although the various levels go by different names in different countries: bureaux, directorates, divisions, etc. However, the significance and effects of this hierarchical model may vary considerably from one system to another or even within a single administration.

1. Some Ministries are placed under the direction of a single individual, the Minister, who is both a political leader and the head of his department. In other cases, by reason of the size of the Ministry or the political need for a distribution of portfolios, the ministerial department is functionally divided so that responsibility for various sections may be allocated to a number of different officials. Some Ministries may thus be divided between two, three, or even four Ministers of unequal status. One of them is set above the others, but although he holds superior authority, the running of the department differs from that of one placed directly under a single head. In the European democracies, ministerial authority is frequently divided in this way, essentially for political reasons to do with the proliferation of ministerial posts and those of Junior Ministers (up to 100 in Britain and Italy), or the constraints imposed by coalitions (in Germany, France, and Italy).

2. Communication between the political summit of the pyramid and the bureaucracy may take a direct form or may be effected through an intermediary political office. In the first case, the Minister has direct contact with the officials in his service. But even here variations occur: a British Minister may not choose his own subordinates but must generally accommodate himself to those already in harness, whereas an American or German Minister can make his own appointments to posts of high responsibility, choosing officials whose views are close to his own (in Germany), or his own political friends from either the public or the private sector (in the USA). In contrast, in France and Italy, a special office (the *cabinet*) mediates between the Minister, the administration, Parliament, and the various interest groups involved. The office is both political (through the ideological or party affinities between its members and the Minister

himself) and administrative (through its composition, since most of the office staff are drawn from the top echelons of the civil service). These *cabinets* have their roots in the historical mistrust—which endures even today—that politicians feel towards the administration, for the latter is suspected of distorting or failing to apply the Minister's directives. But it is worth noting that, in a country such as Britain, where relations between Ministers and the administration rest upon the principle of the latter's strict neutrality, a minority of voices (but a considerable number, for all that:[4] for example, a minority in the Expenditure Committee of the House of Commons for 1977–8) have been arguing for an 'injection' of political appointments within the upper administration.

3. A third organizational difference or variation may stem from the presence (or absence) of a top official (Secretary-General) who heads the administration and is answerable to the Minister. Such an official is responsible for co-ordinating the activity of the various branches of the Ministry, preparing ministerial decisions and supervising their implementation, issuing directives, and so on. Such officials, where they exist, are very powerful, for they can lay claim either to a stability and experience that lend considerable weight to their authority, as in the case of a Permanent Secretary in Britain, or to a wealth of administrative experience backed up by the trust of the Ministers who selected and appointed them, which is the situation of the German *Staatsekretäre*. In some cases, stability and political confidence can both be there, as when the same coalitions govern in rapid succession (e.g. in France, under the Fourth Republic, or in Italy). In such circumstances, a Secretary-General may become just as influential as his Minister—or even more so: under the Fourth French Republic, the Secretary-General of the Ministry of Education certainly wielded more influence than the numerous Education Ministers who succeeded one another in his time. That is no doubt why the Fifth Republic has gradually been eliminating ministerial Secretaries-General, who are such symbols of bureaucratic power. At the Quai d'Orsay, however, the post of Secretary-General survives and remains a highly prestigious one. In Italy, the Ministries of Foreign Affairs and Defence have also retained this structure.

4. The extremely variable size of ministerial departments constitutes another factor of differentiation between them. The size of an administrative apparatus depends upon the types of tasks and responsibilities allotted to the Ministers concerned. Ministries of the Environment (again, in the sense of environmental protection, as opposed to the former British Department of the Environment which included the former Ministries of Housing and Local Government) are always tiny compared to the giant structures of Ministries of Defence or the Postal Services (where the latter are set up as Ministries). For example, both in Italy and in France, the Ministry of Education is the major State employer, representing one-third (in France) and one-half (in Italy) of all civil servants dependent upon the central administration; in Britain and Germany, on the other hand, the education system is (at least notionally) controlled by local and regional authorities. In a comparison between different systems, variations in the size of Ministries provide an interesting indication of the degree to which tasks are dispersed (by assigning them to lateral agencies or organizations of a more or less autonomous nature) or

responsibilities are decentralized (by being transferred to local authorities that lie outside the hierarchical central Ministry). When that happens, pyramidal administrations that outwardly resemble one another may, in reality, operate quite differently.

Local and regional authorities: field services or local autonomy?

Implementing decisions and raising finance are activities that employ ever-increasing numbers of administrative staff, who must perform the most diverse functions and remain in constant touch with the public. Governments may opt for one of two main strategies. Either they can make use of a local administration that is dependent upon the central authorities; or, alternatively, they can depend on local authorities that are autonomous but remain under the ultimate control of the central Ministries. The first of these two solutions was—and still is—exemplified best by the French (together with the Italian) model. The second solution is that adopted—albeit in very different ways—by Britain and Germany.

We should, however, note that in practice neither model is implemented in a pure form: mixed solutions are the general rule.

The French model, on paper at least, is certainly the closest to a hierarchical pyramid. The quasi-military concept of organization and the aim—or illusion—of producing a strategy of general application and transmitting directives and information via a whole series of agents working for the central authorities provides an idealized model of the rationalist and centralist inspiration of the governments of the *ancien régime*, the Revolution, and the Empire. It is a model that has been followed—either deliberately or willy-nilly—by many European States such as Belgium, Italy, and Spain, at one point or another in the course of their histories. The prefect is positioned at the centre of the local organization. He is the representative of the State and is—in theory at least—responsible for co-ordinating all external services. This 'strange animal from the French menagerie' (to borrow the words of a British observer, Howard Machin) was certainly a powerful instrument of a centralized administrative system. However, for different reasons, neither in Italy nor in France does the reality fully correspond to that theoretical description. Italian prefects have never wielded as much power and influence as French ones, if only because of the inadequacy of the external services provided by the State over which, from the very start, they soon lost control. Italian prefects, responsible as they were for organizing elections and for law and order, and consequently compromised by Fascism, have been unable to resist post-war democratic tendencies and the growing influence of the parties. As Sidney Tarrow shows,[5] it is now the latter that have become the true intermediaries between the centre and the periphery.

Virtually the only real justification for the model of a prefect surrounded by external services was the central authorities' claim to control a web-like system that covered the entire territory and encompassed all administrative activities. This system was a powerful instrument in the construction of nation states in much of mainland Europe. The fact that it has survived, in particular in France, is due to the weakness and fragmentation of local systems. However, the system has evolved, under the pressure of two similarly oriented tendencies: in the first place, the prefect and the external State services (or field services), which were in theory supposed to ensure the overall authority of the central government, have been taken over at local levels. Numerous sociological studies undertaken in the 1960s succeeded in demystifying the rhetoric of the supremacy of the central hierarchy and revealed that relations between prefects and the notables surrounding them were on the whole a matter of compromise and collusion. Furthermore, the urbanization and massive expansion of services in towns during the 1960s showed that, while the field services may have been well suited to rural localities, they were certainly unable to cope with the more general development of the Welfare State. Today, public services (apart from education) have for the most part passed into the control of local authorities, although the field State services have preserved certain prerogatives which make it essential for local and the central authorities to collaborate. The 1982 decentralization reform, which transferred power from the prefects to the local élites, was not a revolution but in many instances the legalization of a quasi-*fait accompli*.

A second solution is to rely upon autonomous (and elected) local or regional authorities. Apart from Britain, with its two local levels (county and district) and plans to reduce this number to one, most European countries operate with at least three main strata of local authorities: regions, provinces, and communes in Italy; *Länder*, *Kreise*, and *Gemeinden* in Germany; regions, *départements*, and communes in France. But in Germany, as in France, this pattern is further complicated by many other bodies whose task is to mediate or to organize co-operation.

The degree of importance, numbers, and strengths involved at these major levels is by no means identical in the various countries. The weak link in the chain tends to be the *Kreis* in Germany, and the region in France, although the balance of power in the 1990s began to move towards France's regions at the expense of the *départements*. In Italy,[6] a better balance is maintained between on the one hand the 20 regions, which discharge a number of important responsibilities and which long afforded a haven for the Italian Communist Party (excluded from the central system) and, on the other, the 95 provinces which, in the last analysis, remain the structure upon which the parties and, hence, the political system are based. The provinces are themselves divided into 8,000 communes. The most fragmented system is the French one: 22 regions, 96 *départements*, 36,500 communes, and in addition several thousand (more than 15,000) *ad hoc* organizations set up to liaise between local authorities. In Germany, the 16 *Länder* are divided into 543 *Kreise* and 8,500 communes (*Gemeinden*), 117 of which operate simultaneously as both communes and *Kreise*. It is worth pointing out that in West Germany, following the reforms introduced in the mid-1960s, the number of communes was cut by two-thirds. This was a fine example of concerted action in an effort to decentralize, for the movement was a general one, despite the fact that each *Land* was in principle free to decide when, to what extent, and how to introduce reforms. On unification the East was, however, more fragmented.

In Britain too, the number of local authorities has been drastically cut, in fact reduced by two-thirds, as it was in West Germany. Here, operations have been even more spectacular, amounting, if not to 'permanent revolution', at least to regular reform. Of the 1,500 old units in the previous system, the 1974 reform retained in England and Wales only 47 non-metropolitan counties and 6 metropolitan counties, subdivided respectively into 333 and 36 districts. As well as these, there remained the Greater London Council, divided into 32 boroughs, plus the City of London. As from 1 April 1986, and following a long battle between Margaret Thatcher and the Labour Party, the Government abolished the Greater London Council and the 6 metropolitan counties. Finally, a further reorganization process commenced in 1996 left Scotland and Wales with just one tier of local government, covering the whole range of sub-central-government tasks: Scotland has 29 of these 'unitary authorities' and Wales 22. England, where the latest reforms have been introduced more gradually, could end up with some 40 unitary authorities by the end of the process.

Various pressures favouring devolution of responsibilities to infra-State authorities have led to a complex redistribution of tasks virtually everywhere. In Germany, for example, the *Länder* have been recognized to hold certain legislative powers, but their exclusive responsibilities do not amount to much: the police force, education, and the organization of local authorities. Moreover, in the cases of police and education, the 'exclusive' aspect of the powers of the *Länder* gave way in the pre-unification West to a system of collaboration and mutual agreement with the federal government. For the rest, the lion's share of power remains with the Bund—though it should be remembered that, for over half of federal legislation, the agreement of the *Bundesrat*, the upper house consisting of *Land* delegates, is necessary.

But, to see how the *Länder* can determine or direct policies, we should look not so much at the legislative level but rather at the processes through which decisions—in particular those taken by the federal government—are executed and implemented. For the *de facto* legislative quasi-monopoly held by the Bund is counterbalanced by the undisputed supremacy of the *Länder* in the administrative sphere. By and large, federal policies and *Länder* policies are all implemented either by the civil servants of the various *Länder* or in a sectorial fashion, under the supervision of a kind of prefect: these *Regierungspräsidenten* are each placed at the head of an administrative area intermediate between the *Land* and the *Kreis* (it is, in effect, composed of a collection of *Kreise*). This important post to a certain extent makes up for the lack of legislative power at *Land* level, but it also means that power and influence are channelled away from local politicians and pass to the bureaucrats: in 1989 there were 1.5 million *Länder* civil servants in the West, as opposed to 300,000 federal ones. In order to make the system work, co-operation between various levels of government is absolutely necessary.

There can, however, be no denying that 'co-operative federalism' in West Germany encouraged a centralization of the system to the advantage of the federal authorities, and that unification has reinforced this process. It is they who hold the key powers (defence, the Mint, foreign affairs), control the largest funds, and are best placed to respond to citizens' demands for fair treatment and to the concentration of economic forces. The centralization of Germany is not primarily a political matter. Rather, it stems from a combination of 'the due process of law' or *Rechtsstaat* and imperatives of an economic and commercial nature. The federal institutions that provide the best guarantees for an egalitarian respect for citizens' rights (the supreme courts) and the exercise of economic liberties are also the focal point for pressures exerted by interests of the most diverse nature: trade unions, economic forces, and even institutional interest groups such as local authorities, which frequently band together in competition between the federation and the federated in an attempt to divert power from the central authorities.

The United Kingdom had a partially federal system in the past: for half a century after 1922, Northern Ireland had its own parliament and executive (the head of which had the title of Prime Minister) and substantial autonomy. These institutions were abolished in 1972, and replaced by direct rule from Westminster, after their monopolization by the Protestant majority had helped bring the province to the brink of civil war. While a peace settlement in Northern Ireland would be likely to include plans for regional autonomy, possibly with a role for the Republic of Ireland, the main focus for discussions of regional government in Britain since the 1970s has been Scotland and Wales. Here, the Callaghan Government passed Acts in 1978 providing for a devolution of powers to both countries subject to referendums. But the plan was seen as a tactical move to retain the parliamentary support of the Welsh and Scottish nationalists on whose support Callaghan's parliamentary majority depended; the Labour party was itself divided over the question; and by the time the referendums were held in March 1979 (in Scotland and Wales only, the English not being consulted about the issue), the government was deeply unpopular. Wales voted four to one against having an Assembly, Scotland 52 per cent in favour—but on a turnout of 74 per cent, this Yes vote did not pass the hurdle of 40 per cent of the electorate which the government had set as a condition for implementing the law. Both countries therefore remained without devolved institutions, though this did not mean that they were not given special treatment. The Scottish and Welsh secretaries, both of them Cabinet ministers, headed an impressive range of deconcentrated institutions at both official level (the Scottish Office, with offices in Edinburgh, corresponding to the functions of nine English ministries, and the Welsh Office), and at parliamentary level (the Commons Grand Committees for Scotland and Wales, and the select committees that monitor the activities of the Scottish and Welsh Offices).

Despite these devices, most of them dating back to early in the century, and despite the tendency of Scottish and Welsh Secretaries to fight in Cabinet in favour of cash for their respective countries, the Conservatives became less and less popular in both countries: in 1992, for example, Wales was left with 6 Conservative MPs out of 38, and Scotland with 11 out of 72. And the aspiration to regional autonomy, or even to national independence, grew. It was partly to satisfy this that the 1997 Labour election manifesto pledged devolution if there were a favourable referendum (with no hurdles this time). The referendums held in September 1997, four months after Labour had returned to power, were successful—overwhelmingly in Scotland (where the yes vote was 74.3 per cent on a 60.2 per cent turnout, with 63.8 per cent voting yes to a second question as to whether the Parliament should have tax-raising powers); very narrowly in Wales (where the turnout was 51.3 per cent and the yes vote 50.3 per cent). The result will be a 129-member Scottish Parliament, elected in 1999 and taking office in 2000, with a Scottish Cabinet and First Minister, responsible for education, health, planning, agriculture, fisheries, and part of the economy. Wales will have a 60-strong Assembly with more limited powers. Prior to the referendums, it had been suggested that England should also have regional assemblies, but plans for these have now been shelved.

The scope of the administrative tasks and even legislative powers that fall to the German *Länder* make the responsibilities and means of the Italian regions—and, *a fortiori*, those of the French ones—seem very modest indeed: the latter look extremely light-weight in comparison. The legislative powers of the Italian regions are generally slight, but greater in the five with special status (Sicily, Sardinia, the Trentino–Alto-Adige region, the Aosta Valley, and the Friuli–Veneto–Julian Alps region), particularly in the economic and cultural sectors. However, in both the regions with special status and those with ordinary status, the quantitative proliferation of statutes has not always been accompanied by any qualitative improvement in the standards of government. Nowadays, regional laws can frequently be seen to be quite simply subject to a time-lag, compared with national laws or other regional laws adopted in the past. This is not really surprising, for the regions' small measure of autonomy restricts their means of adaptation. Furthermore, the responsibilities allotted to the regions by the 1947 Constitution relate to relatively secondary sectors: commune boundaries, social assistance, crafts, tourism, hunting, fishing, and so on. The more important sectors are those concerned with health and agriculture, but the regions have no autonomous financial means to cope with health problems and have to a large extent been 'relieved' of their responsibilities as regards agriculture by the transfer of agricultural policy-making to the EEC. The regions have had to fight tooth and nail to prevent the transfer of responsibilities, which has been taking place since 1970, from totally whittling away their means of intervention in the various areas attributed to them by the Constitution. For example, Article 117 of the Constitution is worded in such a way as to make it easy to manœuvre the introduction of restrictive interpretations. It runs as follows: 'In the following matters, the region fixed the legislative rules *within the limits of the fundamental principles fixed by State law, and on condition that those rules do not oppose the national interest or that of the other regions*' (our italics). Given a measure of ill will on the part of central institutions, it is clearly easy to play games with such dispositions. This is exactly what happened in the early 1970s: either isolated powers were excised from the 'body of responsibilities' attributed to the regions, leaving them with no autonomy at all (an operation known as *ritaglio*, 'redefinition'), or the adoption of the general principles that were supposed to make it possible for the regions to act on their own initiative was quite simply blocked. The first of those two obstacles was removed, owing to the political climate of 1977, particularly as a result of pressure from left-wing regions and the Communist Party (whose tacit support the Christian Democrats were courting in connection with their policy of what was known as 'National Union'). The second was swept away by the Constitutional Court, which ruled that, in default of a specific national law, the general principles mentioned in the Constitution could be regarded as following from the whole body of legislation already in effect.

The Italian regions are also active at the administrative level, although that is not the purpose for which they were originally designed. According to the Italian Constitution and the national legislature, the regions were originally conceived as intermediaries, centres of co-ordination and initiation, operating between the central and the local levels. Accordingly, the regions ought to have delegated most managerial tasks to the provincial and communal levels. But that never happened since, given an institutional climate in which they were at a disadvantage, the regions were anxious to hang on to whatever meagre powers they might possess. That is why the regions, originally planned as quite light structures, today employ some 60,000 officials. At the same time, it is only fair to point out that this body represents no more than 2 per cent of civil servants as a whole, despite the fact that the regions manage around 10 per cent of all public expenditure. But in this area, too, regional autonomy is limited, since 90 per cent of the resources available to the regions are provided by the State, and most of them come already earmarked for specific purposes. The room for manœuvre is thus extremely limited. This last point helps us to compare the degrees of regional autonomy in Italy and in France. The French regions have limited funding (63 billion francs in 1993) and discharge relatively few responsibilities (in comparison with the massive central institutional apparatus) and the staff available to serve them is very small (4,490 in 1990). They have often been able to exert a leverage out of all proportion to such slight resources, however, notably by adding small but vital 'top-up' subsidies to other local authorities' investment projects. Since the first direct election of regional councils in 1986, the regions' political clout has increased significantly, their resources have grown faster than those of any other level of government (they quadrupled between 1984 and 1993, albeit from a low base), and they have become involved in areas like university education that are well outside their official remit.

Given the interdependence between central and local authorities regarding the implementation of policies, the choice of solutions is a relatively simple one: either to adopt an authoritarian and centralizing policy so as to ensure that decisions taken at the top are carried out satisfactorily; or, alternatively, to set up instruments of collaboration designed to promote consensus and interdependence. Margaret Thatcher's beliefs—that local-government spending and borrowing, like those of central government, had to be brought under tight control, and that local authorities should be providing many fewer services directly—set her on a collision course with the established local government system. It was a confrontation that the central government, armed with a monopoly of statutory powers, could only win—but not without political cost. The metropolitan counties (London and six elsewhere) were Labour-controlled, unreceptive to reform, and considered to be overspending. The solution was simple: as from 1 April 1986, the Government abolished them, leaving Britain as the only country in Western Europe without an elected authority for the capital city. To reduce local spending, the Thatcher Governments passed the Local Government Planning and Land

Act (1980) and the Local Government Finance Act (1982), strengthened controls (in particular by creating the Audit Commission in 1983), and forced local authorities to put out to tender for public services through the Housing Act (1980), the Education Act (1980), and the Health and Social Security Act (1983). Localities that overspent were subjected to financial penalties by having their central government subsidies cut. Compulsory competitive tendering of council services cost municipal jobs, but ended (as it was meant to) the inefficiency of some local government direct line services. Furthermore, for the first time since the creation of rates in 1601, the Rates Act authorized the government to fix the levels of all local rates (rate-capping). After her third consecutive election victory in 1987, Mrs Thatcher radicalized her policies further. The Queen's Speech of June 1987 announced a redistribution of responsibilities, channelling them away from local authority control, and effectively towards central government, in the domains of housing and education. Housing reform had begun before 1983, with legislation allowing tenants in council-owned housing to buy their homes. Councils were obliged to spend the capital thus raised on debt reimbursement rather than new housing. Public housing may also, on the request of tenants, be taken over by independent organizations from the local authorities. The way is thus effectively clear for a phasing-out of council housing as traditionally understood. In the area of education, citizens can now request that local schools 'opt out' of control by local education authorities and enter under the direct authority of the Minister of Education. As in the case of housing, such requests are likely to be looked on favourably unless very strongly resisted at the local level. But the most dramatic reform was the replacement, in 1990, of the old business and domestic rates, calculated on the basis of an antiquated property value assessment, by a new Uniform Business Rate, fixed by central government, and a Community Charge, levied by each local authority at a flat rate per head of population. More than any other single issue, the unpopularity of the profoundly regressive Community Charge, or 'Poll Tax', was responsible for the plummeting popularity of Margaret Thatcher and her party in 1989–90, and for her resignation in November 1990 after many Conservative MPs had withheld their support from her in the leadership election. Thatcher's successor, John Major, moved fast to limit the political damage. For 1993, he announced the replacement of the Poll Tax by a Council Tax, again based on property values. For 1991, he announced that central government would supply the money—raised by a 2.5 per cent increase in Value Added Tax—to reduce Poll Tax bills. This, of course, had the effect of further raising the share of local government spending financed by central government; the proportion stood at over 70 per cent in 1992, compared with some 45 per cent in the mid-1970s. The destruction of large swathes of local government power, and acute conflict between central and local authorities in Britain under Thatcher, constitute the principal and most striking exception to the tendency towards 'co-operation' which seems to prevail in most of the other Western countries.

In the United States and Germany, the term 'co-operative federalism' has been used to refer to the increasingly close collaboration that has taken over from the principle of classic federalism in which each separate level was autonomous. But it is a phenomenon that is not restricted to strictly federated systems. Non-federated systems also resort to a similar type of co-operation, using specific methods and instruments of their own but not differing fundamentally from those used by federal systems. These administrative, financial, and sometimes political instruments may be formalized to varying degrees from one country to another, but in all cases their overall effect is to substitute co-operation for the traditional situations of separation or supervision.

1. In West Germany before 1990, and Germany since, particularly numerous and important formalized instruments of co-operation have been introduced. One of the most long-standing forms of collaboration evolved in the Conference of Education Ministers, an institution that comprises a whole collection of structures (a plenary assembly, various committees, and a general secretariat). It is chaired by each of the *Land* Ministers in turn, and the chairman also acts as spokesman and representative, most importantly in the Bund and in meetings with foreign counterparts. Similar conferences operate in other ministerial sectors, above all at the level of the *Land* Prime Ministers.

Furthermore, hundreds of committees of every kind have been set up to enable the Bund and the *Länder* to discuss, negotiate, and come to agreement on problems of common interest. Among the best known of these are the Science Council (Wissenschaftsrat), the Education Council (*Bildungsrat*), and the Council for Economic Affairs (*Finanzplanungsrat*). Frequently, the consensus reached is formalized by treaties or agreements of a political or administrative nature, which have full juridical force.

A further step in this process of institutionalization was taken in 1969 with the revision of the Constitution that recognized and 'authenticated' these practices by introducing the concept of 'common tasks' (*Gemeinschaftanfgaben*) in a number of sectors such as the building of universities, regional economic policy, agricultural policy, and the construction of dikes. The federal government was authorized to intervene and co-finance projects, thereby contributing to a better distribution of resources and fairer treatment for the less advantaged *Länder*. Unification placed new strains, both constitutional and financial, in the pattern of inter-*Länder* and *Länder*–federal government relations. In April 1991, for example, four eastern *Länder* chose to ignore a decision of the Conference of Education Ministers. The governments of the five eastern *Länder* plus Berlin now meet regularly to discuss the demands they intend to make both of their western counterparts and of the federal government.

Italy and France have not set up such a comprehensive body of formal agreements, but both countries also make use of mechanisms designed to make for co-operation between central and local authorities. In France, the means most favoured has been contracts—not that they are always concluded between perfectly equal partners, but at least they betoken a switch to dialogue instead of relations of a hierarchical nature. They constitute agreements between the State and local authorities on planned spending programmes over a period of years. Over the last twenty years, all kinds of contracts have been drawn up and have multiplied: contracts with regions, with medium-sized towns, with suburbs, and other planning contracts too. The juridical validity of these agreements is by no means assured, but that is not the important point. First and foremost, these agreements between the centre and the periphery testify to a new mode of government and a new relationship. In Italy, the modalities of co-operation between the State and the regions are, according to Sabino Cassese, similar to the practices adopted in Germany, but on a rather more modest scale. He writes:

In many different sectors, which range from aid for financing the building of universities to cultural measures, employment, agriculture, health, housing, and so on, committees composed of representatives of both the State and the regions are at work. There are at least a hundred of these bodies, many with their own staff, and they operate in sectors that are the responsibility of the State as well as in those that are the responsibility of the regions. Their functions are to mediate between interests, to avert conflict, to exchange information, to deliberate, and so on.[7]

2. These formal agreements are reinforced (or in some cases superseded) by informal relations which may not be as solid and stable but nevertheless constitute essential links between the central and the local authorities. They take many forms: the intertwining of responsibilities and the politico-administrative so-called 'honeycomb structure' in France; communication between the centre and the periphery established by party organizations, in Germany and Italy; the appointment of local or regional spokesmen to keep in touch with the central or federal authorities (associations of mayors, or regional presidents, in France and Italy respectively); 'Missions' from the *Länder* in Bonn, each one headed by the *Minister für Bundesangelegenheiten*, that is to say the Minister for co-operation with the federal government. More specifically, the policy networks that we have identified as characteristic of relations between bureaucracies and interest groups nationally also operate at regional and local level (in Germany as elsewhere), both on a sectoral basis and vertically, between different levels of government. Such a network might include representatives of certain central or federal departments, and from various states or localities, and economic or social groups that are concerned by the particular policy in question (for example, the Industry Ministry, the local or regional authorities for areas affected by the steel crisis, the employers seeking aid, and the trade unions anxious to preserve jobs). Moreover, collaboration of this kind tends to be made easier by the fact that, despite all efforts at rationalization, the distribution of responsibilities is never altogether strict and clear. Overlaps and confusions are the rule rather than the exception and occasion countless problems that can only be resolved through co-operation, unless, that is, increasingly authoritarian solutions are adopted; but these are not necessarily effective anyway.

3. Co-operation between central and local authorities also involves funding from both sources, subsidies, and other fiscal and financial devices that create interdependence. For one important fact needs to be recognized: with very few exceptions, local fiscal autonomy is an illusion in the contemporary world. As Rémy Prud'homme has remarked, 'there are no good local taxes', for the simple reason that local resources never match local needs, particularly when, as in France, the country is divided into so many separate units. There are several possible ways of resolving this problem. One is to 'nationalize' all revenue, as is done in Italy and Holland; but the danger is that the

process of redistribution may turn into something of a free-for-all. Another is to make various adjustments and piecemeal arrangements, as in France and the United States. Yet another is to rationalize the system and make it more equitable, as in West Germany, where the best balance of central and local resources was achieved, although even this system provoked criticisms within the country (which were, however, slight compared to the discontent provoked by the dawning realization of the sums that would have to be transferred to the East following unification). The system depends upon each of its various levels dividing up virtually all its fiscal revenue on the basis of percentages that may be revised when necessary. With this system, everyone benefits or suffers from the general economic situation, since every level receives a fraction of the revenue as a whole, whether it comes from high- or low-yielding taxes, from taxes that are elastic or taxes that are not (whereas in other countries the central governments tend to retain a monopoly over the most modern and high-yielding taxes, leaving what amounts to the crumbs to the lower levels). For example, in 1982, the Bund obtained 48.7 per cent of the revenue, the *Länder* 34.6 per cent, the communes 13.2 per cent, and the remainder went to the EEC. This is probably the model towards which the archaic and complex French system will eventually evolve, but it will mean first overcoming the extra problem of the country being divided into an excessively large number of local authorities.

4. A further dimension to the relationship between sub-national authorities and the State has been added by the growth in importance of regional policy at the European level. By 1995 this had led some 300 regional and local authorities to join the burgeoning hosts of Euro-lobbyists and set up offices in Brussels in the hope of attracting a share of the available funding, either on an individual basis or as part of a national or even cross-national grouping of regions. Some political parties deliberately stress direct links that bypass the nation state; the Scottish National Party and the Northern League, for example, both seek independence, for Scotland and for 'Padania', but within the EU. The idea of a 'Europe of Regions' found expression, under the Maastricht Treaty, in the creation of the European Union's Committee of the Regions, which offers them formal representation and consultation, though with little formal power. But the more powerful regions—certainly the German *Länder*—had achieved a status as the direct interlocutors of the Commission and the Council of Ministers well before the Committee was set up. As the attribution of European money is generally linked to the existence of a viable regional development plan on the ground, politically strong regions as well as those enjoying a positive relationship with central governments willing to back their claims in Brussels tend to be rewarded.

Despite profound institutional differences between the various States, it is possible to detect a number of meaningful convergences. In the federal States, the politico-administrative processes are certainly undergoing a measure of centralization, for the reasons mentioned above (though this process was more or less halted in post-unification Germany). The most centralized States are equally certainly moving towards decentralization and regionalization. An inextricable mixture of rules, conventions, and practices has evolved, tending mutually to compensate for or correct each other's excesses, and creating a system of complex relations in which central and peripheral power are not in truth separate, as the metaphor would suggest, but are on the contrary linked through mechanisms, some formal, some not, devised to encourage co-operation, interaction, and joint or mixed processes of decision and finance. Only Britain has been an exception in this general evolution. Here, centralization was reinforced under the Conservative governments to the point of becoming a fetish. Tension between the central and the local authorities has grown, constituting one expression of the deepening antagonism between the majority and the opposition. The consensus and conventions that traditionally used to link the local authorities to the government and Parliament were dislocated by the radicalism of Thatcherite policies and the (initially) no less radical reactions of Labour local authorities. The traditional political and administrative centralization of the United Kingdom is no longer counterbalanced by its 'local government'. And it was the Conservatives, the traditional defenders of local autonomy, who brought about this evolution, first through their 1974 reforms (which reduced the number of local authorities by two-thirds, making it easy for the government to impose its own control over each that remained), and subsequently through the reforms of the 1980s, which have had the effect of tightening the Government's grip on them. For the Tories themselves, the results at grass-roots level were disastrous; before losing power nationally in 1997, they had been all but eradicated from local government, holding half as many council seats as the Liberal Democrats (it is also significant that not one Conservative MP was elected for Scotland or Wales in 1997). This is likely to prove an obstacle to their electoral recovery. Their Labour successors, on the other hand, will be torn between their declared intention to devolve power away from central government and their at least equally strong determination to keep public spending under tight control at all levels. It will be a hard balance to maintain.

Specialized bodies

All Western bureaucracies share a proliferation of *ad hoc* organizations and parallel institutions whose statutes, structures, and modes of action are extremely diverse. The reasons for this state of affairs are simple enough. On the one hand, the distribution of increasingly specialized services has produced a need for better-adapted means of intervention. On the other, given the difficulties of undertaking a radical reform of the cumbersome classic administrative machinery, the tendency has been to set up parallel structures.

Here again, at the risk of over-simplification, it is possible to distinguish three main types of specialized administration: regulatory and monitoring bodies; those responsible for the management of public services; and those engaged in productive activities—although these do not, strictly speaking, constitute true administrations. A major feature of the 1990s has been the privatization in almost all European countries of many productive activities, and even some utilities such as water (where not already private), electricity, or telecommunications. This certainly represents a shrinkage of the public sector, in terms of manpower and resources; but it has also, in many cases, produced a new need for regulatory bodies to monitor services henceforth delivered by private companies.

Regulatory and monitoring bodies are a new type of autonomous administration which has been most widely developed in the United States (where it is sometimes referred to as the 'headless fourth branch' of the government). It takes the form of what are generally known as Independent Regulatory Commissions.

The relative depoliticization of these regulatory bodies—or, at the very least, their emancipation from government or party control—proved attractive to the European States, which had hitherto experimented either with classic modes of State regulation or with the more controversial methods of corporatism. In France, a number of commissions have thus come into being which, although less powerful and less autonomous than their American counterparts, nevertheless adopt a similar approach: the Commission des Opérations de Bourse, the Commission Informatique et Libertés, the Commission de la Communication des Documents Administratifs, the Haute Autorité de l'Audiovisuel, which later became the Commission Nationale de la Communication et des Libertés, then, in 1989, the Conseil Supérieur de l'Audiovisuel.

In Britain too, commissions with either regulatory or consultative powers play a similar role: the Monopolies and Mergers Commission, the Commission for Racial Equality, the Civil Aviation Authority, etc. Others, conversely, more closely resemble the corporatist model of organizations designed to serve specific interests: the Higher Education Funding Councils, the Research Councils, and the Arts Council. The most recent crop results from the wave of privatizations under the Thatcher and Major Governments: Ofgas, Ofwat (for water), Oftel (for the telecommuniations industry), and comparable organizations have the power—which they have been increasingly ready to use—to dictate aspects of pricing and service policies to privatized utilities enjoying a monopoly or near-monopoly over the services they provide. In West Germany, the 1970s and 1980s were marked by the spread of regulatory bodies, despite the reservations expressed—as in France—by the German juridical establishment in relation to this 'dismemberment' of the State. In particular, the Commission responsible for commercial competition and monopolies (*Bundeskartellamt*) in principle holds considerable powers in the sphere of commercial mergers.

Fewer examples spring to mind in Italy, but two of them are CONSOB, responsible for monitoring Stock Exchange activities, and the Istituto per la Vigilanza sulle Assicurazioni Private.

As can be seen, one of the characteristics of contemporary administrations is the transfer of regulatory tasks to autonomous organizations. This process of fragmentation is a feature every bit as important as the practices of 'deregulation' that tend to attract so much more attention.

Regulatory and monitoring bodies generally carry national or federal status and are few in number. But organizations responsible for the management of services are present at all levels of administration and defy statistical measurement. The most we can do is make a few approximate estimates. For example, there are estimated to be several thousand public organizations of this kind in France, about 40,000 *enti pubblici* in Italy, and about 500 quangos (quasi-autonomous non-governmental organizations) at national level in Britain.

To get some idea of the complexity of the situation, one has only to think of the vast miscellany, in France, of public administrative or industrial and commercial establishments, the mixed-economy companies, the agencies, commissions, and offices, not to mention the thousands of organizations funded with public money and camouflaged by their anodyne appearance as associations set up under the law of 1901.[8] It must be pointed out that this seemingly uncontrollable proliferation is the price that has had to be paid for administrative, budgetary, and financial procedures quite unsuited to the realities of the contemporary world and today's need for efficient management. It is often a particularly heavy price, however, because of the frequent lack of a clear distinction between public and private interests in the running of such bodies. That has made them attractive vehicles for corruption. Italy's *enti pubblici* and France's *sociétés d'économie mixte* have been vital tools for the plundering of public money to finance political parties (and, at times, the lifestyles of politicians).

The administrative confusion is further compounded by the absence of any logical relation between function and status. For example, in France and Italy, the description 'public establishment of an economic nature' in many cases has very little to do with the said establishment's activities: it is simply a device to leave it with a free hand. This gives rise to quarrels of Byzantine complexity, the juridical resolution of which frequently simply leads to further confusion. Why, for instance, should an administrative judge consider the port of Genoa to be an *ente pubblico economico* when the port of Naples is classed as an *ente pubblico non economico*?[9]

Finally, it is worth pointing out that the degree of autonomy possessed by all these agencies, establishments, and quangos varies considerably, ranging from subjection through strict supervision to almost total independence. It depends upon the conditions in which the organization was created, the source of its funding, the type of tasks it is supposed to carry out, and the ability of its managers to shake off supervision from other quarters.

Public management of productive activities

The shrinking but still sizeable public economic sector is not a part of the administration in the strict sense of the expression, for the problems, the management methods, and the status of the personnel involved are different from those of the classic type of administration. It would therefore be natural enough to exclude from the administrative domain firms that are nationalized or that are controlled by the national or local public authorities. However, such an exclusion would not necessarily make sense in countries such as Britain which, unlike France and Italy, do not assign all public agents a body of rules and guarantees that confer upon them the status of civil servants. The gap that exists in France between a salaried employee in a nationalized industry and a local or State civil servant on the one hand, and an employee of the private sector on the other, does not exist in Britain, where the majority of these employees are bound by contractual rules that resemble those of the private sector. Only the situation of part of the Civil Service bears comparison with the circumstances of the French public sector.[10] Furthermore, the distinction between 'service' and productive activities is becoming increasingly blurred in economic systems that create intermediaries between the two and are characterized by the establishment of increasingly close links between them. However, some productive activities, whether at local or at national level, are organized according to methods that are closer to those of the administration than to those of the private sector, although this is becoming less and less common. For example, the situation of an employee of Électricité de France, France Télécom, or the Régie Autonome des Transports Parisiens resembles that of a civil servant (with job security) more closely than that of his or her counterparts in the private sector (which helps to explain the deep hostility of the workforce to privatization). Finally, the historical aspect is also important. Economic sectors taken over by the State some time ago are much closer to administrations than those nationalized more recently. Postal services and railways are in many cases tantamount to administrations, despite efforts to render their management more flexible, whereas nationalizations of more recent date have had no more than a limited impact upon the running of the businesses concerned.

Throughout Europe, however, the public sector has shrunk more or less dramatically since 1980. The pioneer in this respect was Britain, where 18 years of Conservative rule led to the privatization not only of the obviously competitive sector (such as the Rover Group, which was sold to BMW), and of national flagships like British Airways, but also of the whole range of public services and utilities: telephones, water, gas, electricity, and rail, with only the Royal Mail being kept by public demand in the public's hands. At local level, compulsory competitive tendering has pushed local authorities down a similar path, leading them to buy in an increasing proportion of the services they provide to the public rather than supplying them directly themselves.

What had initially appeared, in a world grown accustomed to the continuous expansion of the public sector, as a piece of eccentric far right-wing radicalism became, in little more than a decade, standard practice for most Western governments. This was so even in France, scene of Europe's last great wave of nationalizations (by the Socialists, in 1982), and in Italy, where the pre-war Fascists had created the basis of an enormous public sector, nationalizing major banks and creating the big State industrial holding company, IRI. In these two countries, the public sector in the mid-1980s included not only munitions factories and postal services (public industries of often ancient pedigree), but also railways, electricity, coal, steel, air transport, oil, gas, and large chunks of broadcasting, motor manufacture, banking, and insurance. France departed first along a Thatcherite road, which it has pursued—at varying speeds, it is true— despite three changes of governing majority. The 1986–8 Chirac Government began a vast privatization programme, including both key industries nationalized by the Socialists in 1982 and banks that had been in the public sector since 1944. Its Socialist successors announced that they would freeze the boundaries between public and private sectors, but in practice found this impossible to do, and modified their policy to the extent of being ready to sell off 49-per-cent shares to private firms. With the Right's election victory in 1993 Prime Minister Balladur resumed the privatizations he had masterminded as Finance Minister seven years earlier. And while the Socialists who returned to power in 1997 adopted a more cautious approach, they were prepared, for example, to sell off 20 per cent of France Télécom, hitherto considered very much as a public service to remain in public ownership. That privatization in Italy was long delayed resulted more from the role of the public sector in a corrupt political system than from ideological factors (though the Alleanza Nazionale, no doubt in tribute to their Fascist predecessors, resisted privatizations under Berlusconi in 1994). As President of IRI up to 1989, Romano Prodi offloaded a number of public holdings, notably selling Alfa Romeo to Fiat, and provoked polemics between the Christian Democrats (most of whom supported him) and the Socialists (who did not) as a result. The Amato and Ciampi governments sold two major banks and part of a third between 1992 and 1994, and reorganized the big public-sector shareholdings as joint stock companies ready for sell-off. The national insurance company and tranches of other big state-owned firms, including ENI, the petroleum products company, were sold off between 1994 and 1996. But Prodi as Prime Minister found some difficulty in pursuing what he had begun as IRI President, chiefly because of the determination of Rifondazione Comunista, not necessarily to block all privatization plans, but to exact a price for its acquiescence. Although Rifondazione Comunista had stayed out of the government, Prodi was obliged to bargain with them: the only alternative was to open up his majority rightwards, a step with potentially disastrous political consequences. Hence, for example, the job creation package announced as part of the 'price' for the privatization of Telecom Italia in the autumn of 1997. The large Italian public sector will be sold off, but probably not at the speed seen in Britain or France.

Germany, finally, is a special case owing to unification. In the West, the public sector was never very large, being more or less confined to utilities and public services rather than extending to industry or banking. In the East, on the other hand, it accounted for the whole economy before 1990. Following unification a new institution, the Treuhandanstalt, was created to undertake the difficult, often painful disposal of a host of ailing, run-down nationalized firms. By November 1994, of 12,370 firms that had passed through its hands, 7,853 had been privatized and 3,713 closed down, for a total net expenditure of 130 billion deutschmarks.[11] The cost of the operation, which laid the foundations for an economic recovery that made the East into Germany's fastest-growing area, was not only financial. With great suddenness, East Germany experienced mass unemployment for the first time since the 1930s, with the level rising to 15 per cent by 1993; and the process was used as justification for almost the last flourish of left-wing terrorism in Germany, when the Treuhand's first chief was murdered. Beyond the remnants of the Red Army Faction, however, the privatization process was the object of little fundamental opposition, at least so long as it concerned firms that were clearly in the market sector. For administrations had signally failed to prove that they could do better in this area than private firms.[12]

The civil service

The development of modern bureaucracies has been characterized by a progressive but incomplete abandonment of notions of hereditary posts and practices of clientelism, involving patronage and corruption. Instead, a legal-cum-rational model has been adopted, one of the most important aspects of which is that the recruitment of staff, their training, and their promotion obey specific rules that are generally applied. This way of organizing the bureaucracy was initiated in France at the time of the French Revolution which, while taking over the administrative heritage of the monarchy, modernized it and conferred a new legitimacy upon it. Prussia also undertook a 'revolution from above', following the defeats that it suffered from Napoleon. This was known as the Stein-Hardenberg Reform and it established an administrative system that managed to survive all three of the political disasters of 1918, 1933, and 1945. Britain and Italy were slower to take steps to eliminate corruption, clientelism and political control over the administration. Britain did not introduce reforms until 1855, following the Crimean War (which revealed that the administration had attracted only men 'without ambition, indolent and incompetent') and Northcote and Trevelyan's extremely critical reports urging that the principles still observed in the Civil Service until the 1990s should be brought into operation. In Italy, it was not until 1908 that Giolitti, under pressure from civil servants, agreed to a 'status' that would put an end to 'the monstrous coupling' of politics and the administration and would provide guarantees (regarding employment and careers) for employees whose southern origins no doubt—in view of the dearth of other employment—explained their anxiety and claims.

Today, the principles that govern the recruitment, training, and careers of civil servants tend to create similar situations in all the Western countries. Recruitment is meritocratic; there are guarantees concerning careers, rights, and duties, and these, substantially or formally, constitute a definite 'status' that is different from the situation of employees in the private sector. Differences nevertheless remain from one system to another, on account of their respective histories and traditions.

There are thus both similarities and differences not only in the manners in which public administrations are organized but also in the relations between the bureaucrats of the various systems and their politicians, particularly those in positions of top responsibility in the State.

Recruitment, training, and careers

Before attempting to compare the existing systems in the Western democracies, we must define their respective interpretations of the expression 'public employee'. In France and Italy, it tends to include the entire body of civil servants, whether national or local, and despite differences in status. However, the equivalent expressions in general have a more restricted meaning in the other countries, if only because of the greater degrees of autonomy possessed by peripheral bodies in Germany, and the distinction that exists between central and local employees in Britain.

The second point to be taken into consideration has to do with the internal differences between one 'public administration' or 'Civil Service' and another. Even in its most limited sense, the concept of a public administration may cover a wide variety of employees: permanent ones, contractual ones, clerks, manual workers, etc. For example, in 1989 the 360,826 federal government employees of West Germany were divided into three groups: 114,789 civil servants in the strict sense (*Beamte*), 88,779 clerks (*Angestellte*), and 107,258 workers (*Arbeiter*). In Italy, the 450,000 employees of the *Aziende Autonome* (autonomous public companies) must be included with the 1,500,000 State officials, and so on. In Britain, roughly 100,000 of the 600,000 civil servants of the late 1980s were 'industrial workers'. Since then, the situation has been complicated by the 'federalization' of the Civil Service, with more and more tasks being either contracted out or privatized altogether.

Thirdly, it should be stressed that the particular traditions of each country and the existence or absence of a distinction between private law and public law result in the establishment of different mechanisms. The countries of mainland Europe offer their civil servants constitutional and statutory guarantees and generally fix the terms of their employment according to the techniques of public law. On the other hand, Britain, the land of common law, resorts in the main to rules and procedures that are close to those used in the private sector (such as contracts). But there are other points of similarity: administrations on the Continent are adopting practices followed by the English and American administrations. (For example, in Italy, contracts have now been introduced (*contratti del pubblico impiego*) especially for the purpose of determining salaries, and nearly everywhere wages are negotiated with the public authorities.)

In all the Western democracies that we are considering, the recruitment of civil servants, especially at the senior level, is based upon the merit system, in particular upon competitive examinations. However, the significance and procedures of this type of selection vary. In Italy, France, and Germany, the competitive mode of selection tends to favour those with particular kinds of training (particularly legal training). Tests of an abstract and general nature are followed by probationary periods (in Germany) or by oral tests and interviews designed to evaluate the candidate's personality. But there are many exceptions to this process of selection (as the Constitution in Italy indeed recognizes) and alongside the standard competitions there are many other methods of recruitment that allow the administration considerable discretionary room for manœuvre. (They can organize competitions for particular posts, make temporary appointments, draw up contracts, etc.) In practice, in Italy and in France, at both national and local levels, a large proportion of civil servants gain security of tenure when their contractual posts are confirmed, without ever having entered any real competition. In Britain, more emphasis is laid on tests, exercises, and interviews designed to reveal the candidate's aptitude for his future functions.

Systems also differ with regard to the degree of centralization that characterizes the processes of selection. In Italy and Germany, recruitment is essentially organized by the various Ministries (or other specialized public bodies) on the basis of their own particular needs. In France, on the other hand, since the Second World War, centralization in the recruitment of ministerial personnel has been the rule (although there are many exceptions). In particular, the competitions held by the ENA (École Nationale d'Administration) and the IRA (Instituts Régionaux d'Administration) are major instruments for interministerial recruitment placed under the aegis of the Minister of Public Administration. In Britain the selection process was also extremely centralized, being placed under the authority of the Civil Service Commission. By 1991, however, all but the most senior posts—95 per cent of the total—were being filled by the agencies and departments directly responsible for them; the Commission itself had been broken up into the Office of the Civil Service Commissioners, with a largely supervisory role, and the Recruitment and Assessment Services Agency; and it had become accepted practice to hire at least a minority of civil servants even at the highest level directly from other organizations.

What training do civil servants receive before and, if they are successful, after they take up their duties? In general, there are two main categories of civil servants: those who have received a 'general' training and those who have received a 'specialized' one. Those with a general training, who are responsible for decisions and management, outnumber the rest and assume the most traditional of the administration's tasks. Methods of recruitment (through competitive examinations) are in most countries still marked by a preference for generalists. However, these fall into two groups: the French, Italian, or German type, most of whom have received a legal training; and the English type, whose university degrees are usually in the humanities. For example, in the early 1970s, civil servants who had been trained as lawyers represented 54 per cent of the total in Italy, 67 per cent in West Germany, but only 4 per cent in Britain.[13] The British civil service has often been criticized as an 'administration of amateurs'. It does not lack skilled technicians: in the mid-1980s, the scientists' civil service union, the Institute of Professional Civil Servants, numbered 85,689 members out of a total of half a million non-industrial civil servants. But the ethos at the very top remains that of the generalist, limiting the career prospects open to such people. The Fulton Report (1968) declared, 'The Civil Service is not a place for amateurs. It must be composed of men and women who are true professionals.' Similarly, in Italy, the formalistic and idealistic legal training of Italian civil servants has often been denounced as being—at least in part—the source of the Byzantine complexity and inefficiency of the country's administration.[14] However, the lack of technical expertise at the top of the Italian and British administrations (and, to a slightly lesser extent, Germany's) needs qualification. In the first place, in Britain and Germany, most administrative services, in particular those for which a technical training is necessary, are organized at the local level. Furthermore, when administrations lack the necessary technical experts, they can either themselves provide the specialized training needed (as often happens in Germany, for instance) after recruiting their personnel, or else turn to parallel specialized institutions (and this is common practice in most countries). Some countries, like France, allow more room for specialists (chiefly drawing upon the *grandes écoles* such as the Polytechnique, the École des Mines, the École des Ponts, etc.). But this does not necessarily make for a clearer distinction between generalists and specialists. Very often, the functions of management and administration, which are in principle the major domain of generalists, are assumed by technical experts, particularly in France, where the division of territory between graduates from the ENA and those from the Polytechnique gives rise to covert but intense struggles for influence.

The French schools responsible for preparing the administrative élite (the École Nationale d'Administration (ENA), the Polytechnique, etc.) or the intermediate personnel (the IRA) have no counterparts in the other Western countries, which rely essentially upon the universities for the training of their future public administrators. In West Germany, for example, the Speyer School of Administrative Sciences, founded in 1947 in the French zone under the Allied occupation, was partly inspired by the example of the French ENA, but its functions and methods are very different.[15] It is much more like a centre for the continuing training or perfecting of the skills of civil servants already in office than an instrument for selecting, training, and classifying candidates, in the manner of ENA. The Scuola Superiore dell'Ammistrazione Pubblica in Italy plays a similar role to that of Speyer's Hochschule, but has never acquired a reputation sufficiently prestigious for it to be considered the equivalent of one of the French *grandes écoles*. The Civil Service College created in Britain in 1970 on the recommendation of the Fulton Committee is also a centre providing continuing and intermittent training for civil servants. It offers courses of 4, 12, and 28 weeks, designed for civil servants from the upper echelons when they first enter the Service and during the third and the fifth years of their appointments. A feature of the Thatcher years was the greater stress in training on management and information-technology skills, and its spread to levels very much closer to the summit of the Civil Service, with innovations like the Top Management Programme, though it is not certain that such training radically improved the skills or career prospects of those who underwent it. Unlike in the private sector—in theory, at least—the careers of civil servants follow a relatively smooth and predictable evolution, though, again, this remark now needs qualification in the case of the more fragmented British civil service. Practically speaking, three main questions arise: how are civil servants' careers organized? How much vertical and horizontal mobility can they expect? What rights and guarantees do they enjoy?

1. The answer to the first of these questions is that in general there exists a (variable) balance between promotion on the grounds of merit and promotion on the grounds of seniority. Nearly all countries provide a body of statutory or conventional rules guaranteeing promotion in line with seniority. That is certainly true of mainland Europe, where the matter is strictly codified and institutionalized (by commissions to establish parity, and superior councils in France; committees on federal personnel in

Germany; hierarchical and jurisdictional controls, etc.). But it also applies to countries such as the United States, which is often unfairly represented as being a province of discretionary, or even arbitrary power. To regard it as such, however, is to forget that, as a reaction to such abuses as do occur, the principle of seniority is defended with particular vigour and tenacity. It should also be pointed out that, even when merit does override seniority, strict procedures have to be followed: internal competitions (in France and Italy), or promotions made on the basis of profiles made by the hierarchy. But these strict regulations are applied mainly at the lower or middle levels of the bureaucracy (except in Italy, where the principle of seniority tends to be strictly observed right up to the top of the ladder).

For top civil servants, the principle of promotion on the grounds of merit applies more generally. That is certainly the case in Britain, where the 'high-flyers', mostly products of Oxford or Cambridge, enjoy a series of rapid promotions right at the beginning of their careers. Later, however, promotion comes more slowly, and as political preferences are excluded, most of the top 500 or so civil servants employed in Grades 1 to 3 are relatively mature (generally about 50 years old). In Germany, the situation is quite similar, except that the possibility of promotions or sackings for political reasons sometimes upsets the bureaucratic pecking order.

2. The problem of vertical and horizontal mobility is partly connected with the question of merit. Incentives for mobility are clearly less strong the more the system is based upon seniority. A comparison between the various countries underlines the lack of mobility, either horizontal or vertical, that exists in most administrative systems. In France (and, since 1980, in principle also in Italy), vertical mobility is ensured through internal competitions. The procedure presents the advantage of an incorporated quota system (civil servants who already hold appointments are sure of obtaining a number of the new promotions). Its drawback, though, is its inflexibility, not to mention the fact that it is sometimes deflected from its object of social promotion (as in the internal competitions of the ENA). In Britain, following the criticisms of the Fulton Committee, a single-tiered structure was introduced (to replace the tripartite division into administrative, executive, and clerical classes). Its purpose was to make it possible for any competent civil servant, regardless of his or her initial grade, to get to the top. By authorizing 'leap-frogging' in the case of the most able, this was supposed to introduce a considerable element of democratization. However, the scheme, like much of Fulton, was less successful in this respect than its promoters had hoped.

The opportunities for horizontal mobility are hardly any better. A study carried out in Britain revealed that, in 1971, 72 per cent of the upper administration had spent their entire careers working in the same department—though a big department may offer considerable variety of experience, and high-flyers are now considerably more likely to have experience in more than one department, or on a Minister's staff, or even outside the Civil Service altogether. The normal pattern of career-long attachment to a single Ministry holds good in general for Germany, Italy (especially), and France, but in the last case there are two qualifications to be made. In the first place, all French administrators are expected to move around somewhat (although their mobility is in some cases more apparent than real, as they may move no further than some institution attached to their original Ministry). Secondly, the most brilliant careers are invariably marked by considerable mobility inside—and sometimes outside—the administration. In some countries, the relative immobility of public officials is offset by some movement between the national and the local administrations. In Germany, this type of exchange is quite common between all levels (local, *Land*, federation). However, it is rare in France, despite measures taken in the 1980s to encourage it, except in the particular case of the Paris city hall, which served for nearly two decades as the seedbed of a politico-administrative network constructed around the city's mayor, Jacques Chirac. And such movement is exceptional in Britain and in Italy (despite transfers of staff to the Italian regions following the 1970 reforms). As for mobility between the civil service and the political, economic, and other sectors, this is strongest in France (as a result of the interpenetration of élites and the role played by the State *grandes écoles*), rarer in Germany, and again, almost unknown in Italy. In Britain, recruitment of civil servants from outside has been episodic, recruitment of former civil servants to outside jobs growing. The wartime civil service recruited large numbers of outsiders, many but not all of them academics, to posts of some responsibility (Oliver Franks and Harold Wilson being two distinguished examples), but divested itself of most of their talents when peace came. More recently, it again become official policy to advertise senior posts and recruit some senior officials, initially a minority, from outside. In 1992, for example, the Permanent Secretary to the Treasury, Sir Terence Burns, had come from the London Business School, while both the head of Defence Procurement and the head of the statistical service were imports from Australia. On retirement at 60, on the other hand, or even before, the former servants of the state find a range of company directorships opening before them, something that becomes increasingly attractive as pay differentials between the civil service and the private sector grow.

3. The rights and duties of civil servants are sometimes solemnly established in Constitutions and general laws (Italy, 1957; France, 1958–9; West Germany, 1965), sometimes in isolated written texts, and sometimes through 'conventions' that are more important than the few written rules on the subject. In practice, the anomalies that appear between one system and another are real, but are probably less important than they may seem at first glance. The disorder and multiplicity of regulations in France and Italy lead to just as much confusion as the apparent complexity of the German federal system.

(*a*) The principal rights of civil servants fall into several categories. First there are those related to remuneration and tenure. The first point to note is that everywhere, even in the most 'legal and regulated' situations, contracts play a part of some importance, varying in degree from one case to another. Salaries and conditions of work are sometimes subject to contract in France, Italy (where collective contracts are negotiated every three years),[16] and Germany. Guarantees of employment vary in strength according to whether or not the relations between the administration and its employees are determined by contract but the mechanisms of dismissal or demotion are seldom used.

The situation of employees is, in principle, less securely guaranteed when it is a contractual one, but in practice guarantees of employment are considered an important factor.

Rights affecting trade union and political affiliations depend upon the dominant ethic and specific concept of public service in each country. The right to form trade unions has by now been won in every country, and as a result many more civil servants now belong to trade unions, even in countries where membership used traditionally to be low. In the late 1980s, one-third of civil servants were trade union members in France, 45 per cent in West Germany, and between 50 and 60 per cent in Britain and Italy. But everywhere certain limits to trade unionization are imposed, in relation either to particular categories (the police, the army, the secret services) or to the modes of collective action.

Particularly affected is the right to strike—traditionally the most effective weapon available to trade unions. The right to strike of German civil servants is not recognized, and everywhere it is denied to categories responsible for maintaining the security of the State (the army, the police). However, even where this is the case, public employees are frequently organized into associations that constitute powerful 'lobbies' and that may, furthermore, resort to forms of action (such as the protests of the Paris police and the appeals made by telephone to the Ministry of Defence in Rome by the military, etc.) which make the same kind of impact as a stoppage of work (such as the go-slow strikes of customs officials or air traffic controllers). Finally, the right to strike is subject to a range of 'conventions' and limitations: advance notice is obligatory in France; wild-cat strikes are banned in Italy (by the law of 29 March 1983); and in Britain there is a tradition (not invariably observed) of no striking in the essential State services. Here, the right to strike is linked with the right to form trade unions and does not constitute an infringement of contract provided the legal obligations have been observed (the Trade Union Act of 1984).[17]

Political rights are guaranteed most generously in Germany, France, and Italy with regard both to embracing an ideology or joining a party, and to the possibility of standing as candidate in an election. The regulations at present in force are so generous in France that some observers, such as Ezra Suleiman, consider them positively to encourage members of the administration to take part in politics, and the same applies to Germany. Moreover, French and German civil servants have certainly made the most of the situation, making a point of 'colonizing' the political parties and Parliament. In Britain, on the other hand, such a development would be unimaginable, as civil servants above a certain (fairly low) level enjoy no right to open political activity.

(*b*) The duties of civil servants. Set against the rights that are granted them within the limitations noted above are a number of duties that civil servants are bound to accept. Some are fundamental, others of a more formal nature. Let us confine ourselves to two examples: the obligation to serve the State with loyalty, and the obligation of discretion.

The obligation to serve the State with loyalty may be understood in a more or less sweeping fashion. All countries declare that civil servants are employed in the service of the State, the nation (e.g. Article 98 of the Italian Constitution and the law of 1965 in West Germany), or the Crown, not that of any political party that happens to be in power. But the implications of such declarations may vary. In France, the Constitution states bluntly that 'the administration is at the disposal of the Government'. Yet the Fifth Republic was the first regime not to embark upon a purge when it was set up.[18] But in a less obvious way, the administration can always limit the right to compete for employment of those whose opinions (and the ways in which they are given expression) are considered too extreme. Nevertheless, the Council of State (in the Barel decision, 1954) introduced limitations to those possibilities, a step that made the French system more liberal, since it ruled out insistence upon ideological conformism. The situation is much the same in Italy and Britain, even if their methods are different. In contrast, Germany insists upon total loyalty to the established institutions. In the name of the obligatory loyalty of civil servants towards the federal Constitution, certain candidates for employment in the public sector and certain types of civil servant were banned from the administration from the start, at the moment when the Federal Republic was being set up in the West, but no more drastically than in other States. The problem became more pressing when the extreme Left decided that the moment had come for their 'long march through the institutions', that is to say their subversion. To cope with this, the Ministers of the Interior of both the Bund and the *Länder* agreed upon certain methods of inquiry and for the elimination of these subversive elements. They were announced in a document entitled 'Discussion on Radicals' (*Radikalenerlass*) but better known as the 'professional bans' (*Berufsverbot*). Although relatively few bans were passed—a few hundred—it provoked considerable political and legal debate. The Federal Constitutional Court twice pronounced on the matter, in 1975 and 1977, favouring acceptance of the ban. By the late 1980s, application of the *Berufsverbot* had eased in many areas. Unification added a further dimension to the problem in the shape of the large quantity of civil servants who were closely associated with the former Communist regime. Such civil servants were not sacked, but a number were encouraged to take early retirement, or simply moved into jobs where they had little power or influence.

British civil servants, though restricted from certain political activities in many cases, are allowed in principle and in private to belong to the political party of their choice. This tolerance has its limits: party membership is restricted to groups not regarded as subversive, and the right to political activities does not go with the right to party membership; such activities include running for any elective office, and even canvassing. Up until 1985, civil servants who were members or sympathizers of the Communist Party of Great Britain or of any Nazi group were liable to be dismissed from any employment considered vital to State security. In 1985, the definition of subversive groups was widened (while being left vague, allowing room for government interpretation), while restrictions on political activities were extended to non-administrative State employees (such as curators at the British Library). In the previous year, employees of the Government Communications Headquarters at Cheltenham, which provides signals intelligence for the government, were also stripped of the right to belong to a trade union.[19]

A second duty that affects civil servants relates to the expression of their opinions not only on political matters but also on the running of the service or the administration. It involves the duty of being discreet and of maintaining confidentiality and secrecy (see the Official Secrets Act, 1989). This last constraint is imposed very strictly in Britain[20] the major effect of this seemingly being to multiply leaks and scandals in the Press. In other countries, it is imposed more flexibly.[21] Generally speaking, it is fair to say that, in countries where parliamentary committees of control have an active role to play (Italy, Germany, and Britain), combining secrecy with the obligation to divulge any information that members of parliament require is becoming an increasingly acrobatic feat.

Senior civil servants and politics

The embarrassed relations—even clashes—that sometimes arise between administrations and politicians in the liberal democracies testify to the difficulty of reconciling the contradictory principles upon which they are founded and harmonizing the dogmas of the past with the realities of today. Let us briefly recall a few major points. All the liberal democracies place politics first: the principle of the majority will, and respect for the opposition, expressed in free and competitive elections. In other words, the administration is the servant of the political authorities inasmuch as the latter represent the will of the people. But, over and above this, the administration must respect another principle of liberal democracy, namely, that all citizens should receive equal treatment and hence that the administration must be impartial.[22] This is where the first contradiction surfaces, between the principles of representative government (according to which a majority implements its programme using an administration which, whatever its status, is *obliged* to accept the Government's policies and decisions) and the principles of the liberal charters defined by the American and French Revolutions (including that of equality, which implies the rejection of partisan treatment). The obvious solutions to this clash of principles are essentially determined by the particular historical contingencies and politico-social structures of individual countries. Each system to some extent clings to its own national concepts of neutrality, politicization, loyalty, etc. But the particular features of individual systems also tend to be muted as a result of pressures from phenomena that are common to all States, in particular the 'administrative explosion' that has affected not only the Western States but also those of the Third World and the former Socialist countries.

Similarly, one way to escape from the impasse created by arguing about the respective merits of these democratic principles or the bureaucratic evolution of different systems is to undertake a sociological analysis of the élites concerned and the positions that they hold.[23] For although the problem of relations between administrations and politicians may be a general one, and although the question of the politicization of local administrations appears particularly important in certain countries (particularly where the level of local or regional autonomy is high), the essential problem concerns the highest echelons of the State, where decisions, whether political or administrative, are taken.[24] A study of the career paths of administrative élites may help to gain a better understanding of the relationship between the administration and the political sector, and to seize upon the disparities between principles loudly proclaimed (neutrality, independence, etc.) and the realities of the situation. The relations between the political and the administrative spheres may thus be better revealed by studying the ability of each élite group to influence and penetrate the other than by any amount of abstract or formal analysis of the rules by which their relations are officially codified. In this way, we may be more successful in locating the various models of relations that apply in some of our liberal democracies on a spectrum that ranges from independence to subordination.

The authorities in more or less every liberal democracy have been attracted by a policy of separation between the political and the administrative spheres, as if contamination between the two would be bound to produce negative effects. To call a civil servant 'politicized' or describe him as a 'politician' is seldom considered a compliment. Similarly, although perhaps to a lesser degree, the bureaucratic nature of certain political functions tends to give rise to unflattering or even critical comments ('the permanent staff' or the 'professional' of the political sphere). Yet the temptation to seal these two worlds off from one another completely must be interpreted in different ways in different countries, in the light of the process adopted by each one in constituting itself as a State and of its subsequent democratic development.

In some cases, as in Britain, the democratic process antedates the creation of an administration. By the beginning of the nineteenth century, Britain already manifested many of the features of a liberal democracy—though with an extremely narrow suffrage. On the other hand, its administration was embryonic, fragmented, and riddled with clienteles. Not until the Northcote–Trevelyan Report of 1854 were the classical principles of open competitive recruitment, lifetime service, and promotion on merit under the impartial management of the Civil Service Commissioners recommended by an official body; not until the 1870s were they implemented. The classical nineteenth-century Civil Service lasted about 120 years, undertaking unorthodox recruitment in the First and Second World Wars, growing fast during and after each of them, yet remaining very recognizable withal. For the question of advancement that concerns us here, the important point is that it depended not on the once-and-for-all seal of approval earned by a high passing-out ranking at ENA, nor (still less) on political favours, but on the judgement of senior colleagues from year to year. Recruits to the 'fast stream' or the administrative grades, even if Oxbridge products (as at least half of them were, even at the start of the 1990s) would have to go through the hoops, rarely reaching the top three grades much younger than 45. While the career path of high-flyers typically included a stint as a Minister's private secretary, or even on the Downing Street staff, this would not entail strictly political work in the sense of party or constituency matters; that would be handled by the Minister's parliamentary private secretary, generally a young MP. Promotion to the top three grades depended, formally, on the quiet deliberations (rarely interviews) of the Senior Appointments Selection Committee, chaired by the Head of the Civil Service; and, informally, on coming to the favourable notice of superiors in each successive posting. For a civil servant to seek to accelerate this leisurely escalator by using political contacts would have been counter-productive.[25] That informal, cultural block on the exploitation of political affiliations for advancement within the bureaucracy was reinforced by the clear legal separation between civil servants above a certain grade and party politics, of which the most powerful emblem is the requirement for top civil servants to resign before even standing for elective office. There are therefore no civil servants in the House of Commons, and few former civil servants (though this small group, which includes Harold Wilson and Douglas Hurd, may win office fast once elected).

The Conservative governments of 1979–97 changed much (though not all) of that, not so much through a deliberate bid to politicize the Civil Service in a party sense, as through attempts to improve its responsiveness and efficiency. Margaret Thatcher arrived in office determined to diminish the State's economic intervention, to enhance its authority over interest groups, and to enforce the elected government's primacy over the bureaucracy. She was accused of trying to do this by politicizing the Civil Service, and she certainly had ample opportunity to try: eleven and a half years were enough for her to appoint a new Permanent Secretary to head each department at least once. Mrs Thatcher also showed a strong interest in top appointments. But her preference was more for what Peter Hennessy calls 'a hands-on, can-do type of official' than for card-carrying Conservatives. And John Major appeared to revert to a wholly traditional approach to senior Civil Service appointments, telling the Cabinet Secretary, 'You know these people, I don't.' Far more important for the overall structure of the Service than any attempt to stuff it with placemen was the steady succession of measures directed at its habits (such as the Financial Management Initiative) and ultimately at its structures. Crucial to these was the creation of the Efficiency Unit in the Cabinet Office, initially under the former chairman of Marks and Spencer, Sir Derek Rayner. The Efficiency Unit's gains in Mrs Thatcher's first two terms, annual savings of perhaps £1.5 billion, were useful rather than revolutionary. In 1988, however, its proposals for the 'Next Steps' in reforming the machinery of government had a much larger impact. They recommended that many service-delivering activities of the Civil Service be devolved to distinct agencies with much greater autonomy over recruitment, pay, and working methods; and the Efficiency Unit also initiated the 'market testing' of agencies, under which they could be contracted out, privatized, or abolished altogether. These changes gathered momentum in the early 1990s: by 1994 some 350,000 civil servants, or 60 per cent of the 'civil service', were working in executive agencies. This 'federalization' of the service ran in parallel with the decision to open up more senior appointments to outside competition. Sir Robin Butler, the Cabinet Secretary and the head of the Civil Service, quite explicitly stated that these changes spelt the end of the Civil Service in the sense that Northcote–Trevelyan had conceived it—though he added that there were important lines of continuity to retain with the past, including the impartiality of public service.[26]

Politicization was certainly not the declared purpose of the reforms, and the obvious safeguards such as the ban on civil servants standing for elective office remain. Supporters of the changes argued that the import of private-sector methods that they embodied was necessary to achieve goals that the public had a right to expect, such as value for taxpayers' money and achievement of clear performance targets. A reversal of Next Steps by the Blair government is almost unthinkable, and the most recent proposals for greater mobility and exchange between civil servants and the private sector suggest that, in some ways at least, it would like more of the same. Critics of the Thatcher and Major years, on the other hand, have argued that, at senior level, their impact has been harmful in more subtle ways than direct politicization: that a new culture has been engendered which discourages the honest delivery of policy advice by civil servants if they feel it will be perceived as contrary to the political preferences of a Minister; that the slowing or halting of the smooth upward escalator (as a result both of cuts in senior posts and of competition from outside) represents an incentive to civil servants to use less scrupulous methods to achieve promotion than dedication in the performance of public service; and that such methods may include the currying of political favour.[27]

One episode offers ambiguous indications as to the extent of such a cultural change. A few months before the May 1997 elections, the senior civil servants' trade union, the First Division Association, complained that requests had been made by ministers' political advisers for documentation to help present the 'good news' of the Government's policy achievements. They won the media argument, and were never required to fuel the election propaganda of the Conservative Party. That the attempt was made to use civil servants in this way betrays an attitude towards the Civil Service that would have been unimaginable before 1979. That it was quickly and fairly easily resisted, on the other hand, showed that the Conservatives' 18 years in power had scarcely made the administration over in their own image.

In Italy, the mutual isolation of civil servants and the political sphere is part of a radically different historical, political, and social context. In Britain, the separation between the political and the administrative spheres is essentially a matter expressed through rules and conventions, all of which by no means prevent the administration from playing an essential determining role in the elaboration of policies and the taking of decisions. In Italy, in contrast, the isolation of the senior civil servants is a sign of their limited ability to affect the process of decision-making and their desire to protect themselves from involvement in political and party matters.

The Italian administration that was established after the unification of the country was based on the Piedmontese model, itself a reflection of the Napoleonic system.[28] The first senior civil servants (prefects and ambassadors) were men from the north, mostly drawn from the Piedmontese bourgeoisie and aristocracy. But little by little, this political administration of a quasi-colonial nature was superseded by a meritocratic administration, recruited increasingly from south of Rome. The Liberals and the Marxists thought alike on this score: the unification of Italy must be bought at the price of integrating the intellectual *petite bourgeoisie* of the south since, for them, the sole opportunity for a career lay in administration. Today, the public sector is still 'colonized' by southerners and bears the imprint of their particular brand of education: idealist, formalistic, and juridical. As Sabino Cassese emphasizes, the preponderance of southerners (roughly two-thirds of all officials) is not just a territorial phenomenon, and would not be a serious problem if it were. It is also a cultural matter in which the 'productive' north is set in opposition to the 'unproductive bureaucracy' of the south—a favourite recent theme of the Lega Lombarda.[29] The cultural characteristics of the south are also reflected in the pervading nepotism at work in the allocation of administrative jobs. Political string-pulling is certainly not avoided in the business of securing posts in the public sector (particularly at the lower levels, where there is more room for manœuvre for operations of political clientage); but, as careers advance, it is totally rejected, judged inopportune, and prevented by many laws and regulations. An Italian civil servant seeks to obtain maximum legal and statutory guarantees that will enable him to pursue his career safely out of the way of interference from the political parties and the politicians. In other words, he counts upon the principle of promotion by seniority.

The situation is the same even at the level of high public office. It is here that the flow of recruitment and promotion is controlled, in an extremely corporatist fashion. The upper echelons of the public sector (*la dirigenza*), which comes under pressure from sectorial associations and trade unions, is constantly expanding (about 8,000 individuals at present) and civil servants in posts of authority tend to be elderly. Sabino Cassese shows that in 1979 only 10 per cent of these 'directors' fell within the 35 to 50 age group; 33 per cent were between 51 and 55 years of age; 29 per cent between 56 and 60; and 28 per cent between 61 and 65—and these figures were virtually the same in 1960.[30] Despite reforms introduced in 1980 but whose impact remains limited, the Italian system is characterized by a *corporatist* type of isolation. The separation between the political and the administrative spheres is not prompted by the same objectives (neutrality) and necessities (give-and-take) as the British Civil Service. It is not the product of any theory, nor founded upon any system of values. Its only excuses are historical (the Piedmontese domination, Fascism) and pragmatic (the prevailing 'partitocracy'). Nor is the separation between the senior public administration and the political sphere one-way. Senior civil servants certainly resist interference from the political sphere, but at the same time they themselves seldom venture into parliamentary or ministerial arenas. Italian civil servants enjoy statutory advantages that are essentially identical to those of their French counterparts with regard to freedom to take part in trade union and political activities (in other words, conditions that are extremely favourable). Yet the number of employees from the public sector (not counting teachers) elected to Parliament has never exceeded 5 per cent and, in the entire history of the Republic of Italy, no more than three or four senior civil servants have ever become Ministers. The consequence of this inward-looking attitude (also manifested in other ways which we cannot dwell upon now) is that Italian senior civil servants find themselves relatively marginalized. Instead of producing ideas, they simply execute them; instead of making decisions, they adopt a preventative, blocking role: as a result, it is hard to consider senior officials of the Italian public sector as belonging to the country's élite. However, perhaps this picture of mutual distrust calls for some modification, for one way or another the political and the administrative spheres must coexist, if not co-operate.

This situation of distrustful alienation would hardly be viable were it not for a whole collection of palliatives designed to overcome the difficulties. In the first place, the Council of State and the Court of Accounts play the role of an intermediary in establishing communications between the bureaucracy, in the strict sense of the term, and the political system. These two jurisdictional institutions, particularly the former, provide a reservoir of advisers for Ministers anxious to gather competent men around them. Roughly one-third of the members of ministerial offices come from the Council of State alone, equalling the number of civil servants drawn from the Ministries for which those offices are set up. Because the former group consists of able men who are willing to play an active role on the edge of the political arena, obtaining the position of director of a ministerial *cabinet* may, according to Storchi,[31] lead to a 'veritable career', for some remain in their posts for as long as ten or fifteen years, following the fortunes of 'their' Ministers as these move from sector to sector. But the Council of State and the Court of Accounts may also be used for quite the opposite purpose, as fields where individuals whose careers are on the wane, rather than on the rise, may tactfully be put out to grass. They constitute ideal dumping grounds for staff directors whom Ministers wish to be rid of. Cassese reckons that about 10 per cent of the members of these two jurisdictional institutions are former office directors who have been pensioned off in this way. The situation of the two institutions is thus comparable to that of their French counterparts, except that the latter tend to be used more to reward old friends than to get rid of undesirables.

Another way of improving the situation is to turn to the semi-public sector or the universities in order to get round the administration's unwillingness to become involved with politics. The Italian administration, with all its inefficiency and its obstructions, thus finds itself left out when it comes to filling the most dynamic posts in the *enti pubblici* and also appointing staff for them, for preference goes to men from the rest of the public or semi-public sectors. University teachers, for their part, display none of the reticence of administrators. There are few jurists, political experts, or historians of any stature who have not ventured out into the sea of Italian politics in one way or another. In general, the political roles played by Italian university teachers are probably unparalleled elsewhere in the Western world. They become councillors, *éminences grises*, local representatives, Deputies, members of all kinds of commissions, editors of newspapers associated with the various political parties, and so on. Their presence in the political sphere is further encouraged by the general consensus and tolerance of Italian society: it has room for all sorts, whether from the Left or the Right, and all can claim the rewards that are handed out in the political world (prestige, publicity, and means of both an institutional and a personal nature).

In conclusion, some comment is perhaps called for upon the apparent paradox of the isolation of the country's administration, given that Italy is always presented as an example of clientship and patronage, the country of *lottizazione*. In truth, the beneficiaries of the political sinecures handed out were not civil servants (apart from some exceptional cases, in particular at regional level). The allocation of 'jobs for the boys' is a minor phenomenon, which above all concerns office directors in the Treasury. Others affected by it tended to be administrators of the public or semi-public sector, but they are not civil servants in the strict sense of the term. *Lottizazione* and patronage before 1992–4 chiefly benefited what could be called the party or trade union bureaucracies. Nor is it any exaggeration to speak of bureaucracies in this connection: after all, the parties and trade unions employed several thousand individuals, mostly paid out of public funds either directly, through wages or grants provided for by the law, or indirectly, through the distribution of salaries also drawn from public funds. Political life and the public sector were thus funded by a huge, systematic hand-out, distributed proportionally. Up until the 1970s, the Christian Democrats were both the arch-devisers and the major beneficiaries of this policy of distributed funding. Later, the secular parties obtained their slice of the cake, and even the former Communist Party had a share. Needless to say, the allocation of funds engenders furious battles. The administration of every bank and savings bank was the object of constant haggling, and for three years the board of the RAI failed to get itself renewed. In Italy, this was the level at which an osmosis took place between the bureaucracy and the political sphere. It was this, coupled with equally vague distinctions between the public sector and private interests, which was at the heart of the corruption prevalent in Italian politics, which became incompatible with any attempt to bring the public sector's spending under control, and which ultimately brought the party system down in the mid-1990s.

In the two cases of Britain and Italy, the separation of the administration from politics clearly has different causes and radically different effects. In a two-party system, the British administration has managed to avoid the dangers of purges carried out by each succeeding government by proclaiming its neutrality at the same time as retaining effective and virtually exclusive control over policy-making. Senior civil servants do not venture into the sphere of party politics but they do remain the indispensable shapers of policies. In contrast, the Italian upper administration has put itself beyond the reach of dreaded political interference but at the cost of being relegated to the sidelines. The most it can do is be obstructive—and it takes every opportunity to do so—and meanwhile manage its own 'financial interests', in other words preserve its methods of recruitment, its status, and its careers.

At the other end of the spectrum, political and bureaucratic élites belong more or less to the same world. There is more than one way of interpreting confusion between the political and the administrative sectors. At first sight, such an osmosis would seem to be characteristic of totalitarian States. The monarch's religion is forced upon his subjects, the administration must identify with the values, creed, and strategies of the politicians in power.

That is exactly what the embryonic administrations of the late eighteenth century were conceived to be: simply an extension, an arm of the executive. But such a monolithic system could only survive over a long period of time within a dictatorial framework, and its natural corollary, in the event of political changes, would be a purge. That is why no liberal democracies have political administrations, as certain underdeveloped or socialist countries do, however strong the temptations to establish them may have been at some point or other in their histories.

Germany, Italy, Spain, and Greece—to name but a few—are all countries in which, during the twentieth century, attempts have been made to politicize the administration within the framework of a Fascist dictatorship. France, for its part, had already experienced purges first with the bloody episode of the Convention, and later, after each revolution or change in the regime, from the army. Few bureaucracies have undergone so many serious upheavals in the last two centuries—a fact that testifies both to the political sector's distrust of civil servants and also to the ease with which it has been able to penetrate the French administration.

But there is another way of regarding an osmosis between the political and the administrative sectors, and this emphasizes the democratic virtues of such a process. This point of view rests upon a belief that an administration is dependent not only upon the government and the country's elected representatives, but also upon those under its administration. What better way of ensuring this kind of dependence than the election of administrators? This notion was embraced by the first French Constitution of 1791, which instituted the election of civil servants, and it still applies widely in America at the level of individual states and localities. In France, election as a mode of recruiting civil servants has completely disappeared, but a few traces of this concept of administrative democracy are still detectable both within the administration itself (with all its committees to monitor parity and so on) and in sectors that have not been completely taken over by the traditional administration (social security, professional sectors under 'shared management', etc.).

Here the 'politicization' of the administration and its elected employees is particularly ambiguous. It is neither monolithic nor uniform. The degree of politicization achieved is bound to depend largely upon the links that candidates for administrative posts and those who are elected maintain with the political parties. Such tends to be the situation in particular in systems known, sometimes disparagingly, as 'consociational',[32] that is, countries in which civil peace and political equilibrium result from a meticulous sharing-out of responsibilities in all sectors—economic, cultural, political, administrative, etc. Consensualism in these cases is in reality usually the product of the pacification of many antagonisms. The Netherlands, Israel, Belgium, and Austria have all been or still are prototypes of States in which political and social equilibrium was or is maintained by dint of a judicious and complex system of allocating spoils. In Belgium, for example, where an artificial unity was for a long time guaranteed and maintained by an élite, part Walloon, part Flemish, but totally francophone, the system exploded, revealing all the territorial, linguistic, political, and trade union-based cleavages that have now become familiar.[33] In Austria, a *proporz* system based on an agreement between the Socialist Party and the People's Party quite literally divides up all political and administrative posts between the two main political groups—rendering both of them vulnerable to the populist challenge of Jörg Haider's Freedom Party.[34]

To judge from these experiences, it would seem that total separation between the political and the administrative sectors may come about in two different sets of circumstances. Either it is part of a national situation of such a specific nature that it is impossible to 'export' unless many precautions are taken; otherwise it becomes a source of serious malfunction (as in Italy). The opposite solution, involving osmosis between the political and the administrative spheres, usually leads to one of two impasses: totalitarianism in its blackest guise, or a dismantling of the State in which parties, factions, and interest groups all gain in power. The only remaining possibility is to steer a difficult middle course, attempting to come to terms with the situation by recognizing the ineluctable nature of the links between the two spheres and trying to adapt accordingly. That is the course for which West Germany and France, each in its own way, opted.

Germany, once again, presents a special case owing to the questions posed by unification. The Federal Republic found 1.8 million State employees in post in the East in 1990. Those of any seniority were necessarily compromised by their association with a regime that made no separation at all between the political and the administrative, between those areas of society where the ruling party had the right to rule and those where its jurisdiction did not reach. Some were also directly linked to the Stasi, the secret police. At the same time, the technical competence of many among their number could not be overlooked. The resulting purge, as often in such cases, was fairly modest, with 1,883 senior civil servants and 1,300 university professors removed in 1990. But in 1992 the government admitted that 3,700 former Stasi agents were still working in the East; and that ten of them, including two senior officers, were employed assisting with investigations on the Stasi.[35]

As far as the German system in general is concerned, its main merit is that it tackles the problem of the politicization of the administration by containing it within quite strict limits. Positioned between the political sector and the topmost echelons of the administration are a number of senior civil servants generally known as *politische beamte* (political civil servants). These high-ranking civil servants, who act as the Secretaries-General of Ministries or as directors of ministerial offices, emerge from the ranks of the administration but are selected (and dismissed) on the basis of political criteria. The political aspect of their status stems essentially from the procedure through which they may be appointed and dismissed at the discretion of the government in power. If dismissed, the senior civil servant concerned receives a 'pension',[36] the size of which depends upon his rank and seniority.

In a system that produces many coalitions, this procedure makes it possible to guarantee that the Ministers will be aided in their tasks (to the extent, until the practice was ended in 1969, of having their places taken at Cabinet meetings) by reliable civil servants, while the latter, for their part, benefit from statutory and financial guarantees that are by no means negligible. In many respects, and with only a few variations, the position of senior civil servants in Germany resembles that of those in France. Despite the fact that in both countries the administration is claimed to be at the service of the public rather than of any political party, the neutrality of civil servants, particularly in the upper echelons of the administration, is not always as complete as bureaucratic discourse would suggest.[37] The impingement of politics is manifest in the first place in the requirement that civil servants should support the values of the federal constitutional order. It is thought that, in the course of the 1970s, about 1,000 civil servants or candidates for appointments in the public sector were fired or rejected, while as many as

700,000 employees had their personal files scrutinized by the Office for the Protection of the Constitution.

But connections between the political sector and the administration are also evident from the influence that the political parties in power bring to bear upon the appointment and careers of senior civil servants. In West Germany the politicization of the upper echelons of the public sector until 1969 attracted less attention as a result of the domination of the CDU–CSU. When the Social Democrats came to power (with the FDP) in 1969, they managed to ease out a number of senior civil servants whom they regarded as hostile or lukewarm. In October and November 1969, 11 *Staatsekretäre* and 8 directors of ministerial offices were replaced, as were 70 other senior civil servants whose sympathies lay in the other direction. Between that date and 1982, many more changes took place, provoking considerable criticism from the Christian Democrats (not that this prevented them from acting in a similar way as soon as they returned to power).

Notwithstanding the precarious nature of these top posts in the public sector, civil servants have not been discouraged from aiming for these levels that are subject to the government's discretionary powers. On the contrary: many of them have even become actively engaged in politics either in the parties or in Parliament itself. Kenneth Dyson[38] estimated in 1982 that 41.9 per cent of the members of the Bundestag had emerged from the public sector (about half of them being teachers) and in some of the *Land* Assemblies that proportion exceeded 50 per cent. He also records that in 1978 civil servants accounted for 12.3 per cent of the members of the CDU, and in 1977 for 13.2 per cent of the CSU, 10 per cent of the SPD, and 14 per cent of the FDP.[39] This close coincidence between politicians and civil servants[40] is encouraged by a whole collection of protective rules that are mostly to the advantage of the civil servants: for five years they can make themselves politically available and still draw 75 per cent of their salary; they can be reintegrated into the civil service without difficulty, or move freely between the two spheres; up until 1975, they could be paid as a member of the Bundestag as well as drawing 60 per cent of their civil servant's salary or pension, etc. In short, Ezra Suleiman's[41] appraisal of the situation in France might be equally well applied to the German system: the statutory and financial advantages enjoyed by the public sector in effect subsidize the political system, to the advantage of one particular social group and the parties to which its members belong. The only major difference is that, unlike France, Germany has set up a more strictly codified basis for the relations between the administration and the political sphere and has officially ratified the political status of the civil servants at the top of the State hierarchy.

It is certainly in France that osmosis between the political and the administrative spheres is the greatest, not only because senior civil servants there play a political role, but especially because the civil service is the breeding ground for a large proportion of political personnel. However, the movement of élites between the political and the administrative worlds is but one aspect of a more general phenomenon, namely, the interconnections between the élites that move in and control all sectors: both the public and the private sectors of industry, banks, and insurance companies, cultural activities and international posts, Parliament and the government. Setting the situation in its historical context may help to illuminate the crucial role played by the upper administration and its politicization. The importance of the French upper administration stems from the way in which the élites over whom the State established a virtual monopoly have always been educated and selected. Already under the *ancien régime*, the 'cream' was selected in specialist schools that catered for the needs of the State. The system was further organized and systematized by Napoleon Bonaparte: the École Normale Supérieure, the Polytechnique, the École des Mines, and the École des Ponts et Chaussées have channelled the most brilliant individuals of each generation into the administration. In 1946, the École Nationale d'Administration was created, virtually all its students being drawn from the Institut d'Études Politiques in Paris and the former private École des Sciences Politiques (nationalized in 1945). This brought individuals with a general education in the humanities into the same State-dominated orbit as other specialists and technical experts produced by the *grandes écoles*. The long-standing supremacy of these State schools would not have been so unassailable if their former students had been confined solely to the administration. In reality, being one of the 'happy few' and part of a 'super élite' made one eligible for major posts of responsibility in both the private and the public sectors. The most significant development in recent times is that of the Polytechnique. It was originally set up for the training of military officers, but nowadays this is no more than a marginal function. The 'Polytechnique Mafia', to borrow the title of a book written by one of its former students, now controls many important posts both in the Ministries and in industry.

The other key factor in the politicization of senior civil servants was the creation in 1815 of ministerial *cabinets*. These streamlined structures designed to provide Ministers with advice and assistance were the brain-child of monarchists under the Restoration, who distrusted the Napoleonic administration, which was still in place. The government wanted to be able to turn to reliable, committed advisers, not civil servants who owed their eminence to their loyalty to the fallen Emperor. These small groups of about a dozen individuals, appointed at the discretion of each Minister, were originally composed of dependable civil servants temporarily seconded from their departments in the administration, together with men drawn from outside the administration. Gradually however, they came to be recruited solely from the administration, for civil servants, with their inside knowledge of the workings of the administration, turned out to be more useful than individuals brought in from outside and, besides, they determined to corner for themselves the advantages that accrued from service in these offices. After two or three years of 'worthy and loyal service', these civil servants were indeed—and still are—generally well rewarded: they would either be promoted within the administration, appointed to some prestigious position in the semi-public sector, or else acquire some sinecure in the private sector, unless, that is, they developed a taste for politics and decided to stand for Parliament themselves. Political swings and roundabouts and changes of government render posts in these offices unstable and precarious, but the most prestigious groups in the administration have more or less colonized them. In other words, the *esprit de corps* working to the advantage of each administrative group involved (Polytechnique men, those from the Council of State or the Cour des Comptes, and so on) compensates for the effects of politicization. Civil servants may be divided by their personal political or party loyalties, but they close ranks when it comes to defending the privileges, posts, and strongholds that each of these bodies has managed to make its own.

But it is under the Fifth Republic that the politicization of senior civil servants has reached its peak. General de Gaulle's overt hostility towards politicians as a whole was expressed in particular by his appointment of a whole host of senior civil servants to posts of major importance, starting with some in the government itself. Between 1959 and 1981, on average 41 per cent of French Ministers were drawn from the upper echelons of the Civil Service[42] and about 30 per cent were appointed to the government without being elected Deputies. A similar preponderance of civil servants is noticeable in Parliament. Between 1958 and 1978, 31 per cent of all Deputies came from the bureaucracy, and in 1981 the percentage rose to 53.1 of state employees (but in this instance chiefly teachers). All the political parties including, to a lesser extent, the Communist Party and the FN were affected by this rise of the civil servants: whether governments are left-wing or right-wing, they are all dominated by the technocrats from the *grandes écoles*.[43] The system is fuelled and perpetuated by the considerable facilities that the Civil Service makes available to its employees to enable them to take part in politics, the prestige and influence that accrue from being part of an extremely interventionist State and, finally, the considerable career advantages that stem from political collaboration with government Ministers. The phenomenon became even more noticeable, seemingly almost caricatured, when the Socialists came to power in 1981, to be followed by the Right in 1986. Many were replaced, and the criterion for such decisions tended to be party affiliation rather than professional ability. As a result, too many staff purges took place, non-political civil servants began to feel a certain discouragement, and increasingly severe criticisms were voiced about the political sector's grip over the administration, a grip that was making itself felt ever lower down in the hierarchy (and in local administration, too). The spoils system à *la française* may not have disappeared entirely since the Left's return to power in June 1988; in particular, the Juppé government of 1995–7 attracted accusations of seeking to restore the Gaullist stranglehold of former times. But they were somewhat exaggerated as far as results went (or else the government lacked sufficient time), and the left-wing Jospin government that followed was more determined than its predecessors to resist the temptation of a post-electoral round of musical chairs in the higher echelons of the administration.

This rapid survey shows that, while nobody disputes the ability of civil servants to initiate and implement public policies, because of an unreal notion of their neutrality, they are often criticized for becoming involved in party politics. But in truth the terms of the argument are somewhat obscured, since the accusation of 'politicization' made against the civil servants is so vague. The term can mean different things at different levels:

1. Politicization may be an ideological concept. That is to say it refers to a system of

values to which civil servants subscribe in the same way as other citizens. This kind of politicization is little noticed and seldom criticized provided the civil servants subscribe to the system of values that is dominant or the society concerned is an extremely consensual one. Only parties or groups 'outside the system' attack this kind of involvement in politics on the part of civil servants.

2. Politicization may be to do with the *political parties*: in this case, the fact that individual civil servants support particular political parties is either explicitly or implicitly recognized. But this kind of politicization takes many different forms. In some countries it leads to practices associated with spoils systems, as different governments succeed each other, and this tends to extend to the upper strata of the administration all the antagonisms that arise in political life in general. Such is certainly the situation in the United States, but it is also produced, in specific forms, in Germany and France. Elsewhere, party politicization constitutes a deliberate functional response to the conflicts and rifts that divide the country. In these cases, posts in the public sector are literally shared out between the various political elements of which the country is composed (as in Belgium and Austria). This provides a consensual solution for coping with deep conflicts and antagonisms in a peaceful manner, but it sometimes has the effect of generating even greater tensions, since the agreement achieved concerns not so much means of reducing these divisions, but rather methods that extend them to all aspects of social life.

3. Finally, politicization may be of a structural nature. In this case, politicization is not so much a matter of the choices that individual civil servants make. Rather, it is an effect of the organization of the service as a whole. It would be illusory to imagine that organizations such as the Conseil d'État in France and the individuals who run them can be apolitical or neutral when their very structure and/or their functions are deeply affected by politics.[44] There is nothing shocking or surprising about this. But it is better to face facts and draw the inevitable conclusions—both deontological and organizational—rather than avoid the issue.

It is party politicization that gives rise to the most acute polemics. Other forms tend to pass without comment. This somewhat incomplete appraisal of politicization tends to produce considerable pressure in favour of depoliticizing the public sector. But the idea of eliminating politics from the upper administration is probably utopian. Even in Britain, where the Civil Service is the least open to party influences, the illusion of a 'pure' administration is frequently challenged. Richard Crossman, the former Labour Minister, wrote, 'There is nothing like a civil servant for being a politician and denying that he is one,'[45] and Léo Moulin points out that

mechanisms of politicization are also at work in this somewhat imaginary England that tends to be used as a model but where moving in certain social circles, having been educated at particular schools, speaking with a particular accent, and dressing in a particular style all constitute social criteria that are just as specific and effective as belonging to one political party or another.[46]

The administration's neutrality *vis-à-vis* the political authorities is one of the founding myths of liberal democracy. And they are impressive myths, for they have made it possible to limit the power of the ruler and guarantee as fair and equal treatment as possible to every citizen, thanks to the progressive mutual dislocation and independence of the two spheres.

But the close and continuous collaboration that takes place at their upper levels makes it likely that administrative personnel change along with governments, and this raises problems that cannot be side-stepped merely by expressing disapproval. The way to keep the politicization of civil servants within reasonable bounds is to make changes in the political system rather than in the administrative sphere. Administrations are noticeably more highly politicized where the political sector serves as a clearing-house between various separate spheres. The best route for transferring from the administrative sector to the economic seems to be by way of the political, at least in the United States, Germany, and France. On the other hand, in Britain and Italy (despite the fact that in both countries substantial semi-public sectors exist, just as they do in France), the relative separation between the administrative and the political spheres makes it difficult for civil servants *stricto sensu* to move on to conquer neighbouring domains. The fact that so many differences exist between the various systems suggests that the variable that accounts for the degree of politicization in different civil services should be sought not so much in the characteristics peculiar to each of these administrations, but rather in the structure and organization of the political systems themselves.

Controlling the bureaucrats

Administrations started as servants; but have they now assumed the role of masters? The question is justified by the formidable expansion of the tasks, means, and staff of administrations, an expansion that neither politicians nor citizens seem able to control or check. Means of control do not seem to have kept pace with the quantitative and qualitative evolution that has overtaken bureaucracies. Methods of control have in many cases remained unchanged since the beginning of the century: essentially they are either of a juridical nature or else they amount to no more than 'self-monitoring' systems that are unquestionably necessary but by now quite inadequate. As for strictly political controls, virtually everywhere they play no more than a marginal role.

Political controls

In principle, political authorities can control their administrations in a number of ways. They can make sure that the policies carried out are firmly in line with their directives and with established regulations; they can control the extent and use of the financial means available; and they can often call for the resignation of civil servants in posts of responsibility. Furthermore, liaison between the political authorities and the administration set up to implement their directives is underwritten and reinforced by the fact that the political responsibility of the Minister who heads the administration is at stake when the service is found to be deficient or at fault.

But in all these respects, political controls have been and continue to be of limited effect. The deflections that the intentions of the decision-makers undergo in the course of their implementation are not noticed until too late and, once habits and interests are established and the situation becomes a *fait accompli*, they are hard to rectify—not to mention the fact that frequently the political authorities responsible for initiating a particular policy are no longer there to react to the unexpected effects of their initial decisions or the distortions that these have suffered. Besides, generally speaking, political authorities show little enthusiasm for retrospective evaluations to determine the results and impact of their policies.

The same applies to financial controls, although these could and should constitute a powerful weapon in the hands of the political authorities. Governments and Parliaments are usually content at least to renew the budget of the previous year and in most cases are prepared to increase it without any proper inquiry into the need for funds or the proposed way of using them. The British experience is instructive in this respect. The Thatcher and Major Governments did, at least partially, change the ethos as well as the structures of the Civil Service. Yet this result was achieved through relentless pressure from a Government which knew better than most what it wanted; which also thought it knew how to get it; which did display some willingness to review its past activities and learn from them; and which had the central, and arguably easier, task of spending less money rather than seeing that its positive policies were applied on the ground. Yet John Major still left office in 1997 with public expenditure at the same level, as a share of GDP, as it had been at his first election as an MP in 1979, and taxation rates somewhat higher for most people.

Internal checks can also constitute a way of the executive retaining control provided, that is, there is a genuine desire to make proper use of the existing machinery. Thus, the audit procedures in Britain and the monitoring of the Inspection of Finance and other supervisory bodies in France help to keep a check on the quality and propriety of administrative operations.

There is one other way in which political authorities can retain control over their administrations. It is through the appointment and dismissal of senior administrative officers. This sanction has been used frequently in the United States and also, on occasion, in France and West Germany, but often for political rather than administrative reasons. The administrative 'fuse' blows when it comes to protecting political officials (as happened in 1985 in the *Rainbow Warrior* affair in France). It is also worth pointing out that often—particularly in France and Italy—the sanctions imposed by politicians on civil servants look remarkably like promotions. This is an indication of the extent of the political authorities' timidity where influential administrations are concerned. In truth, in mainland Europe, civil servants are seldom held responsible *de facto* (the administration as a whole tends to assume responsibility for the mistakes of its individual agents). The British case was at least nominally characterized in the past by the principle of ministerial responsibility, under which ministers were responsible for what went on in their Departments, and civil servants were largely immune from scrutiny unless there was clear personal misconduct (as, for example, in the case of George Pottinger, the Scottish civil servant convicted in 1972 of taking bribes from the architect John Poulson). The system, which never worked as well as the principle suggests, has broken down in recent years, largely to the detriment of civil servants. Ministers, with few exceptions, have only resigned when required to do so by the Prime Minister; and they are increasingly disposed to shelter behind the doctrine that 'a Minister is only as good as the briefs his civil servants give him'.[47] At the same time parliamentary select committees, and commissions of inquiry, have been increasingly assertive in summoning and questioning civil servants. Episodes such as the Scott inquiry into the illegal sale of arms to Iraq during the Iran–Iraq War were marked by the spectacle of ministers pleading ignorance or poor briefing, and civil servants claiming to have acted in good faith in the light of what they understood to be ministerial policy. The recent dismemberment of the civil service has also left officials more exposed. In 1996, for example, the Home Secretary, Michael Howard, requested and obtained the resignation of the Director-General of the Prison Service, after a series of lapses in prison security for which many felt the Minister should be held at least as responsible as the official. It is tempting to suggest that Britain has seen an increase in the professional insecurity of officials with no clear corresponding increase in accountability to the public.

Controls through the courts

Everywhere, the administration's responsibility towards the political authorities was established at the outset, but not its responsibility towards citizens. It was only quite late on (the late nineteenth century in Germany, France, and Italy, and not until the twentieth century in Britain) that true control became available to citizens, who could now seek redress by bringing court actions. Through a bizarre historical irony, the very States that strove the hardest to protect themselves against interference from the judiciary by setting up special laws and special tribunals for the administration were the first to have to accept the most stringent controls. But since the Second World War administrative laws and tribunals have also been established in the countries with systems of common law, that is, the United States and Britain (where the influences of both the Scottish juridical system and continental law have made considerable impact).

The model for controls imposed by administrative and financial tribunals was provided by the French Council of State (Conseil d'État) and more recently by the conversion of prefectoral councils (*conseils de préfecture*) into regional administrative tribunals. In Italy, the system is virtually identical: the Consiglio di Stato (which became more or less a court of appeal) was to a large extent supplemented by newly created regional administrative tribunals. In the Federal Republic of Germany, the model has been somewhat complicated by the State's federal structure, both before and since unification. Here, there are three separate levels: the tribunals at local level, the administrative tribunals of the *Länder*, and the administrative tribunal of the Federation as a whole, which sits in Berlin (*Bundersverwaltungsgericht*). In Germany, administrative tribunals are complemented by specialized ones (which, unlike the French specialized tribunals, are not subject to the control of the supreme administrative Court and which are thus autonomous at their own level). Also worth mentioning are the fiscal tribunals (the *Finanzgerichte*), which only exist at *Länder* and Bund levels, and the social tribunals (*Sozialgerichte*), which deal chiefly with social security cases and are organized at three levels, as are the general administrative tribunals. It is interesting to note that France, which provided the original inspiration for this structure, is today, in its turn, adapting to the German type of system in order to cope with its overload of cases. As from 1989, five courts of appeal in part took the place of the Conseil d'État, whose role was thereafter to be limited to pure legal supervision and to checking the most important decisions of central government.

What with the growing number of cases in all countries, these courts are now facing problems, for the dearth of judges is producing a veritable legal bottle-neck so that exercising one's right to seek redress from the administration and obtain due compensation is becoming increasingly fraught with uncertainty. French administrative tribunals are considered to be overstretched (with 9,600 cases brought in 1986 before the Conseil d'État and 59,000 before the regional administrative tribunals, justifying the creation in 1989 of five Courts of Appeal on the German model). But in Italy the situation is even more serious (15,000 cases for the Consiglio di Stato and 40,000 for the regional tribunals).[48] It was worse still in West Germany (in 1978, 98,000 appeals at local level, 14,500 at *Länder* level, and 2,400 at the level of the federal administrative tribunal). Unification compounded the problem, adding to the caseload without supplying a corresponding complement of judges to handle it.

The extent of the tasks facing all these administrative tribunals tends, however, to mask the quite substantial differences between them. In France and Italy, in particular, many of these tribunals' energies are devoted to litigation within the administration itself (47 per cent of all cases in Italy) or to very specific areas of the administration (especially town planning and finance). There are thus many disparities between different sectors, and this throws a rather different light on the role of monitoring the administration that is generally ascribed to the administrative tribunals. Finally the force or quality of the sanctions that a judge may impose depends upon the degree of independence that he has managed to establish for himself in relation to the administration. In this respect, Italian and German judges generally adopt a less deferential attitude towards their administrations than do their French counterparts, who are more intimately linked with theirs (either by reason of their common training in the ENA or through being appointed from within the administration's ranks). German judges and—to a slightly lesser degree—Italian ones are judges of legality rather than judges of the administration (in both senses of the expression) and this has the effect of putting them in the position of essential partners in the administrative process. Paradoxically enough, the relative timidity of French administrative judges towards the administration tends to marginalize their position and get their decisions discounted.

Only the Conseil d'État is unaffected in this respect, but this is not so much on account of its status as a court of appeal but rather because of its position as 'adviser to the throne' and the fact that a proportion of its members (albeit a changing one) is active in both the political and the administrative spheres.

In these three countries, the administrative tribunals are complemented by Courts of Accounts, whose functions are consultative and monitorial. In Italy, for example, all administrative decisions of the State that involve some expenditure must be submitted to the Court for approval. However, given the avalanche of decisions with which it is unable to cope, the effect of this is to render its control illusory or purely formal. In Germany, the Federal Court of Accounts[49] concerns itself only with federal expenses; the *Länder* are monitored by special courts of their own (similar to the new regional audit offices in Italy, except that in Germany these are not subject to their federal counterpart). The German Federal Court of Accounts plays a similar role to the French one and, like the latter, is obliged to produce a report, which it submits to the Bundestag. Also, as in France, the impact made by the Court of Accounts seems somewhat weak, partly because by no means all its recommendations are put into effect and also because its monitoring means are to some extent ill-adapted to the contemporary functions of the administration. The sanction of legality—which in any case could only be a partial one—turns out to be relatively ineffective because it is applied too late. As for managerial monitoring, as in France this remains limited and hesitant, for the judges have few weapons at their disposal and are, moreover, reluctant to impose methods of control that would go beyond their role as judges.

In Britain and the United States, the concept of 'public law' has emerged since the Second World War and special institutions exist for settling disputes between the administrations and individual citizens. Thus Britain nowadays has over 2,000 administrative tribunals that operate in a wide range of sectors (taxes, social security, pensions, etc.). Their name, 'administrative tribunals', is designed to distinguish these first-level institutions from the normal judicial system (where the term 'courts' is used), for the principles on which they are based, their procedure (which is far more informal and less dependent on precedent), and their composition all mark them out from courts of the classic kind. Furthermore, as in the United States, any appeals against the decisions of the administrative tribunals must, in the last resort, be made to the courts. As can be seen, the British administrative tribunals have much in common with the specialized courts at the lowest level in France, such as the Social Security Appeals Commission (Commission de Recours de la Sécurité Sociale). But the proliferation of these tribunals now taking place and the development of public law should lead to further changes and tighter controls. However, the problems involved in incorporating these new tribunals into the traditional juridical system are reflected in the creation, in 1958, of a Council on Tribunals, its purpose being to keep an eye on their progress, methods, and results, with a view to suggesting to Parliament what reforms should be introduced. Meanwhile, for the time being, both in the United States and in Britain, the controls through the courts upon the administration remain necessary and important.

In countries subject to common law, the inadequacies that justified the establishment of embryonic administrative tribunals are to some extent offset by the comparative boldness of judges towards the administration and by the more efficient means that exist for controlling it. The administration has no 'natural judges' of its own, in the first instance, and is subject to the same constraints as those imposed in litigation between private individuals. Furthermore, in the United States in particular, proof of responsibility on the part of the administration[50] may result in its having to pay damages that are not limited (as they are in France) by any concern to preserve public funds. Finally, the courts wield very real powers of constraint over the administrations in these countries: powers of injunction, forbidding or ordering them to proceed (or not to proceed) to issue writs (writ of mandamus, prohibition, or *certiorari*) which, if ignored, may occasion charges of contempt of court followed by increased financial penalties.

Even the most effective juridical controls have their drawbacks: in general, even in the best of circumstances, they are extremely time-consuming and expensive. (The right to dispense with the services of a lawyer in administrative tribunals, in France, is somewhat illusory and tends to look more like a privilege for jurists than a facility for ordinary citizens.) Consequently, despite an increase in the number of appeals, many problems have remained unresolved, or badly resolved, by juridical means. The fact that so many citizens, ill-equipped to defend themselves, were appealing to their Deputies for help constituted one of many indications that litigation was failing to operate satisfactorily in situations that, without being particularly serious, certainly needed to be rectified. One solution seems to have been provided by the Scandinavian countries. They created a new institution to deal with this type of problem: the Ombudsman. Following their example, in 1972 France set up a Mediator, Britain a Parliamentary Commissioner for Administration. However, these two 'mediators' are not as powerful as the model that inspired them, for account had to be taken of the pre-existing mechanisms of litigation and also of the reluctance of members of parliament to relinquish their own traditional function as mediators between ordinary citizens and the administration. Consequently, applications to the French Mediator and the British Commissioner can be made only through members of parliament. Italy and Germany have not introduced any mediators at national level. But it is worth noting that in 1950 West Germany did set up an Ombudsman for military affairs and that some *Länder* (including the Rhineland-Palatinate, which, in 1973, was the first to institute a *Bürgerbeauftragte*) did so at *Land* level. In Italy, eight regions have set up *difensori civici* at regional level, but their powers have been limited both in written texts and in practice and, to date, the results have not been particularly impressive.

A further question has been created, especially in Britain, by the privatization or contracting-out of many public services. What sanctions should be available to users of a private, profit-making organization enjoying a monopoly? The approach of the Conservative governments that undertook the privatizations has been a contractual and regulatory one. Private firms supplying public services commit themselves to a series of performance targets; these are monitored by regulators, with the power to impose fines for non-fulfilment of the criteria; and in some cases, compensation is available directly to consumers under Citizens' Charter provision. Such a system may, depending on the detail, offer the best or the worst of solutions: either real incentives to perform combined with swifter and surer sanctions than could be obtained through the cumbersome means of legal proceedings, or a combination of low or unclear performance targets, regulators without teeth, penalties too small to act as incentives, and users without means of redress.

Conclusion

Western administrations bear the imprint of abstract Weberian models of rational-cum-legal organization. But they have also undergone profound changes that affect both their internal structure and their relations with other organizations or with citizens. In conditions such as these use of the term 'administrations' is justifiable only by virtue of its convenience value. For all administrations have been affected by a fundamental qualitative and quantitative explosion and their modern evolution is characterized by:

- an unprecedented number of public employees;
- a wide range of new kinds of employee, to cope with the increasing diversity of the needs of both the administration itself and the citizens who benefit from its services;
- the heavy public cost of administrative activities, and their increasing inflexibility;
- the trade unionization of civil servants (trade union membership is frequently higher than in the private sector);
- the fragmentation and heterogeneity of administrative bodies, (leading to discrepancies in status, organization, and funding and to rivalry between different departments);
- the growing autonomy of many departments, each committed to its own particular logic;
- increasingly blurred distinctions between the public and the private sectors as a result of privatizations of public services (as well as of productive activities), of co-operation and interpenetration between private interests and parts of the bureaucracy, and of the import—with more or less speed and completeness—of private-sector methods into public organizations where they would formerly have been regarded as quite inappropriate.

Questions

- How do the recruitment, training, and advancement of civil servants affect the character and ethos of bureaucracies?

- Why do the institutional relationships between central and local government vary so much between different West European countries, and with what results?

- Is a wholly 'apolitical' Civil Service a desirable goal, and is it an attainable one?

- How and why have the parameters of the debate over private or public ownership of industries and services changed since 1980?

- Do West European bureaucracies rule or serve?

NOTES

1. This figure includes teachers and professional soldiers.
2. This figure includes only 'civil servants'. It does not include either soldiers or teachers. It should be noted that the Civil Service has lost 260,000 members since Margaret Thatcher came to power; most of these jobs have not disappeared, but have been hived off to non-governmental agencies, local authorities, or in some cases the private sector.
3. On European administrations, see F. Ridley, *Government and Administration in Western Europe* (Oxford: Robertson, 1979); J. Armstrong, *The European Administrative Élite* (Princeton, NJ: Princeton University Press, 1973).
4. In its 1985–6 report, the Treasury and Civil Service Committee again suggested experimenting with 'policy units' (the approximate equivalents of French *cabinets*). The government's response was that ministers who wished to could do so.
5. S. Tarrow, *Between Center and Periphery: Grassroots Politicians in Italy and France* (New Haven, Conn.: Yale University Press, 1977).
6. B. Dente, *Governare la frammentazione* (Bologna: Il Mulino, 1985).
7. S. Cassese, 'États, régions, Europe', *Pouvoirs*, 19 (1981), 19–26.
8. This is an extremely liberal law that makes it very easy to set up an association with a legal status.
9. S. Cassese, *Il Sistema amministrativo italiano* (Bologna: Il Mulino, 1983); D. Serrani, *Il Potere per enti: Enti pubblici e sistema politico in Italia* (Bologna: Il Mulino, 1978).
10. Note, however, that the Civil Service also comprises a category of 'industrial civil servants' that corresponds to State-employed workers (e.g. in munitions factories). Between 1979 and 1985, their number fell by 39%.
11. C. Flockton, 'Economic Management and the Challenge of Reunification', in G. Smith, W. Paterson, and S. Padgett (eds.), *Developments in German Politics 2* (Basingstoke: Macmillan, 1996), 226.
12. See J. Vickers and V. Wright, 'The Politics of Industrial Privatisation in Western Europe', *West European Politics*, 11(4) (Oct. 1988), 1–30.

13. See M. Dogan (ed.), *The Mandarins of Western Europe: The Political Role of Top Civil Servants* (New York: Sage, 1975).

14. See Cassese, *Il Sistema amministrativo italiano.*

15. The Bundesakademie in Bonn also rates a mention.

16. Contracts were introduced in 1968 in the health sector and were extended to public employees generally within the framework of Law no. 93 (1983).

17. But the very fact of forbidding a vital sector to become unionized comes to the same thing as denying it the right to strike.

18. V. Wright, in M. Balluteau, F. de Baecque, D. Lochak, B. Tricot, and V. Wright, 'La Politisation du Conseil d'État: Mythe ou réalité?', *Pouvoirs,* 40 (1987).

19. Y. Fortin, 'L'Administration centrale britannique', in IIAP, *Chronique de l'administration à l'étranger, Administration 1985* (Paris: La Documentation française, 1986, p. 104, and 1987, p. 99). See also R. Thomas, 'Devoirs et responsabilités des fonctionnaires et des ministres: Un défi pour les membres du Cabinet ministériel britannique', *RISA,* 52(4) (1986), 619–53. K. D. Ewing and C. D. Gearty, *Freedom under Thatcher: Civil Liberties in Modern Britain* (Oxford: Clarendon Press, 1990), 130–6.

20. The obligation of secrecy is laid down by the Official Secrets Act (1989), which replaces its predecessor, the Official Secrets Act (1911). Following a leak in the Ministry of Defence in 1984 (when a civil servant, Clive Ponting, passed documents relating to the Falklands War to a member of the opposition), a civil servant was charged in a court of law, but was acquitted. This occasioned considerable friction, which was prolonged in 1986 when the government attempted to stop the publication in Australia of the memoirs of a former Secret Service employee, Peter Wright.

21. In France, despite the law, access to administrative documents is still strongly discouraged by the administration. In Italy, there was no follow-up to a report produced in 1984 urging the adoption of more liberal policies.

22. E. Etzioni-Halévy, *Bureaucracy and Democracy: A Political Dilemma* (London: Routledge and Kegan Paul, 1953).

23. G. Timsit and C. Wiener, 'Administration et politique en Grande-Bretagne, en Italie et en RFA', *RFSP,* 30(3) (1980), 506–32; R. Putnam, *The Comparative Study of Political Élites* (Englewood Cliffs, NJ: Prentice Hall, 1976); Dogan (ed.), *The Mandarins of Western Europe;* J. Aberbach, R. Putnam, B. Rockman (eds.) with the collaboration of T. Anton, *Bureaucrats and Politicians in Western Democracies* (Cambridge, Mass.: Harvard University Press, 1981).

24. See E. Page, *Political Authority and Bureaucratic Power: A Comparative Analysis* (Brighton: Wheatsheaf Books, 1985).

25. A. Doig, 'A Question of Balance: Business Appointments of Former Civil Servants', *Parliamentary Affairs,* 39(1) (1986), 63 ff.

26. R. Rose, 'The Political Status of Higher Civil Servants in Britain', in E. Suleiman (ed.), *Bureaucrats and Policy Making* (London: Holmes and Meier, 1984), 151.

27. P. Hennessy, *Whitehall* (Fontana Paperbacks edn.; London: Collins, 1990), 635–40; C. Campbell and G. K. Wilson, *The End of Whitehall: Death of a Paradigm?* (Oxford: Blackwell, 1995); G. Fry, *Policy and Management in the British Civil Service* (Hemel Hempstead: Harvester Wheatsheaf, 1995); R. Pyper, *The British Civil Service* (Hemel Hempstead: Harvester Wheatsheaf, 1995); W. Plowden, *Ministers and Mandarins* (London: Institute for Public Policy Research, 1994); House of Commons, Treasury and Civil Service Sub-Committee: *The Role of the Civil Service: Minutes of Evidence, 23 November 1993: Sir Robin Butler, GCB, CVO* (London: HMSO, 1993).

28. Cassese, *Il Sistema amministrativo italiano*.

29. S. Cassese, *Questione amministrativa e questione meridionale: Dimensione e reclutamento della burocrazia dall'unità ad oggi* (Milan: Giuffre, 1977). The lower echelons were the first to be taken oven, then the entire Civil Service.

30. S. Cassese, 'The Higher Civil Service in Italy', in Suleiman (ed.), *Bureaucrats and Policy Making*, 35–71.

31. G. P. Storchi, 'Gli "Incarichi esterni" dei magistrati amministrativi', *Rivista trimestrale di Diritto pubblico*, 2 (1977), 596.

32. See, in particular, Arendt Lijphart's classic work, *The Politics of Accommodation: Pluralism and Democracy in the Netherlands* (Berkeley, Calif.: University of California Press, 1968), 197.

33. L. Moulin, 'The Politicization of the Administration in Belgium', in Dogan (ed.), *The Mandarins of Western Europe*, 47 f.

34. G. Lehmbruch, *Proporz demokratie* (Tübingen: Mohr, 1967).

35. H.-U. Derlien, 'Compétence bureaucratique et allégeances politiques en Allemagne', in E. Suleiman and H. Mendras (eds.), *Le Recrutement des élites en Europe* (Paris: Éditions La Découverte, 1995), 70.

36. The Germans describe the position of these civil servants as 'a provisional retirement'. The civil servant is allowed to draw 75% of his salary for five years.

37. See N. Johnson, *State and Government in the Federal Republic of Germany: The Executive at Work*, 2nd edn. (Oxford: Pergamon, 1982).

38. K. Dyson, 'West Germany: The Search for a Rationalist Consensus', in J. Richardson (ed.), *Policy Styles in Western Europe* (London: Allen and Unwin, 1982), 23.

39. J. L. Bodiguel cites the following figures (which include teachers) for France: 30% were civil servants in the governments of the Fourth Republic, 65% under the Fifth; 19.5% of Deputies were civil servants in 1958, 20% in 1968, 33% in 1973, 38.8% in 1978, 51% in 1981 ('Les Relations entre administration et partis politiques dans la France contemporaine', doctoral thesis, IIAS, Louvain, 1985).

40. See R. Mayntz, 'German Federal Bureaucrats: A Functional Élite between Politics and Administration', in Suleiman (ed.), *Bureaucrats and Policy Making*.

41. E. Suleiman, 'From Right to Left: Bureaucrats and Politics in France', in Suleiman (ed.), *Bureaucrats and Policy Making*, 107–35.

42. D. Gaxie, 'Les Ministres de la Ve', *Pouvoirs*, 36 (1986), 61–78.

43. E. Suleiman, *Politics, Power and Bureaucracy in France* (Princeton, NJ: Princeton University Press, 1974); E. Suleiman, *Élites in French Society: The Politics of Survival* (Princeton, NJ: Princeton University Press, 1978).

44. The discretionary appointment of federal judges by the President of the United States politicizes the federal judicial system just as, in France, the appointment of Councillors of State from inside the bureaucracy does, and the intensive practice of secondment within ministerial *cabinets* contributes towards the politicization of this court, whatever the individual behaviour of its members and whether or not they belong to a political party.

45. R. Crossman, *Inside View* (London: Cape, 1972), 78.

46. Moulin, 'The Politicization of the Administration in Belgium', 174.

47. Sir Archie Hamilton, former Armed Forces minister, on the BBC *Today* programme, 26 Feb. 1997.

48. According to S. Cassese, 223,000 applications were pending in 1987 (18,000 of which were

appeals). The average delay is about eight years ('Giudice amministrativo e amministra-zione', *Rivista trimestrale di Diritto Pubblico* section 1/87, p. 113).

49. A law of 20 July 1985 reorganized the federal Court of Accounts, which is defined as a body situated between the executive and the legislature. This is chiefly reflected in the procedures for appointing its President and Vice-President: they are elected by a majority secret vote of the members of the Bundestag, having been proposed by the federal government.

50. However, it should be pointed out that until quite recently in Britain (1977), a judge of legality was not simultaneously the judge of responsibility and this involved individuals under jurisdiction in long, complex and costly litigation.

CHAPTER 8

Constitutions, Politics, and the Judiciary

One of the oldest political demands is that a sovereign be bound by laws. In England, for example, the concept of laws that were open, public, and respected as well as enforced by the King was at the core of Magna Carta, albeit within a fairly limited area of the barons' relations with the monarch. Such a demand has wide-ranging implications: that the sovereign be denied the power to make up laws to suit the needs of the moment; that the law be applied consistently and impartially, to all those under its purview; that the law be seen to be impartial, with recognized processes and independent judges. In some cases, it also included the notion of a higher, divine or natural law, which could not be overturned even by the most solemn legislative processes available. In medieval and Renaissance France, for example, the Salic Law, which required that the succession to the monarchy should always pass, not only to a male, but through the male line (however indirectly), was considered non-negotiable, however disruptive its effects might be.

In practice there was never a truly independent judiciary in, for example, Tudor England or *ancien-régime* France, even if certain courts were able, especially in a context of competition between royal and seigneurial justice, to achieve a degree of autonomy. Nor did the transition to liberal democracy entail a radical transformation in the status of the judiciary; on the contrary. In Montesquieu's triad of legislative, executive, and judicial powers, the third has generally been the weakest. This imbalance in Western institutions, or at least in the European democracies, results from the fact that the democratic principle (of national or popular sovereignty) and the representative principle (that Parliament rules supreme) have long been regarded as more important than the third liberal principle underlying Western political systems, that of the moderation and separation of powers.

France is the extreme case in this respect. The hostility of the French Revolutionaries towards the judiciary had its roots in their desire to break the reactionary opposition of the judges that had been so patent in the last years of the monarchy: far from being guardians of liberties and due legal processes, the judges were seen as the oppressive servants of the King. Hence the Revolutionaries' denial, set out in the law of 17 to 24 August 1790, of any right to judicial control over the administration: 'Judicial functions are distinct and will always remain separate from administrative functions. On pain of breach of faith, judges may not in any way at all upset the operations of administrative bodies nor summon administrators before them for reasons connected with their functions.' This hostility to meddling by an over-mighty judiciary with rules decided by the sovereign people and its representatives persisted until 1958 and even later. The separation of powers, especially as interpreted by Napoleon, meant immunity for the executive from judicial interference in many areas, combined with various forms of hierarchical control emanating from the Justice Ministry that severely limited the judiciary's practical independence. A similar state of affairs prevailed in Italy, which was strongly influenced by the Napoleonic tradition up to and beyond Unification.

There are some points of similarity in the British case. Here, the settlement following the revolutions of the seventeenth century left the judges with several important freedoms: security of tenure 'during good behaviour' (which meant for life under practically all circumstances); the end of royal attempts to set up 'prerogative' courts outside the established judicial system; the preservation of, and right to develop, 'common law', based on jurisprudence; and, technically at least, the right to interpret law and to review the legality of executive acts. But judges also had to give up any right to which they might have aspired to challenge statute law passed by Parliament: the settlement confirmed the superiority of statute over common law. The sovereignty of Parliament (of the monarch, the Lords, and the Commons) was as immune from challenge by judges in Britain as the sovereignty of the 'nation' in France.

Germany, finally, might be seen to present a sharp contrast with the French case: frustrated revolutions, and thus monarchs who owed little if any of their legitimacy to national or democratic sovereignty; constitutions, both of the nineteenth-century States and of the Hohenzollern Empire, that limited the monarchy's powers and stressed the rule of law in the State (the *Rechtstaat*); and an independent judiciary, recruited by the monarchy but on objective criteria, and thereafter responsible solely to the law. This, however, was combined with an absolute prohibition on the right to judicial review of the law itself: ultimately, in other words, a rather similar position to the French on this crucial issue, even if arrived at from the rather different premises of the *Rechtstaat*, as opposed to the General Will.

To find a radically different tradition one must look to America. Not only was the US Constitution the first to implement the separation of powers and establish the fact in a written document; it also declares itself to be the product of a popular consensus and a social pact, and hence to constitute the supreme law of the land. But while the Founding Fathers were democrats of a kind, they were primarily liberals, wary of popular pressures and their expression as law. This explains Hamilton's words in the *Federalist*: 'The Constitution is the fundamental law . . . And when the legislative will, expressed as laws, finds itself in opposition to the will of the people as declared in the Constitution, judges . . . must bring their decisions into line with the laws that are fundamental, not with those that are not.' However, that interpretation in the *Federalist* was still no more than wishful thinking: as yet, nothing in the Constitution subjected judges to the check of constitutionality or granted the last word to the Supreme Court. That had to wait until 1803, when the Supreme Court's famous ruling in the *Marbury* v. *Madison* case, under the inspiration of Chief Justice Marshall, did uphold the superiority of the Constitution to which all are subject—including courts and tribunals, which are thus bound to uphold it. Thirteen years later, in the *Martin* v. *Hunter's Lessee* case of 1816, the Court confirmed that decision by ruling that it was itself the guarantor of the uniformity of judgements throughout the territory of the United States. The interpretations of the lower tribunals, including the Supreme Courts of individual states, were subordinated to those of the highest court in the Union.

We are thus presented with two strongly contrasting situations, two interpretations of the principle of the separation of powers and of the hierarchy of values and norms. Until the mid-twentieth century, the American concept, which stresses the virtues of 'constitutionalism' and the pre-eminent role of constitutional judges, was an isolated and marginal one. The American experience seemed alien to the history, myths, and mores, not just of Britain and France, but of the whole of the old continent. Europeans disregarded the analyses of Tocqueville, preferring Édouard Lambert's lapidary formula of 'government by judges'.[1] But the collapse of classic parliamentarianism in mainland Europe, the trauma of Nazism and Fascism, and the eventual demystification of law as such after the Second World War brought home the truth of Lammenais's lucid but bitter conclusion that 'the law can be oppressive.' In the light of the German courts' acquiescence in the Nazis' destruction of the Weimar Republic, and their subsequent role in applying and legitimizing Nazi laws, it is unsurprising that West

Constitutions, Politics, and the Judiciary

Germany's post-war Basic Law should stress fundamental human rights and the judiciary's duty to enforce them, as well as creating a Constitutional Court with wide-ranging powers to review the legislative and executive acts of the federal government. In the light of the Italian courts' comparable willingness to submit to Fascism, it is understandable that part of the Napoleonic edifice should be modified, and that safeguards for judicial independence as well as provision for a Constitutional Court (finally set up in 1956) should be incorporated into Italy's post-war Constitution. On the other hand, in the two countries that had not generated their own anti-democratic regimes the reappraisal was less fundamental. In France the experience of war produced change in this respect only late and indirectly: the inclusion of a Constitutional Council in the 1958 Constitution was not motivated by the wish to safeguard basic human rights; rather, it was to ensure that the main purpose of the new Constitution, the reinforcement of the executive, was met over the long term, and that there was no slipping back to the *régime d'assemblée* which had served France so ill in 1940 and earlier. In the United Kingdom, finally, war left the system unchanged.

The European countries that did address the problem of constitutional checks and balances in the post-war period adopted different solutions from those of the United States, many of them inspired by the doctrines of the highly influential Austrian jurist, Kelsen.[2] For Europe's constitutional courts had to be grafted on to traditions and a legal apparatus that were already solidly established, whereas in the United States, constitutional supremacy took root at more or less the same time as all the other national institutions and on the heels of a judiciary and a legal system very different from those of Europe.

The importance of the institutional and organizational role played by Constitutional Courts in most Western States (Britain being the major exception) explains and justifies their hybrid, semi-judicial, semi-political nature. They are certainly institutions that interpret laws and pass judgements, and on that account may be described as organs of jurisdiction. But because they operate as mediators, implementing a system of checks and balances, because of the nature of their powers, and because of the manner of their composition, they are also highly political bodies. This description is often rejected, the term 'political' carrying negative connotations of politicians, favouritism, and every sort of corruption. Some strong defenders of Constitutional Courts claim their functions are strictly judicial, while their critics accuse them of being the mere tools of politicians. These simplistic and reductionist views are neither realistic nor borne out by the evidence. Law constitutes an expression of political aims, decisions, and value systems. It is produced mainly by avowedly political bodies such as parliaments and governments whose legitimacy rests upon universal suffrage. But bureaucracies, judges, interest groups, and other actors, too, have a hand in law-making, in their cases without the sanction of universal suffrage. This dimension has to be fully recognized if we are to understand these institutions which are placed at the frontier of law and politics.

What is true of Constitutional Courts can also be said of the ordinary courts, or at least of a section of their activities. While judicial independence has been reinforced in most European countries since the war, this has not entailed an isolation from politics.

Such isolation is impossible, even below the level of Constitutional Courts, for four main reasons. In the first place, many judicial appointments are made by the political authorities, either directly or indirectly. In some countries, notably France, the debate about political influence in such appointments remains very much alive. Secondly, there is a continuous exchange of personnel between the political and the judicial spheres. Some ministers—a continental Justice Minister, a British Lord Chancellor—are at the interface by virtue of their function. Larger numbers may enter politics after a legal training and possibly several years' practice as well. Thirdly, judges are there to interpret laws, even where they cannot rule on their constitutionality, and on certain issues—industrial relations cases, for example—simply cannot avoid giving a judgement, one way or another, which is not only politically charged but is also shaped, with more or less discretion and explicitness, by the judges' political views. They are, in effect, part of the policy-making process by obligation. Finally, in criminal matters, the action of judges may depend on decisions taken (or not taken) by the political executive—typically an Interior or Justice Minister—to prosecute or to investigate a case.

In the complex web of relationships between politics and the judiciary, there is a sense in which elected politicians always have the 'last word': it is always technically possible for them to change the law (or even, ultimately the constitution), after a judicial setback. But such efforts may require an amount of time and a level of political commitment which politicians may not have. To that extent, the judges hold a real, and very political, power. It is, moreover, a power that has tended to grow. While it may be exaggerated to talk of a 'juridification of politics', a number of developments in recent years have given judges more to do, and many of the judges have shown more activism in doing it. These changes can be divided into two broad categories: the political and institutional on the one hand, and the social on the other. The political and institutional developments have been threefold:

The development of the constitutional courts themselves

These did not spring fully armed from constitutional texts; they tended to take several years to assert their authority. Although the German court was making landmark judgements by the 1950s, its Italian counterpart was not even set up till 1956, while the French Constitutional Council, created in 1958, was not fully operational until the 1974 reform giving parliamentarians the right to refer cases to it.

The shifting boundaries of the State

It is a truism to say that the post-war period multiplied the number and range of the State's interfaces with civil society, opening new possibilities of litigation and judicial activity. Some of these have already been discussed in Chapter 7. Less obvious is that more recent attempts to 'shrink' the State, to privatize its activities, or to transform its role from a direct provider of services to an enabler, has had at least a comparable result in its capacity to make work for the courts; for such a transformation requires a clear framework of legal contracts to be effective.

Europe

The European Court of Justice, set up by the Paris Treaty of 1950 and reinforced by the 1957 Rome Treaty, has been active and broadly successful in asserting the primacy of European over national law. In doing this, it has, paradoxically, enlisted the help of national courts. Its role is discussed in Chapter 10 (below, p. 389).

In addition, a wide range of social transformations have generated judicial activity:

Crime

In most Western countries, rising crime rates since the 1960s have brought questions of law and order, policing, judicial procedure, and sentencing to the centre of political debate. In Italy the growth in organized crime, especially from the 1980s onwards, did far more: it raised the question of complicity between the political class and the Mafia; and it brought the judiciary to centre stage in a war that claimed several lives among the investigating judges.

The end of consensus

The end of the post-war boom seriously weakened the political consensus in favour of the social market economy that it had underpinned. At the same time, even in Britain and Germany, the anti-Communism of much of the post-war generation was challenged by extreme left-wing movements from the late 1960s, and by the pacifist movement from the late 1970s. Both had implications for public order, as courts found themselves obliged to give rulings on industrial relations issues or to set limits on the right to demonstrate.

The rights culture

The post-war settlement in most West European countries had superimposed a notion of the collective good, most eloquently expressed in the Welfare State, on the previously existing rights of classical liberalism, essentially the security of persons and goods and freedom of expression. From the 1960s, however, the demand increased for the safeguard and extension of new individual rights and liberties. These included the right to non-discrimination on grounds of race, sex, or sexual orientation; the right to freedom of information; the right to consumer protection; or the right to clean air. Many of these rights were ultimately enshrined in law; but that frequently happened only after they had been asserted in the courts first. And they could become the focus of sharp controversies, especially where the Church opposed reform, as in the case of the abortion issue.

New technologies

The development of new technologies in areas as diverse as telecommunications and artificial techniques of human reproduction has frequently run ahead of legislators. When this happens, it is the courts that have to fill the gap in the law, at least temporarily.

Internationalization

The vastly greater ease of intercontinental transport opened all major European countries to large-scale immigration, whether from former colonial citizens, guest-workers, or asylum-seekers. All four countries have legislated in this area in recent years, usually more than once and usually (though not invariably) with a view to restricting immigration. Once again, it has been the courts who have been called upon to pronounce on the many intractable individual cases, or to ensure that due processes are being followed—a particularly sensitive course, as immigrants may lack their own representatives to defend themselves.

Political corruption

Both in France and Italy, corruption cases in the 1990s have affected not just individuals, but great swathes of the political system. This—combined, in Italy, with the fight against organized crime—has brought judges to the centre of political debate, and into conflict with the political parties that stand to lose from their investigations (that is, with most of them).

This chapter concerns the balance which has been struck, in a changing context, between unrestrained popular or parliamentary sovereignty (often amounting, from day to day, to the prerogatives of ministers) on the one hand, and 'government by judges' on the other. The main focus in the later sections will be on the interface represented by Constitutional Courts. However, as wider sections of the judiciary, both in continental Europe and in Britain (where there is no constitutional court), have also been drawn into the political arena, it is with them that we shall begin.

Ordinary courts in the political arena

There is no British Constitution, in the sense of a body of law set above statutes passed in Parliament, whether it be a Bill of Rights or a set of rules limiting the power of executive or legislature. Restraints on their activities are primarily political; the resistance in public opinion towards the idea of identity cards is a case in point. But such restraints amount to no more than what politicians think they can do with impunity in a given set of circumstances, and those circumstances may change. Northern Ireland is one case where Parliament, with the support of public opinion, has been willing to accept limitations on civil liberties that would not readily be tolerated on the mainland in peacetime. Such limitations needed no more than an Act of Parliament to come into being; for without a Constitution, Britain has not—cannot have—either a Constitutional Court or any form of judicial review of statutes to assess their constitutionality.

This does not, however, mean that judges have no power in the British political system. In the first place, there is a significant body of 'judge-made law', the common law

323

which has evolved over centuries of jurisprudence. This can be overridden by statute law, but significant areas of it remain, especially in the domain of penal law. Secondly, judges retain and use the right, as and when relevant cases come before them, to interpret or 'construct' laws, setting them to work in ways that may vary from what the legislators intended. Thirdly, they regularly do carry out the judicial review, not of laws (as a Constitutional Court would) but of executive acts, to assess their conformity with law. Where an action of the executive branch (whether the national government or a local authority) has exceeded what the law permits, it is considered *ultra vires* and illegal. Fourthly, Britain's growing links with Europe have come to represent a quasi-constitutional limitation on British law. This arises partly through Britain's ratification of the European Convention on Human Rights, but chiefly from membership of the European Union and the activism of the European Court of Justice, which led even judges of a generally conservative bent such as Lord Denning to revise their views about the absolute supremacy of British statute law.

In the absence of a Constitution, the separation of powers between the judiciary and the other branches is assured by ordinary law, or by simple custom. Important institutional links between the branches remain. The most striking of these is found in the person of the Lord Chancellor, who is simultaneously the highest judge in the land, and capable, if he so wishes, of exercising that role in court; a political appointee and a member of the Cabinet who plays an active role, with the Prime Minister, in the appointment of senior judges; and finally (although the function is largely ceremonial) the speaker of the upper house of the legislature. Moreover, the most senior judges are also members of the House of Lords. Among rules intended to ensure a separation between the branches is the ban on senior judges from sitting in the House of the Commons; the custom that 'Law Lords' are expected to sit on the non-party cross-benches in the Lords, and to proffer legal advice but not political opinions in debates there; and the normal practice that politicians are not expected to comment on judicial cases (though they can hardly refrain from doing so where the government announces an appeal against a judicial ruling applying to its own activities). It is also the case that judicial appointments are made after full consultation with senior members of the judiciary itself. This practice, however, has led to another frequent claim: that judges tend to be a narrow, self-recruiting hierarchy, of narrow social origin (the upper middle class, public school, and Oxbridge) and with conservative or reactionary views on all subjects.

One indication among many of the growing extent to which the judiciary in Britain has been drawn into politics is the number of applications for judicial review of executive acts, which grew from 500 in the early 1980s to 2,683 in 1992–3. The record of the courts through much of the 1980s suggests a practice in the settlement of the most politically sensitive cases that was a perfect complement to the right-wing policies of the Thatcher Government. Where prior to 1979 judges had shown a distaste for the legal immunities enjoyed by trade unions, they now chose to enforce the new industrial-relations legislation with rigour. For example, the 'secondary picketing' by striking workers, which the government was at such pains to stop, was punished by fines as high as £200,000, and above all, by the sequestration of the assets of the union concerned;

and the police were authorized to set up roadblocks to prevent striking miners from moving about the country. In another area that proved divisive in the 1980s, that of national security, judges tended to support the government's right both to keep sensitive information secret in the national interest and to define what the national interest was in such a context. Those who leaked such information could and occasionally were sent to prison, and the government's position was defended to absurd lengths in cases such as *Spycatcher*, involving the attempt to ban publication in the United Kingdom of a book that was freely available in the United States. A third area of controversy was the power of local authorities. Here the record is somewhat more balanced, but one historic case, in which the (Conservative-run) London Borough of Bromley successfully petitioned against the Greater London Council's policy of heavily subsidized fares on public transport, was a crucial battle in the government's war with the GLC which ended with the latter's abolition in 1986.

But to view the British judiciary as a mere instrument of Conservative governments would be a serious distortion. In the first place, the judiciary was almost alone among the major national institutions outside Parliament to resist the winds of Thatcherite reformism. Where the Stock Exchange, the universities, and the National Health Service, for example, all experienced more or less painful change, the lawyers managed to bury the reform proposals tabled by the Lord Chancellor, Lord McKay, in 1989. That independence was asserted more and more vigorously against the executive in the 1990s, particularly in the area of penal policy. Here the attempts of Conservative governments, anxious to improve on a poor record on law and order, to codify and prescribe the sentencing of criminals to a far greater extent than ever before, were fiercely (though ultimately unsuccessfully) resisted as striking at the heart of a traditional prerogative of the judiciary. Judicial review also regularly found a succession of Home Secretaries to have acted unlawfully, notably by not having used due legal process in expelling immigrants and asylum-seekers. Rather than political interference, therefore, the record of the British judiciary in the 18 years of Conservative rule shows a combination of conservative instincts with a jealous regard for their own institutional autonomy.

The German case shows some points of similarity with the British, notably in the way in which the courts were drawn into public-order questions in the early 1980s during the demonstrations against the installation of Cruise and Pershing missiles (as well as some particularities, notably the need to reconstruct the whole body of judicial institutions in the Eastern *Länder*). But the political role of the German judiciary is very much structured by the existence of a Constitutional Court with such exceptionally wide powers to handle cases referred to it by both institutions and individuals that the most politically sensitive issues tend, sooner or later, to be funnelled upwards.

The most spectacular confrontations between the ordinary judiciary and the world of politics, however, have arisen from the corruption investigations in France and Italy. The two cases present important points of similarity. Both are civil-law countries with judicial systems springing from a Napoleonic tradition. Central to that tradition have been the subordinate role of the judiciary in relation to the other branches, considered as embodying the General Will of the people; the existence of a separate jurisdiction to deal with the activities of the administration (the Conseil d'État, the Consiglio di Stato); the central role of the examining magistrate in the initial investigation and preparation of cases; and the presence of a public prosecution service, the 'arm of the executive within the judiciary', responsible for assigning briefs to examining magistrates for investigation, and controlled by a Minister of Justice with sweeping powers over the career advancement of the hierarchy of prosecuting magistrates. Such a system did not do away with the idea of an independent judiciary; the principle remained, as did that of the equality of all citizens before the law, and certain judicial institutions, such as France's Conseil d'État, acquired and defended over the years a reputation for competence and impartiality. It was nevertheless a system that offered a series of pressure points for the intervention of the executive, both in deciding on judicial advancement (more or less discreetly in the appointment of examining magistrates and judges, quite openly in that of prosecuting magistrates) and in the use of the Justice Minister's power to issue instructions to pursue, slow down, or halt a prosecution. Careful and unscrupulous use of these pressures could turn the justice system into a tool in the executive's hands.

Yet French and Italian judges in the 1990s have succeeded in confronting their respective political élites, bringing several leading figures to trial, forcing others into exile, and acting as catalysts for very public calls for a 'moralization' of politics and especially of political finance. The French scandals have involved, among other culprits, the Socialist Party, which was found to have set up a nationwide system of illegal finance, siphoning off money from building contracts, at its foundation in 1971; the millionaire and former Urban Affairs minister under Mitterrand, Bernard Tapie, convicted and jailed for bribing football players; the Gaullist Alain Carignon, former Environment Minister and mayor of Grenoble, also convicted and jailed for receiving percentages on the privatization of Grenoble's water services; and Jacques Médecin and Maurice Arreckx, the right-wing mayors of Nice and Toulon, towns in the Var *département* bordering Italy which has a particular reputation for attracting organized crime. Investigations have also produced strong suspicions—though not, so far, major convictions—in the management of the Île-de-France region, of the *départements* of Hauts-de-Seine and Yvelines (the wealthiest in France) and in the City of Paris, where Jacques Chirac was mayor before winning the presidency in 1995; and the murder of Yann Piat, a former National Front Deputy for the Var, has never been elucidated, but has been linked both to organized crime and to politics. In Italy, the first conclusive proof of corrupt practices in the Socialist party, when the Socialist director of a Milanese old people's home was caught in the act of collecting kickbacks in February 1992, led within less than two years to the collapse of all of the ruling parties. They were suddenly both deprived of the illegal funds and (with a change in the law in 1993) the state finance that had sustained them, and decapitated by the arrest or judicial investigation of their leaders: by September 1993, some 2,600 people, including 325 parliamentarians, were the objects of the judges' attentions.[3]

There were obvious parallels between the two cases. In both countries, corruption had reached systemic proportions: although individual politicians grew rich on the proceeds of corruption, the most striking features of the scandals were the regularity of the parties' use of illegal funding to the point of financial dependence, and the practice of *lottizazione*, or spoils-sharing, between several parties. This was standard practice in Italy; in France it was not unknown within a single case (for example, in all probability, the Île-de-France region), and even where it did not apply, there was a tendency for political parties not to exploit to the full each others' difficulties with the courts for fear of provoking an equally damaging reaction. In a context of complicity between parties, an important part of their function of criticism and scrutiny of government disappears—or rather, is left to the judges. In both countries, the judges attracted media attention and popular approval for their role, though their attempts to move into politics themselves (Thierry Jean-Pierre's election on the Goldsmith list at the 1994 European elections, and Antonio di Pietro's brief period in the Prodi government before being put under investigation himself) were inconclusive. In both countries the party politicians tried to protect themselves by smearing the judges' personal integrity or accusing them of political motivations, and by seeking reforms to diminish the gravity of the offence of political corruption (as was attempted by the Amato government, unsuccessfully, in 1993), to alter judicial procedures, or even to grant amnesties (two were passed in France, in 1988 and 1990): expedients which discredited more politicians than they sheltered.

The contrasts between the French and Italian cases are, however, equally striking. Most obviously, where the Italian judges, with help from the voters, brought about the downfall of their country's party system within two years, the French investigations have lasted for nearly a decade, producing patchy results and leaving the established parties weakened and besmirched but still standing. The obvious reason for this difference is that the scale of corruption in Italy (subject to the reservation that France still holds many unconcluded investigations) appears to have been much the greater of the two, reaching the order of ten times the total official income of political parties. French parties have faced financial embarrassment, but not collapse, as a result of losing illegal funding (though the recent generosity of public finance has helped them); and their internal affairs have been less dominated by fundraising and patronage.

But a second explanation of the difference between the course of investigations in the two countries lies in the considerably greater freedom enjoyed by the Italian magistrates to pursue their inquiries. The Napoleonic structures of Italian justice, much abused but never destroyed during the Fascist period, underwent substantial reform after 1945. In particular, the Constitution of 1948 provided for a Higher Council of the Judiciary, two-thirds of whose members would be chosen by the magistrates themselves, and the other third elected by parliamentarians. Its control over judicial appointments would reinforce the separation of powers. In addition, prosecuting magistrates were declared to be full members of the judiciary, with the same right of independence from political intervention as judges; and prosecutions of criminal offences were to be compulsory, rather than at the discretion of the Justice Ministry. Implementation took a decade, but the institution of the Higher Council in 1959 was a major step towards independence; the most important of the 'pressure points' offered by the Napoleonic system to the executive had been removed. Reforms in the 1960s and 1970s then went on to institute promotion through the judicial ranks by length of service rather than by merit. This innovation had the drawback of allowing the rise of potentially incompetent judges, but the advantage of removing them from the political or quasi-political pressures of an established political hierarchy. It was followed, in the 1970s and early 1980s, by notable pay increases for Italy's magistrates (no doubt thanks in part to their having cultivated and been cultivated by party politicians). Finally, the judges had already won widespread public sympathy through high-profile cases involving first the Red Brigades and then the Mafia. The effective declaration of war by the Mafia against the Italian State in the early 1990s, and the assassination of judges Borsellino and Falcone, gave the examining magistrates involved in the *Mani Pulite* (Clean Hands) corruption investigations additional prestige.

In France, on the other hand, the Napoleonic structures had remained more or less intact. The 1958 Constitution, like its Italian counterpart, established a *Conseil Supérieur de la Magistrature* responsible for proposing judicial appointments; but all nine members of the Council were appointed by the President of the Republic (until a 1993 constitutional reform, which shared out the nine appointments equally between the Presidents of the Republic, the National Assembly, and the Senate). Investigations by examining magistrates remain extremely difficult without instruction from the prosecution service, the *parquet*. Members of the *parquet*, while constitutionally independent, remain within a hierarchy controlled by the Justice Minister, who can both issue instructions and move magistrates about. Socialist Justice Ministers such as Michel Sapin and Henri Nallet did not hesitate to send written instructions to the *parquet*. The Gaullist Jacques Toubon made a public virtue of eschewing any such ministerial interventions in corruption investigations, but was ready to use other means to the same ends: for example, he appointed his own former *directeur de cabinet* to head the Paris *parquet*, whose responsibilities included the investigation of the Gaullist party in the capital, where Toubon had been an elected official for nearly two decades. Perhaps unsurprisingly, the inquiry has proceeded at a snail's pace. Toubon's successor, the Socialist Élizabeth Guigou, has made comparable public promises of a 'hands-off' policy. It remains to be seen how far she means it. But in the past, French magistrates have needed fairly unusual conditions to be able to proceed as they wish: either an instruction from an unusually zealous member of the *parquet*, or a Justice Minister willing to use the judicial system to harm political rivals (as was the case in some of the early investigations on the Socialist Party, which resulted from faction-fighting within the party in southern France); or an accumulation of evidence such that no prosecution can ignore it. These are hard conditions to fill. If the results of the French investigations have been more uneven than those of *Mani Pulite*, it was a result, not just of the relative extent of corruption in France and Italy, but also of the different characteristics of the two judicial systems.

Cases of political corruption are perhaps the most accessible tests of judicial independence from politics where the ordinary courts are concerned; and it is in the relatively unreformed Napoleonic institutions of France where the need for a reform of the judiciary is clearest—and most keenly felt among many magistrates. But the most regular and systematic contacts between politics and the judiciary, in France, Germany, and Italy, are to be found in Constitutional Courts.

Constitutional Courts and politics: organization and interconnections

The way in which Constitutional Courts operate should be considered from both an external and an internal point of view. What is their position in the juridical and political organization of the State? And how does their own internal organization reflect their twofold nature and function?

Constitutional Courts in the juridico-political system

The hybrid nature of Constitutional Courts is, at least in part, a consequence of the ambivalence of their terms of reference. Their first role is to 'declare the law' at the very highest level, that of the Constitution. That function could be analysed as pertaining to the traditional role of a judge, and at first sight appears to do so. But the Courts are also supposed to be (or to have evolved into) the instruments of a system of political checks and balances designed to prevent other bodies from exceeding their powers and to ensure that the values expressed in the Constitution are respected. The position of the Courts, as described in constitutional texts, in a sense reflects the initial uncertainty of the Constituents and the difficulty of establishing priorities regarding their twofold functions. For example, the German Basic Law ascribes to the Constitutional Court a type of organization and powers that indubitably stem from a 'political' point of view, but goes on to set out its rules and functions in Chapter 11, 'Judicial Power', where Article 92 states: 'Judicial power is entrusted to the judges; it may be exercised by the Federal Constitutional Tribunal, by the federal tribunals provided for under present fundamental law, and by the *Länder* tribunals.'

By contrast, the provisions of the French and Italian Constitutions reflect a more directly political bias. The 1958 French Constitution contains no suggestion that any real judicial powers should be recognized, let alone that a proper Constitutional Court should be set up. Instead, the primary function of the new Constitutional Council was to shield the executive from parliamentary encroachment. Although this function might adopt juridical means and forms, it was essentially political; the legislative aspect is patently far less important. In the 1948 Italian Constitution, provisions relating to the Constitutional Court were grouped together in Section 6 (magistrates' courts being the subject of Section 4), under the heading 'Constitutional Guarantees', a fact that underlines the particular character of what was, at the time, a new institution in the Italian political system.

If they are to perform their essential role correctly, Constitutional Courts must possess the means to make other constitutional bodies and lower courts respect their decisions. This would appear to be better guaranteed in a system such as that of the United States, where the Supreme Court is recognized as the highest authority within a comprehensive juridical order.

Although the politico-constitutional context of the French Constitutional Council (Conseil Constitutionnel) is very different, its evolution presents certain similarities with that of the American Supreme Court. The French Constitution recognizes that the Council's decisions 'must be observed by the public authorities as well as by all administrative and jurisdictional authorities', but initially this provision was limited in scope: it applied almost exclusively to Parliament; the executive was not affected. As for the Court of Cassation and the Council of State (Conseil d'État), they could refuse to accept the decisions of the Constitutional Council, since there were no means of enforcing the supremacy of its judgements. Although no institutional changes have been made to rectify the Constitutional Council's relative impotence, it has, solely through its jurisprudence, been able to convert its position into one of strength. Its 1971 decision on the freedom of association enabled it to increase its powers of control considerably, by including in the constitutional texts the Preamble to the 1958 Constitution which referred to both the 1946 Preamble and the 1789 Declaration of Rights. From the interpreter of an unexpansive Constitution of ninety-two Articles, the Council now became the guardian of a body of rights and concepts the content, meaning, and scope of which need constant interpretation if the policies of the legislature (or rather, essentially, the government) are to be satisfactorily monitored. At the same time, the Council's chief purpose now became, not so much to guarantee constitutional limits and procedures, but rather to rule on whether government action was compatible with the fundamental principles enshrined in the Constitution of the Republic. By so doing, the Council has increasingly determined the *content* and limits of the decisions of the legislative, administrative, and judicial authorities, although it has not acquired any extra powers to enforce respect for its judgements. In this respect the French Constitutional Council suffers by comparison with the American Supreme Court, which holds general, centralized powers of control. But, more and more, the devices of liberal democracy operate to the advantage of the French Council. The rules of the Constitutional State (*l'État de droit*) and the principle of the limitation of powers are the best possible assurances that its judgements will be respected.

Between the two extremes of the centralized control of the American system on the one hand, and the fragmentation of the French one on the other, there are a number of relatively effective intermediate solutions, as can be seen from the Italian and, especially, the German examples. It would have been perfectly possible for the Supreme Courts of Appeal and the highest administrative tribunals of Europe to acquire as large a measure of control over the constitutionality of their States as that assumed by the Supreme Court of the United States. However, the firmly established principle of the supremacy of the law, the 'timidity' (as Mauro Cappelletti puts it) of judges, and the dual nature of the Courts, each of which is supreme in its own order, all combined to prevent Judge Marshall's illustrious example from being followed in Europe. The problem that remained to be resolved was thus how to guarantee the effective supremacy of a Constitutional Court that had to be fitted into a pre-established judicial system.

Setting up a Supreme Court, as such, would have upset too many deeply rooted traditions and juridical mechanisms, so the Italians and Germans tried to establish bridges between judicial and administrative Courts and constitutional jurisdiction. The first bridge involved deciding that 6 out of the 16 constitutional judges in West Germany and 5 out of 15 in Italy should be drawn from the ordinary courts (as is also traditional in the United States, where a certain number of federal judges are invariably appointed to the Supreme Court). The second bridging device, which we shall consider in more detail later, meant empowering the magistrates of civil, penal, administrative, and financial courts to appeal to the Constitutional Court to rule on all questions of constitutionality that might arise in the course of any lawsuit.

It remained possible to go further. The German example shows that, despite the deep differences between the German and the American modes of monitoring constitutionality, it is possible to achieve equivalent effects. Article 93 of the German Basic Law enables it to monitor the application of laws. The Court may pronounce, in particular, 'upon constitutional appeals that may be brought by anybody who thinks that any of his fundamental rights or any of the rights guaranteed by Articles 20.4, 33, 38, 101, 103, and 104 have been infringed.' Since the Basic Law states that fundamental rights are binding upon all legislative, executive, and judicial authorities, this means that a citizen may attack any legislative, administrative, or court decision that *directly infringes* any of his rights. In practice, this provision affects mainly administrative or Court decisions, for it is quite rare for a law in itself to cause such *direct* infringement. Since the Court insists that all other avenues for seeking redress should have been exhausted, essentially the appeals that private individuals can bring before it are those against the injustice of either administrative or judicial decisions. In 1984, there were over 3,000 appeals against such decisions in West Germany and about 100 judgements were made. That may seem a low figure, but it is enough to guarantee respect for the jurisprudence of the Constitutional Court on the part of all civil, penal, and administrative courts and tribunals.

The juridical–political interface

Another illustration of the hybrid nature of Constitutional Courts is provided by their composition. In France, as in Germany and Italy, the modes of recruitment and the general characteristics of their judges show that, while Constitutional Courts are not purely political bodies, at the same time nor are they quite the same as other courts.

The *political* aspect is manifest chiefly from the nature of the authorities responsible for making appointments. In France, the nine judges are appointed by the President of the Republic and the Presidents of the two Assemblies (and the only individuals to be members of the Council as of right, namely former Heads of State, are of course eminently political figures). In Italy, of the fifteen members of the Constitutional Court, one-third are chosen by the Head of State, one-third by the two Assemblies in a joint session, and one-third by the supreme ordinary and administrative magistracies (three by the Court of Cassation, one by the Council of State, and one by the Court of Accounts). If the political nature of two of the three appointing authorities in Italy needed any stressing, we might point out that the process for setting up the Court was blocked for eight years (not until 30 November 1955 did Parliament manage to agree on five names) and that there was a violent clash between those who favoured discretionary powers for the Head of State (i.e. that he should be free to choose whoever he liked) and those who considered that he should simply ratify the government's choices (a suggestion which Einaudi, the first President of the Republic, and his successors successfully resisted).

In Germany, finally, the rule is that of the sixteen members of the Federal Constitutional Tribunal half should be appointed by the Bundestag and half by the Bundesrat. In practice, the Bundestag elects a proportionally represented commission of twelve, which chooses eight of the sixteen judges. To be elected, a candidate must obtain eight out of twelve of the commission members' votes, and this can only be achieved if the two major parties (the CDU–CSU and the SPD) come to an agreement, to the detriment of the smaller parties. (The Liberal Party can usually elect only one judge, the Greens not even one—at least, as things stand at present.)

The political character of the Constitutional Courts is also evident from the past (and in some cases, future) careers of the judges: in 1987, twelve of the sixteen West German judges belonged to a political party or were closely involved with one, and in Italy the same applied in the case of the judges appointed by Parliament and the President of the Republic. In France, these appointments are also politicized, not only by reason of the authorities who make them, but also because the Constitution lays down no conditions at all, not even regarding the judges' professional qualifications.

In these circumstances, and in view of the prestigious standing of the Courts, it is not surprising to find many leading political figures among the judges: the French Constitutional Council has included a future Prime Minister and President of the Republic, Georges Pompidou, among its members; the last president but one of the Italian Court, Leopoldo Elia, was tipped for Christian Democrat candidate for the Presidency of the Republic; both the German Constitutional Court and the French Council number former Ministers of the Interior and Justice among their presidents. And judges lucky enough to have been appointed sufficiently young are able to continue their careers when their appointments lapse, many returning to political life (this has been the case, particularly in West Germany and in Italy, where Bonifacio, the president of the Italian Court from 1973 to 1975, later even became Minister of Justice).

The *juridical* aspect of the Constitutional Courts is manifested in the nature of the conditions that are sometimes set upon appointments. France does not insist upon any professional qualifications and consequently in principle leaves the way open to politicians. The Council is thus in part composed of 'amateurs'. However, this is an anomaly that is likely to be progressively corrected, for the scope of the Council's jurisprudence is now such that political and party authorities will be increasingly disinclined to regard the function of judge as a sinecure fit to crown a career or as a way of pensioning off politicians considered to be in the way. In Italy and Germany the guarantees of professional competence are stronger. In Italy, the judges are chosen from the ranks of magistrates (or retired magistrates), professors from Faculties of Law, and lawyers who have been in practice for over twenty years. Professionalism here is thus well guaranteed, as it is in federal Germany, where three of the eight judges appointed by each of the two Chambers are recruited from amongst the members of a supreme federal court. The remaining five must possess the qualifications specified for judges by German law. In Italy and Germany, constitutional justice is thus entrusted to professionals; and, furthermore, the appointment procedures guarantee that these will be more than merely technical legal experts.

This balance of the juridical and the political seems a good compromise for the exercise of constitutional justice, for this cannot satisfactorily be entrusted purely to politicians, amateurs, or legal specialists in the narrow sense of the expression. The dream of a Constitutional Court with no political links at all is certainly unrealistic, so, in view of the necessity for a combination of the juridical and the political, we must reject the position adopted by René Chiroux when he writes: 'As regards the—crucial—problem of the appointment of members, the foreign models are not really satisfactory. The choice of constitutional judges in the United States, federal Germany, and Italy reflects political as well as juridical motivation. How can such a Court conceivably be above suspicion?'[4] It is not so much the modes of appointment and recruitment adopted by these countries that should be regarded with suspicion, but rather the absence, in France, of any rules either written or unwritten that would help the Council to function better. Besides, is it not unfair to the judges to suspect them of partiality simply because they were appointed by political authorities? Of course, the possibility is not altogether ruled out, but it is all the greater when the judge owes his appointment purely to favour, without being professionally qualified for the post. If, on the other hand, those selected can rely on their own solid professional capacities over and above political preferences, they will find it easier to resist political temptations and to serve the institution to which they belong, rather than dance to the tune of their original sponsors. How, otherwise, should we explain the illustrious example of Judge Marshall in 1803, that of the French Constitutional Council in 1971, and the even more impressive behaviour of the Italian Court which, though still scarred by the political polemics that surrounded the appointment of its members, had the courage to make its very first judgement a historic one?[5] Or, again, how to explain the fact that Earl Warren, Eisenhower's own nominee in 1953, was nevertheless the architect of one of the most revolutionary policies ever produced by the Supreme Court?

The autonomy that the judges, due in part to their professional abilities, can assert *vis-à-vis* their political partners is reinforced by the independence that they are guaranteed by the tradition of autonomy of the judiciary as a whole—an independence that is structured by the obligations to which they are subject. As they are appointed for a relatively long period (nine years in France and Italy, twelve in Germany), their positions are secure and, as a result, they may, if they wish, enjoy total freedom of decision. That freedom is enhanced by the elevated position of a Supreme Court: the pressures that may be brought to bear within ordinary judicial hierarchies by holding out prospects of promotion scarcely apply here. On the other hand, it would no doubt be helpful to introduce stronger regulations with respect to incompatibility between the functions of a constitutional judge and certain other functions of a political, public, or private nature. In particular, it would be desirable, in France, to ban not only combining the functions of judge with any elective functions (including those connected with local politics) but also standing for election without first resigning (as members of the Civil Service have to do in Britain if they wish to stand as candidates in general elections or by-elections). In other words, while the political and the juridical aspects of constitutional law are intertwined so closely that the notion of absolute 'purity' is impractical and utopian, it is, at the same time, fundamentally important to eliminate, through law or convention, all possibilities of the kind of political manœuvring that still all too frequently takes place in France. The appointments to the Council of former Presidents of the parliamentary Assemblies by their successors are examples of the kind of political 'facilities' that amply justify calls for a purer juridical world.

Political or juridical? submissions, proceedings, and judgements

When defining Constitutional Courts, should the emphasis be placed on the noun or the adjective? Are they first and foremost tribunals, or part of the constitutional machinery? This is not a purely formal question for, logically, the procedures for referring cases to the Courts, the pattern of proceeding, and the style of judgements ought to be determined or at least influenced by the answer. But in practice, logic has very little to do with the matter and, yet again, the conclusion must be that Constitutional Courts are rather like the bats of fable—sometimes mice, sometimes birds.

Modes of submission

Of all the systems operating in Western countries, the French solution is by far the most political and the least judicial in character, as regards both applications and patterns of procedure.

Initially, submissions to the Constitutional Council could only be made by four authorities: the Presidents of the two Assemblies, the President of the Republic, and the Prime Minister. Obviously enough, such a restriction and the nature of the authorities that were empowered to refer were hardly conducive to judicial activism on the part of the Council: between 1959 and 1974, neither the President of the Republic nor the President of the National Assembly had ever appealed to it. The President of the Senate had done so only three times and the Prime Minister only on six occasions, on questions of whether particular laws were or were not in conformity with the Constitution.

The fundamental change was introduced by the constitutional reform of 29 October 1974, which authorized 60 Deputies or Senators to appeal to the Constitutional Council. At the time, the opposition scoffed, calling it a *réformette* (or 'mini-reform'), despite the fact that it was they who were likely to benefit from it (since the majority was unlikely to appeal to the Council over any law that it had itself passed). In practice, however, the 1974 revision proved to be of crucial importance—possibly as important for the long-term stability of State institutions as that of 1962, which had ruled that the Head of State be elected by universal suffrage. The number of applications made to the Council now rose markedly with first the Socialists, then the right, and—after March 1986—the Socialists again, seizing almost every opportunity to appeal to the Constitutional Council. Between 1974 and 1981, 67 appeals were made, 63 of which emanated from Parliament; between 1981 and March 1986, there were 101, 99 of which emanated from Parliament; and between 1986 and 1988 there were 34. Quantitatively, the change was thus considerable. But qualitatively, the political nature of the operation remained unaffected, and it is reinforced by the required timing for applications to the Council, which must be made between the final passage of a bill and its promulgation by the President.

The procedures for referring bills to the Constitutional Council lead to a means of control that is both abstract and a priori (since appeals against a law must be made before it has come into force by being promulgated). It is a means of control that is generally favoured by French jurists, who value its simplicity. In 1981, Jean Rivero cogently summed up this attitude as follows:

To my mind it [the procedure] has one virtue, only one, but of prime importance; it is simple . . . Parliament approves a bill; before it becomes law, the Constitutional Council is requested to pronounce on it; if the bill is declared not to be in conformity with the Constitution, it disappears from the scene, through a trapdoor. It is still-born; the matter is settled.[6]

These methods of appeal in France certainly possess the significant advantages of simplicity and dispatch. But the drawbacks involved offset the benefits. The briefness of the interval of time between the adoption of a bill and the pronouncement of the Council's judgement (between a week and a month) has the effect of turning the Council into a kind of 'third chamber' to which the political minority can appeal and which thus has, as it were, 'the last word', while passions and polemics are still raging. In these circumstances, the Council's decisions tend to be regarded not so much as judgements, but rather as expressing either rejection or approval of the policies that the government has persuaded Parliament to adopt. However, this drawback may be mitigated by the attitude and behaviour of the judges themselves, for the systems used by other countries show that the Courts are not always unaffected by polemics.

Both in Germany and in Italy, modes of application to the Constitutional Court are sometimes political, sometimes juridical. Appeals of a political nature are, however, limited to certain specific questions. For example, in Germany, appeals may be made to the Constitutional Court by the federal government or by the *Länder* governments in cases of disagreement over the interpretation of their powers (West Germany saw thirty or so appeals of this nature between 1951 and 1989), and by constitutional bodies recognized by the Constitution to possess this right, if a clash arises with another constitutional body (twenty-seven such appeals between 1951 and 1983). The Court may also receive from the Bundestag, the Bundesrat, and the federal government appeals aiming to ban a political party for violating the principles of the Constitution. But in none of these cases is it a matter of pronouncing on the constitutionality of laws. The only possibility of a political appeal in this domain is to be found in Article 93.1, which states that the Court may receive appeals from the federal government or from a *Land* government 'in cases where clashes of opinion or doubts arise over the formal and material compatibility with constitutional law of a federal law or a *Land* law, or over a *Land* law's compatibility with any other federal law'. This type of control, known as an abstract control (*abstrakte Normenkontrolle*) is applied relatively infrequently: since coming into being, the Court has been requested to deal with only about fifty cases of this kind.

Similarly, in Italy, the Constitutional Court may receive appeals from the government when regional laws appear to contravene the correct division of tasks between the State and the regions; and it may also be requested by the regions to pronounce upon State laws which appear to infringe their own powers (although the Court has no power to suspend the laws in question). The Court may also pronounce upon disagreements that may arise between different constitutional bodies but, as in Germany, the Court's activities in this area remain marginal.

The essential activities of both the German and the Italian Courts concern appeals of a judicial nature. In both countries, the judges of any court may (whether or not at the request of the parties involved) appeal to the Constitutional Court to rule on the question of any law's constitutionality.[7] Thus, in Italy, over 90 per cent of the appeals heard concern concrete litigations that have been referred to the Court. This was also the case of 765 appeals heard by the West German court between 1951 and 1983.

Finally, in Germany, when the fundamental rights of an individual have been infringed, any citizen concerned may appeal to the Constitutional Court. The appeal may either be lodged directly against a law within one year of its promulgation (this is relatively uncommon), or against an administrative or judicial decision concerning the application of the law within one month of the publication or notification of the decision, but only after first seeking satisfaction from all other courts of appeal. There are more appeals of this nature than any other kind (several thousand every year, 3,382 in West Germany in 1984) and they threaten to overwhelm the Court. To cope with this rising tide of direct appeals, it has been obliged to delegate to a Committee of three judges the task of sifting requests, which they can reject by declaring them to lack motivation. This leaves the Court itself with no more than 100 or so decisions to make on individual appeals. However, this procedure still has considerable significance, for the Court's decisions on concrete litigation and, in many cases, on the judgements involved in it make an important contribution to the task of maintaining the real supremacy of constitutional values and ensuring that they penetrate every branch of the law and every aspect of social life.

As this survey shows, in some countries the modalities of appeal are mixed (Germany and Italy). In others such as France, they are not exactly in conformity with the role that these Courts ought to play or that they claim to play. The political nature of the appeals made to the French Constitutional Council is increasingly at odds with its growing function of pronouncing on the constitutionality of laws.

Procedures

The procedure followed in such actions also testifies to the hybrid nature of constitutional lawsuits. In some respects, it resembles that for normal litigation. But a number of peculiarities are occasioned by the political nature of the Court. Even so, the political nature of the composition of a Court is not directly reflected in the procedure that it follows. This heterogeneity is one of the most unusual peculiarities of Constitutional Courts. The differences between one country and another are most marked in respect of the opportunity for debate (or lack of it) and the degree of secrecy by which actions are affected.

It is in France, where the Council is often accused of being a third Chamber, that the procedure for constitutional 'trials' least resembles the normal practices of Courts. Despite a few slight improvements introduced recently, the procedure remains characterized by its secrecy and the limited opportunities that it affords for hearing both sides of the question.[8] Until Robert Badinter took office as President of the Council in 1986, those appealing were allowed to present their own observations but were not informed of any written comments that had been passed to the Council, in particular those formulated by the Prime Minister's office. Since 1986, the notes produced by the government's General Secretariat have been passed to the applicants, and in response they may present their own arguments, to which the General Secretariat is invited to reply. This undeniably constitutes a measure of progress. But secrecy remains the general rule, from start to finish, as is manifested by the fact that decisions are given collectively, with no hint of dissenting views. On this subject, Laurent Cohen-Tanugi writes as follows:

In order to protect itself against accusations concerning its 'political' nature, and to take up a firmly 'juridical' stance, the Council usually presents its decisions in the traditional manner for conveying judgements in French Courts of Justice: arguments are syllogistic, judgements peremptory, and all underlying disagreements, all considerations of juridical policy, and all dissenting opinions are concealed . . . Yet constitutional law, by its very nature, lends itself even less than other branches of law to arbitrary claims of absolute truth couched in a correspondingly formal style. The Council's determination to express its decisions in the formal language of the French juridical tradition thus sometimes produces *precisely the opposite of the desired effect*, in that it conveys an impression of arbitrariness to the public.[9]

Symptomatic of this confusion was the Council's reaction in 1986 to the criticism that its decisions were provoking. On 12 August it issued a statement that sums up all the ambiguity of its interpretations of the terms 'juridical' and 'political'. The Council drew attention to the fact that 'the Constitution had entrusted it with the *juridical mission* of verifying that the laws submitted to it were in conformity with that Constitution. It therefore declined to become involved in the current argument since this fell within a *political context*'[10] (our italics).

In Italy, on the other hand, the procedure does allow for contradictory debate. All parties involved in the litigation which has given rise to the prejudicial question, and, similarly, the *Avocattura dello Stato*, may submit memoranda and relevant information up until twelve days before the hearing. The hearing is open to the public and, to date, the presiding judge has never needed to close the Court to the public, as he is legally authorized to do—not even in the most polemical of cases, for example, that of the law on abortion. The Court then retires for its deliberations (which may necessitate several meetings), and a vote is taken. Once the decision is made, the President entrusts one judge with the task of formulating it and, as in France, it is considered to have the approval of the Court as a whole.

The German version is an even better example of the hybrid nature of constitutional action. Klaus Schlaich writes as follows:

Procedures before the federal Constitutional Tribunal are characterized by the fact that the circle of individuals empowered to make declarations before the Tribunal is much wider and more flexible than in other judicial procedures. One peculiarity of Constitutional Law . . . is that the business of interpreting, changing, or perfecting Constitutional Law is also part of the political process, in which everyone participates and by which everyone is affected.[11]

However, that participation varies according to the type of appeal and monitoring action involved:

- In the case of the abstract monitoring of laws, the constitutional bodies concerned can only make statements.
- In the case of constitutional appeals made by individuals, the plaintiff and the body affected by the appeal (the legislature, the administration, or some other court) can present all the evidence, statements, and information necessary for an examination of the matter.
- In the case of the concrete monitoring of laws, the Bundestag, the Bundesrat, the federal government, and (if necessary) the *Länder* governments and Assemblies may all take part in the procedure and make their own statements.
- Finally, the court may, on its own initiative, invite any expert or qualified person (e.g. politicians, party representatives, or jurists) to state their views.

In principle, oral debate is the rule, but in practice this is reserved for the most important and most political cases (in which hearings sometimes last for several days), a fact that further strengthens the political image of the Court. On the other hand, the fact that it is possible to challenge a judge strengthens the juridical aspect of the action. At the end of the action, the Court announces its decision and, in some cases, also reports any dissenting opinions.

Judgements: a united front or room for dissent?

This is a particularly delicate point upon which we must briefly dwell, for the countries we are considering resolve the question of concurring or dissenting opinions in quite different ways. France and Italy take shelter behind the principle of secrecy and collegiality. In contrast, West Germany opted for transparency and open debate in 1971, and this has been the rule in the Federal Court both before and since unification. In France, demands for the recognition of dissenting opinions have been few, and meanwhile the secrecy of Council deliberations is in general well maintained (at least, the leaks that occur do not spread beyond a limited circle of initiates). In Italy, by contrast, there exists a strong movement in favour of dissenting opinion and the judges themselves have entered into the debate. For example, in 1971, Leopoldo Elia suggested that minority judges should be able to express their disagreements. However, when he was on the point of being elected President of the Court in 1976, he adopted a much more reserved line on the matter. Furthermore, quite frequently Italian judges who favour the introduction of dissenting opinion make their own opinions on Court decisions known in articles or interviews, thereby implicitly indicating how they will vote. These 'reasoned confessions', as they have been called, are individual and partial substitutes for the expression of dissenting opinion, and at the same time bring pressure to bear in favour of changing the present rules. What disadvantages and what advantages would accompany the recognition of dissenting opinion?

The three main disadvantages may be summed up as follows:

1. Dissent would introduce doubt as to the correctness of decisions and undermine them by diminishing their dignity, solemnity, and authority. To some extent, dissent constitutes 'a worm i' the bud'.

2. Dissent would strengthen the politicization of the Court, for the parties or groups involved would make use of the debate in Court to further their own polemics. As a result, the Court would, as the Italians put it, be 'instrumentalized' by the political forces.

3. By making the judges' votes public, the recognition of dissent would expose them to all kinds of more or less hidden and heavy pressures from many quarters, ranging from the authorities who appointed them, through political parties and interest groups, to public opinion in general as expressed, in particular, by the Press. Secrecy and collegiality, on the other hand, are more likely to guarantee their serenity and independence.

339

However, the advantages of recognizing dissent are by no means slight:

1. It would improve the technical quality of judgements. In the first place, the existence of a majority and a minority would make it unnecessary to look systematically for compromise decisions, designed to give offence to none (the French Constitutional Council's decision on the law establishing new constituency boundaries might fall into this category). Secondly, the existence of a minority opinion certainly makes for more vigorous and better-argued majority decisions. At the same time it rules out amateur judges. Unlike, for example, their counterparts in the French Constitutional Council, the German judges anticipate (and, implicitly, accept) that their decisions will provoke political controversy and criticism, and go to great pains to argue and justify them.

2. Dissent keeps the public informed. It demonstrates that the rule of law— especially in this area—is not inscribed in stone, but is instead the product of an interaction of norms, values, and principles with contingent concrete situations for which there *could* be a different interpretation—and indeed *might* be in the future. The clash of opinion also makes the point that agreement over results takes into account differing views on the means of achieving them. The recognition of dissent involves relying on the intelligence of citizens, who are presented with all the complexities and difficulties inherent in any clash of ideas rather than with the simple virtues of an edict.

3. The expression of dissent may encourage the Courts to produce dynamic jurisprudence, for it constitutes more than simply 'throw-away' remarks on the part of the minority judge or judges. It manifests the kind of cogent and strictly argued debates that stimulate and enrich constitutional reflection. Furthermore, it often constitutes a stage in the evolution of jurisprudence, for with the passing of time a minority view may gather to it enough judges to constitute a new majority.

4. Finally, dissent constitutes a concrete reflection of the reconciliation of the rule of law and democratic principles, at the very highest level, that of the Constitution. Because the Courts are positioned on the borderline between the juridical and the political spheres, within the framework of systems that aim to be democratic, they cannot restrict themselves to pronouncing on the law through some mysterious alchemy that is beyond the understanding of the public. The debate that arises out of a plurality of opinions may prove very beneficial to constitutional jurisdiction. In the first place, it shifts discussion from the field of political suspicions and polemical accusations that may or may not be without foundation to the more fundamental area of values and the more technical one of juridical argumentation. Secondly, judges may derive from the organization of open and pluralistic debate of this kind a substitute for the 'democratic legitimacy' that will never be theirs. Thirdly, the attention that the public pays to the decisions of the Court, and the ensuing debate, framed by the variety of opinion that exists within the Court, constitute the best possible guarantees against tendencies toward 'government by judges'. 'Who will guard the guardians?' is the question often asked, to underline the dangers that the existence of supreme judges might introduce were they subject to no controls at all. And there is really only one

answer to that question: the public, the media can guard the guardians, but only if debate and reflection continue to be enriched and fuelled by a plurality of opinions instead of withering away under the onslaught of sniping attacks and sarcasm, as all too frequently happens.

The juridical and the political: abstract or concrete controls?

The monitoring of laws, whether undertaken a priori or a posteriori, is described as 'abstract' when it does not arise from any litigation over the application of a particular law. The type of monitoring known as 'concrete' (always a posteriori) takes place when a lawsuit or some kind of litigation has arisen. It would certainly be misleading to assimilate abstract monitoring to political controls and concrete monitoring to juridical ones, for the experience of Constitutional Courts amply demonstrates the extent to which the juridical and political aspects are intertwined in both cases. All the same, it is true that abstract controls tend to be more political, concrete ones more juridical. Abstract monitoring is the rule in France, the exception in Germany and Italy, and unknown in the United States. In the last three countries, it is through the concrete monitoring of laws that the Courts generally operate, so the French model is an unusual and isolated case.

There are two possible variants of concrete monitoring:

1. The question of unconstitutionality may be a preliminary issue that any judge whose function is to arrive at the facts of the case himself settles, under the supervision of superior courts or, if necessary, the Supreme Court. That is what happens in the United States.

2. Alternatively, the question has to be settled by the Constitutional Court, to which the judge whose function it is to establish the facts of the case may make application by tabling a preliminary question. This is the solution adopted by Germany and Italy.

Both these solutions have been rejected by the majority of French jurists, even though Italy and Germany have demonstrated that 'teamwork' and collaboration between ordinary courts and the Constitutional Court are perfectly possible.

The French advance various arguments to justify this rejection:

1. They contrast the complexity and slowness of concrete monitoring to the simplicity and speed of the French system of abstract and a priori controls.[12] This argument does not lack force, but a fair rejoinder would surely be that, in the first place, there is no reason why the two modes of control should be mutually exclusive; indeed, if they were both in use, the safeguarding of constitutionality would be considerably strengthened. Secondly, if too much store is set by the virtues of simplicity,

the genuine *complexity* of *real* problems may be missed and a simple system confused with what may actually be an inadequate and rudimentary one.[13] Furthermore, even if the problem of slowness (particularly in Italy) is undeniable, would it not be preferable to try to put that right, rather than to forgo the advantages of a better method of control?

2. Concrete monitoring would choke the Constitutional Courts with appeals that are of secondary importance, misguided, or fantastic, whereas, in France at present, 'the responsible and competent authorities whose duty it is to make applications to the Council do not submit to it laws whose constitutionality is not in any doubt'.[14] It is true, of course, that abuses do occur, as in all social practice. But why does the answer, once again, have to be a hyper-élitist and paternalistic solution? (Is it that appeals on matters of unconstitutionality are considered too important to be entrusted to ordinary judges or to citizens?)

3. The German and Italian solutions turn the Constitutional Courts into 'super-Supreme Courts of Appeal', which, as Louis Favoreu states, are obliged 'essentially, to devote themselves to examining ordinary affairs in which they have to pick out the constitutional questions and then scrutinize them'.[15] And Favoreu goes on to ask: 'Is that really their role? Have they not somehow been "diverted" from their original function?'[16]

Favoreu's criticism seems curious and in contradiction with his other—perfectly correct—thesis that the process of monitoring constitutionality 'upsets' the law, 'progressively projecting over its other branches the shadow of the Constitutional Council'.[17] For what better way of ensuring that constitutional values do indeed permeate not only the law but also the very lives of citizens than by concrete monitoring of the law *as it is applied*? As Mauro Cappelletti remarks: 'In this way, the question of constitutionality is, so to speak, illustrated and made concrete by the episode in real life that is laid before the judge of a lower court.'[18] Far from a constitutional judge demeaning himself by taking the trouble to examine 'ordinary affairs', he may find this to be a way of bringing his authority and full influence to bear and truly making sure that the rule of law (*État de droit*) is respected.

4. Finally, it is argued that declaring a law to be unconstitutional several years after its adoption would undermine juridical stability. The repeal of a law is clearly bound to be upsetting to juridical stability. But the question merits further examination. In the first place, is the juridical stability of an unconstitutional law preferable to the discontent occasioned by its repeal? A politician might answer 'yes', but would a jurist?

Secondly, juridical stability is a relative notion in systems that each year adopt numerous new laws (many of which truly do upset the existing situation—for example, where fiscal matters are concerned) and regulations which, for their part, *are* submitted to a posteriori juridical controls. Now, in a formal hierarchy, laws may be placed above regulations, but that does not necessarily correspond to the 'real' situation. In other words, the content of decrees may be just as (or even more) important than that of certain laws, but the former can nevertheless be annulled after being in force for a few years. So, although the problem of juridical stability is no doubt one that should be taken seriously, let us not delude ourselves: these days, juridical instability is more likely to be caused by volte-faces and instability within the legislature than by any warning shots fired by judges.

Finally, as the German situation shows, it is perfectly possible to correct the drawbacks of total retroactive annulments by resorting to less drastic methods: partial recisions, declaring the law in question to be constitutional provided it is correctly interpreted (i.e. as by the Court), provisional regulations covering a period of transition, declaring a law to be unconstitutional but not retrospectively so, and so on.

Our review of all these arguments has provided an opportunity to indicate the advantages of concrete monitoring. But, as Mauro Cappelletti has pointed out, another of its merits is that it keeps in step with the times: 'This is a modern concept, according to which rights and the law have a life of their own; and it stands in contrast to the static, outdated scholastic concept of a purely a priori system for monitoring laws.' And as Leopoldo Elia, a former president of the Italian Constitutional Court, has pointed out, from a practical point of view this makes it possible to correct old laws that contravene the Constitution. This is an argument of considerable force, when it is remembered that French law still includes dozens of legacies from the past that infringe individual liberties. For the most part they lie dormant but are, unfortunately, always there to be revived for use in particular circumstances. In conclusion, then, it should be emphasized that concrete monitoring makes it possible to revise archaic legislation in a flexible manner that is both in harmony with the problems and spirit of the present age, yet at the same time is based upon superior norms. The use of a concrete and diffused (that is to say, open) system of monitoring to declare antiquated laws to be unconstitutional makes it possible for the legislature to intervene and modernize the legislative apparatus in response to the needs, imperatives, and fundamental values that a particular lawsuit brings to light.

The political and juridical tasks of constitutional judges

The tasks of constitutional judges are in part defined by the supreme law of the State but also, as we have seen, to a large extent by the Courts themselves. It would appear from the written statutes and the praetorian directives of the Courts, taken together, that the Courts fulfil three types of function. The first is to guarantee constitutional equilibrium; the second to protect rights and liberties. Their third task (which we shall not be examining here) varies from country to country and seems to be of relatively secondary importance. It includes functions such as those of monitoring the political scene and the organization of national elections.[19]

Constitutional judges as the
guarantors of constitutional equilibrium

This task may be evaluated from two points of view: territorial and functional. We shall consider the former first.

There is a territorial aspect to the principle of the separation of powers. Constitutions establish a balance between the powers attributed to central authorities and those guaranteed or granted to local ones. Generally speaking, there is more at stake here than simply the technical means of distributing responsibilities. The division of powers reflects an agreement or consensus reached at some particular point, recorded in the Constitution and (in most countries) guaranteed by a Constitutional Court. However, that guarantee is in general directed more to maintaining the fundamental principles upon which the system is based than to insisting on scrupulous respect for the balance initially established. For it is quite clear that, although Constitutional Courts may have been successful in preserving the basic federal, regional, or unitary nature of the German, Italian, and French systems, they have not stood in the way of the progressive centralization that has been taking place, in various forms, more or less everywhere.

In Germany and Italy, the roles of the Constitutional Courts are explicitly defined by the basic law. The German Basic Law (Article 93) makes the Karlsruhe Court responsible for pronouncing judgement on disagreements between the federation and the *Länder* or between one *Land* and another; and the Italian Constitution (Article 134) assigns to the Italian Court a similar responsibility both to monitor regional legislation and also to rule on conflicts between the State and the regions, or between one region and another, over the powers attributed to them. In both countries, the influence of the Constitutional Courts has been useful in preventing excessive inequalities, but has never been anything like as crucial as that of the Supreme Court of the United States. In West Germany, it was originally thought that the Constitutional Court would play a fundamental part in maintaining the balance between the various *Länder* that make up the federation. In the event this appears to have remained a role of secondary importance before the mid-1980s. The Court only had to pronounce judgements on such matters on about thirty occasions, for in general the Bund and *Länder* authorities have preferred to find more practical solutions to their conflicts (special agreements, mixed commissions, negotiation). The famous decision of 28 February 1961, in which the Court denied the federal government the right to set up a national television channel, certainly must have encouraged them to do so. In its pronouncement, the Court drew attention to the unwritten principle of 'friendly behaviour' (*Bundesfreund*) within the federal framework, and specifically declared:

In all cases in which the Federation attempts to set up any agreement with constitutional implications relating to a matter in which all the *Länder* have an interest and by which they are all affected, the obligation to behave in a federal fashion precludes it from acting on the principle of 'divide and rule', that is to say of seeking a solution in dividing the *Länder*, for instance by trying to make agreements with some and then forcing the others to abide by them.

The Court went on to enumerate at length the elements of this code of federal good conduct, which had, in effect, enabled West Germany to construct a new system of co-operative government. On the other hand, the Court did not attempt to discourage the trend toward centralization that has emerged as a result of the overlapping powers of the Bund and the *Länder* in most domains. It has always declined to monitor the (extremely vague) clause in the Basic Law that allows intervention on the part of the Bund in the interests of standardizing living conditions throughout the federal territory. However, from the mid-1980s onwards an increasing number of suits were brought to the Court by *Länder* over financial questions. They took on a new dimension when the Federal Republic absorbed the much poorer East.[20]

The functions attributed to the Italian Constitutional Court in matters concerning the territorial distribution of powers have placed it in a rather difficult position, for in cases of unconstitutionality in regional law (denounced by the regional commissioner for the Republic), the government can make application to the Constitutional Court. At the same time, though for reasons to do with *opportunity* and in cases where conflict arises, the government may also request Parliament to pronounce and decide on the matter. Practice in the 1970s showed that the government manifested a marked tendency to resort to law in its political clashes with the regions, referring to the Court many conflicts that had been artificially dressed up to look like constitutional questions. At the time, the Court was inclined to favour centralization, harbouring reservations regarding the regional experiments then in progress and, as a result, the relations between the regions and the Constitutional Court tended to be marked by distrust. However, as the regional process became more stable and attitudes within the Court changed,[21] the regions came to regard the Constitutional Court as an instrument that guaranteed their autonomy. Their confidence has been increased by instances of jurisprudence that have been more favourable to them. For example, in its decision of 12 October 1983, the Court ruled that even a situation of 'economic emergency' could not justify the violation of a fundamental constitutional principle such as that of regional autonomy.

The question of territorial equilibrium is less acute in France, where the Constitution lays down the unitary nature of the Republic. But even here, the construction of a united Europe coupled with the decentralizing reforms of the Socialists has afforded the Constitutional Council a chance to reaffirm and underline the principle of the indivisibility of the Republic (Decision 76.71 of 30 December 1976) and also to clarify the meaning of national unity in particular in 1982 in connection with the Prefects' powers to monitor territorial authorities and that of decentralization[22] (in 1982, in connection with the special status of Corsica).

Constitutional Courts also take action to rule on certain clashes that arise between one constitutional body and another, or to see that their respective rights to exercise the powers attributed to them are respected. The first point to note in connection with clashes between different constitutional bodies is that constitutional definitions and juridical interpretations of what constitutes such a body vary in scope from one country to another. Germany extends the concept to include the political parties and, in certain circumstances, the various parliamentary groups, or even members of the Bundestag. But, despite its own wide powers, the German Court has demonstrated considerable prudence, as have the Courts of other countries, whenever it came to intervening in clashes between different public authorities. Between 1951 and 1983, the West German Court took action in only twenty-seven cases of this kind. Like the Italian Court, it is careful not to venture too far into the domain of political activities, maintaining that it is not its function to rule upon this type of conflict. Here are a few examples: despite the fact that the conditions in which the Bundestag was dissolved in 1983 were 'suspect' from the point of view of whether they were in conformity with the spirit of the Constitution, the Court did not take steps to rescind the President's decision (on this point, see Chapter 5). The Italian Court, for all that it is sometimes accused of being a co-legislative body, has made no pronouncement on the way in which parliamentary parties and groups have interpreted certain constitutional provisions. (For example, it ruled that it was up to the Senate and the Chamber to decide—each possibly adopting a different solution—on how to interpret constitutional provisions regarding parliamentarians' absenteeism.) Many observers have criticized the Council's failure to impose controls on the French President and have deplored his discretionary powers. But had the Council decided that the Head of State *must* sign the decrees and ordinances that the Council of Ministers presents to him, this would have led to a daunting revision of the practices and spirit of the Constitution which would, in its turn, have placed the French President in the relatively powerless position of his German, Italian, and Austrian counterparts.[23] In the final analysis, Courts refuse to enter into head-on clashes with other constitutional bodies or to become involved in exclusively political questions, for example, in which the executive and the legislative authorities are in conflict. It is a policy that makes perfectly good sense, for a judge lacks the credentials of democratic legitimacy which alone could give him the authority to settle purely political conflicts.

However, the attitude of self-restraint that leads all the Courts to accept the privileges of the executive and the rights of Parliament does not reduce the Constitutional Courts to the role of purely passive spectators. In the first place this is because, as has been noted, they have been given specific powers to control the executive or Parliament. Secondly, on the periphery of the exclusively political core of the powers of public authorities, Constitutions have established rules that it is the Courts' duty to guarantee. Thus, all these Courts are particularly vigilant with regard to procedure (the regulation of parliamentary business, the rights of members of parliament, the right to amendment, etc.) and to ensuring that the powers attributed to each of the constitutional bodies are respected. For example, the German Court has censured the government's practice of exceeding the budgetary limits laid down by Parliament; the Italian Court has ruled that the purely cosmetic reform of a law by Parliament did not justify ruling out the organization of an abrogative referendum; and the French Constitutional Council, responsible for seeing that Articles 34 and 37 are respected, has increasingly acted as the guarantor of all the rights of Parliament (insisting on detailed laws of entitlement, and producing a stricter interpretation of the right of governmental amendment).[24] By indirect means such as these, the Courts are able to keep the activities of constitutional bodies on course and, above all, can prevent excessive imbalances from developing between them.

It is interesting to note that the Constitutional Council, initially regarded as the French executive's 'watchdog', is now increasingly seen as the guarantor of the powers of Parliament (even if, for reasons of political expediency, the Presidents of both Assemblies have, on the contrary, declared that the Council was flouting their rights). It has even been successful in spelling out the manner in which certain presidential prerogatives should be exercised. In short, while the functions of Constitutional Courts are narrowly circumscribed to the extent that they may not pronounce on the rights or wrongs of purely political quarrels, the function that remains to them is one of crucial importance, namely, to ensure that the rules of the game are respected and, when necessary, to clarify them.

Constitutional Courts as the protectors of rights and liberties

This major function of Constitutional Courts is often described, using the German terminology, as 'the protection of fundamental rights'. It is a felicitous formula, for it emphasizes the essential importance of the defence of rights and liberties. But it could be misleading, for it might give the impression that 'less fundamental' rights are not (or are less well) protected. In fact though, the guarantee provided by the constitutional judges affects more than purely concrete rights. It is also, indeed above all, a procedural guarantee. Since no right is absolute, it may be permissible to infringe the right of public assembly or the right to property, but only in certain circumstances and when strict rules are observed in so doing. As Judge Douglas eloquently observed of the United States, in the *Wisconsin* v. *Constantineau* case [1971], 'It is significant that most of the provisions of the Bill of Rights are procedural, for it is procedure that marks much of the difference between rule by law and rule by fiat.'

All Constitutional Courts fulfil that function, but the ways in which each of them operates have been largely determined by history and the particular ideological and institutional context. For instance, the French Constitutional Council had to create efficient instruments of control by including in its terms of reference the Preamble to the Constitution which, in its turn, refers back to the 1946 Preamble and the Declaration of 1789. By contrast, the German and Italian Courts were created largely as a result of the Constituents' desire to set up an instrument for the protection of liberties.

Secondly, the duties of the various Courts are laid down by reference to texts that in some cases go back many years (e.g. to 1789) but in others are of recent date (the end of the Second World War)—texts whose contents vary from one country to another. In some, the provisions are so specific as to resemble legislative rules, in others they take the form of far more general proclamations. Article 1 of the German Constitution declares: 'The following basic rights shall bind the legislative, the executive and the judiciary as directly enforceable by law.' On the other hand, in Italy, where the Constitution is less explicit, a long-standing uncertainty exists as to the proper meaning of 'rights' of an economic or social nature which, unlike classic 'rights', might in truth simply represent political aspirations. In the long run, both in Italy and in France, where uncertainty also arose over the implications of the 1946 Preamble, it has proved necessary to include all preambles and proclamations within the terms of reference even if, by reason of their vagueness or generality, it is not always possible to draw the same concrete conclusions from each and every one.

Thirdly, to cope with provisions that are out of date but nevertheless still affect both those who are currently involved in politics and also the circumstances of the moment, a certain amount of interpretation or 'maieutics' (a term often used in Italy) is called for. This interpretative function of constitutional judges has frequently been criticized, for it obviously implies creative powers that sometimes clash with the views and interests of other public authorities. The situation in Italy is revealing in this respect. Between 1948 and 1956, when the Constitution was finally adopted, the Italian Supreme Courts (the Council of State and the Supreme Court of Appeal) persisted in regarding the rights recognized by the Constitution simply as proclamations that carried no positive juridical force. However, with its very first decision, in 1956, the Constitutional Court ruled that those rights constituted its points of reference and its guiding thread. It is not surprising that the interpretative function of the constitutional judges is frequently condemned: it clashes sharply with two notions that are deeply rooted in the Western democracies, particularly in mainland Europe, namely, the principle of parliamentary sovereignty and that of the 'passive' nature of a judge's role: he may declare the law but not create it.

All the Constitutional Courts have nevertheless embarked upon this course of interpretation—a course so perilous that some fear it could lead to the creation of a 'totalitarian' State. The German Court refers to the theory of 'open constitutional norms', which it may interpret, and to the principle of proportionality, according to which, to be constitutional, actions of the State must be 'necessary, appropriate, and not excessive'. The French Constitutional Council has also embarked upon a course of praetorian interpretation that depends upon reference to 'the fundamental principles recognized by the laws of the Republic', principles which Danièle Lochak has described as 'vague' and 'intangible'. Laurent Cohen-Tanugi rejects such criticisms:

By using its judgements to establish the parameters of a definition of French democratic values, the Constitutional Council has, over the past fifteen years, been filling a gap (compensating for the absence of any founding Declaration of Democratic Rights) and correcting a failure to keep up with the times (France's persistence in regarding democracy as a concept established once and for all rather than a continuing process). Since the Constitution was not founded upon any definition of democratic principles, those principles can only be determined *retrospectively*.

This is a project that should definitely be on the agenda at a time when so much heart-searching is being devoted to the proper functions of the State, the law, and the market, in the context of the French Social Compact.[25]

The effectiveness and the range of the Courts' protection of fundamental rights depend partly upon the degree of boldness displayed by constitutional judges as they interpret and apply the Constitution. But the procedures for eliciting their judgements and monitoring controls (mentioned earlier) are equally important. The advantages of concrete, a posteriori monitoring undeniably outweigh those of abstract controls that may be either a priori or a posteriori, for concrete monitoring makes for a better understanding of the real juridical and social position and guarantees that greater respect for the decisions of the Constitutional Court is shown by the other authorities (legislative, administrative, and jurisdictional).

Conclusion

Throughout this chapter we have been mindful of the ambivalence of Constitutional Courts: they can neither be reduced to mere political bodies nor limited to functions of a purely judicial nature. This hybrid situation is clearly a source of tensions and of both strengths and weaknesses. In short:

1. As political bodies, the Constitutional Courts are, as Robert Dahl has pointed out, policy-makers that have gradually evolved methods of their own which endow them with a very real power not simply of reform but also of decision. Not content with the radical but clumsy and unsubtle weapon of outright annulment, they have developed other techniques: partial annulment, declarations of constitutional conformity within the limits of the Court's own definitions, partial and qualitative annulment as in Germany (the law remains in force, except in certain situations as defined by the Court), deferred annulment (also in Germany), which renders the law precarious and forces the legislature to intervene, judgements that go on to indicate what action should be taken (in Italy and the United States), and so on. But despite all their ingenuity as policy-makers, the Courts are limited by two constraints that are part and parcel of their position within the institutional framework as a whole. In the first place, they cannot implement their own decisions but must rely on other branches of government to put these into effect. Secondly, the Courts can only *react* to the appeals that are made to them in the guise of either direct applications or preliminary rulings. Unlike Parliaments and governments, they can never initiate policies. To pronounce their judgements, they are obliged to wait for a favourable opportunity to arise. This may either take the form of a new law (as in France) or of a legislative, administrative, or judicial decision that gives rise to a judgement of unconstitutionality.

2. This inherent weakness of courts in general and Constitutional Courts in particular explains how it is that the judiciary has sometimes been regarded as 'the least

dangerous branch' as Hamilton put it,[26] despite the fact that nowadays many politicians (from all countries and all parties) and some jurists condemn their praetorian activism[27] on the grounds either of principle (popular legitimacy and sovereignty) or expediency (regarding the judges as 'troublemakers'). It is true that, in spite of their weakness, over the past few decades the Courts have managed to confirm their position as essential partners and have imposed their authority, thanks to the force that one major principle carries in the Western democracies: namely, that the rules that currently apply must be respected and the law of the strongest rejected, even if this means the stronger party climbing down. It is solely by virtue of this provision that Constitutional Courts in the past, and the European Court of Justice today were (or are) able to impose their decisions even upon governments and to do so without weapons and without soldiers: the force of a principle can be enough.

But precisely because the supremacy of the Courts' decisions does not result from force, they have to do their utmost to prevent that reserve of respect and obedience from being eroded. Judges consequently need to be particularly aware that their legitimacy, which stems from their ability to elicit respect for the highest values enshrined in the Constitution, must never be substituted for the democratic legitimacy of other branches of government. This leaves them with scant room for manœuvre but at the same time it makes it possible to replace the Jacobin (and—albeit unwittingly—potentially totalitarian) formula 'You are juridically in the wrong because you are politically in the minority' with another. This is the fine definition of the role of the legislature given by the French Constitutional Council in its judgement of 23 August 1985: 'The law can only express the general will by respecting the Constitution.'

3. A constitutional judge, by reason of his eminent role, operates in a different temporal context from other political protagonists. The body of norms to which he refers is constituted by values that are, so to speak, atemporal (liberty, natural justice, etc.) or at least not confined to that 'present moment' which so much obsesses other political agents, subject, as they are, to the pressure of society's demands and electoral deadlines. However, the judges are not solely oriented towards the past; they must also guarantee that those values continue to be respected in the future, a fact that accounts for and justifies the prescriptive function of their judgements. Faced with a dictator, they would be useless at blocking his progress; but, by virtue of the way in which they strengthen the bases of democracy, they are essential instruments for preventing any dictator from acceding to power.

But there is another temporal aspect that is peculiar to Constitutional Courts, although variations occur from one system to another. It relates to the length of the judges' mandate and the methods employed for replacing them when it has run out. Constitutional judges are in general appointed or elected for longer periods than the members of other constitutional bodies[28] and they are replaced in batches or gradually, either because that is the rule laid down by the Constitution or because individual judges die whilst in office. A number of important consequences ensue. For one thing, the impact of successive political changes is tempered, but without this leading to stagnation even over a short period, since new arrivals and departures amongst the judges are frequent. For another, the mode of recruitment ensures a certain heterogeneity and pluralism. In other words, the situation combines all the ingredients likely to make for a gradual evolution of policies of a less contingent nature than those of other public authorities. Of course, from time to time jurisprudence is affected by profound changes of orientation, but in general the jurisprudential policy of Constitutional Courts is characterized by incrementalism. Finally, we may emphasize the following point: the Constitutional Courts of the Western democracies work to reconcile democratic, representative, and liberal principles (the principles of the popular will, government through representatives, and powers limited by a system of checks and balances). The Courts can accommodate governments of both the left and the right. Their role is to remind them that in fulfilling their mission they must never cease to respect the Constitution and the values that it expresses. In the last analysis, the judges must have enough power to check power without usurping it; this is the source of both the grandeur and the complexity of their role.

Questions

- What factors have reinforced the importance of the judiciary in West European political systems in recent years?

- How and how far can the independence of the judiciary be ensured in practice?

- Why has no West European country chosen to model its constitutional court on the US Supreme Court?

- 'Properly considered, the French Constitutional Council is not a constitutional court at all, but merely a player among others in France's political game'. Discuss.

- Is the 'government of judges' a real or an imaginary danger in political systems with strong constitutional courts?

NOTES

1. E. Lambert, *Le Gouvernement des juges et la lutte contre la législation sociale aux États-Unis* (Paris: Giard, 1921).
2. The jurist Kelsen provided the inspiration for the Constitutionality Controls introduced into the Republican Constitution of Austria between the two World Wars (1920–38).
3. On the judiciary and corruption in Italy, cf. M. Rhodes, 'Financing Party Politics in Italy: A Case of Systemic Corruption', *West European Politics*, 20(1) (1997), 54–80; C. Guarneri, 'The Judiciary in the Italian Political Crisis', *West European Politics*, 20(1) (1997), 157–75; and P. McCarthy, *The Crisis of the Italian State* (2nd edn., Basingstoke: Macmillan, 1997), 139–65.
4. R. Chiroux, 'Faut-il réformer le Conseil Constitutionnel?', *Pouvoirs*, 13 (1986), 107–24.
5. In its first *sentenza* of 5 May 1956, the Court decided that it could rule on all laws, whether

passed before or after the Constitution. This enabled it to sift through the legislation of Fascist inspiration that was still in effect in many sectors.

6. J. Rivero, 'Rapport de synthèse', in L. Favoreu (ed.), *Actes du colloque 'Cours constitutionnelles et Droits fondamentaux'* (Paris: Economica, 1982), 526.

7. There are, however, a number of important differences between the two systems. In Germany, the validity of laws from before the Constitution (and not modified by later laws) is investigated by ordinary tribunals, whereas in Italy, the Court is competent to rule in either case. Furthermore, actions brought before the German Constitutional Court lapse when the main case is over; in Italy, in contrast, once a constitutional action has started it is deemed to have an existence of its own.

8. The rules and practices of the Constitutional Council lend a particular and no doubt unintentional spice to the comments of B. Poullain, its former Secretary-General. He writes: 'The procedure is simple. There is nothing mysterious about it. Clearly defined authorities can submit the law to controls, at a particular moment. The effect of the decision is clear: if the law conforms to constitutionality it is promulgated. If it does not, it never sees the light of day' ('Remarques sur le modèle français de contrôle de constitutionnalité des lois', *Pouvoirs*, 13 (1986), 179–94).

9. L. Cohen-Tanugi, 'Qui a peur du Conseil Constitutionnel?', *Le Débat*, 43 (1987), 58.

10. Cited in P. Avril and A. Gicquel, 'Chronique constitutionnelle française (juillet–septembre 1986)', *Pouvoirs*, 40 (1987), 166.

11. K. Schlaich, 'Procédures et techniques de protection des Droits fondamentaux', in L. Favoreu (ed.), *Les Cours Constitutionelles européennes et les droits fondamentaux* (Paris: Economica, Presses Universitaires d'Aix-Marseille, 1982), 138.

12. Reference is often made to the delays (around two to two and a half years) accumulated by the Italian Court. What is seldom mentioned, however, is the fact that the Court, in its capacity as a High Court, had to hear the cases of the Ministers involved in the Lockheed affair, and this halted all its constitutional work for a period of eighteen months. The smooth processing of applications has never recovered.

13. The irresponsibility of the administration in the 19th cent. was also a simple solution . . . except for the wronged citizens.

14. Poullain, 'Remarques sur le modèle français de contrôle de constitutionnalité des lois'.

15. L. Favoreu, *Les Cours Constitutionnelles*, Coll. Que sais-je? (Paris: PUF, 1986), 127.

16. Ibid.

17. L. Favoreu, 'L'Apport du Conseil Constitutionnel au droit public', *Pouvoirs*, 13 (1986), 17–31.

18. M. Cappelletti, 'Necessité et légitimité de la justice constitutionnelle', in Favoreu (ed.), *Actes du colloque 'Cours constitutionnelles et Droits fondamentaux'*, 499.

19. e.g. the German Court is an electoral tribunal and also a High Court of Justice. The Italian Court also passes judgement on political matters. The French Constitutional Council rules on national electoral operations and also acts in a consultative capacity—which is why it is called a 'Council' (such as the application of Article 16, and the decisions taken in connection with it).

20. See C. Grewe-Leymarie, *Le Fédéralisme coopératif en République Fédérale d'Allemagne* (Paris: Economica, 1981); R. Sturm, 'The Changing Territorial Balance', in G. Smith, W. E. Paterson, P. M. Merkl and Stephen Padgett, *Developments in German Politics* (Basingstoke: Macmillan, 1992), 121–2.

21. e.g. President Lidio Paladin (President from 1985) is one of the most eminent specialists in regional law.
22. See, in particular, L. Favoreu, 'Constitution et décentralisation', *Revue de Droit Public*, 5 (1982), 1259–87.
23. M. Troper, 'La Signature des ordonnances: Fonctions d'une controverse', *Pouvoirs*, 41 (1987), 75–91.
24. G. Carcassonne, 'A propos du droit d'amendement: Les errements du Conseil constitu-tionnel', *Pouvoirs*, 41 (1987), 163.
25. Cohen-Tanugi, 'Qui a peur du Conseil Constitutionnel?', 63.
26. In A. Hamilton, J. Madison, J. Jay, *The Federalist or, The New Constitution*, ed. Max Beloff, 2nd edn. (Oxford: Basil Blackwell, 1987), 396.
27. J. M. Ely, *Democracy and Distrust: A Theory of Judicial Review* (Cambridge, Mass.: Harvard University Press, 1980).
28. The main exception is the French Senate, whose members are elected for nine years, i.e. for the same duration as the judges of the Constitutional Council.

CHAPTER 9

European Integration

The inclusion of chapters on the European Union (EU) in a comparative European politics textbook involves obvious inconsistencies. Until the 1980s, many readers would have seen what was then the European Community simply as a branch, albeit an important one, of foreign policy, an area not systematically covered in this book. Such a view cannot now be sustained: the EU has become a far more complex, substantial entity than any mere international organization. A second objection is that, however far integration progresses and however interesting the insights yielded into its workings by comparative politics, the EU cannot be strictly compared to its own component parts, the member states. It is for this reason that the EU, unlike the four nation states, is largely confined to the background of the preceding thematic comparisons, but is the central theme of the next two chapters.

Despite such formal untidiness, the case for incorporating the EU into any study of Western European political systems remains overwhelming, for three reasons. Firstly, the EU's impact on national policy is now systemic and wide-ranging, covering as much as 60 per cent of what was formerly seen as domestic policy-making.[1] The EU thus defines palpable limits to the sovereignty of member states, encroaching upon the activities of their political, administrative, and judicial systems, despite the vital areas—such as foreign and defence policy, monetary policy, policing, welfare systems, or schooling—that remain, for the moment, largely under national control. Few national ministries can now escape the additional burden of co-ordination, both with other ministries and groups nationally, and at European level, that EU membership necessitates. Furthermore, the EU has reinforced and accelerated a more general tendency towards growing policy interdependence: such areas as environmental policy or drugs control are increasingly difficult to categorize as 'foreign' or 'domestic' policy. Secondly, the EU's impact on the domestic politics of all four member states considered here has been critical. In Britain, divisions over Europe were the harbinger both of Mrs Thatcher's fall in December 1990 and of the Conservative Party's decisive election defeat of May 1997. In France, the decision to remain in the European monetary system in March 1983 entailed a historic economic U-turn by the ruling Socialists; nine years later, the referendum of September 1992 on the Maastricht treaty revealed the extent to which the European issue divided electorates of all mainstream parties. In Germany, European economic and monetary union (EMU) was the central goal of Chancellor Kohl's later years in office, and the convergence criteria for EMU the main source of his travails. In Italy, the EMU-inspired attempts to bring deficits under control dealt a body-blow to the corrupt patronage structures which had underpinned half a century of republican politics, and contributed to the implosion of the party system. Thirdly, the EU has attracted a political science literature of increasing range and sophistication, which has fuelled comparisons with aspects of national systems and led to new perspectives on national as well as European politics.

The very diverse theoretical approaches to the EU can be divided into two main groups: those derived from international relations, and those based on comparative politics.[2] Of the former, intergovernmental or realist models insist on the centrality of interstate bargaining in the 'high politics' of European integration, but suffer from a tendency to see states as unitary and relatively unchanging actors. Neo-functionalists, on the other hand, have paid ready attention to interest groups and other non-State actors, arguing that they help to give the process of European integration a momentum of its own as it 'spills over' from one economic sector to another. Good at explaining periods when integration moved briskly forward, neo-functionalism proved less satisfactory in accounting for those periods when it ground to a halt: hence its fall from favour from the late 1960s and recovery from the mid-1980s.[3]

Comparative-politics approaches focus less on the process of European integration than on how European politics and institutions work: less on the 'high politics' of interstate bargaining, and more on the 'low politics' of day-to-day European policy-making. Rational-choice analysts, for example, have applied game theories to the EU's institutional processes in order to assess their potential for decisions based on consensus, or on the dominance of one or more national actors or institutions.[4] Pluralists draw inspiration from Heclo and other observers of United States in the 1970s, stressing the permeability of European institutions to the activities of an extremely wide range of interest groups, which are able to operate in a context of considerably greater freedom than that prevailing in the more fixed structures of Europe's national systems. Among institutional approaches, some stress the collegiate character of many European decision-making processes, and their layering into those operating entirely at the supranational level, those that work concurrently between the European and the national levels, those that depend on intergovernmental bargains, and those left entirely at the national level: a model that bears resemblances to Germany's 'co-operative federalism'.[5] On the other hand, the 'élite accommodations' that serve to paper over deep national divisions within the EU, and the resulting degree of consensus inside the system despite at times strong dissensus outside, are features shared by models of 'consociational democracy' such as Belgium, Holland, or pre-civil-war Lebanon.[6]

All of these approaches yield valuable insights: but none can be considered as providing a complete analysis. For, as Vincent Wright observes, the EU is many things at once: it

combines elements of an incipient federation, a supranational body, an intergovernmental bargaining arena and an international regime. It is treaty-based yet displays the features of putative constitutionalism (. . .) negotiations may be closed and secret, based on nonpublic bargaining principles rooted in concepts of classical international law between states, or they may be pluralistic and transparent as the result of the development of the Union into an area of interest articulation and aggregation.[7]

To embrace this messy reality we need the approaches both of international relations and of comparative politics. This chapter concentrates on the integration process and the international relations that have shaped it. It includes:

- a narrative account that both demonstrates how unevenly the integration process has advanced, and introduces the major institutions and competences acquired by the EU in its first 40 years;
- a presentation of the international-relations contexts, including the historical legacy of European wars, the opening and closure of the Cold War, and the boom and crisis of European economies, within which integration has unfolded (and, on occasion, almost halted);
- an analysis of the varied and changing approaches to integration of the four major member states covered in this book, concentrating on the Franco-German 'motor';
- an assessment of the impact on integration of leadership at national and European levels;
- a concluding evaluation of two main theoretical approaches to integration.

Chapter 10 covers the functioning of the EU's major institutions, closing with an assessment of the current crisis in the EU and of the difficulties involved in its becoming a fully state-like entity.

European integration: an uneven course

The aim of 'Ever closer union between the peoples of Europe' appears in the preamble to the Rome Treaty which created the European Economic Community. In one limited sense, it has been realized. Since the Treaty's signature on 25 March 1957 (along with a second treaty, creating the European Atomic Energy Commission, or Euratom), European institutions once created, and competences once transferred to them, have become part of an *acquis communautaire* that has never been dismantled or handed back to member states. European integration has never gone into reverse. Nor, though, has it proceeded very smoothly for very long; on the contrary, it has stalled, or slowed down dramatically, on repeated occasions. Signs at the end of the twentieth century, moreover, suggested that the process became more, not less, problematic as it advanced.

From victory in Europe to the Rome Treaty, 1945–1957

The cluster of international organizations set up in Western Europe between 1945 and 1951 were a response both to economic dislocation and to the passage in the space of two years from world war to cold war. The governments of Belgium, the Netherlands, and Luxembourg used plans drawn up in the war years to form the Benelux Customs Union in January 1948. In March of the same year, the Brussels treaty created a seven-member defence pact, the Western Union, that was to form the West European foundation of NATO. A month later, fifteen West European states created the Organization for European Economic Co-operation (later to be transformed into the OECD) to administer the inflow of Marshall Aid from the United States. In 1949 the efforts of a variety of associations, grouped as the European Movement under the patronage of Sir Winston Churchill, were crowned with the foundation of the Council of Europe, which proceeded to draw up a European Convention on Human Rights with a European Commission of Human Rights and a European Court of Human Rights to monitor and (in principle) to enforce its observance. The Council of Europe went on to establish an impressive record of promoting cultural co-operation, while the Court of Human Rights, despite the reluctance of many Convention signatories to accept its jurisdiction, has a substantial caseload and considerable moral authority. Nevertheless, the achievements of the Council of Europe have fallen well short of the (almost unbounded) ambitions of its promoters.

A radically different, though not less idealistic, approach to European integration was embodied in the European Coal and Steel Community, set up by the Paris Treaty of

1951. This was largely the initiative of France's first Planning Commissioner, Jean Monnet, and Foreign Minister Robert Schuman. It responded to a precise problem: how to allow West Germany's steel production to recover while both avoiding the dangers to France's own steel industry of a revived and competitive neighbour, and allaying the fear that political assertiveness would return with West Germany's economic recovery. The ECSC's record of achievement is varied: it had created a common market in coal and steel by 1953 and built thousands of homes for coal and steel workers, but it was territorially circumscribed (Benelux and Italy joined, making six members in all, but Britain, the largest producer at the time, stayed out) and it failed to act effectively against either cartels or the European coal glut of the late 1950s. But the ECSC's importance for the more general process of European integration was considerable, in two ways. Firstly, the ECSC's four main institutions were retained, with certain changes, for what became the EU. They were:

- a supranational High Authority, whose nine members were bound to work 'in full independence for the general interest of the community', with the power to issue binding decisions, and disposing of a budget raised from the turnover of coal and steel firms;
- a Council of Ministers, able to approve or reject the most important decisions of the High Authority, and consisting of ministers of finance, economic affairs, or industry, delegated by member states;
- a Court of Justice (quite distinct from the European Court of Human Rights) to ensure the full and fair application of ECSC decisions;
- a consultative Common Assembly composed of delegates from national parliaments.

Secondly, the Paris Treaty set a pattern that other treaties would repeat: a Franco-German bargain as the centrepiece of the whole; a transfer of some competences to a clearly supranational institution (contrasting with the intergovernmentalism of earlier European organizations); and a gradualist approach which sought to arrive at federalist aims through a succession of limited, practical steps, which would then, it was hoped, create the conditions for further advances. A sign of this last point was given by the appointment of Jean Monnet as the first President of the High Authority.

Two further European initiatives owed their genesis to Monnet. The first, the plan for a European Defence Community (EDC) launched in 1950 by the French Premier René Pleven, responded to another aspect of the 'German question': how to rearm West Germany without recreating Hitler's Wehrmacht. West German rearmament was transformed from a distant issue to an immediate one by the Korean War, and its consequences in terms both of East–West tension and of the strain on America's military resources provoked by the commitment in the Far East. The EDC Treaty, signed in Paris in May 1952, envisaged nothing less than a European army of half a million men with an integrated command structure down to division level, a common budget, and a common uniform. But it failed to win ratification by the French National Assembly in

1954, and was never implemented.[8] This setback owed much to continuing post-war mistrust of Germans under arms, to the unruliness of France's Fourth Republic Parliament, and to the fact that EDC was, to a greater extent than the ECSC, a reaction to short-term events. But it also illustrated the political difficulties inherent in transferring to Europe a policy area which, although limited, has traditionally represented a core attribute of national sovereignty.

The final Monnet initiative, on the other hand, achieved far more than initially envisaged. It opened with a plan to make atomic energy a second area of European sectoral co-operation. This was met in April 1955 with a counter-proposal from Pierre Uri, head of the European department at the Bonn Foreign Ministry, for a United States of Europe and, more practically, for a progressive elimination of European tariff barriers. The two projects, Euratom and the Economic Community, were negotiated in parallel, at Messina in 1955 and Val-Duchesse in 1956, before being agreed by the six ECSC signatories at the Rome Treaties in March 1957.

The institutions set up by the Rome Treaty for the Economic Community were modelled on those of the ECSC, though with the supranational element toned down and with explicit provision for interest group representation. They included:

- a Commission entitled to propose Community legislation, broadly equivalent to the ECSC's High Authority, but with fewer independent decision-making powers (a separate Commission was established for Euratom);

- a Council of Ministers, composed of ministers delegated by each member state, with the power to approve all Community legislation (again, another Council was established for Euratom);

- the same Court of Justice as for the ECSC, but with jurisdiction now extended to all three Communities;

- a single Assembly, with a consultative role, for all three Communities;

- a consultative Economic and Social committee, including representatives from employers' and employees' organizations.

Central to the ambition of the Economic Community was the elimination of tariff barriers and the establishment of a customs union and a common trade policy. The Rome Treaty laid out the necessary steps towards these aims in some detail, providing for a transitional period of eight to ten years. Other goals, however, were present only in outline. These included common policies on transport and provision for the creation of a social fund and an investment bank to be financed by member states. Moreover, the centrepiece of the free trade bargain, that German industrial exports moved freely into France while West Germany opened up markets for cheaper French farm produce, required a common agricultural policy to manage this traditionally very protected and regulated sector, and to protect uncompetitive German farmers from ruin. But this, too, was only included in outline.

What the Six signed at Rome was thus a highly specific treaty in some policy areas, but a framework for future integration in others. The same was true of institutions. Two developments, that of the Assembly of the European Communities from a convention of delegates of national legislatures on the ECSC model into a directly elected parliament, and that of decision-making in the Council of Ministers from unanimity to qualified majority voting,[9] were provided for, but not required, by the Rome Treaty. As with later treaties, much depended on how fast and how far the signatories were prepared to proceed with implementation.

Faltering integration 1957–1984

By 1984, a quarter-century after the first tariff reductions came into force, the European Community could point to a significant record of achievement. The customs union had come into force 18 months early, in June 1968, and the common external tariff had been reduced by 20 per cent. The European Commission's important role as trade negotiator had been confirmed during the Kennedy Round of world trade talks (1964–7). The Common Agricultural Policy, beginning with the cereals market in 1967, had helped to achieve European self-sufficiency in most products: indeed, the wine lakes and butter mountains of the 1970s offered a striking, if embarrassing, contrast to the near-famine conditions that had afflicted parts of Western Europe in the first post-war winters. The Yaoundé Convention of 1963 and the Lomé Convention of 1975 provided for economic co-operation with African, Caribbean, and Pacific countries. The Community had begun to develop policies for the environment, research, and regional aid. The three Communities, Euratom, the ECSC, and the Economic Community, had been merged by a 1965 treaty. The European Parliament (EP) had seen its role reinforced, notably in the control of the budget, and had been directly elected for the first time in 1979. Finally, the original Six had grown to Ten, with the entry of the UK, Ireland, and Denmark in 1973, and of Greece in 1981; Spain and Portugal were scheduled to follow as full members in 1986.

Yet the state of the Community in 1984 fell well short of what federalists had hoped for. One reason for this was that France under the de Gaulle presidency (1958–69) had blocked both the 'widening' of the Community (to new members, in particular the UK) and its 'deepening' (or the transfer to new powers to a supranational level). De Gaulle initially hoped to 'cap' the institutions of the Community with a form of political co-operation that would be strictly intergovernmental and would relegate the Economic Community and its institutions to a subordinate role. This was the essence of the French 'Fouchet Plans' of 1961 and 1962, both of which were rejected by the other member states. In 1965, the Community was thrown into crisis when the French blocked efforts by the President of the Commission, Walter Hallstein, to move to a new phase of integration. Hallstein had proposed a package of reforms under which new arrangements to give the Common Agricultural Policy stable, Community-based financial resources (which the French wanted) would be paralleled by a reinforcement of the powers of the Commission and Parliament, and a move towards qualified majority voting on the Council of Ministers, all of which were resolutely supranational in character. The French responded by an 'empty-chair' policy of boycotting the Community's institutions for six months; and the so-called 'Luxembourg Compromise' which marked their return in January 1966 was more of an agreement to disagree. The French Foreign Minister, Maurice Couve de Murville, registered his country's refusal to accept future Community decisions that threatened 'vital national interests' (which the French themselves would define as and when they arose). His counterparts noted his views without agreeing with them, but in practice the French position meant that unanimity continued as the general rule on Council meetings, and the national 'veto' on Community legislation survived. Hallstein retired as the Commission's first President in 1967; his immediate successors were much less ambitious. The march to a supranational Europe was effectively halted in its tracks.

Nor did it resume after de Gaulle's resignation in April 1969. True, his successor Pompidou readily lifted the ban on enlargement. He was responsible, with West Germany's Chancellor Brandt, for the summit held at The Hague in December 1969 which not only agreed to 'widen' Europe but also made plans to 'deepen' it. But the most ambitious of these, the project to achieve economic and monetary union (EMU) by 1980, was sunk by the collapse of the post-war international monetary system in 1971 and the first oil crisis of 1973–4; while plans for 'political union' were quickly confined to intergovernmental meetings between foreign ministers. Moreover, attempts launched in 1968 by Agriculture Commissioner Sicco Mansholt to rein in the fast-growing budget of the CAP in order to free resources for other projects were only adopted in a watered-down form, preparing the way for severe budgetary difficulties by the early 1980s as the British objected to the size of their net contribution.

The remaining initiatives of the 1970s were of a largely intergovernmental character, though in a manner that was more low-key, and less obviously a threat to the Community's existing institutions, than the Fouchet Plans had been. At Paris in December 1974 the Community's nine Heads of State and of Government (HOGS) agreed to hold regular, informal meetings at least three times annually in future. This institutionalized summitry finally acquired Treaty status (as the European Council) with the Single European Act of 1986, by which time it had been an integral part of Community processes for over a decade, becoming a notable catalyst for enhanced foreign policy co-operation. A major concern of the earlier summits was the search for stable parities between European currencies in the face of international monetary instability. However, neither of the attempts to achieve this, the currency 'snake' (set up as a step towards EMU in 1972, but effectively dead by 1976) and the European Monetary System (EMS) created in 1978, were contiguous with the European Community. Thus Norway was among members of the snake, though not of the EEC, while Britain was a notable absentee from the EMS. And monetary developments were in any case handled on an intergovernmental basis, or between central banks, rather than within a Community framework.

In the light of regular European summits, the direct election of the EP, the growth of political co-operation, the extension of Third World co-operation within the Lomé Convention framework, the beginnings of environmental and research policies, it is no doubt misleading to apply the term 'stagnation' to the European Community of the late 1970s and early 1980s. Equally, though, the federalist momentum of the earliest years still appeared sufficiently stalled for a standard textbook on the Community published in 1985 to argue that 'the prospects for the creation of more common policies are not good'.[10] The federalist revival that followed almost immediately surprised more than one observer.

Revival and crisis, 1985–

Since 1985 Europe has been engaged in an almost incessant run of intergovernmental conferences (IGCs) designed to revise the founding Treaties. The first of these led to the Single European Act (SEA) of 1986, which instituted wide-ranging institutional reform in the wake of its central aim, to complete Europe's internal market. The second IGC produced the Maastricht Treaty of February 1992, which set Europe on a course towards EMU (again), and gave the name 'European Union' to a three-'pillar' structure combining the existing Community with institutionalized intergovernmental co-operation in Justice and Home Affairs and a Common Foreign and Security Policy. Thirdly, the Amsterdam Treaty of June 1997 attempted to prepare Europe's institutions for large-scale future enlargement to the East.

The SEA has so far proven the most successful of the three. Its basis was a Commission White Paper, *Completing the Internal Market*, agreed at the June 1985 Milan summit, which proposed a series of some 300 measures to remove Europe's non-tariff barriers to trade. The plan benefited from a favourable policy environment. Britain's budgetary problems had been settled at the 1984 Fontainebleau summit. France had returned to European monetary discipline in March 1983 after President Mitterrand's two-year attempt to realize 'Keynesianism in one country'. And fears of a revival of world protectionism enhanced the sympathies of member governments for plans to free internal trade, in line with the stated objectives of the Rome Treaty, and to allay outside concerns that Europe was turning into a protected 'fortress'. The great majority of the SEA measures were in place by the deadline set at Milan, 1 January 1993. In addition, however, the SEA incorporated important institutional reforms to achieve this. The most notable of these were the extension of Qualified Majority Voting (QMV) in the Council of Ministers to cover all Single Market measures, and the parallel re-inforcement of the EP's role in some legislation via the new co-operation procedure. The 'veto' did not disappear with the SEA, but its scope was now circumscribed, with wide-ranging consequences for the workings of European institutions.

The aims of the Maastricht treaty were less narrowly focused, and their realization correspondingly more problematic, than those of the SEA. The Commission, under a highly activist president, Jacques Delors (who held the job for a decade, from 1985 to 1995) and with the support of most member states, sought to build on the momentum of the SEA in three areas, and to accomplish further institutional reforms:

- EMU was seen as the logical completion of the internal market and a means to stabilize the European trading environment in a world of monetary instability. It also had political purposes: to lock newly united Germany to its European partners, and to give an irreversible character to European integration. The Treaty agreed both a set of 'convergence criteria' for EMU covering monetary stability, inflation, interest rates, and public finances (a public sector borrowing requirement of no more than 3 per cent of GDP, and a public sector debt of no more than 60 per cent of GDP), and a schedule under which states meeting the criteria would lock their currencies into EMU by 1997 or, at the latest, by 1 January 1999.

- Employee protection was seen as a means to give a 'social dimension' to the Single Market, and to avoid the risk of companies moving about Europe in search of the most deregulated labour markets and the most laissez-faire social legislation, which might result from greater capital mobility. Health and safety provisions had already been included in the SEA, and the European Social Charter, accepted by the Strasbourg summit in December 1989 at the same time as the principle of EMU, became the basis for the Social Chapter of the Maastricht treaty.

- Political union, or the extension of European competence into new areas, notably foreign and security policy and home affairs, was incorporated into the two new 'pillars' of the renamed European Union, which remained intergovernmental in character, though with the provision of institutional procedures (*passerelles*) allowing a greater element of supranationality as and when member states wanted it.

- Of the Maastricht Treaty's institutional reforms, some built on those of the SEA, with a further extension of QMV and another new legislative procedure, co-decision, which for the first time gave the EP something close to a veto over some legislation. The Treaty also gave the EP the right to veto an incoming Commission, created a (consultative) Committee of the Regions, and, on the insistence of the British, for the first time included in the Treaties the principle of subsidiarity, under which different tasks of government should be handled by the most appropriate level of government (Europe, member states, or sub-national authorities).

Maastricht ran into serious difficulties even before being signed, as the British required an 'opt-out' clause allowing the UK to remain outside both EMU and the Social Chapter if its government so wished. The Danes, traditionally almost as reserved about large extensions of supranational power, then rejected the Treaty at a referendum in June 1992, and had to be given their own opt-out before they would say Yes at a second vote a year later. In September 1992 the French voters nearly followed the Danish example, approving the treaty in their ratification referendum by a margin of less than 2 per cent. Britain's Conservative government, despite opt-outs, had to employ the full range of procedural techniques and party pressures to squeeze the treaty past its Eurosceptics in the Commons. Germany, one of the main promoters of the treaty, became the last member state to ratify, in October 1993, owing to difficulties raised by the Constitutional Court.

The political difficulties encountered by Maastricht were compounded by economic ones, as many member states entered a period of recession and monetary instability. Two waves of currency speculation forced the withdrawal of the pound and the Italian lira from the EMS in September 1992, and the loosening of EMS fluctuation bands in August 1993. More seriously, recession and the resulting costs of unemployment pushed the budget deficits of most states above levels set by the EMU convergence criteria. Efforts to reduce them were politically unpopular (costing France's right-wing government its majority in the 1997 parliamentary elections), and unsuccessful. With only 18 months to go before the 1999 deadline set at Maastricht, neither of the two member states at the core of the EMU deal, France and Germany, had brought their deficits below 3 per cent. Indeed, if EMU were to be restricted to states which had respected the full range of convergence criteria from 1992 to 1997, only one, Luxembourg, would qualify.

It was in this difficult environment that the third IGC met to consider further institutional changes to the EU. Its deliberations were prompted by three elements. The first was the gulf between European institutions and European peoples revealed by the Maastricht ratification process. The new treaty aimed to create a 'people's Europe', more transparent and more responsive to popular concerns, and in particular to jobs. The second was the question of bringing the two new 'pillars' under more supranational control, in the light of the poor record of intergovernmentalism in defining a common foreign policy (for example, in relation to former Yugoslavia), or a common immigration and citizenship policy. The third issue was the challenge to Europe's institutions posed by future enlargement. The collapse of the former Soviet bloc had led to the immediate inclusion of East Germany into the European Community as well as into the Federal Republic, and to a wave of new entry applications. Three of these new candidate states, Finland, Sweden, and Austria, entered the EU on 1 January 1995.[11] They had hitherto kept out chiefly because of their neutral status, and were easy partners to integrate by virtue of their wealth and state of development. Far more problematic were the Central and Eastern European countries: Poland, Hungary, and the Czech Republic, and behind them the rest of the former Eastern bloc, plus Mediterranean countries (Turkey, Malta, and Cyprus) and possibly also former Soviet republics, beginning with the Baltic states. Institutions, and a budget, conceived for a community of six, and only partially modified since then, would need a more profound overhaul if they were to absorb such an influx. Changes would cover arrangements for qualified majority voting, the size of the Commission and the EP, and the shape of a budget nearly half of which was still devoted, in the late 1990s, to farm subsidies.

The resulting treaty, however, suffered from the unpromising context prevailing before the Amsterdam IGC. The two newer 'pillars' remained largely intergovernmental, a point symbolized by the reinforcement of the Council's role in the outside representation of European foreign policy; in Justice and Home Affairs the main move forward was the commitment to move towards a common visa and immigration policy. Hopes for a 'people's Europe' were given a largely declaratory answer (with the inclusion of fundamental human rights and freedom of movement for all citizens in the treaty, and the promise of a jobs summit for late 1997, but no budgetary commitments). The EP's future size was capped at 700 members, and its role reinforced by extensions of the co-decision procedure to employment and equal opportunities issues, measures to fight fraud, and customs matters. An initial step to limit the Commission's size was taken by allowing the five largest member states to appoint only one Commissioner, rather than two as in the past. But no agreement was reached on the key issue of how to arrange QMV in the expanding Council of Ministers of the future. In the words of the Commissioner who presented it to the public, this was 'an impenetrable and complex Treaty, timid in the most sensitive areas such as the common foreign and security policy and weak on the institutional aspects'.[12] European integration had seen earlier low points, at which principled opposition combined with political and economic uncertainties to prevent new movement. But the stakes involved, whether they concerned a workable EMU or a viable institutional system for a larger Union, were such as to place a very high cost on possible failure.

The international context

The preceding narrative has stressed the internal determinants of European integration: the manner, for example, in which the SEA built on provisions of the Rome Treaty and was itself the basis for attempts at further integration at Maastricht. But the European ambition alone has clearly been insufficient to achieve its own fulfilment; nothing, after all, came of either the enthusiasms of nineteenth-century figures such as Saint-Simon, Mazzini, or Proudhon, or from the elaborate European Union presented in 1929 by France's inter-war Premier and Foreign Minister Aristide Briand.[13] The following sections seek to explain the genesis of effective integration in post-war Europe, and to account for its uneven fortunes since then, in three ways: through developments in the international context; through the behaviour and perceived interests of the large member states; and through the exercise of leadership by national and European leaders.

The European movements that mobilized after 1945, both at élite level, and, to some degree, at mass level as well,[14] were in the first place movements for peace. In the 80 years preceding the launch of the ECSC project in 1950, its two main participants, France and Germany, had gone to war three times. Moreover, the outstanding lesson of the inter-war years was that the imposition of a punitive peace on a defeated Germany, such as the 1919 Versailles Treaty, would lead to revanchism and a new war. Aside from those (relatively few) among the victorious allies who advocated the complete dismantling of Germany's state and economy,[15] the solution could only be to give the Germans a stake in peace. Internally, this might mean encouraging Germany 'to aim at being a super Sweden, cleaner, better planned and healthier than any state ever was before'; externally, in the words of Léon Blum, France's Prime Minister in 1936–7 and again, briefly, in 1946–7, it meant 'the incorporation of the German nation into an international community sufficiently strong to re-educate it, discipline it, and, if necessary, dominate it'.[16] The 'German question', and the perceived need to encourage Germany's economic recovery but to maintain her political containment, helped to structure not only the generalities but also such specifics of early moves to integration as Monnet's choice of coal and steel, and even, thanks to the nervousness of smaller participants in the ECSC, the national weighting of seats on its different ruling bodies. European integration served the cause of Franco-German reconciliation well, and has been punctuated with symbols, such as the clasped hands of Chancellor Kohl and President Mitterrand at the war cemetery of Verdun in 1984, which have not been lost on voters. When the French were asked, in 1992, to name the major advantages of Europe integration, 55 per cent answered 'peace in Europe'.[17]

The second international 'given' of the founding years was the onset of the Cold War from 1947. The Brussels Treaty of 1948 was dictated by British and French concern to keep 'the Americans in [Europe], the Russians out, and the Germans down'. Europe, and within it, divided Germany, constituted the central stake of early superpower rivalry, as well as being the likely battlefield in the event of hostilities. The United States were prepared to spend much diplomatic effort and money (both openly and, in the form of assistance from the CIA to Christian Democratic and moderate Socialist parties, covertly) to ensure a strong and united Western Europe. Of the three US Secretaries of State to hold office from 1947 to 1959, the first, George Marshall, developed the aid programme that was the catalyst for the OEEC; the second, Dean Acheson, helped to provoke the EDC initiative by announcing that he wanted to see 'Germans in uniform by autumn 1951' in order to release US forces for use in Korea; and the third, John Foster Dulles, was secretary of the US Committee for the United States of Europe.[18] The relationship between the United States and Western Europe was never one of simple tutelage, and the balance between strategic alliance and economic interdependence, and economic competition, grew more complex as Europe's economies recovered.[19] But there was always an implicit alignment between the European Communities and the Western camp. Western Communist parties remained fundamentally anti-European as long as they remained faithful to Moscow. Neutral countries stayed out until the Berlin Wall was safely down.

A third element in the early construction of Europe, explicit in the creation of the Council of Europe, implicit in that of the ECSC, was the defence of liberal democracy. Initially, the focus was once again on Germany: Europe would help democratic values take root (the signs are that it did, in the space of approximately a generation).[20] More broadly, as Gaffney points out, European integration has been an agent of convergence for European regimes, from the pre-war patchwork of democracies, authoritarian states, and downright fascist ones, towards a common pattern of plural liberal democracy which seemed anything but a foregone conclusion to the vulnerable founding states in 1950.[21] A generation later the emergence of Greece, Spain, and Portugal from authoritarian regimes was followed within a decade by their entry into Europe. A distinct, though comparable, argument may even be offered for the cases of Britain and France: their embarkation on the European road coincided with their acceptance of withdrawal from empire.[22]

The importance of these three bases of European integration—the 'German question', the Cold War, and democratization—helps to explain the impact on Europe of the collapse of the Soviet bloc. As Pulzer notes, the Cold War had temporarily suspended the question of Germany's ambiguous geographical position between East and West.[23] Germany lived in a state of 'semi-sovereignty' by virtue of its Nazi past and its division into two states on either side of the Iron Curtain. The Federal Republic remained closely linked to the West through NATO, and through intense commercial ties (80 per cent of West German trade was with the advanced capitalist world). It rapidly built Europe's largest economy, but it was not very much bigger than those of its larger partners. There was therefore a balance between France as the Community's political (and nuclear) heavyweight and Germany's economic strength. Post-unification Germany became, quite unambiguously, Europe's largest country (outside Russia), as well as its largest economy, with both a population and a GDP more than 25 per cent greater than those of either France, Italy, or the UK. The former 'semi-sovereign state' now asserted both a readiness to define many of the specifics of unification on its own terms, and to make independent gestures in foreign policy, notably in relation to former Yugoslavia. These were developments that worried both Margaret Thatcher and François Mitterrand, though they drew radically different conclusions from them. One vital perspective on Maastricht is as a European response to German unification, and a bid to lock Germany to the West, both economically (via EMU) and politically (via the Common Foreign and Security Policy).

The end of the bipolar world of the Cold War also posed the broader question of the place in the world of an entity that would, if united, be the world's largest power in terms of GNP. The definition of a foreign policy commensurate with this economic power now required more than the former recipe of alignment on American positions for strategic fundamentals plus loose voluntary co-operation for the rest. Again, the first of the two new Maastricht 'pillars' should be understood in this light. Finally, the end of the Cold War meant that the demands of newly democratic nations of the former Soviet bloc to join the EU could not be indefinitely resisted without betraying the ideals of a European project based on democratization as well as on economic self-interest.

Economic self-interest, however, was as present in the European project as the strictly political agendas outlined above, and the course of European integration has inevitably been marked by its economic context. Two variables stand out. The first, quite simply, is the difference between the years of steady economic growth and stability and those of slow growth or recession and monetary instability. Not surprisingly, ambitious economic projects have been easier to hatch in the former context than in the latter. The treaty of Paris (creating the ECSC) was signed as Western Europe was beginning to enjoy the first benefits of post-war recovery, those of Rome when the boom known to the French as the *trente glorieuses* was already under way. The SEA was signed, and the Maastricht initiative opened, in a context of recovery from the second oil shock in the mid- to late 1980s. Conversely, the failure to implement EMU in the 1970s, and the extreme difficulties faced in doing so 20 years later, owed much to the economic *atonie* of the major participants and the generally rapid and merciless punishment visited by ever-more-liberalized money markets on currencies of countries whose economic performance appeared doubtful. The timidity of the Amsterdam treaty can be partly explained in terms of the political fall-out of such a context: few of its signatories, and certainly not the economically and financially beleaguered Kohl government, were in a position to take the political risks associated with large steps towards a federal Europe.

The ideological climate of economic policy-making also affected the course of European integration. The ECSC was conceived in a Europe still largely under post-war economic controls, and to some extent bore the *dirigiste* marks of this. The Rome treaty, on the other hand, epitomizes the paradoxical characteristics of Western capitalist economies during the *trente glorieuses*: State interventionism at home (albeit with much variation between different countries), and multilateral economic liberalization abroad (exemplified by the customs union, and by Europe's ready participation in the Kennedy Round of tariff reductions), coupled with a single exception, agriculture, where massive domestic and European intervention was linked by the Common Agricultural Policy to external protectionism.[24] The continued attachment of the EU to this schema into the 1990s is shown by the maintenance of the CAP and the spread of European industrial and research policies: that of its member states by the difficulty encountered by any government attempting to reduce public spending as a proportion of GNP. At the same time it is clear that the shift towards economic liberalism initiated by the Anglo-Saxon economies in the early 1980s has reached the EU. The most systematic manifestation of the liberal impulse has been the SEA and measures that followed from it, such as a newly aggressive competition policy (both of them piloted by former British Conservative ministers). The impact on the European business environment has, it is true, been relatively slight compared with the wider liberalization of world trade. It has also been patchy, with many national exceptions to liberal European rules still being admitted.[25] But the SEA effect has been sufficient to suggest that the EU is not wholly stuck in a time-warp of Keynesian interventionism.

While the international context complements the internal dynamics of European institutions in explaining the course of European integration, the two do not suffice. To understand events such as the 'empty chair' crisis of 1965, the biggest single setback to integration since the Rome Treaties, it is necessary to turn to individual member states.

Europe and its nations

'National interest', writes Helen Wallace, 'is a misleading and mostly unhelpful term': it conceals a rich tapestry of sectional interests, key voter groups, regions, and parties (and factions of parties) in office.[26] The history of European integration is one of movement, which changing national governments and contexts may accelerate, slow down, or halt altogether. It is also a history in which European institutions and other non-state actors have played important roles. That said, the importance for Europe's intergovernmental relations of persistent national approaches, albeit with variations, cannot be ignored. Moreover, the different 'policy styles' which different national systems of government engender, and which national ministers, civil servants, and parliamentarians take with them to Brussels, have affected the EU's internal workings.

France

As one of the two core partners that have constituted the 'motor' of European integration since 1950, France has consistently placed the relationship with Germany at the centre of her external policy. That de Gaulle made time to receive Chancellor Adenauer at length at his private home in September 1958, with a referendum on his new constitution a fortnight away and the Algerian crisis still demanding almost daily attention, testifies to this. More recently, as Haig Simonian remarks, 'French and German leaders since 1974 have visited each other within days of coming to office.'[27] The large policy aims in relation to Germany have not changed very much since Robert Schuman presented the Monnet plan for the ECSC in 1950: to benefit from a reviving German economy that has become increasingly interdependent with that of France; to use European institutions to contain any resurgent political ambitions that Germany might conceive; to ensure that the focus of German policy remains in the West. The prospect of an eastward-looking Germany has tended to provoke a sort of Pavlovian reflex among French policy-makers in favour of closer European integration. Chancellor Brandt's incipient *Ostpolitik*, for example, was one element behind Pompidou's early readiness to relaunch Europe at the Hague in December 1969.[28] Mitterrand's initial alarm at the prospect of German unification in 1989 and early 1990 found expression in a series of speeches calling for the 'reinforcement and acceleration of the construction of Europe', and in the process leading to the Maastricht treaty.[29]

Beyond the containment of an old enemy, packaged in the symbolism of mutual reconciliation, Europe, particularly with West German economic underpinning, has also represented a larger stake for France: a means to 'punch above her weight' in world affairs. De Gaulle's articulation of this view to his junior minister Alain Peyrefitte in 1962 is worth quoting at some length:

What is the purpose of Europe? It should be to allow us to escape the domination of the Americans and the Russians. The six of us ought to be able to do just as well as either of the superpowers. And if France so orders matters as to be the first among the Six, an aim which is within our reach, she can work this lever of Archimedes, and draw her partners after her. Europe is the means for France to regain the stature she has lacked since Waterloo, as the first among the world's nations.[30]

The readiness of de Gaulle's successors, even if they did not quite share his soaring nineteenth-century vision, to use the 'lever of Archimedes' to enhance France's international freedom of manœuvre, helps to explain the disorientation of France's foreign policy at the end of the Cold War. The role of broker between East and West, sought with varying success by all the Presidents of the Fifth Republic, became redundant almost overnight. And there appeared no particular reason why in the long term the continent's spokesman should be France, and not a strong and united Germany whose military defeat was receding into history.

De Gaulle's vision was of a Europe that enhanced and projected French sovereignty rather than limiting it. And herein lies the central ambivalence of much of France's European policy: a wish to draw the benefits of European integration while minimizing the concessions to supranationality. The second half of this approach had deep historical roots. The nation state, painfully constructed over centuries from the medieval Île de France and reasserted with democratic credentials by the Jacobin tradition of the Revolution, had a reality for the French that it lacked, for varying reasons, among other members of the initial Six. Moreover, the central myth to emerge from France's experience of the war years was that of a struggle to preserve national sovereignty through resistance to foreign occupation. That myth fuelled the fortunes of the two parties that dominated the post-war generation in France, the Communists and the Gaullists. Again, France was unique among the original Six in the combined strength enjoyed by the pro-Soviet Left and the nationalist Right, a strength which left rather little space for the political forces that made the European running elsewhere, moderate Socialists and Christian Democrats. The recurrent French allergy to supranationality found early expression in the failure of EDC ratification in the Chamber of Deputies. The recent memory of that setback then dictated caution to the Socialist Prime Minister Mollet as he negotiated aspects of the Rome treaty such as the powers (and even the name) of the Commission. De Gaulle delivered a decisive blow against supranationality through the empty-chair crisis of 1965, and both he and Pompidou blocked direct election of the European Parliament. The election of France's most integrationist President, François Mitterrand, waited until the voting strength of both Gaullists and Communists had fallen below 20 per cent. And even his leadership was barely able to win the French electorate's approval for the Maastricht treaty.

The one area where the French have had little aversion to supranationality, finally, has been agriculture. The economic exchange at the heart of the Rome treaty, that of export opportunities for German industrial firms and for French farmers, meant a high level of price supports to protect farmers in other states, notably West Germany, who would be undercut by cheap French imports. Hence the four central components of the Common Agricultural Policy: a common market for farm produce and common external tariff as for other products, but also centrally set (and artificially high) farm prices, and subsidies for exports to non-European countries. The solidity of subsequent French support for the CAP may be explained partly by its role in making France into the world's second largest food exporter (after the United States), and partly by the French farm lobby, which is the best organized and most powerful in Europe. The strength of that commitment was signalled by the apparent readiness of the French government to prevent any settlement of the Uruguay Round of world trade talks in 1993 rather than allow Europe's negotiators to sign an agreement they considered unacceptable. A similarly intransigent attitude would cause major difficulties for enlargement of the EU to the major agricultural producers from Eastern Europe.

Germany

Germany has proved remarkably accommodating to French concerns through almost the whole history of European integration. Where the French have sought to contain Germany's international ambitions through Europe, the Germans have taken the view that 'the European Community was necessary to save Germany from itself'.[31] Where the French sought reassurance on Germany's European commitment, the Germans actively sought to balance *Ostpolitik* with the 'widening' and 'deepening' of the European Community planned at The Hague in 1969, or stressed, as Kohl did in 1990, that a united Germany and a united Europe were 'two sides of the same coin'.[32] Where the French tried to use Europe to 'punch above their weight', the Germans sought to do the opposite: to present their own proposals, where possible, as Franco-German initiatives; to avoid using their (potentially very large) power as the largest net contributors to the European budget to ease integrationist projects with social payments, rather than to pursue overtly national aims (except in a limited number of cases, for example the halting of ambitious plans for regional aid in 1974); and to avoid clear or assertive diplomatic choices where they could.[33]

The self-effacing character of Germany's European policy owed much to her 'semi-sovereign' post-war status as a defeated nation, unable (and unwilling) to contemplate a conventionally assertive foreign policy, indeed without a foreign ministry till 1951 and a defence ministry till 1955, divided, and wholly dependent on the Western Alliance to defend the frontiers of the Federal Republic and of Berlin. And the defeat also affected internal politics. It did much to discredit the ideas of national sovereignty still current in Britain and France. The new West German political identity would rest on federalism and constitutionalism (and thus diffused and limited sovereignty) at home and Europeanism abroad. After unification it was symbolic that the same Article 23 of the Basic Law which had been changed to integrate the Eastern *Länder* was amended a second time, in December 1992, to assert Germany's commitment to a 'united Europe' through the European Union.[34] Moreover, where France's Europeans were hemmed in by Gaullists and Communists, Germany's were not: the party system that emerged in the Federal Republic of the 1950s held little place for the nationalist Right, and almost none for the pro-Soviet Left, which was banned from 1956. The major governing parties, the CDU/CSU, FDP, and SPD, have not, it is true, been absolute, continuous supporters of a federal Europe. The FDP voted against ratification of the Rome Treaty, whose provisions it found too *dirigiste* (a view shared by the CDU Economics Minister and future Chancellor Ludwig Erhard); the SPD was initially too anxious to build ties with the East to welcome moves to Western European integration. But both had changed their views by the early 1960s. The CDU suffered in the 1960s from disputes between its 'Gaullists', who saw Europe as a means of limiting American tutelage, and its 'Atlanticists', who stressed the continued importance of good relations with the United States. The CSU, initially the Federal Republic's most pro-European party (largely by virtue of its Catholicism), moved in the opposite direction: its European ardour was distinctly cooler by the early 1990s.[35] But those German chancellors who have sought to pursue an integrationist project have not, on the whole, faced the same degree of domestic constraints as their French counterparts.

Self-effacement and the acceptance of limited sovereignty are not the same as selfless renunciation. As Paterson points out, West Germany's European policy was very successful in ensuring a sustained export-led prosperity and, when the opportunity came, in securing more general acceptance of German unification than a more assertive posture would have done. These considerations suggest that French fears of an overt German bid for leadership in the EU are exaggerated—especially as unification entailed the shouldering of new responsibilities immeasurably larger than the new resources that came to Germany with them.[36]

In the problem of resources lies the key to at least part of what unification has changed. Kohl's seizure of the political opportunity of unification took little account of the economic cost, in particular where the parity between Eastern and Western marks were concerned. Similarly, for both Kohl and Mitterrand, EMU was first and foremost a political project: the surest way, if it could be achieved, to make a united Europe irreversible.[37] But, again, large economic costs were entailed by Germany's effort to meet the convergence criteria at a time of low growth, record unemployment, and continued heavy spending in the East. These costs were of a different order to the traditional net contributions to the European budget, or the periodic spending by the Bundesbank in support of beleaguered currencies in the EMS. And they triggered heavy political costs for the Kohl government. This was all the more the case as the purpose of the tax rises and welfare cuts inflicted on German voters after 1992 was to enable Germany to *give up* something as tangible for Germans as ancient symbols of sovereignty were to other European member states: the totem and guarantee of economic success represented by the Deutschmark. At the best of times (for example, during the Maastricht negotiations late in 1991), EMU had attracted only lukewarm support in German opinion polls. More frequently, it was opposed by a margin of two to one. This represented a large flaw in Kohl's European project. By the late 1990s, Germany's all-party consensus on Europe consisted primarily of agreement that the net budget contributions could not go on indefinitely at the same levels and should certainly not rise. The dissensus had come to include the timing of EMU, and even, in some circles, its desirability.

The most probable scenario for future German policy towards Europe is therefore not so much overbearing self-assertion as enhanced caution in the face of new initiatives, and concern about cost. The hesitations of Germany and of all major participants shaped the 1997 Amsterdam Treaty. Such timidity will not, however, necessarily be the best posture from which to face the challenges of the Eastern enlargement to which Germany remains committed.

Italy

Italy's relations with the EU can be treated more briefly. In so far as external policy was a preoccupation of the Christian Democrats who supplied all but two of Italy's Prime Ministers from 1945 to 1992 (and for much of the time it was not), their approach was an ardently European one in every respect except that of the implementation at national level of European legislation. Anti-Communism and Catholicism, two elements of the DC's *raison d'être*, dictated support for a Western Europe that was both cohesive and supportive of the United States (so, for a time, did regular CIA payments to the DC). Italy was a signatory both of the 1951 Paris treaty and of the Rome Treaty six years later. Both were gambles for an unestablished democracy and an undeveloped Mediterranean economy. Both paid off. Although the Italian negotiators might, arguably, have secured a better result for Italian farmers than the CAP which emerged in the late 1960s (and which covered few Mediterranean farm products), Italy was a net budget beneficiary, with the South absorbing its full share of European structural funds. When the Communist Party broke free of Moscow in the 1960s it joined the consensus, favouring Italy's active participation in Europe. Over more than two decades, Eurobarometer polls have shown Italians to be among the most satisfied Europeans with EC/EU membership. And within Europe's institutional negotiations, the Italians, along with the Benelux countries, have been among the most consistent supporters of extensions to supranationality, for example through enhancement of the powers of the Commission.[38]

At the same time, Italy's record of applying Community legislation was one of the worst in Europe. This was partly due to a chaotic and ineffective system of policy co-ordination.[39] But it also resulted from the political clientelism that was at the heart of Italian governance and which in the course of the 1980s pushed the level of public debt above 100 per cent of GNP. The gulf between rhetoric and practice in the Italian approach to Europe became unsustainable with the signature of the Maastricht Treaty. For in committing himself to convergence criteria (including debt at 60 per cent of GNP) which his country could not achieve, Prime Minister Andreotti was effectively sawing off the branch that he and his DC colleagues were sitting on. The financial markets' incredulity as to Italy's ability to join EMU forced the lira out of the EMS in September 1992. And as serious attempts were made to control public deficits, the old patronage-based party system lost the funding that had been its fuel for decades, and imploded in the elections of 1994 and 1996.[40]

The United Kingdom

Alone among the EU's four large states, the UK did not sign the Rome Treaties in 1957. Staying out corresponded to a tradition of aversion to European entanglement as long as trade remained open and no single dominant power threatened to control the continent. Churchill's call for a 'United States of Europe' at Zurich in 1946 clearly envisaged Britain in the role (shared with the USA) of patron and well-wisher, rather than as a participant in a continental federation. Participation in an economic community in the 1950s would have entailed a reorientation of British trade away from imperial partners towards European ones: the British delegates left the Messina talks in 1955 over the central issues of a common market and a customs union (which they thought would never be achieved). Two years later, the British reaction to the signature of the Rome Treaty was one of alarm: de Gaulle records a conversation in which Harold Macmillan likened the nascent Economic Community to Napoleon's Continental System.[41] The British then sought unsuccessfully to merge the EC into a wider and looser free-trade zone, before joining a group of mostly peripheral European countries in the European Free Trade Association (EFTA) in 1960. As preliminaries to Britain's first application to join the EC, in 1961, these steps scarcely amounted to confidence-building. Thanks to de Gaulle's veto, which he justified in terms of (well-founded) doubts as to Britain's European loyalties, the application took over eight years (and two renewals) to be accepted in principle, in December 1969, and a further three years for British membership to become a reality, on 1 January 1973.

Britain's relations with Europe since then have been dogged by both economic and political difficulties. In one respect, more or less spontaneous economic adjustment facilitated and rewarded UK membership: between the 1950s and 1970 Western Europe's share of all British exports grew from a quarter to roughly a half, while that of the Commonwealth shrank in proportion. But Britain still had a major economic concern arising from her small agricultural sector. With few farmers (albeit very productive ones), the UK has drawn relatively little benefit from the CAP, which has until recently accounted for well over half of Community spending. Britain has thus been a net financial contributor to Europe, despite being a smaller economy than either West Germany or France (or, from the 1990s, Italy). Margaret Thatcher won a series of rebates at the summits of the early 1980s, and a more lasting settlement in 1984, but at the price of allowing Britain's European policy to be dominated by this single issue for nearly five years.

Britain's political difficulty is twofold. Firstly, as Ian Ward notes, 'We in the UK are particularly obsessed with sovereignty.'[42] In this respect the UK resembles the other 'old' nation state among the large members, France, rather than Europhile Italy or semi-sovereign and federal West Germany: the whole of Britain's parliamentary and legal tradition is profoundly inimical to transfers of sovereignty away of its ancient repository, the monarch-in-parliament.[43] Secondly, while the UK does have two enthusiastically pro-European parties, both are very small: the Liberals (or the Alliance in the 1980s and the Liberal Democrats in the 1990s) and the Scottish Nationalists (who share with Italy's Northern League a preference for the loose authority of Brussels against the oppressive yoke of Westminster or Rome). Both the Labour Left and the Tory Right have been more or less solidly Eurosceptical, the former because of the undoubted difficulty of 'building socialism' in a single member state of a capitalist Europe, the latter because of Empire and Commonwealth links (in the 1960s), the interventionism of the 'Brussels bureaucracy' (since the 1980s), traditional views about British sovereignty (at all times), or a visceral distaste for 'that un-British combination of high-flown rhetoric and pork-barrel politics which passed for European statesmanship' (in the case of Mrs Thatcher).[44] Labour split in the parliamentary vote on British entry in 1971 (199 MPs opposed entry and 69 voted in favour) and sought to escape divisions with a referendum over 'renegotiated' terms for entry in 1975, before advocating outright withdrawal in the very left-wing 1983 manifesto, turning Euro-enthusiastic in 1989 (after a notable presentation of the Social Charter to the TUC by Jacques Delors), and becoming moderately pro-European on their return to office in 1997. The Conservatives were committed with some difficulty by Edward Heath's leadership to entry in 1971 (they also split in the parliamentary vote, with 39 MPs opposed). After the budget disputes of the early Thatcher years they enjoyed a brief moment of euphoria with the adoption of the SEA and its liberal single-market programme. But even at this 'high point of the Conservative Party's European strategy',[45] Mrs Thatcher opposed the IGC that reformed European institutions. And the late 1980s, despite Britain's ephemeral membership of the EMS, were marked by deepening British isolation, institutionalized by the Maastricht opt-outs. The Conservatives' widening internal divisions over Europe helped to bring down Mrs Thatcher in November 1990 and to weaken her successor, John Major, throughout his premiership.

The stressful character of Britain's relations with Europe should not merely be ascribed to party divisions. Eurobarometer polls have shown that, with the Danes, the British have proved more sceptical than any other citizens about the benefits of EU membership. If British policy has frequently been limited, in the words of Spence, to an exercise in 'damage limitation', in which 'the main priorities lay in renegotiation of existing Community policies of particular high cost to the UK and in preventing the spread of Community competence', this may be what a majority of voters have wanted.[46]

Policy styles

The preceding discussion has focused chiefly on the approaches of different member states to the 'high politics' of European integration, in particular the surrender (or retention) of national sovereignty decided at treaty negotiations from Paris in 1951 to Amsterdam in 1997. An extreme simplification of the different approaches to issues of sovereignty would contrast the cautious attitude of the older nation states, Britain and France, and the more receptive one of Germany and Italy, where the absolute value placed on national sovereignty was limited by military defeat and by the transition from fascism to democracy that followed. This dichotomy is, of course, no more than the most general of frameworks, within which the parties and personalities in power, the salience of different interest groups, and the international context will produce varying outcomes. 'National interest' is a necessary but also a profoundly imperfect guide to attitudes towards European integration.

A quite distinct, albeit connected, difference between national approaches is that of national 'policy styles',[47] the institutional culture that bureaucrats and politicians may take with them into Europe. This type of variation in attitudes affects not so much sovereignty questions as the full range of day-to-day working practices within the EU. It will chiefly affect the national delegates who are the main participants in the Council of Ministers. However, different policy styles may also be expected among the European civil servants of the Commission, who, behind an official role supposed to transcend national loyalties, will often owe their appointment (at senior level, at least) to an informal national quota system, and will make full use of their national connections in order to build the networks on which much of their success in the Commission depends.[48]

Variations in policy styles may have an impact in several areas.

Policy co-ordination

Policy co-ordination within member states is probably the most important of these. Here, too, the major difference is between France and the UK on the one hand, and Italy and Germany on the other. In the former countries, European policy is, at least in principle, closely co-ordinated across ministries from bodies at the centre of the executive (the SGCI in France, the European secretariat of the Cabinet Office in the UK). In Italy and Germany, by contrast, the ministerial autonomy written into the Constitution has produced a more fragmented style of policy-making, compounded in Italy by the poor functioning of the administration, and in Germany by the federal structure of the state. As Wright points out, the British and French systems are not automatically more effective for being better co-ordinated, their main drawback being the lack of flexibility under which national negotiators labour.[49]

The importance of actors other than national government

The importance of actors other than national government also varies between member states. Germany has been notable in this respect both because of the crucial role of the Bundesbank in determining German (and hence, thanks to the EMS, European) monetary policy, and secondly because of the right won by the *Länder* to be consulted on aspects of European policy affecting them. In Denmark, on the other hand, this vigilant scrutiny of the government's European policy is undertaken by the parliament. The power of interest groups also varies from country to country, as do their relations with governments. In all member states, farmers exert an influence out of all proportion to their numbers: but their views are particularly hard to override in France. In member states where government departments have built stable working relationships with leading interest groups (as in France in the case of farmers, but across a wider ranger of groups in Britain and Germany), the ministries have tended to promote the interests of those groups, and use them as sources of information, at the European level. Such mutual aid in Brussels will be more problematic for member states where such relationships have not existed nationally.

The tone of political debate

The tone of political debate is also reflected in the approach to Europe of different member states. The highly adversarial style of British party confrontation is not reproduced, for example, in Holland, where the consensual values of consociational democracy remain strong; nor, on many occasions, in Germany. Consensual values remain very strong in most EU institutions, which perhaps helps to explain why, as Spence notes, 'British policy-making has had an uncanny knack of antagonizing the UK's Community partners at all levels.'[50]

Attitudes to the implementation of EU legislation

Attitudes to the implementation of EU legislation also vary substantially between member states. The record of northern states tends to be better than that of southern ones, with Italy, as we have noted, having an especially poor record. Assumptions about future implementation of proposals will affect the reactions to them of both officials and interest groups. That said, the British have also shown skill in respecting the letter of legislation while clearly contravening its spirit, as in the case of the 1979 Bathing Water Directive.[51]

The strategic location of a country within the EU

Beyond questions of national style, the strategic location of a country within the EU will affect its behaviour on the Council of Ministers and the demands it makes on the EU's resources. A range of cleavages will define this location: budget contributors *versus* budget beneficiaries; North *versus* South; large states *versus* small ones; states with small, low-productivity farmers *versus* those with world-class farm sectors; established member states with a stake in the existing distribution of resources, *versus* new ones anxious to tip it in their favour. The cross-cutting, rather than cumulative, character of most of these differences allows the most successful member states to negotiate package deals with partners on issues that may be quite disparate. That produces a considerably wider range of alliances on the Council than would be suggested by the distinction between reluctance or willingness to surrender sovereignty.[52]

The impact of leadership

One definition of political leadership is the capacity to inspire, persuade, cajole, or bully other people into doing what they would not do spontaneously. De Gaulle's creation and management of the Free French movement, or his simultaneous transformation of France's political system and severing of her colonial links with Algeria, are obvious examples. A second definition, however, might be the ability to seize favourable circumstances to turn long-standing problems into innovative projects. It is this second, less heroic manifestation of leadership that most readily applies to the impact of individuals on European integration. The individuals concerned have rarely made their impact singly: in the collegiate entity of the EU, leadership is more readily exercised in tandems or small groups. Among the leaders of European institutions, Monnet's role in crafting focused plans to serve a larger federal ideal was crucial in ensuring that the ECSC, and then the EEC, produced vastly greater results than the more nebulous idealism that had engendered the Council of Europe. Hallstein, as the first President of the Commission (1958–67), helped ensure the early implementation of the Common Market project at the heart of the Rome treaties, and the fleshing out of the Common Agricultural Policy; Roy Jenkins, in the same office a decade later (1977–81), revived both the Commission's status after a fallow period and the quest for monetary stability, by giving the impulse to the creation of the EMS after the failure of the monetary 'snake'. The role of Jacques Delors (1985–95) in imposing a highly centralized, even personal, style on an activist Commission that prepared the SEA and the Maastricht Treaty, as well as bargaining for Europe in a historically complex set of trade negotiations, has been well documented.[53]

Each of the four European leaders, however, needed support at national level. In the case of Monnet, this was forthcoming from France's foreign minister, Robert Schuman, whose rapid backing for the ECSC project helped ensure its success; from Paul-Henri Spaak, the Belgian Foreign Minister, whose report turned the general conclusions of the Messina Talks into a project that became the Rome Treaties; and from Konrad Adenauer, the West German Chancellor whose Western, Catholic vision of Europe (the view from his house in Rhöndorf, near Cologne, looks westwards across the Rhine)[54] predisposed him to the Monnet plans as an anchor for the identity of the new Federal Republic. The success of the three Commission Presidents depended closely on the solidity of the Franco-German couple, an indispensable condition to any large advances in European integration. Hallstein's aims were in part frustrated by the uncertainties of the tandem. De Gaulle's relations with Adenauer, while remarkable for the symbolism of reconciliation (culminating in the Franco-German friendship treaty of 1963) and for a shared commitment to the Common Market, did not involve a close coincidence of views on other aspects of Europe's future; nor was de Gaulle's vision of a French-led, intergovernmental Europe independent of the US at all close to Hallstein's views; nor did the replacement of Adenauer by Erhard in 1963 improve matters. In the case of Roy Jenkins, the nature of the Giscard–Schmidt couple, characterized by close personal relations and a pragmatic, goal-oriented, and largely intergovernmental view of Europe, was an excellent basis for the EMS project. The projects of Delors, finally, benefited from the support of the most integrationist Franco-German tandem of post-war history in Mitterrand and Kohl. The turning-point of 1995 is instructive in this respect, for thereafter Europe had a deliberately low-profile successor to Delors in Jacques Santer, a French President of erratic European views in Jacques Chirac, and a politically weakened German Chancellor in Helmut Kohl. If Europe's apparent impasse of the late 1990s also owed much to the great intrinsic difficulty of implementing the Maastricht Treaty and the associated economic problems, it is none the less hard to dissociate it from this trio.

The importance of leadership in Europe thus consists first and foremost in the effect produced by the coincidence of an activist Commission President and a French President and German Chancellor strongly committed to Europe. Despite the range of integrationist leaders in other member states, no other combination has had a comparable impact. Nor has leadership yet operated in the opposite direction, in purposeful moves away from integration. De Gaulle's empty chair, it is true, halted the spread of majority voting in Europe, but only for two decades. And Margaret Thatcher's vigorous espousal of an alternative vision of Europe failed to convince her own British Cabinet, let alone her European colleagues.

Conclusion

'There are two competing theories of European integration', writes Tsebelis, simplifying slightly, 'neofunctionalism and intergovernmentalism. Their main point of disagreement is whether governments play the principal role in the process of integration.'[55] In the light of the foregoing discussion, the intergovernmentalist case can be summarized under four main headings.

The uneven character of the integration process over time

If European integration has continued to proceed, it has scarcely done so at the smooth pace that the term 'ever-closer union' would suggest. Measured and purposeful forward steps (the ECSC, the SEA) have been interspersed with spectacular tumbles (EDC), brusque halts (the empty-chair crisis), dead ends (the first attempt at EMU), leaps in the dark (the treaties of Rome, and even more of Maastricht), and inconclusive meanderings (parts of the 1970s, or the later 1990s). This resembles the ordinary vicissitudes of international relations more than the steady construction of a new polity.

The specific character of the international contexts that have favoured integration

Both in 1950 and 1990, European integration was driven by the search, by France and other West European states, for an institutional structure that would restrain a revived Germany and tie its economy and diplomacy to the West. Other contexts, such the economic downturn and monetary dislocation of the early 1970s, have slowed it. Integration may thus be seen as the calculated reaction of governments to changeable circumstance, rather than a process that operates independently of them.

The dramatically varied approaches to integration among member states

At the heart of the process have been the reconciliation and the radically different but frequently interdependent interests of France and the Federal Republic of Germany. Alongside them have been the unreflective Europhilia of the Italians and the caution, pragmatism, or downright Euroscepticism of the British. There is evidence to suggest that these different approaches have structured not only the summit meetings of the European Council, but also the more routine business of the Council of Ministers, and even the behaviour of 'European' civil servants from different member states. Even in the holy of holies of integration, in other words, national identity is alive and well.

The patchiness of European integration across sectors, matching its unevenness over time

The hypertrophy of the Common Agricultural Policy has been accompanied by a single market achieved in two stages, a social and employment policy that barely existed for the first 30 years, and a transport policy that barely exists despite being included in the Rome Treaty. The Amsterdam treaty disappointed hopes that the two new 'pillars' of the EU established at Maastricht would rapidly become as *communautaires* as the Economic Community. On the intergovernmental view, the EU's twisted and unnatural shape, in which prehistoric corporatism coexists with slivers of a neo-liberal regulatory structure and (particularly in the two newer 'pillars') with declaratory policies reminiscent of the UN, is best understood as resulting from untidy package deals negotiated between states—not, once again, from the progressive construction of a 'polity'.

The intergovernmental approach appears an appropriate one for the stalled periods of European integration, readily explicable in the 'realist' terms of conflicting national interest. However, it suffers from a number of defects.

The difficulty of characterizing 'the nation state' as a unitary actor

The policies of member states may vary, not only over time, but in different sectors at the same time. The co-ordination of a complex modern state, problematic at any time (especially where ministerial autonomy has a constitutional basis), becomes more so where government departments are involved in a continuous policy process centred outside the national context. In extreme cases, 'national' policy-makers may come to feel closer to their European counterparts than to their national masters. Moreover, intergovernmentalism cannot easily accommodate other actors, such as interest groups or the Bundesbank, which may affect the course of European integration while operating largely outside the 'state' context.

The 'ratchet' character of European integration

Although it has progressed unevenly, European integration has never gone into reverse. The hopes of British Conservatives, for example, that the inclusion of the 'subsidiarity' principle in the Maastricht treaty would lead to large slices of European Union competence being 'renationalized' have gone largely unfulfilled. Moreover, new steps in integration has usually built incrementally on older ones: the Single Market on the Common Market, for example, or the Single Currency on the Single Market. This suggests that European institutions have built and sustained a dynamic of integration that works, albeit in fits and starts, independently of national governments: the Commission with a handful of deliberate and high-profile initiatives, but also the Court of Justice, which has consistently asserted the primacy of European over national law, and thus furthered *de jure* integration even at times of political stalemate.

The neo-functionalist approaches pioneered by Haas and Lindberg,[56] on the other hand, not only include non-State actors and a European dynamic independent of national governments into their view of integration: they practically depend on them. Central to neo-functionalism are the concepts of 'functional spillover', according to which 'if states integrated one sector of their economies, technical pressures would push them to integrate other sectors'; and 'political spillover', which refers to the political pressures for further integration exerted by interest groups anxious to enjoy its benefits in their sectors and operating at the European level.[57] Integration will then be driven forward, according to the earlier neo-functionalist writings, by the 'constructive disequilibrium' thus engendered. The qualities and drawbacks of neo-functionalism mirror those of intergovernmental approaches. The qualities have already been alluded to:

- Neo-functionalism accommodates a variety of state and non-state actors into the integration process;
- The 'ratchet' character of integration is explicable in terms of an autonomous institutional dynamic;
- Neo-functionalism helps to explain the constant redefinition of member states' positions on European issues, more convincingly than by reference to changing concepts of 'national interest.' It can also explain how some may on occasion be carried to destinations they would not themselves have chosen.

However, while neo-functionalism appears very good at explaining the intense periods of integration, it is a less appropriate theory for times of 'consolidation' or immobility. The drawbacks of neo-functionalism include:

- Its difficulty in explaining the unevenness of integration over time and across sectors, both of which would appear to be impossible according to simple notions of 'spillover';
- Its failure to take into account the vicissitudes of the international context (though George has sought to integrate these into a revised neo-functionalist approach[58]);
- Its failure to explain the consistencies running through the policies of member states over a period of time, which have survived changes of government, and which have served to set the boundaries of possible integrationist projects.

A difficulty with both intergovernmental and neo-functionalist approaches, however, is that they are fundamentally theories of European integration, rather than of European politics. That is, they give relatively little attention to the more regular 'low' politics of the EU's regular functioning. This 'low' politics involves the setting of agendas, the formulation of policies, the debate of legislative proposals, the implementation of policies (at least in outline), and judicial review. These are all things that both the EU and nation states do, albeit in different ways, and as such they invite references to comparative politics. The EU's institutions and their policy-making role will be the subject of the next chapter.

Questions

- Has European integration been primarily an economic or a political project?

- How far can the process of European integration be interpreted as a response to the 'German question'?

- Why have the EU's different member states been unequally willing to surrender sovereignty to supranational institutions?

- What elements in the international context have furthered or hindered the process of European integration?

- To what extent has the process of European integration generated its own dynamic, independently of national governments?

NOTES

1. J. Richardson, 'Policy-making in the EU: Interests, Ideas, and Garbage Cans of Primeval Soup', in J. Richardson (ed.), *European Union: Power and Policy-Making* (London: Routledge, 1996), 3–23: 3.
2. Cf. S. Hix, 'Approaches to the Study of the EC: The Challenge to Comparative Politics', *West European Politics*, 17(1) (January 1994), 1–30, for a full discussion of these approaches.
3. For a fuller treatment of neo-functionalism, cf. S. George, *Policy and Politics in the European Union* (3rd edn., Oxford: Oxford University Press, 1996), 35–56.
4. Cf. e.g. G. Tsebelis, 'The Power of the European Parliament as a Conditional Agenda Setter', *American Political Science Review*, 88(1) (March 1994), 128–42.
5. S. Bulmer and W. Paterson, *The Federal Republic of Germany and the European Community* (London: Allen and Unwin, 1987).
6. P. Taylor, *The European Union in the 1990s* (Oxford: Oxford University Press, 1996).
7. V. Wright, 'The National Co-Ordination of European Policy-Making: Negotiating the Quagmire', in Richardson (ed.), *European Union: Power and Policy-Making*, 148–69: 150.
8. German rearmament took place anyway, within the framework of the Brussels Treaty, the Western European Union, and NATO, from 1955.
9. Qualified majority voting (QMV) is the procedure under which each member state disposes of a number of votes defined in (very) approximate proportion to its size, and a reinforced majority of these votes, typically between two-thirds and three-quarters of the total, is

necessary for a measure to pass. In the fifteen-member EU of 1995, the total number of votes on the Council of Ministers was 87, with the largest members having ten votes and the smallest (Luxembourg) two; the qualified majority was 62. Cf. Table 10.1, p. 451.

10. A rueful self-quotation in the preface to S. George, *Policy and Politics in the European Union* (2nd edn., Oxford: Oxford University Press, 1991), p. v.

11. Norway had also applied, as in 1972, only for the treaty of accession to be rejected at a referendum, again as in 1972.

12. Marcelino Oreja, memorandum presenting the Amsterdam Treaty to European documentation centres, 18 June 1997.

13. M.-T. Bitsch, *Histoire de la construction européenne* (Brussels: Éditions Complexe, 1996), 16–23.

14. Ibid. 27–8.

15. P. Pulzer, *German Politics, 1945–1995* (Oxford: Oxford University Press, 1995), 24–5.

16. Con O'Neill, memo to British War Cabinet, 1945, quoted in W. Paterson, 'Beyond Semi-Sovereignty: The New Germany in the New Europe', *German Politics* 5(2) (August 1996), 167–84: 180; Léon Blum, *A l'échelle humaine*, quoted in M.-T. Bitsch, *Histoire de la construction européenne*, 27.

17. SOFRES, *L'état de l'opinion 1993* (Paris: Éditions du Seuil, 1993), 99.

18. M.-T. Bitsch, *Histoire de la construction européenne*, 84; W. Wallace and J. Smith, 'Democracy or Technocracy? European Integration and the Problem of Popular Consent', *West European Politics*, 18(3) (July 1995), 137–57: 138.

19. For more details on the relationship with the United States, cf. George, *Policy and Politics in the European Union* (3rd edn.), 58–68.

20. Cf. Pulzer, *German Politics, 1945–1995*, 14.

21. J. Gaffney, 'Introduction', in J. Gaffney (ed.), *Political Parties and the European Union* (London: Routledge, 1996), 7.

22. The Mollet government, which signed the Rome Treaty for France, had also set the framework for independence of France's black African colonies—though it was also deeply committed to the war in Algeria. Britain's Prime Minister, Harold Macmillan, delivered Britain's application to join the EC 18 months after his 'winds of change' speech in Cape Town had announced large-scale British decolonization.

23. Pulzer, *German Politics, 1945–1995*, 13, 17.

24. L. Tsoukalis and M. Rhodes, 'Economic Integration and the Nation-State', in M. Rhodes, P. Heywood, and V. Wright (eds.), *Developments in West European Politics* (Basingstoke: Macmillan, 1997), 19–36: 20–1. The paradox can be partly explained by the fact that it was the opposite of the domestic *laissez-faire* and external protectionism which, in the views of the Keynesian orthodoxy of the *trente-glorieuses*, had given the world the depression of the 1930s.

25. Tsoukalis and Rhodes, 'Economic Integration and the Nation-State', 28.

26. H. Wallace and W. Wallace, *Policy-Making in the EU*, 3rd edn. (Oxford: Oxford University Press, 1996), 25, 61.

27. H. Simonian, *The Privileged Partnership: Franco-German Relations in the European Community, 1969–1984* (Oxford: Clarendon Press, 1985), 371. Chirac visited Chancellor Kohl to offer reassurance about his European commitment 48 hours after winning the presidency on 7 May 1995.

28. Ibid. 93–9.

29. F. Mitterrand, *De l'Allemagne, de la France* (Paris: Odile Jacob, 1996), 188–240.
30. A. Peyrefitte, *C'était de Gaulle* (Paris: Éditions de Fallois/Fayard, 1994), 159.
31. T. Garton Ash, *In Europe's Name: Germany and the Divided Continent* (London: Vintage Books, 1994), 389 (1st edn. Jonathan Cape, 1993).
32. T. Banchoff, 'German Policy Towards the European Union: The Effects of Historical Memory', *German Politics*, 6(1) (April 1997), 60–76: 68.
33. T. Garton Ash, *In Europe's Name*, 381.
34. Ibid. 385. Note also (ibid. 386) the resounding European-ness of the conceptions of Germany in the year 2000 offered by new entrants to the 1990 Bundestag.
35. Cf. R. Moeller, 'The German Social Democrats', in Gaffney (ed.), *Political Parties and the European Union*, 33–52; and W. Paterson, 'The German Christian Democrats', ibid. 53–70.
36. W. Paterson, 'The New Germany in the New Europe', 70, 79.
37. Cf. F.-O. Giesbert, *François Mitterrand: une vie* (Paris: Éditions du Seuil, 1996), 693.
38. F. Hayes-Renshaw and H. Wallace, *The Council of Ministers* (Basingstoke: Macmillan, 1997), 177.
39. Cf. D. Hine, *Governing Italy: The Politics of Bargained Pluralism* (Oxford: Oxford University Press, 1993), 288–99.
40. Cf. F. Padoa Schioppa Kostoris, 'Excesses and Limits of the Public Sector in the Italian Economy', in S. Gundle and S. Parker, *The New Italian Republic* (London: Routledge, 1996), 273–93; P. McCarthy, *The Crisis of the Italian State*, 2nd edn. (Basingstoke: Macmillan, 1997), 144–5; M. Bull, 'The Italian Christian Democrats', in Gaffney (ed.), *Political Parties and the European Union*, 139–54.
41. C. de Gaulle, *Mémoires d'Espoir* (Paris: Plon, 1970), 103.
42. I. Ward, 'Identity and Difference: The European Union and Postmodernism', in J. Shaw and G. More, *The New Legal Dynamics of the EU* (Oxford: Oxford University Press, 1996), 15–28: 21.
43. Cf. I. Loveland, 'Parliamentary Sovereignty and the European Community: The Unfinished Revolution?', *Parliamentary Affairs*, 49(4) (October 1996), 517–35.
44. M. Thatcher, *The Downing Street Years* (London: HarperCollins, 1993), 707.
45. P. Morris, 'The British Conservatives', in Gaffney (ed.), *Political Parties and the European Union*, 122–38: 131.
46. D. Spence, 'The Role of the National Civil Service in European Lobbying: The British Case', in S. Mazey and J. Richardson (eds.), *Lobbying in the European Community* (Oxford: Oxford University Press, 1993), 47–73: 70.
47. Cf. J. Richardson (ed.), *Policy Styles in Western Europe* (London: Allen and Unwin, 1982).
48. E. Page, *People who Run Europe* (Oxford: Clarendon Press, 1996), 139; T. Christiansen, 'Tensions of European Governance: Politicized Bureaucracy and Multiple Accountability in the European Commission', *Journal of European Public Policy*, 4(1) (March 1997), 73–90; 83.
49. Wright, 'The National Co-Ordination of European Policy-Making', 59–61.
50. H. Wallace, 'Politics and Policy in the EU: The Challenge of Governance', in Wallace and Wallace, *Policy-Making in the European Union*, 3–36: 27; Spence 'The Role of the National Civil Service', 70.
51. J. Richardson, 'Eroding EU Policies: Implementation Gaps, Cheating and Re-Steering', in Richardson (ed.), *European Union: Power and Policy-Making*, 278–94: 287.
52. Hayes-Renshaw and Wallace, *The Council of Ministers*, 239.
53. G. Ross, *Jacques Delors and European Integration* (Oxford: Polity Press, 1995).

54. Paterson, 'The New Germany in the New Europe', 142.
55. G. Tsebelis, 'The Power of the European Parliament as a Conditional Agenda Setter', *American Political Science Review*, 88(1) (March 1994), 128–42: 138.
56. E. B. Haas, *The Uniting of Europe: Social, Political, and Economic Forces* (Stanford, Calif.: Stanford University Press, 2nd edn., 1968); L. N. Lindberg, *The Political Dynamics of European Economic Integration* (London: Oxford University Press, 1963).
57. Cf. George, *Policy and Politics in the European Union* (3rd edn.), 37–9.
58. Ibid. 57–91.

CHAPTER 10

A European Polity?

'The EU', writes Guy Peters, 'has been conceptualized in a number of different ways, but one important approach to this entity is to think of it as a political system not all that dissimilar to others.'[1] One justification for such an approach is the range of things that the EU does. It regulates the trade of member states, fixing norms for goods exchanged within its borders, setting rules on competition between firms and on subsidies to them, fixing definitions on litigious issues such as what constitutes 'dumping' of produce, or local content, or country of origin, and determining external tariffs in negotiations with world-wide trade partners. It has managed (and protected) Europe's market for farm produce for 30 years under the Common Agricultural Policy. It has overseen the restructuring of what had formerly been a core industry, steel. It sets the framework for the health and safety regulations that apply to every public and private employer on its territory; increasingly, it sets employment regulations too. Its environmental legislation has acquired a stringency beyond what all but a few national governments would have wished. It has sought, with a limited but growing budget, to promote economic 'cohesion' between Europe's wealthier and poorer regions. It has promoted and subsidized mobility among university students and lecturers. It has subsidized a widening range of research and development programmes in such areas as telecommunications and information technology. It co-ordinated economic sanctions against South Africa before 1994, economic aid to Central and Eastern Europe after 1989, and humanitarian aid to Bosnia after 1991. It has sought (with moderate but perceptible success) to limit the vulnerability of Third World trading partners to fluctuations in world commodity prices through the Lomé conventions. It has established a framework policy on immigration and asylum-seeking, allowing the progressive abolition of frontier controls between most member states (with the exceptions of the UK and Ireland). When Jacques Delors predicted that, by the year 2000, some 80 per cent of domestic legislation in member states would be enacted within a European framework, he was guilty of only modest exaggeration. Given the size of this workload, it is unsurprising that, as Wright observes, 'the EU is distinctive amongst international organizations in locking its members into a continuous policy-making process of both an active and reactive nature',[2] and that analysts such as Hix and Lord can state that 'politics in the EU is inherently similar to politics in any "polity" or "system of governance"'.[3]

Such claims nevertheless require qualification. In the first place, as McKay points out, many policy areas that are of great concern to voters remain relatively untouched by EU legislation: they include social security and welfare, health care, elementary and secondary education, defence spending, land-use planning, and law enforcement.[4] Secondly, even apparently highly integrated branches of EU activity such as competition policy or the CAP leave significant room for rule-bending and national variations.[5] Thirdly, recent policy areas brought into the orbit of the EU (such as Foreign Affairs and Security, incorporated as an EU 'pillar' under the Maastricht Treaty), remain under very substantial national control. Fourthly, the implementation of the largest EU initiative of the 1990s, Economic and Monetary Union (EMU), will be in the hands of a new European Central Bank which will be largely free of political control at either national or European level. Finally, the EU is burdened with relatively few of the taxing and spending choices that are an essential dimension of national policy-making: the EU budget is expected to amount to a mere 1.27 per cent of the EU's GDP in 1999. Although a relatively small proportion of this sum is taken up by fixed entitlements, giving the EU significant freedom in its spending choices, the difference between the relative size of the EU's budget and that of a typical member state (anything between 35 and 50 per cent of GDP) is still enormous.

Though indubitably more than an ordinary international organization, the EU is therefore still not equivalent to a state in its policy coverage. This also applies to its institutions. As Helen Wallace remarks, 'precisely because the EC was not established as a state its institutions were in crucial respects not state-like'.[6] Comparisons which carry over institutional arguments and assumptions from member states to the EU, though inevitable and useful, need to be treated with great caution, since the EU remains a unique political system which does not follow any existing constitutional models.[7] In particular, the inter-institutional bargaining identified by many analysts as essential to the EU policy process (to such an extent that the separate roles of Commission, Council, and Parliament are often hard to disentangle) has no precise national-level equivalent.[8]

This central ambiguity of the EU, as an entity that has transcended the status of a mere association of states, without becoming a federal government as its enthusiasts would wish, is a constant of the institutional survey that follows. A second theme is that the 'ever-closer union' envisaged in the Treaty of Rome has proceeded more continuously in the regular workings of European institutions than at the level of formal treaties considered in Chapter 9. If, as Gaffney argues, the EU seems to 'draw [political] parties in and convert them', the same is true of institutions, even those designed as safeguards against federalism.[9] Thus:

- *The European Court of Justice* moved almost immediately from 'holding the ring' between the various institutions of the European Communities to developing a form of European 'Constitution'.

- The work of the *European Council*, begun in 1974 as a simple agreement to hold regular, informal summits at Heads of State and Government (HOGS) level, has become progressively embedded in the other institutions and processes of the EU, and is best seen in this light, rather than as an intergovernmental 'cap' on the development of other institutions.

- The *Council of Ministers*, designed into the Rome Treaty as a means to keep all European legislation under the direct control of ministerial-level delegates from member states (albeit with the possibility of a move to majority voting), has now developed its own bureaucracy, transformed its voting procedures, and embedded itself into a continuous and intense process of consultation with other European institutions.

- The *Commission*, without ever acting as the body of Platonic Euro-guardians imagined by Jean Monnet, has firmly avoided relegation to the status of a mere intergovernmental secretariat envisaged by national leaders like de Gaulle and Thatcher: it has remained at the pivot of all European policy processes, and retains the capacity to play a leadership role as an 'engine of European integration'.

- The *European Parliament* (EP), a merely consultative and delegated body under the

Treaty of Rome, has seen a large accrual of new powers in the two decades following its first direct election in 1979.

- *Interest groups* have followed the shifting locus of decision-making in many areas by massively extending their operations to the European level.

These institutional developments will form the main theme of this chapter. The final section, however, suggests that the unstable equilibrium between its growing range of governmental responsibilities and its retention of a structure falling short of that of a state had, by the late 1990s, plunged the EU into a crisis encompassing the legitimacy and the functioning of its institutions, the nature of the European project they represent, and the EU's relationship to the wider world.

A Constitutional Court? the European Court of Justice

'Its legal system', writes Daniel Wincott, 'is probably the single characteristic of the European Community which most distinguishes it from a conventional international organization.'[10] This does not mean that a body of law, universally respected and un-questioningly implemented in every member state, has sprung fully armed from Europe's treaty-makers and legislative bodies. Mere legalism is no better a guide to politics at European level than it is nationally. The EU contains a variety of legal cultures, more or less inclined to bend general rules to fit specific cases. The legal context is in any case a fluid one, both within member states, where the idea of any constitutional controls on legislation is often recent and controversial, and within Europe as a whole, where the boundaries of EU competence regularly change. But despite those qualifications, the existence of European laws that are enforceable by domestic courts and accessible, at least in principle, to individuals (and thus to firms) clearly distinguishes the EU from, say, an ordinary free-trade or customs agreement. It provides a crucial underpinning to the EU's institutional practices and policies.

The EU's primary legislation is constituted by its constituent Treaties: the Paris Treaty (1951) that set up the ECSC, the two Rome Treaties (1957) that created Euratom and the Economic Community; the Single European Act (SEA) of 1986; the Maastricht Treaty (on European Union) of 1992; and (assuming its ratification) the Amsterdam Treaty of 1997. These texts include preambles containing statements of aims which, after the manner of the Universal Declaration of Human Rights included in the pre-amble to the French Constitution, possess equal status to the rest of the treaty. To these should be added the treaty of 1965 which merged the executive bodies of the three communities; the two treaties of 1970 and 1975, which defined budgetary procedures; the treaties of 1972, 1979, 1985, and 1994 covering the accession of successive new member states; and the 1976 Act providing for the direct election of the EP. The sum total of these documents is a patchwork of extraordinary untidiness (the Maastricht Treaty, for example, consists chiefly of cross-referenced amendments to earlier treaties) but of great importance. For, as Ian Loveland notes, 'The EC Treaties are "constituent" documents. Just as the constitution of the USA creates and limits the powers of the country's federal and state governments, so the EC Treaties create and limit the powers of the EC's various lawmaking institutions.'[11]

Secondary legislation consists of the laws that the EU produces. These include:

- *Directives*, which set out objectives to be translated into law at national level, but leave member states some discretion as to how this should be done;
- *Regulations*, which are directly and universally binding throughout the Union without any requirement for national legislation, and are used in cases where proper implementation would be harmed by the variations that occur in national application of directives, and often, in practice, covering narrow and technical matters, often linked to the CAP;[12]
- *Decisions*, which have the status of administrative acts applying to specific individuals or (more frequently) organizations to whom they are addressed: they may include anti-dumping requirements, or specific exemptions from other legislation for particular member countries;
- *Recommendations and opinions*, which lack binding force, such as memoranda, communications, conventions, programmes, guidelines, or agreements.

One problem of EU law is that, below the level of treaties (all of which are agreed at intergovernmental level and ratified nationally), there is no 'natural hierarchy' that relates the scope and importance of texts to the body deciding them, such as exists in France, for example, between laws (passed by Parliament) and decrees (decided by the executive in application of specific legislation). Directives, regulations, and decisions may all be approved by the Commission, or passed to the Council of Ministers if they are sufficiently important or controversial. The range of legislation is also much narrower than in national law: its chief focus is the EU's central economic pillar and the issues of trade, farms and fisheries, competition, and the environment that are the main stuff of its business. Thus although the EU is a prolific legislator, much of the legislation is of very limited scope indeed.

The guardian of EU law is the European Court of Justice, set up by the 1951 Paris Treaty and the 1957 EC Treaty. The Court, which sits in Luxembourg, consists of one judge for each member state (plus an extra judge if the total number of member states is even), appointed for a renewable term of six years. The judges choose their own president for a three-year period, and are assisted by eight advocates-general, who prepare submissions on cases, as well as a staff of nearly 1,000. They treat upwards of 400 cases annually; a constantly expanding caseload led to the establishment, under provisions of the SEA, of a Court of First Instance, which itself now handles some 600 cases per year. Cases may be brought to the Court of Justice by EU bodies and member states, and by private organizations (typically firms) or individuals able to demonstrate they are directly concerned by a piece of legislation at issue. The most important of such cases typically concern the compatibility of EU laws with the Treaties; the compatibility of national legislation with EU laws; or the failure of member states to act to implement EU legislation. In addition, the Luxembourg Court regularly gives 'preliminary rulings' that interpret points of European law for use by the courts of member states in the cases before them. Since the Maastricht Treaty, the Court has had powers, in specified cases, to impose penalties on member states for non-compliance with its judgements.

Several features of the Court are open to criticism. Its members are required to possess legal qualifications, but not necessarily to have experience as judges. There is no guarantee that the range of their expertise will keep pace with the broadening of the EU's competences.[13] The renewable character of the judges' term makes them vulnerable in principle to pressure from the member states that decide on renewal. The Court's processes are often lengthy (up to 18 months) and costly. And its deliberations take place in secret, without the publication of minutes, voting records, or dissenting opinions, conditions which invite compromise and confusion in rulings.[14]

Despite this potential for fudge, however, a succession of landmark decisions by the Court has displayed an activist thrust comparable to that of the early US Supreme Court under Chief Justice Marshall. In the first place, and on the basis of Article 177 of the Rome Treaty which gave it the right of treaty interpretation, the Court has 'constitutionalized' the basis of EU law by asserting its direct effect within member states, its primacy over national legislation, and the status of Treaty aims as yardsticks by which European and national legislation may be judged. Secondly, the Court's rulings have affected the balance of relations between European institutions. Thirdly, in several areas of public policy, the Court has established a jurisprudence which has either filled gaps left by reluctant legislators, or set the agenda for future legislation.

Direct effect

Direct effect, a legal interpretation set out by the Court rather than a doctrine enshrined in the Treaties, means that European legislation, unlike conventional international treaties, is accessible to individual citizens of the contracting states (which also, indeed more frequently, means firms). It was first established, in relation to the treaties, by the Court in the *Van Gend* ruling of 1962. The ruling is worth quoting at some length, transcending as it does the immediate issue of duties on imports of German urea-formaldehyde into the Netherlands.

The objective of the EEC Treaty, which is to establish a common market, the functioning of which is of direct concern to interested parties in the Community, implies that this Treaty is more than an agreement which merely creates mutual obligations between the contracting states . . . the Community constitutes a new legal order of international law for the benefit of which the states have limited their sovereign rights, albeit within limited fields, and the subjects of which comprise not only the Member States but also their nationals. Independently of the legislation of the Member States, Community law therefore not only imposes obligations on individuals but is also intended to confer on them rights which become part of their legal heritage. These rights arise not only where they are expressly granted by the Treaty, but also by reason of obligations which the Treaty imposes in a clearly defined way upon individuals as well as upon the Member States and upon the institutions of the Community.[15]

A European Polity?

In *Van Gend* the Court used its right to interpret the EEC Treaty of 1957, first to establish that that interpretation could cover general objectives ('to establish a common market') as well as precise details, and secondly to establish that the treaties conferred rights on citizens of contracting states. The Court went on in the 1970s to rule that Treaty articles can be enforced 'horizontally' between private individuals and organizations (in the *Defrenne* v. *Sabena* case, 1976); that EC directives, where not implemented by member states, had direct effect and could therefore be used in court by individuals in disputes with their national governments (in the *Ratti* and *Marshall* cases, of 1979 and 1986); and that the member states which failed properly to implement Community legislation could be made to compensate individuals for any costs that had fallen on them as a result. In 1994, finally, the judges substantially relaxed the criteria necessary for a private individual to prove the 'direct and individual concern' with a legal measure that is a necessary requirement to bring a case to the Court (in the *Cordoniu* case 1994).[16]

The primacy of European over national legislation

The primacy of European over national legislation, which again is not explicitly recognized in the Rome treaties, was asserted in the *Costa* case of 1964. Here, the Court stated that because 'the EEC Treaty has created its own legal system which, on the entry into force of the Treaty, became an integral part of the legal systems of the Member States and which their courts are bound to apply,' it followed that

the law stemming from the Treaty, an independent source of law, could not, because of its special and original nature, be overridden by domestic legal provisions, however framed, without being deprived of its character as Community law and without the legal basis of the Community itself being called into question.[17]

The primacy over national legislation asserted here has two implications. One is that European legislation, albeit within a limited (but ever growing) field, has a quasi-constitutional status in relation to national laws. This was made explicit by the judges in the ruling on *Parti Écologiste Les Verts* v. *European Parliament*, in 1991, when they insisted that 'the European Economic Community is a Community based on the rule of law, inasmuch as neither its Member States nor its institutions can avoid a review of the question whether the measures adopted by them are in conformity with the basic constitutional charter, the Treaty.'[18] Secondly, the primacy of European legislation implied the primacy of the European Court over its national counterparts: for while national courts at all levels had the duty to strike down national legislation that contravened European law, the European court alone can decide on the 'constitutionality' of European legislation, a point made explicit in the *Foto Front* v. *Hauptzollamt Lübeck-Ost* ruling of 1987.[19]

These assertions of the status of the Treaties as the supreme law of the European Union (although still within a limited area of legislation), of the superiority of European law to national law, and of the role of the European Court of Justice's own position as a sort of European Supreme Court, have been neither automatic nor spontaneous. On the contrary, the European Court of Justice has deployed three main strategies in its pursuit of these aims. Firstly, it has taken a 'teleological' approach to the Treaties themselves, arguing that legal interpretation should be based above all on the objectives of the Treaties, for example that of a single market, rather than on their specific legal provisions. Thus, for Wincott,

the Court seeks to give effect to the overall structure and purpose of the Treaty of Rome even if it has to ignore the apparent meaning of the text of particular articles of the Treaty to do so. This method is 'teleological' because it seeks to bring into being the eventual object of the Treaty—a union of the peoples of Europe.[20]

This 'teleological' view has broadened with Community competences over the years: whereas the *Costa* ruling had claimed that 'the Member States have limited their sovereign rights, albeit within limited fields', by the early 1990s, this had become 'in ever wider fields'.[21]

Secondly, in furthering its aim of a fully operative European legal system (with itself at the apex), the Court has often displayed a political adroitness typical of the US Supreme Court in its more creative judgements, and characterized, according to Wincott, by 'purposeful opportunism' (a term first applied to the Commission). That is, many of the Court's rulings have sought to move jurisprudence slowly and progressively towards Europeanizing the legal system, rather than taking all-or-nothing decisions which ran the risk of provoking controversy among the courts or even the publics of member states.[22] This is well-advised: surveys of European public opinion continue to show shaky support for the Luxembourg Court, with regular majorities supporting the Court's abolition 'if it takes too many controversial decisions'.[23]

Thirdly, the European Court of Justice has actively enlisted the support of national courts at all levels, in preference to the confrontation which might readily arise (and on occasion has). In 1967 it even undertook a publicity campaign to attract referrals for interpretation of EC law from national judges.[24] This has been successful: the number of such referrals rose from 32 in 1970 to 194 in 1993, making them the largest single category of cases handled by the Court.[25] The advantage for the Luxembourg Court of this collaboration with national courts is obvious: it gives it allies in every member state and legitimizes it among the judiciary (if not necessarily among the public) throughout the Union. There are also attractions for the national courts. As Renaud Dehousse points out, the invocation of European law may endow ordinary courts with a quasi-constitutional status, permitting them (indeed, obliging them) to disallow national legislation, or grant suspensive relief from its application, if they consider it to infringe a European treaty, directive, or regulation.[26] Perhaps it is not surprising in this light that judicial resistance to the Luxembourg court from member states has come most readily from courts with constitutional or near-constitutional status: during the 1980s, Italy's Corte costituzionale and Consiglio di Stato, as well as France's Conseil d'État showed reluctance to accept Luxembourg rulings on direct effect. So, in the early years after British entry, did the Court of Appeal, though the Master of the Rolls, Lord Denning, came to revise his views within a decade, and in doing so marked a dramatic break with British legal tradition.[27]

Active in promoting the structure of EU law, and thereby its own position, the European Court of Justice has also affected the balance between other EU institutions. The most notable example of this was a series of rulings from the 1980s and early 1990s, which reinforced the position of the EP, both by placing it on a comparable footing as a litigant with the Council and the Commission and, more importantly, by strengthening its role in the legislative process. The *Isoglucose* decision of October 1980 required the Council of Ministers to await the EP's opinion on a legislative proposal submitted to it under the consultation procedure before adopting the legislation, thus granting the Parliament an effective power of delay. The *Titanium Dioxide* ruling of 1991 proscribed the Council's attempt to use the consultation procedure for one of its directives, requiring instead the co-operation procedure (which gives an enhanced role for the Parliament). While the Court has not invariably ruled on the side of the EP, setting limits on its budgetary powers, for example, in 1986, it has on balance acted as its ally, with some of its jurisprudence passing, in modified form, into the Maastricht treaty.[28]

The Court's activism has also found expression beyond questions of institutional competence. With the encouragement of the German Constitutional Court, which had claimed that its constitutional role obliged it to safeguard the fundamental human rights written into the German Basic Law, even against European legislation, the Luxembourg Court began, in the 1970s and 1980s, to develop its own jurisprudence in this area, which had been largely neglected in the European treaties (they were included in the 1997 Amsterdam Treaty).[29] The European Court has also played an important role in securing a minimum level of Europe-wide standards of sexual equality. It did so, for example, in the *Defrenne* vs. *Sabena* case of 1976, where it denied Belgium's national airline the right to dismiss a stewardess on age grounds, when the same rule did not apply to her male colleagues; and in the *Barber* case of 1990, when it ruled that equal-pay legislation applied as much to pensions as to any other part of employee remuneration.[30]

The function of agenda-setting, finally, is a familiar one of the US Supreme Court: *Brown* vs. *Board of Education of Topeka* was important in part for the civil-rights legislation that came, albeit at a decade's distance, in its wake. The European Court's agenda-setting function is best illustrated by the *Cassis de Dijon* decision of 1979. Under this ruling, the West German ban on French blackcurrant liqueur, imposed on the ground that its alcohol content was barely half the German norm of 25 per cent for this type of drink, was struck down by the Court: its view that a clear public-interest requirement had to be demonstrated for this type of trade limitation was to find more wide-ranging expression, six years later, in the White Paper that proposed the abolition of just such non-tariff barriers and led to the SEA.[31]

Perhaps the best confirmation of the Court's importance in the policy-making process is that its activities have attracted the intention of lobbyists, whose representations have probably influenced a number of rulings, for example on sexual equality or (in the case of drinking-water requirements) environmental issues: as Peters remarks, the

Court has thus become an access point to groups in civil society with a European agenda to set.[32] Reflecting the established primacy of European law, this is a major success of the Court, and a necessary but by no means sufficient condition of the EU's eventual transformation into a federal state.

This primacy established, should it be assumed that Court's most active, self-confident period is behind it? Some observers justify this view on three grounds: firstly, a greater caution perceptible in Court rulings from the mid-1990s; secondly, a renewed questioning of the Court's role, for example from the German Constitutional Court; and, thirdly, the regular revision of Europe's treaties, which arguably diminishes the need for jurisprudence to resolve institutional problems.[33] It can also be suggested, however, that treaty revisions may create as many legal issues as they resolve. The Amsterdam treaty, for example, sets out European citizenship rights (such as the right to stand for municipal or European election outside one's country of origin) that are enforceable in the Luxembourg Court. On this view, the continuing institutional fluidity of the EU still guarantees a leading role to the Court, whatever the short-term vicissitudes in its activity.

Organized intergovernmentalism: the European Council

If the Court has a 'natural vocation' as a motor of European integration, the establishment of a body of European law being essential to the expansion of its own role, the same cannot be said of the body that presides over the destinies of all three pillars of the EU, the European Council. As a simple thrice-yearly summit of heads of state and government (HOGS), the European Council, which only came into being in December 1974, nearly 18 years after the signature of the Rome Treaty, has been seen both by its supporters and its opponents as an intergovernmental corrective to Europe's federal tendencies. The latter, in particular, have been tempted to view it as a successor to de Gaulle's 'Fouchet plans', whose more or less explicit intention was to 'cap' the federal progression of the European Community with intergovernmental institutions under French leadership.

The intergovernmentalism of French President Valéry Giscard d'Estaing and West German Chancellor Helmut Schmidt was, however, more flexible and pragmatic than this. The impulse they gave, after winning their respective offices within a few days of each other in 1974, to the institution of regular European summits owed much to a wish to restore the Franco–German axis after the difficulties of the Pompidou–Brandt years. Giscard was also a believer in the value of informal personal meetings to break the deadlocks that had dogged relations between major industrial countries in the early 1970s: hence his simultaneous promotion of OECD summits.[34] In a specifically European context, the main aim of regular summits was to remedy the apparent inability of both the Commission and the Council of Ministers to deliver on the hopes raised at the Hague summit of 1969 (notably on progress to monetary union and on political co-operation), or to frame an adequate European response to the economic and monetary instability of the 1970s.

For over a decade the European Council furnished the outstanding example of a major European institution functioning with no treaty basis at all. The promise of thrice-yearly meetings was kept, on average, since the HOGS met 59 times between March 1975 and December 1994. But their deliberations only acquired official status with the SEA of 1986 and the Maastricht Treaty of 1992.

But regular meetings of the European Community's most powerful politicians could not long remain without institutional consequences. These were essentially fourfold: the agenda of European Council meetings grew in substance and formality; the delegations accompanying the HOGS grew; their preparation became more thorough; and a close link, both logistical and political, was established between the European Council and the presidency of the Council of Ministers. Thus European Council meetings were institutionalized before receiving treaty recognition.

The agenda

The agenda of European Council meetings came to comprise four main elements. The first of these, somewhat on the model of OECD summits, was the economic co-ordination of developed economies in an increasingly unstable world. Such co-ordination was at best relative, as is well illustrated by President Mitterrand's bid to reflate France's economy in 1981 at a time when almost every other European government was doing precisely the opposite. Secondly, European Political Co-operation, the attempt at a common European foreign policy first outlined at The Hague, came within the immediate scope of European Council meetings. They came to discuss issues such as sanctions against South Africa, the recognition of the Palestine Liberation Organization within the context of a European peace initiative in the Middle East, or, later, the West European response to the fall of the Berlin Wall or the break-up of Yugoslavia, as well as addressing more practical matters, such as Europe's position in the GATT talks. Thirdly, the European Council became a sort of 'Court of Appeal' for issues that could not be resolved in the Council of Ministers.[35] In the early 1980s this type of question, and in particular the dreary and recurrent problem of the British budgetary contribution, which the summits had been meant to transcend, threatened instead to engulf them before a final compromise was agreed at Copenhagen in 1984. Fourthly, the European Council has systematically considered the large issues affecting the future of Europe: enlargements, new initiatives such as the Single Market White Paper, and constitutional changes. Thus treaty changes agreed at full Intergovernmental Conferences are invariably prepared at European Council meetings.

The expansion of delegations

The expansion of delegations transformed the summits into large-scale, often ceremonial affairs, with a corresponding loss of informality. As well as HOGS plus their respective foreign ministers (or, in the French case, the President plus either the Prime Minister or the Foreign Minister), financial and economic ministers may hold parallel meetings, as happened in 1992 and 1993. Growing numbers of officials accompany the politicians. From the late 1970s, on the insistence of Roy Jenkins (and despite Giscard's reluctance), the President of the Commission also participated with his delegation. Numbers have also grown with the number of member states (9 in 1974, 15 by 1995). Officials are, it is true, kept at arm's length from the HOGS, only joining their meetings for specific tasks; and the European Council meeting programmes generally build in long mealtime and evening periods for participants to meet informally and engage in the bilateral problem-solving and confidence-building that remain an important purpose of the summits. These provisions offset, albeit only partially, the tendency for greater numbers to mean greater institutionalization.

The preparation of European Council meetings

The preparation of European Council meetings is now undertaken with great care, months in advance. It involves national officials from the state hosting the summit; senior members of the permanent representations of member states in Brussels; and officials from the Secretariat of the Council of Ministers and the Commission. Their preliminary work on the agenda is followed by a foreign ministers' meeting, which confirms the agenda and may open negotiations. Particularly difficult European Council meetings may also be prepared by tours among foreign capitals by ministers of the host country seeking their counterparts' consent to a preliminary agreement.

The link between the European Council and the Council of Ministers

The link between the European Council and the Council of Ministers is first and foremost a logistical one: the Presidency of the Council of Ministers rotates to a different member state every six months, and the member state holding the presidency also hosts the European Council meetings. This engenders a political link. A successful European Council meeting will agree on substantive issues that are of importance to the host state, crowning the months of meetings of the Council of Ministers that have preceded it, enhancing the prestige of the host government, and advancing its European agenda. A European Council meeting that produces no significant agreement, on the other hand, risks turning into a very public display of failure: hence the care with which they are usually prepared. However, such preparation requires the co-operation of other European institutions: the Council of Ministers and its secretariat, and through them the Commission (which formulates the proposals discussed in the Council of Ministers) and the EP (which increasingly has to agree them). Thus the success of the 'intergovernmental' summits depends on the host state's long-term success in furthering its own interests within the full range of European institutions.

A European Polity?

The European Council's inclusion in Europe's treaty structure through the SEA coincided with a reduction in the number of regular meetings from three to two per year, but otherwise did nothing to alter established practice. The Maastricht Treaty was slightly more precise. It defined the European Council's role, in very general terms, as being to 'provide the Union with the necessary impetus for its development' and to 'define the general political guidelines thereof.'[36] It placed the European Council explicitly at the apex of the three 'pillars' of the Union, overseeing the Common Foreign and Security Policy (CFSP) and the Justice and Home Affairs policy (JHA), as well as the central economic pillar. It required the European Council to define occasions where joint action should be taken under the CFSP. And it gave it the very specific task of deciding, on the basis of reports from the European Monetary Institute (the future central bank) and the Commission, on Europe's passage to the final phase of EMU in 1999.

In some senses, the existence of the European Council has placed an intergovernmental 'cap' on the EU's role and evolution. It is the European Council that takes the large decisions about Europe's institutional development, even if other bodies may prepare the decisions and determine the details. Its opposition suffices to kill any policy initiative of really major importance. This sets limits to the powers both of the Commission and of the Council of Ministers to initiate policy and set Europe's agenda; it is noticeable that the behaviour of both of these institutions in the years after 1974 was marked by an increased caution and defensiveness.[37] Moreover, the extension of qualified majority voting has not (with the limited but important exception of the passage to the single currency) applied to the European Council as it has to the Council of Ministers. European Council meetings therefore remain the forum *par excellence* of intergovernmental bargaining, where an individual member state retains the power to prevent agreement. The HOGS who compose the European Council are all accountable to national governments and/or electorates, all of them sensitive, in varying degrees, to their rulers' success in defending 'national interests' within the EU. The European Council's responsibilities to the other institutions of the EU, on the other hand, are largely formal: to present a report to the European Parliament after each meeting, and an annual report in writing on the development of the EU.

However, the intergovernmentalism represented by the European Council, while clearly still dominant in the two newer 'pillars' of the EU, has certainly not given a similar stamp to the rest of the EU's business. In the first place, some European institutions escape the tutelage of the European Council. This is true of the European Parliament, with its increasingly important legislative role; it is also true of the European Court of Justice, except in so far as its judges may depend on national governments for reappointment at the end of six years. Secondly, while the European Council could, in principle, constitute itself as a special meeting of the Council of Ministers, it has never done this. It does not, therefore, have a direct role in the legislation of the Union, though it may influence it indirectly. Thirdly, there is a striking disproportion between the intense, continuous activities of other European institutions and the spaced-out meetings of the European Council, which typically happen every six months and last a mere two days. As we have seen, their preparation is embedded in the other institutions of the EU, whose logic and processes may well be less responsive than the HOGS to national constituencies. A good example is the Commission, which by the 1980s was taking full advantage of its President's recently won right to attend summits. As Rometsch and Wessels write, 'Contrary to initial fears that the European Council would be an instrument for downgrading the Commission to a mere secretariat, it has often proved useful for the Commission's own political strategies. The Commission frequently uses the European Council's declarations and conclusions as a means of setting new goals and developing new initiatives.'[38] European Council meetings frequently require reports from the Commission President. The 1985 White Paper, *Completing the Internal Market*, which led to the SEA, and the two Delors budget 'packages', are all examples of Commission initiatives taken up by the European Council, though the Commission's role in drafting the Maastricht and Amsterdam treaties was rather less important. Finally, while national governments have clearly been able to fix the pace of integration through their control of treaty modifications, this has little bearing on the European Council, strictly speaking, since the treaties are modified by the Intergovernmental Conference. It is therefore more appropriate to see the European Council as a means to improve the EU's responsiveness to its member states than to present it as a brake on all further integration.

Integrated intergovernmentalism: the Council of Ministers

The EU's Council of Ministers fits uneasily into the conventional categories of political institutions. It is a legislature, but one whose members are all ministers, drawn from the political executives of the member states; a European institution, but one initially designed to ensure national control over European policies; a forum for intergovernmental negotiation, but an EU decision-making body; a single institution, but with some twenty different incarnations depending on the policy area being covered. Perhaps the simplest way to conceive of it is as an institution destined by the Rome Treaty to keep the supranational potential of the European Economic Community under tight intergovernmental control, for as long as member states wanted it to: the Community could not, in principle, do anything without the unanimous consent of a group of ministers delegated by national governments. That role lasted longer than many of Europe's founding fathers might have intended. However, since the 1970s, changes in the Council's environment have transformed it into far more of an integrated European institution. This section will consider the Council's evolving political and legal environment before examining the development of its own structures and workings.

The Council and its environment

The essential, though not the sole, activity of the Council of Ministers is legislation, that is, the production of European regulations and directives. Until the Maastricht Treaty, the Council of Ministers had the right of final decision on all European legislation, though this is now shared with the European Parliament for matters falling under the co-decision legislative procedure first set up at Maastricht. The Council of Ministers has always legislated within certain constraints. In the first place, the Commission, not the Council of Ministers, has the sole right to initiate legislation, though in practice this distinction is blurred as the Council frequently invites the Commission to produce legislative proposals on specified issues. Secondly, amendments to Commission proposals can only be adopted either with the Commission's agreement, or with the Council's unanimous support. Despite these constraints, however, the Council is routinely involved in the detailed production of laws; indeed, as Helen Wallace notes, 'the Council rarely discusses general principles as distinct from detailed texts'.[39]

In the first decade or so after the Treaty of Rome, a relatively straightforward model could be applied to the core decision-making process of the EEC: the Commission, the Community organ, proposed, and the Council, the supremely intergovernmental organ, decided, by a unanimous vote. The practice, it is true, was more complicated than this, for four main reasons. First, even within the founding Community of six, the presence of four official languages and the interpreters to cope with them inevitably gave Council meetings a formal and laborious character, ensuring the presence of many more individuals than the half-dozen ministers concerned, and encouraging the use of prepared texts. Secondly, ministers regularly brought two or three officials with them to meetings of the Council; officials from the Commission were also present; and the resulting mêlée of politicians, European and national civil servants, and interpreters came to resemble neither a typical legislature nor a typical ministerial meeting. Thirdly, a growing amount of the Council's work was prepared, and for matters of secondary importance, completed, at official rather than ministerial level. The Council's work rapidly came to be underpinned by the Committee of Permanent Representatives (COREPER), grouping the senior diplomats who head the member states' permanent missions in Brussels, and under it a dense structure of committees and working parties that included officials both from the Brussels missions and from the member states' home civil services. Fourthly, the range of issues within its competence made of the Council a hydra-headed beast, encompassing not one but, by 1975, a dozen groups of ministers. The most frequent and most senior incarnation of the Council is the General Affairs Council, the meeting of foreign ministers which occurs some fifteen times annually. Of almost equal importance are Ecofin, the (roughly) monthly meeting of Economics and Finance Ministers; and Agriculture, also monthly owing to the early importance acquired by agriculture among Community policies. In addition, a range of other Councils, grouping ministers for areas such as Environment, Transport, or

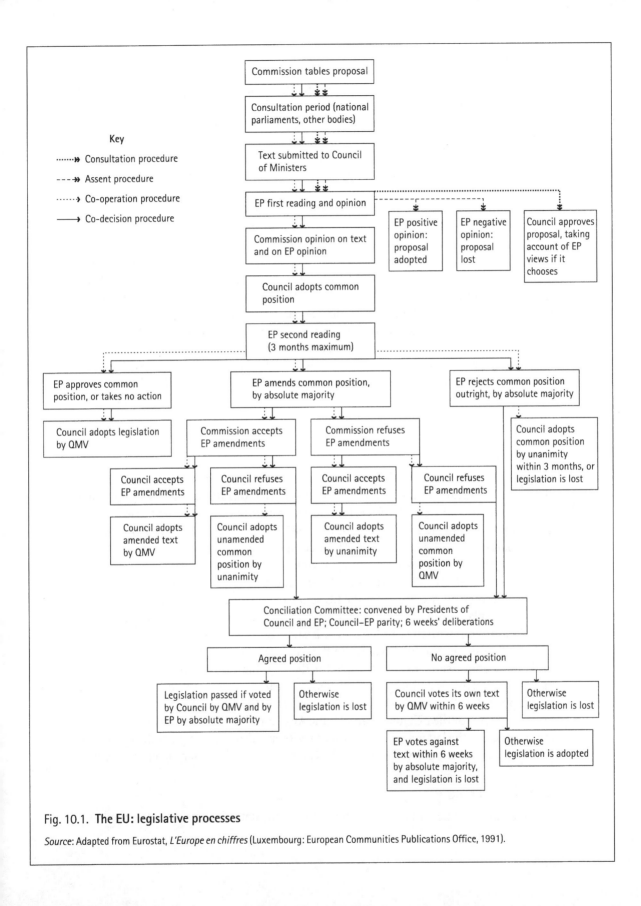

Fig. 10.1. The EU: legislative processes

Source: Adapted from Eurostat, *L'Europe en chiffres* (Luxembourg: European Communities Publications Office, 1991).

Social Affairs, meet between once and four times a year, depending on how 'live' their policy area is within Europe at a given time.

Despite these practical complications, however, the fundamentals of the decision-making process remained relatively simple in the early years: the Council–Commission tandem was the one crucial partnership, and the Council had the final word. The development of this model to allow more majority voting on the Council, or a reinforced role for the Commission, was temporarily frozen by the 1965 Empty Chair crisis and the Luxembourg Compromise that resolved it. The timidity of the Commission's leadership after Walter Hallstein's departure from the presidency in 1967 and the *de facto* continuation of the national veto in Council meetings helped to ensure that Europe's major innovations of the following decade were on an intergovernmental level.

Since the 1970s, however, the tasks and working practices of the Council have been transformed and rendered vastly more complex. Where the early legislative process involved a relatively small number of member states, deciding about rather few things, with the Council as the central decision-maker on the basis of unanimity, the contemporary process embraces a wider range of issues, decided between more member states, with the Council resorting more frequently to votes, and having to co-ordinate its activities with a wider range of institutional partners within Europe. This has resulted chiefly from treaty changes which 'deepened' Europe, widened it to include new member states, and modified the decision-making process itself.

'Deepening' Europe

The growth in the policy-making competence of European institutions has resulted almost automatically in an increase in the legislative workload. According to Fiona Hayes-Renshaw and Helen Wallace, the legislative output of the Council rose from 89 laws adopted in 1965 to 347 in 1970, 601 in 1985, and 738 in 1992, at the height of the Single Market legislative programme.[40] Other aspects of the Council's activity have also taken on greater importance. The budget, which represented less than 0.5 per cent of member states' GDP in 1969, grew to 1.25 per cent in 1995; the distribution of this largesse has become more complex as the EU spends more on a wider range of things. The question of enlargement has rarely left the Council agenda since the 1970s, and took on a new importance with the candidacies of Eastern European countries. The 1980s and early 1990s also saw the EU involved in the vast Uruguay Round of tariff reductions: while the Commission was responsible for the negotiations themselves, the Council played a critical role in defining the Commission's brief—and saying where this had been overstepped. Finally, the Maastricht Treaty also gave the Council a central role in the two new 'pillars' of the EU, Justice and Home Affairs and the Common Foreign and Security Policy. In the latter area, the Amsterdam Treaty also made explicit the role of the President and the Secretary-General of the Council in the EU's external representation.

'Widening' Europe

The addition of 9 new members to the 6 founding states has complicated the basic workings of the Council in rather obvious ways. A simple *tour de table* allowing each member state to speak for five minutes on a legislative proposal might last as little as half an hour among the founding states. With 15 members, and the attendant problems of interpretation (even before the entry of Austria, Finland, and Sweden in the 'EFTA enlargement' of 1995, there were 72 possible combinations of different EU languages), it might take half a day. Unanimity in a Union of 15, given the range of interests represented, is much more difficult to achieve than in a Community of 6.

Changes to the Union's decision-making procedures

These have given the Council a greater range of necessary interlocutors. In the European Community as originally conceived, the Council maintained a continuous dialogue with two partners: the Commission, and the national governments whose ministers constituted the Council's own membership. On a day-to-day basis these relationships were structured by a network of committees, convened by the Commission, that discuss with the Council and with member states future legislative proposals and the implementation of established legislation: they are collectively known under the name of 'comitology'.[41]

The first 'new' interlocutor established by changes to the Community's institutions was the European Council, set up in 1974. The European Council might indeed be seen as a sort of super-Council of Ministers: as Hayes-Renshaw and Wallace note, the Maastricht Treaty sometimes appears to refer to it as such. In practice the European Council has never chosen to meet in this way, or to exercise the legislative function that is the main business of the Council of Ministers. But the work of the Council of Ministers is inevitably structured by the decisions of the European Council, since the latter's clearance is necessary to the passage of any major decision. In that sense a part of the intergovernmentalism that was supposed to be at the heart of the Council's mission has passed 'upwards' to the European Council.[42]

More importantly, formal changes to Europe's legislative procedures, under the Single Act and the Maastricht and Amsterdam Treaties, have greatly reinforced the European Parliament's legislative role (Fig. 10.1), and involved the Council in a new set of negotiations and compromises with a previously neglected partner.

Under the Rome Treaty, Parliament was limited to a purely consultative role in legislation: it had to give its opinion on proposals, but the Council could ignore it. It is true that the European Court's *Isoglucose* decision of October 1980 obliged the Council to await the Parliament's opinion before enacting legislation, thus giving the Parliament an effective delaying power. But this amounted to a somewhat blunt (and possibly unintended) instrument: real modifications had to await the SEA of 1986. Since then, the basic consultation procedure has been replaced in most areas by others: the assent procedure for fundamental issues such as the accession of new members to the EU, and (since the Maastricht Treaty) European citizenship and certain questions relating to EMU; and the co-operation and co-decision procedures (the latter since the Maastricht Treaty) for many other questions.

The assent procedure, which covers such areas as accession of new member states to the EU, association agreements with other countries, questions related to European Monetary Union (EMU), election procedures for the European Parliament, and citizenship issues, consists of a single reading before the Parliament followed by a vote on the text as read. Parliamentary amendments are in principle ruled out of the process, though as Nugent remarks, 'by having the power to say "No" to proposals, the EP also has the power to indicate to what it would say "Yes"'.[43]

The co-operation procedure was introduced by the SEA to allow greater parliamentary involvement in decisions relating to the Single Market. Under this procedure, texts are submitted to the Parliament by the Commission for a first reading. The proposal together with Parliament's opinion then comes before the Council, which produces a 'common position'. This may include amendments to the original text, which may be inspired either by the Parliament's opinion or by the Council's own deliberations, though unanimity on the Council is required to pass amendments with which the Commission does not agree. The common position is then submitted to the Parliament at second reading. If the Parliament approves it, then the legislation is considered adopted by the Council. Rejection of the text, on the other hand (which must be voted by an absolute majority of EP members), means that for the Council to adopt the legislation it must vote it unanimously and within three months. Finally, parliamentary amendments (which must also be voted by an absolute majority of MEPs) are first submitted to the Commission for its opinion. If the Commission refuses an amendment, it can still be adopted by the Council, but only unanimously; amendments approved by Commission can either be approved by qualified majority on the Council or refused unanimously. The co-operation procedure thus replaced the relatively straightforward dialogue between Council and Commission with a more complex three-way game including the EP, in which the formal procedures may be preceded by intense informal preparation and negotiation.

The co-decision procedure, first introduced under the Maastricht Treaty, extends and formalizes this three-way bargaining process. Initially applicable to a limited number of issues including aspects of research, health, and cultural policy, co-decision would become, under the Amsterdam Treaty, 'more or less the general rule', covering a wider range of environmental, transport, employment, social, and regional policies.[44] The co-decision procedure follows a course broadly comparable to co-operation, but with three differences. First, the Council is now obliged to justify its common position to the Parliament, ensuring that parliamentary amendments cannot simply be ignored. Secondly, the refusal of Parliament to adopt a text, or its adoption of amendments which are unacceptable to the Council, leads to the convening by the Commission of a Conciliation Committee composed of equal numbers of MEPs and Council representatives (usually second-rank members of the permanent representations). Thirdly, if the Conciliation Committee fails to reach an agreement within six weeks, or if an agreement is reached but is not accepted by the Council (voting by qualified majority) or by the Parliament (by an absolute majority), then the legislation will be lost. Co-decision therefore removes the Council's right to 'have the final say': even voting unanimously, it cannot override clearly expressed parliamentary opposition to proposed laws.

These changes at the heart of the system of EU legislation justify the observation by Hix and Lord that 'the politics of the EU are structured around *inter*institutional bargaining patterns that make it increasingly unsatisfactory to analyse the Commission, Council and Parliament as separate processes'.[45] Not only must the Council now engage in a continuous dialogue with the EP that was largely unnecessary before the Single Act; in the new triangular legislative process, with the Commission able to choose whether or not to back parliamentary amendments, the Council may find itself aligned either with the Commission against the EP, or vice versa, depending on the issue. Like other European institutions, the Council has also been affected by the growth of lobbying activity since the SEA, with pressure being applied not only through national governments, as it always was, but also through COREPER, and even through the Council secretariat.[46]

The transformation of the Council

Changes in the Council's relationship with the EP and the Commission, and its greater attraction for lobbyists, were closely linked to a transformation of the Council itself and of its decision-making processes. This has involved bureaucratization and institutionalization, and the death or near-death of the unanimity rule that the Luxembourg compromise had preserved.

The bureaucratization and institutionalization of the Council

The bureaucratization and institutionalization of the Council can be illustrated in three ways. First, the full Council meetings at ministerial level are the tip of an ever-larger iceberg. According to Geoffrey Edwards, some 90 per cent of Council decisions are taken at the level of COREPER or below. 'Below' may mean in one of the relatively few formally constituted Council committees (such as the special committee on agriculture, the Article 113 Committee, dealing with commercial policy, or the K4 Committee, covering Justice and Home Affairs matters), or, more frequently, in one of the numerous working groups convened by COREPER which, on the estimate of Hayes-Renshaw and Wallace, settle some 70 per cent of Council business.[47] There are some 50 permanent working groups of this kind, and between 50 and 150 *ad hoc* ones at any given time; on an average day, between 3,000 and 4,000 national officials attend meetings in Brussels. The growing role of officials, and particularly of permanent representatives, while an inevitable response to the need to process a growing volume of Council business efficiently, entails a dilution of the idea that the Council should be the seat of national political control within Europe. Alan Clark's recollections of the Council meetings he attended as a junior minister expresses this view most pungently:

Not, really, that it makes the slightest difference to the conclusion of a meeting what Ministers say in it. Everything is decided, horsetraded off, by officials at COREPER, the Council of Permanent Representatives. The Ministers arrive on the scene at the last minute, hot, tired, ill, or drunk (sometimes all of these together), read out their piece, and depart.[48]

A second aspect of bureaucratization has been the tenfold growth of the Council Secretariat, from 238 staff (many of them interpreters) in 1958 to 2,290 in 1995, organized into ten directorates, a legal service, and an audit office: a small total by standards of most ministries, but large enough, still, to provoke complaints about lack of co-ordination between directorates.[49] While this increase can be partly explained by the arrival of new members and their attendant needs for interpreting and translation facilities, the growth of the secretariat has also been, like the multiplication of working parties, a response to growing responsibilities and volume of business. The result, as Hayes-Renshaw and Wallace remark, has been to create an 'identifiable cohort of decision-makers . . . who have specific common concerns' at the heart of the 'inter-governmental' Council.[50]

Thirdly, the role of the Council presidency, which rotates between member states every six months, has greatly expanded from its initial role of chairing Council meetings. This has happened for a number of reasons. The expansion of Council business has given greater importance to the Presidency's task of fixing the Council's working agenda for a six-month period, allowing the member state concerned significant freedom to press its own positions on some issues, to broker compromises on others, and to consign yet others to benign neglect. A growing awareness of the limitations of the six-month period has, however, led to greater co-operation between successive states occupying the presidency, typically within a 'troika' composed of the current, previous, and future Council presidents, but occasionally within a 'piatnika' which also includes the next two members in the chronological progression. The Presidency's role in convening meetings of the European Council since its creation in 1974 has offered successive member states the opportunity of crowning a successful Presidency with a high-profile summit. The growing importance of the Council's inter-institutional negotiations has given the Presidency an increasingly important role in organizing such contacts. And successive treaties and agreements have given the Presidency a specific role in European activities outside the Economic Community: in the Justice and Home Affairs 'pillar' (albeit in a rather ill-defined way) and in European Political Co-operation and its successor, the Common Foreign and Security Policy, where the current President, assisted by the Secretary-General of the Council, was given the task of representing the EU to the outside world by the Amsterdam Treaty.

Voting on the Council of Ministers

Voting on the Council of Ministers has been transformed by the end of the *de facto* unanimity rule that prevailed on the Council until the early 1980s. The Rome Treaty had provided that unanimous agreement on the Council could be progressively replaced by qualified majority voting (QMV; see Table 10.1) as the member states agreed and as the institutions of the Community took root. But this process was halted in its tracks by the 'empty chair' crisis of 1965 and the 'Luxembourg compromise' that ended it the following year. The 'compromise' was in fact an agreement to differ over what to do when the Council failed to reach unanimous agreement on an issue that remained technically subject to majority voting, but where one state at least felt that 'very important' national interests were involved. The majority view was that the Council members would persist with efforts to find a solution acceptable to all 'within a reasonable time', after which dissenters might be outvoted. The French view was that such discussions should go on indefinitely until agreement was reached, thereby effectively allowing a single member state to block any legislation it wished. The national 'veto' thus enshrined in the Luxembourg Compromise had no treaty status at all, but it became the political baseline for practices which effectively halted the move towards majority voting.

Because it had no treaty status, the Luxembourg Compromise could be undermined by a simple change in mood. This occurred from the late 1970s, for two reasons. First, France, the member state primarily responsible for the Luxembourg compromise, moderated its support for the veto when confronted by the prospect that another member state, Britain, might use it systematically and indiscriminately (a shift in the French position no doubt accentuated by the election of an integrationist President, François Mitterrand, two years after that of Britain's Eurosceptical Prime Minister Margaret Thatcher). The UK's 'veto' was overridden in May 1982 after its representatives had sought, in the name of vital national interest, to link the farm budget to Britain's budget contribution.[51] Secondly, there was a more general awareness among other member states that unanimity had been one of the sources of Europe's relative immobility in the 1970s; that enlargements made unanimity harder to achieve; and that Europe needed the capacity to make more rapid decisions in order to adjust to an increasingly competitive world. That awareness helped ensure that by the mid-1980s, voting on the Council had already become common in some areas.[52]

The 'change of mood' then found clear constitutional expression in the Single European Act of 1986, which included the provision that QMV should apply to legislation designed to implement the Single Market programme. Discussions prior to the Single Act indicated that the new procedures were expected to be used; and from 1987 it became possible for any Council member, not just the President, to call for a vote, which would be taken if a simple majority agreed to one. With the Maastricht Treaty, QMV was extended to environmental policy, development aid, public health, consumer protection, trans-European networks, individual research programmes, some aspects of transport and competition policy, some social policy, and the implementation of the social fund).[53] Under the Amsterdam Treaty QMV would also apply to countering fraud, employment and employment incentives, social exclusion, equal opportunities, and customs co-operation, aspects of data protection, and improving the transparency of the union. It should be noted that these moves to QMV went in tandem with roughly equivalent changes to legislative procedures aimed at giving the Parliament greater involvement, on the principle that measures not unanimously agreed by member states should receive the consent of the EU's directly elected representatives. Thus most policy areas covered by QMV also fall under the co-operation or co-decision procedures.

Unanimity continues to apply in three major areas: first, questions closest to what are commonly considered as the vital interests of member states—key aspects of EMU, joint actions under the Common Foreign and Security Policy, most Justice and Home Affairs questions, and indirect tax harmonization; secondly, to fundamental EU matters (generally subject to the Assent procedure) such as treaty amendments, the accession of new states, the electoral system for the European Parliament, and the appointment of key officials, Commissioners and judges in the European Court of Justice; and thirdly, to a handful of issues which have been subject in the past to sharp dissent along Left–Right lines, or where member states have successfully claimed a special national interest.[54]

The move to QMV is important for three reasons. First, it represents a breach in the intergovernmentalism that was part of the Council's original *raison d'être*. Secondly, it differentiates the EU quite sharply from the normal run of international organizations, where unanimity is the rule, and displays the EU's 'ambition to become a polity', in the words of Hayes-Renshaw and Wallace.[55] Thirdly, by opening up the real possibility that the EU may quite constitutionally legislate in the face of determined opposition from individual member states, it has helped to radicalize debates about Europe's future and its susceptibility to democratic control.[56] That said, there is more continuity than might be supposed in the light of institutional changes between the 'old' Council of the Luxembourg compromise and the 'new' one of the Single Act, and the Maastricht and Amsterdam Treaties. For consensus has remained a common value on the Council in both periods.

The Council and consensus

Observers of the Council agree that in the early years after the Maastricht Treaty, only about a quarter of its legislative decisions were settled by votes. Anthony Teasdale, for example, records that voting occurred in just 72 out of 283 legislative acts between December 1993 and March 1995. In 32 of these cases, voting divided between 'Yes' votes and abstentions; 'No' votes were only cast in 40 cases.[57] Some of these, moreover, may well have been accounted for by the annual farm price round, a routine affair where voting is a matter of course and the time limits are tight. It is true that informal 'sense-of-the-meeting' soundings of opinion in Council may leave no trace in the still-sparse records of Council meetings. Nevertheless, the data available indicate that many, probably most, questions of substance that come before the Council at ministerial level are settled not by votes, but by the informal dealings, whether in the meetings themselves or late at night or during lunch breaks, that permit a variety of available accommodations with reluctant member states: allowances for national interpretation of directives, exceptions to regulations to take account of special national cases, or unminuted declarations giving assurance that a blind eye may be turned to tardy compliance at national level.

Incentives for this consensual approach are present on all sides. For proposers and supporters of legislation, the Commission and members in the majority over any one issue, it is important to ensure effective implementation of European laws. It is also good politics to lock as many states as possible into the majority so as to head off the anti-Europeanism in public opinion that might result from the too-frequent imposition of unwanted legislation on recalcitrant member states. For states in the (potentially) obstructive minority, the prospect of a formal vote hovers over the proceedings, offering incentives for inclusion in the majority: better to exact a price for support than be left in the cold. For a state that consistently finds itself in a minority risks being shut out of the package deals and mutually advantageous arrangements which, as Vincent Wright points out, are the stuff of the interstate politics of the EU.[58]

In the politics of the EU as they are played out in Council, then, the invocation of vital national interest may be a mere bargaining ploy; governments may brandish their veto, or what is left of it, to audiences at home, but hesitate long and hard before using it in Brussels; troublesome member states that could be outvoted under QMV are still accommodated; and representatives of member states, at official and even to some extent at ministerial level, develop a sense of collegiality which might appear from outside to resemble 'going native'. But the search for consensus that is the basis of such practices may appear less strange to continental European (or indeed American) observers of the EU than it does to the British, accustomed as they are to the overweening power of parliamentary majorities. Inter-institutional bargaining is, after all, embedded in Germany's 'co-operative federalism'; Italian politics has been a more or less continuous process of interparty deals necessitated by the absence of majorities; even French governments are condemned to bend rules and to find quiet accommodations with territorial magnates of whatever party. Paul Taylor draws on the consociational model developed to analyse 'pillarized' polities like Holland, where effectiveness in government must take account of diverse sectional interests, to interpret the EU. 'Modified intergovernmentalism', he claims, 'in the special form of consociationalism, was, therefore, the most persuasive image of the European Union in the mid-1990s.'[59]

The Council has neither withered away, as federalists in the manner of Commission President Hallstein might have wished in the 1960s, nor has it been quite the guardian of national interests that de Gaulle would have wanted. Rather, as Hayes-Renshaw and Wallace argue, 'the Council has established an array of procedures and practices that have made it remarkable as a means of pressuring ministers from member governments into a process of sustained collective decision-making'.[60] Many of the forms of intergovernmentalism have been retained even though the outcome differs from that of a typical intergovernmental organization. This apparent inconsistency has a tangible price. The Council's work has been criticized as slow and cumbersome, and the co-ordination between the different Councils as inadequate; the exercise of power has been criticized as both dispersed and unaccountable; the variety of legislative procedures available as baroque in their complexity.[61] But radical alterations to working practices would also entail costs: a purer form of intergovernmentalism would slow down the Council's work to the point of paralysis, while changes in the name of greater 'efficiency' would entail a move to federalism that few member states appear willing to accept.

A government-in-waiting?
the European Commission

If the Council was the most fully intergovernmental institution of the original Community, the Commission was the supremely *communautaire* one. And the Commission's leaders have tended to an elevated view of its federal destiny. Jacques Delors saw it as the 'basis of a European government'. For David Williamson, its Secretary-General, it represented nothing less than 'the future administration of the central institutions of the greatest civil power in the world'; and much of the literature on the Commission argues that its aim transcends the conventional bureaucratic goal of budget maximization, encompassing instead the wider purpose of maximizing the scope of the European Union's competence, and thereby, of course, its own.[62] The founders of the ECSC envisaged that the High Authority (the predecessor of the Commission) would constitute an enlightened European élite, free both of the contingencies of politics and of the selfish preoccupations of member states. These dreams have not been fully realized. The Commission has never enjoyed even the same power, in relation to other European institutions, as that wielded by the High Authority. Many Commissioners have retained, albeit discreetly, a sense of national interest despite their European functions. In some ways, indeed, the Commission resembles a conventional national bureaucracy: it prepares policies for adoption by the elected politicians in the Council and the Parliament, and has limited independent powers of decision. But the Commission is also very much more than the sort of super-Council secretariat that some intergovernmentalists would like it to become. Many commissioners have a high-level political career behind them when they are appointed: and their job allows them to play a far more openly political role than do civil servants. Situated at the interface between politics and bureaucracy, they resemble the 'pure hybrids' delineated in the classic study by Aberbach, Putnam, and Rockman. And the Commission's central power, the power to propose and to persuade, has similarities with that attributed by Richard Neustadt to the American President.[63] This section will open by considering the interplay between the national and the European, the political and the bureaucratic, among Commissioners and the European civil servants who work under them, before examining how the functions of the Commission have endowed it with a power beyond its formal decision-making capacity.

Commissioners and Eurocrats

Nowhere is the uncertain relationship between the demands of nation states and the institutional needs of the EU more evident than in the nomination, appointment, and reappointment of Commissioners. There are 20 Commissioners in the 15-member EU: 2 for each of the 5 largest countries (France, Germany, Italy, Spain, and the UK), and 1 for each of the rest. This total (which has risen from a mere 9 in the original Community) is defined by the wishes of member states (every member wants 'its' Commissioner, and the bigger states want more than the smaller ones), rather than by the intrinsic needs of the Commission. The number is considered as more than enough, and the Amsterdam treaty includes an agreement to move to just one Commissioner for each state, large or small, with the next enlargement. Commissioners, and the President of the Commission, are nominated by the governments of member states; they must be agreed unanimously by the Council; since 1995, the term of office has been for five years, renewable, to coincide with the term of the Parliament. The Maastricht Treaty also subjected the appointment of Commissioners to approval by Parliament (a new duty that the Parliament took very seriously from the outset in 1995, when Jacques Santer's commission came before it).

When nominating Commissioners, governments of member states look first to their own kind. Of the 89 Commissioners appointed between 1967 and 1995, over half (56.2 per cent) had held full national ministerial office: they included 3 former Prime Ministers, 13 former finance ministers, and 7 former foreign secretaries. Two-thirds had previously served in a national legislature, and 22.5 per cent had sat in the European Parliament: a total of 78.7 per cent had some experience of elective office. But some of these politicians had also been bureaucrats: the porous divide between politics and bureaucracy in many member states is reflected in the fact that 55.1 per cent of the Commissioners had served in their national civil services (19.1 per cent as diplomats).[64] Governments also hope (even when, as has been the case of big countries with two posts in their gift, one usually goes to a distinguished opposition politician) that 'their' Commissioners will further the national interest when in post. Hence the lobbying by member states to position 'their' people in jobs to which they attach particular importance, a process which may have as its outcome the awkward division of portfolios to satisfy different candidates: in the 1995 Commission, the EU's external relations were the responsibility of no fewer than four Commissioners (see Table 10.2). There have even been instances of Commissioners incurring reprimand or sanction from their national governments for deviating too widely from national policy: the most notorious case was probably that of Lord Cockfield, the chief author of the Single Market programme, whose failure to win the renomination to the Commission that he wanted was widely attributed to Margaret Thatcher's considering him too enthusiastic a European.

The Cockfield case, though, was the exception rather than the rule, not least because few governments have seen national and European interests as so starkly opposed as did that of Mrs Thatcher. While individual Commissioners maintain close contact with their national governments, and while they have been known to defend national positions against other Commissioners, they are not, on the whole, vulnerable to day-to-day pressures from national governments, and broadly fulfil their Treaty obligation to act on behalf of the whole Union rather than of their member states. Christian Lequesne even cites the case of a Belgian Commissioner who threatened sanctions against his own country's illegal export subsidies.[65]

A European Polity?

Several material circumstances, on the other hand, have helped individual Commissioners to establish a strong record as European policy advocates. Unlike their national ministerial counterparts, Commissioners are untroubled by elections, and relatively immune to public demands for rapid reactions to unfolding events. Their secure five-year term is longer than the period for which most ministers hold a single post. They are able to concentrate almost exclusively on European affairs, they enjoy a near-monopoly of European policy initiatives and, because the Commission is statutorily a collegial body, their personal success in post is linked to that of the Commission as a whole.[66] These considerations do much to balance a Commissioner's dependence on national governments for reappointment and promotion (which about half the Commissioners seek at the end of each term).

Examples of vigorous and (more or less) successful policy advocacy include Étienne Davignon's role in the difficult restructuring of Europe's steel industry in the late 1970s and early 1980s; Lord Cockfield's definition of the 300 measures that made up the Single Market programme; Padraic Flynn's sponsorship of the European Social Charter; Ray MacSharry's dogged pursuit of the first comprehensive reform of the Common Agricultural Policy; Leon Brittan's support for an uncompromising (and, for many member states, deeply unsettling) competition policy; or Carlos Ripa Di Meana's success in tightening Europe's car emission standards. Such cases are, it is true, balanced by those of Commissioners who have seen their jobs as sinecures, or were simply not competent to perform them: George Ross estimates their number at nearly half of the second Delors commission.[67] A Commissioner's impact on policy will thus depend, perhaps to a greater extent than that of a minister, on the activism of the individual concerned.

This is particularly the case because Commissioners lack the electoral mandate which serves, in principle at least, to give direction to the policies of a national government. To some extent, an activist Commission President can fulfil this role. Although formally first among equals in the College of Commissioners, the President has a considerably higher public profile than his colleagues, both inside and outside the EU; and key Commission bodies such as the Legal Service and the Secretariat General come under his direct responsibility. Since the late 1970s the Commission President has appeared at European Council meetings on an equal footing with HOGS; this status now also applies to OECD summits. The presidency offers a 'bully pulpit' (in Theodore Roosevelt's phrase) to an incumbent wishing to use it as such. Jacques Delors clearly did, in a decade-long presidency that moved from the settlement of budgetary difficulties to the establishment of the Single Market to the Social Charter to the EMU project that was the centrepiece of the Maastricht Treaty. As Ross has argued, Delors was adept at 'engineering spillovers' which would further his integrationist purpose.[68] But this leadership did not always favour initiatives from other Commissioners: the inclination of Delors and his private office to bully where they could not cajole often left colleagues and officials demoralized. And the growth in presidential activism has been far from continuous. Each of the three most active Presidents has had a quietist successor: Jean Rey after Walter Hallstein, Gaston Thorn after Roy Jenkins, Jacques Santer after Jacques

Delors. The Delors case may indeed be the exception, and the rule a Commission more inclined to engender a dispersed variety of sectoral measures than a consistent policy thrust.

Commissioners also differ from national Ministers in that they do not head large densely-staffed departments. Indeed, they do not head departments at all: a comparison between Tables 10.2 and 10.3 shows that the portfolios of Commissioners bear only an indirect relationship to the directorates-general into which the bulk of the Commission's civil servants are divided. The Commission's staff in 1995 numbered 19,628 (out of an EU total of 28,501): a figure equivalent to some 80 'Eurocrats' per million EU citizens, against 32,200 national civil servants, or to about half the total number of employees of the City of Paris.[69] The 'bloated Brussels bureaucracy', in other words, exists chiefly in the imaginations of third-rate journalists. The number of civil servants in the senior, policy-making grades runs to about 4,000: again, a tiny number compared with the EU's population.

To some degree, these European civil servants share a sense of mission and a collective identity: one survey in 1988, for example, found that 70 per cent of European civil servants questioned thought it was important to have a 'sense of commitment to the European ideal'.[70] Three elements, however, hold the potential to undermine this. The first is the possibility of poor political leadership, given the rather aleatory relation of Commissioners to directorates-general. Secondly, national divisions apply among civil servants as well as among Commissioners. Although the European civil service operates competitive entry examinations open to candidates from all member states, over half of the most senior posts are occupied by men (and a tiny handful of women) parachuted into Brussels from the upper reaches of national civil services; and at the top three grades, informal national quotas operate.[71] This has certain advantages: civil servants, lobbyists, and politicians of different member states can be reasonably sure of finding a fellow national as an interlocutor somewhere in each of the directorates-general; national governments have fewer excuses to see (or to present) the EU as an alien body staffed exclusively by foreigners. But the drawbacks are equally apparent, such as the over-promotion of second-rate individuals to fill quotas, and the misunderstandings and suspicions between civil servants arising from different national policy styles. Thirdly, the Commission's sense of collective identity is balanced by sometimes deep segmentation and intense competition between different directorates-general. Some directorates-general are almost certain to come into conflict: for example, DGIII, whose main purpose is to ensure the freest possible competition within the EU, and DGIV, which exists to limit and contain the effects of unrestricted competition on vulnerable industries in sensitive regions. DGXI was long regarded as a nest of naïve and irresponsible Greens, whose meddlings were to be contained and resisted by all Eurocrats of good sense.[72] This segmentation and (at times) mutual suspicion is particularly important because, in so far as the EU possesses any technical expertise of its own, it is largely situated within the Commission; and the Commission also acts as the EU's prime target for lobbyists, as the main nodal point for the policy networks that determine so much of European legislation.[73] In other words, we should be aware that 'the Commission' often denotes, not so much a coherent entity operating under a purposeful political leadership, but rather a collection of groups of European civil servants who may entertain more regular contacts with outsiders (from lobbies or the Parliament, for example) than with other civil servants. This relative dispersal is crucial to the way in which the Commission fulfils its functions in the EU.

The Commission and its functions

Although the Commission has not won for itself the status of a government-in-waiting that Commissioners like Hallstein and Delors have wished for it, it retains a very wide scope within which to affect policy. For as Neill Nugent writes, 'One of the key distinguishing characteristics of the system of governance of the European Union (EU) is its considerable dispersal of political power and its associated lack of direct accountability between the governing and the governed.'[74] This dispersal offers considerable scope for the Commission, or its constituent components, to conceive and pursue its own initiatives. These can be classified under three headings: the development of policies and legislation, and a range of both executive and normative functions.

The Commission's legislative and policy-making role

The Commission's legislative and policy-making role is grounded in the treaty provisions giving the Commission the monopoly of legislative initiative, and requiring unanimity on the Council of Ministers in order to amend a Commission proposal in ways to which the Commission is opposed. These early provisions have survived reforms to European institutions more or less intact. For example, although the co-operation and co-decision procedures give an enhanced role to the Parliament in the legislation, they also give the Commission an important role in selecting those parliamentary amendments it wishes to support, and thus how many Council votes would be necessary to carry or reject them. An average year sees the Commission produce 600 to 800 proposals, recommendations, and drafts, and 300 communications, memoranda, and reports.

Two qualifications must be made to this view. First, the monopoly of initiative does not apply to the common Justice and Home Affairs or Foreign and Security policies. Secondly and more importantly, even in the central, Community 'pillar' where it still prevails, the 'monopoly of initiative' is to some extent a matter of form. One survey in 1991 found that only some 6 per cent of 'Commission' proposals really originated with the Commission: among the rest, 28 per cent were linked to international agreements, whether as negotiation guidelines or implementation texts; 21 per cent originated from the Council or from member states; 17 per cent modified existing texts, or followed Court of Justice decisions; 12 per cent followed from programmes (such as research framework programmes) already approved by the Council; 8 per cent were regularly necessary to implement treaty provisions, such as the annual agricultural price round;

and 8 per cent followed from the demands or requests of industry.[75] More generally, as Page remarks, 'proposals are rarely put forward [by the Commission] until they have been negotiated with those whose agreement is essential—above all, member states, sufficient support from which in the Council is a *sine qua non* of major policy change.'[76] Despite such caveats, the Commission's power of initiative remains important. Wherever the initiative originates in the first instance, it is the Commission that controls much of the institutional timing, drafts the initial texts, and decides, in many cases (subject to being overridden by a unanimous vote in the Council and an absolute majority vote in the Parliament), how such drafts may be amended. The very open-ended character of the Rome Treaty has allowed the Commission great freedom to move into new policy areas (such as the environment) and to justify such initiatives in reference to their contribution to achieving a common market. And while its rights of initiative in Justice and Home Affairs and the Common Foreign and Security Policy are limited and certainly not exclusive, the Commission has a 'foot in the door' in these areas, even if as no more than an expert guest.[77] Finally, the Commission is a prolific drafter of subordinate legislation: Page estimates that between 1980 and 1994 the Commission passed 19,603 laws compared with the Council's 8,228. Although the 'comitology' structure ensures, in principle at least, a role for national officials in the drafting of this Commission legislation, and although 61 per cent of it originated with DGVI and consisted chiefly of routine farm price adjustments, the figures remain an indication of how central the Commission is to the regulatory activity that is at the heart of the EU's business.[78]

Because its legislative role is one of proposition rather than of decision, the Commission is bound to exercise its policy-making powers in close co-operation with other EU institutions. First among these is the Council, whose relations with the Commission are as steeped as its own inner workings in incentives to consensus. As Rometsch and Wessels argue, 'it is in the interest of the Commission to push through its proposals and it is in the interest of the Council to have proposals from the Commission which accord with its own views. It is a relationship of give and take in which power plays a central role.'[79] There are several possible models of Commission–Council relations, and while that of 'promotional brokerage', in which the Commission develops and promotes certain policies, but must persuade the Council to accept them, is probably the most commonly applicable, relations may veer between co-operative and conflictual over time.[80] But the potential consequences of institutional deadlock are too dangerous for either side to contemplate prolonged non-co-operation at all seriously: in this respect, the 'empty chair' crisis, though not strictly a Commission–Council dispute, was a salutary lesson.

Secondly, the expansion of the EP's legislative role has led to systematic consultations with parliamentarians, generally within the EP's committees before proposals are formally tabled. In addition, Commissioners now consult the Parliament when drawing up medium-term legislative programmes, and senior officials from the directorates-general regularly appear before parliamentary committees to explain and advocate proposals in the course of the legislative process.

Thirdly, the consultation process goes considerably wider than the formal legislative partners of Council and EP. The Commission must seek opinions from the EU's Economic and Social Council, which groups representatives of employers and trade unions, and from a range of 'expert' committees, composed of national officials who act in an advisory capacity (rather than as the advocates of their national interests), but who may nevertheless offer advance warning on the likely reactions of a national government to a measure, or on the chances of its effective implementation. The Amsterdam Treaty is likely to extend the consultation process further, in the light of new provisions made for the parliaments of member states, and for the EU's Conference of European Affairs Committees of national parliaments, to give opinions on legislative proposals. In addition, the Commission regularly consults a range of formally constituted European interest group federations, of which the archetype is the COPA (Comité des Organisations Professionnelles Agricoles), itself the 'peak' of an elaborate structure of producer groups covering specific agricultural sectors such as cereals, milk, dairy produce, and so on. The circle of consultation also includes the countless individual groups and lobbyists that choose the Commission as their main (though not their only) target within the EU. Research among European civil servants has consistently shown that they place a high value on this type of consultation, not least because the Commission's own human resources and expertise are fairly sparse. As one Dutch official from DGXV told Mazey and Richardson, 'I find that consultation is a very important and very useful source of information in order to guarantee that legislative measures adopted by the European Commission are effective and useful in the "real world".'[81]

However, despite the necessary search for consensus expressed in the endless consultation process, the Commission has on occasion shown, to a greater degree than the Council, breadth and imagination in resolving long-standing problems or setting new policy agendas. The most obvious recent example of this was the chain of initiatives taken under the Delors presidency, including the Single Market programme, the Social Charter, the Maastricht Treaty, and the restructuring of the budget. An essential partner in this succession of initiatives was the European Council, which confounded the fears of federalists (and the hopes of intergovernmentalists) by giving Delors much of the backing he sought.[82]

The Commission's main executive functions within the EU include controlling the implementation of treaties and legislation, managing the EU's finances, and negotiating trade agreements with other states. Part of the task of implementation, the drafting of delegated legislation to flesh out Treaty provisions and legislation passed by the Council of Ministers, has already been referred to. While much of this is routine (and linked to the CAP), some aspects are more sensitive: they include trade questions such as the definition of where subsidies or discounted sales breach competition policy. This subordinate legislation is undertaken within the profusion of advisory, management, and regulatory committees coming under the umbrella of 'comitology'. Comitology has long been a bone of contention between the Council of Ministers on the one hand and Parliament and the Commission on the other, with the Council generally seeking to retain or expand the role of national officials in the committees and Parliament and the Commission to restrain them. A Council decision of 1987, aimed at clarifying the rules governing comitology, succeeded in defining no fewer than seven different types of comitology procedure. So far, the efforts of Parliament and the Commission to simplify this (in one case, through recourse to the Court of Justice) have proved unsuccessful.[83] In a limited number of cases the Commission has been assigned a very direct role in implementation by the member states, most obviously in the highly complex and detailed annual farm-price round. This, though, is very much the exception rather than the rule. More frequently, the Commission attempts to supervise implementation by nation states. Limited resources entail a varying degree of success in this enterprise: standardization of customs and excise procedures and stamps, for example, is a step for which neither member states nor the Commission have so far found the finance, while the Commission (which, after all, lacks its own navy) has found the Common Fisheries Policy almost impossible to police.[84]

The Commission's responsibility for managing the Community budget entails a less critical role than that possessed by the average national finance ministry. This is partly because the budget is so small in relative terms (amounting to under 1.3 per cent of GDP, of which nearly half still goes on farm-price guarantee payments), and partly because the Council has sought to exercise fairly stringent controls, submitting all increases in tax revenue to its consent and requiring all budgets to be balanced. Budgetary difficulties led to a series of crises in the early 1980s. Although these were precipitated by Britain's reluctance to shoulder what Margaret Thatcher considered an unfairly high net budget contribution, they unfolded against a background of low European growth (in which all finance ministries were keen to make savings even from the small shares of national budgets handed over to Europe), and a growing awareness that the farm budget, which at the time represented some 70 per cent of all spending, needed reining in (the EC's farm spending more than doubled between 1975 and 1990, against a GDP growth of just 48 per cent). The resolution of the crises, undertaken largely on the initiative of the Delors Commission, was a series of budgetary reforms which moved the basis of member states' contributions away from a share of VAT receipts and towards a levy based directly on GDP, capped the growth of the farm budget, and allowed a corresponding increase in the Community's structural funds, which accounted for 32 per cent of the 1995 budget. These include the Regional Development Fund, the Social Fund, and the 'Guidance' section of farm spending which assists farmers who move off the land. The Commission also plays an important year-to-year role in the allocation of these funds, as well as in the definition of the EU's various programmes of development aid, whether to African, Caribbean, and Pacific countries or to those of the former Soviet bloc.

The final executive responsibility of the Commission, the handling of trade negotiations, is potentially one of enormous sensitivity. Its importance has grown with the globalization of the world economy and the growing interdependence of other foreign-policy issues (officially still confined to the very intergovernmental 'pillar' of the CFSP, in which the Commission plays a limited role) with trade matters; it was illustrated during the marathon Uruguay Round of trade talks which lasted, with intervals, from 1985 till 1993. For the Europeans, the Uruguay Round was marked by both an institutional and a practical difficulty. The institutional problem was that while the trade Commissioner (Sir Leon Brittan in the final stages) conducts the talks on behalf of the whole EU, the Council is responsible for defining the negotiating brief and for confirming the final agreement: a division of roles that left room for more than one interpretation. The practical difficulty was that of assembling a negotiating position across a wide range of products and services that could both satisfy the conflicting demands of member states and be seen as realistic by the other GATT members. It was the tension between the broadly protectionist instincts of the French (especially on farm produce and cinema and television) and the far more liberal preferences of Sir Leon and of other member states that led to the talks breaking down on several occasions, and only reaching a conclusion at the last possible moment in December 1993.

A final dimension to the Commission's task can be defined as its 'normative' role as the advocate of European integration. In the first place, the Commission has a record as an 'engine of integration'. According to Edwards and Spence, this role often corresponds to a persistent pattern: the use of Article 235 of the Rome Treaty to bring a new area within the competence of European legislation, followed by lobbying to make the same area subject to qualified majority voting. Thus, they argue, 'what the Commission has achieved, with Member State support, of course, has been a sometimes rapid change in the formal, legal basis of Community action'.[85] Secondly, the Commission has maintained certain specific objectives, such as EMU or the Social Charter, on the European agenda even in the face of setbacks or the lack of enthusiasm of member states. Thirdly, the Commission has sought to be a mediator and conciliator, seeking common ground between nation states, and between European groups and institutions.[86] More, perhaps, than any other European institution, the Commission has a vested interest in avoiding a wide-ranging crisis of the EU; this has regularly inclined it to balance bold initiatives with conciliatory gestures and modest incrementalism. Finally, and most tangibly, the Commission is charged with enforcing respect for European law. In some cases the matter at issue, while complex, attracts the Commission's notice as a matter of course. This was true, for example, of the proposed purchase of De Havilland Canada by Aerospatiale, which the Commission blocked on monopoly grounds, by 9 votes to 8; or of the French government's enormous subsidies to Air France or Crédit Lyonnais in the 1990s, to which conditions were set so as to ensure at least a notional respect for competition policy. Other cases are less public: infringements of legislation, or failures to implement it, are difficult to detect for an organization of the Commission's limited resources, and may well be connived at by national governments. Nevertheless, according to Nugent, 'in an average year, the Commission issues around 800 letters of formal notice, delivers 200 reasoned opinions, and makes 80 references to the Court of Justice'.[87] Taking a firm or a member state to the Court of Justice is likely to be a last resort: more frequently, negotiations with a view to ensuring future compliance may be preferred—not least because the sanctions available for imposition on recalcitrant parties are slight, and did not exist at all prior to the Maastricht Treaty. This contrast between the Commission's large powers to frame wide-ranging legislation and its limited ability to ensure that it is complied with is one of several major tensions in its role.

The Commission and its dysfunctions

In so far as the EU resembles a state at all, it resembles a 'regulatory' state. Its main form of policy-making consists of rule-making; its budget is low, and the scope for wealth distribution therefore also low (though not negligible); the costs of policy are externalized, and paid for by member states, individuals, or firms.[88] Growth, for the Commission, means moving into new spheres of competence rather than maximizing its budget. Such growth is backed by interest groups supporting Europe-wide regulation in specific areas (which therefore, as the neo-functionalists would have expected, become agents of European integration).[89] The danger, however, is that the spread of regulation will be piecemeal and unsystematic. For, as Nugent argues,

In many respects the Commission is highly pluralistic, with a divergence of preferences, styles, working procedures and cultures at both College and administrative levels. With Commissioners and DGs enjoying a potentially considerable degree of independence in the exercise of their duties, this diversity can make political and policy dynamism, and overall coherence, difficult to achieve at times.[90]

One cause of the Commission's lack of effective co-ordination and leadership is the very imperfect fit, referred to above (see Tables 10.2 and 10.3) between the portfolios of Commissioners and the directorates-general. This means that directorates-general often lack the clear political direction, and advocacy in the College of Commissioners, that ministries can normally expect from their political heads in a national governmental system. Frequent lack of political direction has allowed culture clashes and turf disputes to go too long unchecked. Member states, which might have sought a remedy to this dispersion, proved reluctant to see a perfectly functional and thus potentially dominant Commission, and so were 'not much moved' to remedy the inevitable intra-institutional rivalries that developed as the individual directorates-general developed their own identities.[91] The result has been characterized by Mazey and Richardson as 'leaderless pluralism', in a Commission that presents a bewildering mix of policy styles between nations and directorates, and an absence of standard operating procedures. In the early years this was compensated to some degree by the 'innovating idealism' of the first generation of Eurocrats; but while this has not disappeared, it is, as Spence argues, inevitably a wasting asset.[92]

Examples of inter-institutional rivalries and differing policy styles abound. The structural conflict between DGIV (Competition) and DGIII (Industry) has already been referred to. To some extent it is replicated in relations between DGVII (Transport)

and DGXI (Environment). Cini, interestingly, describes how DGXI overcame its early marginalization within the Commission by skilfully climbing aboard the bandwagon of the Single Market programme: an example of political leadership overcoming a dysfunction within the Commission.[93] In other cases, however, even clear political leadership is insufficient: the disappearance of DGXXII at the end of the Delors presidency testifies to the failure of efforts to co-ordinate the distribution of structural funds under a single directorate-general.[94] Most bizarrely of all, perhaps, Thomas Christiansen found that 5.7 per cent of the EU's population in the early 1990s lived in regions that were simultaneously eligible for aid from EU structural funds under criteria defined by DGXVI, but denied national or regional aid (to which structural funds are often linked) under the competition rules of DGIV.[95]

The environment of 'leaderless pluralism' has offered ample scope for interest groups to operate: most groups find access to Commission officials easy. This can reinforce the impression of policy incoherence. In more mature bureaucracies this might take the form of individual ministries or directorates forming quasi-independent, exclusive policy communities with selected groups. With the possible exception of DGVI (agriculture) this has not happened in the Commission. Yet the very lack of stable networks of consultative partners can add to the uncertainties of policy-making. As Mazey and Richardson remark, 'The bureaucratic openness is an important cause of the sometimes quite dramatic changes in EC policy as draft Directives are revised following diverse representations from affected groups or because of a bias in the selection of so-called independent experts.'[96]

Linked, albeit indirectly, to the problem of the Commission's lack of co-ordination is that of its legitimacy. For despite attempts by Delors and others to present the Commission as a government in waiting, with the legitimacy and clarity of direction that might be expected to go with it, neither national politicians nor EU citizens have been very willing to accord it this status. Although many Commissioners are former elected politicians, their elevation to the Commission carries with it a tenuous and indirect form of democratic legitimacy: their link to the voters is only through the national governments that nominated them and through the European Parliament which confirmed their appointment. This is the main drawback of the Commissioners' political irresponsibility, and thus immunity from electoral worries, mentioned earlier. It is compounded by the propensity of national politicians, whose electoral concerns may be acute, to blame 'Europe' for unpopular political outcomes.[97] Thus despite Delors' best efforts, a Eurobarometer survey taken in 1992, seven years into his presidency, showed most respondents viewing the Commission as inefficient, too large, static, bad value for money, unclear, bureaucratic, and technocratic; only a bare majority refused to describe it as simply superfluous.[98] Some observers, such as Vernon Bogdanor, have seen a remedy in the forging of a closer relationship between a reformed European Parliament and a Commission which it would not merely vet but choose.[99] But the problem of the relation between the democratic legitimacy of European institutions and their function within the EU's political system is also posed in relation to the European Parliament itself.

The European Parliament and
European political parties

Before the 1980s there were ample grounds for dismissing what was formally known as the Assembly of the European Communities as a weak and unimportant body by comparison both with other European legislatures and with other EU institutions. Until 1979 its members were mere delegates of national parliaments, lacking the sanction of direct election. The Assembly's role in legislation was purely consultative; its opinions could always be overridden by the main European 'legislature', the Council. The 'power of the purse', the tax-raising role that the English House of Commons, for example, had so successfully used in the early assertion of its own power, was limited both by the Rome Treaty and by the small size of the European budget. The Assembly's role as a check on the executive was also severely circumscribed, as none of the bodies which could be seen as constituting the European 'executive'—the Commission, the Council of Ministers, or the European Council—depended on a favourable majority in the EP to remain in office. The EP thus lacked the sanction that lends effectiveness to the range of techniques for parliamentary control of the executive—questions, committees of inquiry, and so on—described in Chapter 5. Moreover, the Council of Ministers in particular was very much a moving target, by virtue of its rotating presidency and its many incarnations.

Since the 1970s, both the treaty texts and, to a lesser extent, European jurisprudence have swung in the EP's favour. In the first place, direct election enhanced the Assembly's legitimacy from 1979, when it also acquired the title of European Parliament (EP): this may be further reinforced from 1999, when the use of a single electoral system throughout the EU should facilitate the constitution of Europe-wide lists of candidates. Secondly, the EP's role in determining the budget has been enhanced by successive texts, starting in 1970. It actually rejected the budget twice, in 1979 and 1984, though with fairly insignificant results. Thirdly, the 1980 *Isoglucose* ruling and, more importantly, the treaty changes made under the Single European Act and Maastricht (which the Amsterdam Treaty would carry one stage further) gave the EP a real role in the legislative process. The treaty changes established the co-operation, co-decision, and assent procedures outlined earlier, and gave the EP the explicit right to request legislative initiatives from the Commission and to be consulted on the EU's legislative programme. Fourthly, the Maastricht Treaty gave the EP a role in ratifying the appointment of the Commission, which it exercised with some energy at its first opportunity in 1995.

None of the old weaknesses wholly disappeared as a result of the changes. Although directly elected since 1979, and thus more than simply national delegates, Europe's parliamentarians (MEPs) do retain a sense of national identity that inhibits the emergence of strong parties at the European level. The 'centrality of parliament' to the legislative process is far from established in the EU, whereas it is taken for granted, at least in formal terms, in member states. The budget is still small. The EP still has no role whatever in the choice of either the European Council or of the Council of Ministers. It remains handicapped by its split location, with its plenary sessions in Strasbourg, committee meetings and party offices in Brussels, and secretariat in Luxembourg (largely because no member state wishes to surrender a share of the EU action); by the language gap which more or less rules out the sort of spontaneous exchanges in plenaries that are the common currency of many national parliaments; by the limited scrutiny of the Council that it can undertake by means of questions; and by the inclination of the Council of Ministers (and of the European Council) to regard it as a nuisance rather than as a partner.[100]

However, the EP's apparent powerlessness in comparison with the parliaments of member states depends in part on the standards by which it is judged: in some ways, MEPs can play more of a policy-making role than their national counterparts. First, while it is true that the absence of strong European party organizations makes for relatively weak and undisciplined party groups in the EP, with a minimal existence outside the Strasbourg hemicycle and the Brussels committee rooms, the case of the US Congress shows that undisciplined party groups with strong sectional loyalties are not invariably the sign of a weak legislature. Secondly, comparison with the US Congress is also useful when considering the political separation of the EP from Europe's 'executive' bodies. Like US Congressmen (but unlike, for example, British MPs, where party binds the fate of the executive to that of majority legislators), MEPs enjoy considerable independence from colleagues in other branches of European governance, and to some extent also from the national party organizations that selected them. Their concern to preserve and extend the prerogatives of their Assembly thus exceeds that of members of the British House of Commons, at least those of its majority. Thirdly, the split-site difficulty is partly compensated by MEPs' relative immunity from constituency concerns (significantly, most constituency mail to the EP has been received by British MEPs, the only ones to have been elected on a constituency system). Unlike US Congressmen, MEPs face neither the constant worry of fundraising nor the need to give the voters an explanation for their every roll-call vote, that go with biennial elections.

The situation of MEPs may perhaps be best summarized as political freedom within institutional constraints. The institutional constraints are self-evident to the casual observer: they mean that even the EP's recently won powers are exercised in close interdependence with other institutions, reinforcing the search for consensus and compromise that we have noted elsewhere. The political freedom is less obvious, not least because of the dreary and impenetrable character of plenary debates in the Strasbourg Parliament. The EP at work, to paraphrase a remark about the US Congress, is very often the EP in committee, and here MEPs do have a chance to affect policy. One sign of the EP's independence (some would say irresponsibility) has been the tendency of interest groups, particularly those seeking to further causes such as equal rights and environmental protection which were not initially well introduced into the EU's other institutions, to beat a path to its door. They have helped make the EP, in George Tsebelis's expression, a 'conditional agenda-setter' for the rest of the EU in some areas.[101]

Elections, Euro-parties, and MEPs

The direct election of the 'Assembly of the European Communities', included as a future option in the Treaty of Rome, was delayed for over a decade by the opposition of member states, and particularly of France under de Gaulle and Pompidou. Decided in principle eight months after Pompidou's death, at the Paris summit of December 1974, direct elections then faced further delays owing to reservations from the Danes and British, and were held for the first time only in May 1979. The resulting enhancement to the democratic legitimacy of the EP, while indispensable in the light of its increased powers, has nevertheless been partial. The EP suffers from a lack of 'readability' for voters that arises from the electoral process itself and the campaigns it engenders; from the (low) political profile of many candidates and MEPs; from the nature of the party groups that MEPs join in Strasbourg; and from the activities of the party groups once constituted.

Turnout at European elections is notoriously low: 62 per cent of eligible voters in 1979, falling to 56.5 per cent in 1994, compared with between 70 and 80 per cent in most elections to national legislatures. One reason for this lack of mobilization, the confusion lent to the contest by a range of electoral systems (of which 13 operated in 1994, on two different days, with separate systems for Northern Ireland and the rest of the UK) is largely technical, and should change with the adoption of one Europe-wide system for 1999. Other factors, though, are more directly political. They arise from mutually reinforcing behaviour patterns on the part of parties, voters, and MEPs. Parties at national level often find European elections embarrassing. If in government, they see them as potentially destabilizing life-size opinion polls between the elections that really matter. Opposition parties, while occasionally sensing an opportunity to flex muscles (the European elections of both 1989 and 1994 delivered famous victories for Britain's Labour Party), may also fear competition from more or less 'anti-system' rivals, particularly where (as in most of the EU) the elections are run on proportional representation. Parties also try to limit the drain on hard-pressed finances caused by European elections, keeping their campaigns low-key to the point, at times, of imperceptibility. And, crucially, they tend to fight the elections, not on European issues, since these are often internally divisive, but on national ones: few attempts are made, beyond rather notional common manifestos for the largest political families such as the European Socialists, to link campaigns to those of sister parties in other member states. Voters respond to (and reinforce) the parties' attitudes by seeing European elections, not as important elections about European issues, but as inconsequential elections about national issues. Polls taken in 1994, for example, indicated that for 55 per cent of European voters, national political issues would count more in voting choice than European ones; only in Holland did a majority expect to vote primarily on European questions, while in five countries the proportion putting national issues first exceeded 60 per cent.[102] Low turnout is complemented by a more or less pronounced tendency to cast protest votes for 'anti-system' parties, especially of the nationalist Right.

The outcome of the electoral process is a body of 626 MEPs, selected with varying degrees of central party control and local autonomy, that resembles national parliamentarians from a social and professional point of view: MEPs are typically dominated by the middle-aged middle classes.[103] The vast majority (many exceptions are apolitical 'personalities' brought in to adorn the lists of some parties) have prior elective experience at local, regional, or national level; some, especially in Italy, France, and Ireland, retain a local or national position; and about 5 per cent—more for the larger parties— have ministerial experience. About a quarter of all MEPs are women—significantly more than in national legislatures: a proportion most readily accounted for by the greater opportunities afforded to parties to put together a (partly) balanced ticket than under most national electoral systems. Yet the career opportunities offered by the EP are generally considered less attractive than those afforded by national parliaments. France is no doubt an extreme case in this respect. French MEPs, according to Hix and Lord, see Strasbourg as 'a nursery school, convalescence ward, or retirement home'.[104] Party leaders like Alain Juppé or François Léotard have readily placed themselves at the heads of electoral lists to enhance their parties' standing, only to resign within weeks or months in favour of more attractive posts. Prominent among Bernard Tapie's reasons for seeking election to Strasbourg was the desire to obtain parliamentary immunity from prosecution for his various business activities and thus avoid a prison cell (he succeeded, but only temporarily). More generally, turnover in the EP is quicker than in national legislatures: only about half of MEPs elected in 1989 had been members of the outgoing parliament.[105] MEPs may already possess the notoriety that politicians crave before they enter the EP, but they are on the whole unlikely to acquire it by staying there. This, in turn, limits the attractiveness of European elections for voters.

A further difficulty for the 'readability' of European elections for voters is the obscurity of party labels. On Kay Lawson's definition of party ('a political party is an organization which nominates and presents to the voters candidates who run on the party label, and which continues to call itself a party after the elections'[106]), there are no European parties. Candidates typically run on lists bearing the names of national parties (or, as in France, on lists carrying ephemeral titles concocted for the campaign), and then join Europe-wide parliamentary groups in Strasbourg with a close or remote connection to their national parties' name, values, and programme. The EP offers incentives, such as secretarial and research back-up, committee posts and possibly chairmanships, and so on, to the formation of groups; these must have 26 members if they come from one member state, 21 if from two, 16 from three, and 13 from four or more. Such incentives appear to be effective, as the tendency in the course of a parliamentary term is towards concentration (though admittedly some groups have also split in mid-term, with the far Right proving especially prone to such schisms). But the price of concentration can be ill-assorted collections of MEPs. Of the three largest groups (see Figure 10.2), the Party of European Socialists (PES) is probably the most coherent as well as the biggest, though even it mixes the Blair Labour Party with Italy's former

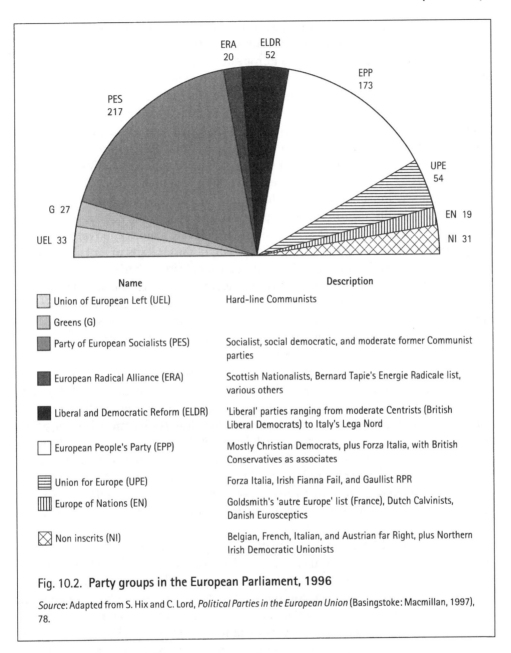

Fig. 10.2. **Party groups in the European Parliament, 1996**

Source: Adapted from S. Hix and C. Lord, *Political Parties in the European Union* (Basingstoke: Macmillan, 1997), 78.

Communists; the broadly Christian Democratic (and pro-European) European People's Party (EPP) also includes Euro-sceptical British Conservatives; while the European Liberal Democrat and Reform Party groups MEPs from the mainstream centre Left, such as Britain's Liberal Democrats, with the anti-system centre Right incarnated in Italy's Northern League).

Under these circumstances, it is perhaps unsurprising that voting behaviour in European parliamentary groups differs significantly from that in most national parliaments, and is less sharply differentiated along European party lines. First, it is coherent where MEPs are united both by party and by country: they tend to vote together, and to organize distinct group meetings alongside the meetings of their Europe-wide groups. Secondly, voting discipline is slighter within the Europe-wide EP groups than it is in groups within national parliaments. Hix and Lord estimate that it has commonly reached between 80 and 90 per cent in the EP groups since 1989, compared with 98 or 99 per cent in many national parliaments; this is as high as can reasonably be hoped for by enthusiasts of discipline, given the rather slight (though not quite negligible) rewards and sanctions available to whips, and the fact that named votes are not recorded. But, thirdly, the three biggest groups vote *with each other* about 70 to 80 per cent of the time, often but not always obtaining an absolute majority and often winning the support of other groups too (though not usually of the far Right or far Left); straight Left–Right votes, on the other hand, are the exception rather than the rule in the EP. Thus the combined effects of proportional representation, which (outside Britain) has lessened the impact of vote swings at European elections in most countries and thereby helped to maintain the EP under a duopoly of moderate Christian Democrats and moderate Social Democrats, together with the absolute majority requirement for many EP votes to be effective, have served to reproduce, within the EP, the incentives to consensus that operate, for rather different reasons, in other EU institutions.[107] The absence of a government to attack or defend, given the Commission's limited powers and limited responsibility before the EP, blunts the edge of debate even where language barriers do not suffice to do so; and the link between holding office and achieving policy goals, so clear at the national level, is much less so at the European level.[108] European groups are not strictly responsible to the national parties that compose them, nor to anyone else: and the loyalty to them of MEPs may be compromised by attachments to particular interest groups, or to issue groups such as Animal Welfare, European Federalism, or Friends of Israel, all of which are represented in the Strasbourg Parliament.

Most observers of European parliamentary groups are therefore fairly damning on their record of achievement. Even Hix and Lord, who argue forcefully that a true, if embryonic, European party system exists, are obliged to conclude that on many criteria, such as organizational cohesion, commitment to office-seeking, policy competition, electoral legitimacy, or recruiting élites and holding them to account for their performance, European parties fail to measure up to national ones: 'the position of European-level parties', they concede, 'is still extremely weak in comparison to parties in most democratic systems'.[109] Peters adds to this the failure of European parties to fulfil the basic function of policy co-ordination, and Gaffney their inability to assure an adequate 'linkage' between citizens and political authority.[110]

Several qualifications, however, may be made to the view that parties are irremediably ineffective, and that the EP is thereby rendered hopelessly weak. In the first place, party groups in the EP are on occasion capable of defining common positions on key issues and sticking to them. Secondly, they can on occasion affect the policies of national parties: Hix and Lord cite the role of the European Socialist Party federation in Strasbourg in converting the British Labour Party to a more positive attitude to Europe in the late 1980s, after Labour's 1983 manifesto commitment to get out of Europe altogether. Thirdly, electoral change can affect the EP's policies: most notably, the change of majority in 1989, thanks chiefly to Labour's impressive reinforcement of the Socialist contingent, did enhance the EP's readiness to legislate on social and environmental issues.[111]

More broadly, criticism of the EP for its lack of highly differentiated, adversarial party groups may, at least in part, be as culturally specific as a distaste for the penchant for package deals and inter-institutional compromises within the EU. That the EP's plenary sessions, aside from brief moments of (restrained) excitement such as the election of the President, the confirmation of the Commission, or the vote of the Budget, are 'chaotic, badly organized, boring, and ill-attended',[112] may seem particularly shocking to observers accustomed to the (relative) drama, and to the sharp party differentiation, of the UK House of Commons. Germans, on the other hand (who provide the largest single contingent to the EP—see Table 10.4), may find more in the EP that is familiar and acceptable to them: the dull plenaries, the search for consensus both within and across party groups. In this respect, the work of the EP's nineteen committees is crucial. The committees are both sectoral, effectively shadowing the Commission's directorates-general (such as foreign affairs, transport, social affairs, or the environment), and horizontal, cutting across a range of policy areas, such as institutional affairs. Committee places and chairmanships are allocated between party groups on a roughly proportional basis, leavened by bargaining, as only half a dozen *national* party groups are big enough to place one or more members in each committee. For chairmanships competition is often acute, especially for committees carrying a big legislative load, such as environment, or those most closely involved with other EU institutions, such as economic and monetary affairs, budgets, or legal affairs. This is particularly true, perhaps, of the Institutional Affairs Committee, described by Westlake as 'Parliament's integrationist hothouse and its strategic command centre', the source of the EP's 'constitutional blueprints' (just enough of which are taken up outside the EP to justify the committee's importance).[113] Beyond the competition for jobs, though, the style of committee work is highly consensual. There are several reasons for this: the duopoly of moderate Christian Democrats and moderate Social Democrats referred to earlier; the parliamentary cultures of some member states; the lack of publicity given to committee work; the interest shared by parliamentarians of all groups (and by the EP's 4,000 or so staff) in the promotion of the EP's role. It is also practically an institutional necessity: as legislative amendments and other EP measures have to be voted in plenary sessions by an absolute majority of all MEPs, and since absenteeism from plenaries is widespread, committee proposals require very broad-based support to have a good chance of passing. The strategic position of committees in the EP's processes invites comparisons with the US Congress, which is very clearly a legislature of strong committees and weak parties—the major difference being that the EP has a great deal less cash to disburse than the Congress and enjoys less freedom in distributing it.[114]

A functioning legislature?

The EP undertakes many of the basic functions of a national legislature: it processes legislation, debates the budget, and scrutinizes the executive. It is also, however, left out of some important sectors of EU activity. This is true of the Common Foreign and Security Policy, though it could be argued that few national legislatures are given much of a role in foreign policy either. But the EP has also been left out of the EU's central political and economic project of the 1990s, that of EMU. Even in the areas where the EP has a clearly established role, it can seem a scaled-down one compared with national parliaments: the right to legislate is, at best, shared with the Council of Ministers and the Commission; the budget is small; and the executive is diffuse and often recalcitrant to control. Against that, though, should be set the considerable recent growth in the EP's powers, and the independence with which it often uses them.

The expansion of the EP's legislative role

The expansion of the EP's legislative role, chiefly since the 1980s, and the main procedures through which it is exercised (assent, co-operation, and co-decision) have been outlined earlier (pp. 403–5). To these procedures should be added the EP's explicit right, recognized at Maastricht, to request legislative initiatives of the Commission, and the increased role played by the EP in the legislative planning process. It is significant that the EP won these new powers not through its own spontaneous initiatives, but by seizing the chances offered by other institutional reforms. The EP's own draft treaty on European Union, for example, which was voted by a comfortable majority and presented in February 1984, was not even examined by the Council of Ministers.[115] Barely two years later, however, the extension of QMV on the Council included in the Single European Act, and the perceived need for an additional source of legitimacy for measures voted in this way opened the opportunity to extend the EP's role through the co-operation procedure. The fact that interest groups, which had hitherto neglected the EP, began to give it more attention after the Single Act indicates the importance of the change.[116] Similarly, the quite widespread extension of the co-decision procedure, and thus of the EU's role, in the Amsterdam Treaty, owed much to a general sense in the IGC that met at Amsterdam that the EU's 'democratic deficit' needed to be remedied, and that one way to do this would be to reinforce the authority of Europe's only directly elected institution.

Does the EP exercise its new powers effectively? In purely quantitative terms, it would appear so: even under the co-operation procedure (which still allows Council the last word on legislation) about half of the EP's amendments to legislative proposals have been adopted, the great majority of them at first reading (when absolute parliamentary majorities are not required). Earnshaw and Judge also consider that some, at least, of these amendments have been qualitatively important. They add that the institution of co-decision has 'tipped the balance [of the EP's legislative role] from influence to power': the creation of the Conciliation Committee, and the EP's ability to halt legislation even after the Committee has met, have made the EP practically an equal partner on the legislative path. This was a partnership that could be pursued with either or both of the other two players; some of the EP's amendments were adopted by the Council against a negative opinion of the Commission.[117] The EP has also, it is true, suffered significant reverses: for example, its attempt in 1994 further to tighten standards on vehicle emissions (after a major success in this area in 1989) led, after intensive lobbying, not only to an adverse Council vote, but even to defeat for the Environment Committee's view within the EP itself.[118] It is also clear that the exercise of its powers under co-decision rapidly led the EP to press further against its institutional limits, notably by seeking its own role in the comitology structures that cover implementation and subsidiary legislation. Just as important as alterations to the formal legislative processes, however, were the wider changes that co-operation and co-decision wrought: the EP increasingly had to be brought into the more or less informal consultation processes that precede any initiative of major importance. The EP's role as 'conditional agenda-setter', according to Tsebelis, stemmed from the Single European Act's combination of QMV and co-operation.[119] The co-decision procedure opened the doors of informal consultation wider: the Council, notably, could no longer be 'off-limits' to MEPs as it had been before Maastricht. The combination of political independence from the executive, relatively lax voting discipline, and a real legislative role, albeit a shared one within limited areas, justify the view that MEPs wield more substantial policy-making powers, but with a narrower scope than their national counterparts, and enjoy a freedom to give issues such as human rights, equal opportunities, and the environment a higher profile on the European agenda than they possess in many national parliaments.[120]

The EP's budgetary role

The EP's budgetary role was reinforced as early as 1970 and 1975 by two treaty changes. They gave the EP powers to propose increases to the Commission's spending plans: if these concern the 'compulsory' budget lines (spending items, chiefly agriculture, made automatic by treaty), the Council can overrule the EP's proposals by a qualified majority; but on other, non-compulsory items, the EP is able to insist on its proposals at second reading. On the other hand, the upward revision by the Council of compulsory budget lines is subject to EP approval. The treaties also empowered the EP, by a two-thirds majority (if this also represented an absolute majority of MEPs), to reject the budget altogether and to submit a new draft from the Commission, though the two occasions when this power was used, in 1979 and 1984, proved inconclusive. It is the President of the EP who holds the formal power to sign the EU budget into law, and the EP may also make observations on the execution of a completed budget before granting it 'discharge'.[121] More recently, the EP has been a partner in the inter-institutional budget planning agreements of 1988 and 1993: these have fixed the overall perspectives within which all spending plans must be made, allowing for a limited increase in the EU's own resources but balancing it both with tighter controls on the farm budget and with an increase in the contributions from member states based directly on GDP. Finally, it was in part thanks to pressure from the EP that the EU's structural funds were classified as non-compulsory from 1993.

There remain, however, significant limits on the EP's budgetary role. The first, simply, is the size of the budget itself; for as we have seen, the EU regulates much but spends little. The most recent inter-institutional agreement expects a budget of 87.5 billion écus (about £59 billion sterling) for 1999, or less than one-fifth the budget of the UK, which accounts for 15.5 per cent of the EU's population. Much of the cost of implementing EU legislation appears in national budgets, over which the EP has no control. Secondly, the EU has been in broad agreement with the general direction of budget reforms since the 1980s—limiting farm spending in favour of 'non-compulsory' outlays—and so has simply not sought to become a loudly dissenting voice in the negotiations on interinstitutional agreements. Thirdly, as Westlake notes, 'Since 1970 the European Parliament has gained increasing power over expenditure, but the European Union's revenue has remained largely beyond its grasp.'[122] Europe's parliamentarians would like to change this by levying a direct 'Union Tax' rather than having the EU rely for the bulk of its resources on the less-than-transparent negotiations between the Commission, the Council of Ministers, and the European Council. Such a change is highly unlikely, given the concern of all member states to control taxation and spending. It might, however, be added that no measure would do more to concentrate the minds of voters on the EP and its activities.

The EP's role in scrutinizing and questioning the activities of the executive

The EP's role in scrutinizing and questioning the activities of the executive is often exercised in similar ways to that of a national parliament. Parliamentarians address some 4,000 written questions a year to other EU institutions, mostly the Commission, and mostly in a genuine attempt to obtain information. Parliamentarians can also address oral questions to Commissioners, a procedure most readily used by British MEPs raising constituency matters. Commissioners also now quite frequently answer questions before the EP's committees, in sessions generally regarded as informal and positive. The EP also plays a part in the appointment of the EU's most senior officials. It must be consulted on the choice of the Commission President. It must ratify the President and member states' choice of Commissioners (the hearings prior to this in 1995 produced pointed criticism both of Jacques Santer and of other Commissioners, and led to two of the latter having to switch portfolios). It may pass, by a two-thirds majority if this is also an absolute majority of MEPs, a vote of censure against the whole Commission (though of seven censure motions tabled since 1979, five have been defeated and two withdrawn). It must discuss the annual report of the Commission.

And it has a right to be consulted over nominations to the Court of Auditors and of the President of the European Monetary Institute.

In undertaking the scrutiny of the executive's activities, the EP faces the usual problems of any national legislature facing a comparable task—a lack of resources adequate to the proper investigation of an executive that is itself often profoundly disinclined to co-operate. Other difficulties, though, are specific to Europe. Executive responsibility is divided between the Commission, the Council of Ministers, and the European Council. The Council of Ministers does usually supply a representative (usually the Foreign Minister of the country occupying the Presidency) to attend meetings of the EP and of its committees. But the Presidency rotates every six months; the Council's composition changes with each national election; and the national governments whose delegates make up the Council, already reluctant to face scrutiny by their own legislatures, are doubly so in relation to the EP. Moreover, the implementation of laws, often a fruitful area for parliamentary scrutiny in national systems, is largely beyond the EP's reach. European parliamentarians know this; hence the wish for more involvement in the comitology structure. But implementation on the ground is in the hands of the national governments, and thus largely inaccessible. The European Council, finally, is largely immune to EP scrutiny, though the EP President may address its summits; indeed, the European Council exerts its own 'scrutiny' over the Council, which is taken more seriously than that of the EP.

A final limitation on the EP's activities is that it does not entirely escape the symbiotic relationship with parts of the executive that characterizes national parliaments (or at least, national majorities) in relation to their governments. To a small degree, this may result from party links between Council or Commission members and EU parliamentarians. Just as important, however, is the mutual interdependence that characterizes the EP's relationship with other institutions, and particularly with the Commission. This relationship is structured by 'a framework of rules and conventions lying outside and beyond the Treaties, with a resultant premium on mutual understanding and goodwill'.[123] The EP needs the Commission to secure support for its legislative amendments, and to provide the expertise which, given its limited staff, it does not have. The Commission (or parts of it), on the other hand, increasingly needs the EP to legitimize its proposals. This interdependence is reinforced by the shared 'integrationist vocation' of two institutions which both depend primarily on further European integration to extend the scope of their activities. A set-piece example of this was the network that succeeded in tightening standards for vehicle emissions in 1989, which included an activist Commissioner and directorate-general working closely with both interest groups and the EP's environment committee. This type of collaboration is necessary in order to establish the legislative record referred to earlier. But as Martin Westlake argues, it also means that, 'Parliament's theoretical constitutional independence is heavily compromised, Parliament frequently preferring to sacrifice the weight of its institutional prerogatives in favour of shorter-term policy aims.'[124]

The ethos of consensus that characterizes the EP as much as it does any other European institution is profoundly worrying to some observers. Vernon Bogdanor, for example, considers that

The European party system bears less resemblance to that of the typical democrat (*sic*) legislature than it does to Giovanni Sartori's model of polarized pluralism in which physical occupation of the centre leads to centrifugal drives, with party competition increasingly coming to take place between an immobile centre and two incompatible extremes, so benefiting anti-system parties and irresponsible oppositions.[125]

At least in relation to the EP, his concerns appear overdramatized. They are so not only because the 'anti-system parties and irresponsible oppositions' are actually quite weak—fewer than 15 per cent of MEPs on the most generous estimate, and thus hardly sufficient to threaten the EP with paralysis—but also because in the EP, they matter rather less than in national parliaments. If the EP has made impressive headway in carving out a legislative role for itself since 1980, it is still far from achieving the 'centrality of Parliament' that was the all-important context of Sartori's model. It remains tempting, and not wholly inaccurate, to regard MEPs as a group of elected officials who are just outside the mainstream of their countries' politics (or, who if they are inside the mainstream, cannot spare enough time for their European duties), are treated with benign neglect by their national party organizations (at least between elections), are given considerable freedom to disport themselves as they wish within the EU's institutions, but are kept out of the really crucial matters such as EMU. Because MEPs arrive in Strasbourg bound by few, if any, electoral commitments, and are subject to rather loose party discipline once there, they readily fall in with the dominant socialization of their institution. This inevitably favours the enhancement of EP prerogatives, and thence both the reinforcement of the EU and the cultivation of good relations with other institutions in it: an ethos that permeates, but also transcends, the dominant groups in the EP. And it would be remarkable if the EP were the only institution within the EU not to favour internal and inter-institutional dialogue and consensus-building against partisan or institutional confrontation.

The role of the EP becomes more problematic, on the other hand, if it is seen as a future base of democratic legitimacy for a federalized EU. For the record of election turnout and of public views on European elections suggest that the EP is very far from enjoying an equivalent legitimacy to that of a national parliament. This is hardly surprising. Democratic legitimacy requires the possibility of choice and of accountability. But choice in EP elections is profoundly skewed, as we have seen, by the interference of national politics. And MEPs are difficult to hold to account as long as their activities lack a stake that is readily comprehensible to voters. None of the piecemeal increases in the EP's powers since the 1970s have supplied that: the EP neither 'chooses' the executive (even in the notional sense of a typical parliament of a European state) nor enjoys the freedom of the US Congress to legislate, tax, and spend almost as it pleases. Nor, largely for these reasons, does it represent any sort of a focus for democratic debate about European or any other issues. MEPs most readily present their own records to voters, not as European policy-makers, or even as European tribunes, but as defenders of national interests.[126] To give legitimacy and 'centrality' to the EP would require not just the Europe-wide electoral system and Europe-wide lists that may come in 1999, but also the attribution of powers commensurate with a discernible stake: the power to tax, to choose the Commission, or both. In other words, the European 'polity' would have to become something much closer to a federal state.

Interest groups and the European Union

If political parties at the European level are weak, even invisible, for much of the time, interest groups are ubiquitous. In Brussels alone, according to Mazey and Richardson, about 3,000 groups, whether European or national, and 100 specialized consultants keep some 10,000 lobbyists gainfully employed seeking to influence European policy-making.[127] In the EU as in nation states, the observation of group activity offers insights into the locus of power in a political system. But several factors render the exercise a particularly complex one in the EU. The policy process is diffused through the whole range of European institutions; the EU's links to the political systems of member states, and thus their systems of group representation, are complex; the (partial) aggregation of interests by parties that occurs in nation states occurs hardly at all in the EU; and the European institutional picture is a dynamic and changing one. This section will define the parameters of group activity in the EU before considering possible models for such activity and how it may be expected to develop.

Parameters of group activity in the EU

The complexity of group activity in the EU is a function of the diversity of the groups themselves; of the range of points within the political system at which groups can exert pressure; of the patchiness of the EU's policy-making capacity; of the segmentation of EU policy-making; and of the diversity of national styles of lobbying.

The diversity of the groups themselves

The diversity of the groups themselves is dictated by the range of EU policy-making. As Mazey and Richardson observe, 'While theorists may debate the precise labels to be used, if one is running an environmental pressure group in France, a chemical company in Germany, or hoping to build a motorway in Spain, the EC will play a very important role in what one is allowed to do.'[128] Some European 'peak' interest groups are actively encouraged, and even subsidized, by the EU: this is true of the European Trade Union Confederation (ETUC), of the Union of Industrial and Employers' Associations (UNICE), or of the Comité des Organisations Professionnelles Agricoles (COPA), all of which are automatic and sought-after policy-making partners of European institutions, especially of the Commission. Below the 'peak' level comes a profusion of Europe-wide producer groups, such as the very well-organized European Chemical Industry Council and, less importantly, the Rubber Industries Liaison Bureau; the Committee of Mayonnaise and Condiment Sauce Manufacturers EEC; the European Assembly of Poultry, Pigeon, and Rabbit Breeders; or the European Natural Sausage Casings Association; and an increasing range of promotional groups, such as Friends of the Earth or the European Union Against Aircraft Nuisance. National-level interest groups may also lobby at the European level, whether they are from EU member states, like France's General Assembly of Chambers of Agriculture, or from elsewhere, like the associations (and firms) grouped under the highly effective umbrella of the American Chamber of Commerce. For most large firms, membership of one or more European interest groups is just one of several avenues through which to exert pressure: the motor manufacturers BMW, Ford, Daimler, Fiat, GM, Peugeot, and Renault were among some 200 firms with their own Brussels offices in 1992. They were joined by local and regional authorities from within the EU, 40 of which, including, for example, 16 of France's 22 regions, had Brussels offices in the early 1990s; in 1995, the Assembly of European Regions (AER) represented some 300 local and regional authorities (compared with just 100 in 1987).[129] Rather less present, except in ETUC, are trade unions, largely because many of them were both nationally powerful and anti-European in the crucial early years, and failed to take full advantage of the corporatist opportunities offered within European institutions such as the Economic and Social Council. It should be added that an office in Brussels is not the sole or indispensable indicator that pressure is being exerted in Brussels. Thus, observes Page, 'Volkswagen, for example, did not have a Brussels office until the early 1990s, and used to direct its lobbying effort, which included chauffeuring the French chairman of the influential *ad hoc* committee on emissions around Brussels, from its Bonn office.'[130]

The range of points at which groups can exert pressure

The range of points at which groups can exert pressure adds to the complexity of analysing their behaviour at European level. The Commission, as drafter of legislation, has traditionally attracted the most intense lobbying efforts in Brussels, whether to its directorates-general or to the *cabinets* of Commissioners: a process likened by Mazey and Richardson to a 'garbage can', an unpredictable and uncontrollable ferment in which lobbyists with solutions seek Commissioners and officials with problems, and vice versa.[131] But lobbyists will also direct their attention to the Economic and Social Committee, to the Commission's various compulsory consultation committees, to the Secretariat of the Council of Ministers, to the committees of the European Parliament (increasingly), and even to the Court of Justice. Moreover, most ministers and senior officials participating in Council meetings will already have been the target of lobbying efforts at national level: thus, according to Hayes-Renshaw and Wallace, lobbyists' activity 'pervades' the atmosphere of the Council of Ministers' deliberations, and may even penetrate the European Council.[132] For a large firm, Europe presents a multiplicity of avenues though which to exert influence, all of which ideally require some attention. The firm can act independently, through one or more national associations, or through one or more European associations; and it can make its representations, whether direct or indirect, through several channels: at national level (and thence to the Council of Ministers); to one or more Commission directorates; to the Commissioners or their *cabinets*; to the committees of the EP; and, in rarer cases, to the European Court of Justice. Alternatively, it can hire a professional lobbying firm to deploy this range of strategies, a practice that has aroused mistrust within the Commission, but which is growing (Brussels counts over 100 such firms).

The patchiness of the EU's policy-making capacity

The patchiness of the EU's policy-making capacity makes possible a wide variety of relations between groups and EU institutions. From the point of view of the Commission, a group may be seen as a useful partner in proportion to its ability to deliver relevant and reliable information, both political (relating to the acceptability of a policy within member states) and technical (relating to the feasibility of implementation), and to deliver consent to policies. But the EU does not handle the full range of policies managed by a nation state, and has not handled them all for the same period of time. In some policy areas the EU has been present from the earliest years, and has built up either its own expertise, or a stable partnership with certain groups, or both. In agriculture, in particular, the EU has long managed a fairly complete spread of policies including the distribution of money. Here, patterns of interest-group consultation are stable and institutionalized, give or take the occasional farmers' demonstration in front of the Commission building in Brussels. In other domains, however, the EU is a more recent arrival in the policy arena, plays a regulatory rather than a distributive role, and is in more need of information and guidance and more inclined to cast its net wide in search of advice. Patterns of interest-group activity vary between the two types. In addition, the EU is also engaged in regular reflection about its own institutional future. This type of strategic thinking would, at first sight, appear to be 'high politics' par excellence, and thus a typical area for intergovernmental bargaining rather than interest-group pressure. Yet there is evidence to suggest that groups have sought to influence this type of negotiation as well as the more day-to-day areas of activity.

The segmentation of policy-making

The segmentation of policy-making also gives rise to wide variations in patterns of relations between the EU and groups. Different groups gravitate to different institutions: while many environmentalists, voluntary organizations, and promotional groups have found the EP more attractive and more open than the Commission, especially since the SEA, most producer groups have been more inclined to see the EP as a second-rank lobbying target after the Commission: thus, as Helen Wallace observes, 'The institutions impact on policy and vice versa, producing different policy modes.'[133] But as we have seen, distinct institutional cultures also coexist between the Commission's directorates. This may require a single group to direct its lobbying to several targets within the Commission at once. And where environmentalists may find regular and respectful listeners in DGXI, scientists in DGXIII, or ETUC in DGV, business interests are more dominant in other directorates.[134]

The diversity of national styles of lobbying

The diversity of national styles of lobbying inevitably affects the process of lobbying within the EU. Just as legislators of some member states will feel better prepared than others, by virtue of their own national parliamentary experience, for the working styles of the EP, so interest groups from different states will be better or less well equipped for 'the essentially low-key, consensual, insiders' approach characteristic of the European environment.'[135] Relations with interest groups also affect the behaviour of national delegations in the Council of Ministers, COREPER, and their subsidiary institutions. On the whole, civil servants and ministers who come from countries with an already intense practice of group consultation, such as the UK, Holland, Germany, Sweden, and Denmark, have found advantages in the additional authority that this gives their representations in Brussels. Prime Minister Édith Cresson actually encouraged French interest groups to organize more at the European level, while Crouch and Menon argue that 'while pluralist systems have not been altered fundamentally by the impact of the EU, more *étatiste* systems such as the French are increasingly experiencing the need for far wider consultation with interests than was previously the case.'[136]

Models of interest group representation in the EU are both diverse and changing

Models of interest group representation in the EU are both diverse and changing as a result of these varying conditions. On the one hand, the Treaty of Rome set up systems of representation in some areas that were deliberately intended to be corporatist. These include the Economic and Social Committee and a range of dispositions connected with agriculture. The official status of COPA and the farm unions that make up its membership allows them both a systematic and largely exclusive involvement in the basic exchange between groups and bureaucrats—knowledge and expertise in return for consideration in drafting legislation—and a role in implementing the CAP. On the other hand, such arrangements coexist in the EU with others, more akin to pluralist models, which are often analysed as policy networks, that is, as more or less close alliances of interest groups, bureaucrats, parliamentarians, and possibly scientific or academic policy specialists ('epistemic networks') covering a particular policy area and intervening at national and European levels. As David Coen observes, 'It is questionable whether empirical observation would support either model [corporatism or pluralism] in its pure form over a broad sample of policy domains.'[137] Moreover, 'policy networks' is itself a term that encompasses wide variations. At one extreme is the rather closed 'policy community', in which bureaucrats and selected groups are able to control most of what happens in a given policy area, and to exclude interlopers—whether other groups or other institutional participants—from their deliberations: information technology and fusion research are among the policy areas that have been characterized in this way. At the other end of the spectrum are impermanent and relatively open 'issue networks', whose participants mobilize towards one specific policy outcome before moving on, absorbing new partners, or possibly dispersing. The same players readily switch interlocutors between different issues: for example, DGXI (Environment), which had proved receptive to the arguments of environmentalists on vehicle emission standards, later collaborated closely with producer groups in consultations about implementing targets for CFC reductions. That inconstancy has led Mazey and Richardson to characterize the European bureaucracy as 'adolescent and promiscuous', capable of relationships with a wide variety of partners, and to conclude that, although no single model of group relations dominates in the EU, 'most [groups] are involved in ill-defined and rather loose "issue networks" of the type identified in the US by Heclo'.[138]

But before concluding simply that group activity within the EU is intense, anarchic, and unpredictable, it is also important to note that not only has group activity grown exponentially since the foundation of the EU (or, more accurately, since the 1980s), but also that it has, in turn, helped shape the EU's development, rather as neofunctionalists said it would. This process needs closer consideration.

The development of
group activity in the EU

The pivotal event in the development of interest groups at European level has been the Single European Act. Prior to the 1980s, group activity was limited by three main elements. First, the range of activity of the European Community was itself limited. The big common policy was agriculture, in which European institutions played a central role in making policy and distributing subsidies, and attracted the participation of farm unions. But in most other spheres, as long as the implementation of the economic integration envisaged in the Treaty of Rome was envisaged in essentially negative terms—the removal of tariff barriers—the extent of European interventionism was fairly small. Secondly, the general rule of unanimity in the Council of Ministers meant that most lobbying efforts could safely be directed towards national governments, particularly if they were intended to stall proposals; a single Council member was enough to do this. Thirdly, as the Council of Ministers had the final decision on all legislation, no return could be expected from lobbying the EP—and only a limited one from the Commission. In this context, as David Coen argues, many interest groups, and notably many large firms, took a largely defensive attitude towards Europe: they aimed to resist European regulation, but did so via their national governments. The small number of business groups, such as the chemical industry, that did establish a strong presence at European level, were exceptions—even if, in their dependence on a fully integrated European market, they were also pioneers.[139]

The change of the 1980s took place in the context of the 'paradigm shift' in West European policy-making, away from the Keynesian models that had nourished the Christian Democratic/Social Democratic consensus of the post-war generation and towards monetarism and the neo-liberal drive to free market forces. This change was accompanied with much rhetoric from its enthusiasts about 'rolling back the State', ultimately involving not so much a 'retreat' of the State as a redefinition of its role away from redistribution and towards the regulation of market forces to ensure their effective working.[140] In Europe, this meant the Single Market programme. Europe-wide regulation offered such a clear prize to major firms, in terms of greater facility to compete within a larger area, with an attendant fall in costs, that it was actively sought by many companies, especially those with transnational bases. At the same time they had an equally clear stake in defining the nature of the Europe-wide regulation so as to correspond most closely to the environment they had been accustomed to in their most important markets. 'The net result,' argues Helen Wallace, 'was to coopt the outside clients of policy as the architects and engineers of policy.' Thus, according to Caporaso and Keeler, when political leaders in Commission and Council sat down to consider the Single European Act they found that much of the work had already been done for them.[141]

The institutional changes brought about by the Single European Act, then, entailed an explosion in interest-group activity at the European level, with the number of officially recognized interest groups rising from 500 in 1985 to 1,500 in 1990.[142] This happened for several reasons. In the first place, the passage to qualified majority voting (QMV) for Single Market legislation removed the former guarantee, more or less effective as long as unanimity had applied in the Council, that national lobbying would produce results in terms of European policy. Interest groups turned to the Commission as the place where legislation was framed in the first instance. And while they could not afford to abandon national lobbying, given the continued importance of the Council of Ministers, they were readier, where necessary, to bypass national governments. Thus Coen's study of the lobbying efforts of major European firms between 1984 and 1994 found that most began to talk less to their national associations, to their national civil services, to their governments, and to their MPs (with whom contact had always been slight), and more to their European federations and to EU institutions. The firms sought to influence not only 'low-politics' questions, such as regulatory structures, but issues of 'high politics' such as enlargement or institutional reform.[143] National governments, meanwhile, found it increasingly difficult both to choose which groups would be allowed into the policy-making circle and to co-ordinate the activities of those that were.

Secondly, far from being an unwilling partner for groups, the Commission found itself increasingly in need of expert advice in view of the enormous broadening in the scope of its job. This was particularly the case as the increased workload involved more regulation rather than more spending. This created ample scope for partnerships between the Commission and a broad swathe of both promotional groups and producer groups seeking Europe-wide regulation.

Thirdly, the enlarged role of the EP as a result of the Single European Act, in an increasingly triangular legislative process, meant that effective lobbying inside the Commission or with the Council could no longer guarantee results. Indeed, the spread of decision-making locations within the EU meant that other institutions, such as the European Court, could also become lobbying targets.

Fourthly, the institutional changes themselves had indirect consequences that also fuelled the explosion in lobbying at European level. The ease of access to European institutions that most groups encountered was an incentive in itself: some groups found in Europe a place in policy-making that they had been denied at national level. There was also a snowball effect, as lobbying by some groups (such as environmentalists) provoked others (such as businesses whose activities might be restricted by environmental regulation) to mobilize.

Fifthly, although business was particularly well placed, by virtue of the resources and lobbying experience it commanded, as well as its international reach, to mobilize across a wide range of policies, it was far from enjoying a monopoly of 'insider' status with EU policy-makers. In part this was because of its own frequent negligence in following some of the most basic ground rules for lobbyists. But it also resulted from the swiftness of institutional change, from the accessibility of policy-makers in the Commission and the EP, and from a diffuse style of policy-making within the EU that has made it difficult for a single group to gain a stranglehold on a policy-making process for long. Pluralism, for Mazey and Richardson, is thus 'the defining characteristic of the EU interest group system', to the point where 'new ideas and proposals can emerge from nowhere with little or no warning, simply because the Commission has seen fit to consult a particular group or a particular expert'—and then, possibly, be reversed following further consultations with other groups. Not only multinationals, but also Friends of the Earth, not only the American Chamber of Commerce, but also the World Wide Fund for Nature, have won a reputation as effective lobbyists in Europe. Hence there exists a series of EU standards on many health and safety questions and environmental issues ranging from drinking water to beaches to packaging to lead-free petrol that have been innovative, and often tighter than most national regulatory structures. Hence too, according to Pollack, a range of possibilities for the representation of 'diffuse interests', such as women or consumers. These, he argues, have so far prevented the free movement of capital within the EU, effective since 1 July 1990, from leading to a 'race to the bottom' in which firms, free to locate where they like, can dictate the stripping-down of regulatory structures to European 'worst-practice' levels.[144]

It is not certain that the intense ferment of group activity triggered by the Single European Act will continue indefinitely in its present form. Several signs since the early 1990s have pointed towards a more ordered but less inclusive system. Firstly, large firms have developed new, often informal, Europe-wide structures to represent their interests: these are typically more flexible than traditional trade associations, and less democratic because they exclude small firms. Secondly, Commissioners and Commission officials, concerned both at 'access overload' and at the unregulated nature of European interest-group activity (which has on occasion led to abuses, such as the sale of draft policy documents to interested parties), have sought ways to restrict access to policy-making to 'natural partners'. Thirdly, the convergence of these two processes in the 1990s led to the establishment of several round-table forums, such as the Automobile Workshop, the Steel Panel, and the Maritime Forum, that bring together Commission officials and large firms. Some of these enjoy effective control of policy-making at a high level: for example, the Bangemann group, named after the Industry Commissioner who convenes it, formulates European telecommunications policy with the participation of eighteen leading European telecommunications firms. Coen sees such contacts tending towards what he calls 'élite pluralism', 'a system where access is generally restricted to a few policy players, for whom membership is competitive and strategically advisable, but not compulsory or enforceable as the corporate model.'[145] Fourthly, large firms have increasingly developed a 'high-politics' agenda covering institutional reform (the streamlining of EU policy processes), monetary policy (EMU without any change to agreed timetables and conditions), and external relations (the establishment of a North Atlantic Free Trade Area), which they have pressed in such forums as the preparation of the 1996–7 IGC.[146]

There are also, however, some grounds for scepticism regarding the early realization of the type of 'élite pluralist' system imagined by Coen. In the first place, the preferences of large firms can themselves be contradictory. For example, there is no guarantee that a more streamlined decision-making process in the EU, which business wants (if only because it would simplify lobbying), would lead to deregulation, which business also wants; the past record suggests that the reverse might be the case. Secondly, the fact that the Commission and leading firms have tried to structure policy-making in round tables does not necessarily mean that they will succeed in producing legislation that satisfies both all the round-table participants and the interested parties on the ground. Such attempts are not unprecedented, but, as McLaughlin and Jordan note, past forums have split apart on national or product lines, leaving the Commission to bargain with individual firms.[147] Thirdly, a large-scale 'rationalization' of the system of group representation in Europe would involve not only the creation of 'inner circles' of policy-making, such as the various round tables, but also the closure of access to many of the players who flooded into the 'market' after the Single European Act. But the exclusion from the policy process of a well-established group (which several environmental groups, for example, clearly are at European level), normally requires a clear, and inevitably controversial, political decision: a classic national example was the Thatcher government's closure of both informal and formal avenues of trade-union representation in government. This, however, is precisely the type of decision that the EU finds most difficult: its ethos, as we have seen, is consensual, and its policy-making structures, even after the Amsterdam Treaty, are diffuse. The issue of the EU's capacity to take clear and thus controversial political decisions is at the heart of the questions about Europe's institutional future, and are addressed in the concluding section.

The crisis of the European Union

The EU possesses four state-like qualities that distinguish it from a mere international organization. It has laws which the Court of Justice has more or less succeeded as establishing as both supreme over the laws of member states and directly accessible to private individuals and companies. It has a directly elected Parliament, which now plays a significant role in legislation. It encompasses an exceptionally wide range of policy areas. And, especially in recent years, it has attracted a vast number of interest groups, which see it at the very least as a decision-making structure to rival, if not to surpass, member states in influence over policy-making.

At the same time the EU can only be conceived of as 'a political system not all that dissimilar to others', as Guy Peters invites us to do (see above, p. 386), in a very limited sense, for it lacks many of the most basic attributes of a state. The EU commands a pitifully small budget, and has no truly independent power to generate revenue because it cannot tax directly. The EP may play a significant role in legislating, but it is not a legislature in the same sense as a national parliament is. The policy areas covered by the EU, wide as they may be, leave important gaps. Not only are important sectors, such as welfare or secondary education, largely left out, but coverage is partial even among sectors that fall more or less within the EU's purview. This is notably the case of the 'regalian' functions included within the Maastricht Treaty, the Common Foreign and Security Policy, and Justice and Home Affairs. As Hayes-Renshaw and Wallace observe, 'the record of the second pillar has been erratic and of the third very thin'.[148] EU foreign policy has barely progressed beyond the declaratory stage: productive of communiqués and harmless in quiet times, but pathetic and vacuous in harsher ones, as the 'EU response' to the collapse of Yugoslavia amply demonstrated. European defence forces, while no longer quite insignificant, remain of largely symbolic importance.[149] There is no European police force and no question of the EU wielding that monopoly of the legitimate use of violence which Max Weber identified as a defining characteristic of a modern state. The EU's policy-making machinery has neither a single institution capable of supplying clear central direction, nor a bureaucracy of remotely comparable size to that found in a modern nation state. Co-ordination not only between, but also within, European institutions is patchy, and policy-making has been called 'loosely knit, headless, porous, inefficient, often unpredictable and occasionally chaotic'.[150] The inadequacy of the EU's performance is perhaps best illustrated by the levels of corruption and fraud of which it is a victim. Most estimates put the cash losses owing to fraud at some 8 to 12 billion écus annually, or roughly 10 to 15 per cent of the total EU budget. While some aspects of fraud are difficult to detect, others are not: perhaps a quarter of Italy's notional olive groves, on which CAP subsidies are paid, are quite visibly non-existent; the subsidies have benefited organized crime, which itself for long enjoyed the active or tacit connivance of the Italian state; and the EU has not chosen to end this state of affairs, partly owing to its lack of enforcement machinery but also because the subsidies form a part of the 'side payments' made to more peripheral players in order to secure consensus on the EU's broader goals.[151]

One interpretation of the EU's lack of basic state-like qualities is that it is simply a matter of time before it develops them: that Europe is a 'nascent polity', in a state of becoming. Several considerations support this view. Of the four state-like qualities outlined above, none was clearly present in the Economic Community of the Rome Treaty: not the superior status of European law, nor the directly elected Parliament, nor the range of policies receiving effective coverage, nor the extraordinary attractiveness to interest groups. All of these arrived later: partly as a result of the intergovernmental bargaining which has supplied the qualitative leaps, via treaties, towards European integration, but also through a series of continuous pressures, exerted both by institutions and, crucially, by interest groups, which corresponds at least approximately to the models developed by the neo-functionalists.

There are also, however, significant difficulties with the 'nascent polity' view of Europe. One of these concerns public opinion; for since the early 1990s it has been clear that the 'permissive consensus' among Europe's voters in favour of continued European integration, a consensus generally shared by politicians, can no longer be taken for granted.

The 'permissive consensus' was based on a combination of general public support for the European ideal (especially in so far as it involved peace and reconciliation within Europe) with relative indifference about the technical means of its achievement. It had underpinned an élite-centred process of European integration which had been more or less sought by Europe's founding fathers, and notably Monnet. They had pursued integration through piecemeal practical steps, justified on technical grounds. This they preferred to grandiose (and thence possibly unrealistic) projects, and to open political debates that risked rekindling precisely the flames of nationalism that they sought to put out for ever: far better to generate reasoned support through quiet and concrete achievement. At the same time, European institutions, once created, quickly begat their own constituency, most notably within the Commission but also in the EP, committed to integration but more intent on mobilizing governments and interest groups behind it than in rallying a public opinion that did not exist, in any structured sense, across European member states. Governments of member states also helped to limit the political scope of Europe in policy debates by treating it as an aspect of foreign policy—a policy area traditionally opened only with great caution to the scrutiny of legislatures and of the public. And they were capable, on occasion, of perfidy towards the institutions they had helped to create: as Helen Wallace remarks, where Europe is concerned, 'Policy gains are frequently claimed by member governments, while policy failures are readily attributed by national politicians to the European level.'[152] That at times, as with de Gaulle's empty chair crisis or Thatcher's budget deadlocks, they sought to halt the integration process and even to call into question the 'permissive consensus', did little to broaden public debate on Europe, which was readily presented as the conflict between stateless technocracy and national sovereignty. Largely absent from the debate has been the usefulness of European integration as a means, largely beyond the capacity of individual member states, to manage the process of globalization in such a way as to preserve some of Europe's specificities, notably the ambition to combine the economic dynamism offered by capitalism with the social justice and public service offered by a strong public sector.

The content of the 'permissive consensus' was perhaps well expressed by the two early referendums on Europe, in France (in 1972) and in Britain (in 1975): both produced a clearly favourable vote, but on a very low turnout, indicating unenthusiastic, and therefore potentially unreliable, support. It is true that European opinion 20 years later, as measured in the twice-yearly *Eurobarometer* polls, remained broadly favourable to the EU: 48 per cent of respondents in the autumn of 1996, for example, thought their country's membership of the EU was a good thing, against 17 per cent who thought it was positively bad. Clear, and in some cases overwhelming, majorities took this view in every country of the EU except Sweden. It is also the case that majorities of Europeans, albeit less substantial ones, carried this general support over to particular issues, supporting common European policies not only in relatively established areas such as agriculture, the environment, scientific research, or fighting unemployment, but also in defence, foreign policy, immigration, and political asylum—and the single currency, supported by 54 per cent against 40 per cent of respondents.[153]

But these generally favourable indices should be set against a gentle but clear decline in support for Europe over the 1990s: in 1990, for example, nearly 64.5 per cent of European respondents had thought their country's membership of Europe was a good thing, and 57.6 per cent had favoured the single currency.[154] Moreover, there is evidence to suggest that the 'permissive consensus' is easily punctured if pressed on particular issues. In this respect the public reactions to the Maastricht Treaty constituted a watershed. The No vote at the Danish referendum of June 1992, while unremarkable in some ways (Euroscepticism has traditionally run as strongly among the Danes as among the British) was both institutionally inconvenient and unprecedented: no people of an existing member state had refused a European policy in this way before. Perhaps more politically unnerving was the minute margin of France's Yes vote the following September: at a referendum whose favourable outcome was at first seen as a foregone conclusion, the citizens of a core member state came within fewer than a million votes of wrecking the European Community's central project. In other states, too, support for EMU ebbed away between the signature of the Maastricht Treaty in February 1992 and its final ratification in October 1993. In Britain, a roughly even balance between support and opposition moved towards a comfortable majority opposed. In Germany, a lukewarm level of support when the treaty was signed gave way to a majority opposed to giving up the Deutschmark for a less-sure European currency.

Several reasons can be put forward for the Maastricht upset, some but not all directly related to the European project. First, a single currency involves a limitation of national sovereignty that is far more visible and tangible to every citizen than anything entailed by, say, a common environmental policy or even the Single Market: the technical debate on EMU is an easy one to turn into a political confrontation about issues of sovereignty and national identity. Secondly, the behaviour of the money markets, which inflicted successive crises on Europe's currencies (notably in September 1992 and August 1993) underlined the project's difficulty, or, as some said, its unrealistic ambition. Thirdly, general popular support for European integration in any case tended to ebb in years of low growth, which 1992 and 1993 certainly were in Europe.[155] The Maastricht Treaty was perceived as remote from the central concern of European electorates, which was unemployment; or, worse, it was seen to cause unemployment, via the high interest rates applied to all European currencies so as to maintain parities with the Deutschmark in the context the Bundesbank's tight money policies after German unification. Fourthly, economic recession also affected the general standing of governments among voters: the deep unpopularity of François Mitterrand and France's Socialists, quite independently of Maastricht, was certainly a factor in the French referendum result. Despite its multiple causes, however, the difficulty of the Maastricht ratification process delivered one simple message: where Europe's élites led, the voters would not automatically follow. That message lent new urgency to a debate, opened some years earlier, about the need to remedy a series of institutional ills known collectively as Europe's 'democratic deficit'. The rest of this section will consider these, the reforms suggested to address them, and Europe's capacity to face the challenges of 'deepening' and 'widening' that will confront it at the turn of the millennium.

The democratic deficit and institutional futures

Europe's 'democratic deficit' can be presented under three headings. First, Europe's institutions lack some of the basic safeguards commonly regarded as indispensable to democratic systems at national level. Secondly, Europe's decision-making processes are cumbersome and impenetrable to the non-specialist. Thirdly, Europe lacks both a popularly elected forum for debate, and clear accountability from governing institutions to citizens.

Europe lacks basic democratic safeguards

For example, as Majone remarks, the legislative role of the Council and the Commission, both of which hold important executive functions, clearly breaches the doctrine of the separation of powers. The governments of member states, meeting in the Council of Ministers, actually control their own parliaments in a sense, rather than vice versa, because the European law decided by the Council will take precedence over the national laws decided by the national legislatures. The Council's meetings, despite recent reforms, tend to hide from the public gaze: a form of behaviour quite appropriate, or at least habitual, in a national government, but far less so in a legislature. Their outcome, moreover, is often fixed in advance by the bureaucrats of the permanent representations, which may distort and diminish the Council's role as the guardian of the interests of the member states. And the bureaucratic branch of the executive, the Commission, holds quite abnormal unofficial and official powers, including its near-monopoly of the legislative initiative.[156]

Europe's decision-making processes are cumbersome and impenetrable

While the institutions of the Community do not lack checks and balances to hinder the abuse of power, they, and the culture of consensus among EU 'insiders' that they help to promote, help to render European institutions incomprehensible to outsiders. According to Wright, for example, the combination of possible variations in Council voting procedures with different legislative paths incorporating a greater or lesser role for the EP has produced no fewer than 25 different legislative procedures.[157] EU law also lacks a proper 'hierarchy of texts' that might distinguish primary from secondary legislation. One result is that the Parliament can be inundated with texts of a detail and technicality that are largely incompatible with clear public debate. Implementing legislation is itself particularly complex: seven distinct procedures come under the umbrella of 'comitology'. Even for insiders, the lack of a common organizational culture and the weakness of policy co-ordination at the centre make the workings of the EU appear arcane at times. For most outsiders, they are a mystery. Among respondents to the autumn 1996 *Eurobarometer* polls, for example, 67 per cent thought they were rather or very poorly informed about the EU, compared with 28 per cent who thought they were quite well informed, and a mere 2 per cent who considered themselves very well informed.[158] As Fries observes, the problem is less due to a lack of information as to information overload, and a consequent lack of 'legibility' of the EU, accentuated by the absence of landmarks in Europe's institutions and processes that have ready equivalents in national politics. This difficulty has grown as the EU has taken on more tasks and added additional processes to existing ones without attempting a general institutional rationalization.[159]

The EU lacks effective channels of popular representation and accountability

The recent growth in the EP's powers to amend or block legislation has been felt almost exclusively in its committees. By contrast, the EP remains extremely weak as a forum for public debate about the major issues of the day. This failure to fulfil one of the major functions of a democratic legislature is all the more striking because of the absence of other institutions which, at national level, have complemented (or even, at times, taken over) the work of legislatures in this area: neither political parties nor the mass media exist at a European level in a meaningful way. The readiness of EU decision-makers to talk to, and to mobilize, interest groups may be seen in this light: interest groups are almost the only Europe-wide institutions outside the EU itself. But they are poor conveyors of popular legitimacy, and tend to reinforce the EU's predilection for low-key, technical, problem-solving approaches over open political debate.[160]

Closely linked to the issue of representation is that of accountability. The diffusion of decision-making through the EU's institutions makes it impossible to identify a European 'government', let alone hold it to account. Most importantly, perhaps, the direct elections which were intended to reinforce the legitimacy of the EP and thence the EU do not serve, as elections in most member states do, as a chance for voters to judge the performance of a government and choose either to renew its mandate or to replace it.

That the EU's 'democratic deficit' exists is a received orthodoxy. But no available corrective commands an equivalent consensus. Broadly speaking, proposals to remedy the 'democratic deficit' fall into two groups. Federalists would like to pull the EU's institutions into structures comparable to those of a nation state. The Commission would become the government: it would be chosen by the EP after each European election, would be responsible to it thereafter, and would manage a full range of policies commonly associated with states, including justice and home affairs and the common foreign and security policy. The EP, elected on the basis of Europe-wide lists to encourage the development of European parties, would become the lower house of Parliament, the chief centre of legislation, and the raiser of European taxes; the Council of Ministers would be an upper house, probably a strong one on the model of the German Bundesrat, with members nominated by the majorities of member states; and the European Council would become a largely ceremonial collective presidency. Confederalists, on the other hand, would move in the opposite direction: handing back powers from the EU to the member states in the name of the subsidiarity principle; downgrading the Commission to the largely executant status of a secretariat serving the principal intergovernmental organs, the European Council and Council of Ministers; and reinforcing control over legislation, not by the EP, but by national parliaments. In addition to these opposed general views about how to bring Europe's governors closer to the governed are ideas intended to settle which policy areas Europe should cover. One of these, much favoured by the former Major government, is of a Europe 'à la carte', in which a small core of European policies common to all member states would be complemented by a second, larger set of policy areas which different member states could join, or not join, as they chose. A variation on this is the idea of a 'multi-speed Europe', in which all member states, while committed to the same range of common policies as ultimate goals, would enjoy more or less freedom to choose the time of their adopting them: an arrangement which, if the delays allowed were long, might come to resemble a Europe 'à la carte'.

So far, institutional reforms to European institutions have been marked by a refusal to choose between these options, and thus by fudged, though apparently inevitable compromises (in the tradition of the Treaty of Rome itself). This happened at Maastricht, where Britain was allowed to opt out of the Social Chapter and EMU (thus offering a preview of Europe 'à la carte'), and where justice and home affairs and the common foreign and security policy were brought into the EU's purview, but on an intergovernmental basis which has coexisted uneasily with the more *communautaire* methods of the Economic Community. Institutional fudge was also in evidence at Amsterdam in 1997, with the simultaneous extension of the co-decision procedure, reinforcing the EP's role, and the inclusion of a six-week period for the Commission's legislative proposals to be considered by national parliaments; and with the recognition of the need for an individual to 'represent' the EU to other countries, but the offer of the job to the President and Secretary-General of the Council of Ministers, which therefore appeared to reinforce intergovernmentalism. Such compromises, while unsurprising in view of the need to accommodate the sharply contrasting views of member states, are not merely untidy: they run the risk of enhancing the democratic deficit by accentuating the already baroque complexity of Europe's institutions.[161]

Each of the more clear-cut proposals for reform, however, presents serious drawbacks. The 'renationalization' of Europe of which intergovernmentalists dream would run the risk of replacing the 'ever-closer union' envisaged in the Rome Treaty by a mere free-trade area. Europe 'à la carte' and a multi-speed Europe present comparable difficulties, if to a lesser degree: in so far as the underlying purpose of the Treaty of Rome was to promote real European union, underpinned by a common European identity, this is unlikely to be furthered by the encouragement of institutional diversity. There is also no evidence that a majority of Europe's citizens, whatever their caution about Maastricht or other specific policies, wish to roll back European integration.[162] Radical federalism also entails grave dangers. Most obviously, there are no guarantees that institutional reform will bring in its wake the popular sense of belonging to a polity that is part of political legitimacy. As Gaffney argues, 'The problem for those trying to push political activity onto the European level, and given that this is the level at which economic activity principally operates, is that politically the nation state still possesses decisive vitality, both as a site of activity and as a player in IR.' Weiler's allusions to the absence of a European 'Demos' refer to a comparable difficulty, albeit not one that Weiler considers insuperable. Anthony Smith, on the other hand, gives the same problem a deeply emotional connotation:

The sacred and heroic places are the shrines of Europe's warring religions, the battlefields of its rival nations and the grim fields of a continent-wide European slaughter, recounted by each of the European ethnies, nations and religions in their own national history textbooks and liturgies, and revisited today in the fields and on the mountains of Bosnia. Without a heritage of binding symbolism, mythology and ritual, the European ideal lacks the ability to present itself to 'the people', to impress itself on their hearts and minds with its feasts and ceremonies.[163]

The threat posed by a European federation, on this analysis, is that Europe's ancient divisions, if denied the outlets currently available in the culture of nation states, would find more sinister forms of expression in the populism of the nationalist far Right: France's Front National, Belgium's Vlaams Blok, or worse. On a more practical, but related, view, the pursuit of accountability in Europe at the expense of other goals contains potential for diminishing as well as for increasing the EU's popular legitimacy. Accountability is best achieved where government commands a clear-cut majority. The majority principle, however, assumes the regular outvoting, and thus the effective impotence, of minorities. This has not so far been considered acceptable in a union composed of states still inclined to see themselves as at least semi-sovereign.[164] It is true that some nation states, if prey to deep and intractable internal divisions, have gone some way to limit the excesses of majority rule through the various arrangements known as consociational democracy. But the drawbacks of consociational democracy

—a diminished level of accountability and a consensus within the political élite that cuts it off from ordinary voters—resemble those of the EU rather closely.

Should this cursory survey of the various options for radical reform to the EU therefore place the indecisive record of Amsterdam in a more favourable light, as the least offensive deal available to Europe's nervous governments and cautious Commission? Such a view would probably not have been shared by Commission President Hallstein, who held that European integration, like a bicycle, must move forward if it is not to topple and fall. More importantly, there are clear practical reasons for nervousness about the choice of no change, or even of slow change, to Europe's structures, in the light of the forward commitments the EU has already made to enlargement and to EMU: for these are likely to place unprecedented stresses upon European institutions.

Enlargement, EMU, and the wider world

Enlargements face Europe with three 'routine' issues. One is that of adjusting Europe's policies and budget to accommodate the newcomers without upsetting long-standing members. This may involve transitional measures to cushion the impact on existing states of unaccustomed competition (for example, from the Mediterranean farm produce of Greece, Spain, and Portugal), or temporary or permanent changes to the structure of the budget to ensure that new entrants neither pay an excessive net contribution nor drain the resources of other member states. The second issue concerns representation in institutions, notably the EP and the Commission. This has been fairly simple in the past: the EP has grown, large states have two Commissioners each, and other states have one. The Amsterdam Treaty has capped the growth of both institutions: the EP will be limited to a maximum of 700 MEPs, and member states to one Commissioner each from the next enlargement. The third problem is the more general one of decision-making processes. In the absence of a more thoroughgoing reform, changes to accommodate new members take place along one dimension only: the numbers for required qualified majority voting in the Council of Ministers. This presents a classic dilemma of consensus versus effectiveness. If the blocking minority of votes required to defeat a proposal remains unchanged after enlargement, the qualified majority necessary to adopt it must be larger, more composite, and more difficult to achieve; consensus is thus favoured at the risk of policy paralysis. If the blocking minority of votes is raised substantially, the adoption of proposals will become easier, but also more controversial, as the size of outvoted and potentially disgruntled minorities on the Council will be increased; effectiveness is favoured at the expense of consensus. This problem was posed by the negotiations for the 1995 'EFTA' enlargement (see Table 10.1), when Britain sought to keep the blocking minority at the low level of 23 out of 87 votes; the 'Ioannina compromise' fixed the new blocking minority at 26, but linked this to a promise to seek all possible means to achieve consensus with the minority when it had more than 23 but fewer than 26 votes. This, it should be noted, was a relatively 'easy' enlargement, concerning four (finally three) small, fairly wealthy countries.

Future enlargements are likely to pose these difficulties with ever greater acuity, because the candidates are both numerous and, in most cases, poor: they include Poland, Hungary, and the Czech Republic in the first wave, with Slovakia, Slovenia, Bulgaria, Romania, Cyprus, Malta, Liechtenstein, Lithuania, Latvia, Estonia, and possibly Turkey, Belarus, Moldova, and Ukraine more or less ready to follow. Structural adjustments to policies are likely to be large, or transition periods long, or both. In purely budgetary terms, the extension of current EU policies to ten countries of Central and Eastern Europe would require an increase in budget contribution equivalent to 0.4 per cent of GDP from each of the fifteen member states of 1995, chiefly in order to subsidize East European peasants.[165] This sum could be found given the political will to do so. It is nevertheless unlikely that it will be forthcoming, given the concern of all member states to control both deficits and taxation, and the unprecedented concern voiced in 1997 by Europe's paymaster, Germany, about the level of its contributions (which had represented 29.1 per cent of the EU budget in 1995). The alternative is large-scale and difficult budget reform, with the possible disappearance of the CAP. More important, perhaps, is the huge disparity in labour costs and living standards between the fifteen-member EU and its eastern neighbours. This will either pose a danger to more recently established EU policies, and notably the Social Chapter, or it will require a lengthy transitional period including unprecedented restrictions on the free movement of persons within the EU. Achieving 'convergence' with the countries of Central and Eastern Europe will thus pose unprecedented political dilemmas for the EU both during and after enlargement negotiations.

The institutional problems will be just as thorny, in the absence of large-scale reform. If the size of the EP and the Commission is unlikely to pose major difficulties for the initial enlargements, the same cannot be said of the Council of Ministers. Increased numbers and more linguistic combinations will add to the labour of meetings, and encourage delegation of more decisions to COREPER and the structures dependent on it. And Europe's poorer countries, those with less than 75 per cent of the EU average in per capita GDP, will see their voting power grow steadily, from a clear blocking minority after the initial enlargement to Poland, the Czech Republic, and Hungary, to something close to an absolute majority in a 25-member EU.[166] At the very least, such changes would diminish the power of the Paris–Bonn axis in setting the European agenda, and necessitate the development of new coalitions. At the most, such an attempt to maintain consensus and intergovernmentalism in a much enlarged and far more diverse union, without a wider institutional reform, would lead to the paralysis of the Council.

EMU poses institutional and political problems of a comparable order to enlargement. For although Tsoukalis and Rhodes were right to argue, in 1997, that Europe's member states had surrendered more economic sovereignty to the market than to the EU since the 1970s, this view will be harder to sustain in a Europe with a single currency.[167] The difficulties that this large transfer of sovereignty are likely to pose are of three types. First, public opinion in several countries has remained reserved about EMU, whether because of the loss of sovereignty entailed (chiefly in Britain), the sacrifices involved in respecting the convergence criteria (in France), or the loss of one of the world's three benchmark currencies (in Germany). The major disagreement in the months before the final decision to proceed with EMU was between France's concern to see the convergence criteria managed flexibly by politicians, and Germany's anxiety to guarantee the replacement of the mark by a 'strong euro' through a strict application of the criteria to all countries seeking to join the single currency. The convergence criteria could continue to be an issue after the definitive launch of EMU in 1999, since they will be indefinitely prolonged as the 'stability pact' and enforced, if necessary, by means of fines against member states. The indefinite continuation of such disputes over the criteria after 1999, and the resulting impact on public opinion, would further damage public support for EMU and thence, possibly, a wider range of European institutions. Secondly, the European central bank might almost have been invented to widen the democratic deficit, entrusted as it is with the control of monetary policy in the framework of an anti-inflationary mission, and effectively accountable neither to the Council of Ministers nor to the EP in the use of this power. Thirdly, the future implications of EMU are potentially very wide-ranging indeed. Some critics argue that, in the absence of the inter-state or inter-regional migrations which Europeans, unlike Americans, tend not to practise on a large scale, once member states have lost the right to adjust to economic setbacks through devaluation the only remedies to the devastating effects of uneven growth will lie in handouts from the European budget.[168] This would introduce a new and highly charged element into European policy-making. It is far from certain that the existing institutions of the EU would be able to absorb the extra political strain that such a new dimension would entail.

The present and future challenges facing the EU are therefore likely to strain to breaking-point not only the present institutional arrangements, but also the tradition of compromise, package deals, and incrementalism that has marked earlier institutional reforms. But more radical steps, whether to accelerate or to reverse the process of integration, have scarcely reached the European agenda. Part of the problem is one of leadership. As Hayward writes of the option of further integration,

The current challenge to Europe's leaders is to persuade their peoples that what most of their representatives regard as indispensable should be implemented in the coming years. It is a matter of concern that so many of them have for the present chosen to lie low, a reflection of the contemporary crisis of representation.[169]

Linked to the problem of leadership, however, is that of purpose. The original rationale for European integration was a threefold one: to settle old quarrels, particularly between Germany and France, to reconstruct a prosperous economy, and to shore up democratic institutions in enough Western countries to ensure the containment of the Soviet bloc. These, by and large, were achieved. To define new goals for further enlargement and integration is not impossible. They would include the reinforcement of democracy, and of its material underpinnings, in Central and Eastern Europe; the definition of a new relationship between Russia and its European neighbours; and above all the accumulation of a degree of global political power sufficient to ensure the survival of political systems committed to balancing the play of market forces with social and environmental protection. For in an increasingly interdependent world where the fifteen-member EU counts for barely 6 per cent of the global population, the 'cost of non-Europe', to use a favoured phrase of the Single Market programme, may prove to be more than a merely commercial one.

Appendix

Table 10.1. **Voting in the Council of Ministers of the 15–member EU, 1995[a]**

Member states	Number of votes for each state	Total
France, Germany, Italy, UK	10	40
Spain	8	8
Belgium, Greece, Netherlands, Portugal	5	20
Austria, Sweden	4	8
Denmark, Ireland, Finland	3	9
Luxembourg	2	2
Total		87
Qualified majority[b]		62
Blocking minority[b]		26

[a] Under Qualified Majority Voting (QMV), each member state is given a number of votes in (very) approximate proportion to its population, and the proportion of the total number of votes necessary to carry a proposal is fixed at substantially more than one half—nearer in fact, to three quarters.

[b] Before the entry of Austria, Finland, and Sweden in 1995, the total number of votes was 76, the qualified majority was 54, and the blocking minority 23. In negotiations prior to enlargement the UK had sought to keep the blocking minority unchanged after the entry of the new member states, and thus to raise the qualified majority to 65. Under the so-called 'Ioannina compromise' of 1994, other member states agreed, in deference to the UK, that while a minority of 23 would be insufficient to block a proposal in the enlarged Union, extended efforts would be made to resolve the point at issue over time if a minority between 23 and 26 was opposed to a proposal.

Table 10.2. **The European Commissioners, 1995**

Name	Country	Responsibilities
Jacques Santer	Luxembourg	President
Sir Leon Brittan	UK	Vice-President: trade policy; relations with OECD countries and with World Trade Organisation
Manuel Marin	Spain	Relations with South Mediterranean countries, Middle East, and South Asia
João de Deus Pinheiro	Portugal	Relations with African, Caribbean, and Pacific countries; Lomé Convention
Hans Van Den Broek	Netherlands	Relations with Central and Eastern Europe, former Soviet Union, Turkey, Cyprus, Malta; common foreign and security policy
Martin Bangemann	Germany	Industrial policy; information technology; telecommunications
Karel Van Miert	Belgium	Competition policy
Padraig Flynn	Ireland	Employment and social affairs
Édith Cresson	France	Education, science, research and development
Ritt Bjerregaard	Denmark	Environment, nuclear security
Monika Wulf-Mathies	Germany	Regional policy, cohesion funds
Neil Kinnock	UK	Transport
Mario Monti	Italy	Internal market, customs; financial services
Emma Bonino	Italy	Consumer affairs; humanitarian affairs; fisheries
Yves-Thibault de Silguy	France	Economic and financial affairs; monetary affairs; credit and investment; Statistical Office
Christos Papoutsis	Greece	Energy; Euratom; small and medium businesses; tourism
Anita Gradin	Sweden	Immigration; justice and home affairs; anti-fraud measures; relations with ombudsman
Franz Fischler	Austria	Agriculture, rural development
Erkki Liikanen	Finland	Budget, personnel, administration, translation and computer facilities

Source: Eurostat, *L'Europe en chiffres* (4th edn., Brussels: European Communities Statistical Office, 1995).

Table 10.3. **Structure of the European Commission, 1995**

DG I[a]	External economic relations
DG IA	External political relations
DG II	Economic and financial affairs
DG III	Industry
DG IV	Competition
DG V	Employment, industrial relations, and social affairs
DG VI	Agriculture (and Veterinary and Phytosanitary Office)
DG VII	Transport
DG VIII	Development
DG IX	Personnel and administration
DG X	Information, communication, culture, and audiovisual
DG XI	Environment, nuclear safety, and civil protection
DG XII	Science, research, and development (and Joint Research Centres)
DG XIII	Telecommunications, information market, and exploitation of research
DG XIV	Fisheries
DG XV	Internal market and financial services
DG XVI	Regional policies
DG XVII	Energy
DG XVIII	Credit and investments
DG XIX	Budgets
DG XX	Financial control
DG XXI	Customs and indirect taxation
DG XXII	Education, training, and youth
DG XXIII	Enterprise policy, distributive trades, tourism, and cooperatives

Secretariat General
  Forward Studies Unit
  Inspectorate-General
  Spokesman's Service
  Joint Interpreting and Conference Service
  Security Office
  Statistical Office
  Translation Service
Legal Service
Informatics Directorate
Consumer Policy Service
European Community Humanitarian Office (ECHO)
Euratom Supply Agency
Office for Official Publications of the European Communities

Attached agencies

European Foundation for the Improvement of Living and Working Conditions
European Centre for the Development of Vocational Training (CEDEFOP)
EUROBASES (EC Database)

[a] DG: Directorate General

Source: H. Wallace and W. Wallace, *Policy-Making in the European Union* (3rd edn., Oxford: Oxford University Press, 1996), 49.

Table 10.4. Members of the European Parliament, by country, 1995

Austria	21
Belgium	25
Denmark	16
Finland	16
France	87
Germany	99
Greece	25
Ireland	15
Italy	87
Luxembourg	6
Netherlands	31
Portugal	25
Spain	64
Sweden	22
UK	87
Total	626

Source: Eurostat, *L'Europe en chiffres* (4th edn., Brussels: European Communities Statistical Office, 1995).

Notes

1. G. Peters, 'Agenda-Setting in the European Union', in J. Richardson (ed.), *European Union: Power and Policy-Making* (London: Routledge, 1996), 62.
2. V. Wright, 'The National Co-Ordination of European Policy-Making: Negotiating the Quagmire', in J. Richardson (ed.), *European Union*, 150.
3. S. Hix and C. Lord, *Political Parties in the European Union* (Basingstoke: Macmillan, 1997), 203.
4. D. McKay, *Rush to Union: Understanding the European Federal Bargain* (Oxford: Clarendon Press, 1996), 98.
5. On competition policy, cf. L. Tsoukalis and M. Rhodes, 'Economic Integration and the Nation-State', in M. Rhodes, P. Heywood, and V. Wright (eds.), *Developments in West European Politics* (Basingstoke: Macmillan, 1997), 27–8; on the CAP cf. E. Rieger, 'The Common Agricultural Policy: External and Internal Dimensions', in H. Wallace and W. Wallace (eds.), *Policy-Making in the European Union*, 3rd edn. (Oxford: Oxford University Press, 1996), 97–124.
6. H. Wallace, 'Politics and Policy in the EU: The Challenge of Governance', ibid. 26.
7. D. Rometsch and W. Wessels, 'The Commission and the Council of Ministers', in G. Edwards and D. Spence, *The European Commission* (Harlow: Longman, 1994), 202.
8. Hix and Lord, *Political Parties in the European Union*, 119.
9. J. Gaffney, 'Introduction', in J. Gaffney (ed.), *Political Parties and the European Union* (London: Routledge, 1996), 14.
10. D. Wincott, 'The Role of Law or the Rule of the Court of Justice? An "Institutional" Account

of Judicial Politics in the European Community', *Journal of European Public Policy*, 2(4) (December 1995), 599; cf. also D. Wincott, 'The Court of Justice and the European Policy Process', in J. Richardson (ed.), *European Union: Power and Policy-Making* (London: Routledge, 1996), 170–84.

11. I. Loveland, 'Parliamentary Sovereignty and the European Community: The Unfinished Revolution?', *Parliamentary Affairs*, 49(4) (October 1996), 517.

12. Cf. S. Weatherill, *Law and Integration in the European Union* (Oxford: Clarendon Press, 1995), 81–2.

13. Ibid. 280.

14. Cf. N. Nugent, *The Government and Politics of the European Union*, 3rd edn. (Basingstoke: Macmillan, 1994), 231.

15. Quoted in Wincott, 'The Role of Law', 588; and Weatherill, *Law and Integration in the European Union*, 98.

16. Loveland, 'Parliamentary Sovereignty and the European Community', 524; Weatherill, *Law and Integration in the European Union*, 122–4, 197; Wincott, 'The Role of Law', 590–1.

17. Quoted in Wincott, 'The Role of Law', 589, and Weatherill, *Law and Integration in the European Union*, 103.

18. Weatherill, *Law and Integration in the European Union*, 184.

19. Ibid. 199.

20. Wincott, 'The Role of Law', 585.

21. Weatherill, *Law and Integration in the European Union*, 53.

22. Wincott, 'The Role of Law', 584–5.

23. European Commission, *Eurobarometer: Public Opinion in the European Union*, 46 (May 1997), B. 57.

24. Wincott, 'The Role of Law', 596.

25. Nugent, *The Government and Politics of the European Union*, 228.

26. R. Dehousse, 'European Integration and the Nation-State', in M. Rhodes, P. Heywood, and V. Wright (eds.), *Developments in West European Politics* (Basingstoke: Macmillan, 1997), 49. The *Simmenthal* ruling of 1978 first asserted the duty of national courts to remedy the violation of European legislation by national laws (Weatherill, *Law and Integration in the European Union*, 98–9, 106).

27. Wincott, 'The Role of Law', 592; Loveland, 'Parliamentary Sovereignty and the European Community', 526–7.

28. M. Westlake, *A Modern Guide to the European Parliament* (London: Frances Pinter, 1994), 44–6; J. Usher, 'The Commission and the Law', in G. Edwards and D. Spence, *The European Commission* (Harlow: Longman, 1994), 150; Weatherill, *Law and Integration in the European Union*, 191–3.

29. Wincott, 'The Role of Law', 594.

30. S. Mazey and J. Richardson, 'Introduction: Transference of Power, Decision Rules, and Rules of the Game', in S. Mazey and J. Richardson (eds.), *Lobbying in the European Community* (Oxford: Oxford University Press, 1993), 15; H. Wallace, 'The Institutions of the EU: Experience and Experiments', in H. Wallace and W. Wallace (eds.), *Policy-Making in the European Union*, 3rd edn. (Oxford: Oxford University Press, 1996), 62.

31. Wallace, 'The Institutions of the EU', 61; Weatherill, *Law and Integration in the European Union*, 234.

32. Peters, 'Agenda-setting in the European Union', 66.

33. Wallace, 'The Institutions of the EU', 62; Wincott, 'The Role of Law', 595; Weatherill, *Law and Integration in the European Union*, 185.

34. Giscard's penchant for contrived informality is well illustrated by both the style and the illustrations of his memoirs. Cf. V. Giscard d'Estaing, *Le Pouvoir et la vie*, 2 vols. (Paris: Compagnie des Douze, 1988 and 1991).

35. G. Edwards, 'National Sovereignty *vs.* Integration? The Council of Ministers', in J. Richardson (ed.), *European Union: Power and Policy-Making* (London: Routledge, 1996), 138.

36. Quoted in Nugent, *The Government and Politics of the European Union*, 154–5.

37. Wallace, 'The Institutions of the EU', 51.

38. Rometsch and Wessels, 'The Commission and the Council of Ministers', 219.

39. Wallace, 'The Institutions of the EU', 59.

40. F. Hayes-Renshaw and H. Wallace, *The Council of Ministers* (Basingstoke: Macmillan, 1997), 63. Hayes-Renshaw and Wallace note that immediately after the completion of the Single Market programme, the volume of legislation proposed by the Commission diminished somewhat. The less important legislation did not go through the Council procedure. According to Edward Page, the total amount of legislation rose from 1,908 regulations, 252 directives, and 1,769 decisions in 1969, to 37,822 regulations, 2,750 directives, and 14,603 decisions in 1994. Most of these consisted of implementing or administrative legislation passed by the Commission and drawn up by officials in the Commission's Directorates General. Cf. E. C. Page, *People who Run Europe* (Oxford: Clarendon Press, 1996), 143; Nugent, *The Government and Politics of the European Union*, 304.

41. For details on comitology, cf. Hayes-Renshaw and Wallace, *The Council of Ministers*, 183, and C. Docksey and K. Williams, 'The Commission and the Execution of Community Policy', in G. Edwards and D. Spence (eds.), *The European Commission* (Harlow: Longman, 1994), 117–45.

42. Hayes-Renshaw and Wallace, *The Council of Ministers*, 159–63.

43. Nugent, *The Government and Politics of the European Union*, 321.

44. European Union, *Amsterdam, June 17, 1997: A New Treaty for Europe*, 12.

45. Hix and Lord, *Political Parties in the European Union*, 119.

46. Hayes-Renshaw and Wallace, *The Council of Ministers*, 21.

47. Ibid. 75; G. Edwards, 'National Sovereignty *vs.* Integration? The Council of Ministers', in J. Richardson (ed.), *European Union: Power and Policy-Making* (London: Routledge, 1996), 135–6.

48. A. Clark, *Diaries* (London, Phoenix Paperback edn.: 1994), 139.

49. Hayes-Renshaw and Wallace, *The Council of Ministers*, 105, 111, and 131.

50. Ibid. 279.

51. As Britain was at the same time soliciting the support of her European partners against Argentina during the Falklands war, she was not in a position to protest very strongly.

52. Edwards, 'National Sovereignty *vs.* Integration? The Council of Ministers', 130; Hayes-Renshaw and Wallace, *The Council of Ministers*, 49.

53. Mazey and Richardson, 'Introduction', 14.

54. A. Teasdale, 'The Politics of Majority Voting in Europe', *The Political Quarterly*, 67(1996), 113.

55. Hayes-Renshaw and Wallace, *The Council of Ministers*, 44–5.

56. Teasdale, 'The Politics of Majority Voting', 113.

57. Ibid. 105.

58. Wright, 'The National Co-Ordination of European Policy-Making', 153.

59. P. Taylor, *The European Union in the 1990s* (Oxford: Oxford University Press, 1996), 96.

60. Hayes-Renshaw and Wallace, *The Council of Ministers*, 69.

61. Nugent, *The Government and Politics of the European Union*, 151–2.

62. D. Spence, 'Structure, Functions and Procedures in the Commission', in G. Edwards and D. Spence, *The European Commission* (Harlow: Longman, 1994), 90, 102. Perhaps surprisingly, Williamson had been Britain's trusted permanent representative under Mrs Thatcher.

63. J. Aberbach, R. Putnam, and B. Rockman, *Bureaucrats and Politicians in Western Democracies* (Cambridge, Mass.: Harvard University Press, 1981); R. Neustadt, *Presidential Power and the Modern Presidents: The Politics of Leadership from Roosevelt to Reagan* (New York: File Press, 1991).

64. Page, *People who Run Europe*, 118–20.

65. C. Lequesne, 'La Commission européenne entre autonomie et dépendance', *Revue Française de Science Politique*, 46(3) (June 1996), 405.

66. N. Nugent, 'The Leadership Capacity of the European Commission', *Journal of European Public Policy*, 2(4) (December 1995), 611; C. Lequesne, 'La Commission européenne entre autonomie et dépendance', 402.

67. G. Ross, *Jacques Delors and European Integration* (Cambridge: Polity Press, 1995); quoted in Page, *People who Run Europe*, 122.

68. Ross, *Jacques Delors*, 244.

69. Eurostat, *L'Europe en chiffres*, 4th edn. (Brussels: European Communities Statistical Office, 1995), 60. The kingdom of France already employed more than 20,000 people by the mid-sixteenth century.

70. Page, *People who Run Europe*, 136.

71. Ibid. 49, 139.

72. Nugent, *The Government and Politics of the European Union*, 95; M. Cini, 'La Commission européenne: lieu d'émergence de cultures administratives. L'exemple de la DGIV et de la DGXI', *Revue Française de Science Politique*, 46(3) (June 1996), 457–73.

73. Nugent, 'The Leadership Capacity of the European Commission', 608.

74. Ibid. 603.

75. F. Fries, *Les Grands débats européens* (Paris: Éditions du Seuil, 1995), 27.

76. Page, *People who Run Europe*, 141.

77. Nugent, 'The Leadership Capacity of the European Commission', 605–6; Rometsch and Wessels, 'The Commission and the Council of Ministers', 220.

78. Page, *People who Run Europe*, 105, 131. These figures should be treated as a rough guide, as they includes multiple entries for single laws.

79. Rometsch and Wessels, 'The Commission and the Council of Ministers', 202.

80. Hayes-Renshaw and Wallace, *The Council of Ministers*, 179.

81. S. Mazey and J. Richardson, 'Faire face à l'incertitude: stratégies des groupes de pression dans l'Union européenne', *Pouvoirs* (79), 1996, 52; cf. also S. Mazey and J. Richardson, 'The Logic of Organization: Interest Groups', in Richardson (ed.), *European Union: Power and Policy-Making*, 201.

82. Cf. above, p. 399.

83. Docksey and Williams, 'The Commission and the Execution of Community Policy', 125; D. Earnshaw and D. Judge, 'Early Days: the European Parliament, Co-Decision and the European Union Legislative Process Post-Maastricht', *Journal of European Public Policy*, 2(4) (December 1995), 634–6.

84. Docksey and Williams, 'The Commission and the Execution of Community Policy', 118; G. Edwards and D. Spence, 'The Commission in Perspective', in G. Edwards and D. Spence (eds.), *The European Commission* (Harlow: Longman, 1994), 4. Cf. also J. Richardson, 'Eroding EU Policies: Implementation Gaps, Cheating, and Re-Steering', in Richardson (ed.), *European Union: Power and Policy-Making*, 278–94.

85. Nugent, 'The Leadership Capacity of the European Commission', 609; Edwards and Spence, 'The Commission in Perspective', 17.

86. Nugent, *The Government and Politics of the European Union*, 119–20.

87. Ibid. 114.

88. Lequesne, 'La Commission européenne entre autonomie et dépendance', 402.

89. S. Mazey and J. Richardson, 'The Commission and the Lobby', in G. Edwards and D. Spence (eds.), *The European Commission* (Harlow: Longman, 1994), 180.

90. Nugent, 'The Leadership Capacity of the European Commission', 612.

91. Wallace, 'The Institutions of the EU', 48.

92. S. Mazey and J. Richardson, 'La Commission européenne: une bourse pour les idées et les intérêts', *Revue Française de Science Politique*, 46(3) (June 1996), 413, 419; D. Spence, 'Structure, Functions and Procedures in the Commission', 91.

93. J. Peterson, 'Policy Networks and European Policy Making: A Reply to Kassim', *West European Politics*, 18(2) (April 1995), 398; Cini, 'La Commission européenne: lieu d'émergence de cultures administratives', 457–73.

94. A. Smith, 'La Commission européenne et les fonds structurels: vers un nouveau modèle d'action', *Revue Française de Science Politique*, 46(3) (June 1996), 474–95.

95. T. Christiansen, 'Tensions of European Governance: Politicized Bureaucracy and Multiple Accountability in the European Commission', *Journal of European Public Policy*, 4(1) (March 1997), 78–80.

96. Mazey and Richardson, 'The Commission and the Lobby', 178.

97. Wallace, 'The Institutions of the EU', 58.

98. Edwards and Spence, 'The Commission in Perspective', 20.

99. V. Bogdanor, 'The European Union, the Political Class, and the People', in J. Hayward (ed.), *Elitism, Populism, and European Politics* (Oxford: Clarendon Press, 1996), 119.

100. Hayes-Renshaw and Wallace, *The Council of Ministers*, 201–10.

101. G. Tsebelis, 'The Power of the European Parliament as a Conditional Agenda Setter', *American Political Science Review*, 88(1) (March 1994), 128–42.

102. P. Bréchon, B. Cautrès, and B. Denni, 'L'évolution des attitudes à l'égard de l'Europe', in P. Perrineau and C. Ysmal (eds.), *Le Vote des Douze: Les élections européennes de juin 1994* (Paris: Presses de Sciences Po, 1994), 158.

103. The tendency for the total number of MEPs to rise with the entry of each new group of member states should be halted by the Amsterdam Treaty, which fixes the maximum at no more than 700, whatever the size of the EU.

104. Hix and Lord, *Political Parties in the European Union*, 87.

105. M. Westlake, *A Modern Guide to the European Parliament* (London: Frances Pinter, 1994), 103.

106. K. Lawson, 'Partis politiques et groupes d'intérêt', *Pouvoirs*, 79 (1996), 35.

107. Hix and Lord, *Political Parties in the European Union*, 136–7, 158.

108. Ibid. 22.

109. Ibid. 228–33.

110. Peters, 'Agenda-Setting in the European Union', 67; Gaffney, 'Introduction', 17.

111. Hix and Lord, *Political Parties in the European Union*, 72–3.

112. Westlake, *A Modern Guide to the European Parliament*, 201.

113. Ibid. 203.

114. Hix and Lord, *Political Parties in the European Union*, 153.

115. M.-T. Bitsch, *Histoire de la construction européenne* (Brussels: Éditions Complexe, 1996), 225.

116. Mazey and Richardson, 'The Logic of Organization: Interest Groups', 202.

117. D. Earnshaw and D. Judge, 'From Co-Operation to Co-Decision: The European Parliament's Path to Legislative Power', in Richardson (ed.), *European Union: Power and Policy-Making*, 101, 108–9, 121.

118. Earnshaw and Judge, 'Early Days: The European Parliament', 632.

119. Tsebelis, 'The Power of the European Parliament as a Conditional Agenda Setter', 140–2.

120. Westlake, *A Modern Guide to the European Parliament*, 150, 209. The prominent place accorded to human rights in the Amsterdam Treaty is worth noting in this light.

121. Cf. Westlake, *A Modern Guide to the European Parliament*, 123, 130–1. Failure to agree on a budget did not have the same dramatic consequences for the EU as it did in 1995 for the United States, partly because the budget and the number of people who depend on it to live are so much smaller, and partly because the 'provisional twelfths' system allowed the month-by-month prolongation of the previous year's budget receipts to meet current needs.

122. Westlake, *A Modern Guide to the European Parliament*, 121.

123. M. Westlake, 'The Commission and the Parliament', in G. Edwards and D. Spence, *The European Commission* (Harlow: Longman, 1994), 247.

124. Ibid. 247.

125. Bogdanor, 'The European Union, the Political Class, and the People', 114.

126. M. Franklin, 'European Elections and the European Voter', in Richardson (ed.), *European Union: Power and Policy-Making*, 198.

127. Mazey and Richardson, 'Faire face à l'incertitude', 58.

128. S. Mazey and J. Richardson, 'Conclusion: A European Policy Style?', in S. Mazey and J. Richardson (eds.), *Lobbying in the European Community* (Oxford: Oxford University Press, 1993), 253.

129. S. Weyand, 'Inter-Regional Associations and the European Integration Process', in C. Jeffery (ed.), *The Regional Dimension of the European Union: Towards a Third Level in Europe?* (London: Frank Cass, 1997), 166.

130. Page, *People who Run Europe*, 89.

131. Mazey and Richardson, 'The Commission and the Lobby', 172.

132. Hayes-Renshaw and Wallace, *The Council of Ministers*, 21.

133. Wallace, 'The Institutions of the EU', 42.

134. Mazey and Richardson, 'Introduction: Transference of Power', 8; Wallace, 'Politics and Policy in the EU: The Challenge of Governance', 32; Wallace, 'The Institutions of the EU', 39.

135. Westlake, *A Modern Guide to the European Parliament*, 207.

136. C. Crouch and A. Menon, 'Organised Interests and the State', in M. Rhodes, P. Heywood, and V. Wright (eds.), *Developments in West European Politics* (Basingstoke: Macmillan, 1997), 165.

137. D. Coen, 'The Evolution of the Large Firm as a Political Actor in the European Union', *Journal of European Public Policy*, 4(1) (March 1997), 91–108.
138. Mazey and Richardson, 'The Commission and the Lobby', 170.
139. Coen, 'The Evolution of the Large Firm', 92–4.
140. W. Müller and V. Wright, 'Reshaping the State in Western Europe: The Limits to Retreat', in W. Müller and V. Wright (eds.), *The State in Western Europe: Retreat or Redefinition?* (London: Frank Cass, 1994), 1–11; Wallace, 'The Institutions of the EU', 53.
141. Quoted in Mazey and Richardson, 'Faire face à l'incertitude', 63.
142. S. Hix, 'Approaches to the Study of the EC: The Challenge to Comparative Politics', *West European Politics*, 17(1) (January 1994), 13.
143. Coen, 'The Evolution of the Large Firm', 100–5.
144. W. Grant, 'Pressure Groups and the European Community: An Overview', in Mazey and Richardson, (eds.) *Lobbying in the European Community*, 44; Mazey and Richardson, 'The Logic of Organization: Interest Groups', 204; Mazey and Richardson, 'Introduction: Transference of Power', 20–2; Mazey and Richardson, 'The Commission and the Lobby', 178; Mazey and Richardson, 'La Commission européenne', 419; G. Majone, 'A European Regulatory State?' in Richardson (ed.), *European Union: Power and Policy-Making*, 266; M. Pollack, 'Representing Diffuse Interests in EC Policymaking', in *Journal of European Public Policy*, 4(4) (December 1997).
145. Coen, 'The Evolution of the Large Firm', 96–8.
146. S. Mazey and J. Richardson, 'Policy Framing: Interest Groups and the 1996 Intergovernmental Conference (IGC)', *West European Politics*, 19(4) (October 1997).
147. A. McLaughlin and G. Jordan, 'The Rationality of Lobbying in Europe: Why are Euro-Groups so Numerous and so Weak? Some Evidence from the Car Industry', in Mazey and Richardson (eds.), *Lobbying in the European Community*, 157.
148. Hayes-Renshaw and Wallace, *The Council of Ministers*, 281.
149. The Eurocorps, under the command of the Western European Union, numbered 50,000 troops from France, Germany, Belgium, Luxembourg, and Spain, and the Eurofor 10,000. Cf. Bitsch, *Histoire de la construction européenne*, 272–4.
150. J. B. Christoph, quoted in Peters, 'Agenda-Setting in the European Union', 69.
151. F. d'Aubert, *Main basse sur l'Europe: enquête sur les dérives de Bruxelles* (Paris: Plon, 1994), 292–300, 448; Y. Mény and M. Rhodes, 'Illicit Governance: Corruption, Scandal and Fraud', in M. Rhodes, P. Heywood, and V. Wright (eds.), *Developments in West European Politics* (Basingstoke: Macmillan, 1997), 111.
152. Wallace, 'Politics and Policy in the EU: The Challenge of Governance', 29.
153. European Commission, *Eurobarometer: Public Opinion in the European Union*, 46 (May 1997), B.12–B.13, B.32–B.33.
154. *Eurobarometer*, quoted in McKay, *Rush to Union*, 162–3.
155. A. Gamble, 'Economic Recession and Disenchantment with Europe', *West European Politics*, 18(3) (July 1995), 158–74.
156. Majone, 'A European Regulatory State?', 272.
157. Wright, 'The National Co-Ordination of European Policy-Making', 152.
158. *Eurobarometer*, 46 (May 1997), B.54.
159. Fries, *Les Grands débats européens*, 40–2.
160. Dehousse, 'European Integration and the Nation-State', 46; M. N. Franklin, C. van der Eijk, and M. Marsh, 'Referendum Outcomes and Trust in Government: Public Support for

Europe in the Wake of Maastricht', *West European Politics*, 18(3) (July 1995), 122–4; J. Weiler, with U. Haltern and F. Mayer, 'European Democracy and Its Critique', *West European Politics*, 18(3) (July 1995), 8.

161. Commissioner Marcelino Oreja, in his memorandum presenting the Amsterdam Treaty to European documentation centres on 18 June 1997, the day after its signature, pointedly dissociated himself from the institutional changes. 'Believe me,' he wrote, 'I am the first to regret all this complexity. I must point out that I did not draft the Treaty: that was the work of those who negotiate on behalf of governments.'

162. Quite the reverse, in fact. According to *Eurobarometer* (May 1997), B.18, 20 per cent of Europeans thought that European unification was proceeding on one of the three fastest available speeds on a 7-point scale, but fully 50 per cent said they wanted Europe to progress at this rapid pace.

163. Weiler, 'European Democracy and Its Critique', 16–20; Gaffney, 'Introduction', 17; A. Smith, 'The Nations of Europe after the Cold War', in J. Hayward and E. Page (eds.), *Governing the New Europe* (Oxford: Polity Press, 1995), 61.

164. Franklin, van der Eijk, and Marsh, 'Referendum Outcomes and Trust in Government', 126–31.

165. G. Falkner, 'Enlarging the European Union', in Richardson (ed.), *European Union: Power and Policy-Making*, 240.

166. W. Paterson, 'Beyond Semi-Sovereignty: The New Germany in the New Europe', *German Politics* 5(2) (August 1996), 174.

167. Cf. L. Tsoukalis and M. Rhodes, 'Economic Integration and the Nation-State', in M. Rhodes, P. Heywood, and V. Wright (eds.), *Developments in West European Politics* (Basingstoke: Macmillan, 1997), 19–36.

168. McKay, *Rush to Union*, 151.

169. J. Hayward, 'Preface', *West European Politics*, 18(3) (July 1995), 3.

CHAPTER 11

Challenges to Democratic Systems

Political rhetoric, legal tradition, and ideological manifestos have often contributed to an abstract and monolithic view of government as 'the State', especially in continental Europe. Such analyses, based as they are upon reductionist theories, preclude any but the most misleading of representations. Admittedly, once 'rational' and 'logical' interpretations are abandoned, doubt and disorder set in: there turns out to be no 'great clock-maker', no puppeteer pulling the strings, after all; nor can any clear dividing lines be drawn between the public and the private sectors, Parliament and government, the centre and the periphery. A quite different picture emerges from an analysis of the concrete functioning of the democracies, for what it reveals are the complexities of the mechanisms of power, the interaction of the agents involved, and the vast number of influences and decision-makers at work. The panoramic view certainly becomes more blurred, the certainties less assured. But that is the price that has to be paid for a more accurate appreciation of the situation. Robert Dahl's question: 'Who governs?' turns out to be more apposite and fundamental than ever. The task of identifying and studying those who hold power is an unending quest for understanding never to be completed.

However, this picture of a multiplicity of agents, a jungle of decisions, and a tangled web of actions should certainly not lead us to unqualified acceptance of the pluralistic theories which regard such dispersal and fragmentation as proof of truly democratic life. True, power is more widely distributed in democracies than in other systems of government, but that is not to say that it is divided equally. All citizens are equal, but some are more equal than others. Is it the case, then, that, in accordance with the 'iron law' defined by Robert Michels, democracies must inevitably be oligarchies controlled by a handful of political, social, and military élites? The criticism is a serious one, and liberal and élitist schools of thought have been sparring for years over the question of whether the Western political systems are pluralistic or oligarchic. The right position to adopt on this is probably the intermediate one which Dahl, after a long investigation, proposes: certainly it is the élites who govern, but they fall into many different, and competing, groups; and this prevents power from falling into an excessively limited number of hands.

To that extent, democracy can be said to have been 'achieved' in the West—since the Second World War in Italy and West Germany, since the First World War in Britain, since 1871 (for men, at least) in France, since 1990 in East Germany. Its development has been far from smooth or even. It has been punctuated by civil wars, internal conquests, and the creation and collapse of (wholly undemocratic) colonial empires. It has been interrupted, in Italy and Germany, by the Fascist and Nazi dictatorships, in East Germany by the 40 years of Communist rule. And liberal democracy faced, for nearly half a century, the challenge of the alternative model offered, with more or less military encouragement, by the Soviet Union and its satellites.

What is new about the end of the twentieth century is that the direct political challenges, whether external or internal, have all but disappeared. Islamic republics, or more or less authoritarian systems based on 'Asian values', have no very serious claim (as Communism did) to represent an alternative world model to liberal democracy, whatever their attractions in particular countries. On the other hand, democracy has been the ideal to which peoples emerging from dictatorships have turned, whether in Eastern Europe, Latin America, or the Philippines. In China, to name but one case, people have died for it. Within the prosperous Western countries, the open competition that democracy faces as a system of government is negligible. Even extremist parties and movements have to join the electoral game and profess allegiance to its rules if they wish to escape complete marginalization. Revolution as a means of change has been rejected by all but a tiny minority. In default of unanimous agreement on the subject of change, there is broad consensus on the right procedures for bringing about its realization.

Does that mean that democracy has 'won', that it is the end point to which all other systems tend, that we are witnessing the 'end of history', in Francis Fukuyama's phrase? Such views are imprudent. History has shown that it is possible to destroy democracies as well as to create them. The experience of former Yugoslavia has shown that it is possible to be geographically at the heart of Europe but politically a million miles from the pluralism and tolerance considered essential to democratic values. Just as important is the civic self-doubt to which established West European democracies have been prone. Even without the temptation offered by complete alternative political 'models', voters have tended to vote less, to give more of their support for populist or extremist parties (the Front National in France, the Leagues in Italy, the Freedom Party in Austria, the Vlaams Blok in Belgium), or to take a pessimistic view of parties in general and of their capacity to effect significant political change. These types of disaffection have been prompted not so much by challenges from those opposed to democracy, as from the contradictions within which West European democracies find themselves enmeshed. These include the difficulty of reconciling the representative institutions of liberal democracy with the demands of big government; the sustainability of the Welfare State; and the diminished independence of the nation state in relation to the global economy.

The gulf between those who rule and the citizens who are the source of their legitimacy has been a common feature of European democracies. That is all too understandable where the existence of large-scale political corruption is common knowledge, as in Italy before 1993 or, to a lesser extent, contemporary France. But even where corruption has been limited to individual cases, the democracies face a more structural problem. They were conceived and developed on the basis of the idea that those legitimate decision-makers should be visible and elected—parliaments and governments: and that they should be reasonably responsive to the wishes of their voters. That has never been wholly true, but the gap has now widened between such mechanisms of classic democracy as are still in place and the real mechanisms of contemporary political systems. On the ground, what is supposed to be mere 'implementation' of decisions taken by elected officials turns out to be a complex, messy process in which bureaucracy takes on a life of its own. The growth of big government has not been sufficiently accompanied by that of administrative democracy. Progress has been made in this area. The due processes of law now afford the people better protection and more guarantees than in, say, 1950. But the public has also become more demanding of such guarantees, and much remains to be done in order to set up not an ideal, unattainable perfection, but simply a system that shows more respect for the rights of individuals.

Some observers see the problem as lying not with the difficulty of adjusting classical liberal States to an era of big government, but with big government itself. For economists and philosophers of the New Right such as Hayek, Friedman, and Nozick, the Welfare State is a monster that threatens to destroy Western democracy from within. A State with tentacles everywhere, which assumes responsibility for the redistribution of wealth and seeks the well-being of its citizens through interventionism, is regarded by these critics as the very antithesis of the democratic ideal. The neo-liberal solution they propose lies in restoring full value and importance to the individual, the only subject who really matters (for society as such has no right to lay claim to a will of its own), and to the market—the only regulatory mechanism capable of respecting the freedom of choice of the individual. This fundamental critique has not eradicated the Welfare State. But its has drawn attention to the performance of big government and its failure to deliver the general well-being it promised; and it has spread well beyond the ranks of the Right, contributing to a new consensus, shared by the British Labour Party, France's Socialists, or Italy's former Communists, that the growth of the public sector should be reined back, halted, or even reversed. The difficulty, however, is that in a context of rising demand for welfare or education services (whether as a result of an ageing population, a rise in the number of single-parent families, high unemployment, or simply higher public expectations), the containment of public spending, even when accompanied by efficiency gains, may still appear as a cut in the service supplied. On the other hand, no West European government has succeeded in reducing public spending enough to allow large and durable tax cuts. Since European publics have been attached both to low taxation and to the generous provision of public services, the Right's inability to deliver the former and the Left's failure to safeguard or extend the latter have been characteristic sources of voter frustration.

A third explanation for popular disaffection in the West European democracies lies in the decline in the real independence of nation states. De Gaulle's view that 'democracy is congruent with national sovereignty'[1] is hard to contest in a purely empirical sense. Electoral turnout is almost invariably highest in national elections; the chance to change the national government (or, in France, the President) is the centrepiece of every democracy's political calendar; European elections, as we have seen, attract many fewer voters and in any case are fought on national issues; and there is no pretence that international organizations like the United Nations have any direct links with voters. But individual nation states can do less and less on their own, and in particular they can do less and less to manage their own economies. The accelerated globalization of the world economy has resulted from four more or less simultaneous developments: the rise of technologies that allow electronic currency and securities markets to shift billions of dollars across the world in seconds, making them extremely difficult to regulate; the diminution of transport costs, whether by surface or air; the progressive dismantling of barriers to world trade; and the emergence of new low-wage producer countries in the 'Third World', hitherto regarded as bad risks but now doing their best to attract inward investment and develop their own industries. In the resulting environment, firms can more readily move out of countries whose business environments they distrust, whether because of taxation rates or labour-market regulation. Indeed, they have an obligation to their shareholders to do so. That the governments of major democratic states, fully integrated into the world trading environment, should turn their backs on these developments and retreat into protectionism on any significant scale is an almost inconceivable option, and one that would itself entail massive economic dislocation. But the only alternative, as France discovered in 1982–3, is to accept the constraints of the global market. That means that the range of economic options that governments can offer their voters is increasingly limited—and so is the voters' ability to exercise real choice. That limitation of choice, and the subordination of large swathes of policy-making to the imperatives of the global capitalist economy, may generate frustration not just with particular governments of one or another political complexion, but with democracy itself.

The European Union could, in principle, remedy the relative weakness of its individual member states in relation to the global economy. Monetary union, for example, is intended to offer a return on the financial disciplines it has entailed by giving all member states that join it the benefits of possessing one of the world's strong currencies, and the relative immunity from speculation that should result. But for this, or the still largely unfulfilled plans to develop a 'social Europe', to be more than a merely technical project, the EU badly needs to reinforce its democratic legitimacy, with more ambitious changes than the institutional tinkerings of the Amsterdam Treaty. Until that is achieved, Europe is likely to be perceived by its peoples as at least as much of a constraint as an enabler.

Two other domains in which nation states have very limited capacities to act alone to any major effect are the environment and North–South relations. True, individual governments can achieve impressive small-scale results in both of these areas. But an exercise of political will is necessary at a global level to deal with the larger issues: climate change, the developed countries' prodigal use of natural resources, the developing world's population explosion, and the grotesquely inequitable distribution of the world's wealth. These are not questions which have hitherto mobilized voters in the West European democracies to any very large extent. Left untreated, however, they will weigh increasingly heavily on the future politics and the budgets of developed countries, at the very least in the form of the costs of correcting environmental damage or adjusting to global warming, and a steady increase in migratory pressures towards the wealthy nations.

Democracies are in some ways ill-equipped to face the new global challenges, and their record to date is not encouraging. Democratic politicians have to work within the confines of the nation state and of the single term of office, which is never longer than seven years and more generally four or five. Such a time-scale may, with luck, allow particular domestic policies to bear fruit. But it is quite insufficient to achieve tangible results from measures to limit carbon dioxide emissions, or to limit Third World debt, even where global initiatives are taken. That said, it cannot be claimed that other systems would do better: as a model of environmental conservation or Third World development, Soviet-style socialism, for example, left even more to be desired. If the democracies dispose of one asset that leaves ground for optimism, it is the (relative) flexibility afforded by their (relative) pluralism. On their success in putting that flexibility to good use, and accepting sacrifices on a large enough scale to meet the challenges, will depend both their own future and that—increasingly threatened—of human life on the planet.

NOTE

1. C. de Gaulle, *Discours et Messages*, vol. 1 (Paris: Plon, 1970), 194.

BIBLIOGRAPHY

Introduction: General and national studies

ALLUM, P., *State and Society in Western Europe* (Oxford: Polity Press, 1995).

ALLUM, P. A., *Italy, Republic without Government?* (London: Weidenfeld and Nicolson, 1973).

ALMOND, G. A., and POWELL, B. G., *Comparative Politics: A Developmental Approach* (Boston: Little, Brown, and Co., 1966).

BAYLISS, J., and SMITH, S., *The Globalization of World Politics* (Oxford: Oxford University Press, 1997).

BULL, M., and RHODES, M. (eds.), 'Crisis and Transition in Italian Politics', *West European Politics* (20.1), special issue (January 1997).

CONRADT, D., KLEINFELD, G., ROMOSER, G. K., and SØE, C. (eds.), *Germany's New Politics* (Oxford: Bergbahn Books, 1995).

DAHL, R., *A Preface to Democratic Theory* (New Haven: Yale University Press, 1956).

EISENSTADT, S., and ROKKAN, S., *Building States and Nations* (Beverly Hills, Calif.: Sage, 1977), i.

FLORA, P., and HEIDENHEIMER, A. (eds.), *The Development of the Welfare State in Europe and America* (New Brunswick: Transaction Books, 1981).

GRAWITZ, M., and LECA, J. (eds.), *Traité de science politique*, 4 vols. (Paris: Presses Universitaires de France, 1985).

GREENSTEIN, F. I., and POLSBY, N. W. (eds.), *Handbook of Political Science*, 8 vols. (Reading, Mass.: Addison-Wesley, 1975).

GUNDLE, S. and PARKER, S. (eds.), *The New Italian Republic* (London: Routledge, 1996).

HALL, P., HAYWARD, J., and MACHIN, H. (eds.), *Developments in French Politics*, 2nd edn. (Basingstoke: Macmillan, 1994).

HINE, D., *Governing Italy: The Politics of Bargained Pluralism* (Oxford: Oxford University Press, 1993).

JONES, B., GRAY, A., KAVANAGH, D. *et al.*, *Politics UK*, 3rd edn. (Hemel Hempstead: Harvester Wheatsheaf, 1998).

KAVANAGH, D., *British Politics; Continuities and Change*, 3rd edn. (Oxford: Oxford University Press, 1996).

LANE, J.–E., and ERSSON, S., *Politics and Society in Western Europe*, 3rd edn. (London: Sage, 1994).

LIJPHART, A., *Democracies: Patterns of Majoritarian and Consensus Government in 21 Countries* (New Haven: Yale University Press, 1984).

—— *Democracy in Plural Societies: A Comparative Exploration* (New Haven: Yale University Press, 1977).

—— *The Politics of Accommodation: Pluralism and Democracy in the Netherlands* (repr. 1975; Berkeley: University of California Press, 1968).

McCARTHY, P. *The Crisis of the Italian State*, 2nd edn. (Basingstoke: Macmillan, 1997).

PULZER, P., *German Politics, 1945–1990* (Oxford: Oxford University Press, 1995).

RHODES, M., HEYWOOD, P., and WRIGHT, V. (eds.), *Developments in West European Politics* (Basingstoke: Macmillan, 1997).

Bibliography

SARTORI, G., *The Theory of Democracy Revisited*, 2 vols. (Chatham, NJ: Chatham House, 1987).

SMITH, G., PATERSON, W. E., and PADGETT, S. (eds.), *Developments in German Politics*, 2nd edn. (Basingstoke: Macmillan, 1996).

SPOTTS, F., and WIESER, T. (eds.), *Italy: A Difficult Democracy* (Cambridge: Cambridge University Press, 1986).

STEVENS, A., *The Government and Politics of France*, 2nd edn. (Basingstoke: Macmillan, 1996).

WRIGHT, V., *The Government and Politics of France*, 3rd edn. (London: Unwin Hyman, 1988).

Chapter 1. Politics and society: cleavages

ALMOND, G. A., and VERBA, S., *The Civic Culture: Political Attitudes and Democracy in Five Nations* (Princeton: Princeton University Press, 1963).

—— —— *The Civic Culture Revisited* (Boston, Mass.: Little, Brown, 1980).

BARNES, S. H., and KAASE, M. (eds.), *Political Action: Mass Participation in Four Western Democracies* (Beverly Hills, Calif.: Sage, 1979).

BERGER, S., *Religion in West European Politics* (London: Frank Cass, 1982).

CROUCH, C., and PIZZORNO, A. (eds.), *The Resurgence of Class Conflict in Western Europe*, 2 vols. (London: Macmillan, 1978).

EASMAN, M. I. (ed.), *Ethnic Conflict in the Western World* (Ithaca, NY: Cornell University Press, 1977).

INGLEHART, R., *The Silent Revolution* (Princeton: Princeton University Press, 1977).

FRANKLIN, M., MACKIE, T., VALEN, H., *et al.*, *Electoral Change: Responses to Evolving Social and Attitudinal Structures in Western Countries* (Cambridge: Cambridge University Press, 1992).

LIJPHART, A., *Democracy in Plural Societies: A Comparative Exploration* (New Haven: Yale University Press, 1977).

LIPSET, S. M., *Political Man: The Social Basis of Politics*, 2nd edn. (Baltimore, Md.: Johns Hopkins University Press, 1981).

—— and ROKKAN, S. (eds.), *Party Systems and Voter Aligments* (New York: Free Press, 1967).

ROKKAN, S., *Citizens, Elections, Parties* (Oslo: Universiteit Forlaget, 1970).

—— and Urwin, D. W. (eds.), *The Politics of Territorial Identity: Studies in European Regionalism* (London: Sage, 1982).

TILLY, C. (ed.), *The Formation of National States in Western Europe* (Princeton: Princeton University Press, 1975).

Chapter 2. Political parties

ANDEWEG, R., 'The Reshaping of National Party Systems', *West European Politics*, 18(3) (July 1995), 58–78.

BARTOLINI, S., and MAIR, P. (eds.), *Party Politics in Contemporary Western Europe* (London: Frank Cass, 1984).

BELL, D. S., and CRIDDLE, B., *The French Socialist Party: The Emergence of a Party of Government*, 2nd edn. (Oxford: Clarendon Press, 1988).

BLACKMER, D. L. M., and TARROW, S., *Communism in Italy and France* (Princeton: Princeton University Press, 1975).

BLAKE, R., *The Conservative Party from Peel to Thatcher* (London: Fontana, 1985).

BOGDANOR, V. (ed.), *Liberal Party Politics* (Oxford: Clarendon Press, 1983).

BRAUNTHAL, J., *The West German Social Democrats, 1969–1982* (Boulder, Colo.: Westview Press, 1982).

BUDGE, I., and FARLIE, D., *Voting and Party Competition* (London: Wiley, 1977).

CASTLES, F. G. (ed.), *The Impact of Parties: Politics and Policies in Democratic Capitalist States* (London: Sage, 1983).

COLE, A. (ed.), *French Political Parties in Transition* (Aldershot: Dartmouth Publishing, 1990).

DAALDER, H., and MAIR, P. (eds.), *Western European Party Systems: Continuity and Change* (London: Sage, 1983).

DI PALMA, G., *Surviving without Governing: The Italian Parties in Parliament* (Berkeley: University of California Press, 1977).

DUVERGER, M., *Les Partis Politiques* (Paris: Colin, 1951).

FREARS, J., *Parties and Voters in France* (London: C. Hurst, 1991).

HANLEY, D. (ed.), *Christian Democracy in Europe: A Comparative Perspective* (London: Pinter, 1994).

IRVING, R. E. M., *The Christian Democratic Parties of Western Europe* (London: Allen and Unwin, 1979).

KATZ, R. S., and MAIR, P., 'Changing Models of Party Organization and Party Democracy: The Emergence of the Cartel Party', *Party Politics*, 1(1) (1995), 5–28.

KIRCHNER, E. (ed.), *Liberal Parties in Western Europe* (London: Croom Helm, 1988).

KNAPP, A., *Gaullism since de Gaulle* (Aldershot: Dartmouth, 1994).

LAVER, M., and SCHOFIELD, N., *Multiparty Government: The Politics of Coalition in Europe* (Oxford: Oxford University Press, 1990).

LAWSON, K., *The Comparative Study of Political Parties* (New York: St Martin's Press, 1983).

LAYTON-HENRY, Z. (ed.), *Conservative Politics in Western Europe* (London: Macmillan, 1982).

MAIR, P., 'Political Parties, Popular Legitimacy, and Public Privilege', *West European Politics*, 18(3) (July 1995), 40–57.

—— (ed.), *The West European Party System* (Oxford: Oxford University Press, 1990).

——and SMITH, G. (eds.), *Understanding Party System Change in Western Europe* (London: Frank Cass, 1990).

MERKL, P. H. (ed.), *West European Party Systems: Trends and Prospects* (New York: Free Press, 1980).

MÜLLER-ROMMEL, F. (ed.), *New Politics in Western Europe: The Rise and Success of Green Parties and Alternative Lists* (Boulder, Colo.: Westview Press, 1989).

PADGETT, S., and BURKETT, T., *Political Parties and Elections in West Germany* (London: C. Hurst, 1986).

PADGETT, S., and PATERSON, W., *A History of Social Democracy in Post-War Europe* (New York and London: Longman, 1991).

PANEBIANCO, A., *Political Parties: Organization and Power* (Cambridge: Cambridge University Press, 1988).

PATERSON, W. E., and THOMAS, A. H., *The Future of Social Democracy: Problems and Prospects of Social Democratic Parties in Western Europe* (Oxford: Clarendon Press, 1986).

PRIDHAM, G., *Christian Democracy in Western Germany* (London: Croom Helm, 1977).

RICHARDSON, J., 'The Market for Political Activism: Interest Groups as a Challenge to Political Parties', *West European Politics*, 18(1) (January 1995), 116–39.

ROKKAN, S., and URWIN, D. W. (eds.), *The Politics of Territorial Identity: Studies in European Regionalism* (London: Sage, 1982).

Bibliography

Rose, R., *Do Parties Make a Difference?* (London: Macmillan, 1980).

Sartori, G., *Parties and Party Systems: A Framework for Analysis* (Cambridge: Cambridge University Press, 1976).

Sassoon, D., *One Hundred Years of Socialism: The West European Left in the Twentieth Century* (London: Fontana, 1997).

Seyd, P., and Whiteley, P., *Labour's Grass Roots: The Politics of Party Membership* (Oxford: Clarendon Press, 1992).

Von Beyme, K., *Political Parties in Western Democracies* (Aldershot: Gower, 1986).

—— *Right-Wing Extremism in Western Europe* (London: Frank Cass, 1988).

Waller, M., and Fennema, M.(eds.), *Communist Parties in Western Europe: Decline or Adaptation?* (Oxford: Basil Blackwell, 1988).

Ware, A., *Parties and Party Systems* (Oxford: Oxford University Press, 1996).

Whiteley, P., Seyd, P., and Richardson, J., *True Blues: The Politics of Conservative Party Membership* (Oxford: Clarendon Press, 1994).

Chapter 3. Interest groups

Bentley, A. F., *The Process of Government* (Evanston, Ill.: Principia Press, 1949).

Berger, S. (ed.), *Organizing Interests in Western Europe: Pluralism, Corporatism and the Transformation of Politics* (Cambridge: Cambridge University Press, 1981).

Castles, F. G., *Pressure Groups and Political Cultures* (London: Routledge and Kegan Paul, 1967).

Dahl, R., *Who Governs? Democracy and Power in an American City* (New Haven: Yale University Press, 1963).

Harrison, R., *Pluralism and Corporatism: The Political Evolution of Modern Democracy* (London: Allen and Unwin, 1980).

Hayward, J. (ed.), 'Les groupes d'intérêt', *Pouvoirs*, 79 (1996).

Hirschman, A. O., *Shifting Involvements: Private Interest and Public Action* (Princeton: Princeton University Press, 1982).

Jordan, A. G., and Richardson, J. J., *Government and Pressure Groups in Britain* (Oxford: Clarendon Press, 1987).

Labbé, D., 'Trade Unionism in France since the Second World War', *West European Politics*, 17(1) (January 1994), 146–68.

Lecher, W. (ed.), *Trade Unions in the European Union: A Handbook* (London: Lawrence and Wishart, 1994).

Lehmbruch, G., and Schmitter, P., *Patterns in Corporatist Intermediation* (London: Sage, 1982).

Marsh, D., and Rhodes, R. (eds.), *Policy Networks in British Government* (Oxford: Clarendon Press, 1992).

Miller, C., *Lobbying Government: Understanding and Influencing the Corridors of Power* (Oxford: Clarendon Press, 1987).

Olson, M., *The Logic of Collective Action* (Cambridge, Mass.: Harvard University Press, 1965).

—— *The Rise and Decline of Nations* (New Haven: Yale University Press, 1982).

Richardson, J. (ed.), *Pressure Groups* (Oxford: Oxford University Press, 1993).

Rush, M., *Parliament and Pressure Politics* (Oxford: Clarendon Press, 1990).

Schmitter, P., *Patterns of Corporatist Policy-Making* (Beverly Hills, Calif.: Sage, 1982).

—— 'Corporatism is Dead! Long Live Corporatism!', *Government and Opposition*, 24(1) (1989), 54–73.

SMITH, M. J., *The Politics of Agricultural Support in Britain: The Development of the Agricultural Policy Community* (Aldershot: Dartmouth, 1990).

STREECK, W., and SCHMITTER, P., 'From National Corporatism to Transnational Pluralism: Organized Interests in the Single European Market', *Politics and Society*, 19(2) (1991), 133–64.

TAYLOR, R., *The Trade Union Question in British Politics: Government and Unions since 1945* (Oxford: Blackwell, 1993).

TRACY, M., *Government and Agriculture in Western Europe 1880–1988*, 3rd edn. (New York: New York University Press, 1989).

TRUMAN, D., *The Governmental Process: Political Interests and Public Opinion* (New York: Knopf, 1951).

WILSON, F. L., *Interest-Group Politics in France* (Cambridge: Cambridge University Press, 1987).

WILSON, G. K., *Interest Groups* (Oxford: Basil Blackwell, 1990).

Chapter 4. Voters, elections, and the elected

BOGDANOR, V., *What is Proportional Representation?* (Oxford: Martin Robertson, 1984).

—— and BUTLER, D. (eds.), *Democracy and Elections: Electoral Systems and Their Political Consequences* (Cambridge: Cambridge University Press, 1983).

BUTLER, D., PENNIMAN, H., and RANNEY, A., *Democracy at the Polls: A Comparative Study of Competitive National Elections* (Washington, DC: American Enterprise Institute, 1981).

DENVER, D., *Elections and Voting Behaviour in Britain* (London: Philip Allan, 1989).

—— and HANDS, G., *Issues and Controversies in British Electoral Behaviour* (Hemel Hempstead: Harvester Wheatsheaf, 1992).

DI PALMA, G., *Apathy and Participation* (New York: Free Press, 1970).

DUNLEAVY, P., and HUSBANDS, C. T., *British Democracy at the Crossroads* (London: Allen and Unwin, 1985).

HARROP, M., and MILLER, W. L., *Elections and Voters: A Comparative Introduction* (Basingstoke: Macmillan, 1987).

HEATH, A. *et al.*, *Understanding Political Change: The British Voter, 1964–1987* (Oxford: Pergamon Press, 1991).

HUNTINGTON, S., and NELSON, J., *No Easy Choice: Political Participation in Developing Countries* (Cambridge, Mass.: Harvard University Press, 1976).

ROKKAN, S., *Citizens, Elections, Parties* (Oslo: Universiteit Forlaget, 1970).

ROSE, R. (ed.), *Electoral Behaviour: A Comparative Handbook* (New York: Free Press, 1974).

—— *Electoral Participation: A Comparative Analysis* (Beverly Hills, Calif.: Sage, 1980).

—— *The Loyalties of Voters: A Lifetime Learning Model* (London: Sage, 1990).

VERBA, S., NIE, N. H., and KIM, J., *Participation and Political Equality: A Seven-Nation Comparison* (Cambridge: Cambridge University Press, 1978).

Chapter 5. Parliaments

ADONIS, A., *Parliament Today*, 2nd edn. (Manchester: Manchester University Press, 1993).

BLONDEL, J., *Comparative Legislatures* (Englewood Cliffs, NJ: Prentice Hall, 1973).

Bibliography

BOGDANOR, V. (ed.), *Representatives of the People? Parliamentarians and Constituents in Western Democracies* (Aldershot: Gower, 1985).

BRAND, J., *British Parliamentary Parties: Policy and Power* (Oxford: Clarendon Press, 1992).

COLLIARD, J. C., *Les Régimes parlementaires contemporains* (Paris: FNSP, 1978).

DALE, S. W., *Legislative Drafting: A Comparative Study of Methods in France, Germany, Sweden and the United Kingdom* (London: Butterworths, 1977).

DI PALMA, G., *Surviving without Governing: The Italian Parties in Parliament* (Berkeley, Calif.: University of California Press, 1977).

ELDRIDGE, A., *Legislatures in Plural Societies* (Durham, NC: Duke University Press, 1977).

HIRSCH, H., and HANCOCK, M. D., *Comparative Legislative Systems* (New York: Free Press, 1979).

KOLINSKY, E. (ed.), *Opposition in Western Europe* (London: Croom Helm, 1987).

LEIGH, D., and VULLIAMY, E., *Sleaze: The Corruption of Parliament* (London: Fourth Estate, 1997).

MEZEY, M. L., *Comparative Legislatures* (Durham, NC: Duke University Press, 1977).

NORTON, P., *Does Parliament Matter?* (Hemel Hempstead: Harvester Wheatsheaf, 1993).

—— *Parliaments in Western Europe* (London: Frank Cass, 1990).

—— (ed.), *Legislatures* (Oxford: Oxford University Press, 1990).

OLSON, D. M., *The Legislative Process: A Comparative Approach* (New York: Harper and Row, 1980).

RYLE, M., and RICHARDS, P. G., *The Commons under Scrutiny*, 3rd edn. (London: Routledge, 1988).

SULEIMAN, E. (ed.), *Parliaments and Parliamentarians in Democratic Politics* (New York: Holmes and Meier, 1986).

WELSH, H., 'Parliamentary Elites in Times of Political Transition: The Case of Eastern Germany', *West European Politics*, 19(3) (July 1996), 507–24.

Chapter 6. Presidents and governments

BLONDEL, J., *Government Ministers in the Contemporary World* (London: Sage, 1985).

—— *The Organisation of Governments* (London: Sage, 1982).

—— *World Leaders* (London: Sage, 1980).

—— and MÜLLER-ROMMEL, F. (eds.), *Cabinets in Western Europe* (Basingstoke: Macmillan, 1988).

BOGDANOR, V. (ed.), *Coalition Governments in Western Europe* (London: Heinemann, 1983).

BUTLER, D., *Governing without a Majority* (London: Macmillan, 1983).

HENNESSY, P., *Cabinet* (Oxford: Basil Blackwell, 1986).

—— and SELDON, A., *Ruling Performance: British Governments from Attlee to Thatcher* (Oxford: Basil Blackwell, 1987).

JOHNSON, N., *State and Government in the Federal Republic of Germany: The Executive at Work*, 2nd edn. (Oxford: Pergamon Press, 1982).

JONES, G. W. (ed.), *West European Prime Ministers* (London: Frank Cass, 1991).

KING, A., *The British Prime Minister* (Basingstoke: Macmillan, 1985).

LAVER, M., and SCHONFIELD, N., *Multiparty Government: The Politics of Coalition in Europe* (Oxford: Oxford University Press, 1990).

LIJPHART, A., *Democracies: Patterns of Majoritarian and Consensus Government in 21 Countries* (New Haven: Yale University Press, 1984).

MARSHALL, G. (ed.), *Ministerial Responsibility* (Oxford: Oxford University Press, 1989).

RICHARDSON, J., *Policy Style in Western Europe* (London: Allen and Unwin, 1982).

ROSE, R., *The Postmodern President: The White House Meets the World* (London: Chatham House, 1988).

——and SULEIMAN, E. (eds.), *Presidents and Prime Ministers* (Washington, DC: American Enterprise Institute, 1980).

VON BEYME, K., *Policy and Politics in the Federal Republic of Germany* (Aldershot: Gower, 1985).

——*The Political System of the Federal Republic of Germany* (Farnborough, Hants: Gower, 1985).

Chapter 7. Local and central bureaucracies

ABERBACH, J. D. *et al.*, *Bureaucrats and Politicians in Western Democracies* (Cambridge, Mass.: Harvard University Press, 1981).

ARMSTRONG, J., *The European Administrative Elite* (Princeton: Princeton University Press, 1973).

ASHFORD, D. L., *British Dogmatism and French Pragmatism: Central–Local Policymaking in the Welfare State* (London: Allen and Unwin, 1982).

CAMPBELL, C., and WILSON, G. K., *The End of Whitehall: Death of a Paradigm?* (Oxford: Blackwell, 1995).

COCKS, R., and BENTLEY, R., *£300 Billion: Government Spending: The Facts* (Reading: Databooks, 1996).

CROUCH, C., and MARQUAND, D. (eds.), *The New Centralism: Britain out of Step in Europe?* (Oxford: Blackwell, 1989).

DOGAN, M. (ed.), *The Mandarins of Western Europe: The Political Role of Top Civil Servants* (New York: Sage, 1975).

DUPUY, F., and THOENIG, J. C., *Sociologie de l'Administration* (Paris: Colin, 1983).

DYSON, K. H. F., *Party, State and Bureaucracy in Western Germany* (Beverly Hills, Calif.: Sage, 1977).

FLORA, P., and HEIDENHEIMER, A., *The Development of the Welfare State in Europe and America* (New Brunswick: Transaction Books, 1981).

FRY, G., *Policy and Management in the British Civil Service* (Hemel Hempstead: Harvester Wheatsheaf, 1995).

HANF, K., and SCHARPF, F. W., *Interorganizational Policy-Making* (Beverly Hills, Calif.: Sage, 1978).

HAYWARD, J. (ed.), *De Gaulle to Mitterrand* (London: Hurst, 1994).

HENNESSY, P., *Whitehall* (London: Fontana, 1990).

JONES, C. (ed.), *New Approaches to the Study of Central–Local Relationships* (Farnborough, Hants: Gower, 1980).

JONES, C., and THOMAS, R., *Public Policy-Making in a Federal System* (Beverly Hills, Calif.: Sage, 1976).

LAGROYE, J., and WRIGHT, V., *Local Government in Britain and France* (London: Allen and Unwin, 1979).

MACHIN, H., *The Prefect in French Public Administration* (London: Croom Helm, 1977).

MAYNTZ, R., and SCHARPF, F. W., *Policy-Making in the German Federal Bureaucracy* (Amsterdam: Elsevier, 1975).

Bibliography

MÉNY, Y., and WRIGHT, V.(eds.), *Centre–Periphery Relations in Western Europe* (London: Allen and Unwin, 1985).

PADGETT, S. (ed.), *Adenauer to Kohl: The Development of the German Chancellorship* (London: Hurst, 1994).

PAGE, E. C., *Political Authority and Bureaucratic Power: A Comparative Analysis* (Brighton: Harvester Press, 1985).

PYPER, R., *The British Civil Service* (Hemel Hempstead: Harvester Wheatsheaf, 1995).

RHODES, R. A., *Control and Power in Central–Local Government Relations* (Farnborough, Hants.: Gower, 1981).

RIDLEY, F. F. (ed.), *Government and Administration in Western Europe* (Oxford: Robertson, 1979).

ROSE, R., *Public Employment in Western Nations* (Cambridge: Cambridge University Press, 1985).

—— *Understanding Big Government* (London: Sage, 1984).

—— *Understanding the United Kingdom: The Territorial Dimension in Government* (London: Longman, 1982).

SHARPE, L. J., and NEWTON, K., *Does Politics Matter? The Determinants of Public Policy* (Oxford: Clarendon Press, 1984).

STERN, S. (ed.), *Meet United Germany* (Frankfurt: Frankfurt Allgemeine Zeitung, 1991).

SULEIMAN, E. (ed.), *Bureaucrats and Policy Making* (New York: Holmes and Meier, 1984).

—— and MENDRAS, H. (eds.), *Le Recrutement des élites en Europe* (Paris: Éditions La Découverte, 1995).

TARROW, S., *Between Centre and Periphery: Grassroots Politicians in Italy and France* (New Haven: Yale University Press, 1977).

Chapter 8. Constitutions, politics, and the judiciary

BLAIR, P. M., *Federalism and Judicial Review in West Germany* (Oxford: Clarendon Press, 1981).

CAPPELLETTI, M., and COHEN, W., *Comparative Constitutional Law: Cases and Materials* (New York: Bobbs-Merrill, 1979).

COHEN-TANUGI, L., *Le Droit sans l'État* (Paris: PUF, 1985).

DELLA PORTA, D., and MÉNY, Y. (eds.), *Democracy and Corruption in Europe* (London: Cassell, 1997).

FAVOREU, L. (ed.), *Les Cours Constitutionnelles et les droits fondamentaux* (Paris: Economica, 1982).

GRIFFITH, J. A. G., *The Politics of the Judiciary*, 4th edn. (London: Fontana, 1991).

—— *Judicial Politics since 1920: A Chronicle* (Oxford: Blackwell, 1993).

GUARNERI, C., 'The Judiciary in the Italian Political Crisis', *West European Politics*, 20(1) (January 1997), 157–75.

HARRISON, M., 'The French Constitutional Council: A Study in Institutional Change', *Political Studies*, 38(4) (December 1990), 603–19.

HOLLAND, K. M. (ed.), *Judicial Activism in Comparative Perspective* (Basingstoke: Macmillan, 1991).

KIMMEL, A., 'Une Crise de la cour constitutionnelle fédérale?', *Pouvoirs*, 79 (1996), 147–52.

KOMMERS, D. P., *Judicial Politics in West Germany: A Study of the Federal Constitutional Court* (Beverly Hills, Calif.: Sage, 1976).

RENOUX, T., 'La Liberté des juges', *Pouvoirs*, 74 (1995), 55–70.

STONE, A., *The Birth of Judicial Politics in France: The Constitutional Council in Comparative Perspective* (New York: Oxford University Press, 1992).

WATERS, S., ' "Tangentopoli" and the Emergence of a New Political Order in Italy', *West European Politics*, 17(1) (January 1994), 169–82.

ZAGREBELSKI, G., *La Giustizia Costituzionale* (Bologna: Il Mulino, 1977).

Chapters 9 and 10. The European Union and its development

ALTER, K. J., 'The European Court's Political Power', *West European Politics*, 19(3) (July 1996), 458–87.

BANCHOFF, T., 'German Policy Towards the European Union: The Effects of Historical Memory', *German Politics*, 6(1) (April 1997), 60–76.

CHRISTIANSEN, T., 'Tensions of European Governance: Politicized Bureaucracy and Multiple Accountability in the European Commission', *Journal of European Public Policy*, 4(1) (March 1997), 73–90.

COEN, D., 'The Evolution of the Large Firm as a Political Actor in the European Union', *Journal of European Public Policy*, 4(1) (March 1997), 91–108.

DEHOUSSE, R., 'Constitutional Reform in the European Community: Are there Alternatives to the Majoritarian Avenue?', *West European Politics*, 18(3) (July 1995), 118–36.

EARNSHAW, D., and JUDGE, D., 'Early Days: The European Parliament, Co-Decision and the European Union Legislative Process Post-Maastricht', *Journal of European Public Policy*, 2(4) (December 1995), 624–49.

EDWARDS, G., and SPENCE, D. (eds.), *The European Commission* (Harlow: Longman, 1994).

FENNELL, R., *The Common Agricultural Policy: Continuity and Change* (Oxford: Clarendon Press, 1997).

GAFFNEY, J. (ed.), *Political Parties and the European Union* (London: Routledge, 1996).

GAMBLE, A., 'Economic Recession and Disenchantment with Europe', *West European Politics*, 18(3) (July 1995), 158–74 (165).

GARTON ASH, T., *In Europe's Name: Germany and the Divided Continent* (London: Vintage Books, 1994) (1st edn. Jonathan Cape, 1993).

GEORGE, S., *Policy and Politics in the European Union* (3rd edn., Oxford: Oxford University Press, 1996).

GRANT, W., *The Common Agricultural Policy* (Basingstoke: Macmillan, 1997).

GREENWOOD, J., and RONIT, K., 'Interest Groups in the EC: Newly Emerging Dynamics and Forms', *West European Politics*, 17(1) (January 1994), 31–52.

HAYES-RENSHAW, F., and WALLACE, H., 'Executive Power in the European Union: The Functions and Limits of the Council of Ministers', *Journal of European Public Policy*, 2(4) (December 1995), 559–82.

—————— *The Council of Ministers* (Basingstoke: Macmillan, 1997).

HAYWARD, J. (ed.), 'The Crisis of Representation in Europe', special issue of *West European Politics*, 18(3) (July 1995).

——*Elitism, Populism, and European Politics* (Oxford: Clarendon Press, 1996).

——and PAGE, E. C. (eds.), *Governing the New Europe* (Oxford: Polity Press, 1995).

HESSE, J. J., and WRIGHT, V. (eds.), *Federalizing Europe?* (Oxford: Oxford University Press, 1996).

HIX, S., 'Approaches to the Study of the EC: The Challenge to Comparative Politics', *West European Politics*, 17(1) (January 1994), 1–30.

Bibliography

HIX, S., and LORD, C., *Political Parties in the European Union* (Basingstoke: Macmillan, 1997).

HOLLAND, M., *European Integration: From Community to Union* (London: Pinter Publishers, 1994).

HOOGHE, L., 'Subnational Mobilisation in the European Union', *West European Politics*, 18(3) (July 1995), 175–98.

JEFFERY, C. (ed.), *The Regional Dimension of the European Union: Towards a Third Level in Europe?* (London: Frank Cass, 1997).

JONES, B. and KEATING, M. (eds.), *The European Union and the Regions* (Oxford: Clarendon Press, 1995).

KASSIM, J., 'Policy Networks, Networks and European Policy Making: A Sceptical View', *West European Politics*, 17(4) (October 1995), 15–27.

LAFFAN, B., *Integration and Co-operation in Europe* (London: Routledge, 1992).

MAZEY, S., and RICHARDSON, J. (eds.), *Lobbying in the European Community* (Oxford: Oxford University Press, 1993).

————'Faire face à l'incertitude: stratégies des groupes de pression dans l'Union européenne', *Pouvoirs*, 79 (1996), 51–67.

————'Policy Framing: Interest Groups and the 1996 Intergovernmental Conference (IGC)', *West European Politics*, 19(4) (October 1997).

McKAY, D., *Rush to Union: Understanding the European Federal Bargain* (Oxford: Clarendon Press, 1996).

NORTON, P. (ed.), *National Parliaments and the European Union* (London: Frank Cass, 1996).

NUGENT, N., 'The Leadership Capacity of the European Commission', *Journal of European Public Policy*, 2(4) (December 1995), 603–23.

——*The Government and Politics of the European Union* (3rd edn., Basingstoke: Macmillan, 1994).

PAGE, E., *People who Run Europe* (Oxford: Clarendon Press, 1996).

PATERSON, W. 'Beyond Semi-Sovereignty: The New Germany in the New Europe', *German Politics*, 5(2) (August 1996), 167–84.

PERRINEAU, P. and YSMAL, C. (eds.), *Le Vote des Douze: Les élections européennes de juin 1994* (Paris: Presses de Sciences Po, 1994).

PETERSON, J., 'Policy Networks and European Policy Making: A Reply to Kassim', *West European Politics*, 18(2) (April 1995), 389–407.

POLLACK, M. 'Representing Diffuse Interests in EC Policymaking', *Journal of European Public Policy*, 4(4) (December 1997).

RICHARDSON, J. (ed.), *European Union: Power and Policymaking* (London: Routledge, 1996).

SBRAGIA, A., *Euro-Politics: Institutions and Policy-Making in the 'New' European Union* (Washington, DC: Brookings Institution, 1992).

SHAW J., and MORE, G., *The New Legal Dynamics of the EU* (Oxford: Oxford University Press, 1996).

SMITH, A., 'La Commission européenne et les fonds structurels: vers un nouveau modèle d'action', *Revue Française de Science Politique*, 46(3) (June 1996), 474–95.

TAYLOR, P., *The European Union in the 1990s* (Oxford: Oxford University Press, 1996).

TEASDALE, A., 'The Politics of Majority Voting in Europe', *The Political Quarterly*, 67 (1996), 101–13.

TSEBELIS, G., 'The Power of the European Parliament as a Conditional Agenda Setter', *American Political Science Review*, 88(1) (March 1994), 128–42.

VAN SCHENDELEN, M. (ed.), *National Public and Private EC Lobbying* (Aldershot: Dartmouth, 1993).

WALLACE, H. and WALLACE, W., *Policy-Making in the European Union*, 3rd edn. (Oxford: Oxford University Press, 1996).

WALLACE, W., and SMITH, J., 'Democracy or Technocracy? European Integration and the Problem of Popular Consent', *West European Politics*, 18(3) (July 1995), 137–57.

WEATHERILL, S., *Law and Integration in the European Union* (Oxford: Clarendon Press, 1995).

WEILER, J. H. H., with HALTERN, U. R., and MAYER, F. C., 'European Democracy and Its Critique', *West European Politics*, 18(3) (July 1995), 4–39.

WESTLAKE, M., *A Modern Guide to the European Parliament* (London: Frances Pinter, 1994).

WINCOTT, D. 'The Role of Law or the Rule of the Court of Justice? An "Institutional" Account of Judicial Politics in the European Community', *Journal of European Public Policy*, 2(4) (December 1995), 583–602.

INDEX

Index

Index

Index

Index

Index

Index